History of Cazewell County

and Southwest Virginia

1748-1920

Wm. C. Pendleton

Alpha Editions

This edition published in 2019

ISBN : 9789353802172

Design and Setting By
Alpha Editions
email - alphaedis@gmail.com

HISTORY

OF

TAZEWELL COUNTY

AND

SOUTHWEST VIRGINIA

1748-1920

BY

WM. C. PENDLETON

With Illustrations

1920
W. C. Hill Printing Company
Richmond, Va.

LOAN STACK

DEDICATED

To the memory of my beloved son

JAMES FRENCH PENDLETON

*He was pure in heart, faithful in service, and
the embodiment of truth*

W.O.Barns   S.C.Graham

S.L.Graham   A.St.Clair   Jno.C.St.Clair

R.O.Crockett   A.S.Higginbotham

Executive Committee. Tazewell Historical Society,
A. St.Clair, President.

Executive Committee, Tazewell Historical Society,
Jno. S. Bottimore, Secretary.

PREFACE

When I was first requested by certain gentlemen, who are descendants of the pioneer settlers of the Clinch Valley, to write a history of Tazewell County, it was intended to be a purely local history. But, after giving the proposition careful deliberation, I conceived the scheme which has made it a history of the Settlement, Development, and Civilization of Southwest Virginia, with Tazewell County as the central figure. The reason for the adoption of this plan will be obvious to every person who is sufficiently interested to read the volume, for the history of the entire Southwest Virginia, Tazewell County included, is, practically, identical. And their history is intimately identified with that of Virginia and of the Nation, as the people who have lived in this region have had much to do with forming and developing the political thought and social character of the State and Nation. In executing this plan, I have separated the book into six distinctly marked Periods, and they are as follows:

1. The Aboriginal Period, which is devoted to that branch of the human family that occupied or roamed over this section of the continent before men of the white race came here to make their homes. And in this Period the origin of the American Indians, together with their social organizations, tribal relations, religious characteristics, et cet., are discussed.

2. The Period of Discovery and Colonization, in which the Spanish Discoveries and Conquests, the French Discoveries and Settlements, and the English Discoveries and the Settlement at Jamestown in 1607, are concisely narrated.

3. The Pioneer Period. This is the most extended Period of the book; and is used to tell who the pioneers were, from whence they came, how they got here, and how they wrought mightily to reclaim this wonderful country from a wilderness waste. The Period begins with the first settlements made west of the Blue Ridge Mountains in 1732, and terminates with the creation of Tazewell County in 1799, thus comprising the settlements made in the Shenandoah, Roanoke, New River, Holston, and Clinch valleys, and Kentucky.

4. The Ante-Bellum, or Formative, Period, which begins with
the organization of Tazewell County in 1800, and concludes with
the commencement of the Civil War in 1861. Of the various events
mentioned in this Period, the one which treats of the forming and
developing of the political, social, and industrial thought and character of the people is, possibly, the most interesting.

5. The War and Reconstruction Period, which embraces the
eventful years 1861-1869. In this Period I relate and discuss the
potential causes that provoked the Civil War. Detailed accounts
of the four raids made by Federal soldiers into and through Tazewell County, and the battles these raids occasioned, are herein
written into history for the first time.

6. The Post-Bellum, or Development, Period tells, in brief form,
about the immense development of the mineral, agricultural, and
other natural resources of Tazewell County and adjacent sections
of Southwest Virginia and Southern West Virginia.

In prosecuting this work my chief aim has been directed to
gathering and preserving, in the form of written history, many
interesting events connected with the performances of the pioneer
settlers of the Clinch Valley and Southwest Virginia, that have
been handed down by reasonable tradition, or are to be found in
authentic records. But I have found it very difficult to select from
the great mass of available material only that which I deemed the
most important and essential for the proper accomplishment of my
task. To that end, I have earnestly examined the records of Tazewell County, and of other counties with which Tazewell was civilly
connected before it was organized as a distinct county. I have also
acquired many facts from the valuable archives, of manuscript or
printed form, that are deposited in the Virginia State Library, and
have carefully studied many local and general histories that are
recognized as reliable sources of information.

My cordial thanks are due, and are hereby given, to the President and Secretary, and to the Executive Committee of the Tazewell Historical Society; and to the following named gentlemen,
who became my financial backers and made it possible to procure
the publication of my manuscript in book form:

S. C. Graham, A. St.Clair, R. O. Crockett, J. W. Chapman,
W. T. Thompson, Jno. S. Bottimore, Jno. P. Gose, R. M. Lawson,
H. P. Brittain, H. G. McCall, H. G. Peery, Chas. R. Brown,

Wm. E. Peery. A. S. Higginbotham. W. O. Barns, W. T. Gillespie.
Geo. R. McCall. G. S. Thompson. A. S. Greever. Barnes Gillespie.
E. L. Greever. C. H. Peery, J. D. Peery, Henry A. Bowen. Henry
S. Bowen. J. Ed. Peery. R. C. Chapman. C. B. Neel. Jeff Ward.
A. G. Kiser. J. A. Greever. H. W. Pobst. O. E. Hopkins. C. P.
Harman. B. I. Payne. Jno. H. Thompson, J. G. Barns. W. R.
Bowen. S. S. F. Harman, M. J. Hankins.

I wish to acknowledge my indebtedness to certain gentlemen
who have given me valuable assistance, in various ways. in the
prosecution of my work—Mr. E. G. Swem. who was for years and
until recently the popular and most capable Assistant Librarian of
the Virginia State Library. and Mr. Morgan P. Robinson. the
polite and efficient Archivist of the Library. These two gentlemen
responded so generously to every call I made upon them for assistance or information. that I can hardly estimate the extent of my
obligation to them.

I am also heavily indebted to Messrs. H. P. Brittain. County
Treasurer; A. S. Greever. Superintendent of County Schools; S.
M. Graham. A. St.Clair. C. H. Peery and Jno. S. Bottimore for
helping to gather material used in my work; and to Messrs. W. O.
Barns. Wm. E. Peery and Henry A. Bowen for special substantial
favors.

The history has been arranged in as nearly chronological order
as it was possible for me to place it. It is hardly necessary for
me to say that it has been truly a labor of love to write about the
deeds and accomplishments of the splendid men and women who
were the pioneer settlers of the Clinch Valley and other sections
of Southwest Virginia. And it has been a pleasant task to compile
and relate the ways and means that have been used by their descendants and successors to bring this section of Virginia to its present
social and industrial high position. My earnest hope and desire
is, that its people shall continue to advance on these lines until
they have attained the most exalted stage of Christian civilization
and human freedom.

WM. C. PENDLETON.

June 1st, 1920.

NOTE—The book has been published under very trying circumstances, produced. in the main. by unsettled labor conditions. This

has not only occasioned delay in getting the history ready for publication, but is, possibly, responsible for most of the typographical and mechanical errors that appear on its pages. These will be easily detected and corrected by the careful and intelligent reader. There is, however, one error in a date to which special attention is called. It occurs in the sketch of Captain Henry Bowen, Tazewell's most distinguished son, on page 636. He was born December 26th, 1841, and not in "1815" as appears in the sketch. The lines that immediately follow the incorrect date in the sketch fully expose and correct the error.

CONTENTS

CONTENTS

LIST OF ILLUSTRATIONS

The Aboriginal Period

Which Treats of the Origin of the American
Indians, their Forms of Government,
Civilization, Religion, etc.

History of Tazewell County and Southwest Virginia

ABORIGINAL PERIOD

CHAPTER I.

ORIGIN OF THE RED MEN, THEIR DISTRIBUTION,
CIVILIZATION, CHARACTER, ETC.

There is one thing connected with the discovery of America which has been settled beyond dispute by historians; and that is that the American aborigines received their name from Christopher Columbus. When the great navigator started out from Palos with his three little ships, manned with one hundred and twenty men, his main purpose was to travel to India by sailing a westward course. After a trying and thrilling voyage of seventy-one days, on the 12th of October, 1492, Columbus landed on one of the Bahamas, took possession of the island for Spain, and named it San Salvador. He there found a tribe of natives whom he called Indians, believing he had reached the shores of the Asiatic Continent and had landed upon the eastern coast of India.

Much has been surmised and a vast deal written about the origin of the Red Men who were the primitive inhabitants of the American Continent. All historians have agreed that they are one of the older races of mankind, but whether they are indigenous to this continent, or are the descendants of an Asiatic race is still not only a matter of dispute but seems likely to remain for all future time an unsolved problem.

Some of the most profound and ardent students of mankind have confidently asserted that the American Indians are a distinct variety of the human race. Among these are Blumenbach, the eminent German naturalist, and Samuel George Morton, the distinguished American ethnologist. On the other hand quite a number of able and celebrated ethnologists, philologists and anthropologists have asserted with equal positiveness that the Indians of both North and South America are descendants of the Mongolian family and came here from Asia. But when they reached this continent or by what route they traveled is completely enveloped in mystery.

Dr. Robert Brown, who has been regarded as one of the most accomplished, as he is one of the latest writers on the subject, in his "Races of Mankind" expresses firm conviction that the American race is of Asiatic origin. He says:

"Not only are the Western Indians in appearance very like their nearest neighbors, the Northeastern Asiatics, but in language and tradition, it is confidently affirmed there is a blending of the people. The Eskimo, on the American, and the Tchuktchis, on the Asiatic side understand each other perfectly."

Modern anthropologists, who uphold the theory of Asiatic origin, are of opinion that the ancestors of the greater part of the American race came here from Japan, the Kuriles and the regions thereabout. Baron Humboldt, one of the greatest scientists the world has ever produced, after traveling extensively in South America, Mexico, Cuba and parts of the United States, said this about the aboriginal inhabitants:

"The Indians of New Spain bear a general resemblance to those who inhabit Canada, Florida, Peru and Brazil. We think we perceive them all to be descended from the same stock, notwithstanding the prodigious diversity of their languages. In a portrait drawn by Volney of the Canadians we recognize the tribe scattered over the Savannahs of the Apure and the Caroney. The same style of features exists in both Americas."

It is a notable fact that the Mongolian cast of feature is most pronounced in the Indian tribes nearest the Mongol coasts, that is on our Pacific coast; and becomes less distinct as we trace the tribes eastward to the shores of the Atlantic. And it is a generally accepted historic fact that the tribes on the eastern seaboard gave as one of their traditions that their ancestors came from the West, while the Western tribes claimed that their progenitors came from regions still further West. Though there were at the period about which Humboldt was writing hundreds of tribes among the American Indians, all of them bore a striking similarity of physical structure, personal characteristics, and languages. This similarity of languages led Albert Gallatin to say:

"Amidst that great diversity of American languages, considered only in reference to their vocabularies, the similarity of their structure and grammatical forms has been observed and pointed out by the American philologists. The result appears to confirm the opinions already entertained by Ponceau, Mr. Pickering and others; and to prove that all the languages, not only of our own Indians, but of the native inhabitants of America, from the Arctic Ocean to Cape Horn, have, as far as they have been investigated, a distinct character common to all, and apparently differing from any of those of the other continents with which we are most familiar."

That all the Indians of both American continents were of common origin is indicated not only by similarity of the structure and grammatical forms of their languages, but by the strong resemblance of their physical characteristics. These have been described as follows:

"A square head, with low but broad forehead, the back of the head flattened, full face and powerful jaws; cheek-bones prominent, lips full, eyes dark and deeply set; the hair long, not absolutely straight, but wavy, something like a horse's mane, and like that, of a glossy hue; little or no beard, where it does appear carefully eradicated with tweezers; color of the skin reddish or copper, height of the men about the average, but looking taller from their erect posture and slender figure; the women rather shorter and more inclined to obesity, but many of them with symmetrical figure and pleasing countenance; hands and feet of both men and women small."

Though the learned men who have carefully studied and investigated the aborigines of America have differed sharply as to how this peculiar race originated, some holding that it was indigenous and others that it was of Mongolian descent, all such ethnologists and philologists have agreed that it had a common origin. Therefore it has been a matter of surprise to those who have been interested investigators of its history to find that but three of the many nations of the American race had attained any considerable degree of civilization when they first became known to the white men.

When Hernando Cortes, in 1519, with his cruelly avaricious but desperately courageous band of Spaniards, invaded Mexico, he found there a large and intelligent nation, ruled over by an emperor, living in walled cities, with sumptuous residences, splendid palaces, and magnificent temples. This people, called the Aztecs, had a code of fixed laws, and were skilled in some of the arts and sciences, especially astronomy. They were excellent argiculturists, engaged extensively in mining the precious metals, and exhibited much skill in the manufacture of both useful and ornamental articles. Historians, from what they deem satisfactory record and traditional evidence, affirm that the Aztecs wandered into Mexico in the twelfth century, and succeeded the Toltecs, another tribe of the mysterious American race. The Toltecs are said to have entered Mexico in the seventh century. Both of these tribes or families had come from the same hive in the North, just as the Saxons, Danes, and Normans, successively, journeyed from Scandinavia and ultimately landed in England.

The Toltecs, the predecessors of the Aztecs, judging from the monuments and other indicia they left behind them in Mexico, and the immense architectural remains of the temples they built in Central America, were more advanced in civilization than were their successors, the Aztecs.

The Toltecs were so skilled in architecture that the name Toltec has been pronounced the synonym of architect. They were skillful agriculturists and introduced maize and cotton into Mexico. In making record of events they used hieroglyphics, and left ample monuments to prove that they were skilled in the arts and sciences. They knew how to fuse metals, to cut and polish the hardest stones, to manufacture earthenware, and weave many kinds of fabrics. It is an astonishing fact that they had knowledge of the causes of eclipses, made wonderful sun-dials, had a simple system of notation, and measured time by a solar year of 365 days. The Toltecs were a people of a gentle, peaceful disposition, but very industrious and enterprising. Their laws were simple but justly administered, and their religion was of a mild form. Why and when they left Mexico has not been definitely settled; but it seems certain that they migrated to Central America, perhaps impelled by the nomadic instincts inherited from their Asiatic progenitors.

In the matter of religion the Aztecs were very much fiercer and more barbarous in their practices than their predecessors, the Toltecs. They believed in one supreme creator and ruler of the universe, but this sublime faith was strangely mingled with a belief that hundreds of inferior divinities existed under the control of the supreme divinity. Not only were the Aztecs heathenish, but they were cannibalistic in the practice of their religious ceremonies; and they were the only family of the American race who offered up human sacrifices. It is related by historians that in the immediate years preceding the Spanish invasion and conquest of Mexico, the Aztecs sacrificed twenty thousand human beings annually upon their altars. The sacrificial ceremonies were performed by their priests on the summits of their temples, and in the presence of vast throngs of worshipers. A victim was bound to the sacrificial stone, the breast was cut open and the heart torn out. This vital organ of the human sacrifice was either placed before an image of their gods, or, after being cut into small pieces and mingled with maiz, was distributed to the assembled worshipers to eat. It was a kind of sacramental ceremony. This strange admixture of a high conception of the Supreme Ruler of the Universe and a sanguinary superstition which induced them to sacrifice human beings to their plural gods puts the Aztecs in a distinct class among the numerous tribes of the American race called Indians.

THE CONQUEST OF PERU BY PIZARRO.

Peru, now one of the Latin Republics of South America, was enjoying its second phase of civilization when Francisco Pizarro, the Spanish adventurer, in 1531, invaded that country with his reckless band of freebooters. There were only one hundred and eighty men in his expeditionary force, of whom twenty-seven were cavalry. Pizarro had been incited to make the daring attempt to conquer a native empire from knowledge of what Cortes had accomplished in Mexico. He had accompanied Balboa when he crossed the Isthmus of Panama in 1513, and was with that cavalier when he first viewed from a mountain top the great ocean which he named the South Sea, but which Magellan a few years later called the Pacific. Pizarro's ambition had also been greatly excited by rumors that came to him of a wonderful country still further South, where silver and gold were found in as great abundance as iron in Spain. Inspired by these reports, with a small company of followers, he made a visit to Peru in 1526 for the purpose of spying out that country; and had returned to Panama with satisfactory evidence that the immense wealth of the land in precious metals had not been exaggerated. The generous natives, who had never seen a white man until Pizarro and his companions visited them in an assumed friendly way, gave him valuable and beautiful ornaments made from gold and silver; and also liberal specimens of fine cloth, of brilliant

hue, made from the wool of llamas and alpacas. Very soon after
this visit of discovery Pizarro traveled to Spain and exhibited these
specimens to Charles V. and his ministers; and revealed to them
what he had seen of the enormous wealth in the land of the Incas.
The Spanish monarch and his court were so deeply impressed with
the glowing representations of Pizarro, he was invested with numerous honorable titles, among them being that of governor and captain general of Peru. Having so successfully accomplished his
mission to the Spanish Court, the first governor of Peru returned to
Panama, accompanied by a band of adventurers who had been lured
to his banner by reports of the large quantities of gold and silver
possessed by the Incas and their people. At Panama the intrepid
adventurer gathered together one hundred and eighty men, twenty-
seven horses for his cavalry, and a fairly good equipment of arms
and ammunition. These were gotten aboard three small vessels,
and the eventful expedition to the country of the Peruvians was
started. Upon arrival in Peru with his small but well equipped
force of soldiers, the Spanish conquerer promptly revealed his
treacherous nature to the people he had visited a few years previously with seeming friendly intention. He proceeded to torture,
kill, and rob the natives until he succeeded in crushing the spirit of
the nation. Thus was the splendid empire of the Incas brought
under Spanish rule, as had been that of Montezuma in Mexico by
the ruthless conquest of Hernando Cortes.

The civilization of the Peruvians in many respects was of a
higher type than was that of the Aztecs. From traditions of the
aboriginal inhabitants it is known that Manco, the first Inca, with
his wife, Mama Oella, mysteriously appeared to the superstitious
natives on the shores of Lake Titicaca. Manco told the astonished
natives that he and his wife were children of the Sun, and declared
that they had been sent by their god Ita (the Sun) to instruct and
rule the people who dwelt in that region. They accepted his statements as true, and willingly became his subjects. Manco kept his
word by instructing the people in agriculture and the arts. He gave
them a pure religion and established an excellent social and national
organization. Mama Oella taught the women to spin, weave and
sew, and trained them in what is now called domestic science.
Investigators and historians are convinced that Manco and his wife
were white persons. That they could have reached a country so
remote, separated by broad oceans that no mariner had then ever

crossed from the continents where the white races lived, seems not only improbable but impossible. If, however, the traditions of the aborigines are substantially true as to the appearance of Manco and Mama Oella, they were of a race entirely different from the natives, and must have been white. The simple and superstitious natives were even disposed to believe that Pizarro and his cutthroat band were children of the gods, because of their personal appearance.

The government which Manco established was in the nature of a mild but positive despotism. It constituted the Inca head of the priesthood, gave him authority to impose taxes and made him the absolute source of all governmental power. His empire was divided into four very extensive provinces, each of these being presided over by a viceroy or governor. The nation was further divided into departments of ten thousand inhabitants, and each of the departments had a governor. In fact, the subdivisions were so extended as to embrace within the least departments as few as ten persons.

There was also an advanced agrarian principle engrafted upon the government which Manco founded. No private ownership of land was permitted. All the lands were allotted each year, one-third of the territory of the empire being set apart for the Sun, the Inca, and the people, respectively. The lands allotted to the Sun were for the support of the temples of this god, to defray the expenses of the costly religious ceremonials and maintain the multitude of priests who had charge of the temples and conducted the ceremonies. Those lands set apart for the Inca were to support his royal state and household, and defray the general expenses of the government. The remaining third of the lands was apportioned, *per capita*, in equal shares among all the people. The allotments made to heads of families were apportioned according to the number of persons in each family. It is stated that this system of annual distribution developed such excellent agricultural methods that the soil was made more productive instead of depleting its fertility. The sandy lands along the seacoast, that originally were of no agricultural value, were transformed into productive fields and rich pastures. This was accomplished by a system of artificial irrigation of such magnitude as the world has never seen equaled. Water was conveyed from mountain lakes and streams to the sandy waste lands by the use of aqueducts, and distributed through canals similar to those used by the ancient Egyptians, and like those now employed in the arid sections of the United States east of the Rocky Mountains.

Several of the Peruvian aqueducts were between four hundred and five hundred miles long. The ruins of some of them still attest the marvelous skill and energy of the people who constructed them without the aid of iron or steel tools or machinery of any kind. How they performed such stupendous tasks is likely to remain as great mystery as the building of the Egyptian pyramids.

The religion of the Peruvians, though of pagan form, was of a higher type than that of most heathen nations. They worshipped, as did the Aztecs and as still do the unconverted tribes of North America, a Great Spirit, whom they adored as the Author and Ruler of the Universe. He, they piously believed could not be symbolized by an image nor be made to dwell in a temple erected by mortal men. They also believed in the immortality of the soul and the resurrection of the body after death. Like the Aztecs, however, they worshipped secondary gods, of whom they recognized the Sun as chief.

That the Peruvians had some very skillful goldsmiths and silver-smiths was attested by the many beautiful ornaments they made from the precious metals to adorn their palaces and temples. Many of these ornaments were exquisitely designed representations of human and other forms, and of plants, all fashioned with accuracy as to form and feature. They also had highly skilled cutters and polishers of precious stones, and used them to fashion images of brilliantly colored birds, serpents, lizards and other things, the stones being cut and arranged with as much skill as the most accomplished artists of Paris and Amsterdam have ever exhibited.

Previous to the advent of the Incas there was another large and highly civilized nation that occupied Peru. Historians and ethnologists have never found the name of this people, know nothing of their origin, and have to rest satisfied with referring to them as the pre-incarial nation, or nations. They had a civilization, a language, and a religion that were different from those of the incarial nation. That they lived in large cities is proven by the splendid architectural remains, sculptures, carvings and other specimens of art that have been viewed with amazement by archeologists who explored the ruins of these ancient cities. The most diligent efforts of scientific investigators have failed to disclose from what regions these pre-incarial nations came and from which race of mankind they sprang. Therefore they will have to be classed as a prehistoric race, just as have been the cave-dwellers of the Rocky Mountains and the mound-builders of the Mississippi Valley.

The Mexican and Peruvian aborigines, like the ancient Egyptians, made use of hieroglyphics instead of letters to record events and give expression to their languages. It is what has been termed picture writing, and the pictures used were representations of natural or artificial objects—such as celestial bodies, animals, fishes, reptiles, flowers, plants, the human form, works of art, and a numerous variety of things. Among the Aztecs the women as well as the men were taught the art of reading and writing the hieroglyphics. The women were also instructed in ciphering, singing and dancing, and even taught the secrets of astronomy and astrology. Their method of writing was so crude and grotesque and the system of notation so imperfect as to make them very inadequate for practical purposes.

When it is known that the Mexican and Peruvian Indians acquired so many of the elements of civilization, it is hard to understand why their attainments were not extended to some of the many other tribes of their race that occupied or roamed over all sections of the North and South American continents. The various tribes, especially the Toltecs, who inhabited Central America, were evidently a useful connecting link for uniting the civilizations of Mexico and Peru; and it is probable that the Central American tribes imparted more than they received from their kindred nations of the Northern and Southern continents.

The civilizations of these three great nations of the American aborigines, the Toltecs, the Aztecs and the Peruvians, partook more of the nature of a refined barbarism than of the type of civilization that developed in Europe after the Christian era began; and they were very deficient in intellectual and moral force. There were several potential causes for these deficiences. One of these was the forms of their religions, which were fundamentally mythological and consequently active breeders of superstition. The religions of the native Mexicans and Peruvians were intensely superstitious; and conspired to make them seclusive or hermit nations, similar to Japan before its policy of isolation was destroyed by Commodore Perry in 1853.

Another reason for the restriction of the civilization of the Mexicans and Peruvians to their own nations was their failure to invent and make use of an alphabet, and their resultant inability

to express themselves with words or a phonetic written language.
Without an alphabet and a written language they could make no
satisfactory record of important events that occurred in their national
life; and, therefore, could not communicate what they had accumulated to neighboring tribes, or even transmit it to their own posterity,
except by tradition.

Another very substantial reason why the Mexicans and Peruvians did not reach a higher standard of civilization, nor impart
what they had to other tribes of their race, was that they had no
monetary system, no medium of exchange in the shape of metallic
tokens that represented specific and intrinsic values.   The vast
quantities of silver and gold these peoples had accumulated during
the centuries that preceded the Spanish conquests were used almost
exclusively for ornamentation of their temples and palaces, for
making images of their gods, and for ornaments for their persons.
The Peruvians had no knowledge whatever of money and no medium
of exchange; but the Aztecs had a kind of currency which they used
in connection with their barter transactions.   It consisted of small
pieces of tin stamped with a character like a T, bags of cacao
(chocolate seeds), valued according to the size of the bags; and
small transparent quills filled with gold dust.   This currency system was not superior to that of the North American tribes who used
shells and beads, called wampum, for money; and was no better
than the coon-skin currency of the pioneer settlers of this country.
Neither of the nations had any knowledge of numerals or figures
for keeping accounts and business transactions, nor did they have
a system of weights and measures.

The highest forms of civilization that existed among the nations
of the Old World were developed by the peoples that were imbued
with a spirit of commercialism; and who possessed the requisites
for conducting business transactions, that is a written language, a
monetary system and a knowledge of numerals.   All historians who
have studied and written about the ancient nations of the world have
agreed that the Phoenecians were the first to become noted as a
great commercial and maritime people, and to engage extensively
in foreign commerce.   At a very early period their trade in manufactured articles and other products extended over the best known
parts of the continents of Asia, Africa and Europe.   It is conceded
that the Phoenecians were the first nation that invented and made
practical use of an alphabet, which was destined to become the

model for all European and American alphabets. Being the first
to have an alphabet, the Phoenecians were the first nation to have
a written language and a literature. These acquisitions served to
stimulate invention, give impulse to industry and generate a commercial spirit, thereby supplying the most essential factors for the
building of a high and progressive civilization. The aboriginal
inhabitants of Mexico and Peru did not have these indispensibles.
Consequently the form of civilization they acquired was very imperfect. It was purely instinctive, the outcome of natural impulse,
rather than the evolvement of mental processes ; and tended to make
these greatest nations of the American Indians physically and
mentally weak.

Three thousand years before the Spaniards invaded Mexico
and Peru the Phoenecians had established intimate commercial relations with the Iberians and Celts who then inhabited Spain. A number of colonies from Phoenecia were established on the seacoast
of Iberia, now Spain. Thus there was infused into the inhabitants
of Spain the elements of civilization that had made the Phoenecians
rank first among the nations of ancient times. At the time Columbus
became the discoverer of America, Spain was the leading commercial and maritime nation of Europe, and was the greatest military and naval power of the world. In addition to that which Spain
had procured from the Phoenecians, she had received from the
Arabs what are known by the distinctive name of *Arabic Numerals,*
the nine figures or digits and the zero that have been used for centuries by nearly all civilized nations in their arithmetical calcu-
lations.

The civilization of the Spaniards was of a very strong type,
having been created by the intellectual development of its people,
while that of the three greatest nations of the American race was
superficial and weak, of spontaneous or instinctive growth. When
these two entirely different forms of civilization met in mental and
physical conflict the stronger, with its higher developed mental
faculties, and trained soldiers, who were armed with cannon, guns,
and swords and spears of tempered and polished steel, easily
defeated the weaker people, burdened with pagan superstition and
who were fighting with the same simple weapons their ancestors
had used many centuries before.

It will not be amiss for the writer to here make known his reason
for so freely discussing the types of civilization that existed among

the aborigines of Mexico and Peru when in their zenith. This has been done with a view of directing equal attention to the best forms of civilization that were found among some of the leading tribes of Indians who inhabited the North American Continent previous to its discovery and settlement by men of the white race. This will give opportunity, by comparison, to analyze and exemplify the wonderful accomplishments of the pioneer settlers, and the steady progress made by their descendants since Tazewell County became an organized society.

CHAPTER II.

Philologists and historians have, without a dissenting voice, agreed that the North American Indians were divided into a number of distinct families; and that each of these families was subdivided into numerous subordinate tribes. Every subordinate tribe had its own dialect; and it is known that more than five hundred different dialects were used by the aborigines. There were also many differences in traditions, habits, and social forms among the numerous tribes.

THE ESKIMO.

So far as has been ascertained, the Eskimo ever since their tribal or family organizations were established have inhabited the Arctic regions of the North American Continent. They have had very sparse settlements above the sixtieth parallel of latitude, are scattered across the continent from Labrador to Alaska, and even extending to Siberia. The Eskimo also inhabit the Asiatic side of Behring's Strait; and the people on both sides of the strait are pronouncedly Mongolian in feature. Being the only family common to both continents, they are claimed by many ethnologists to be an indisputable link connecting the Mongols of Asia and the Indians of America.

The Eskimo are of medium stature but are very strong, and have great powers of endurance. Their skin is of a light brownish or yellow color and tinted with red on the exposed parts. They have small, well formed hands and feet, and their eyes, like nearly all the American tribes, have a Mongolian character, which confirms most ethnologists in the belief that they are of Asiatic origin. Their permanent settlements are so located as to be near the best hunting and fishing grounds. In summer time they hunt caribou, musk-ox, and different kinds of birds; and in the winter they subsist mainly on fish and sea mammals, principally the seal that abound in the Arctic regions.

The Eskimo are of a very peaceable disposition, are very truthful, and remarkably honest, but are extremely lax in their practices of sexual morality. Their dwellings in the summer are made of deer or seal skins stretched over poles, and in the winter they make shallow excavations in the earth and use either wood or whale ribs for a framework, which they cover with turf. Many of their winter huts are built with snow.

The social organization of this peculiar people is very loose, the village being the largest unit, while in matters of government each settlement is independent, a pure form of local self-government. There are no chiefs as found with the tribes of the American natives who lived south of the Eskimo. The men give their time to hunting and fishing, and the women perform all the hard labor. Though they are without anything like culture or education, they are said to be good draftsmen and carvers, and the people about Behring Strait do some painting.

The Eskimo have a strange religion. They believe that spirits exist in animals and even in inanimate objects. Their chief deity is an old woman who lives in the ocean and who controls storms and causes the seals to visit or stay away, as she may direct, from the shores these sea animals frequent. Many other ridiculous beliefs are held in connection with this old woman of the sea. The larger portion of the Eskimo of Greenland and Labrador have been converted to Christianity by Moravian and Danish missionaries; and Russian missionaries for over a century have been working among the natives of Alaska. The Eskimo have been of great service to all explorers of the Artic regions. Recent estimates of the number of Eskimo living in North America place them at nearly thirty thousand.

THE ALGONQUIAN FAMILY.

When the Europeans first discovered the North American Continent and began to explore and make settlements on its coasts the Algonquians were one of the most prominent and powerful families of the red men. They occupied and roamed over an extensive territory south of that inhabited by the Eskimo, including the greater part of Canada and nearly all that portion of the United States which lies north of the thirty-seventh parallel of latitude. Their territory is said to have reached from the eastern shore of Newfoundland to the Rocky Mountains, and from Churchill River, in British North America, to Pamlico Sound. The population of the various tribes or nations of this family of the aborigines has been estimated in the aggregate at a quarter of a million when they first became known to men of the white race. Among the tribes of the

Algonquians were the Shawnees, and also all the tribes that occupied
Virginia east of the Blue Ridge Mountains, including those of the
Powhatan Confederacy. Most of the Algonquian tribes were of an
exceedingly nomadic disposition; and were constantly moving from
one hunting ground and river to others to indulge their passionate
fondness for hunting and fishing, as well as to make sure of their
supplies of food.   The Shawnees were the most ardent rovers
of the various Algonquian tribes; and, consequently, gave very
little attention to agriculture or home-building.   It is said that
when the French and other Europeans began to settle in and about
the territory of the Algonquians that this large family of the
American race had already begun to decline in numbers; and was
being greatly reduced by deadly diseases that practically wiped out
entire subordinate tribes.   This family of the aborigines is also
reputed to have suffered more than any of their kindred nations
from contact with the white men.   They were easily duped and
debauched by the unscrupulous white traders who gave them "fire-
water" in exchange for their furs and lands.

THE HURON-IROQUOIS NATION.

A great nation known as the Huron-Iroquois inhabited territory
within the bounds of that occupied by the Algonquian tribes when
America was discovered by Columbus.   It was a confederation of
tribes of Algonquian origin.   In the zenith of their power the
Hurons exercised dominion over territory that extended from
Georgian Bay and Lake Huron to Lakes Erie and Ontario, and
south of these lakes extended on down to the Upper Ohio Valley,
and eastward to the Sorell River.

The Huron-Iroquois Confederacy originally was composed of
the following tribes, the Hurons (afterwards known as the Wyandots) who lived north of Lake Erie; the Eries and Andestas, who
resided south of that lake; the Tuscaroras who went from North
Carolina and rejoined their kindred in the north; the Senecas,
Cayugas, Onondagas, Oneidas and Mohawks.   The last mentioned
five tribes constituted what was known as the Five Nations of New
York, and later called the Six Nations after the Tuscaroras joined
them in 1712.

The Six Nations occupied the central and western sections of
the State of New York, and had an estimated population of fifteen
thousand.   They were pronounced one of the most intelligent, enter-

T.H.-2

prising and warlike aboriginal nations that occupied the northeastern portion of the continent. Their villages were of respectable size and character, and each tribe was divided into families, and governed by sachems or chiefs. All matters that affected the general interests of the confederated tribes were considered and settled by a conference of all the chiefs of the confederacy. When the English colonists in 1776 revolted against the British Government, and while the war of the Revolution was in progress, the Iroquois became the allies of the British. They were influenced to pursue this course by the very unjust and cruel treatment they had received from the colonists. Led by Joseph Brant, the Mohawk chief, and Red Jacket, chief of the Senecas, the Iroquois inflicted some terrible blows upon the white settlements and gave much valuable assistance to the British armies that the American colonies were struggling against.

Toward the close of the eighteenth century most of the Iroquois tribes sold their lands in New York and gradually moved away. The Mohawks settled in Canada, and were afterwards joined there by a part of the Tuscaroras and parts of other tribes. Other portions of the several tribes eventually moved to western reservations or to Canada. A part of the Senacas went to the Indian Territory, now the State of Oklahoma. In 1917 there were 435 Senecas in that State under Federal Supervision. There were about 5,500 Iroquois living as an independent community in New York State in the year 1890. The report of the Commissioner of Indian Affairs for 1916, shows that the number of Indians then living in New York was 6,245, of whom 5,585 were under supervision of the New York Agency of the Federal Government.

South of the country inhabited by the Alogonquian tribes were the Cherokees. This nation and that of the Shawnees had so much to do with the history of the pioneer settlers of Southwest Virginia, and of Tazewell County, that it will be necessary for the writer to give these two more particular attention than any of the tribes mentioned. For this reason, that which shall be written about the Cherokees and Shawnees will be put in the closing chapters of the Aboriginal Period.

THE MUSKHOGEAN FAMILY.

In the country which now constitutes the extreme Southern States of the United States east of the Mississippi River, dwelt the

Muskhogean family of the North American Indians. The principal tribes of this family were: the Creeks, the Choctaws, the Chickasaws and the Seminoles. Although members of the same family, there were many distinct dissimilarities in both their physical and mental characteristics. All of the tribes were fond of agriculture, and they all lived in villages of comfortable log houses. Their villages that were exposed to attack from an enemy were protected by palisades. They were all brave warriors, but the Choctaws were disposed to fight entirely in self-defense, while the Creeks and the Chickasaws were inclined to engage in offensive wars. The Creeks and the Choctaws, each, had a confederacy, with smaller tribes attached thereto. These confederacies were political organizations erected on kinship, real or fictitious, and the principal object of the confederation was mutual defense. The Muskhogean people numbered 50.000 when first known to the white men.

THE CREEKS.

Of the four tribes of the Muskhogean family, the Creeks have been regarded as the leader. Their name was given them by the English on account of the numerous small streams of water in the country they occupied. They first came in contact with the white race when De Soto invaded their country in 1540. At that time they held the greater portion of Alabama and Georgia, and had their chief villages on the Coosa, Tallapoosa, Flint and Chattahoocha rivers. The Creeks became treaty allies of the English colonists in the Apalachee wars of 1703-08, and from that time were the faithful friends of the colonists of South Carolina and Georgia, with two exceptions, but were bitter foes of the Spaniards. They were allies of the British Government in the Revolutionary War. In 1790 they made a treaty of peace with the United States, but in 1812 were seduced by England's emissaries, broke the treaty and committed a number of bloody outrages upon the white inhabitants of Georgia, Alabama and Florida. The British sent Tecumseh, the celebrated Shawnee chief, in the spring of 1812 from Ohio to the Creeks and other Indian tribes of the South to enlist their support in the war against the United States. Tecumseh used his savage eloquence with telling effect, reminding his kindred of the South of the seizing of their lands by the whites, called attention to the continued encroachments of the pale faces and to the diminution and probable destruction of the Indian race. The Creeks and Seminoles were infuriated by Tecumseh's appeals, and in September, 1812, began war against the white inhabitants of the South. They were soon overawed by General Andrew Jackson, who marched against them with twenty-five hundred Tennessee volunteers. Incited by British agents, the Indians renewed their war against the whites in 1813. About four hundred inhabitants in the most exposed situations on the Alabama River gathered at Fort Mimms for protection. The Indians made a surprise attack upon the fort at noon on the 30th of August, 1813. There were about six hundred warriors who were led by their chief, Weatherford. The whites were driven into the houses, the torch was applied to the buildings, and most of those who escaped the flames became victims of the tomahawk. Only seventeen persons escaped to carry the news of the frightful disaster to other stations.

General Jackson and other military leaders began ruthless war against the Creeks, desolated their country and killed two thousand of their warriors. After two years of desultory war the Indians were brought into subjection, but continued to give trouble to the white people of the surrounding country until they were removed to the Indian Territory in 1836. At the time of their removal they numbered 24,594. The Creek Nation is now a part of the Five Civilized Tribes in Oklahoma; and in 1916 the nation numbered 18,774. Of these 11,965 are Creeks by blood, while 6,809 are freedmen, descendants of the negro slaves the Creeks took with them when they were sent to the Indian Territory.

THE CHOCTAWS.

When first known to Europeans the Choctaws were occupying Middle and Southern Mississippi, and their territory extended at one time east of the Tombigbee River, as far as Dallas County, Georgia. The meaning of the name Choctaw is unknown, but is believed to signify a separation, that is, separation from the Creeks and Seminoles who were once united with the Choctaws as one tribe. As before stated, they were a branch of the Muskhogean family, and were the leading agriculturists of the Southern Indians. The Choctaws were a very brave people, but their devotion to agriculture seems to have led them to go to war in most instances on the defensive. From the narratives of De Soto's expedition, it is known that the Spanish explorer came in contact with the Choctaws in 1540. He had several very fierce encounters with these Indians and found them splendid fighters.

About the year 1700 the Choctaws became very friendly with the French, who were then settling colonies at Mobile, and New Orleans. Although they were of their own kindred the Choctaws were constantly engaged in war with the Creeks and Chickasaws. In 1786 they acknowledged their allegiance to the United States; and rendered the Government very efficient service in the war with England in 1812, and also in the Creek war. Although they were given special privileges by Georgia, that State going so far as to invest them with citizenship, they gradually emigrated beyond the Mississippi River and finally settled in the Indian Territory. In the Civil War they cast their fortune with the Confederate States, but after that war was ended renewed their allegiance to the United States. They are now one of the principal nations of the American natives living in Oklahoma, and one of the members of the Five Civilized Tribes Confederation of that State. According to the 1916 report of the Commissioner of Indian Affairs, the Choctaw Nation numbers 26,828. They are divided as follows: By blood 17,488; by intermarriage 1,651; Mississippi Choctaw 1,660; freedmen 6,029, the latter, as in the case of the Creeks, being the descendants of slaves owned by the Choctaws at the close of the Civil War.

THE CHICKASAWS.

From their traditions we learn that the Chickasaws were closely related to the Choctaws both by blood and language. Notwithstanding this fact, the two tribes were very hostile and were constantly engaged in armed conflict. According to their traditions the Chickasaws and Choctaws came originally from the West, and settled east of the Mississippi River. Fernando De Soto and his ill-fated followers found them there in 1540 and passed the winter of 1540-41 in the country of these Indians. The Spaniards had many encounters with them and greatly terrorized the poor natives; but in the spring of 1541 the Chickasaws inflicted a very heavy blow to De Soto and his followers. The Spaniards undertook to force the natives to accompany their expedition as guides and baggage-carriers. They refused to be thus enslaved, burnt De Soto's camp and their own villages, and concealed themselves in impenetrable swamps. Forty of the Spaniards perished in the conflagration and a large part of their baggage was destroyed.

The Chickasaws were from the earliest times noted for their courage and independent spirit; and were almost incessantly fighting some of the neighboring tribes. They had wars with the Choctaws, the Creeks, the Cherokees, the Shawnees, and even with the Iroquois. The latter once invaded their territory and the invading band was almost destroyed. The Chickasaws were always the bitter foe of the French, this feeling of enmity being encouraged by the English traders and intensified by an alliance of the French with the Choctaws. In 1736 they defeated the French in several battles, and successfully resisted an attempt to conquer them in 1739-40.

In 1786 the United States established friendly relations with the Chickasaws by a treaty, which is known as the treaty of Hopewell; and they gave valuable assistance to the white inhabitants in the Creek War of 1813-14. Early in the nineteenth century the Chickasaws ceded a part of their territory in consideration of certain annuities provided for them by the Federal Government, and a portion of the tribe moved to Arkansas. In 1832-34 the remainder, numbering about 3,600 ceded the 6,642,000 acres which they still claimed east of the Mississippi, removed to the Indian Territory, and became incorporated with the Choctaw Nation. By a treaty made in 1855 their lands were separated from those of the Choctaws, and they acquired thereby their present very valuable holdings in Oklahoma. In the war between the States, 1861-65, the Chickasaw Nation gave its support to the Confederate Government, as they owned a number of negro slaves and were in entire sympathy with the Southern people. The tribe is now one of the Five Civilized Tribes Confederation in Oklahoma. They numbered 10,966 in 1916, divided as follows: By blood 5,659; by intermarriage 645; freedmen, 4,662. The freedmen are the descendants of the slaves held by the Chickasaws when slavery was abolished by President Lincoln.

THE SEMINOLES.

There were several small tribes that were offshoots of the larger* tribes of the Muskhogean family; but the Seminole is the only tribe, in addition to the three already mentioned, that is of sufficient historic importance to be considered by the writer. The Seminoles were originally a vagrant branch of the Creeks, and the name, Seminole, signifies wild or reckless. They moved from the Lower Creek towns on the Chattahoochee River to Florida after the Apalachee tribe. also a branch of the Muskhogean family, was driven from that country. The Apalachees were friendly to the Spaniards; and the English Government of Carolina sent an expedition against the Spaniards and Appalachees in 1703. The army of Governor Moore was composed of one company of white soldiers and one thousand Indian allies, mostly Creeks. They invaded the Apalachee's country and destroyed their towns, fields and orange groves, killed 200 of the Apalachee warriors and made captives of 1,400 of the tribe, who were made slaves. The following year the English and Indians made a second invasion and totally destroyed the Apalachee tribe in Florida. The Seminole branch of the Creeks took possession of the territory formerly occupied by the Apalachee tribe. While Florida remained under Spanish rule, the Seminoles were very hostile to the United States. They were identified with the Creeks in support of the British in the Revolutionary War and the war with England in 1812. Still later, through British influence, they gave the Federal Government a great deal of trouble. This was during the first administration of President Monroe. The Seminoles began to make violent attacks upon the white settlers in Florida; and General Andrew Jackson, who had already become famous as an Indian fighter, was sent there with general and ample powers to suppress the hostiles. British emissaries were going among the Indians, and were inciting them to the commission of frightful outrages upon the whites. With an army composed of eight hundred regulars, one thousand Georgia militia, the same number of Tennessee volunteers, and fifteen hundred friendly Creek Indians, General Jackson entered upon his task of crushing the Seminole uprising. He accomplished his purpose so effectually that Spain abandoned its claim to the territory, and in 1823 ceded Florida to the United States.

In 1832 the United States made a treaty with a part of the Seminole chiefs, which provided for the removal of the whole tribe to a section west of the Mississippi. Osceola, one of the chiefs of the tribe, and who afterwards became famous, persuaded his people to repudiate the treaty and refuse to vacate their homes in Florida. This provoked a war with the United States which lasted for eighteen years. Though but a very small band of the Seminoles, lead by the fearless Osceola, were engaged in it, the war cost the United States thousands of lives and twenty millions of dollars. At the conclusion of the war, Osceola having finally been made a captive, the greater part of the tribe was located on a reservation on the borders of Arkansas. The story of the long confinement of Osceola in the old fort at St. Augustine, and his refusal to go out with the other Indians who made their escape, is full of pathos and romance.

In the report of the Commissioner of Indian Affairs for the year 1916, it is stated that 574 Seminoles still live in Florida. The men are reported to be splendid specimens of physical manhood by persons from this section of Virginia who make visits in the winter

The above is a portrait of Osceola, and is made from a print furnished the author by the Bureau of American Ethnology, Smithsonian Institution. In 1835 he was treacherously seized by General Jesup, and made a prisoner, while holding a conference under a flag of truce. Broken in spirit from brooding over the manner in which he had been betrayed, he died a prisoner in Fort Moultrie, Florida, in January, 1838.

to the Land of Flowers. From the same report of the Commissioner of Indian Affairs it is learned that the Seminoles exist as a separate nation in Oklahoma, and is a member of the confederacy of the Five Civilized Tribes. They number, 3,127 souls, of whom 986 are called freedmen, being the descendants of former negro slaves.

THE SIOUX OR SIOUX FAMILY.

When the Europeans began to plant colonies on the eastern coasts of the North American Continent there were several large and powerful nations of the American aborigines then occupying that portion of the United States which lies west of the Mississippi

River. The largest and best known tribe of the Siouan family is the Dakotas, now commonly called the Sioux. They exercised dominion over a vast territory that extended from the Arkansas River at the South to the country of the Eskimo in the North; and reached westward from the Mississippi River to the Rocky Mountains. There were several principal and a number of subordinate tribes of the Dakotas, with different languages, customs, and social organizations. The first time the Sioux ever came in contact with the white man was when De Soto reached the Quapaw villages in Eastern Arkansas. The Quapaw were a subordinate tribe of the Dakotas. One of the chroniclers of the De Soto expedition relates that one portion of the Quapaw tribe was found living in a strongly fortified village, which he said was, "very great, walled and beset with towers." He also says: "Many loopholes were in the towers and walls, a great lake came near into the wall, and it entered the ditch that went around about the town, wanting but little to environ it. From the lake to the great river (Mississippi) was made a weir by which the fish came into it." This report is pronounced by American investigators a very great exaggeration, as is also the statement: "And in the town was a great store of maiz and great quantity of new in the fields. Within a league were great towns, all walled."

The Dakotas were first met by the French explorers in 1640, near the headwaters of the Mississippi River; and in 1689 Nicholas Perrot took possession of their country for France. In subsequent wars the French drove them down the Mississippi and they located on the plains of the Missouri. During the Revolution and the War of 1812, the Dakotas were the allies of the British.

The social organization of this nation was originally based upon the plan of groups or bands, of which there was a large number. Each group had a chief who was selected by the members thereof and was chosen for the position because of his personal fitness. His authority was controlled and limited by the band, and he could do but little in matters that affected its interests, without the consent or approval of the members. Marriage outside the group was encouraged, for the purpose of introducing new blood, and polygamy was commonly practiced.

After the United States acquired the territory occupied by the Dakotas, or Sioux, frequent treaties were made with these Indians; by which extensive and valuable boundaries of land were ceded to the United States. Nearly all of these treaties were indifferently observed by the Federal Government, and several wars with the Sioux resulted. The last war with these Indians was fought in 1876. Rich discoveries of gold were made in the Black Hills, the greater part of which region belonged by treaty to the Sioux. A desperate and greedy horde of white gold-hunters and adventurers rushed into the Black Hills, regardless of the wishes and rights of the Sioux. This so enraged the Indians that, under the leadership of Sitting Bull, they broke away from their reservations, roamed through Wyoming and Montana, burned houses, stole horses, and killed all persons who offered resistance. The National Government took immediate steps to force the Indians back to their reservations, sending out for that purpose a large force of regulars under Generals Terry, Crook, Custer, and Reno. Sitting Bull and his three thousand warriors had been driven back against Bighorn Mountain and River, and Generals Custer and Reno were sent forward with the Seventh Cavalry to locate the enemy. These generals divided their forces into two columns and separated. Sitting Bull had prepared an ambush and led Custer and his small body of cavalry into a position where they were forced to charge the large force of Indians. This was on the 25th of June, 1876. In the bloody battle General Custer and every man in his command was killed.

After the battle, the Indians separated into two parties. Sitting Bull was in command of the western party, and was overtaken and attacked and routed by General Miles. A large number of the Indians surrendered, but the remainder of the band, with their chief, escaped to Canada. They remained there until 1881, when Sitting Bull returned with his band to the United States, and under promise of amnesty surrendered at Fort Buford. He was confined at Fort Randall until 1883. In 1888 the Government tried to buy the lands of the Sioux, but under the influence of Sitting Bull they refused to sell. He organized a Ghost dance on the reservation, which meant another revolt. A demand was made for his arrest, and when an attempt was made by some of his people to rescue him he was shot and killed by Sergeants Red Tomahawk and Bullhead of the Indian police, on December 15th, 1890.

The great body of the Sioux had been persuaded to return to their reservation in 1880. They ceded a part of their lands to the United States in 1889. About 17,000 of this formerly fierce and unruly nation are now living quietly, under Government supervision, on their reservation in South Dakota.

THE COMANCHES.

South of the Dakotas lived and roved the wild and fierce Comanches. They were one of the Southern tribes of the Shoshone family and the only one of that group that lived exclusively on the plains. Philologists affirm that from their language and traditions it is evident they are an offshoot from the Shoshones of Wyoming. Both of these tribes have practically the same dialect, and have always maintained the friendliest relations toward each other. They originally occupied, or rather roamed over, the territory now embraced in the States of Texas, New Mexico, Oklahoma, Kansas, Colorado, and possibly parts of other adjacent States. When they first became known to Europeans they lived in the regions between the upper Brazos and Colorado, on one side, and the Arkansas and Missouri on the other. The Comanches were great nomads, were constantly moving about, and lived in tents that were covered with buffalo skins and that were portable. Their great delight was hunting the buffalo, and they were acknowledged the best horsemen of the plains. Originally they were divided into twelve distinct divisions or bands. Only five of these are now said to be in existence.

The Comanches disliked the Spaniards very much and were constantly at war with them when the Spanish Government controlled Mexico. They were very friendly with Americans until they were driven from their hunting grounds in Texas by the settlers in that State. In 1835 they made their first treaty with the United States, and by a treaty, known as the treaty of Medicine Lodge, made in 1867, they agreed to settle on a reservation between the Washita and Red Rivers in Southwestern Oklahoma. But the Indians failed to comply with this treaty until 1875, when they consented to setttle on the reservation. Until that time the Comanches were a constant menace to the settlers in Western and Northwestern Texas. The 1916 report of the Commissioner of Indian Affairs shows that the Comanche tribe in Oklahoma numbers 1,568 persons, who are leading a quiet and orderly life.

THE PACIFIC COAST INDIANS.

West of the Rocky Mountains, in that section of the United States called the Pacific States, lived what have been named by some historians the Nations of the Plains. When the Spaniards extended their discoveries up the Pacific coast and made settlements in California there were about 150,000 aboriginal inhabitants then living in that State. At the present time there are a little more than 15,000 located in California. The majority of them are living as squatters on the land of white citizens or of the Government, while others are on land allotted them by the Government, and some own the land they occupy.

The Indians the white men found on the Pacific coast were divided into a large number of groups, with at least twenty-one linguistic families, or about one-fourth of the entire number found in North America. Of these the Shoshonean and Yuman at the South, and the Athapasean and Klamath at the North, were the principal families. These families were, each, divided into a number of subordinate tribes or units; and they occupied all the Pacific Slope from Lower California up to and into British Columbia.

The California aborigines are among the least known of the groups or tribes of the race that inhabited the North American Continent. They were a timid and indolent people, and the white men experienced very little trouble in depriving them of their lands. The various tribes had no social organizations, and culturally were, perhaps, the rudest and simplest of the several nations of the American race that lived on the continent. They gave no attention whatever to agriculture, but subsisted entirely on fish and game and a wild vegetable diet. Their main vegetable food consisted of different varieties of acorns, and seeds which they gathered from grasses and herbs.

The Commissioner of Indian Affairs states in his 1917 report that there are 15,362 Indians living in California, 6,612 in Oregon, and 11,181 in Washington, or a total of 33,155 in the three Pacific Coast States. Historians and investigators have not suggested any specific cause for the singularly large reduction of the Indian population of California. It may be that two reasons can be reasonably assigned for this peculiar condition, migration and depletion from contact with the evil habits of white men.

THE CHEROKEES.

When the first white settlers came and built their cabins in Tazewell the Cherokees and Shawnees were rival claimants of the territory now embraced in the bounds of the county; and of the entire

Clinch Valley. In fact, both tribes asserted title to all the territory that lies between the Clinch Valley and the Ohio River. Therefore the writer deemed it appropriate to say very little about the Cherokees and Shawnees, until after all other tribes to be chronicled were disposed of. I have made diligent effort to procure all information obtainable about the Cherokees and the Shawnees, so as to be prepared to write a complete but condensed narrative of these two tribes whose history is so interwoven with that of the pioneer settlers. A number of histories have been carefully studied. the Bureau of American Ethnology has been consulted, and correspondence conducted with the Commissioner of Indian Affairs. From these best known sources the most reliable information has been procured and is now used.

The philologists and archeologists who have made the most recent investigations of the traditions and life of the aboriginal inhabitants of America designate the Cherokees as a powerful detached tribe of the Iroquoian family who came originally from the North and settled in the Alleghany region. They first became known to men of the white race when De Soto came in contact with them in 1540. At that time they were occupying the entire mountain region of the Southern Alleghanies. in Southwest Virginia, Western North Carolina and South Carolina. Northern Georgia. Eastern Tennessee, and Northeastern Alabama. and made claim to territory in Virginia and Kentucky that reached as far as the Ohio River and as far east as the Peaks of Otter. George Bancroft, the eminent American historian and statesman, in his splendid history of the United States. thus speaks of the Cherokees and the beautiful country they inhabited:

"The mountaineers of aboriginal America were the Cherokees, who occupied the upper valley of the Tennesee River as far west as Musele Shoals. and the highlands of Carolina. Georgia, and Alabama, the most picturesque and salubrious region east of the Mississippi. Their homes were encircled by blue hills rising beyond hills, of which the lofty peaks would kindle with the early light, and the overshadowing ridges envelop the valleys like a mass of clouds. There the rocky cliffs, rising in naked grandeur, defy the lightning, and mock the loudest peals of the thunder storm; there the gentler slopes are covered with magnolias and flowering forest trees, decorated with roving climbers. and ring with the perpetual note of the whip-poor-will; there the wholesome water gushes profusely from the earth in transparent springs; snow-white cascades glitter on the hillsides; and the rivers, shallow but pleasant to the eye, rush through the narrow vales, which the abundant strawberry crimsons, and copices of rhododendron and flaming azelea adorn. At the fall of the leaf, the fruit of the hickory and chestnut is thickly thrown on the ground. The fertile soil teems with luxuriant herbage, on which the roebuck fattens; the vivifying breeze is laden with fragrance; and daybreak is ever welcomed by the shrill cries of the night-hawk and the liquid carols of the mocking-bird. Through this lovely region were scattered the villages of the Cherokees, nearly fifty in number, each consisting of but a few cabins, erected where the bend in the mountain stream offered at once a defence and a strip of aluvial soil for culture."

What a wonderfully beautiful pen-picture is this of the homeland of the Cherokees, so exquisitely drawn by America's word artist historian. But the gifted writer might have added much lustrous beauty to his painting, if he had, with corresponding skill, portrayed the primitive hunting grounds of these Indians, located in our own delightful valleys of the Clinch and the Holston. What a field for brilliant imagery the word-painter could have found here. The wondrous scenic beauty of Southwest Virginia, generally, and of Tazewell County in particular, has spread their fame both far and wide. Here in primitive days the lofty mountains and towering peaks, clothed with living green in summer time, and clad with fleecy snow and icy pendants in winter season, stood as silent sentinels above and around the magnificent forests of oak, poplar, walnut and sugar maple, that transformed each mountain hollow and valley into a sylvan palace. In these sylvan homes the nightingale, thrilled by the soft moonbeams, warbled its liquid melodies; and the mocking-bird, thrush and oriole, screened from the scorching rays of the noonday sun by the refreshing shade of the sugar tree, carolled their richest and sweetest songs. And here Diana and her companion nymphs might have discovered thousands of crystal springs, in whose pellucid depths they could have seen their ravishingly beautiful forms reflected as no highly polished hand-made mirror could present them. If the fabled gods had once drunk of these sweet, sparkling waters, they would have thrown aside their cups of nectar and declined to quaff again their beverage of distilled honey. Here, too, as natives to the soil, luxuriantly grew the sweetest and most nutritious herbage for animals the wide-world has ever known, the wild pea vine and nature's richest pasturage, the bluegrass. Instinctively, from all regions, east, west, north, and south, came the ponderous buffalo, the heavy antlered elk, and the fleet-footed deer to feed and fatten upon the succulent herbage that was of spontaneous growth in this wonderful country.

Is it strange that every tribe of Indians that ever visited the valleys of the Holston and Clinch on hunting expeditions, or had ever heard of the abundance of game that gathered here, made claim of ownership to this great natural game park? When the white men first came to this section they found not only the Cherokees and Shawnees, but even the Iroquois tribes of New York, asserting ownership of the territory. It was truly a debatable land, to which no one tribe had other than an assumed or fictitious title. This gave to that class of white men known as "Long Hunters" equal right with the nomads to enter and enjoy this Hunter's Paradise. And surely it gave to the pioneer settlers, who were eager to make homes for their families upon its fruitful soil, an undisputed natural right to enter and make proper use of "God's Country," which the aborigines had for so many centuries left a wilderness waste.

Philologists have decided that the tribal name, Cherokee, is a corruption of *Tslagi* or *Tsaragi*, and is said to be derived from the Choctaw, *chiluk-ki*, "cave-people." This name alludes to the many caves that are found in the mountain country where the Cherokees then lived. The Iroquois, their Northern kindred, called them *Oyatage ronon*, which means inhabitants of the cave country. From traditions of the tribe and the character of their language, and from the findings of archaelogists, it has been decided that the Cherokees were originally from the North; but it has been impossible to fix definitely the locality from which they migrated or to determine why they moved to the South.

From investigations made by students of the Indian race, it has been ascertained that the Cherokees were anciently divided into fourteen clans, and that eight of these have become extinct by absorption or from other causes. The names of the seven existing clans are as follows: Ani-waya (Wolf), Ani-Kawi (Deer), Ani-Tsiskwa (Bird), Ani-Wadi (Paint), Ani-Sahani, Ani-Ga'tagewi, Ani-Gilahi. Philologists have not been able to find with certainty translations for the names of the last three clans. The Wolf clan is first in importance and the number of its people; and all the clans are recognized in the printed laws and ritual prayers of the nation.

About one hundred and fifty years after De Soto's disastrous expedition relations between the Cherokees and the English colonists of the Carolinas began; and for a period of nearly fifty years thereafter these red men adhered faithfully to their white friends. In 1729 the two Carolina provinces were separated and named, respectively, North Carolina and South Carolina. The proprietary government, that had been conducting the affairs of both since the colony was founded, was superseded by the appointment of a royal governor for each of the provinces.

As soon as the royal government was established in the Carolina provinces, Sir Alexander Cumming was sent as a special envoy to the Cherokee Nation for the purpose of negotiating a treaty which would make them allies, or rather subjects of Great Britain. The chiefs of the tribe were summoned, and assembled at Nequassee, in the Tennessee Valley, where they were met by the English envoy in April, 1730. They formally acknowledged the King of England as their sovereign, and in token thereof presented the English envoy a chaplet made with four scalps of their enemies and five eagle tails. The Cherokees were then induced to send seven of their chiefs as deputies to England, where they were persuaded to sign a treaty adroitly drawn, which the Indians thought was merely a treaty of alliance—offensive and defensive. One of the provisions of the treaty was that no white men, except the English, should be permitted to build cabins or cultivate the soil in the territory of the Cherokees. The seven chiefs were then presented to King George and his court; and were coolly informed that, by the treaty, their nation had become subjects of England; and that their lands were the property of the British Crown. This was the beginning of a series of deceptions practiced by the white men upon the Cherokees that ultimately deprived them of their cherished homes in the Southern Alleghanies. The Indians, however, for a quarter of a century stood faithfully to their treaty pledges.

In 1755 the Cherokees ceded territory to the British Government and permitted the erection of English forts thereon. About this time the whites began to make serious encroachments upon the tribe; and the wrongs inflicted became so galling to the natives that in 1759, under the leadership of Chief Oconostota, they started a war against the Carolinians. In 1760, Governor Lyttleton of South Carolina sent an invitation to some of the chiefs to meet him in con-

ference for the purpose, if possible, of so adjusting their differences
as to prevent a continuance of hostilities between the colonies and
the Indians. During the conference misunderstandings arose among
the conferees over some matters in dispute; and Governor Lyttleton,
unwisely and treacherously, seized the chiefs and put them in prison.
This conduct of the governor of South Carolina was very justly
resented by the Indians as an act of bad faith. Upon their release
the chiefs returned to their country, and their people were so provoked by the indignity that war against the whites was urged and
was begun. The South Carolinians were so hard pressed by the
Indians that they had to call for assistance from other colonies.
Colonel Thomas Montgomery was sent from New York with two
thousand men to aid the Carolinians. In a short time after his
arrival in Carolina, the militia of the colony, under the command of
Moultrie and Marion, joined his army, and he began immediate
operations against the Cherokees. He invaded their country, burned
a number of their towns and villages, destroyed their growing crops,
and had a number of small engagements with the hostiles. In the
last battle twenty of the whites were killed and seventy were
wounded. The condition and size of Montgomery's army were of
such a character as to render it hazardous to advance further into
the Indian country, and orders were sent him to retreat. This was
done, and Colonel Montgomery returned to New York with his
forces, except four companies that were left as part of a guard on
the frontier to prevent an invasion of the colonies by the Indians.

In 1756 Governor Dinwiddie, of Virginia, made a treaty with
the Cherokees in which it was agreed to build them a fort and place
a garrison there to protect them against their aboriginal enemies,
with the understanding that the Indians would send a number of
their warriors to assist the English in their war against the French
and the Northern Indians. Governor Dinwiddie gave orders to
Major Andrew Lewis, of Augusta County, to raise a company of
sixty men and go with them to the Cherokee country and build a
fort. Major Lewis promptly executed the orders of the governor,
by building a fort on the Tennessee River at a point about thirty
miles from where the splendid city of Knoxville is now located, and
it was named Fort Loudon. During the progress of the war between
the Indians and the Carolina colonies, in 1760, the Cherokees
invested Fort Loudon with a large force and continued to besiege
it until the garrison, from a lack of provisions and ammunition,

T.H.-3

was forced to surrender. It was agreed that the soldiers should
return to the settlements armed and unmolested; but, while on their
homeward march, they were suddenly and violently attacked by a
band of Cherokees and about twenty of the whites were killed.
The remainder, about two hundred, were again made captives and
were held until they were ransomed. The following year, 1761,
Colonel Grant, with the four New York companies and a large
force of militia from the Carolina provinces, invaded the Cherokee
country and made ruthless war against its inhabitants. He gave
them a crushing defeat in battle, laid waste their villages, and
destroyed their crops. The natives who escaped death were driven
into the mountains and were compelled to make an ignominious
peace. Francis Marion, who had accompanied Colonel Montgomery
on his expedition the year previous, was also with Colonel Grant;
and the gallant South Carolinian afterwards wrote a very pathetic
account of the horrors of the Grant invasion. From that time until
after the Revolution the relations between the English colonies and
the Cherokees continued very strained.

Friendly intercourse with the Cherokee Indians had been cultivated and maintained by the Virginia Colonial Government previous
to the time that the pioneer settlers began to press across New
River and locate in Southwest Virginia. Before that period the
Indian traders and parties of hunters from Southside and Tidewater
Virginia had journeyed through or hunted over this section; and
had traveled in many instances on to the Cherokee settlements in
East Tennessee and Western North Carolina, where they were
hospitably received by the Indians.

The Loyal Company, which had obtained a grant for 800,000
acres of land, to be located west of the Alleghanies and north of
the North Carolina line, had sent its explorers and surveyors into
Southwest Virginia. Dr. Thos. Walker, who was chief surveyor
and agent for the Loyal Company, had made repeated expeditions
to the Holston and Clinch valleys, and had surveyed more than
two hundred thousand acres of the most desirable lands of this
section, located at many different points. Many boundaries had
been sold by the company, and the purchasers were rapidly settling
upon them. The Cherokees grew very jealous of this movement
to deprive them of their great hunting grounds and began to manifest a hostile disposition toward the settlers in the Holston Valley.

The Six Nations (Iroquois) of New York also claimed these

hunting grounds, and in fact asserted ownership to all the Virginia territory west of the Blue Ridge Mountains, including the great Valley of Virginia. It was determined by the British Government to secure by treaties a cession of the territory in dispute, claimed by both the Iroquois and the Cherokees. In accordance with this plan, a treaty was made at Fort Stanwix on the 5th day of November, 1768, with the Confederacy of the Six Nations, whereby they ceded to the King of England a vast territory, including the disputed lands in Virginia. The treaty was negotiated by Sir William Johnson, who was Agent and Superintendent of Indian Affairs for the Northern Department of America. Dr. Thos. Walker, Agent of the Loyal Company, was, by appointment, Commissioner to represent Virginia, and as such signed the treaty. As before stated the Loyal Company had sold a number of boundaries of land to settlers in the disputed territory west of New River, and was anxious to have both the Iroquois and the Cherokees renounce all claim to the territory. A number of boundaries in Tazewell County had been sold to different persons, among the purchasers being William Ingles, who had bought lands in Burke's Garden, Abbs Valley, and several boundaries on the headwaters of Clinch River from the Loyal Company. The Iroquois claimed title to the ceded territory by right of conquest. Nearly a hundred years previous to the making of the Fort Stanwix treaty they had invaded the country of the Southern Indians, and had conquered all the Southern tribes, from the Ohio River down as far as Georgia and east of the Mississippi. This included the Cherokees; and that was the reason why the Shawnees, who were a detached tribe of the Iroquois, disputed the right of the Cherokees to hunt in the Clinch Valley about the time the pioneer settlers began to arrive there.

On the 13th of October, 1768, about three weeks previous to the treaty made at Fort Stanwix, John Stuart, Commissioner of Indian Affairs for the Southern District of North America, had met the chiefs of the Upper and Lower Cherokee Nations, at Hard Labor, South Carolina, and had concluded a treaty with them, which fixed the boundaries of their territory or hunting grounds in Virginia. By this treaty the Cherokees acquired undisputed ownership of all the region west of New River, from Colonel Chiswell's mine (lead mines in Wythe County) to the confluence of the Great Kanawha with the Ohio River.

This treaty was very unsatisfactory to the Loyal Company and its agents, and to a number of persons who had purchased lands from the company and settled with their families thereon. These settlers began to contest the right of the Cherokees to enter this section and assert ownership, claiming that the title of the Six Nations was superior to that of the Cherokees and that it had been transferred by the Northern Indians to the British Government. Steps were taken, however, to make a new treaty with the Cherokees; and this was accomplished by Stuart at Lochaber, South Carolina, on the 22nd of October, 1770. By the provisions of this treaty the lines fixed by the treaty at Hard Labor were so changed as to cede to Virginia the territory now known as Southwest Virginia. The lines were afterwards run by Colonel Donelson, who was appointed for that purpose by Lord Botetourt, then governor of Virginia; and the Indians accepted the lines as established by the Donelson survey.

From the date of the Lochaber treaty to the beginning of the Revolutionary War the Cherokees remained at peace with the Virginia Colony. While the war, historically known as Dunmore's War, was in progress, in 1774, there was grave apprehension among the settlers in the Holston Valley that the Cherokees would again make war upon the whites. This alarm was occasioned by a small lawless band of white men led by a man named Crabtree. While on a hunting expedition on the Wautauga River in Tennessee, Crabtree, without provocation, killed a friendly Cherokee who had been given the English name Billey. Major Arthur Campbell, who then had his fort at Royal Oak, just east of Marion, the county seat of Smyth County, and who was commander of all the militia of Fincastle County west of New River, reported the incident to Colonel William Preston, through a letter written in June, 1774. In part, Major Campbell said:

"Sir—Since the rash action of Killing a Cherokee on Wattaugo, the lower settlement on this, and Clynch Rivers, is greatly alarmed. Some preparing to move off, and indeed from the behavior of the Squa & Indian fellow, that Was in Company with the one that was Killed; we may expect a reprisal will be made shortly, if there is not some Men sent to cover the inhabitants, until the matter can be made up with the Chiefs. * * * One Crabtree is generally suspected to be Principal, in the late dispatching of Cherokee Billey. However let the consequence of the affair be what it will, I am persuaded it would be easier to find 200 Men to screen him from the Law, than ten to bring him to Justice; Crabtrees different robberies, the Murder of Russell, Boons & Drakes Sons is in every ones mouth."

The intimation made by Major Campbell that Crabtree might be screened from punishment for his dastardly crimes by a majority of the frontiersmen shows that a very peculiar condition existed on the frontier at that time. Evidently there were either many bad men on the border, or hatred for the red men was so intense with the border men that they would extenuate any offense, no matter how grave and cruel, committed against the savages. The danger apprehended by the settlers in the Holston Valley was happily averted by convincing the Cherokees that the sober-minded men on the Virginia border detested the conduct of Crabtree and his profligate associates. Messengers were sent to the Cherokee towns; and when they returned to the Watauga settlement, it was with the assurance that the Indians would remain peaceful if Crabtree and his associates were repressed. This was done, and peace was maintained with the Cherokees until they were incited by the British to join them in the War of the Revolution.

As soon as the British Government became convinced that it was the purpose of the American colonies to throw off the English yoke and establish an independent government, it was determined by the Royal Government to solicit and organize the Indians as allies to prosecute war against the colonies. Agents were sent to all the Southern tribes to arouse them against the adjacent colonies; and in the spring of 1776 the Cherokees and the neighboring tribes had enlisted in the service of the British Government.

Alexander Cameron was then the British agent with the Cherokee Nation; and it was through his nefarious influence and by his procurement that these Indians became active allies of the British Government. The chiefs and warriors were assembled together, and the desires of the British Government disclosed to them; and they were urged to make ruthless war on the white settlers. Cameron promised them many valuable presents and abundant supplies of arms and ammunition, told them they would be at liberty to plunder the whites who had settled on lands that had been taken from the Indians; and that their hunting grounds should be restored to them. It is not strange that these alluring promises enlisted the support of the rude natives, who felt they had been cruelly robbed by the white men.

Three weeks after the adoption and promulgation of the Declaration of Independence, on the 22nd of July, 1776, President Rutledge of South Carolina notified the Virginia Council, which then had charge of the affairs of the colony, that the Cherokees had begun hostilities against the Georgians, and the Carolinians. On the 26th of July, the Council of Safety of North Carolina sent notice to the Virginians that the Indians were preparing to make an attack on Colonel Chiswell's Lead Mines, in Wythe County, for the purpose of cutting off the Southern colonies from the supply of lead they were receiving from these mines. The Virginia Council determined to act promptly against the Cherokee tribes, and sent orders to Colonel William Preston, county lieutenant for Fincastle County, to erect a fort at the Lead Mines, which was done as promptly as possible. Another step taken by the Virginia Council was the organization of two battalions of militia to send into the Cherokee country. Colonel William Christian was made commander-in-chief of the military expedition as well as commander of the first battalion. Colonel Charles Lewis was placed in command of the second battalion.

In October, 1776, Colonel Christian assembled his small army at Long Island on the Holston River. His entire force numbered but 2,000 men, of whom 400 came from North Carolina. With but little delay the march was commenced toward the Indian towns in the mountains of North Carolina. The expedition was uninterrupted until the army arrived at a crossing of the French Broad River. There a force of about 3,000 Cherokees, with a few Creeks and Tories, were waiting to give battle to Colonel Christian's forces. From fear, or for some other cause, the Indians retreated in the night time and returned to their homes. Colonel Christian followed them to their towns, where he remained for two weeks, and had his men burn the cabins and destroy the corn and other supplies of the Indians. The Cherokees were thoroughly cowed and sued for peace. They proposed to surrender all the prisoners they were holding, to restore the horses and other property they had taken from the white settlers, and to relinquish all claim to the lands the settlers were already occupying. On these terms a truce was effected, and Colonel Christian returned with his forces to Virginia. The following spring a treaty of peace was concluded between the Upper

Cherokee Nation and Virginia and North Carolina at the Great Island of Holston River.

After the making of the treaty at Great Island there were sporadic outbreaks against the settlers that continued at intervals until the Revolutionary War terminated. During this period several bands of the Cherokees moved down the Tennessee River and formed settlements at Chickamauga and at different points on the Tennessee-Alabama line. In 1779 the British agents persuaded one of the Chickamauga bands, who were led by Chief Dragging Canoe, to commence preparations for attacks on the frontier settlements of North Carolina and Virginia. To meet these threatened attacks the two States jointly organized a force of volunteers; and Colonel Evan Shelby was put in command of them. He assembled his army at the mouth of Big Creek on the Clinch River, near where Rogersville, Tennessee, is now located. There, Shelby was joined by a regiment of men, commanded by Colonel John Montgomery, and who had been enlisted to be used as a reinforcement to General Clark, then operating against the British in the Illinois country. Shelby built canoes for his small army and traveled in that way down the Tennessee River until he arrived at Chickamauga. The arrival of Shelby and his army was a great surprise to the Indians. A large amount of supplies that had been furnished the Indians by the British, valued at one hundred thousand dollars, was captured, the towns were destroyed, and the horses and cattle of the Indians were driven back to the settlements. Shelby then destroyed his fleet of canoes and marched his army back to the settlements on foot. This was the last expedition of note made by the Virginia settlers exclusively against the Cherokees.

At last the mountaineer Indians of the Southern Alleghanies were subdued and made to acknowledge the sovereignty of the United States. This was accomplished by a treaty made on the 28th of November, 1785. Under this treaty the Cherokees were given assured unmolested possession of their hunting grounds. "Then began the ever-recurring story of white man's encroachments and red man's resistance, with the ultimate advantage on the side of the intruders." By treaties made in 1791 and 1798 the Cherokees were forced to surrender large portions of their territory to greedy white men and many of their people emigrated west of the Mississippi.

Just about the beginning of the eighteenth century Moravian missionaries began their work among the Cherokees and the Indians

were rapidly becoming civilized and Christianized. but. regardless
of the fact that the Cherokees had rendered valuable service to the
United States in the war with England in 1812-15, the white men
of Georgia demanded the removal of those of the tribe who still
remained in that State.   Drastic laws against the treaty rights of
the red men were enacted by the Legislature of Georgia; and the
Federal Government proclaimed its inability to maintain its treaty
obligations.   Gold had been discovered within the territory of the
Cherokee Nation near the present Dahlonega, Georgia.   This discovery greatly increased the clamor of the white men for the removal
of the Indians to another section of the country.   After a prolonged
but hopeless struggle, which was led by John Ross, the great chief
of the Nation, they were compelled to submit to the white man's
greed and give up their lands and homes.

On the 28th of December, 1835, a treaty was made by which the
Cherokees sold the entire territory they still possessed, and they
agreed to move to the country set apart for them in the Indian
Territory.   The removal took place during the winter of 1838-39;
but was not accomplished without much resistance on the part of
the unwilling Indians, and the infliction of many cruelties by the
white men.   They were driven from their homes by military force;
and in the progress of their tragic exodus, by estimate, lost in
various ways one-fourth of their entire tribe.   Upon their arrival
in the Indian Territory they reorganized their government, which
had first been formed in 1820 and modeled after the government
of the United States.   At the time the main body of the tribe was
removed, several hundred of the unfortunate and persecuted people
fled to the wildest mountain sections of North Carolina, where they
remained unmolested until 1842.   Then, at the earnest solicitation of
a trader named William H. Thomas, the refugees were granted
permission to remain in Western North Carolina, and lands were
set apart for their occupation and use.   A number of their descendants are now living in Swain and Jackson counties of that State on
what is known as the Qualla Reservation.

Since the Cherokees settled upon their reservation west of the
Mississippi they have made marvelous advancement in education
and material prosperity.   In 1821 a mixed blood. Sequoya by name,
invented a Cherokee alphabet, and gave his nation a position in the
literary world, as their books and newspapers have since been
printed in their own language.   Sequoya was the son of a white

man and a Cherokee woman of mixed blood. She was the daughter of a chief. Sequoya was born in the Cherokee town of Taskigi, Tennessee, about the year 1760, and was, therefore, more than three score years old when he made the splendid invention for his people.

The above is a portrait of Sequoya, and is made from a photograph of the bronze statue of the great Indian that was placed in Statuary Hall in the National Capitol, and unveiled June 6th, 1917. The statue was placed there to represent Oklahoma. On the left is a marble statue of Daniel Webster, representing Massachusetts, and on the right a marble statue of Stephen Fuller Austin, who was the founder of the State of Texas. Austin was born in Wythe County, Va. The author is indebted to Senator Robt. L. Owen, of Oklahoma, for the photograph from which the above cut was made.

When the Civil War began, a majority of the Cherokees enlisted in the service of the Southern Confederacy. Many of them were slave owners and were, therefore, under Southern influence; and they may have remembered that the United States Government had repeatedly violated its treaty obligations, and had finally driven them from their cherished homes in the Southern Alleghanies. Some of the tribe adhered to the National Government. Their territory was overrun by both Confederate and Federal military forces, and, as a consequence, they were in a very prostrate condition at the close of the war. By a treaty made in 1867 the Cherokees were again brought under the protection of the Federal Government.

In 1867 the Delawares, and in 1870 the Shawnees, who had been living in Kansas, moved to the Indian Territory. Combined, the two tribes numbered 1,750 souls, and they incorporated with the Cherokee Nation. The Cherokee Commission was created in 1889 for abolishing the tribal governments and opening the Territory to white settlers. Negotiations to that end were carried on for fifteen years before a final arrangement was made by which the government of the Cherokee Nation was abolished on the 3rd of March, 1906. Following this, the Indian lands were divided, and the Cherokees, both native and adopted, were made citizens of the United States. The Cherokee Nation now numbers 41,824 persons, and is composed as follows: By blood, 36,432; by intermarriage, 286; Delawares, 187; Freedmen, 4,919. Of these 8,703 are full blood, 4,778 one-half or more, and 23,427 less than half blood.

THE SHAWNEES.

A concise narrative of the origin and performances of the Shawnee tribe of Indians should be of special interest to the people of the Clinch Valley, and to all persons who have been connected in any manner with this historic section of Virginia. Though the Cherokees asserted superior title or right to this region, and may, possibly, have occupied it for a considerable period to the exclusion of all other tribes of the aborigines, the Shawnees included, there is no satisfactory evidence, visible or tangible, which proves that the Cherokees ever used it for any other purpose than a hunting ground. It is also an undisputed fact that the Shawnees never visited the Clinch Valley with the intention of making their homes there.

The Shawnees were for a long while a difficult problem to investigators of the different families and tribes of the North American Indians. Many theories have been advanced as to their origin, their earliest location, and their relationship and associations with other tribes of their race. But on account of the indefinite character of their name, their innate disposition to wander and to confine their wanderings to the unexplored interior, none of the theories of the investigators have been accepted with perfect confidence. Philologists have agreed that linguistically the Shawnee belongs to the Central Algonquian dialect; and all investigators have confidently announced that the tribe is a branch of the great Algonquian family which at one time occupied the larger portion of the present territory of the United States lying east of the Mississippi River and south of Canada. The Shawnees have been called "The Southern advance guard of the Algonquian stock." Beyond this it has been found useless to try to trace the origin of the tribe or to place them in a location other than that they occupied when they first became known to men of the white race, or in which their indefinite traditions may locate them. Their known history has been traced back pretty clearly to 1660-70. They were then divided into two distinct colonies or bands. One of these was located in the Cumberland Basin in Tennessee, and the other on the Middle Savannah in South Carolina. These two divisions remained separate until nearly a century later, when they got together as one band in Ohio, prior to Dunmore's War in 1774. This peculiar separation of an Indian tribe into two divisions, living so widely apart, has puzzled and confused most of the students of the Indian race. The only reasonable explanation offered for this anomalous condition is that the country situated between the two colonies of the Shawnees was inhabited by the Cherokees. At that time the two nations were enjoying the friendliest relations as neighbors and kinsmen. It is also known that the Cherokees had in the past exercised dominion over the territory in Tennessee and in South Carolina on which the two divisions of the Shawnees were living, and had invited the nomads of their race to cease their wanderings and make settlements on these lands. This view of the matter is strengthened by knowledge of the fact that there is substantial evidence that the two nations intermingled freely and intimately for many years, both in South Carolina and Tennessee. It is further sustained by the fact that the Cherokees resumed possession, under claim of former ownership, of the country in South Carolina and in Tennessee vacated by the Shawnees when they were forced to again become homeless wanderers and traveled toward the North.

The Shawnees who lived in South Carolina were there in 1670, and were there when the first settlement was made by the whites in that province. They were known to the colonists as the Savannahs, and for a long period were the friends of the white settlers. In 1695 Governor Archdale spoke of them as "Good friends and useful neighbors of the English." Their principal village was situated on the Savannah River, and was called Savannah Town. They gradually moved away from South Carolina on account of the unjust treatment they were receiving from the white men. Adair, in his history, says that the Shawnees lived on the Savannah River "Till by our foolish measures they were forced to withdraw Northward in defense of their freedom." And further says: "By our own misconduct we twice lost the Shawnee Indians, who have since proved very hurtful to our colonists in general." In 1690 they began to move from South Carolina. Some of them settled in the Valley of Virginia about where Winchester is located, and others journeyed on to the Cumberland Valley in Maryland. Subsequent to their arrival at these places, they each built villages, one on the present site of Winchester and the other at Oldtown, near Cumberland, Maryland. A part of the tribe that migrated from South Carolina joined the Mohicans, and became identified with them. Others, who had settled on the Delaware, removed to the Wyoming Valley in Pennsylvania. A short time thereafter they were joined by a small band who had located at a point on the Susquehanna River in the present county of Lancaster, Pennsylvania. In 1740 the Quakers began missionary work among the Shawnees at Wyoming; and in 1742 Zinzindorf, the zealous Moravian missionary, joined the Quakers in their effort to convert and civilize these restless aborigines. Under the gracious influence of these excellent Christian workers the savage impulses of the Shawnee warriors in Pennsylvania were suppressed; and for a long time they remained neutral in the French and Indian War, which began in 1754, though their kindred in Ohio were actively engaged as allies of the French against the English.

Owing to the fact that the Western Shawnees were inhabiting the Cumberland Basin, a region that was isolated and not in the usual course traveled by the European explorers, this branch of the tribe was but little known to white men until after the year 1714. In that year a French trader by the name of Charleville went among them at one of their villages located near the present Nashville, Tennessee. They were then being gradually driven from the Cumberland region by the Cherokees and the Chickasaws, with whom, for some unknown cause, they had become involved in war.

Soon after Charleville arrived among them in his capacity of trader, they abandoned the Cumberland Valley, and again became wanderers. They roamed around in Kentucky for about fifteen years. That country, being unoccupied by any other tribe, was an ideal hunting ground. It was peculiarly suited to the Shawnees, who were passionately fond of hunting and greatly averse to agriculture. Blackhoof, one of their most noted chiefs, was born while they were living at a village near where Winchester, Kentucky, is now located. About 1730 they began to cross over into Ohio and to make settlements on the Ohio River, in Ohio and Pennsylvania, their settlements extending from the Alleghany down to the Scioto. They built a number of villages along the river, among them being Sawcunk, Logstown, and Lowertown. In 1748 the Shawnees on the Ohio, by estimate, had 162 warriors or about six hundred persons in that division. A few years later their kindred left the Susquehanna in Pennsylvania and joined them in the Ohio Valley. The two divisions, one formerly located on the Savannah River, and the other in the Cumberland Basin of Tennessee, were united into one tribe for the first time after they became known in history.

Following their reunion on the Ohio River, the history of the Shawnee tribe became a part of the eventful history of that portion of Virginia lying west of the Blue Ridge Mountains and south of the Ohio River; and also of the splendid Northwestern domain, extending north to the Lakes and westward to the Mississippi, which was presented to the United States by Virginia in 1783.

From the middle of the eighteenth century until the treaty of Greenville, made in 1795, the Shawnees were almost constantly hostile to either the English or the Americans. In 1754 what has always been called the French and Indian War by historians was begun. The Shawnees in that war were most efficient allies of the French, who were engaged in a mighty struggle with the English for supremacy in North America. They were the most vital force of the French army that gave such a humiliating defeat to the British army, commanded by General Braddock, in a battle fought near Fort Du Quesne on June 19th, 1755. George Washington participated in the battle as aide-de-camp to General Braddock; and he was singled out by a Shawnee chief and his band of warriors as a special target for their rifles. They fired a number of volleys at the intrepid young Virginian, killed two horses under him and put four bullets through his coat, but Washington made a marvelous escape from death to afterwards become the beloved "Father of his Country."

The French and Indian War was not finally concluded on land until 1760; and the Shawnees were hostile to the English all through the protracted conflict. After France, in 1763, ceded her entire possessions in North America east of the Mississippi, save New Orleans, to the English, the Indian tribes of the North, including the Shawnees, ceased for a brief period making attacks upon the English colonies. But the acquisition of New France by Great Britain gave only temporary rest to the western frontiers of Virginia. Reckless frontiersmen, both from Virginia and Pennsylvania, persisted in committing outrageous depredations upon the Indians who lived in the Ohio Valley; and the pioneer settlers continued to invade and appropriate the hunting grounds of the natives. The treaty of Fort Stanwix, in 1768, and that of Lochaber, in 1770, had accorded the red men lawful possession of all the lands in Virginia beyond the Cumberland Mountains and north of the Ohio River. Encroachments by the white men and reprisals on the part of the exasperated red men finally brought on the war called Dunmore's War. It was almost exclusively a war between the Shawnees and the Virginians who lived west of the Blue Ridge and Alleghany Mountains, and was of short duration. There was but one battle and it was fought at Point Pleasant, where the Ohio and the Kanawha rivers come together. The Virginians were commanded by Colonel Andrew Lewis, and one company was composed of pioneer settlers from the Clinch Valley, who were under the command of Captain William Russell.

A little less than two years after the battle at Point Pleasant the momentous struggle between the American colonists and the mother country began, and the British Government experienced very little difficulty in enlisting the support of the Shawnees against the colonies. During the Revolutionary period, and for some years thereafter, these Indians were the implacable foes of the Virginians; and wrought bloody havoc upon the settlers in the Clinch Valley and in Kentucky. Nearly all the expeditions sent by the Americans across the Ohio while the Revolution was in progress were directed against the Shawnees. With British guidance and support they made stubborn resistance to the Americans, but finally were driven from the Scioto Valley and retired to the head of the Miami River, from which region the Miami tribe had withdrawn a few years previous. After the Revolution was over, having lost the support of the British, a large band of the Shawnees joined the Cherokees and Creeks in the South, these two tribes then being very hostile to the Americans. Another small band united with a part of the Delawares and accepted an invitation from the Spaniards to settle at a point near Cape Girardeau, Missouri, between the Mississippi and Whitewater rivers. Those who remained in Ohio continued to give the American Government much trouble through the years 1791-92-93. In 1791 General Arthur St. Clair, then governor of the Northwestern Territory, found it necessary to undertake an expedition with the intention of destroying the Indian villages on the Miami. On the 4th of November, 1791, he came in contact with the hostiles at a point about fifteen miles from their villages. The Indians had a large force and gave General St. Clair a crushing and humiliating defeat. The American loss in the engagement was thirty-eight officers and five hundred and ninety-three men killed, and twenty-one officers and two hundred and forty-two men wounded. This frightful reverse was a severe shock to both the Government and the American people. General St. Clair, who had made a brilliant record in the Revolution, was so humiliated by his terrible defeat that he resigned as governor of the Territory. General Anthony Wayne was appointed to the vacancy caused by the resignation of St. Clair. In August, 1794, "Mad Anthony," at the head of three thousand men, marched against the Indians on the Miami. On the 14th of the month he arrived with his army at the Rapids, and made an ineffectual effort to negotiate a peace with the Indians. They were so inflated with their success over General St. Clair that they rejected General Wayne's proposition with contempt. On the morning of the 20th the Americans made a rapid advance upon the Indians and soon routed and put them to flight. For three days General Wayne kept his men busily engaged destroying the houses and corn fields of the enemy in that vicinity, and a few days later he proceeded to lay waste their entire territory. Wayne's signal victory so thoroughly cowed the Indians that he had no difficulty in making a satisfactory treaty with them in 1795, by which they were forced to surrender their lands on the Miami and retire to the headwaters of Anglaize River, still further to the northwest. The more hostile part of the tribe left Ohio, crossed the Mississippi and joined their kindred who had settled at Cape Girardeu, in Missouri.

The Shawnees still held the position of leading tribe of the American aborigines inhabiting the country between the Ohio and the Wabash. Tecumseh was their chief, and he was, beyond a doubt, the greatest leader the tribe had ever produced. He had a brother, Tenskawatawa, who was called the Prophet, and who pretended to be in communication with the spirit-world and to receive revelations therefrom. The Prophet secured the confidence of the superstitious members of his own and of neighboring tribes, and gathered a large number of followers in his village at the mouth of the Tippecanoe River. Tecumseh and his brother had originated a plan for uniting all the tribes of the Northwestern Territory in a desperate effort to throw back the invading white settlers, and prevent further encroachments upon the territory of the Indians.

In September, 1809, General Harrison, then governor of the Indiana Territory, gathered the chiefs of several tribes together and purchased from them three million acres of land. Tecumseh not only refused to sign the treaty, but declared he would kill any of the chiefs who affixed their names to the paper. He was encouraged in this course of resistance by the British, as England was then involved in a controversy with United States which eventuated in the War of 1812. In 1811 Tecumseh, at the instigation of the British Government, made a visit to the Cherokees and other Southern tribes to enlist their support of his announced purpose to drive back the white settlers, who seemed determined to keep driving the Indians further and still further west. Demands had already been made by Tecumseh and the leaders of other tribes for an abrogation of the Fort Wayne treaty and a relinquishment of the lands ceded thereby to the United States. This demand was promptly rejected by Governor Harrison. Every movement of Tecumseh and the Prophet showed that hostilities could not be avoided by the Americans, and the Government ordered General Harrison to take immediate steps for the protection of the frontiers from attack. He promptly assembled a force of three thousand men, composed of regulars and militia, at Vincennes; and marched into the Indians' country. On the 6th of November he appeared before the town of the Prophet, and on the following morning, the 7th of November, 1811, the celebrated battle of Tippecanoe was fought and a glorious victory was won by the Americans. After destroying the town of the Prophet, General Harrison marched his victorious army back to Vincennes. The power of the Prophet was broken, and the Indians submissively sued for peace.

Upon his return from the South, Tecumseh found all his plans had been wrecked by the premature battle of Tippecanoe; and he remained in comparative seclusion until the breaking out of the War of 1812. He then gathered his forces, some two thousand in number, and joined the British army in Canada. There he was received most cordially and was distinctly honored by being made

Above is shown a portrait of Tecumseh (properly *Tikamthi* or *Tecumtha*, meaning "Crouching Panther" and "Shooting Star"). He was born in 1768 at the Shawnee village of Piqua, about six miles southwest of the present city of Springfield, Ohio. The portrait is made from a print furnished the author by the Bureau of Ethnology; and Tecumseh is dressed in his uniform of a British brigadier general. He was killed at the battle of the Thames on October 5th, 1813. The shot that killed Tecumseh was fired by Richard Mentor Johnson, a native Virginian, but then a resident of Kentucky. He was Vice-President of the United States 1837-1841.

a brigadier general in the British army. He proved himself a most valuable ally of the British, and fought gallantly at Frenchtown, The Raisin, Fort Meigs, and Fort Stephenson. After Commodore Perry defeated the British on Lake Erie, Tecumseh covered the retreat of General Proctor very effectively, but insisted when the army arrived at the Thames that the British general should make a stand at that river. This was done, and on the 5th of October, 1813, the battle of the Thames was fought, resulting in the overwhelming defeat of the allied English and Indian forces by the

T.H.-4

Americans, who were under the command of General William Henry Harrison.

Tecumseh had a presentiment that he would be killed in the battle. This caused him to discard his general's uniform and to array himself in the deerskin dress of an Indian chief. The presentiment came true, and Tecumseh, the greatest Indian character in American history, fell in front of his warriors while urging them on to battle with the Americans. The war spirit of the Shawnees, and other Northwestern tribes who had come under his influence, was completely crushed by the death of Tecumseh; and very soon thereafter most of the tribes accepted the terms of peace offered by General Harrison.

The division of the Shawnee tribe which had settled some twenty years previously in Missouri did not participate in the War of 1812; and in 1825 they sold their lands in Missouri and moved to a reservation in Kansas. In 1831 the small band who had remained in Ohio sold their lands and joined those who had migrated to Kansas. The mixed band of Shawnees and Senecas at Louiston, Ohio, also moved to Kansas about the same time. About the year 1845 the larger part of the tribe left Kansas and settled on the Canadian River in the Indian Territory (now Oklahoma) where they are known as the "Absentee Shawnees." In 1867 that part of the tribe that was living with the Senecas moved from Kansas to the Indian Territory, and they are now known as the "Eastern Shawnees." The main body of the tribe in 1869, by an intertribal agreement, was incorporated with the Cherokee Nation, with whom they are now residing in the State of Oklahoma.

In 1910 the Eastern Shawnees numbered 107; the Absentee Shawnees 481; and those who became a part of the Cherokee Nation were about 800, making a total of about 1400 for the entire tribe in Oklahoma. The latest estimates given in the 1916 report of the Commissioner of Indian Affairs show that the Eastern Shawnees numbered 152, of whom only 4 are full blood, 26 one-half blood or more, and 122 less than half blood. From this same report it is seen that the number of Absentee Shawnees is 569, of whom 472 are full blood, 80 are half blood, or more; and 17 less than half blood. The 800 Shawnees who were incorporated with the Cherokees in 1869 seem to have lost their identity as a tribe, and from intermarriage or adoption are now regarded as Cherokees.

The latest Government estimate places the entire Shawnee population in Oklahoma at 3,752. Of these 2,746 speak the English language, 2,535 read and write the English language, 3,031 wear citizen's clothing, 3.053 are citizens of the United States, and 846 are voters. These things show that the once fierce wandering tribe is beginning to yield to the force of European civilization, and is gradually becoming absorbed by the American Nation. This happy result has come from proper treatment of the nomads by the Government, and is largely due to supplying them with schools.

VIRGINIA INDIANS—THE PAMUNKEYS.

It may be said that too much space and effort have been given to the Aboriginal Period of a history that was intended primarily to be local in character. However, my work will be incomplete if no mention is made of the tribes that were living in Virginia east of the Blue Ridge when the English settlement was made at Jamestown.

Captain John Smith, who was undoubtedly the most important figure and character among the first settlers at Jamestown, is considered by all historians very accurate in what he wrote about those portions of Virginia of which he had knowledge. He states that there were forty-three tribes in that part of the present Commonwealth that lies east of the Blue Ridge. Of these numerous tribes there are now only remnants of three left in the State, the Pamunkey, the Chickahominy, and the Mattapony; and none of the members of these tribes are of full blood.

The scholarly men who have investigated the origin and names of the various tribes of the American race say that the name Pamunkey is derived from *pam*, which means sloping, or slanting; and *anki*, which means hill, or rising upland. This refers to a tract of land in what is now King William County, Virginia, beginning at the junction of the Pamunkey and Mattapony rivers. There is a sloping hill or rising upland on this tract, and from this the Pamunkeys received their tribal name. Captain Smith said: "Where the river is divided the country is called Pamunke."

At the time the settlement was made at Jamestown, in 1607. the Pamunkey Indians were the leading tribe of the Powhatan Confederacy; and they were then living about the junction of the Pamunkey and Mattapony rivers in the present King William County. Captain Smith then estimated their number at nearly 300 warriors or a total of 1,000 persons. Their principal town, which was destroyed

by the English colonists in 1625. was near the present West Point,
Virginia, at the junction of the two rivers. In 1722 they numbered
about two hundred, and in 1781, Thomas Jefferson estimated them
at about sixty persons of tolerably pure blood.

They were very hostile to the English colonists after the death
of Powhatan. until the death of their chief Opechancanough. and
their frequent conflicts with the white men greatly reduced their
numbers. But in 1654 they assisted the English in repelling an
invasion made by the tribes from the mountains; and in this war lost
their chief. Totopotomoi. and one hundred of their warriors. In
1675, their queen, who bore the title of "Queen Anne," widow of
Totopotomoi, aided Governor Berkeley against the rebels in Bacon's
rebellion. For this service the Indian queen received special recognition from the English Government. In 1722 they numbered only
about 200, and by a treaty were put upon a reservation of three
hundred acres in a bend of the Pamunkey River in King William
County, opposite the historic place known as White House. They
still occupy this same reservation and maintain their tribal organization under State supervision. The population is entirely of mixed
blood and numbers about one hundred and fifty of both sexes. They
live chiefly by hunting and fishing. but engage in farming in a
small way.

THE CHICKAHOMINY INDIANS.

The Chickahominy tribe was one of the strongest and most
important in Virginia when the settlement was made at Jamestown
in 1607. It was connected with the Powhatan Confederacy. but
was not as much subject to the control of the so-called emperor as
were the other tribes that recognized him as their ruler. They were
living on the Chickahominy River when the colony was planted at
Jamestown, and the tribe then had about 250 warriors. or. perhaps.
some nine hundred persons of all ages and sexes. As early as 1613
they formed an alliance with the English settlers and assumed the
name of *Tassantessus*, or Englishmen. There is now a band of mixed
blood, numbering about 225 persons, who are the descendants of the
ancient tribe. but with no regular tribal organization. They live on
a reservation on both sides of the Chickahominy River in the counties of New Kent and Charles City; and are intimately associated
with the Pamunkey and Mattapony tribes. Their principal pursuits
are hunting and fishing.

THE MATTAPONY.

There was a small tribe living on the river which is now called Mattapony, in Virginia. This tribe had the same name as the river upon which they lived. Captain John Smith on his map gave the name "Mattapanient" to the town in which they lived, and it was located in the upper part of the present James City County, near the mouth of Chickahominy River. It was a very small tribe but a member of the Powhatan Confederacy. In 1608, the year after the settlement at Jamestown, the tribe had only thirty men, or a total of perhaps one hundred persons. In 1781, according to Jefferson, they numbered only fifteen or twenty and were largely of negro blood. According to the last census there were about fifty persons of mixed blood living on a small State reservation on the south side of the Mattapony River, in King William County. They are closely related to the Pamunkey tribe, whose reservation is only ten miles distant.

THE INDIANS IN TAZEWELL COUNTY.

In that Chapter of his history entitled "Introduction To Indian Wars of Tazewell," Bickley says:

"I have thought proper to trace the history of the Indians, who have, since 1539, inhabited Southwestern Virginia. These have been the Xualans, Shawnees, and Cherokees, the latter of whom will not be noticed at length. History, indeed, throws but little light on this interesting subject, yet, I imagine, more than is generally supposed."

Dr. Bickley permitted his imagination to get away with him when he asserted that a mythical tribe called Xualans and the Shawnees, in succession, inhabited Southwest Virginia since 1539, until the coming here of the whites. He also drew largely on his imagination by asserting that De Soto with his band of explorers visited the Upper Holston and Clinch Valley regions, that is, "the counties of Tazewell and Washington, Va., as early as 1540." The Bureau of American Ethnology, which, in the Handbook of American Indians, gives the names of the hundreds of tribes and thousands of subordinate tribes that inhabited the North American Continent during the many centuries preceding the coming of the white men to the continent, makes no mention of the Xualans. The Handbook is compiled from the investigations made by numbers of the most learned and diligent ethnologists, archaeologists, and investigators of the Indian race, and none of these found any traces of the so-called Xualan tribe. Bancroft, the diligent researcher and America's greatest historian, says not one word about the Xualans. There is no existing reliable evidence to prove that a tribe called Xualans ever inhabited Southwest Virginia. Nor is there anything to show that any part of Tazewell County was occupied at any time by any portion of either the Cherokee or Shawnee tribes for other purposes than hunting grounds. The Cherokees were chiefly an agricultural people, and they built their permanent homes in a milder climate, where the land was easier cleared of the forests and the soil more easily tilled than in this section of Virginia. When the first settlers came to the Clinch Valley they found the whole region a dense forest, abounding in trees that were of five hundred or a thousand years' growth. No marks were discovered on the soil showing that it had ever been cultivated by the Indians, and no implements, even of the rudest kind, have been found here that were used by the aborigines for agricultural purposes.

To support his claim that an extinct tribe called the Xualans, once occupied the Clinch Valley, Bickley says: that traces of many forts and towns were to be seen in 1852 in Southwest Virginia. He says:

"These cannot be Cherokee forts, though they captured the Xualans, and hence became masters of the country, for they do not build forts in the same manner; beside, the trees growing on some of them, prove, beyond doubt, that they have been evacuated three hundred years. That they were towns as well as forts, is proven by the existence of many fragments of earthenware, etc., found on or around them, and from their shape and general location they were certainly forts."

"They were circular, varying in size from three hundred to six hundred feet in diameter. An embankment of earth was thrown up some five or six feet, and, perhaps, this mounted by palisades. A few of these towns or forts were built of stone and sometimes trenches surrounded them. A stone fort of great size, stood in Abb's Valley, in Tazewell County, Virginia, and has but lately been removed. * * * The remains of a remarkable fort are to be seen on the lands of Mr. Crockett, near Jeffersonville, having evident traces of trenches, and something like a drawbridge. This fort has been evacuated, judging from the timber on it, over two hundred years."

These forts or fortifications were either built by the Cherokees or some one of the tribes that contested with them the right to use the Clinch Valley as a hunting ground. More than two hundred years before the time Bickley was engaged in writing the history of Tazewell County, the Iroquois had driven the Cherokees from their hunting grounds in what is now known as Southwest Virginia; and the Northern Indians held dominion over this territory for many years. In fact, they claimed it by right of conquest until they ceded it to Great Britain by the treaty of Fort Stanwix in 1768. Both the Cherokees and the Iroquois built just such fortifications as Bickley describes and of which there were remains seen in 1852. The Cherokees built similar forts in Ohio before they migrated to the South; and the Iroquois built them in New York. The prehistoric remains mentioned by Bickley were, no doubt, originally fortifications constructed by hunting parties of one or the other of these tribes, while they were hunting here in the summer or fall season.

In the eighteenth century the Cherokees and Shawnees asserted very fiercely rival claims to the Clinch Valley; and, no doubt, had many bloody encounters over the question as to who should occupy it. The last encounter between these two tribes took place in 1768; and the battle was fought on the top of Rich Mountain just west of Plum Creek Gap, and about three miles southwest of the town of Tazewell. Tradition says that about two hundred Cherokee warriors participated in the battle; and the inference is that the Shawnees had a superior force, as they were the attacking party. On the occasion of this battle the Cherokees protected their position on the top of the mountain with a temporary breastwork or fort. Bickley says: "It consisted of a simple embankment, about three or four feet high, running east and west along the top of the mountain about eighty yards, and then turning off at right angles to the north or down the mountain side. The Shawanoes commenced the ascent of the mountain before night of the first day, but finding their enemies so strongly fortified, withdrew and posted themselves in a position to commence the attack early the following morning."

The emergency fort built by the Cherokees on the top of Rich Mountain was so similar in feature to the fort in Abb's Valley and

the one on Mr. Crockett's place near Jeffersonville, that it warrants
the belief that these two were also emergency forts, that they were
built by the Cherokees to protect themselves against a superior foe,
and not for permanent occupation. This was the last battle between
the Indians that took place in Tazewell, and the last in which the
Cherokees and Shawnees were engaged as foes. Though the battle
was fought one hundred and fifty years ago, traces of the breastworks, hastily erected by the Cherokees, are still plainly discern-

   The above scene is a historic one. It is made from a photograph of
Plum Creek Valley, as it now appears, where the first settlements were
made in Tazewell County. The camera was placed a short distance
north of the residence of the late T. E. George; and Thomas Witten,
the first settler, built his cabin in 1767 about half a mile west of the
hay rick shown in the picture. Looking southward, Rich Mountain is
seen; and the little black cross marks "Battle Knob", where the Cherokees and Shawnees fought their last battle in 1768. Some two miles
west of Battle Knob can be seen "Morris' Knob", which has an elevation
of 4,510 feet above sea level. The view from Morris' Knob is one of
the grandest on the North American Continent.

ible. This strongly substantiates the theory that the forts mentioned
by Bickley were built for emergency defence by either the Cherokees or the Iroquois, who, no doubt, engaged in frequent encounters
for the possession of the splendid hunting grounds in the Clinch
Valley region.

   Bickley says: "Both parties were well armed and the contest
nearly equal, the Shawanees having most men, while the Cherokees
had the advantage of the breastworks. Through the long day the
battle raged with unabated vigor, and when night closed in, both

parties built fires and camped on the ground. During the night the Cherokees sent to Butler and Carr for powder and lead, which they furnished. When the sun rose the following morning the battle was renewed with the same spirit in which it had been fought the previous day. In a few hours, however, the Shawanees were compelled to retire. The loss on both sides was great, considering the numbers engaged. A large pit was opened and a common grave received those who had fallen in this last battle fought between red men in this section."

Dr. Bickley further states that he received an account of the battle from a person who received it from Carr, an eyewitness. Dr. Bickley was misinformed as to who furnished powder and lead to the Cherokees after their ammunition became exhausted. Thomas Witten was then living with his family at the Crabapple Orchard; and he was the man who supplied the Indians with powder and lead. This statement is made from substantial traditions that have come down through three several branches of Thomas Witten's descendants. Samuel Cecil was a grandson of Thomas Witten, the pioneer settler, and was born in 1788 at a point within less than a mile of where his grandfather lived. He was told by his grandfather, and by his mother, who was Nancy Witten previous to her marriage with William Cecil, that Thomas Witten gave the powder to the Indians. Samuel Cecil was the grandfather of the author, and I received this information through him. Judge Samuel C. Graham's grandfather was William Witten, a grandson of Thomas Witten, and Judge Graham got a similar account through his grandfather. John S. Bottimore is a grandson of Thomas Witten 3rd, who was a grandson of Thomas Witten, the first settler; and Mr. Bottimore has received the same tradition from his grandfather. Carr was a professional hunter and trapper, still lingering in the Clinch Valley, and may, possibly, have witnessed the battle between the Indians.

CHAPTER III.

THE INDIANS, THEIR CIVILIZATION, GOVERNMENT, MANNERS AND RELIGION.

The civilization of the aboriginal inhabitants of the North American Continent was not only very crude but very diverse from that which was brought here by the Europeans. Man, wherever he has been found. even in the wildest forms of life, has disclosed a sociable nature. and a disposition to have a home somewhere, of some kind. This natural love of man for society and companionship caused the North American aborigines to have both families and communities. As a natural sequence, every Indian community had its social organization and a form of government. The Handbook of American Indians. issued by the Bureau of American Ethnology, has this to say about the social and other organizations of the aboriginal inhabitants:

"The known units of the social and political organization of the North American Indians are the family, the clan or gens, the phratry, the tribe, and the confederacy. Of these, the tribe and the confederation are the only units completely organized. The structures of only two or three confederations are known, and that of the Iroquois is the type example. The confederation of the tribes was not usual, because the union of several tribes brought together many conflicting interests which could not be adjusted without sacrifices that appeared to overbalance the benefits of permanent confederation, and because statesmanship of the needed breadth and astuteness was usually wanting. Hence tribal government remains as the prevailing type of social organization in this area. In most tribes the military were carefully discriminated from the civil functions. The civil government was lodged in a chosen body of men usually called chiefs, of whom there were commonly several grades. Usually the chiefs were organized in a council exercising legislative. judicial, and executive functions in matters pertaining to the welfare of the tribe. The civil chief was not by virtue of his office a military leader. Among the Iroquois the civil chief in order to go to war had to resign his civil function during his absence on the warpath."

Every structural unit which composed the tribal organization was invested with and exercised authority to hold councils for the consideration and determination of its own affairs. They had family councils, clan councils, tribal councils, and confederation councils, each of them exercising a separate and independent jurisdiction. Sometimes the Indians held grand councils, at which questions of vital interest to the tribe were considered and determined. A grand council was composed of the chiefs and sub-chiefs, the matrons, and the head-warriors of the tribe. With a very few exceptions the chiefs of the various tribes were merely the leaders and not the rulers. Most of the chiefs were elective and were chosen because of some particular qualification, such as courage and skill in war, oratorical powers, wisdom in council, and so forth.

The Indians had no written language, and, therefore, could and did not have any written code of laws. Their forms of government were the outgrowth of their instincts and wants as individuals and communities; and were conducted with as little restraint upon personal liberty as possible. Savage opinion sanctioned no laws that restricted the exercise of their passions and restrained personal freedom. Their simple forms of government were established upon the basal concept "that freedom is the law of nature."

A historian has said: "The most striking characteristic of the race was a certain sense of personal independence, wilfulness of action, freedom from restraint." Consequently slavery was unknown among the aboriginal tribes who occupied the regions east of the Mississippi. A mild form of bondage, however, did exist with the primitive tribes that inhabited the region that bordered on the Upper Pacific Coast. With the exception of this area, no traces of real slavery have been found among the Indians who lived north of Mexico. The early French and Spanish historians fell into the error of using the terms "slave" and "prisoner" interchangeably, thereby leaving the impression that certain of the tribes of whom they were writing did make slaves of their enemies, those who were made prisoners in the inter-tribal wars. It is true that the men, women, and children who were made captives were always considered spoils of war, but they were not enslaved. They were either killed or adopted into an Indian family, the institution of adoption being very general among the numerous tribes. "When a sufficient number of prisoners had been tortured and killed to glut the savage passions of the conquerors, the rest of the captives were

adopted, after certain preliminaries, into the several gentes, each
newly adopted member taking the place of a lost husband, wife, son,
or daughter, and being invested with the latter's rights, privileges,
and duties."

The chief motive of the red men for the exercise of the custom
of adoption was to replace the losses their tribes suffered in men
killed in battle, and women and children who were killed or captured
by their enemies. This was done to keep the tribes from dwindling
away, as did most of the Virginia tribes that the white men found
east of the Blue Ridge. The custom was also used by the Indians
toward their white captives. John Salling, who was made a prisoner
in 1726 by a Cherokee hunting party, at or near the Lick where the
city of Roanoke is now located, was afterwards captured from the
Cherokees by the Illinois Indians, and adopted by a squaw of that
tribe, to take the place of her son who had been killed in battle.
Thomas Ingles, who was captured when a small boy at the Draper's
Meadows massacre in 1755, was adopted into a Shawnee family in
Ohio. He lived with the Indian family for thirteen years, and
became so attached to his Indian father, mother, sisters, brothers,
and little squaw sweethearts that he refused to leave them when his
white father sent a man by the name of Baker to Ohio to ransom
and bring him home.

James and Polly Moore, and Martha Evans, who are known in
history as the "Captives of Abb's Valley," after they were taken
to the Shawnee towns in Ohio were similarly adopted. They were
so kindly treated by those who made them members of their families
that they always spoke in affectionate terms of the Indians after
their return from captivity. Bickley says: When Martha Evans and
Polly Moore were among the French, they fared much worse than
among the Indians. The French had plenty, but were miserly and
seemed to care little for their wants. The Indians had little, but
would divide that little to the last particle."

INDIAN EDUCATIONAL SYSTEMS.

After stating that the Indians had no written language and no
code of laws, it may seem paradoxical to say that they had systems
of education. Yet they did educate their young with as much care
along certain lines as any civilized nation gives to the training of
its children. The Indian children were instructed in vocational or
economic pursuits, such as hunting, fishing, handicraft, agriculture

and household work. And in some of the tribes they were taught oratory, art, customs, etiquette, social obligations, and tribal lore.

The red men had a system that in modern parlance would be called kindergarten. At a very tender age the children were put to work at serious business, the girls to household duties and the boys to learn the most important pursuits followed by the men. The children were supplied with appropriate toys or models, which they were required to use as patterns for fashioning similar articles; and, unconsciously, they would develop into basket-makers, weavers, potters, water-carriers, cooks, archers, stone-workers, and agriculturists. The range of instruction was regulated by the pursuits and customs of the tribe to which the children belonged.

When the aborigines came into intimate contact with the white men, the Spaniards, the French, the English, the Dutch, and the Swedes, a new era of secular and industrial education was introduced among the Indians. Christian missionaries commenced their work in Florida, in Canada, in the Mississippi Valley, in Virginia, in New England, in New York, and in New Jersey. The main purpose of the missionaries was to convert the heathen natives to Christianity. Though they failed to accomplish much in that direction, they did succeed in infusing into the Indians many of the industrial processes of the Europeans. From the colonists of the different nationalities that made settlements in North America the red men obtained and learned how to use firearms, metal tools, and domestic animals—horses, sheep, cattle, goats, hogs, and poultry. Possession of these caused a gradual change to take place in the Indian system of education. One of the objects in colonizing Virginia, mentioned in the charter of 1606 and repeated in that of 1621, was "to bring the infidels and savages to human civility and a settled and quiet government."

Henrico College, which was founded in 1618, was intended to be used as much for the education of Indian youths as for the whites. In 1619 the council of Jamestown declared its desire and purpose to educate the Indian children in religion, a civil course of life, and in some useful trade. But the benevolent professions and intentions of the early settlers at Jamestown were destroyed by greed; and a cruel policy of extermination of the natives was substituted for that of education and regeneration of the poor "infidels and savages." The pioneers who settled beyond the mountains in Virginia imbibed this spirit of extermination from the inhabitants who lived east of the Blue Ridge, and drove the natives from the country they had so long loved and occupied as hunting grounds.

After the government of the United States was organized, various Christian organizations established secular day and boarding schools among the Indians. The Roman Catholics, Moravians, and Friends were the pioneers in this work. Later on the Baptists, Methodists, Episcopalians, Presbyterians, and other less prominent denominations also took up the work. When the War Department was created in 1789, Indian affairs were committed to that department of the Federal Government, and remained there until 1849, when the Indian Bureau was transferred to the Department of the Interior.

General Knox, Secretary of War under Washington's administration, made an urgent appeal for industrial education of the Indians; and President Washington united with Knox in the recommendation. It seems that the Knox plan was adopted on a small scale; and, in a message to Congress in 1801, President Adams mentioned the success of the effort "to introduce among the Indians the implements and practices of husbandry and the household arts." In 1819 Congress made its first appropriation of $10,000 for Indian education, and provided that superintendents and agents to distribute and apply the money should be nominated by the President.

In the year 1825 there were 23 Indian schools receiving government aid. The first contract school was established on the Tulalip reservation, in the State of Washington, in 1869, but not until 1873 were government schools proper provided. The Handbook of American Indians, edited by Frederick Webb Hodge, says: "In the beginning there were only day schools, later boarding schools on the reservations, and finally boarding schools remote from them. The training in all the schools was designed to bring the Indians nearer to civilized life, with a view to ultimate citizenship by enabling them to assimilate the speech, industrial life, family organization, social manners and customs, civil government, knowledge, modes of thinking, and ethical standards of the whites."

More than three centuries have passed since the benignant promise of bringing "the infidels and savages to human civility and a settled and quiet government" was written into the first charter for Virginia issued by James I; and the promise is now being successfully carried out by the Federal Government. This is accomplished through government schools for the Indians. The scheme being used by the Indian Office is "to teach the pupils English, arithmetic, geography, and United States history, and also to train them in farming and the care of stock and in trade as well as gymnastics." For this training, day, boarding, and training schools are maintained, numbering in the aggregate 253, with 2,300 employees, and an annual expenditure of $5,000,000.

INDIAN MARRIAGE CUSTOMS.

There was much diversity in the marriage customs of the aboriginal tribes of North America. Though they were so completely removed from what is known as refined civilization, their marital practices were of unusual merit, much superior to those of other barbarian nations. Whilst polygamy was permissible with a few of the tribes, monogamy was almost the universal practice with the nations who inhabited that part of the continent east of the Mississippi. The clan or gentile systems prevailed among all these tribes. These systems were adopted to prevent the physical and mental deterioration of a tribe which would follow the repeated marriage of those who were of near kinship.

When a youthful Indian wanted to get married he would seek a girl who was a competent housewife, and the girl would select for her mate one who was a skilled hunter. Courtship in all the tribes of the Algonquian family were practically conducted alike. The parents of the young couple would generally arrange the marriage, though the young men in some instances were allowed to conduct their own courtship. Among the Delawares the mother would take the presents of game killed by her son to the parents of the girl and receive gifts in return from them. Then, a conference would take place between the relations of the young lovers, and, if a marriage was agreed upon, the exchange of presents would be continued for some time. It is more than probable that all these rude ceremonials were merely formal; and that the lovers had frequent happy meetings before and while their relations were arranging for the marriage.

Marriages among the Iroquois were arranged by the mothers without the knowledge and consent of the young folks. Though the marriage bond was loose, adultery was held to be a serious crime. Divorce was easily effected, but was not considered creditable. A husband could put away his wife whenever he found fault with her, and a wife could separate from her husband with like ease. If the divorcees had children, the offspring went with the wife. Divorces were not as common among the savages as they are now among the English-speaking nations, the American Nation in particular, which boasts of superior Christian civilization.

Like all other races the Indians had both happy and unhappy marriages. Infidelities of a husband sometimes drove his ·faithful wife to suicide; and the faithless wife was without protection, and if her husband insulted or disfigured her, or even killed her, no protest was made by her relations or other members of the tribe.

AMUSEMENTS.

The primitive Indians were of sombre mien and sedate manner. but they had their amusements just as the white races have always had theirs. The dance was almost universal with the American tribes. Their dances were mostly ceremonial, of religion and of war, but they also had the social dance. When not engaged in hunting or on the warpath, much of their time was occupied with dancing, gaming and story-telling. From Hudson Bay to the Gulf of Mexico, and from the Atlantic to the border of the plains, the great athletic game was the ball play, now adopted among the civilized games under the name of *lacrosse*. Athletes were regularly trained for this game. both for tribal and intertribal contests. Roosevelt. who got his information from John Bartram, the great American botanist who visited the Cherokees in 1773, says this about the game:

"The Cherokees were a bright, intelligent race, better fitted to 'follow the white man's road' than any other Indians. Like their neighbors they were exceedingly fond of games of chance and skill, as well as of athletic sports. One of the most striking of their national amusements was the kind of ball play from which we derive the game of lacrosse. The implements consisted of ball sticks or rackets, two feet long, strung with raw-hide webbing, and of a deer-skin ball, stuffed with hair, so as to be solid, and about the size of a base ball. Sometimes the game was played by fixed numbers, sometimes by all the young men of a village; and there were often tournaments between different towns and even different tribes. The contests excited the most intense interest, were waged with desperate resolution, and were preceded by solemn dances.

"The Cherokees were likewise very fond of dances. Sometimes these were comic or lascivious, sometimes they were religious in their nature, or were undertaken prior to starting on the war-trail. Often the dances of the young men and maidens were very picturesque. The girls, dressed in white, with silver bracelets and gorgets, and a profusion of gay ribbons, danced in a circle in two ranks; the young warriors, clad in their battle finery, danced in a ring around them; all moving in rythmic step, as they kept time to the antiphonal chanting and singing, the young men and girls responding alternately to each other."

The warriors and boys of nearly all the tribes amused themselves at target practice with arrows, knives, or hatchets, thrown from the hand, and with both the bow and rifle. Games resembling dice and hunt-the-button were played by both sexes, most generally in the wigwams during the long winter nights.

The women had special games, such as shinny, football, and the deer-foot game. Football was not played by the Rugby Rules, but the main object was to keep the ball in the air as long as possible by kicking it upward. The deer-foot game was played with a number of perforated bones that were taken from a deer's foot. They were strung upon a beaded cord, with a needle at one end of the cord. The bones were tossed in such a way as to catch a particular one upon the end of the needle. The children also had ample amusements. They had target shooting, stilts, slings and tops for the boys, and buckskin dolls and playing house for the girls, with "Wolf" or "catcher", and several forfeit plays, including a breath holding test.

RELIGION OF THE INDIANS.

"The fool hath said in his heart, *There* is no God." This emphatic proclamation by the Psalmist of the mental deficiency of the atheist was not and is not applicable to the North American Indians. They did not strive through mental processes to establish the existence of a first Great Cause, or a self-existent Supreme Being; but with simple, child-like faith they believed that an invisible Almighty Person controlled the heavens and the earth. To him they directed their spiritual thoughts as the source of all power, and they worshipped him as the Great Spirit. They believed that this Great Spirit entered into, directed and dominated everything throughout the Universe; and that he was present everywhere, all the time; ruling the elements, protecting and caring for the obedient and good, and punishing the disobedient and wicked.

Though the traditions of none of the Indian tribes or families

T.H.-5

tell of any direct revelation made to men by the Great Spirit, their faith was as strong in the existence of a Supreme Being and a future life for man after death as is that held by any of the races who worship the God of Abraham, or the God Man, Jesus Christ. To the Indians the mysteries of Life and Light were emblems of Life Eternal. In an address delivered at Boston on the 4th of July, 1825, Charles Sprague, in protraying the characteristics of the North American Indians, thus eloquently spoke of their religious instincts:

"Here, too, they worshipped, and from many a dark bosom went up a fervent prayer to the Great Spirit. He had not written his laws for them on tables of stone, but he had traced them on the tables of their hearts. The poor child of nature knew not the God of Revelation, but the God of the universe he acknowledged in everything around. He beheld him in the star that sank in beauty behind his lonely dwelling; in the sacred orb that flamed on him from his midday throne; in the flower that snapped in the morning breeze; in the lofty pine that defied a thousand whirlwinds; in the timid warbler that never left its native grove; in the fearless eagle, whose untired pinion was wet in clouds; in the worm that crawled at his feet; and in his own matchless form, glowing with a spark of that light, to whose mysterious source he bent in humble though blind adoration."

Moralists and scientists have tried in vain to fathom the depths of the moral and religious tenets of the untutored American aborigines. These simple children of nature, who were as ferocious as the beasts of the jungle when grappling with their foes, in the presence of the God whom they worshipped were as humble and reverent as the most cultured and devout expositors of the enlightened religions of the world. The moral law was given to the Israelites by direct revelation from Jehovah; and was transmitted through his son, Jesus Christ, to the Gentile nations. It was given to the Indians by the inspiration or visitation of the Holy Spirit; and this was why the wild red men of the American forests and plains recognized God's presence in every grandly mysterious or beautiful thing in nature. It was a faith that emanates from the contact of spirit with spirit, the spirit of the Living God touching and enlivening the spirit of the creature, man. Truly has it been written:

"God moves in a mysterious way,
His wonders to perform."

The religious concepts of the North American tribes were more materialistic than rationalistic. They tried to reach the supernatural through the natural, impelled to this by a belief that there is a magic or inherent power in natural objects more potent than the natural powers of man. This idea of a magic power is a fundamental concept of all the Indian tribes; and they believe that the strange power exists in visible and invisible objects, in animals, men, spirits, deities, and so forth. The Algonquian tribes called it *manito,* or *manitou;* with the Sioux tribes it is known as wakanda; and the Iroquois call it orenda.

The aborigines used the word manito to express the unknown powers of life and of the universe. In the vocabulary of the white man manito means spirit—either good, bad, or indifferent. To the Indians the name also signifies, god, or devil, guardian spirit, and so forth.

Most of the tribes believed in tutelary or patron spirits—a belief which strongly resembles the Christian concept of guardian angel. The manito of the individual Indian is supposed to invest him with magic power, and with it abilities to become a successful hunter, warrior, priest, or to imbue him with power to acquire wealth and success in winning the love of women. And the means used by the red men to control or influence the powers of nature were very much like those adopted by the white races. One of these was the use of charms, as still employed by superstitious and ignorant white persons. Another medium was prayer, which the Indian either directed to his individual protecting spirit, or to the supreme powers of nature. They also used ceremonial songs of a peculiar rhythm when making appeals to the supernatural, just as the Jews sing psalms and the Christians sing hymns and anthems in their services.

Among the Indians generally there was a strong conviction that if the supernatural powers were offended by the sin or sins of a particular individual, the powers could be propitiated by punishment of the offender. This was accomplished by driving the offending individual from the tribe, by killing him, or the appeasement could be effected by a milder form of punishment. The milder form was most generally used.

The Indians believe that disease is caused by the presence of a material evil object in the body of the diseased person, or is due to absence of the soul from the body. Such a belief will not appear so unreasonable when we remember that Christ healed maniacs and

epileptics by casting out the devils that were in the poor unfortu-
nates. In their efforts to cure diseases, the Indians employ their
medicine-men, who claim to procure their powers for healing from
or through their guardian spirits. The medicine-man, or shaman
works himself into a state of excitement by singing, by using a drum
and rattle, and by dancing. The Indians, who are very superstitious,
also believe in witchcraft, and that hostile shamans can bring disease
to the bodies of their enemies, and may even abduct their souls.
So believing, the aborigines made witchcraft a great crime; and
punished the witch, but not more severely than did the Puritan
fanatics of New England.

The Indians as a race have rejected the great spiritual verities
that Christ planted in his Church nineteen hundred years ago. Why
have they refused to accept a religion that is so exalted in its purity,
and that awakens not only the holiest emotions but is pillared on
the profoundest reason of which man is capable of exercising? Why
do the red men scornfully turn away from a religion that teaches
the highest moral standards, and that is filled with the elemental
principles of truth, justice, charity and righteousness? There is
not much trouble in finding an answer to these questions. The white
men came among the Indians professing to have a religion that had
been revealed to them by the Great Spirit. They tendered the simple
natives the Ten Commandments, the Sermon on the Mount, and
the Golden Rule as divine revelations to men. These the white men
professed to believe and to practice. Naturally the aborigines made
the practices of the so-called Christians the touchstone by which
to test not only the sincerity of the white man's professions, but
to fathom the quality of the new religion that was brought from
beyond the seas. The Spanish discoverers and conquerors, and the
French and English colonists, each and all, came to the New World
proclaiming their desire and purpose to convert the heathen natives
to Christianity. But the great human passions—greed of gold, and
lust of pleasure in its most sensuous forms—not only caused them to
desecrate the holy banner they bore aloft, but to violate every
precept of the Decalogue, the Sermon on the Mount, and the Golden
Rule. They murdered and robbed the Indians, destroyed and drove
them from their homes, and dishonored their women. Their crimes
were not confined to the poor natives; but they oppressed, killed
and robbed each other; frequently assigning their fanatical religious

beliefs as a justification for committing the vilest crimes against men and women of their own race. Menendez, the Spanish brute, massacred the entire colony of French Huguenots on the St. John's River in Florida, offering as an excuse for the crime that they were Protestants, or heretics; the Cavaliers of the Anglican Church in Virginia outlawed the dissenters, the Baptists and Presbyterians, and drove them from the colony to North Carolina and Maryland; and the Puritan Calvinists of Massachusetts and the other New England colonies organized at Boston a military force which was sent to Nova Scotia to destroy the homes and drive into exile the French inhabitants of Acadia. Bancroft says: "Seven thousand of these banished people were driven on board ships and scattered among the English colonies from New Hampshire to Georgia; one thousand to South Carolina alone." Their houses and barns were destroyed with the torch, and large numbers of cattle, hogs, sheep, and horses were forcibly taken and divided as spoils among the English officers. The annals of the human race record no fouler crime than the one which the men of England and New England committed upon the defenceless French inhabitants of Acadia, who were made objects of cruel vengeance, because as they declared: "We have been true to our religion, and true to ourselves." The Christian religion is pure and holy, and should be accepted by all men; but is it any wonder that the North American Indians rejected, and still reject it, after witnessing its perverted exemplification by the brutal white men who claimed to be Christians?

Period of Discovery and Colonization

Relating the Discoveries and Conquests of the
Spaniards, and the Discoveries and Settlements of the French and English
in America.

PERIOD OF DISCOVERY AND COLONIZATION

CHAPTER I.

In the preparation of a purely local history much trouble is experienced by a writer in selecting, from many collated facts, the things most important and only essential as a prelude to the discussion of the particular subject of which he intends to write. This difficulty has confronted the writer while preparing to write the Pioneer Period of Tazewell County. Most of the local historians of this country have considered it necessary to introduce in the opening chapters of their books a considerable amount of information about the first discoveries of the North American Continent; and also to write much of the performances of the first settlers on its shores. Our historians in Virginia, both State and local, have followed this course with such thoroughness and so admirably that it seemed useless for another to repeat what they have already done so well. But I have found it necessary to enlarge upon the plan outlined in my "Announcement" and have added another Period, which I will call "The Period of Discovery and Colonization." This will be seen to be an important necessary link to connect the Aboriginal with the Pioneer Period.

As to those who have been reputed the very first discoverers of the New World, there is as much of fable as of reasonable fact. It has been claimed, and generally accepted as true, that the first white men who ever caught sight of the Western Continent were with a Norse navigator who had the name of Herjulfson. He was sailing from Iceland to Greenland A. D. 986, was caught in a storm, and was driven westward to Newfoundland or Labrador. Herjulfson saw the shores of a new country but made no attempt to go on shore. Upon his return to Greenland, he and his companions told wonderful stories of the new land they had seen in the west.

E. Benjamin Andrews in his history of the United States says: "It is a pleasing narrative, that of Lief Ericson's sail in 1000-1001 to Helluland, Markland, and at last to Vineland, and of the subsequent tours of Thorwald Ericson in 1002, Thorfinn Karlsefue, 1007-1009, and of Helge and Finnborge in 1011 to points still farther away. Such voyages probably occurred. As is well known,

Helluland has been interpreted to be Newfoundland; Markland, Nova Scotia; and Vineland, the country bordering Mount Hope Bay in Bristol, R. I. These identifications are possibly correct, and even if they are mistaken, Vineland may still have been somewhere upon the coast of what is now the United States."

As these stories are said to have been taken from Icelandic manuscripts of the fourteenth century, without any substantial supporting evidence being found on this continent, there is grave doubt whether the sea-rovers from the North ever made any prolonged stay on American soil. Therefore it is claimed that Christopher Columbus should be accorded the honor of being the first discoverer of America. Columbus made his first voyage of discovery in 1492, and landed on the island he named San Salvador on the 12th of October of that year. Before returning to Spain he discovered Cuba and Hayti and built a fort on the latter island. In 1493 he made a second voyage from Spain, starting out from Cadiz. This expedition was not completed until 1496, and during its progress he discovered the Lesser Antilles, Porto Rico, and Jamaica. In a third voyage, made in 1498-1500, he found Trinidad and reached the mainland of South America at the mouth of the Orinoco River. On his second voyage he had established a colony in Hayti and appointed his brother governor. Upon his return from the South American coast he found the colony in Hayti in a badly disorganized condition. He was attempting to restore order when he was seized by Francisco de Bobadilla, who had been sent from Spain to investigate charges of maladministration against Columbus. The great navigator was put in chains and sent back to Spain but the king repudiated the act of Bobadilla, set Columbus free, and started him on his fourth voyage in search of the Indies. This voyage resulted in nothing more than explorations along the southern coast of the Gulf of Mexico. Disappointed with the results of his last undertaking, he returned to Spain and found that Queen Isabella, his great friend and patron, was dead. Friendless and neglected, he died May 20th, 1505, and became famous to future generations. It is a remarkable fact that Columbus never placed his feet on the North American Continent. He died without knowing that he had discovered a new continent, and claimed till the last that he had reached the coast of India. Columbus had, he believed, accomplished the chief purpose of his perilous voyages, that is, gained access to the rich treasures of the Indies. He was a devout Catholic and a cordial hater of the Turk, whom he wished to drive from Europe and the Holy Land. John Fiske in his very interesting book, "Old Virginia And Her Neighbors", says:

"The relief of the church from threatening dangers was in those days the noblest and most sacred function of wealth. When Columbus aimed his prow westward from the Canaries, in quest of Asia, its precious stones, its silk stuffs, its rich shawls and rugs, its corals and dye-woods, its aromatic spices, he expected to acquire vast wealth for the sovereigns who employed him and no mean fortune for himself. In all negotiations he insisted upon a good round percentage, and could no more be induced to budge from his price than the old Roman Sybyl with her books. Of petty self-seeking and avarice there was no more in this than in commercial transactions generally. The wealth thus sought by Columbus was not so much an end as a means. His spirit was that of a Crusader, and his aim was not to discover a New World (an idea which seemed never to have once entered his head), but to acquire the means for driving the Turk from Europe and setting free the Holy Sepulchre. Had he been told upon his melancholy death-bed that instead of finding a quick way to Cathay he had only discovered a New World, it would probably have added fresh bitterness to his death."

At the time Columbus was preparing for a second voyage to the New World, Amerigo Vespucci, a native of Florence, was at the head of a Florentine mercantile firm in Seville. He was a naval astronomer of considerable attainments; and, having heard of the wonderful discoveries made by Columbus, he became very eager to enter the field of discovery. On the 20th of May, 1499, he sailed with an exploring expedition, commanded by the Spanish Admiral Hojeda, from Cadiz. This expedition first landed on what is now the Venezuelan coast of South America. He made explorations in the Bay of Paria, which lies between the Island of Trinidad and the mainland, and he also sailed several hundred miles along the South American coast. Admiral Hojeda returned to Spain with his squadron in the early autumn of the same year.

Another expedition was promptly fitted out, and Vespucci, in December, started on his second voyage. This time his only accomplishment was the discovery of groups of small islands on the south of the Gulf of Mexico. After his return to Spain from the second voyage, Emanuel, King of Portugal, persuaded Vespucci to quit

the service of Spain and enter that of Portugal; and he made two
voyages, beginning the first on the 10th of May, 1501, and the
second on the 10th of May, 1503. The chief purpose of the Florentine was to sail westward with a view of discovering a passage to
Malaca, which was then the extreme point on the Malay coast that
had been reached by European navigators. His fleet for the last
voyage consisted of six ships, but one of these was lost in a storm.
After encountering and escaping many perils, Vespucci at last
reached safety with his five vessels in what is now called "All Saints
Bay" on the coast of Brazil. Then it was that the Florentine
realized that he had discovered a new continent, and upon his
return to Europe he so reported. Columbus having made the mistake of claiming to have reached India when he landed on the South
American coast; and the Cabots having announced that they had
reached the continent of Asia on their several voyages to the coasts
of North America, it was reserved for Amerigo Vespucci to first
make known to Europe the fact that the continent which the Norse-
men, and Columbus, and the Cabots had repeatedly visited was not
a part of Asia, but was a newly discovered and distinct continent.
It was, therefore, very natural that when Amerigo published a
narrative of his voyages the new continent should be given his
name, America, as an honor justly due him. There has been much
adverse criticism of the Florentine, because of the belief that he
cunningly appropriated an honor that belonged of right to Christopher Columbus. It was also charged by his enemies and detractors
that he was a man of inferior ability, with very limited knowledge
of the sciences necessary to make him a successful navigator. Baron
Humboldt and other distinguished scientists, who made investigations, defended him against these aspersions; and assert that it was
his excellent knowledge of various branches of science that caused his
selection as naval astronomer for the several expeditions he conducted or accompanied across the Atlantic. It is also a notable fact
that Christopher Columbus and Amerigo Vespucci were intimate
friends after they had each made voyages, though Columbus disputed until the day of his death that a new continent had been discovered.

The discovery of America not only created intense interest
among the scientific and scholarly men of the Old World, but
excited in the countries of Western Europe an unusual spirit of

enterprise and adventure. This was especially manifest in Spain, occasioned, no doubt, by the fact that the discovery had been accomplished with the liberal aid and patronage of Spanish sovereigns. Within the space of ten years after the death of Columbus the larger islands of the West Indies had been explored and Spanish colonies established upon them. The first continental colony planted by the Spaniards was on the Isthmus of Darien in 1510, and three years later the governor of that colony, Vasco Nunez De Balboa, made his way across the Isthmus and discovered the mighty ocean that covers about two-fifths of the entire surface of the world.

There was a succession of explorations and colonizations made by other Spaniards in ensuing years. Juan Ponce De Leon started out from Porto Rico, of which island he was governor, in 1512 in search of a mythical fountain of youth, which was believed to be located somewhere in the Bahamas. Being an old man, he was ambitious to be made young again; and was foolish enough to have faith in the fabulous tales he had heard about this fountain of youth. Having failed to find the fountain in the Bahamas, he sailed toward the coast of Florida, and on Easter Sunday, the 27th of March, he looked upon an unknown beautiful shore. A few days later a landing was made a short distance north of where the city of St. Augustine was started about a half a century later. Ponce De Leon was so charmed with the many beautiful flowers that abound in that land, he named the country Florida, the "Land of Flowers." Afterwards the King of Spain made Ponce De Leon governor of Florida; but he did not return to the new province until the year 1521. Upon his arrival he found the natives in a very hostile mood. Shortly after they had landed the Spaniards were furiously attacked by the Indians, and a number of the white men were killed. The remainder fled to their ships, taking with them their leader who had been mortally wounded with an arrow. Ponce De Leon was carried back to Cuba, where he died from the wound.

In the year 1517 Fernandez De Cordova discovered Yucatan and the Bay of Campeachy. His company was attacked by the natives and he received a mortal wound. The following year Grijalva, assisted by Cordova's pilot, made extensive explorations of the coast of Mexico; and in 1519 Hernando Cortes began his famous conquest of the Aztec empire.

The next discovery of importance was made by Fernando De Magellan, the famous Portuguese navigator. He had petitioned the

King of Portugal in vain for ships to make a voyage in search of a
southwest passage to Asia. The court of Portugal gave such deep
offense to Magellan that he traveled to Spain, accompanied by his
countrymen, Ruy Falero, who was an excellent geographer and
astronomer. He succeeded in interesting Charles V., King of Spain,
in his plans for seeking a southwest passage, and procured ample
assistance from that monarch. Magellan sailed in September, 1517,
with five ships and two hundred and thirty-six men. Heading
direct for the South American coast, he arrived safely at the mouth
of the La Plata River. Thence he sailed along the coast of Pata-
gonia, passed through the strait which has since borne his name,
entered the southern Pacific Ocean, giving it that name on account
of the beautiful weather which prevailed when he sailed into its
waters. He then started out to complete his voyage around the
world; but was prevented from accomplishing in person his ardent
desire by his unfortunate death, which occurred on one of the
Philippine Islands in a fight with the natives. in April, 1521. A
new captain took charge of his ship and carried it back to Spain by
way of the Cape of Good Hope, arriving at home in September,
1522. Thus was completed the first voyage around the world.

In the year 1520 a very disgraceful expedition was undertaken
by Lucas Vasquez De Ayllon, who had become very rich as a
Spanish judge in San Domingo. The object of this expedition was
to kidnap the natives from the Bahamas to be used as slaves by
De Ayllon and other unscrupulous planters on their plantations in
San Domingo. De Ayllon sailed with two vessels for his proposed
destination, but a storm drove them out of their course and onto the
coast of South Carolina. The ships were sailed into St. Helena
Sound, and their anchors lowered at the mouth of the Combahee
River. De Ayllon gave the name Chicora to the country, and called
the river the Jordan. The natives were exceedingly timid but kind
and friendly to the strange visitors, and gave them presents of their
simple food, and rude trinkets. Their curiosity was aroused, and
a sufficient number to crowd the ships were lured on board, when the
brutal commander of the expedition ordered the anchors to be
weighed and started on the return voyage with his slaves to San
Domingo. A heavy storm was encountered, one of the ships found-
ered, and the poor creatures, who had been imprisoned under the
hatches of the ship, were rescued by death from the horrible fate
that awaited them as slaves in San Domingo. This was the first

effort of the Spaniards to make slaves of the Indians. The discovery of Chicora was reported to Charles V., King of Spain, and he appointed De Ayllon governor of the newly discovered country, granting him the right to make conquest thereof. De Ayllon returned with a small fleet to his province in 1525, but his best ship was grounded in the Jordan when he entered that river. The Indians recalled the cruel outrages they had suffered on the previous visit of the Spaniards, their timidity was replaced with desperate courage, and they made a furious attack upon the occupants of the grounded ship, killing a number of the invaders. The survivors were glad to escape with their lives, and hastily started back to San Domingo. De Ayllon was greatly humiliated by the failure of his expedition, and he was ruined in fortune and favor with the Spanish Government.

Pamphilo de Narvaez was appointed governor of Florida in the year 1526 by Charles V., King of Spain, with the privilege of conquest, as had been given Cortes, Pizarro and other Spanish adventurers who brought expeditions to America. A very extensive territory both east and west of the Mississippi was included in his commission. He went to Florida with three hundred soldiers, of whom forty were cavalrymen. The object of the expedition was more for hunting gold than for colonization. In some way the natives found out the motive of the invaders, and practiced a shrewd deception upon them. The Indians exhibited small gold trinkets and pointed to the North. This greatly excited the avaricious Spaniards, who inferred that the natives were telling them that there were rich gold fields and large cities in the North, like those Cortes had found in Mexico, and Pizarro in Peru. The Spaniards started out through the dense forests in search of the great wealth they believed would be found in the North. Instead of finding cities and gold, they came to impenetrable swamps and encountered small bands of savages who lived in squalid villages consisting of a few rude huts. After many days travel in what is now Georgia and Alabama, they were so fatigued and scant of food that they determined to return to their ships on the coast; and finally arrived at St. Marks harbor. But the ships they expected to find were not there. Desperately situated, the remnant of the band built some small boats, which they entered, and started out with the hope of reaching a Spanish settlement in Mexico. Storms came upon them, they were driven out of sight of land and then thrown back upon the coast. Some were drowned, others were killed by the Indians, and some were starved to death. The boat in which Narvaez was traveling was sunk near the mouth of the Mississippi and he perished there. Only four of the entire expeditionary force succeeded in reaching Mexico; and they wandered across the continent to the village of San Miguel on the Pacific Coast. From that place they ultimately found their way to Mexico.

One of the most distinguished Spanish cavaliers who accompanied Pizarro to Peru was Ferdinand De Soto. He was of noble birth, was an intimate friend of Pizarro, and had returned from Peru to Spain with vast wealth he had gathered in the land of the Incas. His great popularity in Spain made it easy for him to secure an appointment as governor both of Cuba and Florida, with ample authority granted for making conquest of the Land of Flowers. A very large number of wealthy and high-born Spaniards made eager application for enlistment under De Soto to accompany him on his expedition to Florida. From the numerous applicants he carefully selected six hundred, whom he considered the most gallant and be: fitted for the service and hardships he knew would have to be endured. These cavaliers were splendidly equipped with the finest suits of armor, made after the pattern of those worn by knights in the days of chivalry. Careful preparations were made to have this excel in splendor all other expeditions that had gone from Spain to make conquests in the New World. Arms in abundance and large stores of supplies of the first quality were assembled; trained artisans, with ample tools for forges and work-shops were added; and bloodhounds to chase down the fleeing natives and chains to bind them when made captives were also made part of the equipment. A herd of swine, to be fattened on the corn of the natives and the acorns and nuts that grew in the vast forests that were to be explored, was also provided. Twelve priests of the Holy Catholic Church were enlisted to look after the spiritual welfare of the gay cavaliers, and to make converts to Christianity of the heathen natives. It is possible these priests were sent by the Spanish Inquisition, hence the trained bloodhounds to chase the poor Indians and the shackles to bind them with when made captives.

A year was occupied by De Soto in extensive preparation for his wonderful expedition of discovery and conquest. In the spring of 1539 his squadron of ten vessels sailed from the harbor of San Lucar with his eager and impatient six hundred followers aboard. It required but a few weeks to make the voyage to Havana. There he left his wife in charge of his own and the island's affairs until he could return with greatly added wealth and glory from his exploration of Florida. He sailed from Havana after a brief stay there, and in the early part of June sailed into Tampa Bay. A number of Cubans had joined the expedition, but a part of these were so terrified by the awful gloom of the forests and swamps they saw in Florida that they separated from De Soto and returned to Cuba. De Soto and his intrepid followers made but little delay in beginning what proved a disastrous march into the interior in search of the mystic El Dorado they confidently hoped to reach. The months of July, August and September were fully occupied with an energetic march toward the North. The explorers struggled through almost impenetrable swamps, swam rivers and had frequent encounters with the Indians, whom De Soto found were much bolder and more effective fighters than the aborigines he had helped to conquer in Peru. In the month of October they reached Flint River in Georgia, and there came in contact with the Appalachian Indians, with whose several tribes they were to have many experiences in the future. De Soto concluded to winter there; and, having done this, in the early spring of 1540 the march was resumed and was turned into an almost senseless wandering over the territory now constituting the States of South Carolina, North Carolina, Georgia, Alabama, Mississippi, and Tennessee, east of the Mississippi River; and Missouri, Arkansas and Oklahoma on the west of the river. In the spring of 1541 the Indian guides brought the Spaniards to the Mississippi; and the great "Father of Waters" was revealed for the first time to white men, as De Soto and his followers gazed upon it. In the latter part of May the Spaniards crossed the Mississippi. They began their roving journey over the territory west of the river and did not return to its western banks in the neighborhood of Natchez until 1542. The spirit of the ambitious leader was completely crushed. He was stricken with a malignant fever which soon caused his death, and he was buried in the great river which has ever since been historically and dramatically associated with the name of De Soto.

Previous to his death, De Soto had selected as his successor Moscoso, one of his most trusted lieutenants. Under his leadership the depleted band of ragged and starving adventurers resumed their journey in search of the riches for which they had already expended two years of fruitless endeavor. They wandered back in a westwardly course until they came to the upper waters of Red River on

the northern borders of Texas. Then they turned northward and
wandered through the territory occupied by the Pawnee and
Comanche tribes of Indians, still hunting for gold. At last they
came to such rugged and barren mountains, and were so discouraged
that they turned back and again came to the Mississippi River, a
short distance above the mouth of Red River. Overcome with
despair, the remnant of De Soto's gay band of cavaliers decided to
build boats and travel down the Mississippi to the Gulf, and then
try to reach a Spanish settlement in Mexico. In pursuance of this
resolution, they cut trees from the forests, and sawed them into
lumber, built forges and turned all the iron and steel they had,
including the fetters of the captive natives, into nails and other
iron pieces necessary for the construction of their boats. In this
way they succeeded in making seven brigantines and on the 2nd
day of July, 1543, they began their voyage down the river. Seventeen days were necessary to reach the Gulf. They then headed their
boats westward, and in fifty-five days after entering the Gulf they
came to the Spanish settlement at the mouth of the River of Palms.

More than twenty years passed away after the disastrous De
Soto expedition before Spain made another attempt to plant a colony
in Florida. In 1565 an enterprise for that purpose was entrusted
to Pedro Menendez de Aviles, a soldier of notorious criminal character and vicious disposition. At that time Philip II. was King of
Spain, having succeeded his father, Emperor Charles V. Philip had
adopted his father's policies for the government of his kingdom and
empire, the chief of which policies were the maintenance and extension of absolute rule throughout his dominions and a zealous support
and propagation of the Catholic religion. Like his father, he was
an ambitious despot and fanatical supporter of the Spanish Inquisition. He hated the Protestants and was anxious to destroy a colony
of French Huguenots who made a settlement in Florida on the St.
Johns River, about thirty-five miles above its mouth. This settlement was within the limits of the territory claimed by Spain. In
fact, Spain asserted title to all of North America, by virtue of a
bull issued by the Pope of Rome, who assumed to exercise temporal
as well as spiritual power over the entire world. Philip was determined to apply not only his principle of absolutism to his American
dominions, but to enforce the decrees of the Inquisition here as well
as in Spain. Hence the selection of the brutal fanatic Menendez,
who was given a commission to explore and make conquest of

Florida and establish a colony there. In compensation for his base performances, Menendez was to receive an annual salary of two thousand dollars and two hundred and twenty-five square miles of land to be located in proximity to the colony. The spirit of adventure and the hunger for gold were still rampant in Spain, and with very little trouble Menendez assembled twenty-five hundred persons, many of whom were married men with families, that were eager to accompany the expedition. He started out from Spain with his large fleet in July, 1565, reached Porto Rico early in the month of August, and on the 28th day of the same month arrived on the Florida coast. It was St. Augustine's day when the coast came in view, but a landing was not effected until the 2nd of September. When a location for the colony had been selected, the Spanish leader named it St. Augustine, in honor of the Saint of that name. This was the first permanent settlement made by people of the white race within the present bounds of the United States. It was destined to become one of the most historic spots in our land. Subsequent to its founding, the place was the scene of many tragic events. The French and hostile Indians repeatedly attacked it; in 1586 it was captured and pillaged by England's most renowned sea-rover, Sir Francis Drake, and by pirates in 1665. Frequent assaults were also made by the English and Huguenot colonists of the Carolinas. Great Britain acquired St. Augustine under a treaty with Spain in 1763, and made use of it as an important military station during the Revolutionary War. It was afterwards possessed by Spain, and in 1819 was ceded to the United States.

With but little delay after making a landing and starting his colony, Menendez began to execute his plans for the destruction of the French heretics. The Huguenots thought the Spaniards would bring their vessels up the St. Johns and make an attack; and committed the serious mistake of sending their few ships and nearly all their men down the river to anticipate the enemy by making an attack upon them. After the French got their ships out on the sea a very heavy storm burst upon them; their ships were driven on the coast, and all but two of the vessels were dashed to pieces. Most of the men, however, reached the shore in safety. Menendez, having found out the unprotected condition of the Protestant colony, gathered his forces together, and made a secret and rapid march through the swamps, fell upon the surprised and helpless colony and slaughtered men, women and children without mercy. About two hundred persons were slain by the Spanish butchers, only a few members of the colony escaping, among these their leader, Laudonniere. Then Menendez turned his attention to the men who had escaped when their vessels were wrecked. They were induced to surrender to the Spaniards, with assurance that they would be humanely treated and their lives protected. Immediately after their surrender, each captive had his hands bound behind him and two prisoners were then tied together. They were then marched toward St. Augustine; and as they approached the Spanish fort a trumpet was sounded. This was a signal for their slaughter; and the seven hundred unhappy prisoners were killed by the cut-throat minions of Menendez. With this terrible tragedy and the permanent establishment of the colony at St. Augustine, the period of Spanish voyage and discovery as to the North American Continent seems to have been terminated. Spain does not now own or exercise control over a foot of land in either of the Americas. This looks like retributive justice visited upon the Spanish Nation for the barbarous cruelties practiced upon the aboriginal inhabitants and the Protestants who came from France and other countries of Europe that they might enjoy religious freedom in the New World.

CHAPTER II.

FRENCH DISCOVERIES AND SETTLEMENTS.

The discoveries made by Columbus and other navigators aroused great interest in France. John Cabot's discovery of Newfoundland attracted the attention of the fishermen of Normandy and Brittany. They had heard of the wonderful fishing banks found about the shores of Newfoundland, where the schools of cod and other varities of fishes were so great that it was difficult to steer a ship through them; and in 1540 these fishermen began to sail across the ocean to try the fishing grounds that are still famous. An adventurous Frenchman by the name of Denys made a map of the Gulf of St. Lawrence in the year 1506, a hundred years before the English settlement was made at Jamestown.

In 1518 Francis I., King of France, became interested in the colonization of the New World; and six years later, in 1524, a voyage of discovery was started out with John Verrazzano, a native of Florence, in command. The object of this expedition was to search for a northwest passage to Asia. Verrazzano began his voyage in January, 1524, with a fleet of four vessels. Three of the ships were so badly damaged in a storm that they were compelled to return to France, but the determined navigator continued the voyage in his remaining vessel, the Dolphin. After a very rough and dangerous voyage of fifty days' duration, on the 7th of March the mariner came in sight of land near Wilmington, North Carolina. He changed his course south and hunted for a good harbor. Finding none, he returned northward and anchored for a few days at a point between the mouth of Cape Fear River and Pamlico Sound. Verrazzano and his crew went on shore and met some of the native inhabitants, who were found to be of a kind and peaceable disposition. After a few days' stay at that place, he again sailed northward, exploring the coast, and entered the harbor of New York. Thence he sailed to the present port of Newport, Rhode Island, and made a stay of fifteen days, viewing and outlining the coast thereabout. Leaving Newport, he continued his course along and up the coast of New England, passed to the east of Nova Scotia, and arrived at Newfoundland in the latter part of May. In July he returned to France and upon his arrival at home published an account of his discoveries which caused much excitement among his countrymen.

The entire country whose seacoast he had explored and mapped was claimed by right of discovery to belong to France.

On account of the distracted condition of the country, not until ten years after the Verrazzano expedition did any French explorers again visit America. In 1534 Chabot, Admiral of France, succeeded in awakening the interest of Francis I. in a scheme for exploring and colonizing the New World. James Cartier, a trained mariner of St. Malo, in Brittany, was selected to conduct the expedition. With two ships he left the harbor of St. Malo in April, and reached the shores of Newfoundland in May. Without delay he sailed around the island, crossed the Gulf of St. Lawrence and anchored in a bay, which he called Bay of Chaleurs. Failing to find the westward passage, that all the voyagers had sought without avail, he then sailed along the coast as far as the inlet of Gaspe; and there, upon a point of land, raised a cross with a shield and the lilies of France thereon. This was to notify other nations that the discoverer had taken possession of the country for France. In August, Cartier left the Bay of Gaspe and discovered the St. Lawrence River. On the ninth of August he started back to France and arrived safely at St. Malo. The report of his discoveries made him popular and famous in his country.

Friends of Cartier urged the king to give the discoverer another commission and provide him with ships to make a second voyage. A new commission was given him, and three ships were furnished by the king. A number of the young nobles became volunteers to accompany Cartier on this voyage. The company sailed for the New World in May, 1535, and after a difficult and stormy voyage arrived on the coast. The gulf Cartier had discovered on his first voyage was given the name of St. Lawrence, in honor of the Saint of that name. Afterwards the same name was given to the great river which is by far the largest body of fresh water in the world. The St. Lawrence River, under the name of St. Louis, has its source in the same extensive plateau which starts the Father of Waters on its lengthy journey to the Gulf of Mexico and the Red River of the North towards Hudson Bay. It is 2,200 miles from its source to where the river enters the Gulf of St. Lawrence. The St. Louis River flows into Lake Superior and goes on through a succession of lakes—Lake Huron, Lake Erie and Lake Ontario—until its mighty volume pours out of Ontario and becomes the wonderful St. Lawrence River. It is four hundred miles from where

the St. Lawrence issues from Lake Ontario to the splendid gulf that
bears the same name.

After entering the river Cartier sailed up stream to an island,
afterwards called Orleans. There he came in contact with a tribe
of Indians of the Algonquian family. From these natives he
received the information that farther up the river there was an
Indian town on the Island of Hochelaga. This excited his curiosity,
he sailed up the river in a small boat, and found a beautiful native
village nestling at the foot of a hill. He climbed the hill, and the
view from its summit was so magnificent that he immediately called
the place Mont-Real. Upon this site the splendid city of Montreal
now stands. Returning to his ships, Cartier and his men passed
an unpleasant winter where they were anchored. In the spring a
cross was put up on a point of land, bearing the emblem and the
arms of France, and with an inscription declaring that the country
was a possession of Francis I. The name of New France was given
to the country. Cartier then sailed for home, and on the 6th of
July arrived at St. Malo. His report of the character of the St.
Lawrence regions, the very cold climate and failure to find any indi-
cations of silver and gold, discouraged the people of France from
further early attempts to plant a colony there.

After a lapse of four years, under the title of viceroy and lieutenant general of New France, in 1540, Francis de la Roque, Lord
of Roberval, was commissioned by the King of France to establish
a colony, with regal authority in land, territories, and islands that
were bordering on the St. Lawrence. He selected Cartier, who was
familiar with the country, to take charge of the expedition as captain
general and chief pilot. Cartier started out from St. Malo in the
spring of 1541; he made a safe voyage to the St. Lawrence and
built a fort near the site of Quebec. There the colonists remained
through the winter, and nothing of moment having been accomplished, Cartier with his ships and men returned to France. About
the time of his departure, Roberval arrived upon the scene with a
number of colonists. He did nothing more than to verify the reports
of former discoverers, and returned to France.

The repeated unsuccessful attempts to found colonies on the
St. Lawrence so discouraged the French Government that a period
of fifty years elapsed from the failure of Roberval before another
effort of importance was made by the French to plant a colony in
America. There were, however, several private enterprises that
tried to make settlements in Florida and Carolina. The most

notable of these was conceived by Admiral Coligny, the Protestant admiral of France. He resolved to do something for the persecuted Huguenots of his country. In 1562 he secured from his sovereign, Charles IX., the privilege of planting a Protestant colony in America. He selected John Ribault, a practical seaman, to take charge of the Huguenot expedition. It started from France in February and first touched on the Florida coast, and entered the St. Johns River. Thence the ships were sailed up the coast until they arrived at Port Royal on the Carolina coast. It was determined to make a settlement there, the colonists were landed on the island and a fort was erected. In honor of Charles IX. the place was called Carolina. A century afterward the English adopted the name and gave it to all the country which lies between the Savannah River and the southern boundary of Virginia. Ribault returned to France for more supplies and colonists, leaving twenty-six men in the fort as a garrison. He failed to return with reinforcements and supplies, and in the spring the dissatisfied men of the garrison united and killed their captain, who was trying to hold them at the post. The mutineers constructed a rough boat they thought would prove seaworthy and made a desperate attempt to cross the ocean with the hope of getting back to France. They were tossed about on the sea for many weeks, and when nearly dead from starvation were rescued by an English ship and taken to the coast of France.

Two years later Coligny, who was still hopeful of establishing a Protestant colony in America, started out another expedition in charge of Landonniere. The colonists located on the banks of the St. John's River in Florida, fifteen miles west of St. Augustine. This colony was afterwards brutally destroyed by Menendez, the Spaniard, as has been related in a previous chapter.

Again, in 1598, the government of France decided to assert its claims of discovery by colonization. The Marquis of La Roche, under a commission from the king, undertook to locate a colony on Sable Island, Nova Scotia. The site was most unfavorable and the colonists were chiefly criminals, who had been turned out of prisons upon promise of enduring the hardships of a settlement in Northeastern America. After establishing the settlement, La Roche returned to France to get additional supplies and more emigrants, but he died shortly after arriving home. He had left about forty criminals at the settlement on Sable Island. They suffered frightful hardships on the gloomy island for seven years, but were at last rescued by some passing ships and conveyed to France.

The time it seems had arrived when France was to plant a successful and permanent colony in the northeastern section of America. In the year 1603 the King of France gave a commission to De Monts which granted him sovereign control of that part of the continent which lies between the latitude of Philadelphia and one degree north of Montreal. In the spring of 1604 he came to America with a number of colonists to take possession of the magnificent domain that had been given him by his generous monarch. He reached the coast of Nova Scotia, and the captain of one of his ships, whose name was Poutrincourt, was so delighted with a harbor he discovered on the west coast that he requested the privilege of locating there with his family. His request was granted and he was given the harbor and many acres of land adjacent thereto. De Monts, with the remainder of the colony, crossed the Bay of Fundy, and built a fort at the mouth of the St. Croix River. In the spring of 1605 De Monts and his colony returned to the harbor where Poutrincourt had located. At that place, on the 14th of November, 1605, the first permanent French settlement on American soil was established. The fort and harbor were named Port Royal and the country was called Acadia. They are now called Annapolis.

In 1603, two years before the settlement was made at Port Royal by De Monts, the most noted and successful of all the French explorers, Samuel Champlain, made a voyage of exploration to the St. Lawrence country. He was the son of a sea captain, was a trained soldier, and had on one occasion accompanied a Spanish expedition to the West Indies. A company of Rouen merchants had become impressed with the idea that great wealth could be won from the fur trade of the St. Lawrence regions; and they employed Champlain to go to that country and establish a trading-post for them. He made the trip and chose as a site for the post and fort the locality where the great city of Quebec was afterwards built. Champlain returned to France in the autumn of 1603, made report to his employers, and his choice for the site of the trading-post was accepted. He made a second trip to the St. Lawrence for the merchants in 1608, and in July of that year laid the foundation for the city of Quebec. The next year he explored the great lake which bears his name and that will make him famous as long as civilization stands. Later on the intrepid explorer began to investigate the entire lake regions of the North and even extended his travels into the great unknown West. He died at Quebec in 1635.

ENGLISH DISCOVERIES AND SETTLEMENTS.

The discovery of the New World by Columbus excited as intense interest in England as it had provoked in Continental Europe. A Venetian by the name of John Cabot was then residing in Bristol. He was an accomplished navigator and was seized with a desire to make a voyage to the newly discovered continent. On the 5th of March, 1496, he was commissioned by Henry VII., King of England, to make explorations in the Atlantic and Indian Oceans under the English flag. The commission empowered Cabot and his three sons, or either of them, to sail east, west or north, with authority to take possession, in the name of the King of England, of all continents or islands he, or they, might discover. John Cabot had been a sailor from his boyhood, and was a man of adventurous disposition and daring spirit. In May, 1497, with a fleet of five vessels, he sailed from Bristol on a voyage of discovery in the Atlantic Ocean, accompanied by his three sons, Ludivico, Sebastiano, and Sanzio. On the 24th of June he came in sight of the mainland of the North American Continent at a point somewhere on the coast of Labrador. It was on St. John's Day when he sighted land, and was thirteen months and one week previous to the day on which Columbus first discovered the mainland of the American Continent at the mouth of the Orinoco River, South America. This is why many writers have insisted that John Cabot was the first discoverer of the American Continent. Cabot, however, was as much in error as to the character of his discovery as was the illustrious Genoese navigator. Columbus thought he had certainly reached India when he landed on the eastern shores of America, and that by traveling a westerly overland course the Ganges could be reached. Cabot believed the land he discovered was the eastern shore of the Asiatic Continent and was a part of the dominion of the Cham of Tartary. He explored the shore lines for several hundred miles. Finding no people inhabiting the land when he went on shore, he raised the English flag and took possession of the country in the name of Henry VII., King of England. After making such investigations as he thought necessary to determine the character and extent of the country, Cabot sailed for England, and arrived at Bristol, after a voyage that covered a little more than three months. The people of Bristol received him with joyous acclaim, and Henry VII. not only made him a very liberal donation of money, but urged the successful navigator to make a second voyage. Subsequently, another fleet was provided and a new commission, with far more liberal provisions, was given him, but, for some reason that has not been explained, John Cabot never made a second voyage. He disappeared from public notice; and where and when he died history does not record.

In May, 1498, the same month in which Columbus started on his third voyage to discover the mainland of America, Sebastian Cabot, second son of John, sailed from Bristol with two ships on another exploring expedition. His company was composed largely of young English volunteers, the expense of the expedition being borne chiefly by young Cabot; and his object was to discover a northwest passage to Cathay and Japan. The voyage was uneventful until he arrived west of Greenland, in July, where icebergs were so thick and dangerous that the bold navigator was forced to change his course. He first went ashore at a point near where his father had landed the year previous. From that place he directed his course southward and crossed the Gulf of St. Lawrence. In succession the coast lines of New Brunswick, Nova Scotia, and Maine were explored; and he then sailed along the Atlantic coast from Maine to a point as far south as Cape Hatteras. All the country which bordered on the Atlantic coast as far as Cabot navigated was formally claimed by him for the Crown of England. For some reason the discoveries of the Cabots were not utilized by Henry VII. It has been suggested by a few historians that the repeated failures to discover a passage to the Indies and inability to find gold and other precious metals, in part, made the English Government lose interest in the New World. Others have accounted for the strange neglect by citing the fact that Henry VII. was a devout Catholic and was unwilling to contravene the wishes and decrees of the Pope of Rome. At that time all the Catholic monarchs of Europe accorded the Pope as full power and authority in temporal matters as they did in spiritual affairs. The Pope, who was especially favorable to Spain, because it was the most zealous friend of the Church of all the Catholic countries, had published a bull which gave Spain first and complete title to all of North America, and practically all of South America. No matter what was the cause, the King of England withdrew his attention from America and made no further effort to assert title to any part of the New World by right of discovery. At his death he was succeeded as monarch by his son, Henry VIII., and one of the earliest acts of the young king was to surrender to his father-in-law, the King of Spain, the services of Sebastian Cabot.

During the reign of Henry VIII., there were sundry attempts made by English mariners to discover the mythical northwestern passage to Asia. When the strangely constituted English monarch repudiated his Spanish wife, Catharine of Aragon, and abandoned the Roman Church, he entered his country as a vigorous rival of Spain for control of the New World. Then came the incipient movement to crown England "Mistress of the Seas" and make her supreme in the commerce of the world.

Upon the accession of Edward VI. to the throne of his father, Henry VIII., there was an added impulse to the maritime spirit of England, and that spirit was more thoroughly aroused by the recall from Spain of the venerable navigator, Sebastian Cabot. For "good service done and to be done" he was made grand pilot. But Cabot seems to have lost interest in the Western Hemisphere and directed his energies to establishing trade relations with China and with the theretofore unknown country of the Muscovites. It was an English ship that entered the icy harbor of Archangel in 1553 and disclosed Russia to Southern and Western Europe. Though Sebastian Cabot did so much for England as a discoverer, and continued her faithful servant until he reached an extremely old age, like that of his father, his death was obscure; and his burial place is not only unmarked, but, to the shame of the country he served so well, is actually unknown.

After the death of Edward VI. his half-sister, known in history as "Bloody Mary", became Queen of England. In 1554 she married Philip, son of Charles V., heir to the Spanish throne, much against the will of her ministers and the Protestant element of the Nation. Queen Mary was the daughter of Catharine of Aragon, a devout Catholic and fierce supporter of the Papacy; and an intolerant foe of Protestanism. The barbarous persecutions of Protestants that disgraced the latter part of her reign were not sufficient, however, to completely check the growing passion of Englishmen for maritime adventure. Upon her death, in November, 1558, her half-sister, Elizabeth, the great "Virgin Queen," ascended the English throne. Her reign was a long one, lasting nearly forty-five years; and in accomplishment was, possibly, the most noted and splendid England has ever known. During the Elizabethan Period the literature of the world was enriched by the productions of Shakespeare, Spencer, Bacon, and other brilliant and profound English writers. Martin Frobisher and Francis Drake created a new spirit of maritime enterprise, and laid a foundation for building the wonderful commercial and naval power England has ever since enjoyed. The greed of gold, that had given inspiration to all the former explorers of America, still existed and manifested itself in the performances of Frobisher and Drake, but it was under the patronage of Queen Elizabeth that Englishmen first made earnest effort to establish colonies in America.

While Drake was occupied with his daring naval adventures, which Bancroft says "were but a career of splendid piracy against a nation with which his sovereign and his country professed to be at peace," Sir Humphrey Gilbert was maturing plans for planting colonies in North America. He was a half-brother of Sir Walter Raleigh by his mother's side, and it is said bore a striking resemblance to him in character. In June, 1578, Gilbert obtained letters patent from Queen Elizabeth, investing him, his heirs, and assigns with authority to discover, occupy and possess such remote "heathen lands not actually possessed of any Christian prince or people as should seem good to him or them." He succeeded in enlisting quite a large company of young men, among them Walter Raleigh; and, largely at his own expense, made preparation for a voyage to America. After he had assembled his ships and company, dissensions arose, which caused a good many of the men to withdraw from the expedition. But, with a reduced number of ships and men, Gilbert persisted in his enterprise; and on the 19th of November, 1578, he sailed from England, accompanied by Raleigh, for the New World. In the way of accomplishments the expedition was a complete failure, as no report of where it went and what it did is found in history. Gilbert returned with his fleet to England in the summer of 1579. Undaunted by the failure of his first undertaking he launched a second expedition, assisted again by Walter Raleigh. The queen tried to dissuade him from the second voyage, but failing in that effort, commanded Raleigh, who had become a favorite of Elizabeth, to not accompany his brother. However, she sent Gilbert a letter on the eve of his departure, in which she wished him "as good hap and safety to his ship as if she herself were there in person."

The fleet, consisting of five ships, sailed from Plymouth on the 11th of June, 1583; but on the 13th one of the vessels, that had been built and equipped at Raleigh's expense, deserted and returned to port. Gilbert proceeded with his voyage, and on the 5th of August landed on the coast of Newfoundland. He took formal possession of the country for his sovereign; and some of his men

found in the adjacent hills pieces of mica which a mineralogist, who
was in the company, pronounced silver. The crews of the ships
became insurbordinate and one of the vessels was so unfit that it
had to be abandoned. Samples of the supposed silver ore were
taken aboard, and, with his three remaining ships, Gilbert started
southward to make further explorations; but a storm was encountered and the largest ship was lost near Cape Breton. It was then
determined to return to England, with what was left of the fleet. as
speedily as possible. At midnight, on September the 9th, a raging
storm came upon the two little vessels. and the *Squirrel*, on which
Gilbert was sailing, suddenly went down and he and his crew
perished.

Walter Raleigh then resolved to accomplish that which his gallant brother, Sir Humphrey Gilbert, had striven so hard to do but
had so unfortunately failed to perform. He obtained from Queen
Elizabeth a patent which was more ample in its provisions than the
one which had been issued to Sir Humphrey Gilbert. It constituted
Raleigh lord proprietor of an extensive region in the New World.
He concluded to profit by the failure of those explorers who had
vainly sought a northwest passage to Asia. or to make settlements
in the northern section of the continent. His scheme was to seek
the more congenial clime of the South Atlantic coast, and there
plant a colony. In pursuance of this plan, he fitted out two ships
with ample crews and provisions and placed them under the command of Philip Amidas and Arthur Barlow. On the 27th of April.
1584, they started on an exploring voyage to the southern mainland
of the North American Continent. They sailed over the same cir-
cuitous route that had been used by Columbus and other explorers—
that is, by way of the Canaries and the West Indies. A short stop
was made at the West India Islands, and, then, the expedition
sailed northward. In due time, on the 4th of July, 1584, it reached
the Carolina coast, where explorations were made for a distance of
a hundred miles or more along the shores; and on the 13th of July
the ships were anchored in a small convenient harbor. After piously
returning thanks to Almighty God for the safe voyage and their
happy arrival on the delightful coast, the commanders and their
men went on shore and took possession of the country for and in
the name of the Queen of England. This occurred on the Island
of Wococken, since known in history as Roanoke Island. It was
midsummer and the Englishmen were completely enraptured with
the luxuriant and gorgeous vegetation, the excellent wild fruits,

and the salubrious climate. Amidas and Barlow explored the island, which is twelve miles long, to the northern end. There they found, as reported by them, an Indian "village of nine houses, built of Cedar, and fortified round about with sharpe trees to keep out their enemies, and the entrance to it made like a turne pike very artificially." This evidently was a village fortified with a stockade of similar character to those found by De Soto among the Choctaws and Chickasaws while he was exploring in their regions.

After the commanders of Raleigh's ships had explored Pamlico and Albemarle Sounds and Roanoke Island, and had gathered from the Indians such information as could be obtained about the interior country, the homeward voyage was begun. They took with them to England two of the Indian chiefs, Manteo and Wanchese. Upon their arrival in England, Amidas and Barlow gave such highly colored descriptions of the land they had seen that the people of the country again became greatly interested in America. Queen Elizabeth was so gratified with the success of the expedition and charmed by the reported beauties of the newly discovered land, she named the country Virginia, to commemorate her virgin life.

On account of his great service to the English Nation and Crown, Raleigh was knighted by Queen Elizabeth; and he was also honored by being elected to Parliament as the representative of the county of Devon. In the spring of 1585 the then Sir Walter Raleigh determined to send out a colony for settlement in the territory of which he was lord proprietor. One hundred or more men were selected for the company of settlers; and these were placed in charge of Richard Lane, who had been selected for governor of the colony. The expedition sailed from Plymouth in April and was escorted by seven armed ships under the command of Raleigh's cousin, Sir Richard Grenville. The reason, no doubt, for this protective escort was, that trouble was then brewing between Spain and England, which culminated in a declaration of war between the two nations in July following. The colonists arrived safely at their selected destination, but a series of blunders and misfortunes made this first attempt to plant an English colony on the South Atlantic coast a deplorable failure. Lane and Grenville, accompanied by Thomas Cavendish, the distinguished navigator, and Hariot, historian of the expedition, went ashore and made an excursion of eight days among the Indians and along the coast. The excursionists were most hospitably treated by the natives; but while the party was visiting an Indian town a silver cup was stolen from them, and this trivial incident was treated so unwisely by Grenville that it was, possibly, the primal cause of the disasters that finally broke up the colony. The Indians were slow about restoring the cup to its owner, and Grenville, either from revenge or to intimidate the Indians, had the village of the natives burned and their growing corn destroyed. Shortly after this the colony was located on Roanoke Island, and Grenville sailed with his ships for England.

The climate agreed with the men and the health of the colony was excellent, but its first year was uneventful, though Lane explored the country a short distance to the south, and he sailed as far north as Elizabeth River where it connects with Hampton Roads. The colonists had been chiefly engaged in a mad hunt for gold when their first year spent at Roanoke Island had expired. They had grown weary while looking for supplies from England. About this time Sir Francis Drake, who was returning from one of his piratical excursions to the Spanish Main, entered Roanoke Inlet with his fleet of twenty-three ships. The colonists made piteous appeals to Drake to take them to England and he complied with their request. In a little over two weeks after the departure of the colonists, Sir Richard Grenville appeared on the coast with three ships and an abundance of supplies. He made a vain search for the colony, and, having no knowledge of its departure, left fifteen men on the Island of Roanoke to hold its possession, and sailed back to England. This practically ended the first effort to form a permanent English colony in America.

Sir Walter Raleigh was so much encouraged by the reports of Hariot, the historian of his first expedition, as to the fertility and beauty of his province, that he resolutely set to work to gather a new colony for starting and developing an agricultural community in Virginia. Therefore, in selecting emigrants he chose men who had wives and families. John White was appointed governor of the new colony, and Raleigh directed that the settlement should be made on Chesapeake Bay, where it was known ample harbors could be found. The company sailed from England in April, 1587, in a fleet prepared at the expense of Raleigh, and reached the coast of North Carolina in July. Search was made for the fifteen men Grenville had left there as a garrison. The houses were tenantless, the fort had been destroyed by the Indians, and human bones were lying around, indicating the fate of the fifteen men who composed the garrison. The order of Raleigh for locating the colony at a designated point on the Chesapeake Bay was brought to naught by the conduct of Fernando, the naval officer of the expedition. He refused to join White in exploring the coasts, and sailed for the West Indies, leaving only one vessel with the colony. Lane, the governor of the first colony, had built a fort, with a group of dwelling houses about it, at the northern end of Roanoke Island. White and his company availed themselves of these buildings, that had been occupied by the fifteen unfortunate men Grenville had left on the island as a guard.

The Roanoke Indians had become very suspicious and jealous of the white men. Manteo, one of the chiefs that had accompanied Lane to England, remained friendly; and as a matter of policy Raleigh had him invested with the title of an English baron, as the Lord of Roanoke. This, however, did not pacify the unfriendly natives, nor delay the disasters that followed; and repeated difficulties and bloody encounters occurred between the Indians and the colonists. Conditions became so alarming that White determined to go to England to procure succor in the way of men and much needed supplies. Before he started on this mission, his daughter, Eleanor Dare, wife of Ananias Dare, gave birth to a daughter, on the 18th of August, 1587. She was the first child born of English parents on the American Continent, and she was named Virginia. About ten days after this interesting event Governor White embarked on his journey to England, little thinking that he would never again see his daughter and grandchild, or any member of the colony he was leaving in Virginia. At the time of White's departure the colony was composed of eighty-nine men, seventeen women, and two children, all of whom disappeared during the governor's absence. When he arrived in England he found intense excitement prevailing, occasioned by a threatened invasion from Spain. King Philip was then building a large fleet, which he was pleased to call the "Invincible Armada", to be used for crushing the English navy and transporting the Spanish army to England; and which was to destroy Protestantism and dethrone Queen Elizabeth. All the noted military and naval leaders, among them Sir Walter Raleigh, were busily occupied with preparation to repel the intended Spanish invasion. But Raleigh found time and occasion to provide White with two ships and supplies for relief of the Roanoke colony. A company of men was gathered and were started out with the two ships on a relief voyage, but while en route became engaged with hostile ships in a bloody engagement. The ships were boarded by the enemy

T.H.-7

and robbed of all their supplies. This forced the expedition to return to England. The unfortunate circumstance prevented the sending of any succor for the Roanoke colonists until after the destruction of the Invincible Armada was accomplished by England's great sea-kings, Drake, Hawkins, Winter, Frobisher and Howard.

It was in August, 1587, that White parted from the Roanoke colony and went to England to crave assistance. The prolonged Spanish-English War prevented him from returning to the colony until March, 1591, and he was forced to travel there as a passenger on a West Indian vessel. When he landed at Roanoke Island, it was nearly four years after the birth of his grandchild; but he did not find little Virginia Dare and her mother there, or any member of the colony, to give him welcome. On his departure for England he had directed that if anything occurred during his absence making it necessary for the colonists to move to some other spot, a record should be left by carving on a tree the name of the place to which they had removed; and if they were in distress, a cross was to be added to the inscription. The grief-stricken man found grass growing in the fort, and the houses grouped about it were tenantless. On the bark of a large tree standing near the fort he found the word "Croatan" carved, but no cross. Croatan was the name of a neighboring island where an Indian settlement, known to White, was located. In response to his entreaties, the captain of the ship consented to take him to Croatan Island, where White hoped to find the entire body of colonists. A violent storm was encountered, like those that frequently come about Cape Hatteras. The ship was tossed about on the sea for several days, and the captain, despite the pleadings of his unhappy passenger, turned the prow of his ship toward the east and sailed for England. This was the last opportunity White had to seek his missing loved ones. Ever since, the fate of Virginia Dare, of her mother, and the Roanoke colony has been a topic for much speculation. Sir Walter Raleigh made five attempts to ascertain the fate of the colony but failed to find even a trace of it. He had already spent forty thousand pounds, the bulk of his fortune, in vain efforts to establish colonies in Virginia. Discouraged by these failures, he transferred his patent to a company of merchants and capitalists, some of whom were afterwards identified with the settlement of Jamestown.

CHAPTER III.

There are few things in history so edifying and pleasing to the investigating human mind as the birth of a nation. That great Semitic family known as the Hebrews, of which the Chaldean patriarch, Abraham, was the progenitor, for nearly four thousand years has been a fruitful source of pleasure and profit to students of mankind, though the Hebrews no longer exist as a nation. No matter when or where a Jew is met or seen by men of intelligence, he is quickly associated with the pledge given by the Great Jehovah to Abraham, then old and childless, that his seed should become a great nation, and as such inherit the Land of Canaan.

When Romulus and Remus, the twin sons of a Vestal Virgin, began to build a rude wall around their little town on the Tiber, 753 years before the Christian era, they never dreamed that they were laying the foundation of what would become known in history as the "Eternal City". Nor is it probable that they had the remotest idea that from the small community of refugee murderers and slaves they gathered within the walls of their citadel, a mighty nation would be evolved and a splendid empire created, to stand for centuries as the sovereign master of the then known world.

No epoch in the written or traditional history of our Sphere has been more potent in shaping the destiny of the human race than the birth of the marvelous American Nation. The small company of Englishmen who, at the beginning of the seventeenth century, originated a crude plan for planting an English colony in Virginia, never imagined that from such a small business venture there would issue a great nation of one hundred million people. But within a period of three centuries following the settlement at Jamestown, the magic, giant nation was in existence, and is still here, growing and taking on new form and feature. It is a strangely composite nation, the offspring of mingled nationalities and races. The intermixing of Teutons, Celts, Latins, Greeks, Franks, Huns, Slavs, Bulgars, Turks, Armenians, Jews, and other races and nations, representing the continents of Asia, Africa and Europe, is producing that peculiar type of man, the American. Even the aboriginal race of the North American Continent seems destined to gradually disappear in this mixing process, not by extermination of the Indians as decreed by the pioneer settlers, but by benevolent absorption. In the coming centuries the most astute ethnologists will find themselves hopelessly entangled and puzzled when they try to trace the origin of the Americans. It will be impossible to find a common paternity for this conglomerate race, except by turning back to the primal origin of man. This is truly a novel method for nation making; and one may well inquire, What will be the ultimate outcome or product? Will the American Nation be welded into a homogeneous race, in which the altruistic spirit will be so dominant as to bring to pass the Utopian hope for the perfection of human laws and the complete establishing of the brotherhood of man? Shall this Nation be a city set upon a hill, a beacon to illumine the way for other peoples as they press forward to the goal of national excellence? Or shall there be a realization of the gloomy apprehensions expressed by certain learned men of Europe more than a hundred years ago, that the discovery of America by Christopher Columbus and the finding of a new ocean route to Asia by Vasco da Gama may prove a curse rather than a blessing to mankind?

At the beginning of the seventeenth century events that materially affected the colonization of America by the English people began to occur. The protracted war with Spain had come to a conclusion, with complete satisfaction to England, and with the Spanish power, both on land and sea, very greatly impaired, if not broken. Elizabeth Tudor, England's great queen, passed away in 1603, after a magnificent reign of nearly forty-five years. She was succeeded on the throne by King James of Scotland, who, as James I., became sovereign of England, Scotland and Ireland. Scarcely had King James mounted the English throne, when a foul conspiracy, lead by Robert Cecil and Henry Howard, was formed to excite the animosity of the king against Sir Walter Raleigh. The conspirators were successful in their malignant designs; Raleigh was arrested for an old trumped-up offence, was confined in the Tower, and after a season was beheaded by the order of the crafty and vain little Scotchman, the unworthy successor of the great Virgin Queen. No blacker crime tarnishes the reign of any of the cruel or dissolute monarchs of England than the vicious murder of Sir Walter Raleigh, who was undeniably the Father of Virginia. But other strong men were destined to take up the work which Raleigh had so heroically begun of founding a mighty nation in the Western Hemisphere. The Earl of Southampton was released from the Tower of London about the same time Sir Walter Raleigh had entered its gloomy portals as a prisoner. Southampton had been connected with Essex's rebellion in 1600, and had narrowly escaped death, though the noble Essex was, on the 25th of February, 1601, beheaded for his foolhardy-effort to excite an insurrection against Queen Elizabeth, whom he had for years served so faithfully and gallantly.

Southampton had become greatly interested in making a settlement in Virginia, and began to formulate plans for this undertaking. In 1602, though then confined in the Tower, he sent Bartholomew Gosnold, on a voyage of exploration to Virginia. Its territorial limits then extended north as far as the St. Lawrence River. Gosnold, with this, his first, expedition, merely visited that portion of the territory then known as North Virginia, now the present New England.

In 1603, a company of Bristol merchants dispatched Martin Pring on a trading expedition to North Virginia; and about the same time, Bartholomew Gilbert, son of Sir Humphrey Gilbert and the nephew of Sir Walter Raleigh, made a voyage to the Chesapeake Bay. While coasting along its shores, young Gilbert and some of his companions were killed by the Indians. Another expedition under command of Captain George Weymouth, and of which the Earl of Southampton and Sir Ferdinando Gorges were patrons, visited the present New England, then North Virginia, in 1605. He spent a month exploring and investigating that region, and then returned to England, taking with him five Indians, members of a tribe with whom a profitable trade had been opened. Upon his arrival at home, Weymouth made a report so favorable as to the commercial value of the country that renewed interest in America was aroused. This was the last voyage of exploration or preparation made by Englishmen prior to the planting of the colony at Jamestown.

Bartholomew Gosnold, who had been very much pleased with the soil, climate and apparently valuable resources of that part of the North American Continent he had visited, went actively to work to procure aid from other prominent men of his country for establishing a colony in Virginia. After a time, he succeeded in getting Edward Maria Wingfield, a merchant, Robert Hunt, a clergyman, and John Smith, a soldier of fortune, in sympathy with his views as to the proposed enterprise. He next secured the influence of Sir

Ferdinando Gorges, who was a man of large wealth, and Sir John Popham, Chief Justice of England, to obtain from King James a patent, authorizing a company to settle a plantation in Virginia.

On the memorable 10th of April, 1606, King James I. issued patent letters to certain of his subjects empowering them to enter and possess all that region of North America lying between the thirty-fourth and forty-fifth parallels of latitude, and extending inland from the Atlantic coast one hundred miles. The territory granted by the patent stretched northward from the mouth of Cape Fear River to the dividing line between the State of Vermont and Canada, and it was set apart for occupation by two rival companies. These companies were called, respectively, The London Company, and The Plymouth Company; and they were proprietary associations, each member thereof being invested with a joint and several proprietary interest in the domain granted their respective companies. The names of but four men were mentioned in the charter of the London Company, as follows: Rev. Richard Hakluyt, Sir Thomas Gates, Sir George Somers, and Captain Edward Maria Wingfield. This company was assigned the southern zone of the territory for the establishing of its settlements. The Plymouth Company was authorized to locate its colony in the northern zone. Raleigh Gilbert, William Parker, Thomas Hanham, and George Popham were the four persons named in the charter of the Northern Company. The first colony was to confine its settlements to the territory between the thirty-fourth and the thirty-eighth degrees of latitude; and the second colony was to occupy the territory between the forty-first and the forty-fifth degrees, thus leaving a strip of three degrees width open to both colonies, upon certain conditions. There was a provision in the patent prohibiting either company from making a settlement within a hundred miles of any other settlement already established by a rival company. This plan virtually divided the granted territory into three zones, the middle one being made neutral.

As the subsequent doings of the Plymouth Company will have but little connection with the history of Tazewell County, which I am writing, I will confine myself to a brief recital of the performances of the London Company.

The charter members of the London Company, and the associate shareholders of that proprietary body, fitted out three small vessels to be used for transporting a number of colonists to Virginia. Cap-

tain Christopher Newport, one of England's most skillful sailors
and esteemed naval officers, was selected for commander of the
expedition.

Spain, though terribly weakened by her disastrous wars, still
asserted ownership of all the region embraced in the then defined
bounds of Virginia; and resented the announced purpose of England
to make encroachments upon that territory. Zuniga, the Spanish
ambassador to England, having heard rumors of the plans that
were being matured by prominent Englishmen, to establish colonies
in Virginia, forwarded a dispatch to his sovereign, Philip III, warning him of "an unpalitable scheme" of the English, "to send five or
six hundred men, private individuals of this kingdom, to people
Virginia in the Indies, close to Florida." Sir John Popham, Lord
Chief Justice of England, was known to be one of the promoters of
the movement for sending "people to Virginia;" and it appears that
the Spanish ambassador made complaint to Popham about the
threatened encroachments upon the American dominion of his
sovereign. Zuniga reported that, in reply to his protests, the Lord
Chief Justice lightly declared, that the object of the undertaking
to establish a Virginia colony was to relieve England of a lot of
thieves and worthless fellows, and probably get them drowned in
the sea.

These incidents occurred a short time previous to the issuance
of the letters patent to the two companies. The seemingly jocular
reply of Chief Justice Popham to the protest of the representative
of Spain may have been intended to be taken seriously, as the
majority of the men who came with the first band of colonists to
Jamestown were so worthless that England could well afford to be
rid of them. It is truly astonishing that the intelligent men who
promoted the London Company undertook to establish a successful
colony with such indifferent material; and it is no wonder that
disasters which threatened the life of the enterprise were encountered from the very beginning. No women and children accompanied the colonists, and they brought with them no domestic animals
or fowls. Evidently it was more of a treasure-hunting adventure
than an agricultural and home-making enterprise. This conclusion
is supported by the fact that while the charter gave the company
authority to own and operate mines, it contained a provision which
required payment to the king of one-fifth of all the gold and silver
and one-fifteenth of all the copper that was found and mined. An
impression then prevailed in England that the precious metals,

though undeveloped, were as abundant in Virginia as the Spaniards had found them in Mexico and Peru. There was an absurd belief existing over there that nature furnished such abundant supplies of food over here, that men could live luxuriously without toiling. A poem written by Michael Drayton, afterwards poet laureate of England, addressed as a farewell message to the London Company's colonists, gave expression to the ridiculous fancy of these Englishmen. Thus spoke the poet in three of the stanzas:

> "And cheerfully at sea
> Success you still entice,
> > To get the pearl and gold.
> > And ours to hold
> Virginia,
> Earth's only paradise!

> "Where nature hath in store
> Fowl, venison, and fish;
> > And the fruitfull'st soil
> > Without your toil,
> Three harvests more,
> All greater than your wish.

> "And the ambitious vine
> Crowns with his purple mass
> > The cedar reaching high
> > To kiss the sky,
> The cypress, pine,
> And useful sassafras."

The charter which King James issued to each of the American colonies was very ample in its provisions for their government. A Royal Council, consisting of thirteen members, and appointed by the king, was placed in general control of the two companies; and the local management of each colony was fixed with a local council also of thirteen members. The members of the local councils were appointed by the Royal Council, resident in London, and it also selected the presidents of the two local councils for the first year. After the first year had expired, the local councils were invested with power to select their own presidents each year, and remove them for misconduct or inefficiency. These local councils were authorized to supply vacancies in their own membership caused by death, removal, or resignation. A number of other important powers were given the local councils. Fiske, in his "Old Virginia and Her Neighbors," says:

"Power was given the colonial council to coin money for trade between the colonies and with the natives, to invite and carry over settlers, to drive out intruders, to punish malefactors, and to levy and collect duties upon divers imported goods. All lands within the two colonies were to be held in free and common socage, like the demesnes of the Manor of East Greenwich in the county of Kent; and the settlers and their children forever were to enjoy all the liberties, franchises and immunities enjoyed by Englishmen in England, a clause which was practically nullified by the failure to provide for popular elections or any expression whatever of public opinion. The authority of the colonial council was supreme within the colonies, but their acts were liable to veto from the Crown."

A few days before Christmas, or to be exact as to date, on the 19th of December, 1606, the first colonization expedition of the London Company started from Blackwalls, England; and dropped down the Thames to cross the Atlantic Ocean and settle a colony in Virginia. The fleet consisted of three ships, with the commander, Captain Christopher Newport, sailing on the *Susan Constant*. The *Godspeed* was commanded by Bartholomew Gosnold, and the *Discovery* by John Ratcliffe. On board the three vessels, besides the crews, were congregated one hundred and five colonists. On account of "unprosperous winds" the little fleet was detained for more than a week in the Downs, off the Southeast coast of the county of Kent, a large natural harbor in which outward and homeward bound vessels took refuge to escape dangerous storms, or to await favorable winds. New Year's day, 1607, the fleet got away on its eventful and momentous voyage, which was eventually to terminate at a peninsula on James River, and where the cradle of the American Nation was decreed to be placed.

Newport was familiar with the course or route which Columbus and the other first explorers of America had followed; and sailed his ships by way of the Canaries and West Indies. During the progress of the voyage very serious dissensions arose among some of the leading spirits of the expedition; and these troubles were much aggravated when it became known that no one among the company was clothed with sufficient authority to quell the disturbances. King James had placed his instructions for the government of the colony, with the names of the men who were to constitute the local council, in a sealed box; and had given positive orders that the box was not to be opened until the expedition reached its destination. This left the colonists without any designated leader to act when emergencies came. Trouble arose between Edward Wingfield and John Smith, and Wingfield made an accusation against Smith of plotting a mutiny. Smith was put in iron fetters, which he was forced to wear until the fleet arrived in Virginia.

After a tedious voyage of four months' duration, Captain Newport entered the Chesapeake Bay and landed with a small party at the southern cape, which was named Cape Henry, in honor of the Prince of Wales, eldest son of King James. The northern cape was afterwards named Cape Charles, from the second son of James I., and whose reign, as Charles I., and as the successor of his father, was the most tragic and eventful in the record of England's monarchs. Captain Newport took the sealed box on shore with him, and, when opened, the names of the local council were disclosed. Six persons only were named, though the charter had provided for thirteen members of this council. Those appointed were Bartholomew Gosnold, John Smith, Edward Wingfield, John Ratcliffe, John Martin and George Kendall. The malignant Wingfield and his associates refused to permit Smith then to act as one of the council, but continued to hold him a prisoner until after their arrival at Jamestown. At Cape Henry the colonists had their first encounter with the Indians. Hon. George Percy, a brother of the Earl of Northumberland, and a member of Newport's landing party, in a graphic account of the occurrences after entering the Chesapeake thus describes the incident:

"At night when we were going aboard, there came the Savages upon all fours, from the Hills like Bears, with their Bowes in their mouths, charged us desperately in the faces, hurt Captain Gabrill Archer, in both his hands, and a sayler in two places of the body very dangerous. After they had spent their Arrows and felt the sharpenesse of our shot, they retired into the woods with great noise, and so left us."

These natives belonged to the Chesapeake tribe, and were not a part of the Powhatan Confederacy. According to Jefferson's Notes, published in 1809, their principal village was located on Lynhaven River, in Princess Anne County, a small stream which flows northward into Chesapeake Bay. Stith says in his history, that they were living on the Elizabeth River, which flows into the Chesapeake below Norfolk. They belonged to the Algonquian family of Indians; and in 1607 were estimated at one hundred warriors, or about three hundred inhabitants. The tribe disappeared as a distinct nation about the year 1669.

The colonists remained for several days in the vicinity of Lynhaven Bay, and Captain Newport, accompanied by small parties, made short excursions both inland and along the shores. On the 28th of April he launched a shallop and with several companions started out on a trip of investigation. They discovered a point which put them in such "good comfort", that they named it "Cape Comfort". It is now known as Old Point Comfort, is at the entrance to Hampton Roads, and the historic Fort Monroe is located there. On April 30th they brought their ships to "Cape Comfort" and continued their explorations from that point, visiting the rude natives and partaking of their hospitality.

Before the expedition sailed from England the Royal Council had Rev. Richard Hakluyt prepare lengthy written instructions for the guidance of the officers after their arrival in America. In these instructions the officers were urged to select a site for the permanent settlement that was healthful in its surroundings and that could be easily defended against attacks made by the natives or the Spaniards. It was thought that Spain might possibly resent and resist the planting of an English colony in Virginia. Therefore the instructions to the Local Council, in part, said:

"You must take especial care that you choose a seat for habitation that shall not be overburthened with woods near your town, for all the men you have shall not be able to cleanse twenty acres a year, besides that it may serve for a covert for your enemies round about.

"Neither must you plant in a low or moist place, because it will prove unhealthful. You shall judge of the good air by the people, for some part of that coast where the lands are low have their people blear eyed, and with swollen bellies and legs, but if the naturals be strong and clean made it is a true sign of a wholesome soil".

On the 13th of May, after a number of locations had been visited and inspected, the leaders chose the little peninsula as the proper spot for permanently establishing the colony. In most respects the site was the very opposite of that which the letter of instructions

urged the officers to select. It was so low and damp that it was
necessarily a breeder of malaria; and at high tide one half the
point of land was covered with water. There was no running water
on or about it, except the river, which was so brackish at high tide
that it was unfit to drink. Possibly it might have been deemed well
situated for defence against the Indians, but that was later shown
to be not true. This peninsula, which is called Jamestown Island,
is situated on the north side of James River, in James City County,
and is thirty-two miles above the mouth of that river. It contains
about seventeen hundred acres, and averages two and a half miles
in length and three-fourths of a mile in width. On the east, west
and south sides it is surrounded by James River, and on the north
by Back River, the latter separating the peninsula from the mainland. From its founding, in 1607, until 1698, Jamestown was the
seat of the Virginia Colonial Government. In 1698 the government
was removed to Williamsburg.

As soon as Captain Newport had landed the colonists, the members of the council, with the exception of John Smith, took the oath
of office and organized, electing Edward Wingfield president for the
first year. On the following day, it is said, the council put the men
to work to build a fort and houses for the settlers. The work
accomplished in that direction appears to have been in keeping with
the indolent and thriftless character of the greater number of the
emigrants. In one of his narratives about the settlement, Captain
John Smith said: "When I went first to Virginia, I well remember
we did hang an awning which is an old sail to three or four trees
to shadow us from the sun; our walls were rails of wood, our seats
unhewed trees till we cut planks; our pulpit a bar of wood nailed
to two neighboring trees; in fine weather we shifted into an old
rotten tent for we had no better. The best of our houses were of
the like curiosity but for the most part, much worse workman-ship
that neither could well defend wind or rain." Captain Smith
in his narrative said nothing about the fort. It is likely that the
experienced soldier was either so amused or disgusted by the thing
Wingfield and his associates called a fort that he scorned to mention it. Henry Howe, in his History of Virginia, thus speaks of
the so-called fort: "The President, who seems to have been a
very weak man, and ill suited for his station, was too jealous of his
own men to allow exercises at arms or a fortification to be erected;
and the only protection provided, was a sort of half-moon formed
of the boughs of trees."

In the written instructions given by the London Council was one which said: "You must observe if you can whether the river on which you plant doth spring out of mountains or out of lakes. If it be out of any lake the passage to the other sea will be the more easy."

The minds of the best informed men of England, as well as of Continental Europe, still clung to the fatuous belief that the distance from the Atlantic to the other sea (the Pacific Ocean) was not very great; and that a water route across the North American Continent, connecting the two oceans, would surely be found. This was one of the chief motives the English merchants had for identifying themselves with exploring expeditions that came to America. All commercial Europe was then eagerly reaching out for the trade of India and other Asiatic countries.

In obedience to the instructions of the Royal Council, Captain Newport took prompt steps for exploring the noble James and finding the source of the river. Though the local council, under the control of Wingfield, still refused to allow Captain Smith to enter upon the discharge of his duties as a member of the council, Newport had become impressed with Smith's ability, and took him along on the trip up the James. The exploring party, in addition to Newport and Smith, consisted of four other gentlemen, four skilled marines, and fourteen common sailors. Six days were occupied by Newport and his company in making the voyage from Jamestown to the head of tidewater at Richmond. They found an Indian village at the falls of the river, and learned that the name of the village was Powhatan (that is "Falling Waters"). The village consisted of about a dozen houses "pleasantly seated on a hill", and the buildings were large clan houses, framed with wooden beams, the roofs and sides being covered with bark. Newport and his companions were kindly treated by these natives, and learned from them that Powhatan was the head-chief of a confederacy, consisting of a number of tribes or clans; and that his principal town and place of residence was called Werowocomoco, which was afterwards found to be situated on the north side of York River in the present county of Gloucester.

Upon their return from their trip up the river, Newport and Smith found that during their absence the colonists had been attacked by hostile Indians; and that one Englishman had been killed and eleven wounded. For two weeks or more after this attack the settlers were greatly annoyed by the red men. They would conceal themselves in the tall grass near the fort, and with their bows and arrows pick off a white man at every opportunity. Relief was offered by friendly natives of the Powhatan tribe, who made the proffer of an alliance with the Englishmen to drive away the hostiles. The Powhatans also suggested that security could be obtained by cutting and burning the grass near the fort. This was done, and present relief resulted. The hostiles were not of the Powhatan Confederacy, and it is likely were a band of the Chesapeake warriors.

Captain Smith, who had waited so patiently for a trial on the charges Wingfield had made against him, demanded that he be given an opportunity to have a hearing before a jury of his peers. Wingfield objected very strenuously to a trial, but it was accorded, and Smith was honorably acquitted of all the charges. Thereupon, on the 10th of June, he was sworn in as a member of the council and became the most efficient and useful member of that official body. The fort was completed on the 15th, and Captain Newport sailed for England on the 22nd, carrying back on his ships a cargo of sassafras and fine wood for wainscoting. At that time sassafras was very much in demand in England for its supposed medicinal qualities, and for preparing a pleasant beverage from the bark or roots of the shrub. The beverage was sold at daybreak by venders in the streets of London, under the name of Saloop.

When Captain Newport sailed for home he promised to return to Virginia in twenty weeks. It was found that there was barely enough food on hand, and that of a very poor quality, to sustain the colony for fifteen weeks. This made it necessary to put every one on reduced rations until Newport's return. By an order of the London Company all supplies sent over from England, and all produced by the labor of the colonists, were to be kept in a common stock, from which each member of the colony was to share equally. This community system was to continue for five years; and the lazy and worthless were put upon the same footing as the industrious and helpful. Under such conditions, it is no wonder that horrible suffering followed and continued until Newport returned from England with fresh supplies. The most of the settlers were too indolent to avail themselves of the abundant supplies which nature had placed about them. That there was an abundance, which a Trans-Alleghany pioneer would have used to advantage, is shown by Hon. George Percy, one of the gentlemen of the colony. In a letter sent by him to a relative in England, he said:

"This river which we have discovered is one of the famousest Rivers that was ever found by any christian, it ebbes and flowes a hundred and three score miles where ships of great burthen may harbour in safetie. Wheresoever we landed upon this River, we saw the goodliest woods as Beach, Oke, Cedar, Cypress, Walnuts, Sassafras, and Vines in great abundance, which clusters on in many trees, and all the grounds bespread with strawberries, mulberries, Rasberries, and Fruits unknown, there are many branches of this River which runne flowing through the Woods with great plentie of Fish of all kinds, as for Sturgeon, all the World cannot be compared to it. There is also a great store of Deer both Red and Fallow. There are Beares, Foxes, Otters, Beavers, Muskrats and wild beasts unknowne."

The same gentleman, Mr. Percy, who wrote the above about the famous river and country, was one of the number who endured the terrible sufferings through which the colony passed while Newport was over in England; and he afterwards wrote this about it:

"There were never Englishmen left in a foreigne Countrey in such miserie as wee were in this new discovered Virginia. We watched every three nights, lying on the bare ground what weather soever came; and warded all the next day; which brought our men to be most feeble wretches. Our food was but a small Can of Barlie sodden in water to five men a day. Our drink cold water taken out of the River, which was at floud very salt; at a low tide full of slime and filth; which was the destruction of many of our men. Thus we lived for the space of five months in this miserable distresse, not having five able men to man our Bulwarkes upon any occasion. If it had not pleased God to have put a terrour in the Savages hearts, we had all perished by those wild and cruell Pagans, being in that weak estate as we were; our men night and day groaning in every corner of the Fort most pitiful to heare. If there were any conscience in men, it would make their harts bleed to heare the pitifull murmerings and outcries of our sick men without relief, every night and day for the space of six weeks; some departing out of the World, many times three or foure in a night; in the morning their bodies being trailed out of their Cabines like Dogges, to be buried. In this sort did I see the mortalitie of divers of our people."

This eccentric but graphic account of the miseries of the unfortunate colonists shows clearly their unfitness for the work they had been selected to perform. And it emphasizes the hateful greed and criminal carelessness of the London Company for thus placing these incapable men in such a deplorable situation. There were but very few of them who had been trained to work in any way, most of them being of the then idle class called gentlemen. They didn't know how to work, and, if they had known how, they were so inadequately supplied with implements and tools for doing agricultural or mechanical labor that they could have accomplished but little. It is not surprising, with so little food, of such a poor quality, and located as they were at a place reeking with miasma, that the colonists became the victims of deadly diseases. In August, Captain Gosnold died from fever, and thereupon the quarrel between Wing-field, president of the council, and Captain Smith was renewed.

Shortly thereafter charges were made that Wingfield was concealing and taking from the scanty stores various luxuries, including wine and spirits, for the use of himself and friends. This and other unpopular acts caused the council to depose him, and John Ratcliffe was elected president in his stead. A short time afterwards, Wingfield and Kendall were accused of trying to escape from the colony in a pinnace, and they were removed from the council. This left only three of the council in office, Ratcliffe, Martin and Smith. Though the charter of the London Company authorized and directed them to fill vacancies in the official body, they declined to exercise that power. It seems that Ratcliffe and Martin were both very unpopular with the colonists, and Smith was looked to as the leader and controller of the affairs of the settlement. He accepted the responsibilities of leader, and succeeded in getting affairs in order. The men were put to work, and built more comfortable dwellings; and Smith secured a supply of corn from the Indians, which relieved the people from a continued period of starvation.

Being again supplied with ample provisions, the indolent and thriftless remnant of the colony returned to their former habits of idleness and wastefulness. Captain Smith saw that more supplies would have to be secured from the Indians, and he made several trips in the pinnace up the Chickahominy, and possibly the James, and purchased an abundance of corn from the natives. Cold weather came on and supplies of game were obtained. Smith again ascended the Chickahominy, this time chiefly on an exploring expedition, and it was then he was made a captive and was rescued from imminent death by the Indian girl, Pocahontas. He was in captivity some five or six weeks, and upon his release returned to Jamestown. On the day of his return, which was the 8th of January, 1608, Captain

Newport with his relief ship reached the landing at the settlement, bringing what was called the First Supply of men and provisions. Of the 105 colonists Newport left there in June, there were only 38 surviving, sixty-seven had died from disease and want during his absence of six months. The First Supply added 120 to the colony, bringing the entire number up to 158 persons. Smith and Newport realized that the supplies brought over from England, with the corn on hand added, would not be sufficient to feed the colony through the winter; and they determined to try to purchase more corn from Powhatan. A party consisting of Smith, Newport, and others not mentioned, paid a visit to the old Indian chief at his home, Werowocomoco, where they were cordially received and hospitably entertained. The Englishmen, Smith and Newport, succeeded in getting a good supply of corn, exchanging therefor glass beads and other trinkets that struck Powhatan's fancy.

In the spring Newport sailed for England again, taking with him Edward Wingfield, the deposed and disgraced first president of the council. Captain Smith spent the summer of 1608 making explorations of the Chesapeake Bay and the Potomac, Patapsco, and Susquehanna rivers. During his absence from Jamestown the affairs of the colony again got in a wretched condition, owing, it is said, to the incompetency and unpopularity of Ratcliffe, who was the successor of Wingfield as president of the council. On his return in September, Smith was chosen president of the council, and put things in pretty good shape by the time Newport got back from England with the Second Supply of men and provisions. Newport arrived on the 8th of September, and brought over 70 persons. The colony had lost 28 of its members, leaving only 130 of the 158 left by Newport in the spring. With the 70 new arrivals the colony then numbered 200. There were two women in the last company, a Mrs. Forrest and her maid, Anne Burroughs. The maid soon gave up her maidenhood by marrying John Laydon. This was the first recorded English marriage solemnized on the American Continent.

Newport on this trip brought instructions from the London Company which proved that its members were not satisfied with the progress of their get-rich-quick scheme. In promoting the Virginia colony they believed they were embarking in a very lucrative enterprise; but instead it was proving a grave trouble, and a heavy loss as a financial proposition. So, Newport was ordered to discover a new passage to the South Sea, to find a large lump of gold, to trace the lost Roanoke colony, or not to dare to return to England. When

T.H.-8

Newport showed these instructions to Captain Smith, the valiant captain very aptly pronounced the London Company a lot of fools. There was another absurd instruction given Newport, which the historian Fisk says: "Was grotesque enough to have emanated from the teeming brain of James I. after a mickle noggin of his native Glenlivat." This ridiculous instruction was to the effect that Powhatan should be crowned as a king, and be made a vassal of the King of England. Smith and Newport, after preliminary arrangements with the Indian chief, went to Werowocomoco and there, in the chief's wigwam, performed a burlesque coronation ceremony. They put a scarlet robe on the greasy old man, and placed a tinsel crown on his head. The newly crowned forest monarch sent his old raccoon-skin cloak as a present to his royal brother, King James I. Smith and Newport were very elaborately entertained by King Powhatan. A wonderful masquerading performance that was presented before the English visitors was described as follows by one of the party:

"In a fayre playne field they made a fire, before which we sitting upon a mat, suddainly amongst the woods was heard * * * a hydeous noise and shrieking. * * * Then presently we were presented with this anticke; thirtie young women came nearly naked out of the woods, their bodies all painted, some white, some red, some black, some particolour, but all differing; their leader had a fayre payre of buck's horns on her head, and an otter's skin at her girdle, and another at her arm, a quiver of arrows at her back, a bow and arrow in her hand; the next had in her hand a sword, another a club, * * * all horned alike * * * These fiends with most hellish shouts and cries, rushing from among the trees, cast themselves in a ring about the fire, siging and dauncing with most excellent ill varietie; * * * having spent near an houre in this mascarado, as they entered in like manner they departed. Having reaccomodated themselves, they solemnly invited us to their lodgings, where we were no sooner within the house but all these nymphes more tormented us than ever, with crowding, pressing, and hanging about us, most tediously crying, *Love you not me?* This salutation ended, the feast was set, consisting of fruit in baskets, fish and flesh in wooden platters; beans and peas there wanted not, nor any salvage dainty their invention could devise. Some attending, others singing and dancing about us; which mirth and banquet being ended, with firebrands for torches they conducted us to our lodging."

These impersonators of the wood nymphs were Pocahontas and other maidens of the tribe. The Indian princess was then just entering her teens; and had no thought at the time she was "Mascaradoing" for the amusement of a company of English adventurers, that she would very soon thereafter become a leading character in a drama, with a continent for its stage and a mighty nation its theme. She saved the life of Captain John Smith by placing her own head upon his to shield him from the impending blows of Indian bludgeons; and helped him save the life of the Jamestown colony when threatened with destruction from starvation and other perils. Nor did the dusky maiden dream when cooing to a pale-faced guest of her father, "Love you not me?" that in a little while she would be made the bride of a white gentleman and have introduction to proud Albion's nobility and royalty; and would become the historic ancestress of some of Virginia's most distinguished sons, and even of the beautiful wife of a President of the United States.

Captain Newport made an ineffectual effort to discover a route to the Salt Sea that was believed to be not far beyond the mountains. Although Smith tried to dissuade him from the attempt he went upon a trip of discovery above the falls of James River, but returned with his party without even reaching the Blue Ridge Mountains. Smith went energetically to work to provide a cargo to send to England, which was composed of tar, pitch, glass and boards; and Newport again started on a home voyage, taking along Ratcliffe, the second deposed president. Captain Smith sent by Newport a letter to the Royal Council in London in which he set forth the mistakes that prevented the success of the colony. In part, he said:

"When you send again I intreat you to send but 30 carpenters, husbandmen, gardeners, fishermen, blacksmiths, masons, and diggers up of trees, roots, well provided, rather than 1,000 of such as we have; for except we be able both to lodge them and feed them, the most will consume with want of necessaries before they can be good for anything.

* * *

"These are the causes that have kept us in Virginia from laying such a foundation as ere this might have given much better content and satisfaction; but as yet you must not look for any profitable returns; so I humbly rest."

Captain Smith had a very quaint style of expressing his views, but he managed to inform the Royal Council that they were respon-

sible for the ill success of the colony; and also to tell them they
should expect no profitable returns from their venture until a change
was made in the character of the emigrants that were being sent
across the waters to Virginia. He put all the men to work with
the assurance that: "He who would not work, might not eat;" and
Jamestown began to assume an appearance of life and thrift. We
are told that they "digged and planted" twenty or thirty acres in
corn, and cultivated it under the instructions of two friendly Indians.
This was a pretty big job, especially the digging of thirty acres
with hoes; and it shows how impractical and careless the Royal
Council had been in not providing horses or oxen to plow and cultivate the land.

————————

At the request of the London Company a new or second charter
was, on the 23rd of May, 1609, granted the company, which changed
its form of management and made material alterations in the boundaries of Virginia. The company was changed from a proprietary
organization to a corporate body, to be known as the "Treasurer and
Company of Adventurers and Planters of the City of London for
the First Colony in Virginia." All the power of control which was
reserved by the king in the first charter was transferred to the company, and the management of the Virginia Colony was committed to
a Supreme Council to be chosen by the shareholders and to reside in
England. This Supreme Council had authority to legislate for the
colony and to appoint a governor and council to conduct its local
affairs. The new charter gave to the corporate body "all those
Lands, Countries and Territories situated, lying and being in that
part of America called Virginia, from the Point of Land called Cape
or Point Comfort, all along the Sea Coast to the Northward 200
miles, and from said Point of Cape Comfort, all along the Sea Coast
to the Southward 200 miles, and all that space and circuit of Land,
lying from the Sea Coast of the Present aforesaid, up into the land,
throughout from Sea to Sea, West and Northwest, and all the islands
lying within 100 miles along the coast of both Seas of the Precinct
aforesaid." This extended the territory of Virginia to the Pacific
Ocean, and to the Great Lakes.

Upon its reorganization the company selected Sir Thomas
Smith, a prominent London merchant, for treasurer of the corporation, and Thomas West (Lord Delaware) for governor of Virginia.
Smith and Lord Delaware were both men of very fine character,
and their appointment to these high executive offices bespoke better

days for the Jamestown colony. As soon as the new charter was secured steps were taken to organize another expedition; and some 500 persons, men, women, and children, were induced to cross the ocean and become settlers in Virginia. A fleet of nine vessels, with ample supplies, was assembled, and Captain Newport, the able mariner, was placed in charge. He sailed with his fleet from England in June, 1609, and in August the Third Supply, 300 or more persons, reached Jamestown. The balance of the emigrants were on the ship *Sea Venture,* along with Sir Thomas Gates and Sir George Somers, who were sent out by the company to give personal supervision to the colony. Their vessel was separated from the balance of the fleet and was wrecked by a storm on the coast of the Bermuda Islands. This part of the expedition had to remain in the Bermudas for nearly a year. They built small vessels and succeeded in getting to Jamestown on May 10th, 1610.

The failure of Gates and Somers to reach Jamestown with the main part of the expedition left the control of the colony in the hands of Captain Smith. He soon found out that the newly arrived emigrants were very much inferior to the former ones, of whose quality he had complained to the London Company. The newcomers were largely of the shiftless vagabond class, whom Smith described as "unruly gallants packed thither by their friends to escape ill destenies."

President Smith had never approved of the Jamestown site for the colony, because of its unhealthy, marshy surroundings; and he determined to hunt a better situation. With this end in view, he sailed up the James to the Indian village called Powhatan, and purchased from the Powhatan tribe a tract of land close to where the city of Richmond now stands. Because of its beautiful and pleasant location he named the place "Nonesuch". While he was returning to Jamestown, Smith was severely injured by the accidental explosion of a bag of gunpowder. The wounds he received were so severe that he was compelled to go to England for surgical treatment, and early in October he sailed on the home voyage; and this severed finally his official connection with the first Virginia colony. Smith left George Percy in command, but that gallant gentleman did not have the executive ability or the qualities of leadership needed to control the 500 colonists, most of whom were unruly vagabonds. Trouble arose with the Indians and the red men slew the settlers at every opportunity. The disreputable

Ratcliffe and thirty of his associates were killed at one time while on a trading visit to the Pamunkey village.

When winter came on more cabins were needed, but the men were too worthless to build them, and some of the colonists died from exposure. Then, what was afterwards called "The Starving Time" came on. The supply of food became exhausted, Percy was sick, Smith was in England, and famine, in most horrid form, took possession of the settlement. For a short time the people subsisted on herbs and roots. Then they resorted to the horrible practice of cannibalism. A slain Indian was boiled and eaten, and starving men began to cook and eat their own dead. One brute killed his wife, salted her down, and had eaten a part of her body when his fiendish act was discovered, and he was burned at the stake by outraged though starving citizens. McDonald in his "Life in Old Virginia," says:

"Smith left in Virginia three ships and seven boats, a supply of commodities ready for trade with the Indians, a goodly supply of corn newly gathered, provisions in store for the colony, three hundred muskets with other arms and ammunition, nets for fishing, tools of all sorts for work, apparel to supply their wants, six mares and a horse, more than five hundred hogs, as many hens and chickens and some sheep and goats."

It is almost incredible that nearly five hundred persons could have been gathered together from any part of the world, and especially from England, as incapable and helpless as these colonists. There were four hundred and ninety persons in the colony when Captain Smith left in October, 1610; and when Gates and Somers arrived in May, 1611, only sixty were left. Vice, sickness, indolence, and famine had accomplished their deadly work; and if relief had been delayed a few days longer there would have been none left to tell the deplorable fate of the settlement. Gates and Somers were struck with horror by the conditions they found, and readily consented to take the miserable people back to England. Tearfully the captains realized that Virginia must be abandoned, and they got the people aboard their small vessels, with the intention of sailing to the coast of Newfoundland, to get a supply of fish, and then cross the ocean to England. On the 7th of June they dropped with the tide down James River and spent the night at Mulberry Island. The next morning anchors were weighed and the expedition started again on the homeward journey; but at noon, when they were entering Hampton Roads, they discovered in the distance a small boat approaching. It proved to be the longboat of Lord Delaware, who was coming to take up his work as the first governor of Virginia. He had with him three ships well stocked with supplies, and the colonists were easily persuaded to return to Jamestown and resume the effort to make a permanent settlement in Virginia. On the morning of the 8th they were landed at the desolate place so recently deserted; and Lord Delaware fell upon his knees, raised his hands toward heaven and devoutly thanked God for permitting him to reach Virginia in time to save the life of the colony.

The first act of Lord Delaware upon landing was to have a religious service held. After a sermon had been preached, the governor read his commission and made a speech to all the people, in which he censured the old settlers for their vanities and idleness, and gave them to understand that under his administration the vicious and slothful would receive no mercy. He put the men to work building new fortifications and repairing the houses, and the little church was made neat and attractive again. A bell was hung at a convenient point, to take the place of a clock, and was rung to regulate the hours of work; and system and order were established in the settlement. The winter of 1610-11 was in many respects a hard one for the colony, but was not as severe as the previous one. Still, about 150 of the settlers died during the winter, and Lord Delaware's health was so greatly impaired that he was compelled to return to England. For a short time George Percy was again left in command. Captain Newport made another trip to the colony in March, this time bringing 300 emigrants who were more shiftless and worthless than any of the previous supplies. Sir Thomas Gates was appointed deputy governor, but for some reason could not at that time come to Jamestown; and Sir Thomas Dale, with the title of High Marshal of Virginia, was sent over to take charge.

For the next five years Dale ruled the colony, Lord Delaware, the governor, remaining in England during the time. The High Marshal proved himself well suited for the task given him. By his great energy, indomitable will and splendid common sense, he brought order out of chaos, and put the Virginia colony once more on the road to permanency. When he reached Jamestown he found the men idling away their time playing games, instead of planting and cultivating the soil. A severe code of laws was immediately prepared and put in force to stay the idle and vicious dispositions of the men; and a number of offenses were punished with death. A plot to overthrow and kill Dale was formed by Jeffrey Abbot and other desperate characters. The plot was discovered and Abbot and four of his companions were executed. In the fall of 1611, six months after Dale took charge, another supply of settlers was brought over, and the colony then numbered about eight hundred persons. A good stock of cows, oxen and goats was also added to the increasing resources of the colony. The idea of expansion from the Jamestown colony followed, and a settlement was made at the mouth of James River where the present town of Hampton is now located. This is the oldest continuous settlement, save two, in the United States, St. Augustine, Florida, and Santa Fe, New Mexico. It seems that Sir Thomas Dale thought, as did Captain Smith, that a more favorable site should be selected for the colony. So believing, he selected the Dutch Gap peninsula farther up the James and built a town there. He called the place Henricus, after the then Prince of Wales, and erected fortifications and houses for three hundred persons. Other settlements were made at Bermuda and Shirley Hundreds on James River, and at Dale's Gift near Cape Charles on the Eastern Shore of Virginia. The establishment of these new settlements was a strong assurance that the colonization of Virginia had become permanent.

The London Company applied to King James for a new charter. and on the 12th of March, 1612, it was granted by the king, and is known as the Third Charter. The company wanted to get possession of the Bermuda Islands and to secure for its members fuller and more direct management of the affairs of the corporation; and these two things as well as many others of importance were secured by the Third Charter. In this same year another important event in the history of Virginia occurred, it being the marriage of John Rolfe, the English gentleman, to Pocahontas, the uneducated Indian girl, the daughter of Powhatan. Rolfe and his English wife were among the emigrants who were cast on the Bermuda Islands when the *Sea Venture* was wrecked on the coast of those islands. They came from the Bermudas to Jamestown with Gates and Somers in May, 1610. Soon after they arrived in Virginia, Mrs. Rolfe died; and later on her widowed husband became the lover of the dusky Indian girl, who had been made a captive by Captain Argall and held as such at Jamestown. Rolfe did not wish to marry a heathen; and Pocahontas was baptized into the Christian faith and given the Bible name, Rebekah. The marriage was celebrated in the church at Jamestown, and witnessed by a mixed company of Indians and Englishmen.

It is said that Rolfe was the first Englishman who cultivated tobacco for commercial purposes. He and his Indian wife went to England in 1616 in the same vessel with Sir Thomas Dale after he vacated the office of High Marshal of Virginia. Pocahontas became a popular society rage in London, where she was entertained and banqueted by English royalty and nobility. In 1617, when Argall was appointed deputy governor of Virginia, Rolfe was made secretary for the colony. On the eve of his sailing for Virginia, Pocahontas became suddenly ill and died at Gravesend, and was buried in the parish church at that place. She had one child, Thomas Rolfe, who remained in England with an uncle until he attained his manhood. He then came to Virginia and settled permanently, and became the ancestor of some of the most prominent families in the State.

In 1616 George Yeardley was in Virginia as deputy governor, and succeeded Sir Thomas Gates as acting governor; and administered the affairs of the colony until Captain Samuel Argall was appointed deputy governor in 1617. Argall's administration was brief and very unsatisfactory. He ruled with as much severity as his predecessor, Dale, but his conduct of the office was unscrupulous and dishonest. After serving one year, Argall was recalled by the company, and Lord Delaware was directed to again take personal charge of the colony. Delaware sailed from England in the spring of 1618 to resume his duties as governor. He was accompanied by 200 emigrants and traveled by way of the Azores. While they were making a short stay at St. Michael Island, Lord Delaware and thirty of his companion voyagers became violently ill and died. There was a strong suspicion that they were poisoned by the Spaniards who entertained them at St. Michael's.

Up to 1612, no member of the colony was permitted to enjoy private ownership of land. Sir Thomas Dale then became convinced that the community system, which had been enforced since the founding of the colony, had proved the principal cause of the suffering from starvation, in that it discouraged the industrious and encouraged the lazy in their indolent habits. Acting upon this belief, he made distribution of small portions of land to each settler to work for his own benefit, but required that a certain portion of the products should be turned into a general store to be used for the common benefit in an emergency.

George Yeardley was knighted and appointed governor of Virginia to succeed Lord Delaware. In 1619 the colony had increased to 2,000 persons; and the people demanded that they should be accorded local self-government, and the request was granted. Governor Yeardley was directed to issue writs for the election of a General Assembly in Virginia. Writs were issued for an election of representatives from eleven local constituencies or boroughs, which were designated as City, Plantation, and Hundred; and each constituency was given two representatives, who were called burgesses. This gave the name, House of Burgesses, to the Assembly, which name continued in use from 1619 until the Revolutionary War in 1776. The eleven boroughs that sent representatives were James City, Charles City, the City of Henricus, Martin Brandon, Martin's Hundred, Lawne's Plantation, Ward's Plantation, Argall's Gift, Flowerdien Hundred, Smith's Hundred, and Kecoughtan. Soon afterwards the name of Smith's Hundred was changed to Southampton Hundred and Kecoughtan was changed to Hampton. The assembly, in addition to the twenty-two elective members, had an upper house, which was composed of the governor, deputy governor and an assistant council, and altogether they constituted a General Assembly. The body was invested with both legislative and judicial functions and had full authority for legislating for the colony; but its acts had to be approved by the General Court of the London Company before they were enforced. On July the 30th, 1619, the General Assembly of Virginia met for organization and business in the church at Jamestown, and was the first legislature that assembled in the English colonies of America.

During the year 1619, other events of importance affecting the future of the colony and Virginia occurred. One of these was the introduction of African slaves, which came soon after the right of local self-government had been accorded the colony, and a short time after the first sitting of the General Assembly. John Rolfe, who was then secretary of the colony, said: "About the last of August there came in a Dutchman of warre that sold us twenty negars." Five years later a census showed that there were only twenty-two negroes in the colony, and the increase of slaves came very slowly in Virginia.

The next most important event was the bringing of a ship-load of young women-spinsters, selected with care as to character and in charge of matrons, to become wives for the unmarried men who were greatly in the majority in the colony. These young women were left free to select their own husbands, and had no trouble finding plenty of suitors; but no accepted suitor could marry his girl until he had paid the company 120 pounds of tobacco to cover the expense of transporting her to Virginia. This matrimonial experiment resulted so happily that the practice of bringing over wives for the bachelors was continued; and the following year "Sixty young maids of virtuous education, young, handsome, and well recommended", were imported. This resulted in the establishing of many pleasant homes, and naturally increased immigration. In 1622 the population had become four thousand, the cultivation of tobacco had been made an important and profitable industry, domestic ties were strengthened, habits of thrift superseded the indolent and wasteful customs that had prevailed, and cheerful comfort chased away the gloom and squalor that threatened the life of the colony.

Other incidents of importance in this eventful year of the colony occurred. A college was established in Henrico for the purpose of educating and converting the native children to Christianity. King James, through the various Bishops of England, collected a fund of fifteen thousand pounds for endowing the institution; and the London Company donated 10,000 acres of land to enlarge the design of the college by providing for the education of the white children of the colony.

Cordial relations had existed between the Indians and colonists for several years previous to 1622. Powhatan died in 1618, and was succeeded as head-chief of the confederacy by his brother Opechancanough. The latter was never friendly to the whites, but had been held in restraint by Powhatan. Early in 1622 Opechancanough secretly planned the destruction of the colony. He and his people had become very restless and resentful as they witnessed the growing strength of the colony and saw the best lands of the Indians appropriated by the white settlers. An Indian chief, to whom the English had given the name of Jack of the Feather, killed one of the colonists, and he was killed by the whites in requital. Opechancanough and his associates then formed a conspiracy to destroy the entire colony on a certain day. On the 22nd of March, 1622, the Indians made a concerted attack upon the colonists, and killed 347 persons. The red men failed to accomplish their fell purpose, as two thousand five hundred persons were saved from the general massacre. However, the colonists were so fearful of another attack that they abandoned seventy-two of their plantations and huddled together on eight. They also abandoned their college and their infant manufacturing establishments, and confined their cultivation of the soil to such a limited area that enough food could not be produced to support the people. Again much sickness and want prevailed in the colony. But the London Company came to the partial relief of the colony by sending over supplies of food, and King James sent them a lot of old muskets. In a short while the colonists recovered from their panic, and sent a military expedition of three hundred men to punish the Indians for the brutal massacre of the settlers. The natives fled from their homes on the approach of the avenging expedition, taking with them most of their corn; but the whites destroyed many of their villages and a great deal of their property. At the following session of the General Assembly a law was enacted which directed that at the beginning of the next July the inhabitants should attack and kill all savages in their respective neighborhoods. This war of extermination, or driving back of the natives to the wild forests, was continued without intermission until a peace was concluded with the Indians in 1632. By the provisions of this treaty the whites retained all the habitations and cleared lands they had taken from the natives, who were forced to take refuge in the forests and marshes.

In 1623 the London Company realized that the affairs of the colony had not been successfully managed, and sought to correct the management by a reorganization of the corporation. During the sixteen preceding years ten thousand persons had been transported to Virginia and only a little more than two thousand remained after the massacre by the Indians. From a business standpoint the colony had proved a decided failure, as the annual exports amounted to no more than one hundred thousand dollars. King James, who was greatly displeased with the liberal democratic government the company had given the colonists, determined to annul the charter and establish a royal government in Virginia. His plans to this end were carried out through the employment of five commissioners, who were sent to Jamestown to investigate the management of the colony from the time the first settlement was made. These commissioners were appointed by the king, and were: John Harvey, John Pory, Abraham Piersey, Samuel Matthews and John Jefferson. They were instructed: "To make more particular and diligent inquiry touching divers matters, which concerned the state of Virginia; and in order to facilitate the inquiry, the governor and council of Virginia were ordered to assist the commissioners, in this scrutiny, by all their knowledge and influence." Thus began the artful scheme of the crafty king to take from the Virginia colony its right of self-government.

The commissioners, as appointed, came to Jamestown and tried to get the General Assembly to petition the king for a revocation of the charter of the company. Failing to secure the petition from the General Assembly, the commissioners returned to England and made a false and defamatory report as to existing conditions in Virginia. To this report the General Assembly made a spirited denial and drafted a petition to the king in which it was prayed, "that the governors may not have absolute power, and that they might still retain the liberty of popular assemblies, than which, nothing could more conduce to the public satisfaction and public utility." This petition, however, never reached King James, as Mr. Pountis, a member of the Colonial Council, to whose care it was entrusted, died while on his passage to England to deliver it to the king. The king instituted *quo warranto* proceedings in the King's Bench for the purpose of divesting the London Company of its corporate privileges and powers, and for the dissolution of the company. The cause was tried at the Trinity Term of the court in 1624, and all the demands of King James were granted by a decree of Lord Chief Justice Ley, who was a mere creature of the king. Dissolution of the company occasioned very little change in the government of the colony. A committee was appointed by the king to exercise the functions previously performed by the London Company. Sir Francis Wyatt was reappointed governor, and he and his council were empowered to govern the colony "as fully and amply as any governor and council resident there, at any time within the space of five years last past". Strange to relate, King James refused to appoint as members of the new council for Virginia any of the extreme partisans of his court faction, but selected men of conservative views for the government of the colony.

The dissolution of the London Company did not weaken the colony, but upon the contrary strengthened it by making it more self-reliant and independent in action. Factional fights for its control by antagonistic leaders of the company had been continuous from the date of the first settlement at Jamestown; and the selection of incapable, and in some instances very corrupt, men to administer its affairs had greatly retarded its success. At first the colonists were greatly alarmed by the dissolution of the company, fearing that it might take from them their House of Burgesses and deprive them of the already cherished form of representative self-government. The General Assembly was invested with both legislative and judicial authority and had not failed to exercise freely these important functions. Fiske, in "Old Virginia and her Neighbors", writes very interestingly about the first American legislative body; and among other things says:

"The place of meeting was the wooden church at Jamestown, 50 feet in length by 20 in width, built in 1619, for Lord Delaware's church had become dilapidated; a solid brick church, 56 by 28, was built there in 1639. From the different plantations and hundreds the burgesses came mostly in their barges or sloops to Jamestown. In 1634 the colony was organized into counties and parishes, and the burgesses thenceforth represented counties, but they always kept their old title. At first the governor, council, and burgesses met together in a single assembly, just as in Massachusetts until 1644, just as in England the Lords and Commons usually sat together before 1339. A member of this Virginia parliament must take his breakfast of bacon and hoe-cake betimes, for the meeting was called at the third beat of the drum, one hour after sunrise. The sessions were always opened with prayers, and every absence from this service was punished with a fine of one shilling. The fine for absence during the whole day was half a crown. In the choir of the church sat the governor and council, their coats trimmed with gold lace. By the statute of 1621, passed in this very church, no one was allowed to wear gold lace, except these high officials and the commanders of hundreds, a class of dignitaries who in 1634 were succeeded by the county lieutenants. In the body of the church, facing the choir, sat the burgesses in their best attire, with starched ruffs, and coats of silk or velvet in bright colours. All sat with their hats on, in imitation of the time-honoured custom of the House of Commons, an early illustration of the democratic doctrine, 'I am as good as you'. These burgesses had their speaker, as well as their clerk and sergeant-at-arms. * * * From sweeping principles of constitutional law down to the pettiest sumptuary edicts, there was nothing which this little parliament did not superintend and direct."

During the first years of its existence the House of Burgesses. in the exercise of its very ample powers, enacted a number of peculiar laws. Some of these laws were fundamentally sound, some were absurd in their intendment, and others sharply in conflict with the principles of democratic government, toward which the colony, even in its early life, seemed to be traveling. The tax question was then, comparatively, as momentous as it is today with the average citizen and the aspiring politician. One of the first acts of the General Assembly, which was passed without a dissenting voice, was a declaration, "that the governor shall not lay any taxes or impositions upon the colony, their lands or commodities, otherway than by the authority of the general assembly, to be levied and employed as the said assembly shall appoint." This was a wise protection of the functions of the legislative branch of the government from encroachments by the executive branch thereof.

Moved by a humane and philanthropic spirit, the assembly passed a law looking to the conversion and education of the young savages. The act provided for the procurement from each borough of a certain number of Indian children to be educated "in true religion and a civil course of life; of which children the most towardly boys in wit and graces of nature are to be brought up by them in the first elements of literature, so as to be fitted for the college intended for them, that from thence they may be sent to that work of conversion." This was conforming to the scheme of 1619 for establishing a college in Henrico for the Indians, to which enterprise the Bishops of England had contributed fifteen thousand pounds and the London Company 10,000 acres of land; and was completely at variance with the laws passed by the assembly, after the frightful massacre of 1622, encouraging the extermination of the Indians.

Very rigid laws were enacted to prevent drunkenness, forbidding extravagance in dress, and to suppress flirting, the latter being considered a very grave social crime. For the first offence, a drunkard was privately reproved by the minister; the second time he was publicly admonished; for the third offence he was put in irons and made to pay a heavy fine; and for subsequent violations of the statute he was placed at the mercy of the governor and the council, who were to punish him severely in their discretion. Extravagance in dress was made a misdemeanor, for which an unmarried man was taxed for public purposes "according to his own apparel," and a married man "according to his own and his wife's apparel." In these days, when women have acquired the right to vote in many of the States of the Union, with the prospect of soon obtaining the exercise of suffrage in every State, the average male legislator would be slow in voting for a measure to regulate the dress of women, but would hastily cast himself in the midst of the great temperance wave that is sweeping over our country and the entire civilized world.

The law against flirting declared that "every minister should give notice in his church that what man or woman soever should use any word or speech tending to a contract of marriage to two several persons at one time   *   *   *   as might entangle or breed scruples in their consciences, should for such their offenses either undergo corporal correction (by whipping) or be punished by fine or otherwise, according to the quality of the person so offending." Possibly this law was suited to the times, but it would now be regarded as a disgrace to any civilized community; and the act was particularly obnoxious for the reason that the punishment to be inflicted was measured "according to the quality of the person so offending." The common folks were to be whipped and the gentle people were to be fined.

To say anything offensive about the governor or a member of the council was a misdemeanor, for which the offender was placed in the pillory. The planters were not allowed to sell any part of their tobacco crops until they had put aside a certain portion for the minister's salary. There was a law which said "No man shall disparage a mynister whereby the myndes of his parishioners may be alienated from him and his mynistric prove less effectuall upon payne of severe censure of the governor and councell." From the class of "mynisters", then inflicted upon the colony it would seem that they were worthy subjects for disparaging remarks. At least the General Assembly must have thought so, as it was necessary for that august body to give warning to the clergyman by a statute which said: "Mynisters shall not give themselves to excess in drinking or ryote, spending their time idelie by day or night playing at dice, cards, or any unlawfull game." Evidently the "mynisters" were more at home in the tavern or at the gambling table than in the pulpit.

In recent years there has been much controversy over the question of government regulation of the sale of food products and other articles. The General Assembly of the Virginia colony exercised that power without its authority to do so being questioned. A law was made fixing retail prices for wines and other liquors. The preamble of the act said: "Whereas there hath been great abuse by the unreasonable rates enacted by ordinary keepers, and retaylers of wine and strong waters", and the assembly proceeded to fix maximum prices for these commodities. The penalty for a violation of the law was a fine of double the rate charged by the venders.

The House of Burgesses also passed a very stringent law to suppress the speculators, or as they were then called "forestallers", in foodstuffs and other necessary articles. The act said: "Whatsoever person or persons shall buy or cause to be bought any marchandize, victualls, or any other thinge, comminge by land or water to markett to be sold or make any bargaine, contract or promise for the haveinge or buyinge of the same * * * before the said marchandize, victualls, or other thinge shall be at the markett readie to be sold; or make any motion by word, letter or message or otherwise to any person or persons for the enhansing of the price or dearer sellinge of any thinge or thinges above mentioned, or else disswade, move or stirr any person or persons cominge to the markett as aforesayd, shall be deemed and adjudged a forestaller. And if any person or persons shall offend in the thinges before recited and being thereof duly convicted or attaynted shall for his or theire first offence suffer imprisonment by the space of two monthes without baile or maineprize, and shall also loose and forfeite the value of the goods so by him or them bought or had as aforesayed; and for the second offence * * * shall suffer imprisonment by the space of one halfe yeare * * * shall loose the double value of all goods * * * soe bought * * * and for the third offence * * * shall be set on the pilorie * * * and loose and forfeit all the goods and chattels that he or they then have to their owne use, and also be committed to prison, there to remayne duringe the Governors pleasure."

This act was very drastic but not too severe. It was directed against monsters concealed in human forms, vampires who dared to call themselves men, but who did not scruple to sacrifice the comfort and life of men, women, and children to gratify their greed of gold. The greatest present menace to the life and happiness of the American people comes from "forestallers"—speculators and extortioners—who infest our land, and who are plying their wretched trade, despite any feeble endeavor made by the Federal and State governments to fasten punishment upon them. It would be well for the suffering public if the Old Virginia House of Burgesses could return to exercise its legislative functions and supply the Congress of the United States with quaint but effective laws to suppress the worst of criminals.

T.H.-9

CHAPTER IV.

FROM DEATH OF JAMES I TO 1676.

On the 27th of March, 1625, King James I. died, after an unpopular reign of twenty-two years. He was succeeded by his son, Charles I., who had no more regard for the political rights and privileges of the Virginia colonists than he showed for his subjects in England. But the General Assembly, when informed of the death of King James, sent Sir George Yeardley, then a member of the council, as an envoy to England to present their respects to King Charles; and to give him assurance that the Virginians were satisfied with the government his father had given them. The request was presented that no change be made in their very liberal form of government; and in 1626 Sir George Yeardley was appointed governor of Virginia, which satisfied the colonists that their request had been favorably received by their sovereign. All through his reign of twenty-five years, Charles was involved in such bitter strife with Parliament and his Scotch and English subjects that he could give but little attention to the Virginia colony.

Within a period of twenty years the colony had three forms of government. When the settlement was first made at Jamestown its nature was that of a Proprietary Government, and it so remained until the second charter was obtained in 1609 by the London Company. It then became a Corporation, and continued as such under the third charter until the company was dissolved by a decree of the Court of King's Bench in 1624, when it was made a Royal Province. Soon after ascending the throne, Charles I. appointed William Claiborne secretary of state for the colony, and in Claiborne's commission designated it "Our Kingdom of Virginia." It may be gratifying to some Virginians of this day, who are charmed with royalty and the degenerate European nobility, to know that for about a quarter of a century Virginia was recognized as a Kingdom by an English monarch.

The administration of justice when the colony was first established was lodged with the president and council; and after a governor was substituted for the president all judicial authority was vested in the governor and his council. This was a very dangerous power to place with a single man, who might prove himself either a knave or a fool and trample upon justice, rather than uphold and vindicate the rights of the people. In 1628-29, commissions were

issued to justices or magistrates to hold monthly courts in each of
the boroughs or hundreds. These courts were the origin of the old
county courts that administered justice in the counties of Virginia
until the Constitution of 1870 was put in operation.

From "Acts made by the Grand Assemblie Holden at James
City the 21st. August, 1633," we find that the colony had then so
extended its limits and had become so permanently planted as to
require the establishment of a county or shire system of government.
Consequently an Act was passed by the "Grand Assemblie", creating eight shires and they were given the following names: James
City, Henrico, Charles City, Elizabeth City, Warwick River, War-
rosquyoak, Charles River, Accawmack. These shires were to be
organized and governed in the same manner as the shires in England; and they were subsequently designated and conducted as counties. Their original boundaries cannot be ascertained, despite the
most diligent researches of archivists and historians. But their
location is known from the counties that now bear the same name,
to-wit: James City, Henrico, Charles City, Elizabeth City, Warwick,
York (Charles River) and Accomac. At a Grand Assemblie, Holden
at James City, the 2nd day of March 1642-3, the following act was
passed: "Be it further enacted and confirmed that the plantation
and county knowne now by the name of Acomack shall be knowne
and called by the county of Northampton. It is likewise enacted
and confirmed that Charles River County shall be distinguished by
this name (County of York). And that Warwick River shall be
called the County of Warwick." From that time all counties in
Virginia were created by special acts of the General Assembly.

Early in 1642 Sir William Berkeley was appointed governor of
Virginia by Charles I. About the same time the London Company
sought to regain control of the colony by a petition directed to
Parliament. The General Assembly met and made a strong protest
against the restoration of the company, avowing that control by
the corporation would be very detrimental to the welfare of the
colony. Speaking of the written protest sent by the assembly to
the king, Howe, in his History of Virginia, says: "This paper is
drawn with great ability, and sets forth the objections to the petition in very strong and striking terms. They enlarge especially
upon the wish and the power of the company to monopolize their
trade; the advantage and happiness secured to them by their present
form of government, with its annual assemblies and trial by jury;
the fact, that a restitution of the power of the company would be an
admission of the illegality of the king's authority, and a consequent

nullification of the grants and commissions; and the impossibility of men, however wise, at such a distance, and unacquainted with the climate or condition of the country, to govern the colony as well as it could be governed by their own Grand Assembly." The king was so favorably impressed with the spirit and force of the protest that he refused to consent to any change in the form of government that had brought so much happiness to the colonists.

The above shows all that remains of the city of Jamestown—the ruined tower of the brick church built in 1639.

In 1644 the colony suffered from another massacre by the Indians. The natives had been driven away from their homes on the borders of the rivers in the tidewater section, where the lands were fertile and easily tilled, and were forced to struggle for a precarious existence in the highlands, where the soil was thin. They had been greatly reduced in numbers by the policy of extermination which the House of Burgesses had inaugurated shortly after the dreadful massacre of 1622. Those who had fled to the interior for safety had become more skilled in warfare, and were made desperate by the continued encroachments of the settlers, who were forcing them still further away from the homes they and their fathers had occupied so happily for many years. Opechancanough, Powhatan's brother and successor, had grown so old that he had to be carried about on a litter, and he was so weak that he could not raise his eyelids without assistance; but his mental faculties were so well preserved that he was able to gather all the tribes of the confederacy together, without being discovered, and make a concerted attack on the colonists. On the 18th of April, 1644, the day appointed for the massacre, the Indians made their attack on the frontier settlements and killed three hundred persons. Owing to their greatly reduced number of warriors and the increased number of the colonists, the strength of the hostile Indians was soon broken. Recalling the terrible reprisals the whites had made upon them following the massacre of 1622, the natives fled in dismay to the remote thick forests. Opechancanough was made a captive by Sir William Berkeley, who had run the Indians down with a squadron of cavalry. The old chief was imprisoned at Jamestown, where he was brutally murdered by a cowardly soldier who was guarding him. Soon after this deplorable incident Governor Berkeley sailed for England, where he remained for a year, and upon his return to Jamestown he negotiated a treaty in 1646 with Necotowance, who had succeeded Opechancanough as chief of the remnant of the Powhatan Confederacy. The Indians made a complete submission to the whites and ceded such lands as were demanded. From that time, being at peace with the natives, with an abundance of fertile lands, and free markets for their tobacco, the colony was very prosperous and grew rapidly. Their ports were visited by the ships of the leading commercial nations, and historians say that, "At Christmas 1648, there were trading in Virginia ten ships from London, two from Bristol, twelve Hollanders and seven from New England."

The number of the colonists had grown to twenty thousand, but they were so much occupied with their own affairs that they could give but little attention to the bitter and bloody struggles that were taking place in England between the royalists and the Parliament. But when Charles I. was beheaded, in 1649, the Virginia Government recognized his son Charles II. as their sovereign; and "Virginia was whole for monarchy, and the last country belonging to England that submitted to obedience to the commonwealth." Being struck with horror at the monstrous crime of the Parliament that had beheaded their king, numbers of the nobility, gentry, and clergy fled from England and found generous welcome and safe asylum in Virginia. "The mansion and the purse of Berkeley were open to all, and at the hospitable dwellings that were scattered along the rivers and among the wilds of Virginia, the Cavaliers, exiles like their monarch, met in frequent groups to recount their toils, to sigh over defeats, and to nourish loyalty and hope." Thus were the English Cavaliers introduced into Tidewater Virginia in such numbers as to win for the State in coming years the name of Land of the Cavaliers.

Sir William Berkeley, in recognition of his loyalty, was recommissioned governor by Charles II. The fidelity of the Virginians to the royal cause was resented by Parliament; and the Council of State, of which Oliver Cromwell was the leading spirit, was ordered to take steps for bringing the rebellious colonies into obedience to the authority of the new republican English Government. Parliament passed a law to prevent foreign ships entering and trading at any of the ports "in Barbadoes, Antigua, Bermudas and Virginia." This law would have practically destroyed the foreign trade of the colony; but it was found so damaging to commerce that it was repealed before the authority of the Parliament was acknowledged in Virginia. The Virginians were so confident of their ability to defy the authority of Parliament that Governor Berkeley, speaking for the colonists, wrote to Charles II., then in exile at Breda, inviting him to come to Virginia and establish his Kingdom in America.

Parliament determined to bring into subjection the colonies that were adhering to the royalists. A large fleet and a considerable number of soldiers were sent out to make the rebellious colonists acknowledge allegiance to the Commonwealth. The fleet sailed first to Barbadoes and Antigua, and after bringing those two colonies into submission, unannounced, arrived at and anchored before Jamestown. Anticipating such a movement, Governor Berkeley and the colonists had made preparations to resist the Commonwealth's military and naval expedition; but the commissioners sent by Parliament along with the fleet offered such fair and liberal terms that the Virginians accepted the proposed articles of surrender. So far as self-government was concerned the colony was placed in a better situation than it had ever occupied under the royal governments.

Sir William Berkeley, who remained a royalist in heart, declined to hold the governorship under the Parliament, and Richard Bennett, a Roundhead. and who was one of the Virginia Council, was elected governor. A council was also elected by the assembly, with powers to conform to any instructions they might receive from the Parliament. Bennett's conduct of the government was so honest and liberal that it was approved by both the colonists and the Parliament; and when he retired from office in 1655, Edward Diggs was elected his successor. It is a notable fact that Cromwell never made any appointments of officers for Virginia during his protectorate; but encouraged the colony to become as nearly self-governing as possible.

On the 20th of April, 1653, Oliver Cromwell dissolved, or rather dispersed with his soldiers, the notorious Rump Parliament, and thence forward he became supreme ruler of England until his death in 1658. He grasped power and ignored the exasperating assumptions of Parliaments, only because he sought to promote in the speediest and surest way the prosperity, happiness and glory of his country. Under his administration as Lord Protector, he proved himself England's greatest ruler. His home policies were liberal and just, ever looking to the elevation of the masses, while his foreign policies were of such a nature as to secure for England a more commanding position among other nations than she had ever occupied. Virginia, and all the English colonies in America, made wonderful progress under Cromwell's liberal and able rule. He died on September the 3rd, 1658, and was succeeded as Lord Protector by his son, Richard. The General Assembly of Virginia, after maturely considering the matter, recognized Richard Cromwell as their ruler. He was a man of mediocre intellect, idolent by nature, and entirely unqualified to occupy the position his father had filled with such distinction. During his feeble administration, which was for a little more than seven months, Virginia was left free to conduct her own affairs. The General Assembly had elected Samuel Matthews governor in 1658, and he died shortly after Richard Cromwell was removed as Lord Protector.

Sir William Berkeley was re-elected governor in 1660, and the General Assembly by enactment declared "that the supreme power of the government of this country shall be resident in the assembly; and all writs shall issue in its name until there shall arrive from England a commission, which the assembly itself shall adjudge to be lawful." This action was taken to prevent the governor from assuming authority to control the conduct of the General Assembly as Governor Matthews had previously attempted.

After the death of Cromwell the desire of the English people

for a settled government lead to the restoration of the House of
Stuart; and Charles II, returned to England, landing at Dover on
the 26th of May, 1660. He ascended the throne amid the joyful
acclamations of the royalists, and for twenty-five years the profligate
monarch gave his country the most disgraceful government it ever
had to endure. Virginia promptly after the restoration announced
allegiance to the new king; and one of his first acts in connection
with the colony was to give recognition to Sir William Berkeley by
re-appointing him governor. Berkeley made himself as abnoxious
to the colonists during his second term of office as he had been
popular with them when first serving as governor. It was largely
due to his arbitrary and haughty conduct that Bacon's Rebellion
was brought about in 1676, which occurred just one hundred years
before the Revolution. In fact, the more appropriate name for
the uprising of Nathaniel Bacon and his fellow-colonists against
the oppressions of the royal and local government is revolution.
It was essentially a revolt against the despotic course of King
Charles, supplemented by that of the local government. Virginia
had reached a stage where she was content to have the protection
but not the despotic control of England. Parliament had, by its
commissioners, pledged a preservation of all the privileges and
immunities the colony had acquired under the protectorates of
Oliver Cromwell and his son Richard. There were a number of
grievances that aroused popular discontent. One was the enactment
of a navigation law which prohibited the colonists from trading
with foreign countries, and requiring them to confine their trade
exclusively to England. The object of this law was to enrich the
English merchants and increase the revenues of the king, at the
expense of the colony. This was an early manifestation of England's insatiable commercial greed; and it is as pronounced today
as it was when Charles II. had his mean navigation act foisted upon
the American colonies. A remonstrance against the outrageous
measure was prepared and dispatched to King Charles. Failing
to secure a repeal of the obnoxious measure, the colonists had the
will and courage to trade with all foreign ships and merchants who
were willing to take the risk of having their cargoes captured on
the high seas by English cruisers.

There were other grievances which were even more potential
for inciting revolt against the English and the Colonial governments. These were burdensome and unequal taxation and arbitrary
restrictions of the right of suffrage. The taxes were so levied as

to bear heavily upon the poorer members of the colony; and by an
act of the House of Burgesses, passed in 1670. the rights of suffrage
and of membership in the legislature were restricted to freeholders.
Speaking of these unjust and oppressive laws, Howe, in his interesting History of Virginia, says:

"But these evils in domestic legislation were trivial, compared
with those produced by the criminal prodigality of Charles, who
wantonly made exorbitant grants to his favorites of large tracts of
lands, without a knowledge of localities, and consequently without
regard to the claims or even the settlements of others. To cap the
climax of royal munificence, the gay monarch, in, perhaps, a merry
mood, granted to Lords Culpeper and Arlington the whole colony
of Virginia, for thirty-one years, with privileges effectually royal
as far as the colony was concerned, only reserving some mark of
homage to himself. This might be considered at court, perhaps.
as a small bounty to a favorite, but was taken in a very serious
light by the forty thousand people thus unceremoniously transferred.
The Assembly in its extravagance, only took from them a great
proportion of their profits; but the king was filching their capital,
their lands, and their homes, which they had inherited from their
fathers, or laboriously acquired by their own strenuous exertion."

CHAPTER V.

BACON'S REBELLION, AND DISCOVERY OF SHENANDOAH VALLEY.

Nathaniel Bacon, then about twenty-eight years old, was living on his plantation on the James, near Curl's Wharf. He was an Englishman by birth and raising, had been educated as a lawyer, and had emigrated with his young wife to Virginia a few years previous; and had shown such talent that he had already been made a member of the Colonial Council. Bacon was a man of resolute purpose, fine personal appearance, and of republican convictions. The Susquehannock Indians, from Maryland and Delaware, who were of the Iroquoian stock, had been making incursions into Virginia and attacking exposed settlements. This had made Bacon very hostile to the Indians, and in a moment of anger he had declared: "If the redskins meddle with me, damn my blood but I'll harry them, commission or no commission." Governor Berkeley on the other hand was anxious to stay at peace with the Indians, and had announced that he would not give a commission to any one to march with an armed force against the savages. In May, 1676, the Indians made an attack upon Bacon's upper plantation, where Richmond is now located, and killed his overseer and one of his servants. When it became known at Curl's Wharf, the planters in the vicinity armed themselves and offered to accompany Bacon on an expedition against the Indians. He dispatched a messenger to Berkeley and requested a commission to lead the expeditionary force, and received from the governor an evasive answer. Bacon sent him a courteous note, thanking him for the commission, and without delay started with a mounted force of the planters to make war on the redskins. They had marched but a few miles when they were overtaken by a messenger with a proclamation from Governor Berkeley, commanding the party to disperse. A few of the men obeyed, but Bacon and the others continued their march, came upon the Indians, and gave them a severe defeat. In the meantime Berkeley had started with a troop of cavalry in pursuit of the Bacon party, but the governor was recalled to Jamestown by intelligence that the planters of the York peninsula were in revolt. Upon his return to Jamestown, the governor dissolved the House of Burgesses, then in session, and issued writs for the election of a new assembly. Bacon became a candidate to represent

Henrico County, and he was elected by a heavy majority, the people being in sympathy with his views on the several vital questions then engaging the attention of the colony. When the time came for the assembling of the House of Burgesses, Bacon, with thirty followers, journeyed to Jamestown; and upon his arrival he was arrested by orders of the governor and taken before that dignitary, who rebuked and then pardoned the young rebel. In a spirit of compromise, Bacon was reluctantly induced to admit at the bar of the assembly that he had acted illegally in marching against the Indians without a commission from the governor; whereupon, Berkeley extended his forgiveness to Bacon and all the men who had accompanied him on his expedition against the Indians.

The General Assembly had not been long in session until a struggle began between that body and the governor, the latter demanding that the assembly confine its legislation exclusively to Indian affairs. But the assembly, defiantly and resolutely, went to work to relieve the people from the evils that had been oppressing them. They restored universal suffrage; repealed an odious law which exempted councillors and their families and the families of clergymen from taxation; abolished trade monopolies; made provision for a general inspection of public expenses and the careful auditing of public accounts, and enacted a number of other reform measures.

Nathaniel Bacon had been an active worker for reform legislation, and had also made insistent application for a commission to resume hostilities against the unfriendly Indians, who continued to make depredations upon the outlying settlements. These acts of the young patriot so angered Governor Berkeley that he not only refused to give Bacon a commission but made secret plans for his arrest and trial upon a charge of treason. Friends warned Bacon that his life would be endangered if he remained longer at Jamestown, and he secretly left that place in the night time. He repaired to his plantation at Curl's Wharf and organized a force of six hundred men. With this small but resolute band of followers he marched upon Jamestown; and on the afternoon of a sultry day in June halted his men on the green in front of the State House. With a small detail of soldiers he advanced to the door of the building in which the governor and council and the burgesses were then sitting. The governor, in a towering rage, presented himself at the door, and pulling open his lace shirt front to bare his bosom, cried out to Bacon: "Here I am! Shoot me! 'Fore God, a fair mark, a fair mark—shoot!" Bacon stood calm, and politely replied: "No, may it please your honor, we have not come to hurt a hair on your head or of any man's. We are come for a commission to save our lives from the Indians, which you have so often promised, and now we will have it before we go." It seems that Bacon's calmness was self-enforced, for as soon as Berkeley retired with his council for a conference, the angry young rebel declared he would kill them all if the commission demanded was not forthcoming. His squad of soldiers pointed their guns at the windows and shouted: "We will have it! We will have it!" In response to the cry of the soldiers, one of the members of the assembly waved from a window "a pacific handkercher" and called out, "You shall have it." The General Assembly prepared and gave Bacon a commission as general of an army, and also addressed a memorial to the king, setting forth the wrongs Bacon and his adherents were seeking to get rid of, and heartily commending the intrepid young patriot for the valuable services he had rendered the colony. On the following day the governor was constrained to affix his approving signature to the commission and also to the memorial to the king.

Governor Berkeley promptly issued a proclamation declaring Bacon and his associates rebels and traitors. He then went to Gloucester County, where he expected to find sufficient loyal sentiment among the people to enable him to cope with and suppress the Bacon rebellion. He found the sentiment in Gloucester as pronounced for the rebels as it was at Jamestown and in other localities of the colony. The infuriated old man made his escape across Chesapeake Bay to Accomac, where he was protected by loyal supporters.

When Bacon heard of the harsh proclamation of the governor, he was severely shocked by its accusations as to the purposes of himself and his followers. "It vexed him to the heart to think that while he was hunting Indian wolves, tigers and foxes, which daily destroyed our harmless sheep and lambs that he and those with him should be pursued with a full cry, as a more savage or a no less ravenous beast." He quit his hunt for the "Indian wolves" and hastily marched his men to Middle Plantation, the point where the historic city of Williamsburg was afterward located. One of his first acts was the issuance of a manifesto in reply to Berkeley's proclamation. Though written in the peculiarly stilted and obscure style then used by even the most highly educated men, it is an eloquent and fervid defence of the young leader and his companions against the acrimonious attacks of Governor Berkley. From the original manuscript, which is still preserved in the British State Paper office, the following is quoted:

"If virtue be a sin, if piety be guilt, all the principles of morality, goodness and justice be perverted, we must confess that those who are now Rebels may be in danger of those high imputations. Those loud and several bulls would affright innocents, and render the defence of our brethren and the inquiry into our sad and heavy oppressions Treason. But if there be (as sure there is) a just God to appeal to, if religion and justice be a sanctuary here, if to plead the cause of the oppressed, if sincerely to aim at his Majesty's honour and the public good without any reservation or by-interest, if to stand in the gap after so much blood of our dear brethren bought and sold, if after the loss of a great part of his Majesty's colony deserted and dispeopled freely with our lives and estates to endeavour to save the remainders, be treason—God Almighty judge and let guilty die. But since we cannot in our hearts find one single spot of rebellion or treason, or that we have in any manner aimed at subverting the settled government or attempting of the person of any, either magistrate or private man, notwithstanding the several reproaches and threats of some who for sinister ends were disaffected to us and censured our innocent and honest designs, and since all people in all places where we have yet been can attest our civil, quiet, peaceable behaviour, far different from that of rebellious and tumultuous persons, let Truth be bold and all the world know the real foundations of pretended quiet. We appeal to the country itself, what and of what nature their oppressions have been, or by what cabal and mystery the designs of many of those whom we call great men have transacted and carried on. But let us trace these men in authority and favour to whose hands the dispensation of the country's wealth has been committed."

This splendid protest of Nathaniel Bacon against the assumptions and oppressions of a profligate king remained a glowing spark on the plains of Williamsburg for one hundred years; and then burst forth into a consuming flame when George Mason presented to the Virginia fathers the greatest charter of human liberty ever penned by man, the Virginia Bill of Rights. Bacon sounded the first æolian notes for American freedom; and Mason and Jefferson caught up the strain, and in glorious, swelling, undying tones chanted it to an enslaved world.

The manifesto of Bacon was a protest against the oppressive and corrupt acts of the men in authority whom he designated as "juggling parisites whose tottering fortunes have been repaired at the public charge." Grave accusations were made against the official and personal conduct of Sir William Berkeley. He was charged with levying unjust taxes upon the common people for the benefit of his private favorites and for other sinister ends; with failure to protect the colony by fortifications, and neglecting to advance its commercial interests. And he was also accused of bringing "the majesty of justice" into contempt by placing in judicial positions men who were "scandalous and ignorant favourites." Another serious accusation was, that the governor had monopolized the beaver trade, and for the purpose of "that unjust gain," had "bartered and sold his Majesty's country and the lives of his loyal subjects to the barbarous heathen." The manifesto named nineteen of the most prominent men of the colony as Berkeley's "wicked and pernicious councellors, aiders and assisters against the commonality in these our cruel commotions." Some of the names mentioned were those of Sir Henry Chicheley, Richard Lee, Robert Beverly and Nicholas Spencer. The paper closed with a demand that all the persons mentioned be arrested and placed in confinement at the Middle Plantation until further orders. On account of their apparent truth, these charges were very galling to Berkeley, and sharpened his appetite for revenge upon his accusers.

After he had promulgated his manifesto, Bacon called a convention of the most notable men identified with the rebellion to formulate plans for making it effective. The meeting was held at the Middle Plantation on the 3rd of August, 1676, and the convention declared the governorship was vacant because of the abdication of Sir William Berkeley, and that the council should fill the vacancy until action could be taken by the king. Five members of the council also issued writs for the election of a new House of Burgesses. An agreement was drawn up which pledged the signers thereof to stand by and with Bacon until all the matters in dispute between Berkeley and the colonists could be presented to and passed upon by King Charles. For a time some of the leaders refused to sign the paper, because they thought Bacon was going too far in his resistance to the authority of the king, though professions of loyalty to Charles II. were prominently set forth in the document. News was then received of renewed hostile attacks by

the Indians; and this information removed the reluctance of those
who had hesitated in signing the agreement. Bacon took his army
across James River and marched to the town of the Appomattox
tribe, then located where Petersburg now stands, and gave the
Indians a crushing defeat. For several weeks the Indians were
pursued in different localities, the white men killing, capturing and
dispersing them. Bacon then sent an expedition of four armed
vessels, under command of Giles Bland, to the Eastern Shore to
arrest Governor Berkeley; but Bland and his entire party were
made captive by Berkeley through the treachery of the captain of
one of the vessels. Bland was put in irons and one of the captains
hanged, as a warning of Berkeley's intentions to the other leaders
of the revolt. Berkeley then gathered an army of one thousand
men, composed largely of the indentured servants of the planters
who were with Bacon, promising these servants the estates of their
masters if he succeeded in repressing the rebellion. With this
motley force he sailed up the river and again took possession of
Jamestown. At that time Bacon was at West Point with his army,
and he immediately marched to Jamestown, and after a few days
of desultory fighting forced the governor to flee again to Accomac.
The town was then burned, Bacon declaring that it should no longer
"Harbour the rouges." It was but a brief while thereafter when the
rebellion was terminated by the death of Bacon. He had contracted the fever while besieging Jamestown, and died at the home
of a friend in Gloucester County. His remains were secretly buried,
his friends fearing that if Berkeley regained power he would take
the body from the grave and hang it on a gibbet as Charles II.,
after his restoration, had treated the remains of Oliver Cromwell.
A number of Bacon's followers surrendered, placing themselves at
the mercy of Berkeley; and he lost no time in hunting down those
who tried to conceal themselves. Colonel Thomas Hansford was
captured by Robert Beverley. Hansford requested that he should
be "shot like a soldier and not hanged like a dog", but Berkeley
was thirsting for vengeance and Hansford was hanged, being made
"the first martyr to American liberty." Berkeley then made proclamation of a general amnesty to all his enemies who would surrender their arms and restore the property they had taken from his
partisan supporters. Many of the revolutionists availed themselves of these terms, only to find that the perfidious governor had
taken this course to entrap them. Persecutions and prosecutions
were begun against the most prominent men of the rebellion. Heavy

fines were imposed and large estates were confiscated for the private benefit of the governor and his minions. Twenty-three of the leaders were hanged without jury trials, a military court, acting under martial law, imposing the death penalty upon the victims at the dictation of Berkeley. Fortunately, commissioners had been sent from England to investigate the rebellion; and through their effort and at the protest of the General Assembly, Berkeley was prevailed upon to desist from his prosecution of the offending colonists. The commissioners in their report of the trials that took place after their arrival gave severe condemnation to the governor and his subservient military court. They said: "We also observed some of the royal party, that sat on the bench with us at the trial to be so forward in impeaching, accusing, reviling, the prisoners at the bar, with that inveteracy, as if they had been the worst of witnesses, rather than justices of the commission, both accusing and condemning at the same time. This severe way of proceeding represented to the assembly, they voted an address to the governor, that he would desist from any further sanguinary punishments, for none could tell when or where it would terminate."

Strange to tell, the two great-grandfathers of George Washington were partisans of Governor Berkeley in his vindictive persecutions of the patriots. They were John Washington and Colonel Augustine Warren. One hundred years thereafter George Washington, their great-grandson, became the patriot military leader of the Virginians when they revolted against Governor Dunmore's attempted enforcement of the oppressive and unjust tax laws of George III. The despicable Berkeley was forced to return to England with the commissioners, where he found himself so scorned by his fellow-countrymen that he soon died from humiliation and shame.

Some historians have been disposed to condemn Bacon and his associates for making their determined struggle for popular government, upon the theory that a majority of the wealthiest and most aristocratic citizens of the colony were opposed to the revolutionary movement. These aristocrats were averse to democratic ideas and popular government; and were worshipers of monarchy and nobility, even when represented by such debased creatures as Charles II. and Sir William Berkeley. This Cavalier element adhered to the doctrine that "society is most prosperous when a select portion of the community governs the whole." It is the same fatuous doctrine that in these days exudes from the narrow minds of certain political leaders who contend that those whom they call "the best people" shall rule; and that an oligarchy is preferable to the form of popular government which Thomas Jefferson and Abraham Lincoln gave to their country.

Made desperate by the oppressions of his people, heaped upon them by a venal governor, the young leader may on some occasions have been too extreme in expression and in action, but his revolt was the first tragic manifestation of a yearning for personal and political freedom in Colonial America.

The Bacon rebellion was of brief duration and was confined to a small territory, but its influence was far-reaching in connection with other English colonies in America. A number of persons who were connected with the Virginia rebellion fled to North Carolina to escape the persecutions of Governor Berkeley. They found the condition of affairs in that province very much like they had been in Virginia. An obnoxious navigation act, coupled with excessive taxation, and "denial of a free election of an assembly" brought about an insurrection. It was led by John Culpeper, a prominent member of the colony, and he was valuably assisted by the refugees from Virginia. The royalists were as bitterly opposed to popular government in North Carolina as they had been in Virginia. The advocates of self-government were denounced by the royalists as meriting "hanging for endeavoring to set the poor people to plunder the rich." The government was then being conducted by Thomas Miller as president and secretary, and with the added authority of collecting the revenues; and he had a council, as did the governor of Virginia. One of the counsellors joined in the rebellion, but the others, with Miller, were arrested and imprisoned. Culpeper and his associates refused to submit to the odious acts of Parliament, organized a representative popular government, and established courts of justice. The insurrectionists sent Culpeper and another planter to England to effect a compromise with the proprietaries of the colony. After fulfilling his mission, Culpeper started to leave England, but was arrested at the instance of Miller. He was acquitted by an English jury for participating in the insurrection; and from that time the North Carolina colonists were left free to conduct their local affairs.

The sixty-nine years that intervened between the landing of the colony at Jamestown and the insurrection lead by Nathaniel Bacon were pregnant with incidents that were tinged with romance, pathos, and tragedy. They were an appropriate sequel to the sad story of

T.H.—10

the lost Roanoke colony and little Virginia Dare. The small community that had been planted on the Jamestown peninsula in 1607 had expanded until it occupied nearly the entire Tidewater Virginia. Beautiful estates, many of them now historic, were located along the borders of the James, the York and other rivers, and of the numerous inlets that dotted the shores of the Chesapeake Bay. The population had grown to forty thousand souls, and enterprise and abundance had supplanted the slothfulness and destitution which had threatened to destroy the colony during the first years of its existence. The neighboring colonies, Carolina, Maryland, and Pennsylvania, as well as those more remote, New York, and Massachusetts, were also prospering and growing to such form as to forecast the need of a continental government for all of the colonies. From this time onward, until 1776, the trend of the American communities was in the direction of independent republican government.

The thirty years following the Bacon rebellion were stamped with full assurance that the Virginia colony had reached a stage of permanency and stability. Many incidents occurred which showed that all the colonies were entering upon a period of revolution that was to culminate in the formation of a federal government.

———

The year 1710 was an eventful one in the history of Virginia. In the month of June of that year Alexander Spottswood arrived from England to assume charge of the colony as its governor. All historians affirm that he was the best and ablest of the colonial governors. He was descended from an old and distinguished Scottish family, and from his early boyhood had been a soldier in the English army. His valor and ability won for him the rank of colonel at the early age of twenty-eight; and he came to Virginia six years later with a reputation so exalted as to make his reception at Williamsburg, then the seat of government, most cordial by the leading citizens of the colony. He brought with him from England authority from the Parliament to extend to Virginians the privilege or right of habeas corpus, which had previously been denied them, though other Englishmen had enjoyed the sacred right for many years. This one thing made Spottswood very popular with the people.

In a short time after his arrival the new governor became involved in quarrels with the burgesses, occasioned by what he believed to be a lack of public spirit on their part and reluctance to provide revenue for the essential needs of the government. They refused to appropriate money to send armed assistance to the Carolina colonists who were hard pressed by the Indians and were appealing for help; and plead the poverty of the colony as an excuse for their reprehensible conduct. Spottswood was so provoked that he sharply called the attention of the burgesses to the fact that they were greedily taking their pay as members of the assembly without enacting any laws that would be helpful to the colony. And in an address to the assembly he said: "To be plain with you, the true interest of your country is not what you have troubled your heads about. All your proceedings have been calculated to answer the notions of the ignorant populace; and if you can excuse yourselves to them, you matter not how you stand before God, or any others to whom you think you owe not your elections. In fine, I cannot but attribute these miscarriages to the people's mistaken choice of a set of representatives whom Heaven has not * * * endowed with the ordinary qualifications requisite to legislators; and therefore I dissolve you." Commenting on the manner in which Governor Spottswood rebuked the demagogues and time-serving politicians of the assembly, the historian Fiske thus writes of the gallant and honorable gentleman:

"In spite of this stinging tongue Spottswood was greatly liked and respected for his ability and honesty and his thoroughly good heart. He was a man sound in every fibre, clear-sighted, shrewd, immensely vigorous, and full of public spirit. One day we find him establishing Indian missions, the next he is undertaking to smelt iron and grow native wines; the next he is sending out ships to exterminate the pirates. For his energy in establishing smelting furnaces he was nicknamed 'The Tubal Cain of Virginia'. For the making of native wines he brought over a colony of Germans from the Rhine, and settled them in the new county named for him Spottsylvania, hard by the Rapidan River, where Germanna Ford still preserves a reminiscence of their coming."

Spottswood was governor from 1710 to 1723, and his administration was clean, able, and progressive. He introduced the English postal system into the colony, but for a time was antagonized in this movement by the burgesses. They contended that the postal charges were a tax, and that Parliament had no right to lay such a tax upon the people without their consent, given through their representatives.

More than a hundred years had passed since Captain Newport landed the first settlers at Jamestown; and no concerted effort had been made by individuals or the government to explore and occupy that extensive region belonging to Virginia, lying beyond the Blue Ridge Mountains. The belief was still almost universal in the colony that the coast land from Virginia to Labrador was a narrow strip, like Central America, separating the Atlantic Ocean and the one that was known to wash the western shores of the continent. In the fall of 1608, at the command of the London Company, Captain Newport made an ineffectual effort to reach and pass over the mountains, with the confident hope of finding a "salt sea" not far beyond the Blue Ridge. From that time to the coming of Spottswood the settlers were content to confine themselves to the tidewater section, where there was an abundance of everything necessary for their comfort, and where their tobacco crops could be used as money in all commercial transactions. The settlements had been extended far enough to bring the mountains in view, but a strip of forest fifty miles wide still intervened between the frontier and the Blue Ridge.

In 1716 the stalwart and energetic Spottswood determined to explore the region west of the mountains; and for that purpose organized an expedition composed of a number of gentlemen who were eager to accompany the governor. They took along a number of negro servants and some Indian guides, and a train of pack-horses laden with supplies, including an abundance of native and imported wines and liquors. The gay Cavaliers assembled at Germanna, and traveled thence up the Rappahannock River and its tributaries until the mountains were reached. They crossed the Blue Ridge at Swift Run Gap, and entered the great Shenandoah Valley a short distance north of Port Republic, a locality that was afterwards to be made famous by Stonewall Jackson, the greatest military leader America has ever produced, in his brilliant campaigns against the Federal armies. Spottswood and his company discovered a beautiful stream flowing down the valley and he named it the Euphrates, which was soon changed to the more appropriate name of Shenandoah. The party crossed the river at a very deep ford, on the 6th of September, and, on the western bank of the stream, Governor Spottswood formally took possession of the country for George I., King of England. After remaining a few days in the splendid country, which no white man had ever visited before, the governor started back to Williamsburg and arrived there after an absence of eight weeks.

John Fontaine, who was a member of the party, kept a diary from which there has been preserved a partial account of the expedition. He said that the governor had no graving irons and could not grave anything on stone, but Mr. Fontaine said: "I graved my name on a tree by the riverside, and the Governor buried a bottle with a paper enclosed, on which he writ that he took possession of this place in the name of the King George First of England. * * * We had a good dinner (on the 6th) and after it we got the men together and loaded all their arms, and we drank the King's health in champagne and fired a volley, the Princesse's health in Burgundy and fired a volley, and all the rest of the royal family in claret and fired a volley. We drank the Governor's health and fired another volley. We had several sorts of liquors, viz: Virginia red wine and white wine, Irish usquebaugh, brandy, shrub, two sorts of rum, champagne, canary, cherry punch, cider &c." The diarist also relates that bears, deer, and turkeys were abundant, and in the Valley the foot-prints of elk and buffalo were seen in many places.

Governor Spottswood was so delighted with the outcome of his exploring expedition that, upon his return to Williamsburg, he established an Order which he named "Knights of the Golden Horse-shoe." From a letter written by Rev. Hugh Jones, who was then rector of Bruton Church, we learn the reason for the name given the Order. Rev. Jones says: "For this expedition they were obliged to provide a great quantity of horse shoes, things seldom used in the lower parts of the country, where there are few stones, upon which account the governor upon their return presented each of his companions with a golden horse shoe, some of which I have seen, studded with valuable stones, resembling the heads of nails, with this inscription * * * *Sic juvat transcendere montes.* This he instituted to encourage gentlemen to venture backwards and make discoveries and new settlements, any gentleman being entitled to wear this golden shoe that can prove he drank his Majesty's health upon Mount George."

It seems that a party climbed the highest peak that they could find and that Spottswood cut the name of George I. on the summit. In letters which he wrote to the Lords of Trade in London, Spottswood disclosed that the object of his expedition across the mountains was not for pleasure, nor for the discovery of new territory, but was for a military and commercial purpose; and to prevent the French from coming down from the Lake Country and encroach-

ing upon the dominions of Virginia as defined by the several charters given the London Company. After referring to the fact that
the French had in recent years built forts in places that threatened
the possessions of England, he stated, "that the Brittish Plantations are in a manner Surrounded by their Commerce w'th the
numerous Nations of Indians seated on both sides of the Lakes;
they may not only Engross the Whole Skin Trade, but may, when
they please, Send out Bodys of Indians on the back of these Plantations as may greatly distress his Maj'ty's subjects here, And
should they multiply their settlem'ts along these Lakes, so as to
join their Dominions of Canada to their new Colony of Louisiana,
they might even possess themselves of any of these plantations
they pleased. Nature, 'tis true, has formed a Barrier for us by
that long Chain of Mountains w'ch run from the back of South
Carolina as far as New York, and w'ch are only passable in some
few places, but even that Natural Defence may prove rather destructive to us, if they are not possessed by us before they are known to
them. To prevent the dangers W'ch Threaten his Maj'ty's Dominions here from the growing power of these Neighbours, nothing
seems to me of more consequence than that now while the Nations
are at peace, and while the French are yet uncapable of possessing
all that vast Tract W'ch lies on the back of these Plantations, We
should attempt to make some settlements on ye Lakes, and at the
same time possess ourselves of those passes of the great Mountains,
W'ch are necessary to preserve a Communication with such Settlements."

Though he made such intelligent suggestions as to how the
French could be prevented from doing what they afterwards tried
to do, and partially accomplished, he remained very ignorant of
the physical structure and extent of the regions north and west of
the Shenandoah Valley. In another letter addressed to the Lords of
Trade, dated August 14, 1718, he said:

"The chief aim of my expedition over the great mountains in
1716, was to satisfye myself whether it was practicable to come at
the lakes. Having on that occasion found an easy passage over
that great ridge of mountains W'ch before were judged unpassable,
I also discovered, by relation of Indians who frequent those parts,
that from the pass where I was it is but three days' march to a
great nation of Indians living on a river W'ch discharges itself in
the Lake Erie, that from ye western side of one of the small mountains W'ch I saw, that lake is very visible, and cannot, therefore,

be above five days march from the pass afore-mentioned, and that the way thither is also very practicable, the mountains to the westward of the great ridge being smaller than those I passed on the eastern side. W'ch shews how easy a matter it is to gain possession of those lakes."

Spottswood became involved in a quarrel with Dr. James Blair, who was President of William and Mary College. Blair's influence was very great with the English Court, and he procured the removal of Spottswood as governor in 1722. The deposed governor had become so deeply attached to Virginia that he made it his future permanent home. He continued to act as postmaster-general for the American colonies, and by 1738 had a regular mail route established that extended from New England to Williamsburg; and irregular mails were sent by riders on south to the Carolinas. In 1740 Spottswood died at his estate of "Temple Farm" at Yorktown. The surrender of Lord Cornwallis was negotiated in the house where the valiant and noble gentleman died.

Pioneer Period

Embracing Discovery and Settlement of the Shenandoah, Roanoke, New River, Holston and Clinch Valleys and Kentucky.

PIONEER PERIOD

CHAPTER I.

Events that seem of little importance at the time of their occurrence are sometimes followed by consequences of such magnitude as to greatly affect the character and material welfare of a nation. The discovery of the Shenandoah Valley by Governor Spottswood was an event of this kind. His expedition across the Blue Ridge, so far as he was concerned, was executed for purely military and commercial purposes. It was certainly nothing more than a pleasure-seeking excursion on the part of Robert Beverly, Colonel Robertson, and the other Virginia gentlemen who accompanied the governor, judging from the account of the expedition related by John Fontaine in his diary. The handsome jewel Spottswood gave to each member of his illustrious Order of "Knights of the Golden Horseshoe," bore the inscription: *"Sic juvat transcendere montes,"* which translated means: "Thus it is a pleasure to cross the mountains."

When Spottswood buried a bottle on the bank of the beautiful Shenandoah, with a paper in the bottle declaring that the river and newly discovered territory were the possessions of King George I., neither the governor nor any one of his gallant companions took thought that the seed of European civilization was being planted in the strange, vast wilderness lying beyond the Blue Ridge Mountains. Nor could they foresee that this seed of civilization would quickly germinate, and its rich harvest be scattered broadcast, northward to the lakes, and westward until it reached the distant shores of the great "salt sea," which the London Company ordered Captain Newport to seek and find. Spottswood's expedition was the forerunner of the pioneer movement that brought the first settlers to the Clinch Valley and all parts of Southwest Virginia. Writing about this wonderful western movement, Fiske, the delightful historian, says:

"This development occurred in a way even far-seeing men could not have predicted. It introduced into Virginia a new set of people, new forms of religion, new habits of life. It affected all the colonies south of Pennsylvania most profoundly, and did more than anything else to determine the character of all the states afterwards founded west of the Alleghanies and south of the latitude of middle Illinois. Until recent years, little has been written about the coming of the so-called Scotch-Irish to America, and yet it is an event of scarcely less importance than the exodus of English Puritans to New England and that of English Cavaliers to Virginia. It is impossible to understand the drift which American history, social and political, has taken since the time of Andrew Jackson, without studying the early life of the Scotch-Irish population of the Alleghany regions, the pioneers of the American backwoods. I do not mean to be understood as saying that the whole of that population at the time of our Revolutionary War was Scotch-Irish, for there was a considerable German element in it, besides an infusion of English moving inward from the coast. But the Scotch-Irish element was more numerous and far more important than all the others."

A very large portion of the pioneer settlers in Tazewell were of the Scotch-Irish blood, therefore it is proper to inquire at this stage of my work: Who were these peculiar people, with a compound name, and from whence did they come? Fiske very concisely and splendidly gives the desired information by saying:

"The answer carries us back to the year 1611, when James I. began peopling Ulster with colonists from Scotland and the north of England. The plan was to put into Ireland a Protestant population that might ultimately outnumber the Catholics and become the controlling element in the country. The settlers were picked men and women of the most excellent sort. By the middle of the seventeenth century there were 300,000 of them in Ulster. That province had been the most neglected part of the island, a wilderness of bogs and fens; they transformed it into a garden. They also established manufactures of woolens and linens which have ever since been famous throughout the world. By the beginning of the eighteenth century their numbers had risen to nearly a million. Their social condition was not that of peasants; they were intelligent yeomanry and artisans. In a document signed in 1718 by a miscellaneous group of 319 men, only 13 made their mark, while 306 wrote their names in full. Nothing like that could have happened at that time in any other part of the British Empire, hardly even in New England.

"When these people began coming to America, those families that had been longest in Ireland had dwelt there but for three generations, and confusion of mind seems to lurk in any nomenclature which couples them with the true Irish. On the other hand, since love laughs at feuds and schisms, intermarriages between the colonists of Ulster and the native Irish were by no means unusual, and instances occur of Murphys and MacManuses of Presbyterian faith. It was common in Ulster to allude to Presbyterians as Scotch, to Roman Catholics as Irish, and to members of the English Church as Protestants, without much reference to pedigree. From this point of view the term 'Scotch-Irish' may be defensible, provided we do not let it conceal the fact that the people to whom it is applied are for the most part Lowland Scotch Presbyterians, very slightly hibernicized in blood."

In 1698 the English manufacturers became very jealous of the successful Scotch-Irish manufacturers in Ulster, and secured from Parliament legislation that inflicted such damage to the Irish linen and woolen industries that they had to discharge many of their skilled workmen, who suffered grievously from lack of employment. And about the same time the English Church inaugurated disgraceful persecutions against all Protestants who dissented to the doctrines of the Established Church. Similar persecutions were being used in Virginia and were continued for a number of years. The Presbyterians were not permitted to have schools; their ministers were not allowed to perform the marriage ceremony; and if any persons had the courage to violate the law, the marriage was declared invalid. They were also denied the right to hold any office higher than constable. There were other despotic and foolish enactments that were a disgrace to the British Government. Oppressions were heaped upon the Scotch-Irish in Ulster until they became unendurable; and they began to emigrate to America in large numbers about the time Spottswood made his famous exploration of the Shenandoah Valley. This tide of emigration from Ulster continued to flow to America until the Toleration Act for Ireland was enacted by Parliament in 1782. It is known that during one week in 1727 six ship-loads of emigrants from Ulster were landed at Philadelphia; and that in the two years 1733 and 1734 as many as 30,000 came over to America, seeking religious and political freedom. From carefully prepared estimates it is also known that between the years 1730 and 1770—a

period of forty years—half a million of the Scotch-Irish left
Ulster and made their future homes among the American colonies.
Most of them located in Pennsylvania, where they were given
grants of land in the western mountain sections for the purpose of
thus making them a strong defence of the frontier against Indian
invasion of the older settlements, as well as against the French.

The "Knights of the Golden Horseshoe", after their return
to Williamsburg from the famous exploring expedition, were loud
in their praises of the country beyond the mountains. They spoke
in the most glowing terms of its scenic beauty, its fertile soil, and
the abundance of big game. Their brilliant descriptions, however,
did not induce any of the Virginians then living east of the Blue
Ridge to migrate to the Valley, and take the risks and endure the
hardships of pioneers. They preferred to live in safety, and to
enjoy the luxury that had been built upon indentured servitude
and slavery. Thus was the honor of bringing this magnificent
section of America to a high state of civilization given to a hardier
and more intelligent class of men, who came from Ulster and
Germany, via Pennsylvania and Maryland.

———

The General Assembly of Virginia at a session "Begun and
holden in the Capitol in the City of Williamsburg on the second
day of November 1720" passed an act to erect a county to be
called Spottsylvania in honor of Governor Spottswood. The preamble of the bill stated: "That the frontiers towards the high
mountains are exposed to danger from the Indians and the late
settlements of the French to the westward of the said mountains."
In the enacting clause, the boundaries of the new county are thus
given: "Spottsylvania County bounds upon Snow Creek up to a
mill, thence by a southwest line to the river North-Anna, thence
up said river as far as convenient, and thence by a line to be run
over the high mountains to the river on the North-west side thereof,
so as to include the northern passage thro' the said mountains,
thence down the said river until it comes against the head of the
Rappahannock; thence by a line to the head of Rappahannock
river; and down that river to the mouth of Snow Creek; which
tract of land from the first of May, 1721, shall become a county
by the name of Spottsylvania County."

The preamble of the act discloses the primary purpose for the
creation of the new county. It was another invitation to bold
spirits to cross the Blue Ridge Mountains and establish homes

and build forts, as did the pioneer settlers of the Clinch Valley; and erect a strong barrier against the Indians who had previously been making bloody attacks upon the frontier settlements east of the mountains. The Virginia colonists did not respond to this second invitation, following Spottswood's discovery of the Valley; and no settlements were made there until more than ten years after Spottsylvania County was formed. It appears that the entire Valley between the Blue Ridge and the Alleghany Mountains was uninhabited. The aborigines had, though different tribes asserted claim to the territory, set it apart as a hunting ground, just as they had done with all the territory in Virginia west of New River and south of the Ohio. Therefore it became a highway for war parties of hostile tribes as they traveled either north or south to make war on their enemies. The Shawnees, who had settled at the present site of Winchester, Virginia, after their expulsion from South Carolina by the Cherokees in 1690, had joined their kindred either in Pennsylvania or in the Ohio Valley. This is indicated by the fact that the first settlement made in Virginia west of the Blue Ridge was at or near Winchester. Hunters and small exploring parties had, possibly, visited the Valley but no settlements were made there until 1732.

Several local historians state, as a fact, that before any settlements were made in the Shenandoah Valley, John Marlin, a pédlar, and John Salling, a weaver, started out from Winchester to explore the upper country. Waddell, in his Annals of Augusta County, fixes the date of the Marlin-Salling exploration at about the year 1726. They traveled up the valley of the Shenandoah to the divide which separates that valley from the James River Valley, and journeyed on until they reached the Roanoke River. There they were discovered and surprised by a hunting party of Cherokee Indians, possibly, about the "Great Lick," where the city of Roanoke is now located. Salling was captured by the Indians, but Marlin escaped. Salling's experience as a captive was about as thrilling as that of Thomas Ingles, who was captured by the Shawnees at Draper's Meadows in 1755, and James Moore, who was captured by a band of the same tribe in Abb's Valley in 1784. Salling was taken by the Cherokees to one of their towns in Tennessee. While on a hunting expedition in Kentucky with a party of the Cherokees he was captured by a band of Illinois Indians, and was taken to Kaskaskia, where he was adopted into the family of an Indian squaw who had lost a son in battle. The

Illinois Indians sold him to Spanish traders who wanted to use him as an interpreter. They took him to Canada, where he was purchased from the Spaniards by the French governor, and was sent by him to the Dutch settlement at New York. From New York he made his way to Williamsburg, and from thence to Winchester, arriving there after an absence of six years.

In 1730, John and Isaac Vanmeter, who were German Huguenots, and then located in Pennsylvania, procured from Governor Gooch, of Virginia, a grant for 40,000 acres of land to be located in the lower Valley and within the present boundaries of Frederick County, Virginia, and Jefferson County, West Virginia. The Vanmeters sold, in 1731, their warrant for the 40,000 acres to Joist Hite, also of Pennsylvania. He began to survey and locate valuable tracts of land, and offered extraordinary inducements to immigrants . to settle upon the lands. But the strongest inducement was the removal of his own family from Pennsylvania to the Valley. He settled with his family, in 1732, a few miles south of where Winchester is now located; and this is supposed to be the first permanent settlement made by a white man in the splendid Valley of Virginia. Waddell says:

"Population soon flowed in to take possession of the rich lands offered by Hite; but a controversy speedily arose in regard to the proprietor's title. Lord Fairfax claimed Hite's lands as a part of his grant of the 'Northern Neck.' Fairfax entered a *caveat* against Hite, in 1736, and thereupon Hite brought suit against Fairfax. This suit was not finally decided till 1786, long after the death of all the original parties, when judgment was rendered in favor of Hite and his vendees. The dispute between Fairfax and Hite retarded the settlement of that part of the Valley, and induced immigrants to push their way up the Shenandoah River to regions not implicated in such controversies."

About the year 1732 John Lewis, whose descendants afterwards figured so conspicuously in the affairs of Virginia, settled in the Shenandoah Valley. Local historians designate him as the first white settler in that region. He became acquainted with John Salling shortly after the latter returned to Winchester from captivity; and was so pleased with Salling's description of the Upper Valley that he and John Mackey made a visit to the country under the guidance of Salling; and all three of these men determined to

make their homes there. There was an abundance of fertile land
with no one claiming ownership to any portion of it, and Lewis
and his companions were free to choose what they wished.

John Lewis was a native of the county of Donegal, Province of
Ulster, Ireland, was of pure Scotch descent, and came to this country from Portugal, first settling with his family in Pennsylvania.
He had been forced to leave Ireland on account of killing an Irish
landlord from whom he had rented land. The landlord was trying
to evict Lewis from his holdings by force and shot into the house,
killing a brother of Lewis and severely wounding his wife. Thereupon Lewis rushed out of the house, killed the Irish lord, and drove
his retainers away. His conduct was fully justified by the authorities, but he thought it best to leave the country. When he moved
his family to the Shenandoah Valley he brought with him three
sons, Thomas, Andrew and William; and a fourth son, Charles,
was born at the new home. Andrew commanded the Virginians at
the battle of Point Pleasant, and won distinction as a general in
the Revolutionary War. Charles commanded a regiment at Point
Pleasant, and was killed in the engagement. In his Annals of
Augusta county, Waddell says: "Concurrently with the settlement of Lewis, or immediately afterward, a flood of immigrants
poured into the country. * * * It is believed that all the
earliest settlers came from Pennsylvania and up the Valley of the
Shenandoah. It was several years before any settlers entered the
Valley from the east, and through the gaps in the Blue Ridge."
A large majority of the pioneer settlers of the Clinch Valley and
of all Southwest Virginia were of the same stock as those who first
came to the Shenandoah Valley. In fact, Pennsylvania and Maryland furnished nearly all of them, but many located for a time in
the Valley before coming here.

These settlers were not by any means all of the Scotch-Irish
blood. There was a strong element of Germans among them, who
shared equally with the men from Ulster the glory of making
the Shenandoah Valley and Southwest Virginia two of the most
noted and delightful sections of the United States. The Scotch
and German pioneer settlers were, alike, men of great energy and
dauntless courage; and filled with such intense political and religious convictions that they and their descendants have made an
indelible impression upon the social, political and moral life of
America. Fiske, the historian, says: "Jefferson is often called the
father of modern American democracy; in a certain sense the
T.H.—11

Shenandoah Valley and adjacent Appalachian regions may be called its cradle. In that rude frontier society, life assumed many new aspects, old customs were forgotten, old distinctions abolished, social equality acquired even more importance than unchecked individualism. The notions, sometimes crude and noxious, sometimes just and wholesome, which characterized Jacksonian democracy, flourished greatly on the frontier and have thence been propagated eastward through the older communities, affecting their legislation and their politics more or less according to frequency of contact and intercourse." This Jeffersonian democracy of the pioneer settlers of the Appalachian regions, including the Clinch Valley, was scattered by their descendants throughout the West and Northwest. And in the middle of the last century it was given added impulse by Abraham Lincoln, who is the only peer of Jefferson, as a leader and teacher of a pure democracy, the world has ever produced.

In 1734 an event occurred which greatly accelerated the westward movement. This was the creation of a new county to be taken from Spottsylvania. On the 20th of September of that year the General Assembly of Virginia passed an act for that end, and its provisions, in part, were as follows:

"Whereas divers inconveniences attend the upper inhabitants of Spottsylvania county, by reason of their great distance from the courthouse, and other places usually appointed for public meetings, Be it therefore enacted, by the Lieutenant Governor, Council and Burgesses of this present General Assembly, and it is hereby enacted, by the authority of the same, that from and immediately after the first day of January, now next ensuing, the said county of Spottsylvania be divided, by the dividing line, between the parish of St. George, and the parish of St. Mark; and that that part of the county, which is now the parish of St. George, remain, and be called, and known by the name of Spottsylvania county; and that all that territory of land adjoining to, and above the said line, bounden southerly by the line of Hanover county, northerly by the grant of Lord Fairfax, and westerly by the utmost limits of Virginia, be thenceforth erected into one distinct county and be called and known by the name of the county of Orange." The county seat was afterwards located at the site of the present Orange, Virginia.

That the intention of the act was to encourage settlements to the westward of the Shenandoah, called in the act the "Sherrendo" river, is evidenced by the recital: "That all inhabitants that shall be settled there after the first day of January succeeding shall be free and exempt from the *paiment* of public, county, and parish levies by the space of three years, from thence next following."

This act brought into existence the largest county that was ever established in the world. In fact, it was extensive enough in territory to be called an empire, but had no white inhabitants, except the few settlers in the Shenandoah Valley and a few hundreds east of the Blue Ridge. Its bounds extended as far northerly and westerly as the utmost limits of Virginia. The charters given by James I. to the London Company fixed the northern limits at the Great Lakes and the western limits at the Pacific Ocean.

The British Government grew more restless as the French continued to push south from Canada with their forts and trading posts, locating them on Virginia territory; and the policy of advancing the English settlements as far north and west and as rapidly as possible was adopted. In pursuance of this policy, first suggested by Governor Spottswood, the General Assembly of Virginia determined to erect two distinct counties west of the mountains, and to hold out stronger inducements for settlers to locate with their families in the unexplored and indefinite regions. On the 15th of December, 1738, an act was passed by the General Assembly for erecting two new counties west of the Blue Ridge, to be called Frederick, and Augusta, respectively. The title declared it to be: "An Act for erecting two new Counties, and Parishes, and granting certain encouragements to the inhabitants thereof;" and the preamble declared that, "Whereas great numbers of people have settled themselves of late upon the rivers of Sherrendo, Cohongorton, and Opeckon, and the branches thereof, on the northwest of the Blue Ridge mountains, whereby the strength of this colony, and its security upon the frontiers, and his Majesty's revenue of quitrents are like to be much increased and augmented: For giving encouragement to such as shall think fit to settle there, Be it enacted," etc.

After outlining the bounds of the two counties, several important provisions were incorporated in the enacting clauses. One of these provided that the two new counties should remain attached to Orange County and Saint Mark's parish until it was made known to the governor and council that there was "a sufficient number of inhabitants for appointing justices of the peace and other officers and erecting courts therein." The act also provided that the inhabitants should be exempted from "the payment of all public, county and parish levies for ten years." And it was further provided that all levies and officers' fees could be paid "in money, or tobacco at three farthings per pound, without any deduction."

The erection of these two counties confined the bounds of Orange County to a comparatively small area east of the Blue Ridge. As left by the act, which called Frederick and Augusta into existence, its territory was composed of the present counties of Orange, Culpeper, Rappahannock, Madison and Green. All the Virginia territory west of the Blue Ridge, except that portion of the Valley east of Rockingham and Page counties and a small part of the present State of West Virginia, constituted Augusta county. This made the extreme limits of Augusta reach westward to the Pacific Ocean and northward to Canada. Thus did the entire Clinch Valley become a part of Augusta County. By the treaty of Paris, negotiated in 1763, the limits of Augusta were reduced so as to embrace only the present State of Virginia west of the Blue Ridge, nearly all of the present State of West Virginia, all of Kentucky, Ohio, Indiana and Illinois; and Michigan and Wisconsin, except the portions of these two states that lie west of the Mississippi. The county was not regularly organized until 1745. On October 30th of that year Governor Gooch issued "a Commission of the Peace" to twenty-one citizens of the county, namely: James Patton, John Lewis, John Buchanan, George Robinson, Peter Scholl, James Bell, Robert Campbell, John Brown, Robert Poage, John Pickens, Thomas Lewis, Hugh Thompson, Robert Cunningham, John Tinla (Finley?) Richard Woods, John Christian, Robert Craven, James Kerr, Adam Dickinson, Andrew Pickens and John Anderson.

James Patton and John Buchanan, two of the men named in this Commission of the Peace, came from Ireland to the Shenandoah Valley about 1735 or 1736, where they soon became leaders in the affairs of that region, and of Augusta County after its organization in 1745. A few years thereafter they became the leading spirits in the exploration and settlement of the Trans-Alleghany regions. Patton was a seafaring man and had been a lieutenant in the British navy, and was the son-in-law of Benjamin Burden, the latter being the agent of Lord Fairfax in the management of his great "Northern Neck" grant. Buchanan was a skilled surveyor, and was the son-in-law of Colonel Patton. In 1745 Patton was made county lieutenant and commander of the militia for Augusta County; and a little later secured from the Crown a grant for 120,000 acres of land to be located in Virginia, west of the Alleghany Mountains. He organized an exploring and surveying expedition in the spring of 1748 to locate lands under the grant. His party, in addition to himself, consisted of Colonel John Buchanan, Charles Campbell, who was son-in-law of Colonel Buchanan; Dr. Thomas Walker, James Wood, and an ample number of hunters, chain-carriers, cooks, etc. They had pack-horses in sufficient numbers to carry provisions, ammunition and other things that were needed for a long journey and a protracted stay in the wilderness. The late Colonel Thomas L. Preston, a great-grandson of Charles Campbell, in his "Reminiscences of An Octogenarian," thus speaks of the four leading characters of the expedition:

"Colonel Patton was about fifty-eight years old, of a tall and commanding figure and great physical strength and vigor. He was wealthy and well educated, and well fitted for the long and arduous expedition he planned. His party was also well chosen for the same purpose. John Buchanan (his son-in-law) was a surveyor, as was also Charles Campbell, both of whom had the spirit and courage of the early pioneers, with the physical attributes of strength and power of endurance.

"Dr. Thomas Walker, born January 15, 1715, was thirty-three years old and in the prime of manhood. He was richly endowed with every qualification for such an expedition, mentally and physically, and, as physician and surveyor, a great accession to the party."

The expedition started out from Colonel Patton's home, near the present Waynesboro, Augusta County, where he had a splendid estate of 1,398 acres, which had been a part of the historic "Manor Beverley" grant, and which Patton had acquired from William Beverley for the sum of five shillings (83½ cents).

If any diary or written record was made of the movements and accomplishments of this expedition, it was not preserved; and, therefore, such incidents as are of sufficient moment to become written history have to be collected from well authenticated traditions. This was not the first expedition that had crossed the Alleghany Mountains in Virginia; but it was the first that was followed with practical results in the way of introducing settlers into the splendid section now known as Southwest Virginia. It is a well established historical fact that Major Abram Wood, who lived at the falls of Appomattox River, where Petersburg, Virginia, is now situated, made a trip of exploration and discovery to the Upper New River Valley in 1654, and that the stream he then discovered was afterwards known as Wood's River. No written record was preserved of Major Wood's expedition but it is authenticated by traditions and circumstances as substantial, comparatively, as those connected with the expedition of Colonel Patton. Summers in his history of Southwest Virginia says:

"It is reasonable to believe that Colonel Wood made this trip, and, to support this view, three circumstances may be mentioned. First, The House of Burgesses of Virginia had authorized Colonel Wood, along with others, in July of the preceding year to discover a new river of unknown land 'Where no English had ever been or discovered.' Secondly. A gap in the Blue Ridge, lying between the headwaters of Smith river, a branch of the Dan, in Patrick county, and of Little river, a branch of New river, in Floyd county, is to this day called Wood's Gap. Thirdly. The present New river was known at first as Wood's river."

There is but little doubt that Major Wood was hunting for a river west of the Blue Ridge that was believed to exist and flow into the Pacific Ocean, just as Captain Newport, in 1609, and Governor Spottswood, in 1716, had sought and expected to find such a stream. In 1666 another exploring expedition visited the Upper New River Valley. It was composed of Captain Henry Batte, Thomas Wood and Robert Fallen. They acted under a commission issued by Governor Berkeley, had an Appomattox Indian for a guide, and traveled on five horses. On the 1st of September, 1666, the expedition started from the falls of the Appomattox, as did that of Major Wood, twelve years previous. Captain Batte kept a journal, in which he stated that the object of the expedition was "for ye finding out of the ebbing and flowing of ye waters behind the mountains in order to the discovery of the South Sea." The Virginia colonists, even their governors and other officials, still adhered to the belief that the South Sea (the Pacific Ocean) would be found a short distance west of the Blue Ridge Mountains. Batte and his companions failed, of course, to find the South Sea, but they did re-discover New River, then known as Wood's River.

From their brief description of the country about where they came upon the river, historians have been unable to locate the exact, or approximately, correct point. It is possible that it was at or near the place now known as Austinville, in Wythe County, at the Lead Mines. Batte says they found Indian fields with corn stalks in them. There was a heavy flood in New River in 1916, and the river overflowed the bottom lands doing great damage to crops along the shores for a hundred or more miles down the valley. At a point not far from Austinville, in a river bottom, a channel was cut by the flood, revealing an Indian graveyard and exposing a number of skeletons. Evidently there had been a Cherokee village in the locality, and hence the corn fields. Spottswood's expedition was not the first to cross the Blue Ridge, but it was the first to enter the Shenandoah Valley. It is also evident that Colonel Patton's was not the first expedition to cross the Alleghany Mountains, but it was the first that crossed New River, and it was the first to enter the territory now embraced in Tazewell County.

It is claimed by local historians that many years previous to the Patton expedition that traders came from east of the mountains and visited the Cherokee towns in Tennessee. These traders employed Indian guides, and transported their merchandise on packhorses, traveling along the Holston Valley while going to and from the Cherokee country. Many hunters had also made hunting trips from the eastern part of Virginia to the Clinch Valley and Holston Valley previous to the visit of Colonel Patton and his company. They were attracted here by the great abundance of game, which they killed largely for their hides, furs then being very valuable for exportation to Europe. Among these hunters was one William Clinch, whose name was given to the great valley and the beautiful river that has its source in Tazewell County.

But to return to Colonel Patton and his expedition, made in 1748. After leaving his home in Augusta County, Patton traveled through Rockbridge County until he reached the James River Valley. Surveys had been made some ten years previously of valuable tracts of land where the towns of Pattonsburg and Buchanan are now located. Pattonsburg was named in honor of Colonel Patton, and is on the north side of the river in Rockbridge County. Buchanan is on the south side of the James, directly opposite Pattonsburg, in Botetourt County; and received its name from Colonel John Buchanan. These two towns are among the oldest in Virginia,

not ten years younger than Richmond and Petersburg. Patton on
this occasion also located lands in the Catawba Valley and at
Amsterdam in Botetourt County. From thence he went to the
Roanoke Valley, and made surveys on Strouble's Creek, and located
a large boundary at the present Blacksburg, which was first called
Draper's Meadows and afterwards Smithfield, the latter name being
given the place at the time Colonel William Preston became its
owner. Leaving Draper's Meadows, the Patton party crossed
New River at Ingles' Ferry, which is about a mile up the river
from Radford, and traveled on toward the Holston River, or, as it
was then known, Indian River, locating choice lands at different
points on the route. A large survey was made just south of Max
Meadows, in Wythe County, and Colonel Patton named the tract
"Anchor and Hope," and gave it to his daughter, who was the
wife of Colonel Buchanan. A few years later Colonel Buchanan
moved from Pattonsburg, where he had previously settled, and built
himself a home near where the present "Anchor and Hope Church"
now stands.

From "Anchor and Hope," Colonel Patton and his party made
their way to the headwaters of the Middle Fork of Holston River.
In that locality a very fine boundary of land, consisting of 1,300 acres
was surveyed and given the name of "Davis' Fancy." It was
patented to James Davis, who may possibly have gone there with
the Patton party. A large portion of this tract is now owned and
occupied by George W. Davis, great-great-grandson of James Davis.
From "Davis' Fancy," Colonel Patton led his party down the Holston Valley to the beautiful country about the present Seven Mile
Ford, in Smyth County. While camping at that place they were
visited by Charles Sinclair, a hermit hunter, who had built himself
a cabin on the South Fork of Holston River three miles south of
Seven Mile Ford. The Hon. B. F. Buchanan, of Marion, Virginia,
and whose ancestress was a sister of Colonel John Buchanan, had
frequent interviews with the late Colonel Thomas L. Preston; and
from him learned certain interesting facts that transpired after
Sinclair joined the Patton party. As related by Colonel Preston
to Mr. Buchanan, they are substantially as follows:

"Colonel Preston told me that on reaching some point on the
Holston this exploring party was visited by a man named Sinclair,
who told the party that he was well acquainted with this section of
the country and knew the best lands, as he had hunted all over it;

that he was on friendly terms with the Indians and could insure
the party against attacks by them; and proposed to guide them and
show them the choice lands, if they would make a survey and have
the patent issued to him of a tract of land on the South Fork of
the Holston River, where he was located. This was agreed to, the
survey was made, and a tract still known as St. Clairs Bottom,
three miles south of Seven Mile Ford, was surveyed and afterwards
patented to Sinclair."

Colonel Preston, who was the great-grandson of Charles Campbell, one of the explorers in the party, stated, from family traditions,
what transpired after the expedition reached Cumberland Gap. He
said that: "On reaching the summit of the mountain where the three
states of Virginia, Kentucky and Tennessee now join, they pitched
their tents, and Patton, in gratitude for the princely grant which
had been given him, named the mountain and river that rises along
its western base for the Duke of Cumberland." The traditions in
the Preston and Campbell families also held that when the Patton
party returned from Cumberland Gap they were shown the choice
lands on the North Fork of Holston River in the present Smyth
County, and were also conducted to Burke's Garden by the hunter,
Sinclair. These occurrences as related by Colonel Preston are
substantially as follows:

On the return of the party from Cumberland Gap, Sinclair
conducted it across Walker's Mountain into Rich Valley, by way of
Saltville, where they located a tract of 330 acres of land, in the
name of Charles Campbell and named it the "Buffalo Lick." They
then traveled up the North Fork of Holston River, located the
Taylor bottoms near and above the present Broadford, which
included "Campbells Choice," a boundary of 1,400 acres of, possibly, the finest land in Virginia. After surveying "Campbells
Choice," the party went into and through Locust Cove; and all of
the Cove was located for Colonel John Buchanan. He gave this
magnificent boundary, which is underlaid with the finest gypsum
on earth, to his sister, Martha Buchanan, the wife of Captain John
Buchanan. A few years later Captain Buchanan and his wife moved
to the cove, and Archibald Buchanan, a brother of the captain,
also located in that vicinity. The greater part of "Locust Cove"
is still owned and occupied by descendants of Captain Buchanan and
his wife, Martha; and practically all the Buchanans in Tazewell
and Smyth counties are their descendants. From the Cove the party

made its way to Burke's Garden. According to Colonel Thomas L. Preston: "It was late in the fall, and the next morning, after reaching the Garden, a heavy snow had fallen, and they determined to suspend their surveying until the next year. After cooking their breakfast, a man named Burke, who was with the party as an axman or chain-carrier, cleared away the place where their fire had been made, and planted a lot of potato peelings, covering them lightly with brush. The following Spring or Summer, Patton and Buchanan, accompanied by William Ingles, returned to survey lands, and found a large bed of potatoes where Burke had planted the peelings, and they gave it the name "Burke's Garden." Surveys were made in the Garden, and patents issued afterwards to William Ingles and to William Thompson, a son-in-law of Patton."

There can be no question of the fact that Colonel Patton and his party were the first men who ever visited Burke's Garden with a view of locating land and preparing it for settlement by white men. But it is asserted and believed by many, who speak from tradition, that James Burke had previously made hunting trips to the Garden and had built and occupied a cabin on the farm now owned by Rufus Thompson. This matter of dispute, however, will be given more ample notice further on in this volume.

CHAPTER II.

All the lands surveyed by the Patton expedition in 1748 were located under authority of the grant for 120,000 acres that Colonel Patton received from George II. After returning to their homes in the east, Colonel James Patton, Dr. Thomas Walker, and others, organized and incorporated what was known as the "Loyal Company;" and secured from the English Crown a grant for 800,000 acres of land to be located north of the North Carolina line and west of the Alleghany Mountains. Dr. Walker was made agent for this company, and both he and his company played a conspicuous part in the early settlement and development of that portion of Southwest Virginia west of New River. The first land ever surveyed in Tazewell County, so far as existing records show, was under the 800,000 acre grant to the Loyal Company. On October 14th, 1750, a tract containing 650 acres, located at "Crabapple Orchard, Waters of Clinch River," was surveyed for one John Shelton and, on the 16th of the same month and year, another tract of 1,000 acres was surveyed for Shelton on a "Branch of Clinch River." Thomas Lewis was then surveyor of Augusta County, but the surveying of these two tracts was done by Colonel John Buchanan, as deputy for Lewis. The "Crabapple Orchard" tract is the same boundary, which Bickley, in his History of Tazewell County, published in 1852, says was occupied in 1768 by two hunters, Butler and Carr; and that Butler sold it to Thomas Witten in 1771. The 1,000 acre tract was, no doubt, also on Plum Creek; and a part of the lands afterward owned by the sons of Thomas Witten, a goodly portion of which is still possessed by their descendants.

In the spring of 1750, Dr. Walker organized an exploring party at his home in Albemarle County to further explore the Virginia territory west of New River. This was done, apparently, for the purpose of discovering choice lands to be located for the Loyal Company, and to select desirable places for settlements. Dr. Walker kept a record of the route followed by him and the daily performances of the expedition. Walker's journal shows that no effort was made by him, or by any one of his party, to survey lands during the expedition; and that they traveled every day, except when prevented by inclement weather or while resting on the Sabbath, until the journey was completed. The first paragraph of the journal reads thus: "Having on the 12th of December last been employed for a certain consideration to go to the westward in order to discover a proper place for a settlement. I left my home on the 6th day of March, 1749-'50, in company with Ambrose Powell, William Tomlinson, Colby Chew, Henry Lawless & John Hughes. Each man had a horse and we had two to carry the baggage; I lodged this night at Col. Joshua Fry's, in the Albemarle, which county includes the Chief of the head Branches of James River on the east side of the Blue Ridge."

Historians and investigators have been so confused by the peculiar entry in Dr. Walker's journal, "the 6th day of March, 1749-'50," that they have been unable to determine whether it meant March 6th 1749, or March 6th, 1750. However, it has been generally accepted that he started on his expedition the 6th day of March, 1750. This, I believe, is correct. There is one very prominent fact which shows that Dr. Walker and his companions began their journey on the 6th of March, 1750. The "Loyal Company," in whose interest the expedition was made, did not secure its grant for the 800,000 acres until the 12th of July, 1749. The company would hardly have started out an exploring party and promised its agent, Dr. Walker, a valuable consideration, previous to receiving the grant. At that period the British Government was anxious to extend the frontiers of Virginia as far west and north as possible, to block the advances that were being made south from the lakes and east from the Mississippi by the French. To that end large grants of land were given to individuals and companies who would agree to solicit and secure settlers on the frontiers. In pursuance of this policy, the governor and council of Virginia, on the 12th day of July, 1749, granted to the "Ohio Company" 500,000 acres of land and to the "Loyal Company" 800,000 acres. The "Ohio Company" was to locate its surveys south of the Ohio River, and, as previously stated, the Loyal Company was to take up its lands north of the North Carolina line and west of the Alleghany Mountains.

This put two strong, rival companies in the field, both being commercial or financial enterprises. Though there was a vast unexplored region available to entry by the rival companies, each manifested eagerness to get first in the field with exploring and surveying parties. The Ohio Company engaged the services of Christopher Gist, a Marylander and a noted surveyor, as their agent.

He was instructed to hasten with a corps of men to the country bordering on the Ohio, now West Virginia and Kentucky, and search for choice lands along the Ohio River and other tributaries of the Mississippi. His instructions were very ample and urgent; but Gist did not start with his expedition until some time in October, 1750. From this it will be seen that the Walker party started out seven months in advance of the Gist expedition. These facts substantially prove that Walker made his second explorations in Southwest Virginia, in 1750; and it is certainly true that the first surveys in this section for the Loyal Company were made during that year.

Persons who are familiar with the geography of Virginia, and especially of the Southwest portion of the State, can, by inspecting Dr. Walker's journal, easily trace the route pursued by his party until they reached Cumberland Gap. From Walker's home, in Albemarle County, they traveled through the present counties of Nelson and Amherst to the James River, and crossed that stream at or near where Lynchburg is now located on the 12th of March. On the morning of the 13th, Dr. Walker says, in his journal: "We went early to William Calloway's and supplied ourselves with Rum, Thread and other necessaries & from thence took the main Wagon Road leading to Wood's or the New River. It is not well cleared or beaten yet, but will be a very good one with proper management." It seems that the Doctor and his companions thought Rum a necessary article to be taken on the trip, and he, a physician, mentioned it as the first of the necessaries. They then traveled on through Buford's Valley, just east of the Blue Ridge, crossed that mountain at Buford's Gap, pronouncing "the ascent and descent is so easy that a stranger would not know when he crossed the Ridge." The author crossed the "Ridge" at this point in the fall of 1863, and can affirm that Dr. Walker's statement as to the character of the pass is very accurate. After crossing the Ridge the party entered the Roanoke Valley at or near Bonsacks, and from there went to the "Great Lick on a Branch of the Staunton." The Roanoke River was then called the Staunton, as it was a tributary of the Staunton River. At the Great Lick they bought corn for their horses from Michael Campbell; and then proceeded up the river to a point above Salem, where Walker says they "Lodged at James Robinson's, the only place where they had corn to spare." Thence they followed the stream "to William Englishe's." This was William Ingles, who had then settled at Draper's Meadows, and whose family and descendants in a few years became tragically associated with the

history of Southwest Virginia and Tazewell County. Evidently the
Upper Roanoke Valley was then attracting many Scotch-Irish settlers from Pennsylvania and the Shenandoah Valley.

Leaving the home of Ingles, the Walker party passed down the
Alleghany Mountains, crossed New River at, or near, the point
where William Ingles afterwards built a fort, and on the west side
of the river came in contact with a small colony of Dunkards, who
had recently settled at a place which is still known as "Dunkard's
Bottom." Walker and his company remained several days as the
guests of this humble Christian people; and then moved on, by
way of Reed Creek. towards the Holston Valley. On the night of
the 22nd of March they camped at a large spring "about five miles
below Davis' Bottom on Holston River." This is, no doubt, the
large spring at the northeast end of Marion, Virginia, near the passenger station of the Norfolk and Western Railway, and now the
property of that company.

The following day. the 23rd of March, they traveled down the
Middle Fork of Holston River about four miles and again went
into camp; and Dr. Walker wrote in his journal that day: "Mr.
Powell and I went to look for Samuel Stalnaker, who I had been
informed had moved out to settle. We found his Camp and returned
to our own in the Evening. The following day (the 24th) he entered
in his journal: "We went to Stalnaker's. helped him to raise his house
and Camped about a quarter of a mile below him. In April, 1748.
I met the above mentioned Stalnaker between the Reedy Creek
Settlement and Holston River. on his way to the Cherokee Indians.
and expected him to pilot me as far as he knew, but his affairs
would not permit him to go with me."

It is wonderful how in those primitive days persons traveling
through an almost pathless wilderness, could, in some way, learn
that a bold pioneer had plunged into the wilds, with axe and rifle,
to build a home for himself and family. Stalnaker had already cut
and prepared the logs for his rude dwelling when Walker and his
party came upon the scene and helped him "to raise his house."
That was the first "house-raising" that occurred in the Holston
Valley. The exact location of Stalnaker's home has never been
ascertained, but could not have been very far from Seven Mile Ford,
and was near the place where Charles Sinclair joined Colonel Patton and Dr. Walker in 1748. Of the future history of this man
Stalnaker very little is known. Summers, in his valuable history
of Southwest Virginia, says:

"On the 29th of July, 1756, a Council of War assembled at Staunton, by direction of the Governor of Virginia, to determine at what points forts should be built along the frontiers for the protection of the settlers.

"The Council was composed of Colonel John Buchanan, Samuel Stalnaker and others, of which Council Wm. Preston acted as clerk. There can be no doubt that Captain Samuel Stalnaker represented the Holston settlement and that it was at his request that the stockade fort was built at Dunkards' Bottom, on New River, and at Davis' Bottom, at the headwaters of the Middle Fork of Holston River."

It appears that a party of Indians made a hostile visit to the Upper Holston Valley in June, 1755, and made Samuel Stalnaker a prisoner, but he escaped from the savages. In a register of the persons killed by the Indians in this foray the names of Adam Stalnaker and Mrs. Stalnaker appear. They were the wife and son of Samuel Stalnaker.

But to return to Dr. Walker and his exploring party. On the 26th of March, twenty days after starting from Albemarle County, they separated from Samuel Stalnaker, and saw no more settlers until their remarkable circuit journey was almost completed. While going up a creek that is a branch of the Greenbrier River, about noon, July 7th, Dr. Walker notes in his journal, "5 men overtook us and informed us we were only 8 miles from the inhabitants on a Branch of James River called Jackson's River." From Stalnaker's settlement, then the farthest west in Southwest Virginia, they traveled "nigh west" to a large spring on a Branch of the north fork of Holston. Thence they went to Reedy Creek and down that creek to the Holston River. There they found an elm tree of such immense size that curiosity prompted them to measure its girth; and they found it was 25 feet in circumference. They crossed the North Fork of the Holston at a ford about a half mile above where the North and the South Fork come together. From that point they traveled a northwest course, crossed over Clinch Mountain, and got to Clinch River near the present Sneedsville, in Hancock County, Tennessee. This was on the 9th of April, and Dr. Walker states in his journal: "We travelled to a river, which I suppose to be that which the hunters Call Clinche's River, from one Clinch a Hunter, who first found it."

From "Clinches River" they continued their journey toward Cumberland Gap, which seemed to be their objective. On the route pursued they passed over and along a number of streams, some of which had already been given names; but by whom, when and why they were so named Dr. Walker did not state as he did about "Clinche's River." The 11th of April he wrote in his journal, "We came to Turkey Creek, which we kept down 4 miles;" and on the 12th, after crossing over a certain mountain he made a note: "From this mountain we rode 4 miles to Beargrass River." While traveling up this river he found "some small pieces of coal and a great plenty of very good yellow flint, and added: "The water is the most transparent I ever saw. It is about 70 yds. wide." Summers says: "On the 12th day of April they reached Powell's river, ten miles from Cumberland Gap. It is well to note at this point that Ambrose Powell, one of Dr. Walker's companions, cut his name upon a tree on the bank of this river, which name and tree were found in the year 1770 by a party of fifteen or twenty Virginians on their way to Kentucky on a hunting expedition, from which circumstance the Virginia Long Hunters gave it the name of Powell's river, which it still retains." Thus the stream which Dr. Walker called Beargrass River, had its name changed to Powell's River.

On the 13th of April, five weeks after leaving his home in Albemarle County, Dr. Walker with his company arrived at Cumberland Gap, and in his journal called it "Cave Gap." Some of the historians who have written about the expedition hold that this was the first exploring party that reached the gap; and that it was on this occasion that Dr. Walker gave the name, "Cumberland," to the gap, the mountain, and the river that now bear the name. Dr. Hale, in his "Trans-Alleghany Pioneers," and L. P. Summers, in his "History of Southwest Virginia," accept this claim as true; and it is possible that quite a number of writers have, successively, followed each other to that conclusion. Theodore Roosevelt in his "Winning of the West says: "One explorer had found and named the Cumberland river and mountains and the great pass called Cumberland Gap." This explorer Mr. Roosevelt says was Dr. Thomas Walker of Virginia. But Roosevelt states in this connection that Walker had been to the Cumberland region in 1748, at the time Colonel Thomas L. Preston and others have said, that Colonel James Patton, along with Dr. Walker, John Buchanan and others discovered the Gap and named it for the Duke of Cumberland. Colonel Preston based his claim upon information he received by tradition, that came down to him through two preceding generations of the descendants of Charles Campbell and Colonel John Buchanan, who were with Colonel Patton and Dr. Walker in their expedition of 1748. Colonel Preston was a descendant of Campbell and Buchanan, his mother being the granddaughter of Charles Campbell and the great-granddaughter of Colonel Buchanan. Therefore, Colonel Preston's information was as substantially correct as any can be that is derived from tradition. When this is reinforced by the admission that Walker had visited the Cumberland region in 1748 with Colonel Patton, it makes the contention that Colonel Patton discovered and named Cumberland Gap very hard to overthrow.

On the other hand, there is very strong supporting evidence in Walker's Journal of the position taken by the historians aforementioned, that Dr. Thomas Walker named it Cumberland Gap. He passed through the gap, which he then called "Cave Gap," on the 13th of April, 1750, and entered Kentucky, for the first time, as there is no claim that the Patton expedition went through the gap or over the Cumberland Mountains in 1748. After passing through the gap, Dr. Walker says, in his journal: "On the North West side we came to a Branch that made a great deal of flat land. We kept down it 2 miles, several other branches coming in to make it a large creek, and we called it Flat Creek. We camped on the Bank, where we found very good Coal."

On the 14th they traveled down the creek, "5 miles chiefly along the Indian Road." The 15th was Easter Sunday, but that holy day was not observed by the explorers, as they continued their journey for a reason assigned by Dr. Walker in his journal: "Being in bad grounds for our Horses we moved 7 miles along the Indian Road to Clover Creek. Clover and Hop Vines are plenty here." It is known that the common red clover is indigenous to this country, but the hop vine is still pronounced a doubtful native of North America. If these two valuable plants were growing a "plenty" in a Kentucky wilderness, where white men had never dwelt and where no recent aboriginal inhabitants had been even temporarily located, how did the clover and the hops get there?

It rained the 16th and the party remained in camp, the horses, no doubt, feasting on the clover. On the 17th it still rained, and Dr. Walker relates: "I went down the Creek a hunting and found that it went into a River about a mile below our Camp. This, which is Flat Creek and some others joined, I called Cumberland River."

It looks very much like Dr. Walker had concluded to give names to important streams, passes and other landmarks that he found

T.H.—12

while on his exploring tour; and is conclusive evidence that he was the first to name the river the Cumberland. But it does not definitely settle the disputed question of who gave the name to Cumberland Gap. This, however, is an inconsequential matter, and one can take either side of the controversy without detracting from the fame of either Colonel Patton or Dr. Walker. What they, each, accomplished in the way of exploring the regions west of the Alleghanies, and introducing settlers into this marvelously rich territory, will cause their names to be honored as long as the people of Southwest Virginia, West Virginia and Kentucky retain any interest in the local history of their immediate country.

Having discovered the Cumberland River, Dr. Walker on the 18th of April began to explore the river, moving along and down it, on the south side thereof, a distance of seventeen miles. On the 21st of April they determined to cross to the north side of the river, and built a bark canoe to get their baggage over. On the 22nd, which was the Sabbath, one of the horses was unable to walk; and Dr. Walker proposed that he and two others should continue the exploration, and the balance of the company remain in camp until they returned. Ambrose Powell and Colbey Chew were selected for Walker's companions. The entire party crossed the river to the north side; and Walker, Powell and Chew started down the Cumberland. They traveled about 35 miles and then returned to the camp. After breaking camp on the 31st of April, Walker and his companions continued to explore the country west and north of the Cumberland Mountains. Though Dr. Walker was a skilled surveyor, for some reason, he failed to make any note in his journal of the courses they followed; and, consequently, it is almost impossible for any one, though familiar with the section of country traveled, to follow the meanderings of the party. He continued to give names to the new streams he discovered, naming one for each of his three associate explorers, Powell, Tomlinson and Lawless.

Sometime in May, not definitely stated in his journal, Dr. Walker and his party changed their course to the east, and crossed the Cumberland Mountain into the present territory of Virginia, leaving what is now Kentucky. At what point they entered this State is not certainly known, being merely conjectural; and it is impossible to even approximately fix the devious course followed by the expedition previous to its arrival on the west bank of New River, just below the mouth of the Greenbrier. The most reasonable conclusion is, that on the journey from the Cumberland region, they passed through the present counties of Wise, Dickenson, Buchanan and Tazewell, Virginia, and Mercer and Summers counties, West Virginia, all these counties then being a part of Augusta County.

Major Jed Hotchkiss, who was a distinguished civil engineer and mineralogist, and well known throughout Virginia before and after the Civil War, brought to public attention the journal of Dr. Walker. And Major Hotchkiss, after a careful study of the matter, confidently asserted that Dr. Walker was at the present site of Pocahontas, Tazewell County, Virginia, in 1750, and that he was the first man to discover and make mention of the great coal deposits about Pocahontas and in the Flat Top region. If Walker did visit the Flat Top coal region, it is absolutely certain that he and his company passed through Wise, Dickenson and Buchanan counties to get there; and then through Mercer and Summers counties, West Virginia, to get to New River. On the 28th of June Dr. Walker made the following entry in his journal:

"It continued raining till noon, and we set off as soon as it ceased and went down the Branch we lay on to the New River just below the mouth of Green Bryer. Powell, Tomlinson and myself stripped, and went into the New River to try if we could wade over at any place. After some time having found a place we returned to the others and took such things as would take damage by water on our Shoulders and waded over Leading our Horses. The bottom is very uneven, the Rocks very slippery and the Current very strong most of the way. We Camped in Low Ground opposite to the mouth of Green Bryer."

Leaving the New River, Dr. Walker and his companions traveled up the Greenbrier and its tributaries, and crossed the Alleghany Mountains to the headwaters of James River. They visited the Hot Springs, and then passed on down into Rockbridge County. From there they went to Augusta Court House (Staunton), arriving at that place on the 11th of July. The following day, Dr. Walker separated from his company, and started, unaccompanied, to his home in Albemarle County, where he arrived at noon on the 13th of July, 1750. Thus was completed one of the most eventful exploring expeditions ever made to Southwest Virginia. Dr. Walker had occupied four months and one week from the beginning to the completion of the journey; and his journal discloses very little of the real purposes of the expedition. From various entries in his journal, it appears he was hunting for valuable minerals more eagerly than for suitable places for settlements. He made a very difficult and dangerous trip through the rugged region west and north of the Clinch Valley, where there was but little game and a great scarcity of herbage for his horses, when by coming up the Clinch Valley he could have found an abundance of both. On the 21st of June Walker entered in his journal: "Deer are very scarce On the Coal Land. I have seen but 4 since the 30th of April." He was evidently very much interested in the "Coal Land." But he must have had no conception of the unmeasured wealth, in the shape of "black diamonds," that was hidden beneath the surface of the territory lying between the Cumberland Mountain and New River, and then open for entry by the Loyal Company under its 800,000 acre grant. If he or the company had realized its value, they would have lost but little time in locating the entire grant in that seemingly poor and valueless region.

Dr. Walker's report of his discoveries to the Loyal Company must have been satisfactory. Though it was greatly hampered by the Ohio Company, it made strenuous effort to anticipate that company in finding and locating the best lands in the New River territory and in the Clinch and Holston valleys. In fact, in October, following Dr. Walker's return from his exploring tour in 1750, the Loyal Company had one surveyor and possibly others at active work in the Holston and Clinch valleys. As previously stated, John Buchanan, on October 14th, 1750, surveyed the "Crabapple Orchard" tract, at Pisgah, three miles west of Tazewell, for John Shelton, it being the same boundary that Thomas Witten settled on in 1767. And on the 16th of October, Buchanan surveyed another tract of 1,000 acres on a "Branch of Clinch River," for Shelton. Both of these tracts were located under the grant of 800,000 to the Loyal Company. Summers says: "About this time the 'Ohio Company' entered a caveat against the 'Loyal Company,' and the 'Loyal Company' got into a dispute with Colonel James Patton, who had an unfinished grant below where this company were to begin, and no further progress was made until June 14th, 1753."

Notwithstanding these obstructions to its enterprise, Dr. Walker, and other surveyors of the company, by the end of the year 1754 had located 224 tracts of land in Southwest Virginia, aggregating more than 45,000 acres. Most of these lands were sold to prospective settlers, and a goodly number had been promptly occupied by the purchasers.

Though the "Ohio Company" did not get its exploring agent,
Christopher Gist, into the field until October, 1750, after starting
he was quite as energetic in the prosecution of the work for his
company as Dr. Walker had proved to be in his performances for
the Loyal Company. As before related, Christopher Gist set out
on his exploring expedition, from his home on the Potomac River,
in October, 1750. Following the instructions of his employers, he
crossed the Alleghany Mountains, and passed through what is now
West Virginia to the Ohio River and explored the country along
that stream as far down as the Great Falls, where the city of Louisville is now located. He devoted the entire winter of 1750-51 to
exploring Kentucky. In the spring of 1751 he reached the Cumberland Mountain at Pound Gap, and came through that gap to the
southeast side of the Cumberland range, entering the present Wise
County, Virginia. Then he traveled down Gist River (now called
Guest's River) to the Powell and Clinch valleys. From that region
he made his way northeastward, pursuing very nearly the same
route that Dr. Walker had followed the preceding summer. His
course was along what is named on the maps the "Dividing Ridge,"
which divides the watersheds of the Clinch and Sandy valleys.
It is possible that he was also making notes of the coal and other
minerals, and that he was at or in the vicinity of Pocahontas. He
passed through Mercer and Summers counties, West Virginia, and
on Tuesday, the 7th day of May, 1751, crossed the New River at
a point near what is known as Crump's Bottom, one of the finest
boundaries of land in the Middle New River section. This fine
estate is now owned and occupied, by a Tazewell man, George W.
Harman, a descendant of Mathias Harman, the mighty Indian
fighter. Summers says, in his History of Southwest Virginia, that,
after crossing New River, Gist traveled in an easterly direction
and that:

"On Saturday, the 11th, he came to a very high mountain, upon
the top of which was a lake or pond about three-fourths of a mile
long northeast and southwest, and one-fourth of a mile wide, the
water fresh and clear, its borders a clean gravely shore about ten
yards wide, and a fine meadow with six springs in it.

"From this description, it is evident that Gist visited Salt Lake
mountain, in Giles county, Va., as early as 1751, and found the lake
as it now is.

"It is evident from this journal that the traditions that we so often hear repeated about this lake are nothing more than mythical, and that this lake existed as it now is at the time of the earliest explorations of the white man."

Commenting on these assertions of Summers, the late Judge David E. Johnston, in his "History of the Middle New River Settlements," says: "If tradition well authenticated is to be taken when supported by well attested evidence, then Christopher Gist never saw Mountain Lake in Giles county. The earliest settlers in the vicinity of the lake and who lived longest, left the unbroken tradition that when they first knew the place where the lake now exists there was a deep depression between the mountains into which flowed the water from one of the springs which found its outlet at the northeastern portion of the depression, and in this gorge or depression was a favorite salting ground in which the settlers salted their cattle by whose continued tramping the crevices through which the water from the springs found an escape, became closed and the depression began to fill with water. This filling began in 1804 and by 1818 the water in the depression had risen to about one-half its present height."

As late as the summer of 1861, the writer of this volume had intimate association with a gentleman who had owned the basin previous to the existence of the lake in question and while it was forming. This gentleman was Hon. Henley Chapman, the most distinguished citizen Giles County has ever produced, and one of the pioneers of that section. His father was John Chapman, who moved with his family from Culpeper County to the Shenandoah Valley in 1766; and after living in that valley two years came on to New River, where he settled at the mouth of Walker's Creek, in the present Giles County, in 1768. His son, Henley, was born there, where he lived an honored citizen until the year 1864. He was a lawyer by profession, was the first Commonwealth's Attorney of Giles County, one of the first attorneys who qualified to practice law in the county court of Tazewell County after its organization in 1800, and was a member of the convention that framed the Virginia Constitution of 1829.

Mr. Chapman told me that he owned the place where Mountain Lake is now seen, and ranged his cattle, as did other settlers, on the mountain thereabout; and that he and others used the basin as a salting ground for their cattle. His account of the formation of the lake was precisely the same as that given by Judge Johnston.

I was fourteen years old in 1861, and was spending the summer with my uncle, Albert G. Pendleton, who then lived at "Fort Branch", just southeast of Pearisburg, where Judge Martin B. Williams now lives. During this visit I went to the "Salt Pond," as it was then called, with a party of young people, among whom were two grandsons and two granddaughters of Mr. Chapman. Even at that early age I was intensely interested in the local history of Southwest Virginia, and an ardent lover of its great physical beauty. The splendid lake of fresh water on the summit of the lofty mountain made a deep impression upon my young mind and heart. Together with the Chapman boys, I rowed out on the lake in a small boat; and we could see large forest trees still standing erect in the lake, beneath the crystal water. After returning from the expedition to the "Salt Pond" I made a visit of several days at Mount Pleasant, the home of Mr. Chapman, near the mouth of Walker's Creek. The old gentleman was very fond of playing checkers, and was the best player I ever tackled. While we were playing checkers in his room I mentioned the "Salt Pond" and my recent visit to it; and he said the trees I had seen in the lake were there, alive and full of foilage in the summer time, when he salted his cattle in the basin, and before the water began to accumulate in a body.

The testimony I have cited is not tradition, but is given by a man who was born and reared within a dozen miles of "Salt Pond," and had actual personal knowledge of the origin of the lake. It proves beyond a doubt that Gist could not have seen the "Salt Pond," as it was not in existence when he made his exploring trip in 1750 for the Ohio Company. Moreover his description of the physical surroundings of the lake do not correspond with those of the "Salt Pond." The "gravelly shore about ten yards wide," and "a fine meadow with six fine springs in it," are physical impossibilities at the location of "Salt Pond," on "Salt Pond Mountain." The very name fixes the origin of the lake. It was never called Mountain Lake until after the Civil War, when it was purchased by General Haupt, of Pennsylvania, from the heirs of Henley Chapman. I visited the "Salt Pond" again in August, 1871, ten years after my first visit. It then presented the same appearance, and, from a boat, the forest trees were still visible, still standing erect in the transparent water.

When Dr. Thomas Walker made his second exploring visit to that portion of Southwest Virginia which lies west of New River,

a current of immigration had already started in this direction. He
found settlers all along the Upper Roanoke Valley, at Draper's
Meadows, and the Dunkard colony at Dunkard's Bottom on the
west side of New River. On Reed Creek, near Max Meadows, he
lodged with James McCall and bought from him a supply of bacon
for his exploring party. In the Middle Holston Valley, at a point
somewhere between Marion and Seven Mile Ford, he found Samuel
Stalnaker preparing for a permanent settlement, and the Walker
party gave a day to helping the pioneer "raise" his house. Stalnaker, it seems, was then the most advanced settler west of New
River; and when Dr. Walker and his companions separated from
him, Walker wrote in his journal: "We left the Inhabitants."

Dr. John Hale, in his intensely interesting book, the "Trans-
Alleghany Pioneers," states that the settlement at Draper's
Meadows was made in 1748. It is evident that the first settlers
at that place came in the wake of the Patton-Walker exploring
expedition of that year. They consisted, so far as is known, of
Thomas Ingles and his three sons, William, Matthew, and John;
Mrs. George Draper and her son, John, and daughter, Mary;
Adam Harmon, Henry Lenard, and James Burke. Their homes
were built upon the present site and lands of the Virginia Polytechnic Institute, at Blacksburg, the land they occupied being purchased from Colonel Patton. The Ingles, the Harmons and James
Burke were later on prominent figures in the settlement of the
Clinch Valley and Burke's Garden. In the spring of 1749, Adam
Harmon moved from Draper's Meadows to the New River Valley
and settled at the place now known as Eggleston's Springs. Very
soon thereafter Philip Lybrook moved in and settled on New River,
near the mouth of Sinking Creek, about three miles below Harmon;
and a little later on the Snidows, Chapmans and others came from
the Shenandoah Valley and settled near Lybrook. There were
other settlements made about the same time at several points in the
present counties of Pulaski, Wythe and Smyth; but no permanent
settlements were made in the present Tazewell County until nearly
twenty years after Colonel Patton's first visit to Burke's Garden, in
1748, and Dr. Walker's visit to the coal bearing regions about Pocahontas, in 1750.

Colonel Thomas L. Preston, in his Reminiscences of an Octogenarian, says, that in 1749 Colonel Patton and William Ingles
went to Burke's Garden and located and surveyed land there. This
statement, I believe, is incorrect. The records in the Land Office

of Virginia show that Colonel Patton and William Ingles surveyed lands in Burke's Garden for Ingles, acting under the 800,000 acre grant to the Loyal Company, in 1753. In the same year they surveyed tracts for William Ingles on the headwaters of Clinch River and on Bluestone Creek in Abb's Valley. The patent for the Abb's Valley tract was issued to William Ingles on the 5th of July, 1774, and was for 1,000 acres, situated in Abb's Valley on the waters of Bluestone Creek, a branch of New River. The patents for the boundaries in Burke's Garden and on the branches of Clinch River were not issued until November 1783; and were then issued to William Christian and Daniel Trigg, as Executors of William Ingles, deceased. Ingles had not completed his titles to these tracts previous to his death, owing to causes that will hereafter be mentioned. His executors brought a suit in the District Court of Montgomery County to perfect the title of their decedent to various tracts of land. The District Court entered a decree in favor of the executors, and the case was appealed by the opposing litigant to the Court of Appeals of Virginia. On the 2nd day of May, 1783, the Court of Appeals entered a decree confirming the decree of the District Court, and ordered that patents be issued to William Christian and Daniel Trigg, Executors of William Ingles, for two tracts of land, one of 345 acres and one of 200 acres, situated in Burke's Garden, as per surveys made on April 18th, 1753, under order of Council, which gave authority to the Loyal Company to take up and survey 800,000 acres of land west of the Alleghany Mountains. And shortly afterward patents were issued to the said executors of William Ingles for five tracts of 140 acres, 70 acres, 61 acres, 210 acres, and 131 acres, respectively, all situated on the headwaters of Clinch River.

CHAPTER III

FRENCH AND INDIAN WAR

In 1754 what is known in history as The French and Indian War was begun, and it was not concluded until the year 1763. It was the beginning of the final struggle between France and England for supreme control of the North American Continent. The war was occasioned by three distinct causes, and the first of these was the conflicting claims of these two nations for a large part of the territory now embraced in the United States. England claimed by right of discovery nearly all the territory south of Canada, and extending from the Atlantic to the Pacific Ocean, basing her claim upon the discoveries made by Sebastian Cabot. France, however, asserted superior title to the territory because she had been the first to establish colonies on the St. Lawrence River and its tributaries. During the latter half of the seventeenth century, France had pushed her explorations westward along the shores of the Great Lakes to the headwaters of the Wabash, the Illinois, the Wisconsin, and St. Croix rivers; and southward through the Valley of the Mississippi to the Gulf of Mexico. These explorations were begun by zealous Jesuit missionaries, for the dual purpose of converting the natives to Catholicism and to secure the vast territory as a possession of France. Charles Raymbault was the pioneer among these Jesuit explorers. He made his way over the waters of Lake Huron, and passed through the Straits and explored Lake Superior in 1641. For the succeeding thirty years the Jesuits prosecuted their explorations and missionary enterprises with unabated ardor. In 1682 Robert de La Salle descended the Mississippi to the Gulf of Mexico; and in 1684, he brought a colony from France to Matagorda Bay and established it in Texas; and attached that territory to the province of Louisiana. By the year 1688 France had planted colonies, built forts and placed garrisons in them at Frontenac, at Niagara, at the Straits of Mackinaw, and on the Illinois River. And by the year 1750 the French had made permanent settlements at Detroit, at the mouth of St. Joseph, at Green Bay, at Vincennes, at Kaskaskia, at Fort Rosalie, where Natchez is located; and at the head of the Bay of Biloxi on the Gulf of Mexico. The English Government had not pushed its frontiers beyond the Alleghany Mountains, though Governor Spottswood, of Virginia, in 1716 had recommended that the Virginia settlements be advanced to the lakes and westward as far as possible, to prevent the French from joining the "Dominion of Canada to their new colony of Louisiana." All that was necessary for France to do to effect the union of her Dominion of Canada with her Province of Louisiana was to occupy the Ohio Valley. This she was seeking to accomplish, and, in fact, was doing when the French and Indian War was precipitated in 1754.

The second cause for this war was the long nourished hatred between France and England as nations. This bitter animosity was the outgrowth of racial antipathies and religious prejudices. The French people were of the Gallic race, while the people of England were of mingled Teutonic and Celtic blood. France had been for many years the leading Catholic country of Europe, and England was the first among the Protestant nations. When to these racial antipathies and religious prejudices was added intense commercial jealousies between the American colonies of the two nations, war became inevitable. And when the French began to build forts on the disputed territory, and sought to monopolize the fur trade of the Indians, Great Britain realized that she would have to repel the encroachments of her enemy or be forced to confine her territorial possessions to the country east of the Alleghanies. Governor Spottswood had given warning in 1716 that these conditions would arise, unless Great Britain built forts and established settlements west of the Alleghanies, and even on the shores of the Great Lakes.

The third cause of the war was more potent and immediate than either of the other two. It was the jealousy that existed between the French traders of Canada and the traders from Virginia and Pennsylvania, who were competing for the fur trade with the Indians on the Ohio River and its tributaries. As has been repeatedly stated, Virginia made claim under the charters given by James I. to all the territory embraced in the present states of West Virginia, Ohio, Kentucky, Indiana, Illinois, and the portions of Michigan and Wisconsin that lie east of the Mississippi River. Her claim was vindicated by the treaty of Paris in 1763. The French traders continued to invade the territory of Virginia and Pennsylvania. The "Ohio Company" was organized in 1750 for the purpose of taking possession of a part of the disputed territory, and thereby stop the encroachments of France. This company was composed of Virginians, among whom were Governor Dinwiddie, Lawrence and Augustus Washington, and Thomas Lee, the latter then being president of the Virginia Council. The company obtained a grant for 500,000 acres of land to be located between the Kanawha and Monongahela Rivers, or on the northern branch of the Ohio River. One of the provisions of the grant was that the lands should be rent free for ten years, but requiring the company to settle one hundred families thereon in seven years.

In October, 1753, Governor Dinwiddie of Virginia, sent George Washington, then a young surveyor, as a commissioner or messenger with a protest to General St. Pierre, who was commander of the French forces in the West and was stationed at Erie. This action, it is likely, was largely procured by the "Ohio Company," of which Dinwiddie and the two Washingtons were conspicuous members. The official communication which George Washington bore to St. Pierre warned the French authorities against further intrusions upon the territory of Virginia. This mission of the young commissioner was a serious one, and the journey was attended with much danger and severe hardships. Washington's party consisted of himself and four armed companions and an interpreter; and Christopher Gist, agent and explorer of the Ohio Company, acted as guide. They traveled up the Potomac and its tributaries, crossed the mountains to the headwaters of the Ohio River, and followed those streams down to the site of Pittsburgh. Then they proceeded to Logstown and held a council with the Indians, who renewed their pledges of friendship to the English colonists and fidelity to the British Government. From Logstown the party went to the French fort at Venango, and the officers stationed at that post made no concealment of the intention of France to unite the Dominion of Canada with the Province of Louisiana by taking possession of the Ohio and Mississippi valleys. From Venango, Washington traveled through the forest to Fort le Bœuf, which was situated on French Creek, fifty miles above its junction with the Alleghany River. There he found St. Pierre engaged in strengthening the fortifications. He was received courteously by the French general, but the latter declined to enter into any discussion with Washington touching the rival claims of the French and English. St. Pierre informed Washington that he was acting under instructions from the governor of New France and would obey his orders to the letter. A polite reply to Governor Dinwiddie's communication was given to Washington, in which St. Pierre stated that France claimed title to the Ohio country by virtue of discovery, exploration and occupation; and was resolved to maintain its claims by force of arms, if necessary. While at Fort le Bœuf, Washington discovered that the French had built a fleet of fifty birch-bark canoes and a hundred and seventy boats from pine lumber for transporting men and supplies down the river to the junction of the Alleghany and Monongahela. The French had recognized the strategic importance of the spot where Pittsburgh is now located and had determined to build a fort there.

It was midwinter when Washington, with Christopher Gist as his sole companion, started on his return journey to Williamsburg, bearing the answer of General St. Pierre to Governor Dinwiddie. The perils and sufferings of that journey are familiar to all interested readers of Virginia and Colonial history. Garbed in an Indian fur robe, with rifle on his shoulder and knapsack on his back, the young patriot tramped and struggled through the wilderness, enduring sufferings from cold and hunger that it would seem impossible for any man to withstand; but Washington arrived at Williamsburg in due season and delivered St. Pierre's defiant note to Governor Dinwiddie. This was the first public service rendered by the future "Father of His Country," and from that time until the day of his death Washington became a central figure in the affairs of his country, and he still remains the most revered of American patriots.

The Ohio Company, which had earnestly directed the attention of the British Government to the French invasion of the Ohio regions, in the winter of 1753-54 organized a company of thirty-three men and placed it under command of a man by the name of Trent, with orders to proceed as quickly as possible to the source of the Ohio River and build a fort there. This company marched as instructed, and in March, 1754, arrived at the confluence of the Alleghany and Monongahela, and built a rude stockade fort on the present site of Pittsburgh. As soon as the ice gorges in the river were broken up St. Pierre left Venango with his fleet of canoes and boats, and swept down the river and forced Trent and his party to withdraw from the country. The French cleared away the forest and began to build a fort, which later became famous in history as Fort Du Quesne.

In the meantime George Washington had been given a commission as lieutenant colonel, with authority to raise a regiment of volunteers to go to the relief of Trent and his company. He was stationed at Alexandria, but before he could get his regiment organized Trent had been forced to surrender on the 17th of April. Early in May, 1754, Washington set out from Alexandria, with about one hundred and fifty men, to recapture the place surrendered by Trent. He was instructed to march to the source of the Ohio, to construct a fort, and to drive out all persons who opposed the settlement of Englishmen in that region.

On the 26th of May the small force of Virginians arrived at the Great Meadows, about thirty miles south of Pittsburgh. Washington built there a stockade, to which he gave the name of Fort Necessity. His Indian scouts soon discovered that a company of the French was secretly scouting in the vicinity, and Washington determined to surprise and capture the party. Two of the Indians discovered the French concealed in a rocky ravine. The Virginians, with Washington leading them, gun in hand, advanced cautiously upon the enemy; but the French became aware of their approach and siezed their guns, whereupon Washington gave the command, "Fire!" This was the first volley that was fired in the French and Indian War, which did not terminate for nine years. Jumonville, was in command of the French company, and ten of his men were killed and twenty were made prisoners.

Learning that General De Villiers was marching from Fort Du Quesne with a large force to make an attack upon him, Washington fell back to Fort Necessity. On the 3rd of July, De Villiers invested and made an attack upon the fort. The French army consisted of six hundred men besides a large force of Indian allies; but Washington with his gallant little band of Virginians successfully resisted for nine hours the attacking party, though thirty of his men were killed and a number wounded. De Villiers on account of a shortage of ammunition proposed a parley; and Washington, realizing that with his small force he could not hold out much longer, accepted the very honorable terms of surrender which were proposed by the French commander. On the 4th of July, the garrison with all their arms, except artillery, and baggage left the fort and withdrew from the country. This left the entire Ohio Valley in possession of France, and caused great alarm among all the Northern colonies as well as in Virginia.

About this time a congress, to which all the American colonies had been requested to send delegates, had assembled at Albany, New York, for the purpose of urging concerted action against the French and to secure more cordial support from the Indian tribes of New York and Pennsylvania, and, if possible, of the tribes along the Ohio. Benjamin Franklin was the leading and guiding spirit of this convention. Steps were taken to unite all the English colonies into a common government, it being then apparent that their future welfare required the formation of a federated form of government. Franklin drafted a constitution, which, after a manifestation of considerable opposition thereto, was adopted by the commissioners in attendance. Copies of the proposed constitution were transmitted to each of the colonies for ratification or rejection; but it was received with great disfavor nearly everywhere. The copy sent to England for approval was contemptuously rejected, the British Board of Trade declaring that the Americans were trying to establish an independent government of their own. Possibly the Board of Trade was not far wrong in that conclusion, as was shown by the Revolution which came on about two decades later.

In the meantime the French were actively occupied in strengthening their fortifications at Crown Point, at Niagara, and at all their posts along the lakes and in the Ohio Valley. The British Government was at last awakened to the fact that something had to be done to stop the aggressions of France, or submit to the loss of all English territory west of the Alleghanies. Though there had been no declaration of war, England determined to send a large army to America to protect her colonies against the continued invasions of the French and Indians. General Edward Braddock was sent over with six thousand regulars, and the colonies were requested to furnish as many volunteers as they could to unite with the regular troops for the protection of the frontiers. The ministers of France and Great Britain continued negotiations for a peaceful solution of the controversy; but Louis XV., King of France, sent three thousand splendidly equipped soldiers to Canada for reinforcing the army he already had in that province, stationed at various forts on the frontier.

On the 14th of April, 1755, General Braddock held a conference at Alexandria, Virginia, for the purpose of forming and outlining a concerted campaign for checking the advances of the French, and the recovery of the territory already invaded and possessed by the enemy; and it was agreed that there should be no invasion of Canada, but that the French should be driven out of the Ohio Valley and the other territory claimed by England. And it was also planned that Lawrence, lieutenant governor of Nova Scotia, should complete the conquest of that province according to the boundaries as claimed by Great Britain.

Braddock started out from Alexandria with two thousand British veterans to recapture fort Du Quesne. At the mouth of Wills' Creek, a tributary of the Potomac, and where Fort Cumberland was built, he was joined by two companies of volunteers from New York and several companies from Virginia. George Washington also joined the army at Fort Cumberland, and Braddock made the young Virginian his aid-de-camp. The British general's commission contained an order which directed that no provincial officer should be given any rank while serving with the British army. This prescription was so offensive to the colonial authorities that they declined or failed to send the large quotas of troops they could have furnished to assist the English forces. George Washington at first declined to go with Braddock in such an inferior capacity, but from purely patriotic motives joined him at Fort Cumberland. The stubborn and foolhardy British commander refused to accept any advice from Washington, or from any of the colonial officers, as to how the campaign should be conducted against the French and Indians. He persisted in his purpose to fight the Indians according to the rules of military art as it was practiced in Europe, and his stubbornness was followed by terrible disaster.

On the 9th day of June, 1755, Braddock's army was led into an ambuscade, and was nearly destroyed by the combined forces of the Indians and French. There were six hundred and thirty Indians, most of them Shawnee warriors, and two hundred and thirty French soldiers in the engagement. British tactics proved worse than valueless when matched against the skill and daring of the Shawnee warriors in a battle fought in the wilderness. Confusion first came to the trained English veterans, and this was followed by panic, which turned the battle field into a bloody shambles for the British soldiers. Braddock had five horses shot under him before he received a fatal wound. Of the eighty-two English officers, twenty-six were killed and thirty-seven were wounded. Washington was the only mounted officer who escaped injury; and he had two horses killed under him, and his coat was pierced by four bullets. When Braddock sank to the ground from a bullet wound in his right side, Washington rushed to his assistance. Then the haughty Briton turned to the Virginian and inquired: "What shall we do now Colonel?" Washington promptly replied: "Retreat sir—retreat by all means." An order for retreat was then given;

and though but about thirty of the Virginians had escaped slaughter, under the command of our Washington, they effectively covered the retreat of the crushed and ruined army. The French and Indians had three officers and thirty men killed and about the same number wounded. Of the English army, seven hundred and fourteen men of the ranks were killed and wounded. A hasty retreat was made by the remnant of Braddock's army to Fort Cumberland, and a few days later that place was abandoned and the army marched to Philadelphia.

At the convention held by the governors of the colonies at Alexandria on the 14th of April, 1755, it had been ordered that Governor Lawrence should make complete conquest of Nova Scotia, so as to settle the boundaries of that province, which had been ceded by France to England by the treaty of Utretch, made April 11th, 1713. There had been sharp contentions between France and England over the boundaries of the ceded province.

The first permanent settlement made by Frenchmen on the North American Continent was established on the southwest coast of Nova Scotia, at a harbor which had been called Port Royal by the French discoverers. And the whole country thereabout, including the surrounding islands, was called Acadia by the founders of the settlement. After the cession of the province to England, the name of Port Royal was changed to Annapolis, and the name Acadia was changed to Nova Scotia. At the time the province was ceded to Great Britian the population was estimated at about three thousand, and at the outbreak of the French and Indian War their numbers had increased to about sixteen thousand. The French inhabitants outnumbered the English about three to one. Lawrence, the acting British governor, pretended that there was danger of an insurrection, as a very large majority of the inhabitants of the province were French and were dissatisfied with British rule. Bancroft, the great American historian, says of these people:

"Happy in their neutrality, the Acadians formed, as it were, one great family. Their morals were of unaffected purity. Love was sanctified and calmned by the universal custom of early marriages. The neighbors of the community would assist the new couple to raise their cottage on fertile land, which the wilderness freely offered."

These excellent people were placed at the mercy of their military masters, and were denied protection in the civil tribunals. Their property was taken without their consent for the public service and

T.H.—13

"they were not to be bargained with for the payment." They were required to furnish firewood for their oppressors, with an order from the governor: "If they do not do it in proper time, the soldiers shall absolutely take their houses for fuel." Their fire-arms and boats were taken from them, leaving them without means to escape from their oppressors. Orders were given the English officers to punish Acadians at discretion, if they behaved amiss; and if the troops were insulted they had authority to assault the nearest person, whether he be the guilty one or not, taking "an eye for an eye, and a tooth for a tooth."

The British officers and men were taught to believe that the colonies existed for no other purpose than to be exploited for the benefit of the mother country; and they despised the Acadians, even though they were an honest, industrious and virtuous people. So, Lawrence was given full authority to reduce the French popula-tion of Nova Scotia to complete submission; and to assist him in the cruel undertaking a British fleet was sent from Boston.

On the 20th of May, 1755, the fleet, with three thousand troops aboard, under the command of General Monkton, sailed from Boston for the Bay of Fundy. The 2nd of June the British army was landed on the coast of Nova Scotia, and in a campaign of less than a month, with a loss of twenty men, the British had brought into subjection the whole country east of the St. Croix River. The French inhabitants and the garrisons at the two fortified posts that France still held in the isthmus which divides Nova Scotia from New Brunswick, were taken entirely by surprise, as the hos-tile British movement was made before any declaration of war. While this atrocious campaign in Nova Scotia was in progress, Braddock was marching to his doom on the Monongahela.

Acadia, peaceful and helpless, had been easily conquered; but the French inhabitants outnumbered the English three to one. To remove any danger from an insurrection, Governor Lawrence and Admiral Boscawen, upon the advice of the chief justice of the province, determined to deport the French inhabitants. As a pre-liminary to the execution of this great crime, a demand was made that the people should take an oath of allegiance which was so framed that the French, as faithful Catholics, could not subscribe to it. Upon their refusal to take the oath of renunciation, the Eng-lish plotters accused the French of treason and made then surrender all their firearms and boats. The heavy-hearted people were driven from their homes in the villages and hamlets and their houses destroyed by fire. They were forced to assemble in the larger towns and when a sufficient number were collected, they were driven on shipboard for deportation. Ridpath, writing about this horrible transaction, says:

"The wails of the thousands of bleeding hearts were wafted to heaven with the smoke of burning homes. At the village of Grand Pre four hundred and eighteen unarmed men were called together and shut up in a church. Then came the wives and children, the old men and the mothers, the sick and the infirm, to share the common fate. The whole company numbered more than nineteen hundred souls. The poor creatures were driven to the shore, forced into the boats at the point of the bayonet, and carried to the vessels in the bay. As the moaning fugitives cast a last look at their pleasant town, a column of black smoke floating seaward told the story of desolation. More than three thousand of the helpless Acadians were carried away by the British squadron and scattered, helpless, half-starved and dying among the English colonies. The history of civilized nations furnishes no parallel to this wanton and wicked destruction of an inoffensive colony."

At the close of the year 1755 the British armies had nothing to their credit in the way of success, except the disgraceful conquest of Acadia, and a dearly bought victory won by General Johnson over General Dieskau near Fort Edward, New York. The years 1756-57 proved two years of great disaster to the British. In July, 1756, General Montcalm captured the two forts at the mouth of the Oswego River; and the French greatly strengthened their forts at Crown Point and Ticonderoga. The only successes won by the English were scored by the colonial volunteers, called provincials. During the summer the Delawares violated their treaty with the colonies, and made vicious attacks upon the settlers in Western Pennsylvania. Colonel John Armstrong, with three hundred Pennsylvania volunteers, crossed the Alleghany Mountains, and by a twenty days march got to the Indian town called Kittanning, which was situated forty-five miles northeast of Pittsburg. Colonel Armstrong was one of the Scotch-Irish immigrants who had come from Ulster, and his three hundred men were mostly of the same blood. The Pennsylvanians attacked the village at daybreak. Captain Jacobs, the Delaware chief, raised the war-whoop and cried: "The white men are come, we shall have scalps enough." Jacobs was one of the Indians who laid the ambuscade for Braddock's army, and a hearty participant in the scalping carnival that followed Braddock's defeat. On this occasion there was quite a different scene. Jacobs and his entire family and most of his warriors were killed and scalped by the white men. The town was burned, but the Americans lost sixteen of their good men killed, and a number were wounded. Among the wounded were Colonel Armstrong and Captain Hugh Mercer. The Pennsylvania county which includes the battle field is named Armstrong; and the West Virginia county that adjoins Tazewell bears the name of Mercer.

After the defeat of Braddock, the General Assembly of Virginia made an appropriation of money for Colonel George Washington and the other officers and the privates of the Virginia volunteers, to reward them "for their gallant behavior and losses in the late disastrous battle." Colonel Washington was also given command of all the forces raised or to be enlisted in Virginia. He selected for his field officers, next in rank to himself, Lieutenant Colonel Adam Stephens and Major Andrew Lewis. The latter was from Augusta County, was one of the Trans-Alleghany pioneers, and became eminent as an Indian fighter and officer in the Revolutionary War. Washington established his headquarters at Winchester, as the Indians and their French allies were making hostile incursions into the Valley of Virginia, and were spreading consternation among the settlers, many of whom were fleeing with their families for safety across the Blue Ridge Mountain.

Washington made a tour of the outposts, from Fort Cumberland to Fort Dinwiddie, on Jackson's River; and was satisfied that the means he possessed were not sufficient to protect the Valley and the outlying settlements against the Indians. He then determined to go to Williamsburg and urge that more adequate means be furnished; but he was recalled after he reached Fredericksburg by an announcement that the Indians had renewed their attacks upon the settlements. Hurrying back to Winchester he gathered his small forces and drove the savages back from the border. In the spring of 1756 he went to Williamsburg and induced the General Assembly, then in session, to increase his force to fifteen hundred men. After accomplishing this, he returned to Winchester and found that scouting parties of Indians were massacreing the unprotected inhabitants on the border, and were attacking the forts and killing some of his best soldiers. Conditions were so deplorable, and the number of troops so inadequate for the protection of the settlers, that Colonel Washington wrote a letter to Governor Dinwiddie in which he pictured the distressing situation, and declaring that: "The supplicating tears of the women, and moving petitions of the men, melt me with deadly sorrow, that I solemnly declare, if I know my own mind, I could offer myself a willing sacrifice to the butchering enemy, provided that would contribute to the people's ease." The summer and autumn of 1757 were spent by Washington in repairing the old forts and in building a new one at Winchester, which was named Fort Loudoun.

The year 1757 proved equally as disastrous for the English as had the two preceding years. At the close of the year it looked as if the British would be driven out of America, or, at least, be forced to confine themselves to the regions they had so long occupied east of the Alleghanies. France was in possession of twenty times as much American territory as England, and every English settler had been driven from the Ohio Valley. But a great change in the situation came in 1758. William Pitt, the first Englishman to be called the "Great Commoner," was placed at the head of the ministry; and the disgraceful mismanagement of English affairs in America was brought to an end. General Ambercrombie superseded the incapable Lord Loudoun as commander-in-chief; and Admiral Boscawen was put in charge of a splendid fleet of twenty-two ships of the line and fifteen frigates. Able generals and a corps of capable subordinate officers were given the commander-in-chief. Among these were Generals Amherst, Howe, Forbes, and Wolfe, and Colonel Richard Montgomery. The latter was the favorite officer in the brigade of the gallant General James Wolfe, and was with him when he captured Quebec from the French on the 13th of September, 1759, and when he received a mortal wound on the Heights of Abraham. It was a strange decree of fate which placed Colonel Montgomery in command of a Colonial army with which he sought to capture Quebec from the British on December 31st, 1775; and that he should receive a mortal wound, while leading his troops, not far from where Wolfe was killed sixteen years previously.

The war was pressed with vigor during the years 1758 and 1759. Louisburg was captured by General Wolfe on the 28th of July, 1758, and soon thereafter Cape Breton and Prince Edward Island were surrendered to Great Britain. General Ambercrombie made an ineffectual effort to take Ticonderoga on the 6th of July. On the 8th the English army made another assault, a bloody battle ensued, and the carnage was dreadful, the British losing in killed and wounded nineteen hundred and sixteen men. General Montcalm was in command of the four thousand French, and it was due to his skillful and energetic management that the English lost the battle. A short time after the defeat at Ticonderoga, Colonel Bradstreet captured Frontenac after a two days siege, which compensated for the failure to capture Ticonderoga.

Later in the summer General Forbes left Philadelphia with an army of nine thousand men and moved slowly and cautiously in the direction of Fort Du Quesne. Washington was in command of the provincials, and Colonel Armstrong, already famous from his victory over the Indians at Kittanning, commanded the Pennsylvanians. On the 24th of November, Washington, who was in charge of the advance troops, arrived within ten miles of Fort Du Quesne. The French garrison, which numbered only about five hundred men, abandoned and destroyed the fort and made their retreat in their canoes and boats down the river. It was on the following day, November 25th, 1758, that the English flag was raised again on the noted spot and the name Pittsburg given thereto in honor of the "Great Commoner," who had restored the prestige of England in America. Thus was wrested from the French what has since been known as "the gateway of the west."

For the campaign of the next year, General Amherst was placed in full command of the American forces, Parliament voted twelve million pounds for its conduct, and the colonies cheerfully joined the British Government to raise an army of fifty thousand men.

On the 25th of July, 1759, the French surrendered Niagara to Sir William Johnson, and communication between Canada and Louisiana was completely broken. The 26th day of July the French garrison abandoned Ticonderoga and retreated to Crown Point; and five days afterward they deserted that place. General Wolfe gave the final blow to the power of France in Canada on the 12th of September, when he successfully attacked Quebec, though he lost his life in that supreme effort. Montcalm, the gallant French commander, was also mortally wounded in the battle, and when told that he could live but a few hours, said: "So much the better; I shall not live to see the surrender of Quebec." The citadel was surrendered to General Townshend on the 17th of September, 1759.

In the spring of 1760 France made the last great struggle to regain her power in Canada. A few miles west of Quebec the French and English met in a severe battle and the English were forced to retire into the city; but reinforcements were sent to the British and the French were driven back. On the 8th of September,

1760, Montreal, which was the only strong post still held by France in the St. Lawrence Valley, was surrendered to General Amherst. At the time of the surrender of Montreal it had been stipulated that the number of small posts held by the French in the vast territory bordering on the Great Lakes should be turned over to Great Britain. And in the fall of 1760, General Amherst sent Major Robert Rogers with two hundred provincial rangers to receive these outposts from the several French commanders. In November, Major Rogers reached Detroit, the fort was surrendered to him, and he raised the English flag over the fortress, where it continued to float to the breeze until it was hauled down to make place for our own great emblem of freedom, the Stars and Stripes. Then Fort Miami on the southern shore of Lake Michigan, and Fort Onatanon on the Wabash were surrendered to Major Rogers. It was his purpose to travel on and take possession of the forts at Mackinaw, Green Bay and St. Marie, but severe storms prevented him from doing this; and those remote forts were not garrisoned with English soldiers until the summer of 1761.

The fall of Montreal and the subsequent surrender of the French forts placed Great Britain in complete possession of all the disputed territory which had provoked the French and Indian War. While this war was in progress the French, by very kind and considerate treatment, had won the friendship and confidence of their Indian allies; and the hatred of the red men for the English had been greatly intensified. The Indians still believed that France would reconquer the country and expel the detested English; and, so believing, the native tribes continued to make attacks upon the frontier settlements. In the summer of 1761 the Senecas and Wyandots joined in a conspiracy to capture Detroit and massacre the English garrison; but Colonel Campbell, commander of the post, got information of the conspiracy and thwarted the attack. The following summer a similar plot was formed, but it was defeated by the alert English officers.

In the spring of 1763, Pontiac, who was chief of the Ottowas, and who led his warriors at Braddock's defeat, conceived a plan for uniting all the tribes between the Alleghanies and the Mississippi River, to make concerted attacks upon all the forts in the possession of the English, and overwhelm their garrisons. This noted chief had met Major Robert Rogers, when he was on his way to take possession of Detroit for the British, at the place where Cleveland, Ohio, is now located; and had made objection to further invasion of the territory by the English. But when he was informed that the French had been defeated and had surrendered all their forts in Canada, he consented to the surrender of Detroit, and for a time was disposed to be friendly to the British. Later he was deceived by rumors that France was preparing to make a reconquest of her American possessions, and proceeded to carry out his plans for a general uprising of the Indians and the destruction of the English forts and settlements.

The 7th of May, 1761, was the day selected for the general uprising and for the beginning of what is known in history as Pontiac's War. Pontiac was to make an attack upon Detroit, the capture of that place being considered the most difficult task of the Indians' scheme. An Indian girl. who was deeply infatuated with an English officer at the post, the day before the uprising visited the fort and revealed the plot to Major Gladwyn, the commandant. When Pontiac's warriors the following day attempted by treachery to accomplish their design, they found all the soldiers and the citizens under arms and fully prepared to repel any onslaught. A protracted siege followed, but finally had to be abandoned.

At other points the Indians were more successful in the execution of their scheme. On the 16th of May, a band of the Wyandots captured Fort Sandusky. killed all the garrison and burned the fort. A few days later Fort St. Joseph experienced a similar fate at the hands of a number of the Pottawotamie tribe. This was followed by the capture of Fort Mackinaw and nearly all of its defenders were cruelly butchered by the savages. The Indians continued their operations against the forts and settlements until the middle of the summer, by which time they had taken every fort held by the British, except Detroit, Fort Pitt, and Niagara.

For the three years succeeding the surrender of Montreal to the British the war between France and England was continued on the seas, with the British fleets victorious in nearly every engagement. France was so reduced in men and resources that she was forced to come to very humiliating terms; and on the 10th of February, 1763, a treaty of peace was negotiated at Paris between the belligerent nations. By this treaty France surrendered to Great Britain all of the territory claimed by the French east of the Mississippi,

from its source to the river Iberville, and thence through Lakes
Maurepas and Pontchartrain to the Gulf of Mexico. In the same
treaty Spain, with whom England had also been engaged in war,
ceded East and West Florida to Great Britain; and, in lieu of this
cession, France was forced to cede to Spain all of that extensive
and magnificent territory west of the Mississippi, then known as
the Province of Louisiana. Thus was France deprived of all her
possessions in the New World; and thus was concluded one of the
most important wars in the world's history.

The French and Indian War is worthy of much consideration
and study by all persons who are interested in the formation and
development of our splendid American Republic. This war not
only caused extensive and important changes in the map of the
world, but exercised a mighty influence upon its social, political
economic, and religious thought. During its progress a momentous
struggle was going on in Europe between the Protestant and Catholic monarchs. Frederick the Great, of Prussia, was standing almost
alone as the defender of Protestanism against the combined forces
of France, Austria, Bavaria, and the other Catholic countries of the
Continent. Bancroft says: "Among the rulers of the European
Continent, Frederick, with but four millions of subjects, stood forth
alone, 'the unshaken bulwark of Protestantism and freedom of
thought.'" It is known that after George Washington's withdrawal
from the service of Great Britain in 1761, in his retirement at Mount
Vernon, he kept in his library a bust of Frederick, whose devoted
struggles for political and religious freedom he watched with the
keenest interest and profoundest sympathy. And up in New England, the stern Calvinists were constantly sending up petitions to
Almighty God for the success and preservation of the King of
Prussia in his heroic struggle against the Papacy.

To the Americans this war was one of vital import, in that it
directed the attention of the colonies to the fact that, if they became
united in sympathy and purpose, they need be no longer dependent
upon Great Britain for protection against either domestic or foreign
foes. Could the mother country have foreseen that the first volley
fired in the war, at the command of George Washington, was the
beginning of a revolution in American thought and purpose, which
in a few years would constrain the colonies to proclaim their independence, England would not have been so eager to expel the French
and Spaniards from the North American Continent.

In 1742, Baron Montesquieu, the distinguished French jurist

and philosopher, gave notice to the intellectual world that "a free, prosperous and great people was forming in the forests of America, which England had sent forth her sons to inhabit." Jaques Turgot, a distinguished son of France, when only twenty-three years old, in 1750, made accurate prophesy as to what would transpire in America before the close of the eighteenth century, when he exclaimed to the assembled clergy of France: "Vast regions of America! Equality keeps from them both luxury and want, and preserves to them purity and simplicity with freedom. Europe herself will find there the perfection of her political societies, and the surest support of her well being. Colonies are like fruits, which cling to the tree only till they ripen: Carthage declared itself free as soon as it could take care of itself; so likewise will America."

Ample warning was given by other great men as to what results would follow the French and Indian War. Just at the beginning of the struggle, David Hume, England's "great master of historic style," and who exposed "the hollowness of the prevailing systems of thought in Europe," speaking of America, said: "The seeds of many a noble state have been sown in climates kept desolate by the wild manners of the ancient inhabitants, and an asylum is secured in that solitary world for liberty and science."

In 1760 an interesting interview took place between Lord Camden, attorney general for Great Britain, and Benjamin Franklin, who was visiting England in the interest of the colonies. Camden observed: "For all what Americans say of your loyalty, and notwithstanding your boasted affection, you will one day set up for independence." To this Dr. Franklin replied: "No such idea is entertained by the Americans, or ever will be, unless you grossly abuse them." Camden promptly rejoined: "Very true; that I see will happen, and will produce the event."

Dr. Franklin was loyal to the mother country, just as he was true to everything he ever espoused, but he spake truly when he gave notice that he and his fellow-Americans would not submit to further gross oppressions from the British Government. And Lord Camden was equally as sincere when he announced his conviction that such abuses would come during the reign of George III.; and that the American colonies would declare and win their independence. Just after the treaty of peace was made at Paris, in 1763, Vergennes, the French ambassador at Constantinople, declared: "The consequences of the entire cession of Canada are obvious. I am persuaded England will ere long repent of having removed the only check that could keep her colonies in awe. They stand no longer in need of her protection; she will call on them to contribute towards supporting the burdens they have helped bring on her; and they will answer by striking off all dependence."

The French and Indian War was an important event for the Americans, in that it was a training school for a number of the men who became famous as leaders and officers of the armies that won independence for the colonies. It also prepared a number for directing the civil affairs of the United Colonies when the struggle for escape from British misrule was inaugurated. George Washington, Horatio Gates, Andrew Lewis and Daniel Morgan, from Virginia; and John Armstrong and Hugh Mercer from Pennsylvania, were with Braddock when he met defeat and death on the Monongahela. The Virginia and Pennsylvania volunteers, under the leadership of Washington and Armstrong, saved the panic-stricken army from total annihilation by the blood-thirty Indians. Israel Putman, of Connecticut, John Stark, of New Hampshire, and Philip Schuyler, of New York, were equally as conspicuous and useful in the campaigns conducted by the British armies in Western New York and in Canada. And Francis Marion and William Moultrie, two of the most gallant and efficient generals of the Revolutionary War, were with Colonels Grant and Montgomery when those British officers made their invasions of the Cherokee country to bring the Cherokees into submission. These noble patriots and splendid military leaders of the Revolution were products of the French and Indian War. It made them familiar with the tactics and fighting qualities of the British armies; and acquainted them with the methods of the Indians who were the allies of Great Britain.

CHAPTER IV

DRAPER'S MEADOWS MASSACRE AND OTHER TRAGIC INCIDENTS.

To the pioneer settlers who had already crossed the Alleghanies to build homes, and secure for themselves and their children personal and religious freedom, the French and Indian War was a fearful tragedy. Its effect upon them was more immediate and telling than it was upon the older settlements of the colonies, or the powerful European nations that engaged in the war from a desire of conquest and commercial supremacy in North America. For them it introduced the brutal practice of paying a price for each scalp of a white person who was butchered by the Indians. The red men had previously taken the scalps of their dead foes to keep and exhibit as an isignia of valor; but in this cruel war the French paid their savage allies so much for each English scalp they brought in; and the savages reaped a rich harvest from the battle field where Braddock's army was beaten. This caused the British to offer their savage allies a reward for each scalp of their Indian foes that was secured. Perhaps the English were justified in making this cruel reprisal, but they did not stop there in the brutal practice. In the Revolutionary War and the War of 1812, the British Government paid their Indians so many shillings for each scalp they secured from the heads of Americans.

For sometime previous to the commencement of the war, the French and English had been actively competing for the support of the Shawnees and other tribes that inhabited the Ohio Valley. When the Ohio Company sent Christopher Gist on an exploring expedition to the Ohio country in 1750, he was not only instructed to "examine the western country as far as the falls of the Ohio; to look for a large tract of level land; to mark the passes in the mountains; to trace the courses of the rivers;" but he was specially directed to ascertain the strength and numbers of the Indians and to secure their friendship for the English. In obedience to these instructions, he crossed the Alleghanies and first visited a small town of friendly Delawares on the east side of the Ohio; and then crossed the river and traveled down to Logstown. It was then occupied by a mixed band of Senecas, Mohicans, Ottawas, and others, with nearly a hundred cabins. These Indians had become very jealous of the known purposes of the Ohio Company, and told Gist: "You have come to settle on the Indian lands: You shall never go home safe," though they treated him respectfully as an accredited messenger of the English King. Nothing daunted by this manifestation of anger, Gist traveled on to a village of the Ottawas on Elk's Eye Creek, and found its people warm friends of the French. He then visited the town of the Wyandots at Muskingam and found its hundred families about equally divided in sympathy for the French and English. Those who were friends of the English said to Gist: "Come and live with us; bring great guns and make a fort. If the French claim the branches of the lakes, those of the Ohio belong to us and our brothers, the English."

The Shawnees were then located on both sides of the Ohio just below the mouth of the Scioto. When Gist arrived at their towns they made earnest professions of friendship for the Virginians, and expressed deep gratitude for the protection that had been given them by the English against attacks from the Six Nations. After leaving the Shawnee towns, the English envoys next visited the Miamis at their towns on the Miami River. The Miamis were an Algonquian tribe and had the largest and most powerful confederacy in the west. The Virginians and Pennsylvanians were the first white men of the English race to see the splendid country beyond the Scioto. They found the land rich and level, with alternating stretches of magnificent forests of walnut, maple, wild cherry and ash, and beautiful praries carpeted with wild rye, blue grass, and white clover; and fine herds of deer, elk and buffalo grazing thereon. It was the very kind of country Gist had been directed to search for, and he and his companions rapturously declared that: "nothing is wanting but cultivation to make this a most delightful country."

Christopher Gist and his company remained some days with the various tribes of the Miami Confederacy; and, then, on the 1st day of March, 1751, started for Kentucky, with assurance from the Miamis that they would make no terms with the French, and bearing to the English authorities the message: "Our friendship shall stand like the loftiest mountains." The shrewd agent of the Ohio Company had made arrangements for all the friendly tribes of the West to meet the following summer at Logstown to make a treaty with Virginia. After leaving the Miami towns he descended the Little Miami River and crossed the Ohio into Kentucky at a point about fifteen miles above where Louisville is now situated. Thence, as hereinbefore related, he traveled through Kentucky and Southwest Virginia, and on to Williamsburg, where he made report of the accomplishments of the expedition to Governor Dinwiddie and the other members of the Ohio Company.

The following year the Ohio Company, with the approval of the General Assembly of Virginia, determined to place a settlement beyond the Alleghany Mountains; and Christopher Gist was sent out by the company to explore the lands southeast of the Ohio, as far as the Kanawha. He found that the Indians had become very suspicious of the intentions of both the French and the English. The natives had begun to realize that the two great European nations, while each was professing great regard for the Indians, were about to engage in a mighty struggle for permanent possession of an extensive and valuable territory to which neither had any just claim of ownership. It had become very evident that France and Great Britain were both maneuvering to get the assistance of the simple natives in a war which was bound to result in robbing the Indians of their lands, no matter whether the French or English were victors. Therefore it is not surprising that a Delaware chief said to Christopher Gist: "Where lie the lands of the Indians? The French claim all on one side of the river and the English on the other." And about the same time another chief, the Half-King, declared: "We see and know that the French design to cheat us out of our lands. We, therefore, desire our brothers of Virginia may build a strong house at the fork of Monongahela."

The Ohio Company in 1753 built a road by way of Wills Creek into the western valley; and Gist established a settlement with eleven families. He marked out sites for a town and a fort on Shurtees Creek; but the British Government gave no protection to the little colony, and the settlers were forced to flee from the Indians and French in a very short time.

In the meantime, while the Virginians and Pennsylvanias were negotiating with the Indians for the peaceful occupation of the country both north and south of the Ohio, the French pushed on down from the lakes and took possession of the entire region. DuQuesne sent twelve hundred men to occupy the valley of the Ohio. The Delawares, Shawnees, and Mingoes met in council at Logstown, and started an envoy to Montreal to protest against the invasion of their country by an armed force, but he was turned back at Niagara by the French, who told him it was useless to proceed to Montreal.

DRAPER'S MEADOWS MASSACRE.

By shrewd management, with bribes, threats, and promises of protecting them in the possession of their lands, the French secured as their allies nearly all of the Indian tribes that were then occupying the Ohio Valley. They proved very efficient and faithful allies; and were a potential factor in winning the French victory over Braddock. From the date of that disaster to the British arms, the Indians began to send marauding parties to attack the settlers in the Valley of Virginia, the Upper James Valley, the Roanoke Valley, and the few settlements that had been made west of the Alleghanies in what is now known as Southwest Virginia. In fact the scheme of terrorizing the Virginia frontiers with scalping parties was put in motion previous to Braddock's defeat. The first blow that fell upon the pioneers of Southwest Virginia was the attack made by a band of Shawnees on the settlement at Draper's Meadows, at the present site of the Virginia Polytechnic Institute, at Blacksburg. This settlement, as previously related, was started in 1748. Dr. John P. Hale, who was a descendant of Mrs. William Ingles, one of the victims of that horrible tragedy, has given a concise and authentic narrative of the incident in his book, the "Trans-Alleghany Pioneers." He thus relates the story as told to him by his ancestors:

"On the 8th of July, 1755, being Sunday, and the day before Braddock's memorable defeat, near Fort DuQuesne, when all was peace, and there was no suspicion of harm or danger, a party of Shawnees from beyond the Ohio, fell upon the Draper's Meadows settlement and killed, wounded or captured every soul there present, as follows:

"Colonel James Patton, Mrs. George Draper, Casper Barrier and a child of John Draper, killed; Mrs. John Draper and James Cull, wounded; Mrs. William Ingles, Mrs. John Draper, Henry Lenard, prisoners.

"Mrs. Draper, being out of doors, a short distance from the house first discovered the enemy approaching, and under circumstances indicating hostile intent.

"She ran into the house to give the alarm and to get her sleeping infant. Taking the child in her arms she ran out on the opposite side of the house and tried to make her escape. The Indians discovered her, however, and fired on her as she ran, breaking her right arm and causing the child to fall. She hastily picked it up again with her left hand, and continued her flight. She was soon over-taken, however, and made a prisoner, and the child brained against one of the house logs. The other Indians, meanwhile, were devot-ing their attention to other members of the families and camp, with the results in killed, wounded, and captured, as above stated.

"Colonel James Patton, who had large landed interests hereabout, was here at this time and with him his nephew, William Preston.

"Whether Colonel Patton was only temporarily here, or was then making this his home, I do not know. He had command of the Virginia Militia in this region, and had just bought up a supply of powder and lead for use of the settlements, which, I believe, the Indians secured.

"Early on the morning of the attack, Colonel Patton had sent young Preston over to the house of Mr. Philip Lybrook, on Sinking Creek, to get him to come over and help next day with the harvest, which was ready to be cut, and this fortunate absence doubtless saved young Preston's life.

"Colonel Patton was sitting at a table writing when the attack was made, with his broadsword, which he always kept with him, lying on the table before him. He was a man of large frame (he was six feet four inches in height), and herculean strength. He cut down two of the Indians with his sword, as they rushed upon him, but was, in turn, shot down himself by others out of his reach. He was a widower, sixty-three years of age, and full of health and vigor when he met his untimely death."

When the attack was made William Ingles was in a grain field some distance from the house, possibly in the field from which the grain was to be harvested the next day. As soon as he saw the smoke and flames of the buildings, which the Indians had set fire to, he apprehended that something serious had happened, and ran rapidly to the aid of his family. He saw the large number of Indians and realized that it was folly for him, unarmed as he was, to offer resistance, and turned to make his escape; but he had been seen by the Indians and was pursued by two of the warriors. They failed, however, to capture him; and he and John Draper, who was from home when the massacre occurred, went to the settlements farther east to get assistance.

Mrs. Ingles had two small sons, Thomas, who was four years old, and George, three years old, who were also captured. Dr. Hale failed to mention the boys in the above list of captives, but refers to them frequently as he proceeds with his narrative. The Indians collected much valuable booty—guns, ammunition, and household goods. These things were packed on some of the horses of the settlers, and the women and children were placed on other horses; and the march was then started for the Indian towns. Dr. Hale says:

"About half a mile or mile to the west, on their route, they stopped at the house of Mr. Philip Barger, an old and white haired man, cut his head off, put it in a bag, and took it with them to the house of Philip Lybrook, on Sinking Creek, where they left it, telling Mrs. Lybrook to look in the bag and she would find an acquaintance."

It seems that Philip Lybrook and William Preston had left Lybrook's house, and had taken what was called a "near cut" across the mountains for Draper's Meadows, to help in the harvest field the next day. This saved them from encountering the Indians, and, no doubt, preserved their lives. There is no record of the route followed by the Indians and their captives, but it is evident that they traveled down New River, as far as the mouth of Indian Creek. There they crossed the river and followed it to the mouth of Bluestone, passed up that stream a short distance, then proceeded along the route of what afterwards was known as the Giles, Raleigh and Fayette Turnpike to the head of Paint Creek. This stream was followed to the Kanawha River which they crossed to the northeast side, possibly at Witcher's Creek Shoals.

Dr. Hale says that: "On the night of the third day out, the course of nature, which waits not upon conveniences nor surroundings, was fulfilled, and Mrs. Ingles, far from human habitation, in the wide forest, unbounded by walls, with only the bosom of mother earth for a couch, and covered by the green trees and the canopy of heaven, with a curtain of darkness around her, gave birth to an infant daughter. * * * Owing to her perfect physical constitution, health and training, she was next morning able to travel, and did resume the journey, carrying the little stranger in her arms, on horseback."

Upon arrival at the salt spring, just above the mouth of Campbell's Creek, the Indians made a halt of several days to get a supply of game and salt to take to their towns. The pots and kettles that were taken from the houses of the captives were used for boiling the salt water. Mrs. Ingles and the other prisoners did the salt

T.H.—14

making while the Indians were hunting and killing the fine game that came to the "Lick" for salt.

After resting and hunting several days at the salt spring, the Indians and their captives resumed their journey; and about one month after the Draper's Meadow massacre the party reached the Shawnee town at the mouth of the Scioto River. The marauders were received with much glee by all the members of the tribe, and delight was expressed at the success of the bloody enterprise. All the captives, except Mrs. Ingles and her children, were required to "run the gauntlet." It seems that she had, by tact and intelligent service, secured the good will of her captors. Mrs. Draper, though still suffering from the wound in her arm, was made to endure the agony of the terrible ordeal, as did Henry Lenard and James Cull, the two men captured at Draper's Meadows. It is more than probable that these men were killed while passing through the ordeal, as there is no known record of them after the event. A few days afterward, the Indians raiders met for a division and distribution of the spoils, including the captives. The prisoners were alloted to different persons and became widely separated. Mrs. Ingles and her infant remained at the Shawnee town, while her little sons, Thomas and George, were taken to Detroit. George died a short time after he arrived at that place, and Thomas remained with the Indians for thirteen years, when he was at last found by his father and ransomed. As Thomas Ingles was a prominent figure in the pioneer settlement of Tazewell County his interesting life will be given more ample notice in connection therewith.

Mrs. Draper was taken to Chillicothe, where she was adopted into the family of an old chief; and after six years of captivity was ransomed by her husband, John Draper, and brought back to her home on New River. She was kindly treated until she made an unsuccessful attempt to escape, which provoked for her the usual penalty, burning at the stake; but the old Indian, of whose family she had become a member, concealed her until he secured her pardon. Resigning herself to her cruel fate, she resolved to win the confidence and favor of the tribe. She taught the women to sew and cook, and nursed the sick and wounded so tenderly that the Indians pronounced her a "heap good medicine squaw." John Draper had been unwearied in his efforts to find and secure the release of his wife from captivity, but failed in every attempt to locate her, until 1761. In that year a treaty was made between the Indians and the whites and Mr. Draper attended the assembly with the hope of getting some information about his wife. The old Indian chief in whose family she was living was at the meeting, and Draper was at last rewarded with success in his search for his absent wife. A heavy ransom was demanded and paid, and husband and wife were happily reunited after a separation of six years. They returned to their home at Draper's Meadows, but in 1765 Mr. Draper exchanged his land at Draper's Meadows for a splendid boundary west of New River in the present county of Pulaski, to which place he moved, giving it the name of "Draper's Valley." A part of this land is still owned and occupied by Draper's descendants. Seven children were born to John and Betty Draper after she was rescued from captivity. Mrs. Draper died in 1774, the year of Dunmore's War, and John Draper two years afterwards married Mrs. Jane Crockett, a widow, by whom he had two daughters. He was a lieutenant in Dunmore's War and did gallant service at the battle of Point Pleasant.

———

In a little while after the division and separation of the Draper's Meadows captives, a party of Shawnee Indians and several French traders went to Big Bone Lick, which is about one hundred and fifty miles below the mouth of the Scioto River, in the present Boone County, Kentucky. The object of the Indians was to make salt and to hunt the big game that came to the Lick, while the French were along to buy pelts from the redskins. Remembering the efficiency Mrs. Ingles had shown as a salt maker at the salt spring on the Kanawha, the Indians took her with them to assist in the work. They also took along a Dutch woman, who was named Stump, whom they had captured in Pennsylvania near Fort Du Quesne. Mrs. Ingles, after much persuasion, gained the consent of the Dutch woman to join her in an attempt to escape and return, if possible, to their respective homes. The unhappy woman knew that if she made the desperate venture she would have to leave her infant daughter with the Indians; and that meant a sacrifice of her child, either by cruel death or permanent separation from it. But she realized that her first duty was to her husband and an effort to recover her little boys from captivity. So, she decided to abandoned her child. After placing "the dear little babe as cosily as she could in a little bark cradle, gave it her last parting kisses and baptism of tears, tore herself away, and was gone, never to see it again in this world."

The two women started late in the afternoon on their long and perilous journey. They each had a blanket and a tomahawk, but no food or clothing except the scanty apparel they were wearing. With no roads to follow and without compass, they concluded to make their way to the Ohio and follow that stream up to the mouth of the Kanawha; and then journey up that river until they arrived at a point near Draper's Meadows. The route as mapped out was followed pretty closely, though it was rugged and wild, and many severe hardships were encountered. For the forty days that were occupied in making the journey, they had no food but nuts and berries, and a little raw corn. And they had no shelter at night but caves, hollow logs and an occasional deserted Indian camp.

Exposed to dangers innumerable and suffering from hunger almost intolerable, Mrs. Ingles was at last forced to desert Mrs. Stump, because the old Dutch woman was so crazed by starvation that she tried to kill her companion to appease her hunger. This occurred when they reached a point where East River flows into New River. Mrs. Ingles sought to divert the old woman from her murderous intention by proposing that they should draw lots as to which should die, and Mrs. Ingles lost in the drawing. Then began a life and death struggle between the two. Mrs. Ingles succeeded in tearing herself from the grasp of the old woman, who had become exhausted by the struggle, and started again up the river. When she got beyond the vision of the poor old creature she concealed herself under the bank of the river until her dangerous companion passed by. She remained in hiding until night came on. The moon was shining, and she fortunately discovered an old canoe on the river bank. It was half filled with leaves and had no oar or paddle. But the resolute young woman, who had never handled a canoe, resolved to cross the river in the frail boat and pursue her journey on the east side of the stream, and thus avoid further danger from Mrs. Stump. She found a slab that had been torn from a tree by lightning, and using this slab for a paddle she reached the eastern shore of New River in safety. The following morning Mrs. Ingles resumed her journey, and after traveling a short distance saw the old Dutch woman on the opposite side of the river. They were near enough to each other to have a conversation; and the old woman expressed great sorrow for her action the previous day. She plead with Mrs. Ingles to cross the river and continue the journey with her; but the young woman declined, and they continued and completed their journey on opposite sides of the stream.

Mrs. Ingles was now within thirty miles of Draper's Meadows, but was so exhausted from hunger and exposure that she began to despair of ever reaching her desired destination. At many points on the eastern shore of New River the cliffs project very closely to the edge of the water, and it was with great difficulty that she passed along the rocky shore. Struggling on, she at last reached the immense cliff just below Eggleston's Springs. This cliff projects out to and overhangs the river, and is 280 feet high at the highest point. There are no shelving rocks for footholds along the base of the cliff, and Mrs. Ingles was unable to pass around it as she had the cliffs further down the river. There was snow on the ground and the water was icy cold, but the brave woman tried to wade around at the base of the cliff. The water is very deep up to the cliff's edge, and could not be waded. She had to pass the night on the bare ground, shivering and hungry. The following morning, with almost superhuman effort, she climbed over the giant cliff. It took her all day to accomplish what proved to be her final mighty struggle to reach her husband and home. Dr. Hale thus relates what immediately followed the scaling of the cliff.

"Mrs. Ingles, after getting to the bottom of the cliff, had gone but a short distance when, to her joyful surprise, she discovered just before her, a patch of corn. She approached it as rapidly as she could move her painful limbs along.

"She saw no one, but there were evident signs of persons about. She hallooed; at first there was no response, but relief was near at hand. She was about to be saved, and just in time.

"She had been heard by Adam Harmon and his two sons, whose patch it was, and who were in it gathering their corn.

"Suspecting, upon hearing a voice, that there might be an intended attack by Indians, they grabbed their rifles, always kept close at hand, and listened attentively.

"Mrs Ingles hallooed again. They came out of the corn and towards her, cautiously, rifles in hand. When near enough to distinguish the voice—Mrs. Ingles still hallooing—Adam Harmon remarked to his sons: 'Surely, that must be Mrs. Ingles' voice.' Just then she, too, recognized Harmon, when she was overwhelmed with emotions of joy and relief, poor, overtaxed nature gave way, and she swooned and fell, insensible, to the ground.

"They picked her up tenderly and conveyed her to their little cabin, near at hand, where there was protection from the storm, a rousing fire and substantial comfort.

"Mrs. Ingles soon revived, and the Harmons were unremitting in their kind attentions and efforts to promote her comfort. They had in their cabin a stock of fresh venison and bear meat; they set to work to cook and make a soup of some of this, and, with excellent judgment, would permit their patient to take but little at a time, in her famished condition.

"While answering her hurried questions as to what they knew about her home and friends, they warmed some water in their skillet and bathed her stiff and swollen feet and limbs, after which they wrapped her in their blankets and stowed her away tenderly on their pallet in the corner, which to her, by comparison, was 'soft as downy pillows are,' a degree of luxury she had not experienced since she was torn from her home by ruthless savages, more than four months before.

"Under these new and favoring conditions of safety and comfort, it is no wonder that 'nature's sweet restorer' soon came to her relief and bathed her wearied senses and aching limbs in balmy, restful and refreshing sleep."

How tenderly and sweetly has the lineal descendant of Mrs. Ingles told of her dramatic arrival and reception at the cabin home of her former neighbors and friends, Adam Harmon and his two sons. And what a splendid tribute he has paid to the gallantry and kindness of heart of these rugged pioneers of the New River Valley. They were the kindred of the Harmons who were among the first settlers in the Clinch Valley; and hundreds of their relations are still here.

Mrs. Ingles remained several days resting and feasting with her hospitable and delighted friends, the Harmons. The elder Harmon, over the protest of his guest, actually killed a nice young beef, that had been fattened on the wild pea vine, to procure a small piece of meat to make her some beef tea, which he had heard was a particularly good diet for invalids. As soon as Mrs. Ingles thought herself sufficiently recuperated to travel, she was placed on a horse and Adam Harmon mounted another, to accompany and protect her; and they went to Draper's Meadows, some fifteen miles distant. On arrival they found that the settlers at that place had been alarmed by a report of another invasion by the Indians, and had fled to the fort at Dunkard's Bottom for safety. Without delay Mrs. Ingles and Harmon traveled on to Dunkard's Bottom, and got there on the evening of the same day they started from Har-

mon's home. Mrs. Ingles was pleased to meet again a few of her
old friends, but was sadly disappointed at not finding her husband,
and her brother, John Draper, at the fort. The next morning after
Mrs. Ingles arrived at Dunkard's Bottom she prevailed on Adam
Harmon to go in search of the old Dutch woman. He found her
near the mouth of Back Creek, about where the village of Bell Spring
is now situated, and took her up to the fort. Before a great while,
Mrs. Stump found an opportunity to go to Winchester, and from
that point she journeyed on to her home in Pennsylvania.

Some weeks previous to the arrival of Mrs. Ingles at Dunkard's
Bottom, her husband, and her brother, John Draper, had gone on a
journey to the Cherokee towns in Tennessee, to see if they could
get any information through these friendly Indians of their wives
and children who had been captured at Draper's Meadows. Ingles
and Draper failed to accomplish anything by their trip to the
Cherokees, and were returning heavy-hearted to the settlements.
The night Mrs. Ingles reached Dunkard's Bottom, the two disappointed, weary men stayed all night at a point about three miles
west of the fort, near where the town of Newbern, in Pulaski
County, was afterwards located. The following morning they went
very early to the fort to get their breakfast, and were joyfully
surprised to find Mrs. Ingles there. Mr. and Mrs. Ingles had
remained at the Dunkard's Bottom Fort but a short time when
information was received of another impending incursion by the
Shawnees; and they went to Vass' Fort, some twenty miles east
of Dunkard's Bottom, where they believed they would find greater
safety. This fort was located on the east side of the Alleghany
Mountains, on the headwaters of Roanoke River, and about one
mile west of the present village of Shawsville, in Montgomery
County.

It was in the spring of 1756 that Mr. and Mrs. William Ingles
went to Vass' Fort. They had been there but a few weeks when Mrs.
Ingles had a presentiment that the Indians were going to attack
the place. She was so greatly alarmed that Mr. Ingles took her
east of the Blue Ridge to a fort in Bedford County, which was near
the Peaks of Otter. Strange to say, the very day they started
across the Blue Ridge the mental premonition of Mrs. Ingles was
fulfilled. The attack on Fort Vass was made in the summer of
1756, or about one year subsequent to the massacre at Draper's
Meadows, and was even more horrible in its consequences. Dr.
Hale, whose kindred were the chief sufferers in this second tragedy

in what is now Montgomery County, Virginia, from well authenticated tradition thus describes the terrible incident:

"John and Matthew Ingles, the younger brothers of William Ingles, were at this fort. John was a bachelor. Matthew had a wife and one child. Before the attack was made, but after the fort was surrounded, an Indian climbed a tall poplar tree which commanded a view of the interior, to take an observation. He was discovered and fired on from the fort, and it is the tradition that it was the rifle of John Ingles that brought him down.

"Matthew Ingles was out hunting when the attack was made; hearing the firing, he hastened back, and tried to force his way into the Fort, to his wife and child; he shot one Indian with the load in his gun, then clubbed others with the butt until he broke the stock off; by this time the gun-barrel was wrenched from his hands, when he seized a frying-pan that happened to be lying near, and, breaking off the bowl or pan with his foot, he belabored them with the iron handle, right and left, until he was knocked·down, overpowered and badly wounded. The tradition says that he killed two Indians with the frying-pan.

"His bravery and desperate fighting had so excited the admiration of the Indians that they would not kill him, but carried him off a prisoner. He was either released or made his escape some time after, and returned to the settlement, but never entirely recovered from his wounds. He died at Ingles' Ferry a few months later. His wife and child were murdered in the Fort as was his brother John."

From the diary of Colonel William Preston, which is published in the papers of Lyman C. Draper, and from other sources the following appears to be an accurate list of the persons killed, wounded and captured at Fort Vass:

Lieutenant John Smith, John Ingles, John Robinson, and Mrs. Matthew Ingles and child, killed; William Robinson, Thomas Robinson, Samuel Robinson, and Matthew Ingles, wounded; Peter Looney, William Bratton, Joseph Smith, William Pepper, Mrs. Vass and two daughters, James Bell, Christopher Hicks, —— Cole, —— Graham, Benj. Davies, and John Walker, prisoners. It is probable that all the wounded were carried off as prisoners. Some of the captives made their escape, but whether this happened while en route to the Ohio country or after arrival at the Indian towns is

not known. Those who made their escape were: Captain John Smith, Peter Looney, William Bratton and Matthew Ingles.

There are several excellent reasons for giving, as I have done, a somewhat extended account of the massacre at Draper's Meadows. It was the first serious outrage committed by the Indians upon the pioneer settlers of Southwest Virginia; and was typical of quite a number of similar tragedies that were later to be enacted in the New River, Clinch River and Holston River valleys. It also furnished, in the persons and characters of Mrs. William Ingles and Mrs. John Draper, excellent types of the noble pioneer women who came to this section with their husbands and fathers to do their part in transforming a dense wilderness region into a land of beautiful homes, to be occupied by a thrifty and intelligent people.

The Draper's Meadows massacre was also an important event in connection with the history of Tazewell County, as Colonel James Patton was the central and commanding figure of this first murderous assault by the Indians upon the pioneer settlers of Southwest Virginia. He was the first man to organize and bring an exploring and surveying party to the section of Virginia west of New River. This was in 1748, and, as has been previously related, he then visited Burke's Garden, and in 1750 and 1753 had surveying done on the headwaters of Clinch River, and in Abb's Valley. He thus prepared the way for those who came to settle in what is now known as Tazewell County.

CHAPTER V.

In the summer of 1755, just about the time of the attack upon Draper's Meadows, a scalping party of Shawnees made an incursion into the Middle Holston Valley. They attacked the more exposed settlements, killed several settlers and captured others. Captain Samuel Stalnaker, who then had his cabin home some four or five miles west of the present town of Marion, Smyth County, Virginia, was made a captive, and Mrs. Stalnaker and Adam Stalnaker were killed. The presumption is that they were the wife and son of Samuel Stalnaker. He was the man whose house Dr. Walker and party helped to "raise" in March, 1750, while they were en route to Cumberland Gap and Kentucky. Stalnaker and the other prisoners were taken through or across the Clinch Valley by the Indians on their return to their towns in Ohio. This is evidenced by the journal of Colonel William Preston who commanded a company in the expedition of Colonel Andrew Lewis, known in history as the "Sandy Expedition," and which was made in the months of February and March, 1756. While traveling down the stream that Colonel Preston called "Sandy Creek," on Sundy the 29th of February, 1756, he noted in his journal: "This creek has been much frequented by Indians both traveling and hunting on it, and from late signs I am apprehensive that Stalnaker and the prisoners taken with him were carried this way." Captain Stalnaker made his escape from the Indians, but when, where, or how is not recorded in any history, nor is there any record showing what was the fate of the other prisoners.

There were a number of persons killed, wounded, and captured on New River and Reed Creek by the Shawnees who persisted in sending scalping parties to those sections in the summer and fall of 1755, and in February and March 1756. It was to avenge the outrages inflicted upon the settlers in the New River and Holston valleys, as well as the massacre at Draper's Meadows, that the "Sandy Expedition" was projected. The purpose of this expedition was to march to the Ohio River and punish the Shawnees, by killing as many of them as possible, and to destroy their towns.

Colonel Andrew Lewis was commander of the expedition, and his forces consisted of about four hundred men, including one hundred, or more, Cherokee and Chickasaw Indians, who had been induced to become allies of the Virginians in the French and Indian War. This small army was composed of Augusta County militia and four companies of volunteers. The several military companies were commanded by Captains Peter Hogg, William Preston, John Smith, Samuel Overton, and Obediah Woodson; and the four volunteer companies were under the command of Captains Robert Breckenridge, Archibald Alexander, John Montgomery, and —— Dunlap. The Indians had been recruited by Captain Richard Pearis and were commanded by him.

This expedition was assembled at Fort Prince George, afterwards called Fort Lewis, four miles west of where Salem, Roanoke County, is now located. Captain William Preston was placed in charge of the vanguard, and began the march on "Monday ye, 9th day of February, 1756;" and in his journal says:

"In persuance to ye orders of Major Lewis, dated the 9th inst., I marched from Fort Prince George, with my two Lieutenants, 2 Sergeants, 3 Corporals, and 25 Privates." On Wednesday, the 11th, they arrived at New River, at Ingles' Ferry, where they found the Indian allies in camp; and Captain Preston says: "As we marched by the Cherokee Camp we saluted them by firing off guns, which they returned in seeming great joy and afterwards honored us with a war dance."

Major Lewis with the main body of his white force, arrived at New River and reviewed all the troops on Friday, the 13th; and on Saturday, the 14th, Captain Dunlap joined them with a company of twenty-five volunteers. This completed the military force that was encamped at Fort Frederick, which was the name then held by the fort at Dunkard's Bottom. On Sunday, the 15th inst., James Burke, who had fled from Burke's Garden, arrived at the camp and gave information that Robert Looney had been killed by the Shawnee Indians near the home of Alex Sawyers, on Reed Creek.

The expedition had been organized to go to Ohio to look for the Shawnees and destroy their towns; but Major Lewis and his little army were about to come in contact with small bands of these Indians at a point only some sixty miles distant from Fort Prince George, the starting place, and right in the settlements on Reed Creek. As a matter of precaution, on Monday, the 16th, forty Indians and sixty white men were sent out to range the woods about Reed Creek; and on Thursday, the 19th, the army broke camp and started on its perilous and disastrous journey. As this was the first military expedition of white men that entered and passed over the territory now embraced in Tazewell County, it is an event of special interest in connection with the history of the county. Therefore, I will reproduce that part of Captain Preston's journal which shows the route pursued and what transpired while Lewis and his men were marching through this particular region. The following are the entries made by Captain Preston.

"Thursday 19, Left Fort Frederick at 10 o'clock: 27 loaded pack horses, got to William Sawyers: camped on his barn floor.

"Friday 20, Switched one of the soldiers for swearing, which very much incensed the Indian chiefs then present. Advanced to Alex Sawyers, met the Indians who went out with the first division, and Lieutenant Ingles, who informed us of the burial of Robert Looney. Some of our Indians deserted.

"Sat. 21, Major Lewis, Capt. Pearis and the interpreter went to Col. Buchanan's place (Anchor and Hope), where they met the Indians who had deserted us, and induced them to return, which they did.

"Sunday, 22. marched to John McFarlands." (McFarland lived in Black Lick on the head of Reed Creek.)

"Monday, 23, marched over the mountain to Bear Garden, on North Fork of Holston's river. Lost sundry horses.

"Tuesday 24, Crossed two mountains and arrived at Burkes Garden. Had plenty of potatoes, which the soldiers gathered in the deserted plantations.

"Wednesday 25, Remained in Camp.

"Burke's Garden is a tract of land of 5,000 or 6,000 acres as rich and fertile as any I ever saw, as well watered with many beautiful streams and is surrounded with mountains almost impassible.

"Thursday 26, Marched early, crossed three large mountains, arrived at head of Clinch. Our hunters found no game.

"Friday 27, Lay by on account of rain. Hunters killed three or four bears.

"Saturday 28, passed several branches of Clinch and at length got to the head of Sandy Creek where we met with great trouble and fatigue, occasioned by heavy rain, and driving our baggage horses down said creek, which we crossed 20 times that evening. Killed three buffaloes and some deer.

There were no settlers in the territory which now constitutes Tazewell County when the Sandy Expedition passed through Burke's Garden and the Clinch Valley. If James Burke had formed an intention to become a permanent settler, he abandoned such intention when he fled from the Indians, never to enter Burke's Garden again as a resident.

I am at a loss to understand what Captain William Preston meant by the entry made in his journal on the 24th of February, 1756, stating that they: "Had plenty of potatoes which the soldiers gathered in the deserted plantations." This entry would justify the conclusion that there was more cleared and cultivated land there at that time than tradition has placed to the account of James Burke's industry. It might also warrant the belief that other persons had been living there besides Burke. The plantations, however, mentioned by Captain Preston may have been what the first settlers called "patches."

Another very peculiar entry in the Preston journal is one which tells that when the expedition left Burke's Garden it crossed three mountains to reach the head of Clinch River. If this statement is correct, the army did not make its exit through the gap at the west end of the Garden. In the mountain which encircles the Garden there is a low place between the gap and the Bear Town peak. Colonel Lewis evidently took his men through this low place over to Little Creek, then crossed Rich Mountain to a point just west of the divide between Clear Fork and the Clinch Valley. Not being familiar with the country, instead of turning westward, down the valley, the expedition crossed Buckhorn Mountain and came into the valley just west of Dial Rock. Thence the march was continued until the head of "Sandy Creek" was reached.

Local historians have expressed different views as to which branch of the stream was reached and followed. This, however, is unimportant, as Tug River was the main stream followed, and received its name from an incident which occurred during the journey. At one time the provisions were so completely exhausted that the men were threatened with starvation. Johnston, in his History of the New River Settlements, thus relates what occurred: "The weather was extremely cold, snow having fallen the march was a difficult one, and the men stopping at Burning Spring (Warfield) took strips of the hides of the buffaloes and broiled them in the burning gas. They cut them into strips or thugs, hence the name of Tug River. On leaving the spring they scattered through the

mountains and many of them perished, either frozen to death,
starved, or killed by the Indians. They left, however, some marks
by the way, cutting their names on trees on the route pursued by
them, notably at the forks of Big Coal and Clear Fork of that
river, but these trees have been destroyed in recent years."

The remnant of the little army was then returning from its
unsuccessful and disastrous expedition. It did not get as far as the
mouth of Sandy River, the point where it was expected to reach the
Ohio. On the 12th of March the men were so discouraged that they
began to desert; and on the 13th Montgomery's and Dunlap's volunteers left with a view of getting back to their homes, if they could.
It is probable that it was then that the return march was begun.

Colonel George Washington was in command of all the Virginia
military forces in 1756, with his headquarters at Winchester, as
previously related, and he vigorously opposed the Sandy Expedition.
He knew the wild and rugged character of the region through which
Lewis and his men had to travel, and was confident the enterprise
would prove unsuccessful, especially as it was undertaken in the
winter season. Governor Dinwiddie was so provoked at the Shawnees for their repeated savage attacks upon the frontier settlements
that he insisted that the expedition should go forward, and upon
him rested the responsibility for its failure.

The failure of the Sandy Expedition was not only a seriously
alarming blow to the English settlements west of New River, but
was a great incentive to the Shawnees and the other hostile tribes in
Ohio to continue their savage attacks upon the border settlements,
extending from the Holston Valley to the Potomac River. These
incursions of the Indians were encouraged and supported by the
French, who were then engaged in a general war with Great Britain,
and were vigorously prosecuting the French and Indian War against
the English colonies in America. The French were not only furnishing the Indians with arms, ammunition, and other supplies, but
were paying them liberally for the scalps of the English settlers,
and also for the prisoners they captured. These conditions continued until the close of the French and Indian War in 1761, and
the Pontiac War in 1763; and resulted in driving out nearly all
the settlers who had located west of New River. Colonel William
Preston, who, after the death of his uncle, Colonel James Patton,
became the guiding spirit of the Trans-Alleghany Pioneers, in a
letter written from his home at Greenfield, in the present Botetourt

County, on the 27th of July, 1763, thus related the unhappy condition of the settlements along and west of New River:

"Our situation at present is very different from what it was when we had the pleasure of your company in this country. All the valleys of Roanoke river and along the waters of the Mississippi are depopulated, except Captain English (Ingles) with a few families on New river, who have built a fort, among whom are Mr. Thompson and his family, alone remaining. They intend to make a stand until some assistance be sent them. Seventy-five of the Bedford militia went out in order to pursue the enemy, but I hear the officers and part of the men are gone home, and the rest gone to Reed Creek to help in the family of James Davis and in two or three other families there that dare not venture to travel.

"I have built a little fort in which are eighty-seven persons, twenty of whom bear arms. We are in a pretty good posture of defence, and with the aid of God are determined to make a stand. In five or six other places in this part of the country they have fallen into the same method and with the same resolution. How long we may keep them is uncertain. No enemy have appeared here as yet. Their guns are frequently heard and their footing observed, which makes us believe they will pay us a visit. My two sisters and their families are here and all in good health. We bear our misfortunes so far with fortitude and are in hopes of being relieved."

CHAPTER VI.

No settlers came to the Clinch Valley until nearly twenty years after surveying parties had come in and located tracts of land here. John Buchanan, deputy surveyor of Augusta County, had made surveys on the waters of Clinch River, in 1750; and Colonel Patton and William Ingles had surveyed a number of boundaries in Burke's Garden, Abb's Valley, and on the headwaters of Clinch River in 1753. The inquiry has frequently been made why the settlements were so delayed in the Clinch Valley, especially as a number of persons had located with their families on New River and its tributaries, and even in the Holston Valley, as early as 1750.

When Dr. Thomas Walker made his famous expedition to Cumberland Gap in 1750, he found settlers scattered along the route he pursued from the "Great Lick," the site of Roanoke City, to the present Seven Mile Ford, on the Middle Fork of Holston River. These settlers, when they came in, had followed the Buffalo Trail, which the Cherokees had been using for years in making their hunting excursions that were extended as far east as the Great Lick, and even to the Peaks of Otter. It was also the same trail that the traders from Eastern Virginia had traveled when they went on trading expeditions to the Cherokee towns in Tennessee, then North Carolina. The Clinch Valley was then used by the Indians, the Cherokees and the Shawnees, as a hunting ground; and had never been entered by white men, except a few hunting parties, who were, possibly, as anxious to preserve it for a game park as were the Indians.

But for certain causes, which I will mention, settlements would have been made in what is now Tazewell County immediately following the surveying of land here by the Loyal Company, of which company, Dr. Thomas Walker was the active agent. This company had, by an order of the Virginia Council, obtained leave to take up and survey 800,000 acres of land, in one or more surveys, to be located on the north of the North Carolina line, and running westward and northward for quantity; and the company was given four years to complete its surveys and purchase rights for the same. The company began its work of surveying in 1750, and sold a number of tracts west of New River, to purchasers at the rate of three pounds per hundred acres. Some of the purchasers settled on the lands they bought, while others failed to make settlements. The Loyal Company was then interrupted by *caveats* entered by the Ohio Company and other conflicting claimants, which prevented the completion of the surveying within the term of four years prescribed by the order of council. An application was made for a renewal of the grant and on the 14th of June, 1753, an order was made by the council, giving the company four years more to complete the surveys. By this last order the lands granted are described as lands lying on the branches of the Mississippi in the county of Augusta. The company began as soon as possible to locate and sell lands under the renewed grant, but the French and Indian War then came on in 1754, and put an end to the surveying. The Indians commenced their hostile incursions into the settlements west of the Alleghanies; and this not only prevented, for a period of nine years, the making of any settlements in the Clinch Valley, but drove out nearly all the settlers in the New River and Holston valleys.

The Greenbrier Company, organized by Andrew Lewis and other prominent Virginians, obtained a grant from the Virginia Council for 100,000 acres of land, which was to be located west of the Alleghanies, and south of the Ohio. The execution of the surveying of this company had also been hindered by the same causes that had affected the Loyal Company. As soon as the war was terminated these two companies presented a joint petition to the governor and council, representing that they had made a number of actual surveys of lands within their respective grants and made sales of tracts to divers persons. The petition also set forth the fact that the companies had been prevented from completing their surveys and making settlements thereon only by the war; and praying the renewal of their grants for another four years.

In the meantime King George II. had sent instructions to the colonial government to make no more grants upon the western waters. Following this instruction, the governor and council, on the 25th of May, 1763, declared that they were restrained by the royal instructions from granting the prayer of the two companies. On the 7th of October, 1763, the king issued a proclamation prohibiting all persons from settling in that tract of country west of the Alleghanies, which included the territory west of New River; and the proclamation of the king even required those persons who had settled in this region under patents to remove therefrom and take

T.H.—15

up their residence in the interior. This course was adopted by the royal government to pacify the Indians, who, after the French and Indian War was terminated, remained bitterly hostile to the English, because of their manifest purpose to rob the natives of their lands and hunting grounds.

The proclamation of the king not only destroyed every possible hope that the Loyal Company could ever again secure from the royal government a renewal of its grants, but, seemingly, invalidated the titles to all the lands it had sold to settlers or prospective settlers. This latter conclusion was based upon the conviction that the Virginia Council had made a grant to the Loyal Company of lands that did not belong to the English Crown, but were still owned by the Indians. And the order of the king for the removal of all persons who had settled in the forbidden territory placed another obstruction to the settlement of the Clinch Valley which lasted for a period of years.

The Iroquois, or Six Nations, of New York, who had been allies of the British in the war just closed, claimed by right of conquest all the Virginia territory west of the Blue Ridge and south of the Ohio River; and the Cherokees, who were also allies of the British in the war, demanded the withdrawal of all the white settlers from the territory west of New River and south of the Ohio. These demands were recognized by the British Government as just; but gave great concern to the Loyal Company and all persons to whom the company had sold lands west of New River, either for homes or speculative purposes. And the company and its vendees went earnestly to work to secure relief by the negotiation of treaties with the two Indian nations. Quite a number of would-be settlers had congregated in the Upper James River Valley and the Roanoke Valley, eagerly awaiting opportunity to move beyond New River. In response to their appeals, and through the very effective work of Dr. Walker and other members of the Loyal Company, treaties were made with the Indians by which the section west of New River was opened up for settlement.

In the spring of 1768 the British Government instructed Sir William Johnson, of New York, to negotiate a treaty with the Six Nations, and procure from them the relinquishment of their asserted claim of certain territory in the provinces of New York, New Jersey, Pennsylvania and Virginia. He called a congress of the chiefs of the Iroquois Confederacy, which assembled at Fort Stanwix, near Oswego, New York, on the 24th of October, 1768; and four days thereafter, on the 28th of the same month, a treaty was concluded. Dr. Thomas Walker was present, as commissioner from Virginia, and witnessed the signing of the treaty by the six representative chiefs of the Indian confederacy. No doubt the skillful management of the accomplished agent of the Loyal Company had much to do with securing the desired treaty with the Indians. The treaty conveyed to King George Third, Sovereign Lord of Great Britain, France and Ireland, all the Virginia territory claimed by the Iroquois, south of the Ohio River, beginning at the mouth of the Cherokee (Holston) River, where it empties into the River Ohio, and following along the southern side of said River to Kittanning, which is above Fort Pitt. This eliminated for all time the claim of ownership of Virginia territory by the Iroquois.

The British Government had also directed John Stuart, Southern Superintendent of Indian Affairs, to negotiate a treaty with the Cherokees. He met the chiefs of the Upper and Lower Cherokee Nations at Hard Labor, South Carolina, and negotiated a treaty with these Indians on the 14th of October, 1768, just two weeks before the treaty at Fort Stanwix was concluded. This treaty was entirely unsatisfactory, as it failed to secure the very purpose for which it was sought. It left in the possession of the Cherokees all the territory they claimed west of New River, which they had held for many years as their most cherished hunting grounds, the Clinch and the Holston valleys particularly.

Dr. Walker had been appointed commissioner from Virginia to be present when the treaty was made with the Cherokees, but did not attend the meeting. No reasonable explanation was ever given by John Stuart for the negotiation of a treaty whose terms were the very opposite of those sought and intended by the government he represented. Lord Botetourt was then governor of Virginia, and he was induced to appoint Colonel Andrew Lewis and Dr. Thomas Walker commissioners to visit the Cherokees and procure from them another treaty on the desired lines. They proceeded promptly to South Carolina, where they had conferences with some of the Cherokee chiefs, and obtained from them a pledge that the settlers west of New River should not be disturbed in the possession of their homes, pending the negotiations for rearranging the boundary lines of the hunting grounds of the tribe. It was also arranged by the commissioners that a new treaty should be made with the Indians. John Stuart, Superintendent of Indian Affairs, met the principle chiefs and about a thousand of the warriors of the Cherokees at

Lochaber, South Carolina, on the 18th of October, 1770, and on October 22nd, the treaty was concluded.

This treaty seems to have been of as much moment to South Carolina and North Carolina as it was to Virginia, judging from the persons who attended the assembly. From a record of the meeting embodied in the treaty it appears those present besides John Stuart were: Colonel John Donelson, who was there "by appointment of his Excellency, the Right Honorable Lord Botetourt, in behalf of the Province of Virginia," Alex'r Cameron, Deputy Superintendent; James Simpson, Clk of his Majesty's Council of South Carolina; Major Lacy, from Virginia; Major Williamson, Capt. Cohoon; John Caldwell, Esq., Captain Winter, Christopher Peters, Esq., besides a great number of the back inhabitants of the province of South Carolina; and the following chiefs of the Cherokee Nation: Oconistoto, Killagusta, Attacalaculla, Keyatory, Tiftoy, Terreaino, Encyod Tugalo, Scaliloskie Chinista, Chinista of Watangali, Octaciti of Hey Wassie, and about a thousand other Indians of the same Nation."

The following are the most important recitals in the treaty: "The subscribing Cherokee Chiefs and Warriors on behalf of their said Nation in consideration of his Majesty's paternal goodness, so often demonstrated to them, the said Cherokee Indians, and from affection and friendship for their Brethren, the Inhabitants of Virginia, as well as their earnest desire of removing as far as possible all cause of dispute between them and the said inhabitants on account of encroachments on lands reserved by the said Indians for themselves, and also for a valuable consideration in various sorts of goods paid to them by the said John Stuart, on behalf of the Dominion of Virginia, that the hereafter recited line be ratified and confirmed, and it is hereby ratified and confirmed accordingly: and it is by these presents firmly stipulated and agreed upon by the parties aforesaid that a line beginning where the boundary line between the province of No. Carolina and the Cherokee hunting grounds terminates and running thence in a west course to a point six miles east of Long Island in Holston's river and thence to said river six miles above the said Long Island, thence in a ―――― course to the confluence of the great Canaway and Ohio rivers, Shall remain and be deemed by all of his Majesty's white subjects as well as all the Indians of the Cherokee Nation, the true and just boundaries of the lands reserved by the said Nation of Indians for their own proper use, and dividing the same from the lands ceded by them to his Majesty's within the limits of the province of Virginia, and that his Majesty's white subjects inhabiting the province of Virginia, shall not, upon any pretense whatsoever, settle beyond the line, nor shall the said Indians make any settlements or encroachments on the lands which by this treaty they cede and confirm to his Majesty."

The 2nd Article of the treaty provided that there should be no alteration whatsoever in the boundry line established by the treaty, "except such as may hereafter be found expedient and necessary for the mutual interest of both parties."

By the completion of this treaty with the Cherokees the titles to the lands already occupied by settlers, or purchased for future settlement, were quieted, where the purchases had been made from the Loyal Company under its grant for 800,000 acres or from Colonel Patton under his grant for 120,000 acres. It also vacated the proclamation, issued by the king in 1763, forbidding all persons from settling on the "western waters;" and it threw the Clinch Valley wide open, as well as all the territory ceded by the Cherokees, for settlement. The Loyal Company, however, was denied the right of making further locations under its grant, which had expired by limitation in 1763, and had never been renewed. At this time the British Government and the Colonial Government of Virginia were impressed with the wisdom of extending the frontiers of the Dominion as far westward as possible; and earnest invitation was given emigrants to make their homes on the waters of the Mississippi, in what is now known as Southwest Virginia. Very liberal land laws were enacted and new counties were erected as inducements to attract settlers west of the Alleghanies and beyond New River. On the 28th of November, 1769, the General Assembly of Virginia passed an act for dividing the county of Augusta into two counties, thereby bringing the county of Botetourt into existence. As the act is almost contemporary with the first settlements made in Tazewell County I will quote from it very liberally, as follows:

"I. Whereas many inconveniences attend the inhabitants of the county and parish of Augusta, by reason of the great extent thereof, and the said inhabitants have petitioned this General Assembly that the said county and parish be divided:

"Be it therefore enacted, by the Governor, Council and Burgesses of this General Assembly, and it is hereby enacted by the authority of the same, That from and after the 31st day of January next

ensuing the said county and parish of Augusta be divided into two
counties and parishes by a line beginning at the Blue Ridge, running
north fifty-five degrees west, to the confluence of Mary's creek, or
the South river, with the north branch of James river, thence up
the same to the mouth of Carrs creek, thence up the said creek to
the mountain, thence north fifty-five degrees west, as far as the
courts of the two counties shall extend it; and that all of that part
of the said county and parish which lies on the south side of said
line, shall be one distinct county and parish, and called and known
by the name of Botetourt; and that all the other part thereof, which
is on the north side of said line, shall be one other distinct county
and parish and retain the name of Augusta."

The act provided for the payment of officers' fees in tobacco at
the rate of eight shillings and four pence per hundred weight of
gross tobacco, but the most important and interesting features of the
act to the future settlers of the Clinch Valley was the following:

"IX. And whereas the people situated on the waters of the
Mississippi, in the said county of Botetourt, will be very remote
from their court-house, and must necessarily become a separate
county, as soon as their numbers are sufficient, which will probably
happen in a short time: *Be it further enacted by the authority
aforesaid,* That the inhabitants of that part of the said county of
Botetourt, which lies on the said waters, shall be exempted from
the payment of levies, to be laid by the said county court for the
purpose of building a county court-house and prison for the said
county."

In Clause IX. of this act we find an urgent appeal to brave
pioneer spirits to push further into the wilderness, and erect a barrier to furnish additional protection for the people east of the Blue
Ridge from incursions by the hostile natives. There is also a confident prediction made in the act that the invitation would be
promptly responded to by such numbers of persons seeking homes
in the Clinch and Holston valleys, that "in a short time" a new
county would have to be formed.

CHAPTER VII.

THE TAZEWELL PIONEER SETTLERS.

No word that is more expressive than "Pioneer" has ever been written into the English language. It means not only the first to enter any field of endeavor, but signifies unusual achievement in some worthy undertaking by the man or woman who fairly wins the title. The unvarnished narrative I will write about the daring men and loyal women who first came to make homes for themselves and their children in the unbroken forests of this region, now known as Tazewell County, will have little merit if it fails to help procure for these immortals a high niche in the Temple of Fame that will surely be erected some day, somewhere, to perpetuate the memory of the Trans-Alleghany Pioneers. They were of a class entirely different from the adventurers and outcasts that Captain Newport brought to Jamestown in 1607-8-9. They had no wealthy corporate body, like the London Company, to give them supplies of food and clothing, arms and ammunition, and houses to dwell in, nor soldiers of a royal government to protect them from attacks by the hostile natives. Nor were they of an indolent, vagrant class, like those first settlers at Jamestown, who were listed as "gentlemen," but who died from starvation because they were too lazy or too proud to work. They found no fertile fields on the banks of noble rivers and splendid bays, already prepared for cultivation, and which they could wrest by fraud or force from the simple, hospitable natives. But these glorious pioneers of the Clinch Valley were real men and women, with great hearts, strong and willing hands, and inspired with a resolute purpose to do all they could, with the means they had, to secure for themselves and their descendants the political and religious freedom that had been denied them or their fathers in the "Old Countries." In perseverance, in self-command, in forethought, in heroism, in all the virtues that conduce to success in life, the Tazewell Pioneers have never been surpassed. Our ancestors chose well when they selected this beautiful mountain country for their homes and for establishing a civic community for sturdy men and lovely women. Nature, or rather Nature's Almighty Creator, had profusely placed here, for the benefit of the pioneers and their successors, the three greatest essentials for the development and extension of a refined civilization—an invigorating climate, a fruitful soil, and a sublime aspect of nature.

When writing about the first settlers, I shall make no great effort to disclose their antecedents, except for the purpose of showing from whence they came. This will be done as briefly as possible; and then I will strive to show what manner of men and women they were by narrating what they accomplished after they came to the Clinch Valley and other sections of the county. While doing this, equally as much consideration shall be given the first generation born here, quite a number of whom I knew; and from whom I learned much that has inspired me to execute the pleasant task of writing this history. They are truly worthy to be classed with the pioneers, as many of them were co-workers with their fathers and mothers in the excellent preparation that was made for the organization of the civic community which bears the name of Tazewell County.

———

A number of men with their families had collected in the New River Valley, and in sections of Augusta County east of the Alleghany Mountains, eagerly awaiting an opportunity to locate in the Clinch Valley. And immediately following the assurance that they could take up lands unincumbered by claims of the Indians or the Loyal Company, the pioneers began to move in and settle on the waters of the Clinch. There has been much conjecture and many opinions expressed as to the time of the entrance of the pioneers into Tazewell. Dr. Geo. W. L. Bickley, in his History of Tazewell County, published in 1852, places the first permanent settlement here in the spring of 1771. Writing of this event, Bickley says:

"1771.) In the spring of this year Thomas Witten and John Greenup moved out and settled at Crab Orchard, which Witten purchased of Butler. Absalom Looney settled in a beautiful valley now known as Abb's Valley. Mathias Harman and his brothers, Jacob and Henry, settled at Carr's place (on one of the head branches of the Clinch river, two miles east of the present town of Jeffersonville). John Craven settled in the Cove, Joseph Martin, John Henry and James King settled in Thompson Valley, and John Bradshaw in the valley two miles west of Jeffersonville. The settlers, this year, found little annoyance from the Indians, who were living peaceably at their homes in the west and south. The consequence was the settlers erected substantial homes and opened lands to put in corn, from which they reaped a plentiful supply, in the fall.

"1772.) The following persons moved out, this year, and settled at the several places named. Capt. James Moore and John Pogue, in Abb's Valley; William Wynn, at the Locust Hill, (the place that Carr settled) which he purchased from Harman. John Taylor, on the north fork of Clinch, and Jesse Evans, near him. Thomas Maxwell, Benjamin Joslin, James Ogleton, Peter and Jacob Harman, and Samuel Ferguson, on Bluestone creek. William Butler, on the south branch of the north fork of Clinch, a short distance

The small white flag in the centre of the above picture is at the spot where Thomas Witten built his cabin in 1767 on the Crab Orchard tract. On the right is the new Pisgah Methodist Church.

above Wynn's plantation; William Webb, about three miles east of Jeffersonville; Elisha Clary, near Butler; John Ridgel, on the clear fork of Wolf Creek; Rees Bowen, at Maiden Spring; David Ward, in the Cove, and William Garrison at the foot of Morris' Knob.

"1773.) Thomas, John, and William Peery, settled where the town of Jeffersonville now stands; John Peery, Jr., at the fork of Clinch, one mile and a half east of the county seat; Captain Maffit and Benjamin Thomas, settled about a mile above, and Chrisley Hensley, near them. Samuel Marrs settled in Thompson's Valley; Thomas English (Ingles) in Burke's Garden; James and Charles Seaggs, Richard Pemberton, and Johnson, settled in Baptist Valley, five miles from where Jeffersonville now stands. Thomas Maston, William Patterson, and John Deskins, settled in the same valley, but further west; ————— Hines, Richard Oney and Obadiah Paine, settled in the Deskins Valley, in the western part of the county.

"1774-76.) The settlers who came in during the years of '74-'5 and '6, generally pitched their tents near the one or other of the locations already mentioned. Even yet there is a preference manifested for the older settlements. This may be accounted for, from the fact that the first settlers generally chose the most desirable locations; the lands being now better improved, and society more advanced, still render these places more attractive than other parts of the county settled at a later period."

Dr. Bickley in the preface of his history very truly says: "Writing history from tradition is a very different thing from reducing to order a heterogeneous mass of recorded facts. While the one is a sure guide to the historian, and from which he cannot depart; the other is full of uncertainty and apt to betray a writer into error and misrepresentation. * * * * The simple statement of having collected the facts, and written the following pages in the short space of seven weeks, will, I hope, be a sufficient apology for its many imperfections."

In the second chapter of his history, Bickley says: "What little I have gleaned from the obscured pages of the book of the past, has now become little more than mere tradition. For, situated as I am, in an isolated region, the advantages of a public library are denied me; and from a large private library little is to found, throwing any light on this uncertain part of my work. The information here embodied, was received from the grandsons, sons, and even from the men themselves who were the principal actors in the drama to be recorded. Memory cannot survive the decay of the physical system, unimpaired; and hence, caution is necessary, in recording an event told us, even by the chief actors therein. With this fact before me, I have placed more reliance on an incident related to me by a son of a pioneer, than if related by the pioneer himself."

After the Tazewell Historical Society engaged my services to write a history of the county, I received a letter from my friend and kinsman, Judge Samuel Cecil Graham, who was then wintering at City Point, Fla., in which he said:

"Much of the history of our country has become tradition. So were "The Tales of a Grandfather" by Scott, but they bore the stamp of accuracy and are now history.

"Truth as best it can be found; a judicial mind to solve conflicts and get at what human beings might have done—even if they did not do it—will at least satisfy conviction when the real facts are obliterated or beclouded. Fortunately in your undertaking, you know the truth or can get it."

Tazewell's first historian did a wonderful work, in view of the fact that he was only occupied seven weeks in gathering data and writing his interesting and valuable book. The statistics, and other invaluable data he used, were furnished him largely by Dr. Fielding Peery, who at that time was, possibly, the most learned and scientific man in Tazewell County. But for this assistance, Dr. Bickley would have been compelled to occupy as many months as he did weeks in the execution of his task. That he made some mistakes is very evident; and that many valuable facts and interesting incidents connected with the early history of the county were overlooked, or not obtained, is certain. In his preface, Dr. Bickley says he knew he would commit errors. It is to be regretted that he performed his work with so much haste, as it is now very difficult to supply his omissions. This, however, I shall try to do as effectively as I can. He failed to mention some of the earliest settlers, among them the Thompsons, the Cecils, and others, who were closely identified with the pioneer settlement of the county. I am satisfied he was mistaken in the date he gave of the first permanent settlements made here—that is in 1771 and 1772. And he was clearly in error when fixing the date of the first hunting party that came to the Clinch Valley, that is in 1766.

The Loyal Company was not only disputing the claims of the Indians to the territory west of New River, but Dr. Walker, the shrewd and diligent agent of the company, was actively at work all the while to induce settlements on the numerous tracts of land he had surveyed and sold to various purchasers. Colonel John Buchanan and the heirs and representatives of Colonel James Patton were also urging settlers to move in and occupy the tracts that had been surveyed under the grant of 120,000 acres to Colonel Patton. The Virginians who, as officers and soldiers, had served in the French and Indian War felt at liberty to make locations in this section under the grants that had been given them for military service and were making locations. Consequently settlers had been moving into the country, to the Holston Valley and other localities, for several years preceding 1771.

In the year 1765, David Campbell purchased from Colonel John Buchanan a tract of land containing 740 acres, called "Royal Oak," situated on the Middle Fork of the Holston River, just east of the present town of Marion. This boundary of land had been surveyed by Colonel Buchanan in 1748. In the year 1766 Arthur and John Campbell, sons of David Campbell, moved from their homes in what is now Rockbridge County, to the Holston Valley. Arthur built his

The above picture shows the house that Arthur Campbell built at Royal Oak. He surrounded it with a stockade and made it a fort when the Indians began to attack the Holston settlements.

house on the tract his father had purchased from Colonel Buchanan, and turned his home into a stockaded fort in 1773, when trouble with the Indians began. This was afterwards known as Campbell's or "Royal Oak Fort," and will be frequently mentioned in connection with the Clinch Valley, for reasons that will be apparent. Arthur Campbell built a mill near his home, on the Middle Fork of Holston River in 1770, the first mill that was erected on the waters of the Holston. Fortunately I have a picture of the old Campbell home, built in 1766. The house was, unfortunately, torn down a few years ago; and the picture is shown above. Summers, in his History of Southwest Virginia, says:

"Among the settlers that came this year (1768) was Joseph

Martin a daring and enterprising backwoodsman. He was accompanied by a band of from twenty to thirty men, and led them to Powell's Valley, now in Lee county, Virginia, where they erected a fort upon the north side of a creek, near two fine springs of water, which fort and creek were thereafter called Martin's Fort and Martin's Creek. * * * There were some five or six cabins built about twenty feet apart, with strong stockades between, and in the stockades there were port-holes. Here they cleared the land and planted corn and other vegetables. In the latter part of the summer of this year the Indians broke them up, and the settlers returned to the waters of the Holston. Martin's Fort was not occupied after the Revolutionary War."

Reuben Gold Thwaites, in his "Documentary History of Dunmore's War," says that Captain William Russell moved from Culpeper County to Clinch River in 1770, if not earlier.

Thomas Witten, who was, beyond dispute, the first white man to bring his family to Tazewell County and make permanent settlement here, had been living on Walker's Creek, in the present Giles County, Virginia, for a year or more prior to his settlement at the Crab Orchard on the Clinch. He had boldly disregarded the claims of the Indians to the territory west of New River, and had defiantly ignored the royal proclamation of 1763, which forbade British subjects settling in the disputed region. If his intended destination was the Clinch Valley, why should he linger on Walker's Creek until 1771? From well authenticated tradition, which I will in a future chapter set forth, he must have settled in the Clinch Valley as early as 1767, as he was living at the Crab Orchard when the battle between the Shawnees and Cherokees was fought on the top of Rich Mountain, just west of Plum Creek Gap, in 1768.

Though it is stated by Bickley that Rees Bowen settled at Maiden Spring in 1772, it is a tradition with the Bowen family that he located there several years earlier. Lyman C. Draper, in his "King's Mountain and Its Heroes," says: "Rees Bowen was born in Maryland about 1742. He first emigrated to what is now Rockbridge county, Virginia, and, in 1769, to the waters of Clinch, in what is now Tazewell County." The question of when the first settlers came to the Clinch Valley, and also the earliest known visits of hunting parties will be discussed more fully in subsequent pages of this volume.

The route used by the pioneers as they journeyed from New River to the Clinch Valley is well defined. It was the same trail that was made by herds of buffalo as they traveled to and from the regions east of the Alleghanies; and had, no doubt, been trodden many times by hunting and war parties of Indians. Coming from the east, the first settlers crossed New River at a ford opposite Ripplemead, a station of the Norfolk & Western Railway, about one mile below where Walker's Creek empties into New River. A ferry was established just above the ford by the Snidows in the pioneer days; and the log dwelling of Colonel Christian Snidow, built in 1793, is still standing on the east side of the river, opposite Ripplemead. A splendid steel bridge now spans the stream at the ford our ancestors used when they crossed the river. From thence they followed the Walker's Creek Valley to where the Kimberling branch of that creek joins the main stream in the present Bland County. Then they followed Kimberling Creek to its source, crossed over the divide into what has since been known as the "Wilderness," and through that forest to Rocky Gap. Passing through the Gap they came up the Clear Fork of Wolf Creek to the divide, six miles east of the present town of Tazewell; and traveling on one mile came to the head spring of the south fork of the historic Clinch. Tradition, uniformly, tells us that this was the route traveled by the pioneers when they came here.

It is a very reasonable supposition that most of the first settlers came on tours of inspection and investigation before they moved their families out. Thomas Witten had been living with his large family for a year, or more, within fifty miles of the place where he ultimately located; and it is almost certain that he and his oldest sons made trips of exploration to the Clinch before they moved here. His selection of the "Crabapple Orchard" tract for his home, the choicest bit of land on the Clinch, that had been surveyed by Colonel John Buchanan for John Shelton in 1750, and where Bickley says a hunter had built a cabin and cleared a patch for corn, is very strong proof that Thomas Witten knew precisely where he was going when he started out from his temporary home on Walker's Creek. The very judicious selection of land made by the other first settlers shows that they had been on the ground before, or had received reports from some person pretty familiar with the country. Absalom Looney told James Moore of the splendid land he could find in Abb's Valley, and the route he should follow to get there; and Moore abandoned his home in Rockbridge County, then

Augusta, and took up his residence where, a few years later, he met a tragic death at the hands of the Shawnee Indians.

It required wonderful fortitude, perseverance and physical vigor for women and children to make the journey from the former homes of the emigrants to the Clinch Valley. From New River to the points where they located on the Clinch the route was through an unbroken wilderness, and so rugged that it was difficult to travel on foot or horseback. Most of the early settlers seem to have been pretty well supplied with horses; and it is likely that the women and children rode on horseback, and that the few necessary household articles were transported on pack-horses. The men and boys walked, with their rifles on their shoulders, ready for instant use if an enemy, man or beast, appeared. It is probable that some of the settlers brought cows along with their families, as they knew of the rich herbage that was found in the Clinch Valley. The wild pea vine then grew abundantly in the forests; and in places where the forest was free from brush, and in the open places along the streams, the native bluegrass grew in sufficient abundance to furnish good pasturage for horses and kine. Bickley, in writing of the hunters who frequented the Clinch Valley before the advent of the pioneer settlers, and who brought with them a number of pack-horses to take home their peltry, says: "Pasturage for their horses was to be found everywhere; and game in such abundance, that plenty and good cheer were their companions from the time they left their homes, till their return."

Owing to the very meagre transportation facilities they possessed, each and every family had to exercise great care in selecting the amount and the character of the baggage they brought with them to their backwoods homes. The supply of bedding and clothing was reduced to a minimum—barely sufficient for protection from the cold and to keep their persons comfortably and decently clad—these articles being of the plainest and most inexpensive kind. A modern housewife would be shocked and disgusted if she were called upon to begin housekeeping with the few and simple things the pioneer mothers brought with them in the way of house and kitchen furnishings. These consisted of iron kettles, frying pans, pewter spoons and, maybe, a few pewter platters, and in some instances a few steel knives and forks; but the tableware was mostly made of wood, hand-made and home-made. such things as bowls, trenchers, platters and noggins. Crockery and chinaware did not make their appearance on the Clinch until some years after the pioneers had established their homes in Tazewell.

The man who was the head of a family had to assume and exercise a triune personality, that of farmer, of mechanic, and of hunter; and on occasion a fourth was added, that of warrior. Every acre, yes, every foot of land he wished to prepare for use had to be cleared of giant forest trees and thick undergrowth. This was done with an axe, wielded by his brawney arms, and the land was cultivated by him and his family with hoes and such other crude implements as he could improvise. In the role of mechanic he had to be a "Jack-of-all-trades", making wooden vessels for domestic use, rough besteads, cupboards, tables, stools, a loom, shoes and moccasins from buckskins and other animal hides, sometimes the raw hide. His list of tools was very limited—a drawing knife, broadaxe, tomahawk, a tool to rive clapboards to cover his cabin and corncrib and stable, and possibly an auger and a handsaw. With these tools he accomplished wonders as a carpenter. With awl, needle and waxed thread he, or his wife, made the moccasins for himself and family from buckskin he had dressed in the Indian style.

As a hunter the pioneer settler had great responsibility upon him, for his wife and children were dependent upon his skill and success for their supply of meat, generally venison and bear's flesh; and frequently for a substitute for bread. The grain would sometimes give out before the new crop was ready for food, and the breasts of pheasants and wild turkeys were used as substitutes for bread. The pioneer virtually made conquest of this great country with the backwoodsman's axe and his trusty rifle. Men, boys, women, and even girls could and did use, effectively, when occasion demanded, these indispensible weapons of the pioneer.

The pioneers brought with them good supplies of salt, but they soon found that this mineral, so essential to the health and comfort of both man and beast, could be made at the Salt Lick on the North Fork of the Holston River; and from the time they obtained this knowledge until the Saltworks was acquired by the Mathieson Alkali Company, the people of the Clinch Valley got ample supplies from that place. There was another article of food, now considered a great luxury, that the pioneers did not have to bring from the east, but could make at home—that was sugar. In every valley, and in the mountain hollows, the Tazewell pioneers found magnificent groves of sugar maple. Every settler had his "sugar orchard"; and in the late winter or early spring he would tap his "sugar trees" and make an abundant supply of sugar and "tree molasses" for his family needs for the ensuing year.

Seed corn was brought out by the fathers and seeds of different kinds of vegetables—beans, potatoes, squash, turnip, cabbage and others seeds—by the provident mothers, who in those days took most interest in the garden or "truck patch." The settlers moved their families to their new homes in the early spring season. No doubt the trees had been belted in the winter time so as to keep the sap from rising when spring came, and thus prevent the trees from leafing. The clearings were made by chopping down the large trees about the sites of the houses to be erected and using the logs for the buildings. On the adjacent ground the large trees were belted, the saplings cut down and the brush grubbed out; the brush and saplings were then burned or removed, and the loose rich soil was easily prepared for seeding.

After the pioneer had planted his first crop of corn and vegetables there had to be endured by him and his family weeks and months of anxious expectancy as to what the harvest would be. They had several reasons for apprehending that the most important crop, the corn, might be a failure. Bears and other wild beasts might destroy or materially injure it; a hot dry season might come and cause the blades to fire and the shoots to parch and not mature; and, then, "Jack Frost" in those days made early visits and got in his work of destruction. The supplies of corn brought from the eastern settlements, by early summer, were generally exhausted, and the corn pone, though always a necessity, became a luxury. If the season proved favorable, when the early vegetables came in much relief was given; and when the corn reached the "roasting ear" stage the event was welcomed with shouts of joy by the children and the grown-up folks alike. This condition of scarcity, or threatened scarcity, of bread continued for several years after the first settlers arrived, a notable instance occurring in the Clinch Valley while Dunmore's War was in progress, in 1774.

————

The first settlers usually came in groups, or located in groups after they arrived; and fixed their homes in such immediate nearness as would enable them to be of service to each other in times of stress. This established a community of interest in a social and economic sense; and was of the utmost importance as a means of protection against the attacks of hostile Indians. The home of a settler, cen-

trally located, was selected in each neighborhood, where all the
families in the vicinity could flee for protection when the Indians
made hostile incursions into the country. At these central points
forts were built, where safety was assured all who got there before
the Indians made surprise attacks on their cabin homes. The first
forts built in the Upper Clinch Valley were, Thomas Witten's fort
at the Crab Orchard, near Pisgah; Rees Bowen's fort at Maiden
Spring; and William Wynne's fort, at Locust Hill. The latter was

The flag in centre of picture shows where Thomas Witten built his
fort when the hostile Indians began to invade the Clinch Valley settlements.

located on the point just west of Mr. George A. Martin's residence,
one and a half miles east of Tazewell. These three were community
forts and were very similar in form and construction. Indeed they
were like all such places of refuge and defence as were at that time,
or afterwards, erected on the frontiers of the English colonies.
Roosevelt, who carefully investigated all that was written by the
earliest writers about the old frontier forts, gives a description of
them in his "Winning of the West." He says, they were: "A
square palisade of upright logs, loop-holed, with strong block houses
as bastions at the corners. One side at least was generally formed
by the back of the cabins themselves, all standing in a row; and
there was a great door or gate, that could be strongly barred in case
of need. Often no iron whatever was employed in any of the build-

ings. The square inside contained the provision sheds and frequently a strong central block house as well. These forts, of course, could not stand against cannons; and they were always in danger when attacked with fire; but save for this risk of burning they were very effectual defences against men without artillery, and were rarely taken, whether by whites or Indians, except by surprise."

There were no attacks made by the Indians on the Witten or Wynne forts, and none upon the fort at Maiden Spring, although a small band of Shawnees on one occasion, in the absence of Rees Bowen, threatened to make an assault on his fort, but were prevented from so doing by a clever ruse practiced by Mrs. Bowen, who was as fearless and resourceful as her husband. The families of each settlement went to their community fort when Indian wars came on, and remained there until the war was ended, or until winter arrived. The Indians made no incursions in the winter time, when the forests were denuded of foilage, or snow might fall and reveal their presence in the settlements.

When the first detachments of settlers came to the Clinch Valley the Indians in Ohio and in Tennessee were at peace with the Virginians; and the relation continued friendly until Dunmore's War began in 1774. This gave our ancestors several years of opportunity to build their houses unmolested and extend their clearings deeper into the forests. It also made effective the social and economic features of the plan adopted by the settlers for grouping their homes around and about some central point. And when the war commenced there was ample existing evidence that the Tazewell pioneers had utilized the years of peace very well, as they were in a condition to not only defend their own settlements, but to furnish substantial assistance in the military campaign against the Shawnees and other hostile tribes in Ohio. The houses they built to dwell in were nothing more pretentious than log cabins. Some had only a single room, while others were double cabins. Roosevelt, in "Winning of the West", gives a very accurate description of the houses and their furnishings that were built and occupied by the backwoodsmen. Mr. Roosevelt got this description from the celebrated McAfee MSS, and its accuracy is undoubted. Roosevelt says:

"If he was poor his cabin was made of unhewn logs, and held but a single room; if well-to-do, the logs were neatly hewed, and besides the large living and eating-room with its huge stone fireplace, there was also a small bedroom and a kitchen, while a ladder

led to the loft above, in which the boys slept. The floor was made
of puncheons, great slabs of wood hewed carefully out, and the
roof of clapboards. Pegs of wood were thrust into the sides of
the house, to serve instead of a wardrobe; and buck antlers, thrust
into the joists, held the ever ready rifles. The table was a great
clapboard set on four wooden legs; there were three-legged stools,
and in the better sort of houses old-fashioned rocking chairs. The
couch or bed was warmly covered with blankets, bear-skins and deer-
hides."

Shown above is the oldest standing house in Tazewell County. It
was built during the Revolution by John Witten, eldest son of Thomas
Witten, and stands in the yard of John C. St. Clair, four miles west of
the town of Tazewell, and is an excellent type of the pioneer cabin.

All the early settlers knew that in the making of their new
homes self-help must be their chief reliance; but they also realized
that what they, as families, would do could be greatly added to by
the families of a community helping each other. From this idea of
community interest excellent results came; and from it originated
the old-time log-rollings, house-raisings, house-warmings, corn-
shuckings, quiltings and sugar-stirrings. All these were affairs of
utility and were made joyous festive occasions. They served to
unite the pioneers of the Clinch Valley in the strong bonds of neigh-
borly kindness and fellowship, engendering a spirit which was transmitted in such measure to their descendants as to make the hospi-

tality, clanship, and fidelity of the sons of Tazewell proverbial. On such occasions the men, women and children of some particular neighborhood would assemble and do more useful work for a single family in a day than such a family could accomplish unassisted in several weeks, or possibly months. These gatherings were made delightful social and festive affairs. The mothers and daughters, who were the hostesses, would be happily assisted by the mothers and girls of the neighborhood in preparing a bounteous repast for the men who were engaged in the log-rolling, or the house-raising, or whatever work was being done.

At meal time the tables would fairly groan beneath the abundance of meats, of such variety that they would make a modern gourmand chuckle with delight, if he could have a chance to partake of similar viands. There would be bear and venison steaks and roasts, wild turkeys, pheasants, and other small game, prepared in a homely way, but deliciously fragrant and appetizing. For bread they had the wonderful "Johnny Cake" and the corn pone, the making of which is now a lost art, the one baked on a clean board before a blazing log fire, the other baked in an iron oven on the stone hearth. They had no tea or coffee on the frontier in those days, but in most instances had plenty of rich milk, given by cows that grazed on the pea vine and blue grass; and plenty of sparkling water that gushed from the springs that were found near every cabin home; and these were served to the hearty log-rollers and house-raisers by the wives and their rosy-cheeked daughters. Nor had they any desserts at their feasts, worth mentioning, as wheat and flour had not yet been introduced; for there were no mills in the region but small hand mills that were used for grinding the corn. Few persons now living have been so fortunate as to eat meats and other foods similar to those of which the first settlers had an abundance, prepared as the pioneer women cooked them. The author in his boyhood days sometimes ate venison steaks, the Johhny Cake, and the corn pone prepared by the old-time cooks that had been trained by the pioneer mothers or their daughters. Nothing in modern cookery is half as delicious to me as those things that were prepared by "Aunt Trecy," the negro cook that was trained by my grandmother Cecil.

At the log-rollings, house-raisings and corn-shuckings it was the custom of the men to divide into "sides" to see which division could accomplish the most work in a given time, or for the day—each side having a captain to direct its movements. This caused the work to progress more rapidly, as each side put forth its full strength to be first in the contest. At the quiltings the women would frequently divide into parties and work from opposite sides to see which would first reach the centre of the quilt. I attended several corn-shuckings when I was a boy, and greatly enjoyed witnessing the jolly shuckers work and hearing them sing. These shuckings were held at night, and a bountiful supper was always spread and eaten after the work was completed. And when I was a little fellow my mother frequently took me to quilting parties given by her neighbors; and she had many quilting parties herself, that I remember. I always enjoyed the good dinners and took childish interest in the innocent gossip of the ladies.

A description of the apparel of the pioneer men and women has been given by Theodore Roosevelt in his "Winning of the West" and also by Dr. Bickley in his History of Tazewell County. Their accounts are strikingly similar, and were procured from early writers, who were familiar with frontier life. Roosevelt says: "The backwoodsman's dress was in great part borrowed from his Indian foes. He wore a fur cap or felt hat, moccasins, and either loose, thin trousers, or else simple leggings of buckskin or elk-hide, and the Indian breech-clout. He was always clad in the fringed hunting-shirt, of homespun or buckskin, the most picturesque and distinctively national dress ever worn in America. It was a loose smock or tunic, reaching nearly to the knees, and held in at the waist by a broad belt, from which hung the tomahawk and scalping-knife. His weapon was the long small-bore, flint-lock rifle, clumsy, and ill-balanced, but exceedingly accurate. It was very heavy, and when upright reached to the chin of a tall man; for the barrel of thick, soft iron, was four feet in length, while the stock was short and the butt scooped out. Sometimes it was plain, sometimes ornamented. It was generally bored out—or, as the expression then was, 'sawed-out'—to carry a ball of seventy, more rarely of thirty or forty, to the pound; and was usually of backwoods manufacture. The marksman almost always fired from a rest, and rarely at a very long range; and the shooting was marvelously accurate."

The gun described by Colonel Roosevelt was one of Daniel Boone's rifles, which, according to an inscription on the barrel, was made at Louisville, Kentucky, in 1782, by M. Humble. Prior to the Civil War (1861-65) a number of rifles of similar pattern could be found in Tazewell County, and there are some still here.

Garbed in hunting shirts, with tomahawk and scalping knives sheathed in their belts, and armed with rifles like Boone's, a number of the pioneers from the Clinch, under command of Captain Russell, were with General Andrew Lewis at the battle of Point Pleasant; and the gallant Lieutenant Rees Bowen, with his company of sterling patriots similarly garbed and equipped, marched with Campbell to King's Mountain, and in the battle there placed Tazewell's name on the scroll of fame.

In the days of the American Revolution the rifles of the men from the mountain frontiers made the American guns famous. General Howe, a British general, called them "the terrible guns of the rebels." A recent supposed authority on guns and projectiles has written: "In the colonial days the residents of the Atlantic seaboard were the greatest users of guns of their period, and gunmaker's shops were in every city and town. With little knowledge of ballistics, these men perfected the American rifle that was a factor of great moment in the revolution when wielded by the sharp-shooting keen-eyed men of the colonies."

The guns that were made and used on the Atlantic seaboard about the time of the Revolution were principally of the smooth-bore style, while the guns used by the men of the mountain sections were universally rifles after the Boone type; and Roosevelt says this kind of gun "was usually of backwoods manufacture". It was perfected by the gunmakers of the mountains and not in the gunmaker's shops in the seaboard towns. Rifles made in the mountains of Virginia, in the hands of Daniel Morgan's riflemen won the battle at Saratoga and at the Cow Pens, and caused General Howe to speak of "the terrible guns of the rebels." The Mountain riflemen from the Clinch and Holston valleys, with their trusty mountain rifles, under the command of the mountain general, William Campbell, won the battle at King's Mountain and turned the scale for the colonies in the War of the Revolution.

The dress of the pioneer women was limited in the kind of garments used and was of the coarsest and cheapest quality. Roosevelt says the outfit of a well-to-do bride was "not very elaborate, for a woman's dress consisted of a hat or poke bonnet, a 'bedgown', perhaps a jacket, and a linsey petticoat, while her feet were thrust into coarse shoepacks or moccasins". Bickley in his chapter on "Manners and Customs" of the first settlers, quoting from Dr. Doddridge, says: "Linsey coats and bedgowns were the universal dress of the women in the early times." Dr. Bickley thinks this was an excellent description of the dress of the women who first came to the Clinch Valley; and he follows this adoption of the Doddridge description with the following statement as to the resourcefulness and industry of the pioneer women:

"The garments made in Augusta, Botetourt and other older settlements, had worn out, and a different material was brought into use. The weed now known among us as wild nettle (*Urtica dioica*), then furnished the material which served to clothe the persons of our sires and dames. It was cut down while yet green, and treated much in the same manner in which flax is now treated. The fibrous bark, with the exception of the shortness of the fibers, seemed to be adapted to the same uses. When this flax, if I may so term it, was prepared, it was mixed with buffalo hair and woven into a substantial cloth, in which men and women were clothed. It is a true maxim 'necessity is the mother of invention.' "

In the introductory paragraphs of his chapter on the "Manners and Customs" of the pioneers, Dr. Bickley made an apology for the crude state of society that prevailed among the first settlers. This apology was unnecessary, and was based upon what I believe was a false interpretation of the customs and habits of our pioneer ancestors. Tazewell's first historian says:

"I must ask such sons and daughters of the noble people whose habits form a theme of my pen, who are either vain or proud, to forgive me for exhibiting their fathers and mothers, in such a light as I necessarily must. I, too, am of these people, and hope I am as sensitive of my ancestors as the vainest or the proudest.

"The people of all mountain countries have some customs peculiarly their own. The same pastoral simplicity which characterizes the people of the Scotch highlands, the mountainous regions of Europe, and the hill country of ancient Judea, may be clearly traced. The same industry, love for stock, determination to be free, hatred of oppression, pure sentiment, etc., are found here."

Following this apology, Bickley quotes from Doddridge's "Settlements and Indian Wars" a lengthy description of a wedding in the pioneer days, of which he declares "a more faithful picture could not be drawn." Though it does not justify an apology for the supposed unrefined customs of our pioneer ancestors, it is the only description of a frontier wedding written by an eye witness; and I will reproduce it. Doddridge says:

"For a long time after the first settlement of this country the inhabitants in general married young. There was no distinction of rank, and very little of fortune. On these accounts, the first impression of love resulted in marriage, and a family establishment cost but little labor, and nothing else. A description of a wedding from beginning to end will serve to show the manners of our forefathers, and mark the grade of civilization which has succeeded to their rude state of society in the course of a few years.

"In the first years of the settlement of a country, a wedding engaged the attention of the whole neighborhood; and the frolic was anticipated by old and young, with eager expectation. This is not to be wondered at, when it is told that a wedding was almost the only gathering which was not accompanied with the labor of reaping, log-rolling, building a cabin, or planning some scout or campaign. On the morning of the wedding-day, the groom and his attendants assembled at the house of his father, for the purpose of reaching his bride by noon, which was the usual time for celebrating the nuptials; and which, for certain reasons, must take place before dinner.

"Let the reader imagine an assemblage, without a store, tailor, or mantua-maker, within a hundred miles; an assemblage of horses, without a blacksmith or saddler within an equal distance. The gentlemen dressed in shoepacks, moccasins, leather breeches, leggings, linsey hunting shirts, and all home-made. The ladies dressed in linsey petticoats, and linsey or linen bedgowns, coarse shoes, stockings, handkerchiefs, and buckskin gloves, if any. If there were any buckles, rings, buttons or ruffles, they were the relics of olden times; family pieces from parents or grandparents. The horses were caparisoned with old saddles, old bridles or halters, and pack-saddles, with a bag or a blanket thrown over them; a rope or a string as often constituted the girth as a piece of leather.

"The march in double file was often interrupted by the narrowness of our mountain paths, as they were called, for we had no roads; and these difficulties were often increased, sometimes by the good, and sometimes by the ill-will of the neighbors, by falling trees, and tying grape-vines across the way. Sometimes an ambuscade was formed by the wayside, and an unexpected discharge of several guns took place, so as to cover the wedding company with smoke. Let the reader imagine the scene which followed this discharge; the sudden spring of the horses, the shrieks of the girls, and the chivalrous bustle of their partners to save them from falling. Sometimes, in spite of all that could be done to prevent it, some were thrown to the ground. If a wrist, elbow, or ankle happened to be sprained, it was tied up with a handkerchief, and little more was said or thought about it.

"The ceremony of the marriage preceded the dinner, which was a substantial backwoods' feast of beef, pork, fowls, and sometimes venison and bear meat, roasted and boiled, with plenty of potatoes, cabbage and other vegetables. During the dinner, the greatest hilarity always prevailed; although the table might be a large slab of timber, hewed out with the broadaxe, supported by four sticks, set in auger holes; and the furniture, some old pewter dishes and plates; the rest, wooden bowls and trenchers: a few pewter spoons, much battered about the edges, were to be seen at some tables. The rest were made of horn. If knives were scarce, the deficiency was made up by the scalping knives, which were carried in sheaths, suspended to the belt of the hunting-shirt, every man carried one of them.

"After dinner the dancing commenced, and generally lasted until the next morning. The figures of the dances were three and four handed reels, or square sets and jigs. The commencement was always a square form, which was followed by what was called jigging it off; that is, two of the four would single out for a jig, and were followed by the remaining couples. The jigs were often accompanied with what was called cutting out; that is, when either of the parties became tired of the dance, on intimation, the place was supplied by some one of the company, without any interruption to the dance. In this way the dance was continued until the musician was heartily tired of his situation. Toward the latter part of the night, if any of the company, through weariness, attempted to conceal themselves for the purpose of sleeping, they were hunted up, paraded on the floor, and the fiddler ordered to play 'hang out till to-morrow morning.'

"About nine or ten o'clock a deputation of young ladies stole off the bride, and put her to bed. In doing this, it frequently happened that they had to ascend a ladder, instead of a pair of stairs, leading from the dining room and ball room to the *loft*, the floor of which was made of clap-boards, lying loose. This ascent, one might think, would put the bride and her attendants to the blush; but the foot of the ladder was commonly behind the door, which was purposely opened for the occasion, and its rounds, at the inner ends, were well hung with hunting-shirts, dresses and other articles of clothing. The candles, being on the opposite side of the house, the exit of the bride was noticed by but few.

"This done, a deputation of young men, in like manner, stole off the groom, and placed him snugly by the side of his bride. The dance still continued; and if seats happened to be scarce, as was often the case, every young man, when not engaged in the dance, was obliged to offer his lap as a seat for one of the girls; and the offer was sure to be accepted. In the midst of this hilarity, the bride and groom were not forgotten. Pretty late in the night, some one would remind the company that the new couple must stand in need of some refreshment; *black Betty,* which was the name of the bottle, was called for and sent up the ladder; but sometimes black Betty did not go alone. I have many times seen as much bread, beef, pork and cabbage sent along, as would afford a good meal for half a dozen hungry men. The young couple were compelled to eat and drink, more or less of whatever was offered.

"But to return. It often happened that some neighbors or relatives, not being asked to the wedding, took offense; and the mode of revenge, adopted by them on such occasions, was that of cutting off the manes, foretops, and tails of the horses of the wedding company.

"On returning to the in-fare, the order of procession, and the race for black Betty, was the same as before. The feasting and dancing often lasted several days, at the end of which, the whole company were so exhausted with loss of sleep, that many days' rest were requisite to fit them to return to their ordinary labors."

Bickley makes further explanation and apology for adopting the Doddridge wedding story by saying: "I have quoted this account, written by Dr. Doddridge, because nothing could be more correct, and it was beyond my power to tell an original tale so well."

Dr. Doddridge's description is, no doubt, highly colored, as the border annalists were as prone to indulge in hyperbole as the most brilliant modern war correspondent. The kind of weddings the author of "Settlements and Indian Wars" describes did sometimes occur in the backwoods; but they were exceptional, and should not have been adopted as a type for illustrating the manners and habits of our forefathers and foremothers. Occasional weddings of the Doddridge kind may have taken place in the Clinch Valley in the early days after its settlement; but I doubt if any such occurred in the families of the pioneers. The first settlers on the Clinch were dignified, sober-minded men and women, intent upon accomplishing a great work, that of erecting happy and useful homes. They were descended from ancestors who sought asylum in America to escape religious and political persecutions, and their children, the first generation born in Tazewell, were as dignified and refined as any persons now in the land. I knew quite a number of them in my childhood and boyhood, and speak from actual knowledge.

The sons and daughters of the pioneers married while they were very young, frequently before the boys were twenty-one, and when the girls were in their early teens. They inherited and possessed but little of the world's goods to begin their married life with. The groom would have a horse, an axe, and his rifle, the latter was given each boy when he became twelve years old; and in case of an invasion by the Indians he was expected to, and did, fill a man's place at a loophole. And the bride, if she had been industrious and helpful, and her parents were thrifty, would have for her dowry a brood-mare, a cow, a bed well furnished with blankets, quilts and woolen coverlets—the latter woven by herself or her mother—and a chest for her clothes. These chests took the place of trunks, as there were no trunks in those days. They were always made from cedar or black walnut, were neat in appearance, and were capacious and useful. My mother had one, which was given her by her parents, and it is still an heirloom in the family.

There was, however, an abundance of fertile land still unoccupied and unclaimed, from which the young married man could select four hundred acres, and acquire title thereto under the liberal settler's laws then existing in Virginia. After he had selected, and possibly marked out with his tomahawk, the boundary he wished to occupy, he and his bride would choose a location for their future residence. Then the community custom and feeling, that had been happily planted in the beginning of the settlement, would assert itself in most generous form. All the men of the neighborhood would assemble where the new house was to be built; and they would chop the logs and roll them to the proposed site of the building, with their broadaxes they would hew and notch the logs, and raise the house for the young housekeepers. As soon as the chimney was built and the roof of clapboards was placed, the festal joys of a house-warming, with all the social forms of the wedding, were extended by the young housekeepers to their kindred and neighbors. Thus were the homes of the sons and daughters of the pioneers established and the community made stronger and better by the addition of other families. Race suicide was then an unheard of thing in this glorious mountain country; and the Biblical injunction, "multiply and replenish the earth" had not become obsolete. The man cheerfully assumed his duties of armed protector of his wife and children and provider for the family, and the woman, as house-wife and child-bearer, with smiling contentment, carried her many cares and burdens.

In some respects it was a lonely and monotonous, as well as dangerous, life our ancestors led when they first moved into this wild, uninhabited region; but there were many things to stimulate and interest those who were brave, intelligent and industrious. They were constantly experiencing thrills that came from contacts with the ferocious animals that lurked in every mountain hollow and valley; and from the still more exciting experiences that came from actual or anticipated encounters with hostile Indians. And there was an excitement, intense and pleasurable, in their task of home-making. There is no greater pleasure to normal men and women than the work of making a home, where they can be surrounded by their children, and enjoy the comforts and beautiful things that are the products of honest, earnest toil. What a delight it must have been to our ancestors. Like happy birds building nests for their young were the men as they felled the trees and built their cabins; and the good women, no doubt, would joyfully sing the old-time songs, in rivalry of the love-songs of their feathered neighbors, as they placed in position their modest household possessions.

There was still another exciting pleasure enjoyed by the pioneers, as hunters. It combined both business and amusement. At the time the first settlements were made, the Clinch Valley was the most cherished hunting ground of the Shawnee and Cherokee Indians. Both of these tribes were very jealous of its appropriation by white men; and, as rival claimants to the territory, had engaged in many bloody contests for its possession.

Though hunting parties from Eastern Virginia, known as "Long Hunters", had been visiting the Clinch Valley regularly for nearly twenty years previous to the advent of the pioneers, and had killed thousands of splendid animals for their valuable hides; and, though the Indians had made frequent journeys to this favorite hunting ground to procure supplies of meat for winter use, there was an abundance of deer, bears, and smaller game animals left here. Small herds of buffalo and a few elk also wandered in to graze upon the succulent herbage, the wild pea vine and the bluegrass, that was found in profusion everywhere; and it was truly a hunter's paradise for the first settlers. They hunted the animals I have mentioned chiefly for meat for their families; but the skins were also of special value as they were used, together with the hides of the otter, beaver, mink, fox, and other fur-bearing animals, to buy powder and lead, iron and other necessary articles from merchants or dealers in the eastern part of Virginia.

The pioneers were all expert hunters, or soon became expert after they reached the Clinch regions. They acquired all the tricks and arts used by the Indians to lure game within range of their rifles, imitating the call of the turkey, the howling of the wolf and the sounds and calls of other animals and fowls. The keen-eyed hunters could easily distinguish the marks or traces left by different kinds of game, and soon became familiar with the haunts of the deer, the elk, the bear, the wolf, and every kind of animal that abided or roamed in the region. All the men were successful hunters, but some won the distinction of experts. James Witten, son of Thomas Witten, the first settler, who was only fifteen years old when he came with his father to the Clinch Valley, soon after his arrival was admitted to be the most skillful hunter and woodsman in the settlements; and in the time of the Revolutionary War he became the most noted and efficient scout in the entire region. Dr. Bickley, who obtained much valuable information directly from the sons of the pioneers, wrote in his History of Tazewell County the following interesting story of the accomplishments of the early woodsmen:

"Neither was hunting the mere pastime, devoid of skill, which it now is. The hunter might be considered somewhat of a meteorologist; he paid particular attention to the winds, rains, snows, and frosts; for almost every change altered the location of game. He knew the cardinal points by the thick bark and moss on the north side of a tree, so that during the darkest and most gloomy night he knew which was the north, and so his home or camp. The natural habits of the deer were well studied; and hence he knew at what times they fed, etc. If, in hunting, he found a deer at feed, he stopped, and though he might be open to it, did not seek to obscure himself, but waited till it raised its head and looked at him. He remained motionless till the deer, satisfied that nothing moving was in sight, again commenced feeding. He then began to advance, if he had the wind of it, and if not he retreated and came up another way, so as to place the deer between himself and the wind. As long as the deer's head was down he continued to advance till he saw it shake the tail. In a moment he became the same motionless object, till it again put down its head. In this way, he would soon approach to within sixty yards, when his unerring rifle did the work of death. It is a curious fact that deer never put their heads to the ground, or raise it, without shaking the tail before so doing.

"The quantity of game will be apparent when it is known that Mr. Ebenezer Brewster killed, during his life, twelve hundred bears in this county. He died in the summer of 1850, and this statement occurred in an obituary notice."

There was another famous hunter in Tazewell County who was a contemporary of Ebenezer Brester. I refer to 'Squire Thomas Peery. He was called "Squire Tommie" to distinguish him from a number of other Peerys who bore the name of Thomas. His father, William Peery, settled in 1773 where the town of Tazewell is now located, and he was born and reared near the site of the residence of the late Albert P. Gillespie. He was a fine business man and acquired a splendid estate, but was an ardent hunter, bear-hunting being his special delight; and he had a record for the number of bears he killed that nearly equalled that of Ebenezer Brewster. If he had devoted more time to hunting and less to his personal affairs, he would, no doubt, have beaten Brewster's record. As it was, he had a record of more than a thousand bears and killed great numbers of deer and wolves.

THE COUNTY OF FINCASTLE ESTABLISHED.

When the county of Botetourt was established by an act of the General Assembly, passed November 28th, 1769, there were but few inhabitants in that portion of Virginia west of the New River, all of which section was made a part of the new county. They were so remote from the place where it was known the county seat was to be located that the act provided that the people "situated on the waters of the Mississippi," which included the few settlers in the Clinch Valley, "shall be exempted from the payment of levies, to be laid by the said county court for the purpose of building a county court-house and prison for the said county." Another important and substantial reason was recited in the act for the exemption of such inhabitants from the specified taxation. This reason was, that the people living on the waters of the Mississippi: "Must necessarily become a separate county, as soon as their numbers are sufficient, which will probably happen in a short time."

The General Assembly was acquainted with the fact that many men with their families were on the borders, ready to cross New River and settle on the waters of the Mississippi—that is in the Clinch, Holston and New River valleys—and that some settlers had already moved out to the wilderness country. So, it was found necessary, in less than three years after Botetourt County was formed, to verify the prediction that a new county would have to be provided for the inhabitants living on the waters of the Mississippi west of New River. In the winter of 1771-72 the settlers of the Holston and New River valleys presented a petition to the General Assembly, setting forth the inconvenience arising from their remoteness from the county seat of Botetourt, and praying for the erection of a new county. Responding to this petition, the General Assembly, on the 8th day of April, 1772, enacted the following:

"I. Whereas it is represented to this present General Assembly, by the inhabitants and settlers on the waters of the Holston and New River in the county of Botetourt that they labour under great inconvenience, by reason of the extent of said county and their remote situation from the court house:

"Be it therefore enacted, by the Council, and Burgesses of this present General Assembly, and it is hereby enacted, by the authority of the same, That from after the first day of December next, the said county of Botetourt shall be divided into two distinct counties, that is to say, all that part of the said county within a line to run up the east side of the New River to the mouth of Culberson's creek; thence a direct line to the Catawba road, where it crosses the dividing ridge between the north fork of Roanoke and the waters of New River; thence with the top of the ridge to the bent where it turns eastwardly; thence a south course, crossing Little River to the top of the Blue Ridge Mountains shall be established as one distinct county and called and known by the name of Fincastle, and all the other part thereof, which lies to the east of the said line, shall be one other distinct county and retain the name of Botetourt."

The act provided for a justices' court to be held on the first Tuesday of every month after the county was regularly organized, and made provision for the usual county officers and public buildings, but did not designate any location for the county seat. The Colonial Governor ordered that the county seat should be placed at the Lead Mines, in the present county of Wythe, and where the village of Austinville is now situated; and the name of the county, Fincastle, was received from the country seat of Lord Botetourt, in England.

No reference is made in the act to the settlers on the Clinch River, and, apparently, none of the inhabitants of the Clinch Valley signed the petition. These omissions may have been caused by the fact that the Clinch Valley was then so inaccessible and isolated, that the men who promoted the scheme did not undertake to cross the mountains and present the petition to the settlers, who were scattered for more than seventy miles up and down the valley. At the time the petition was prepared and presented to the General Asesembly there must have been several hundred people living in the territory that now constitutes Tazewell County; and as many more were located lower down the Clinch, in the present counties of Russell and Scott. As early as 1770 there was quite a community of settlers in the present Castle's Woods neighborhood in Russell County. The men who formed that settlement were: ———— Castle, from whom the place received its name; Henry Dickenson, Charles Bickley, Simon Oscher, James Bush, William Fraley, Archelous Dickenson, Humphrey Dickenson, James Osborn, William Richie, Jerry Harold, William Robertson, Richard Long, William Bowlin, William Russell, Samuel Porter, Henry Neece, Henry Hamblin and William Wharton.

John Murray, Fourth Earl of Dunmore, was then governor of the colony of Virginia; and was the last royal governor Virginia had. On December the 1st, 1772, he issued a "Commission of Peace" appointing the justices who were to constitute the first county court of Fincastle County, as follows: William Preston, William Christian, Stephen Trigg, Walter Crockett, Anthony Bledsoe, Arthur Campbell, Benjamin Estill, William Inglis, John Montgomery, Robert Doach, James McGavock, James Thompson, William Russell, Samuel Crockett, Alexander McKee.

William Russell, one of the above named justices, was from the Middle Clinch Valley. He then lived at or near Castle's Woods, where he erected a fort in 1774 on the land of one Cowan; and later he became very prominent in both the civil and military affairs of the Clinch Valley and of Southwest Virginia, as succeeding pages of this volume will disclose. The first county court for Fincastle was held at the Lead Mines on the 5th of January, 1773, with the

T.H.—17

following members of the court present and sitting: Arthur Campbell, James Thompson, William Preston, William Ingles, Walter Crockett and James McGavock.

The court elected William Preston sheriff of the county; and Daniel Trigg, John Floyd, James Thompson, and Henry Moore were made his deputies. William Preston was also elected surveyor of the county, with the following as his deputies: John Floyd, Daniel Smith, William Russell, Robert Preston, Robert Doach, and James Douglas. Two of the deputy surveyors, Smith and Russell, were from the Clinch Valley, and were then living in the present county of Russell.

John Byrd was elected clerk of the county, with William Christian, Stephen Trigg, and Richard Madison for his deputies. John Aylett was elected King's Council, which completed the civil organization of the county.

From the showing of the records, it seems that the pioneer settlers of Tazewell County took no active part in the organization of the county of Fincastle. They were too busily occupied with the building of their homes, clearing their fields, and perfecting themselves as woodsmen and frontier soldiers to give much heed to their civil connection with the Virginia Government. The upper Clinch settlements were then the extreme northwestern outposts of the territory occupied by white men west of New River; and were directly at the front of three of the favorite war-paths, or trails, that the Shawnees traveled when they came to this section to hunt or make atacks upon the settlers. Being so perilously located, our ancestors on the Clinch were very wise in preparing to defend their homes and possessions against the attacks they apprehended were coming from the red men; and, in doing this, they were rendering a great service to the inhabitants of the Holston and New River valleys by erecting a strong barrier for their protection from the Indians.

When the first settlers came to Tazewell they knew they were taking a very serious risk of having their families suffer for a time from a lack of proper food; and they realized that a much graver danger would have to be met, that of having their dear ones, and perhaps themselves, murdered by the Indians. The danger of anyone suffering for lack of substantial food, or other creature comforts, in the Clinch settlements had, apparently, disappeared by the time Fincastle County was established; but the perils from Indian invasions had increased considerably, and, in fact, were imminent. For several years previous to 1773 the Northwestern Indians had been exhibiting marked hostility to the Fort Stanwix treaty, by which treaty the Iroquois Nation had assumed the right to cede all the hunting grounds south of the Ohio to the Dominion of Virginia; and the Shawnees were greatly exasperated by the avowed purpose of the Virginians to extend their settlements along the Kanawha River and from its mouth on down into Kentucky.

A number of prominent men, resident both east and west of the Blue Ridge, were anxious to secure large holdings of the splendid, fertile lands that were known to lie in the lower Kanawha Valley, along the southern banks of the Ohio, and in most of the sections of Kentucky, while the settlers in Clinch Valley were more than content with what they had found here, and were intent upon holding the valuable territory they had already acquired. Among the then and subsequently distinguished men of Virginia who were seeking to locate large boundaries of land on the Kanawha and Ohio Rivers, and in the territory of the present State of Kentucky, were: George Washington, Patrick Henry, William Byrd, Andrew Lewis, William Preston, William Russell, Arthur Campbell, and others. George Washington had already won a leading position in the citizenship of Virginia, and Patrick Henry had just emerged from thriftless obscurity and become famous as an orator and tribune of the people. Some of those who were eager to acquire lands in the unsettled territory were real home-seekers, a few were speculators who desired to accumulate large estates, and many were officers and soldiers who had obtained grants from the Virginia Government for valuable service rendered in the French and Indian War.

Small exploring parties had visited the Kanawha, Ohio, and Kentucky regions in 1773, and had returned to the settlements in Virginia with glowing accounts of the wonderful fertility of the soil and the abundant resources of the unappropriated lands they had traversed. The Indians were well informed, through their spies and hunting parties, of these exploring expeditions; and reasonably concluded that they were the precursors of an active movement of the white men to take complete control, for settlement, of the entire country south of the Ohio, and to drive the natives from their splendid hunting grounds. Then began a series of outrages, committed by both the Indians and the whites, that brought a reign of terror to the borders; and the Tazewell pioneers had barely erected their cabin homes when they were required to enter into a desperate

struggle with the most intrepid Indian warriors then living east of
the Mississippi.

———

Small bands of Shawnees began to make hostile incursions into
the Lower Clinch Valley, and during the fall of 1773, according to
reports of Colonel William Preston, county lieutenant of Fincastle
County, eleven persons were murdered by the Indians in the county
of Fincastle. The most notable of the outrages committed was the
killing of James Boone, son of Daniel Boone; Henry Russell, son
of Captain William Russell, and ——— Drake, son of Captain
Drake. Daniel Boone had collected a company of emigrants in
North Carolina and from the Holston and Clinch valleys, and had
started to Kentucky to establish a settlement. The three young
men, or youths, had separated from the party to engage in hunting,
and had secured a large number of valuable pelts which they
intended to take to market. On October 10th, 1773, they were surprised and killed by a mixed party of Shawnees and Cherokees. It
was thought that one Isaac Crabtree, a white desperado and outlaw,
had provoked the attack; and that the three youths were murdered
for purposes of robbery, as all their pelts and other belongings were
stolen by the murderers. Daniel Boone abandoned his migration to
Kentucky for the time being, and brought his party back to the
Clinch and Holston valleys. He remained in this section throughout
1774, and rendered very valuable assistance to the inhabitants of the
Clinch Valley while Dunmore's War was in progress.

Early in the spring of 1774 a number of surveying parties made
their way to the Lower Kanawha Valley and to Kentucky, where
they surveyed a number of large and valuable tracts of land, and
entered them in the names of the several persons who had employed
them to do the work. Among the surveyors were: James Douglas,
Hancock Taylor, Anthony Bledsoe, and John Floyd. The descendants of John Floyd have had so much to do with the making of the
history of Tazewell County that it will be appropriate to give a
brief sketch of the life and career of the pioneer surveyor, which
I take from Thwaites' "Dunmore's War:"

"John Floyd was born in Virginia in 1750, and when about
twenty-two years of age removed to Fincastle County, and engaged
in school-teaching, living in the home of Colonel William Preston.
In 1774 he was appointed deputy sheriff (*also deputy surveyor*)
and in the spring of the same year led a surveying party into Ken-

tucky. Upon his return he joined the Point Point Pleasant expedition, but arrived too late to engage in the battle. The following year he returned to Kentucky as surveyor of the Transylvania Company and remained at St. Asaph's till the summer of 1776. Returning to Virginia he embarked on a privateering enterprise, was captured, and spent a year in Dartmouth prison, England. Having effected an escape to France, Franklin aided him to return to America, where he married Jane Buchanan, a niece of Colonel Preston, and in 1779 set out for his final emigration to Kentucky. There he built a station on Beargrass Creek, but was shot and mortally wounded by the Indians in 1783. His son John became governor of Virginia."

Colonel George Washington had become greatly impressed with the future value of the lands on the lower Kanawha and in Kentucky. Very largely by his work and influence the government of Virginia had issued large grants to the colonial officers and soldiers who had served in the French and Indian War. Washington was anxious to secure patents for some 200,000 acres for himself and his fellow-officers and soldiers. He had been intimately associated with Colonel William Preston during the French and Indian War, and had great confidence in Preston's business integrity and sagacity. This induced the future "Father of his Country", and a number of other distinguished Virginians who were associated with him, to place the matter of locating their grants in the hands of Colonel Preston. At that time John Floyd was living at Colonel Preston's and was both deputy surveyor and deputy sheriff of Fincastle County; and he was selected to conduct a surveying party to Kentucky.

On the 9th of April, 1774, Floyd started on his surveying expedition, with eight men as his companions, whom he had collected together at Smithfield, the home of Colonel Preston, which was situated a short distance west of the present town of Blacksburg. One of the party, Thomas Hanson, kept a journal, in which he entered many interesting incidents connected with the expedition; but which, on account of its length, cannot be reproduced in its entirety in this volume. In the first entry Hanson says:

"We left Col. Wm. Preston's in Fincastle County at one o'clock in high spirits, escorted by the Coln. three miles, eight of us being in company, viz Mr. John Floyd assistant surveyor, Mr. Douglas, Mr. Hite, Mr. Dandridge, Thos. Hanson James Nocks (Knox)

Roderick McCra & Mordecai Batson. We traveled fifteen miles to John McGuffins at Sinking Creek."

Floyd's party, evidently, intended to follow practically the same route the Shawnees pursued in 1755, when they took Mrs. Ingles and the other captives from Draper's Meadows to the Indian towns in Ohio. They overtook Hancock Taylor, assistant surveyor, and his company of seven men on their sixth day out. On the eighth day they passed the Burning Spring, which was situated about fifteen miles above the present Charleston, West Virginia. This spring was then a pool of water, through which natural gas forced its way and kept burning, when ignited, over the surface of the water.

On the 17th day of April the company, then seventeen men, came upon Major John Field and his party of explorers, some nine or ten miles below the mouth of Elk Creek. Hanson says Major Field and his people "informed us, that the Indians had placed themselves on both sides of the Ohio, and that they intended war."

The 19th of April, Floyd and his party saw Thomas Hogg, who was improving a river bottom for cultivation, and Hanson recorded in his journal: "Mr. Hogg confirmed the news we had of the Indians. He says there were 13 People who intended to settle on the Ohio, and the Indians came upon them and a battle ensued. The white people killed 3 Indians (imagined to be chiefs) and then fled. This caused the Indians to hold a council & they are determined to kill the Virginians and rob the Pennsylvanians."

Regardless of the warnings of Colonel Field and Mr. Hogg, the fearless young surveyor and his resolute companions proceeded as rapidly as possible to the mouth of the Kanawha. When they arrived at the point, which in a few months was to be made the scene of the bloodiest battle that had yet taken place between the white men and the Indians, Hanson says in his journal: "At our arrival we found 26 people there on different designs—some to cultivate land, others to attend the surveyors. They confirm the same story of the Indians. * * * Mr. Floyd and the other Surveyors were received with great joy by the people here."

After resting a day at the place, which now bears the historic name of Point Pleasant, the surveying party divided into two groups and proceeded down the Ohio River. In a few days they reached Kentucky, where they again received from hunters and explorers additional warnings of the threatened outbreak of the Indians; and Hanson notes that "the alarm before mentioned occasioned 4 to

return back, viz Mr. Dandridge, Taylor, Holloway & Waggoner."
The remainder of the company, then thirty-three in number, traveled
on down the Ohio for several days until they arrived at a point
opposite the mouth of the Sciota River. This was on Saturday, the
30th of April, and as to what was done on May 1st, the following
day, Hanson relates: "It being Sunday we took our rest, and looked
at an old Fort we found about 4 or 500 hundred yards from the
Banks of the River. It is a square Figure, each side 300 Paces long.
It has 4 gates and Sally Ports, and it is so antient, that the Indians
cannot tell when it was built, or by whome. There has been an
Indian Town there formerly & there is some remains of it to this
Day."

Thwaites undertakes to account for this strange ruin, which
Hanson calls a Fort, by saying that George Croghan, a Pennsylvania
trader, had, some twenty years previously, built a stone trading
house in the locality where Floyd's party saw the ruin. Hanson's
description of its dimensions must be greatly exaggregated, or
Thwaites' theory of its origin is unreasonable.

On the 2nd day of May, Floyd and his companion surveyors
began their surveying in Kentucky. The first survey they made was
a boundary of four or five hundred acres in the name of Patrick
Henry, which included the old Fort and the abandoned Indian town.
It was the town from which Mrs. Mary Ingles made her escape
from the Indians in 1755. Floyd and his company then went
actively to work, making surveys of the best lands in different localities, and continued this work until Daniel Boone and Michael Stoner,
messengers sent out by Captain Russell, reached and informed them
that the Indians had commenced hostilities. Thereupon, Floyd, and
the men who were with him, started on a hasty march to the Clinch
Valley settlements, while Boone and Stoner went on to give warning to Taylor and others who had separated from Floyd's surveying party.

The Floyd surveying expedition was an incident that very
greatly affected the welfare of the inhabitants of the Clinch Valley;
and for that reason I have given it extended notice. It was one of
the certain contributing causes that provoked the Indians to commence hostile attacks in 1774 upon the settlers in the Alleghany
regions—all the way from Pennsylvania to the Cumberland Mountains—and it involved the Tazewell pioneers in a frightful struggle
with the Shawnees, that did not terminate until several years after
the Revolutionary War was concluded.

In the spring of 1774 the Virginians were engaged in two very bitter quarrels, one with the Pennsylvanians over the boundary line between the two provinces, and the other with the Indians in Ohio over the territory south of the Ohio River. The Virginians were determined to take actual possession of the uninhabited lands in Kentucky and in the present West Virginia for establishing settlements, claiming to have acquired the right to do this under the treaty made with the Iroquois Indians. On the other hand, the Pennsylvanians did not wish to disturb the Indians in the possession of the disputed territory. The Pennsylvania traders had for a number of years held control of the trade with the Indians in the Ohio Valley, and had realized heavy profits therefrom; and they openly encouraged the red men to resist further encroachments upon their hunting grounds by the white men, no matter whether they were from Virginia or Pennsylvania.

John Floyd, wrote a letter to Colonel William Preston, dated, "Little Giandot, 26th April 1774," in which he related the following: "Last night Thos. Glen, Lawrence Ordered & William Nash came to our camp who were ordered off the River by a Party of Indians who only saw them across the River. The Shawnees took Darnell & 6 Others prisoners a few weeks ago & held a Council Over them three Days; after which they took everything they had & sent them off: telling them at the same time it was the directions from the Superintendent Geo. Crohon (Croghan) to kill all the Virginians they could find on the River & rob & whip the Pennsylvanians. This they told them in English."

The Virginians were greatly angered by the conduct of such scoundrels as Croghan; and accused the Pennsylvania traders of not only inciting the Indians to commit brutal outrages upon the whites, but charged them with supplying the savages with guns and ammunition to be used in their plundering and murderous forays against the border settlements. But the best element of the backwoodsmen, including the Clinch Valley pioneers, were reluctant to engage in war with the Indians, knowing that a very large percentage of the much-wronged natives were still friendly to the whites and wanted to preserve peaceful relations with them. Availing themselves of several acts of violence and thievery perpetrated by a few of the vicious red men, certain brutal and disorderly white men began to murder, without provocation, innocent men and women of the red race.

A few days after John Floyd made his voyage down the Ohio River from the mouth of the Kanawha, two cruel butcheries of friendly Indians occurred in the Upper Ohio Valley. These acts were so inhuman that even the friendly Indians became frenzied, and war was ushered in. As previously stated, there was an acrimonious controversy going on between the Virginians and the Pennsylvanians over the boundry line. Virginia was claiming title to the country about Pittsburg and the entire Susquehana Valley; and a large number of the Pennsylvania mountaineers were supporting the claims of the Virginia Government. Lord Dunmore, then governor, appointed Dr. John Connolly, a native of Lancaster County, Pennsylvania, to act as agent for Virginia in the boundary dispute. Connolly was a fiery-tempered and rash man; and was not unwilling to bring about strife between the men of Virginia and Pennsylvania, and precipitate war with the Ohio Indians. On April 15th, 1774, three traders in the employ of a man named Butler were traveling in a canoe about fifty miles below Pittsburg when they were attacked and robbed by a band of outlaw Cherokees. John Floyd in his letter to Colonel Preston, written at "Little Giandot" on the 26th of April, thus refers to the incident: "The whites & Indians the 15th Instant had a skirmish at the mouth of Beaver Creek 45 miles below Pittsburg. One white man killed, another wounded & One other yet missing the Wounded man got into Fort Pitt where Dr. Wood Dressed his Wounds. this I have from the second hand & I think may be depended on."

Immediately following this act of violence, Connolly issued an open letter to the white men on the frontier, ordering them to make strong resistance to all attacks made by the Indians, and informing the backwoodsmen that the Shawnees had become hostile. This circular letter was construed by the more desperate white men on the border to be an invitation to make attacks upon the Indians. In fact the letter was interpreted by the white settlers to be a declaration of war against the Shawnees and their allies of the other Ohio tribes; and Roosevelt says: "As soon as they received Connolly's letter they proceeded to declare war in the regular Indian style, calling a council, planting the war-post, and going through other savage ceremonies, and eagerly waited for a chance to attack their foes."

Captain Michael Cresap was then near Wheeling with a company of hunters and scouts, and with them engaged in the savage ceremonies described by Roosevelt. Butler, the trader, whose men had been robbed and killed by the Cherokees, sent two friendly Shawnees in a canoe to the mouth of Beaver Creek to try to recover some of the furs of which he had been robbed by the Cherokees. These two friendly Shawnees were ambushed, and killed, and scalped, by Captain Cresap and his men, on the 27th, of April, near Captina. The better class of the frontiersmen made earnest protest against the outrageous act, but Cresap and his brutal band were proud of their crime. The next day Cresap and his followers made an attack upon a party of Shawnees who were returning from a trading expedition to Pittsburg, and killed one and wounded two of the Indians. One of Cresap's men was also wounded. Among the men who were with Cresap when these outrages were committed was George Rodgers Clark, then twenty-one years old, and who a few years later became famous as an explorer and leader of the military expeditions that won the great Northwestern territory for Virginia.

Cresap's dastardly acts were followed in a few days by the commission of a crime against friendly Indians that was more revolting than anything that had previously occurred on the border. It happened on the 30th of April, three days after the killing of the Shawnees by Cresap; and among the victims were a brother and sister of Logan, the great Mingo chief, who had been a staunch friend of the whites. The scene of the massacre was near the mouth of Yellow Creek, on the east side of the Ohio River, and at the house of a man named Baker. Lord Dunmore, in his report to the Earl of Dartmouth, secretary of state for the colonies, made on the 24th of December, 1774, gave the following account of the deplorable incident:

"A party of Indians, with their women, happening to encamp on the side of the Ohio opposite to the house of one Baker, who, together with a man of the name of Gratehouse, called to, and invited the Indians to come over and drink with them; two men and as many women came accordingly, and were, at first, well received, but Baker and Gratehouse, who by this time had collected other People, contrived to entoxicate the Indians, and they then Murdered them. Soon after two more came over from the Indian Party in search of their Companions, and these met with the same fate. The remainder of the Indian Party growing uneasy at not seeing their friends return, five of them got into a Canoe to go over to the house, but they were soon fired upon by Baker and Gratehouse, and two of the Indians killed and the other three wounded."

Previous to the killing of Logan's sister and brother, a council of the Indians had been held, at which many of the warriors urged that all the Ohio tribes should unite and resist the continued aggressions and intrusions of the "Long Knives," this name then being applied to the Virginians. Logan was present and took a conspicuous part in the council, and urgently insisted that peace should be maintained with the whites. He conceded that his people had been outrageously wronged by the pale faces, but he told the Indians they had also been guilty of many outrages upon their white foes. And he also asserted that the red men could accomplish nothing more than harrass and distress the border settlers; and, that, resenting such acts, the Virginians would come in great numbers and drive the Indians from Ohio. He was an orator, his oratory prevailed, and the hatchet for the time being was buried; but the Yellow Creek massacre turned Logan into a veritable fiend. When he was informed of the foul murder of his brother and sister, he raised his hatchet aloft and made a vow that he would not cease to wield it until he had taken ten white scalps for each one that had been torn from the heads of his kindred. Logan's sister was the Indian wife of Colonel John Gibson, who was born in Lancaster, Pennsylvania, and who had participated in the previous Indian wars. At the commencement of Pontiac's War Gibson was captured, but was saved from being burned at the stake by adoption by a squaw. He was released from captivity by Boquet's expedition in 1764, but continued to have intimate relations with the Indians, even taking Logan's sister for a wife. After Dunmore's War, he espoused the Revoluntionary cause and commanded the 13th Virginia regiment; and after the Revolution was ended he held several important civil offices in his State and in the Nation. His Indian wife had an infant child with her when she was murdered by Baker and Greathouse; and the child was sent to Pennsylvania, where its father was then residing as an Indian trader. What became of the child, history does not relate.

Immediately after the Yellow Creek tragedy the Mingos sent runners to the Shawnees, the Delawares, and other tribes, to inform them of the outrages perpetrated by Cresap and Greathouse; and urging a war of vengeance against the whites. Logan gathered a band of Mingos together and began to make bloody incursions into the settlements. His first scalping expedition was made into Pennsylvania and the Panhandle section of Virginia, now West Virginia; and he took thirteen scalps, six of which were taken from the heads of little children. He and his band were pursued by Captain Francis McClure with a company of Virginia militia. McClure was ambushed by the Indians, who killed and scalped him, and shot Lieutenant Samuel Kinkhead through the arm.

———

While the horrible calamities were happening along and on the Ohio River the inhabitants of the Clinch, Holston and Upper New River valleys were diligently occupied with preparation for the troubles they apprehended would soon come upon them.   Colonel William Preston, as county lieutenant, had command of all the military organizations of Fincastle County; and Major Arthur Campbell, as a subordinate of Colonel Preston, was in charge of all the militia and other military organizations on the west side of New River.   Preston was then living at Smithfield, his home, just west of Blacksburg; and Campbell was living at Royal Oak, just east of the present Marion, Virginia.   Both of these men were eminently fitted for the positions they were called upon to fill, and had acquired much experience with the habits and methods of the Indians in war and in peace.   This was fully proven by the successful manner in which they dicharged their duties in the war that was then imminent with the Indians.   They had to organize the inhabitants of Fincastle County into military bodies, and establish a line of defence reaching from New River, on through the Clinch and Powell's valleys, to Cumberland Gap, on the northwest side of the county; and from Cumberland Gap to the present North Carolina line on the southwest border.   Fortunately the men who were to perform military service, as volunteers or drafted men, were all of the pioneer type, trained hunters and woodsmen, brave and strong, and ready to do or die for the protection of their homes and families.   Of these splendid men none were braver or more efficient than the Tazewell pioneers.

The Ohio Indians, chiefly the Shawnees, made urgent appeals to the Cherokees in North Carolina and Georgia to unite with them in a vigorous war against the whites; and it required very skillful management on the part of Major Campbell of the Holston, and leading men of the Watauga settlements to prevent the Cherokees from entering the war.   As it was, a few of the first outrages committed were by mixed bands of Shawnees and Cherokees, the most notable being the murder of the three young men, Boone and Russell and Drake, in Powell's Valley, in 1773.

It was the belief of all the men of military experience, especially of those who had fought the Indians, that, if the Shawnees invaded Fincastle County with any considerable force, they would come from their towns in Ohio by way of Big Sandy River and its tributaries.

This would be the most direct route, and the one where the savages would encounter no resistance until they reached the Clinch Valley. If they did come the Sandy River route, they would travel up Tug River, or the Dry Fork of Tug, or up the Louisa River; and by following either one of these three streams to their source, they would enter the Clinch Valley on territory now embraced in Tazewell County. For this reason the military authorities of Fincastle County were extremely anxious to make the line of defence in Tazewell County as strong as possible. The Tazewell pioneers had the work pretty well done before the conflict with the Indians began.

The white cross shows the location of William Wynne's fort. The beautiful home of Mr. and Mrs. Geo. A. Martin is shown just east of the white cross.

There were three substantial forts already erected on the headwaters of the Clinch. Thomas Witten's fort at the Crab Orchard, Rees Bowen's at Maiden Spring, and William Wynne's at Locust Hill.

Great excitement, and in some instances consternation, prevailed in all the settlements west of New River. Colonel Preston became deeply concerned about John Floyd's surveying party that was then actively at work in Kentucky; and sent a messenger to Captain Wiliam Russell, urging him to send scouts to warn Floyd and all the surveying parties of the impending danger; and to tell them to come home as quickly as possible.

Captain Russell, who was then at his fort at Castle's Woods, on Sunday, June 26th, wrote Colonel Preston: "I am Sensible good Sir of your Uncommon concern for the Security of Capt. Floyd and the Gentlemen with him, and I sincerely Sympathise with you, lest they should fall a Prey, to such Inhuman, Blood thirsty Devils, as I have so lately suffered by; but may God of his Infinite Mercy, Shield him, and Company, from the present impending Danger, and could we (thro' Providence) be a means of preserving such Valuable Members, by sending out Scouts, such a procedure would Undoutedly be, of the most lasting, and secret Satisfaction to us; and the Country in general. I have engaged to start on the occasion, two of the best Hands I think of, Danl. Boone, and Michl. Stoner; who have Engaged to search the Country, as low as the falls, and to return by way of Gaspers Lick, on Cumberland, and through Cumberland Gap. So that by the assiduity of these men, if it is not too late, I hope the Gentlemen will be apprised of the eminent Danger they are Daily in."

It is needless to say that the two fearless pioneer patriots, Boone and Stoner, lost no time in starting on their rescue mission. They journeyed into the wilderness regions of Kentucky, with which they were already pretty familiar. At Harrodsburg they came upon Colonel James Harrod and thirty men, who were busily engaged in building a village of cabins. This was in July; and on the 14th of the preceding May, according to a note in Hanson's journal, John Floyd and his surveying party had visited Colonel Harrod and his party at this same place. Boone and Stoner informed Harrod and his party of their danger and they made no delay in starting to the settlments east of the Cumberland Mountains. Then the two scouts started out to find Floyd, and came upon another surveying party at Fontaincbleau. After warning them, Boone and Stoner proceeded to the Kentucky River, where they found Floyd, and he started immediately for the settlements in the Clinch Valley. Arriving at Captain Russell's fort and finding that Russell was preparing, with his company, to join the militiary expedition to Point Pleasant, Floyd proceeded to Colonel Preston's home at Smithfield, reaching that place on the 13th of August, 1774. Boone and Stoner proceeded to the falls of the Ohio River, where they found another company of surveyors to whom they gave warning, and then started on the return trip to the Clinch Valley. They arrived safely at Captain Russell's, having traveled eight hundred miles in sixty-one days on foot. There were more than a dozen men, of other surveying parties, that the scouts did not find, and they had to be left to their fate. Two of these, Hancock Taylor and James Strother, were killed by the Indians while they were traveling in a canoe. It is presumed that the others escaped, as Captain Russell reported to Colonel Preston that "John Green and three others of Mr. Taylor's Company have Arrived at Clinch." Two of these were John Bell and Abraham Hempinstall; the other man's name has not been preserved.

CHAPTER VIII.

FRONTIERS OF FINCASTLE COUNTY INVADED BY INDIANS.

In the spring of 1774 Captain William Russell went to Williamsburg to acquaint Governor Dunmore with the serious condition of affairs on the borders of Fincastle County; and he returned with instructions from the governor, directed to Colonel Preston and the other officers of the county, to take proper steps for protecting the borders, and to urge the inhabitants not to abandon their homes on the frontiers.

On the 25th of June, 1774, a council of the militia officers of Fincastle County was held at the county seat, the Lead Mines, and at this council it was determined that Lieutenant Colonel Christian should march with several companies of militia to the settlements on Clinch River, and from thence send out ranging parties to discover and attack any parties of Indians that might possibly come up Sandy River to distress the settlers on the Clinch. This action was taken in compliance with orders from Governor Dunmore, who seemed anxious to protect the inhabitants of the Holston and Clinch valleys from incursions by the Cherokees and Shawnees. In pursuance of this plan of action, Colonel Preston, who was then at Fort Chiswell, in the present Wythe County, on June 27th 1774, sent the following instructions to Colonel William Christian:

"I have given Orders to six Captains to raise twenty men out of each of their Companys either as Volunteers or by Draught; which with what men can be engag'd from other companies, will make up the party One Hundred & fifty men besides Officers.

"You are to take the Command of this party, Captains Crockett & Campbell will go with you & each will have fifty men beside the Necessary Officers, the remaining fifty will be under your Immediate Command as a Company, and as One subaltern will be enough I am in hopes Ensign William Buchanan will answer that purpose.

"You will endeavor to procure ammunition and Provisions for this service. I expect a good many of the soldiers will take their Horses to carry the provisions, for which they ought to be made an allowance, this allowance & the value of the provisions or what ever else may be necessary for this Service you will please to have Settled by two honest men on Oath. *   *   *   *

"I have appointed the Soldiers to meet you at the Town House on Holston early next week, from whence you are to begin your march to Clinch & from thence over Cumberland Mountain by any Gap or pass you think proper that Leades to the head branches of the Kentucky & there Range together or in separate parties & at such places as you judge most likely to discover and repulse the Enemy on their Approach to our Settlements. It is believed there is a large party of Cherokees on their way to or from the Shawnees Towns, if you should fall in with this Company & know them I must leave it to your own Prudence in what manner to treat them, tho it is generally Said that these Indians are about to Join our Enemies, yet as this Report is not reduced to a Certainty, I cannot give any Particular orders herein. You will Probably be able to Judge by the Manner of their approach or rather Circumstances that cannot now be foreseen, what Indians they are & then you will act Accordingly, but upon the whole I would earnestly Recommend the utmost caution and Discretion in this very nice & important part of your duty. Should this party of Cherokees, which is generally said to be about Seventy in number, come in a Hostile manner there is no doubt but they will be Accompanyd by a number of Shawnees or rather Enemy Indians which may render them formidable to your party.

"I would therefore Recommend your keeping out some active men on the right & left, in the front & Rear even to the distance of a mile on Your march and at Camp to keep out a number of Centinals, to prevent a Surprize which is too often attended with fatal Consequences, this above all things ought ever to be Guarded against, nor Should this Part of the duty be Neglected or Relaxed on any occasion whatsoever."

Colonel Preston then recommended that Colonel Christian should consult his officers in connection with important matters connected with the expedition; and expressed the hope that the officers, who were required and commanded to obey their commanding officer, would be alert and obedient in the performance of duty. He also directed that the officers should keep good order and discipline in their companies, and "be unanimous and Friendly amongst themselves that every Intention of Sending out the Party may be fully answered." Colonel Preston closed these orders with the following stirring appeal to the patriotism and military spirit of the officers and men of the expedition:

"As it is expected that you will have none but choice officers & men on this little Expedition: therefore the Eyes of the Country will be upon you: So that I have no doubt but every person in his station will exert himself to answer the wishes & expectations of his Country, and serve it as much as in his power lies.

"That Heaven may give you Success & Safety it is the Sincere wish

  of Sir your most Humble Servant

      Wm. Preston.

Colo. William Christian"

These military orders, issued by the county lieutenant of Fincastle County, will be read with interest, no doubt, by all persons who are descendants of the pioneer settlers of Tazewell County; and should be interesting to those who care to acquaint themselves with its early history. It will be observed that the first military expedition sent to the Clinch Valley, in the first war in which its inhabitants were to take an active part, was ordered to march to the lower sections of the Valley, though the three principal passes used by the Indians when they came by the way of the Sandy Valley were at the headwaters of the Louisa, the Dry Fork, and Tug River. All of these passes were in territory that was subsequently embraced in Tazewell County. This indicates that the inhabitants of the Lower Clinch Valley were more seriously threatened, or were more alarmed than the people on the headwaters of the Clinch, or that they were not as well prepared to resist savage invasions as were our pioneer ancestors.

The exhortation of Colonel Preston to the officers, to be "unanimous and friendly among themselves," warrants the belief that jealousies and rivalries had previously existed, or were then being cultivated, among the officers connected with the expedition. In fact, such a feeling had been manifested by and between certain of the officers from the Holston Valley, and possibly by some of those from the New River and Reed Creek sections. There was nothing of this kind shown among the Tazewell pioneers. None of them were concerned about holding official positions. Their chief concern was the protection of the homes they had struggled to erect in the wilderness country. In a letter written by Captain Russell to Colonel Preston after the arrival of the expedition at Castle's Woods, he showed some feeling, because he thought he and others in the

T.H.—18

Clinch Valley had not received proper consideration in being appointed to commands and regularly enlisted in the service. He said: "I am sorry to find Sir, I can't be Indulged to serve my Country with a Captns Command, as early as others; who are but new Hands." In another part of the letter he said: "Was I to Keep a Commission, in hopes of Benefiting my Country, or selfe, and my hopes was, from a set of Gentlemen; who, were all desireous to serve as well as my selfe; I am assured against such powerful Connexions, as are upon the Holston, and New River Waters, It wood be useless for me to mention one Word about it."

Captain Russell was not much of a speller, and he was ill-versed in the art of punctuation and the proper use of capital letters; but he knew how to politely rebuke what he believed to be favoritism and nepotism. Possibly he had been wrought to this temper by remembrance of the manner in which the county offices had been distributed when the county of Fincastle was organized. Certain families "upon the Holston and the New River Waters" were apportioned all the offices of honor and profit; and Colonel Preston was, at the time Russell wrote him, county lieutenant through appointment by the governor, and both sheriff and surveyor of Fincastle County by election by the county court, of which court he was also a member. In those days certain families in Virginia, under a royal government, were potential in most of the counties, and such has been the case in nearly all the counties of the Commonwealth since a republican form of government was established in 1776. This was a very natural condition, and it always obtains where organized society is found. The organization of what we call civil government has ever been brought about by the energy and zeal of a few dominating spirits, who necessarily become self-constituted leaders of the government, or are made such by the people. This was the case when our Federal and State governments were formed, and the records show that it was the same when the great county of Tazewell was organized as a distinct civil and military community.

The first week in July, 1774, in obedience to orders, Colonel Christian assembled his command of three companies, of fifty men each, besides officers, at Town House. At this point lived Captain James Thompson, who was a grandson of Colonel James Patton. Thompson had a small private fort and the name of his home, "Town House," was given because it had been selected by Colonel

Patton as a suitable place for a settlement or town, just as he had
selected Draper's Meadows for such a purpose. Captain William
Campbell was in command of one of the companies, Captain Walter
Crockett of another, and Colonel Christian, in compliance with
orders, took charge of the third company. Campbell then lived at
Aspinvale, the present Seven Mile Ford, and Crockett lived on the
headwaters of the South Fork of Holston River, both living within
the limits of the present Smyth County.

Soon after commencing his march from Town House for the
Clinch, Colonel Christian deemed it expedient to make a departure
from the specific orders of Colonel Preston to march with all his
force "to the Clinch and from thence over Cumberland Mountain
* * * to the head branches of the Kentucky." From a point
somewhere near Abingdon, on the 9th of July, Christian sent a
messenger, with a written report of the movements of his command,
to Colonel Preston. Among the important matters reported, the
following is found:

"On Thursday last Mr. Doack's letter to Crockett was shown
to me at Cedar Creek about 9 miles on this Side of Stalnakers. I
thought it best to send Crockett off with 40 men to the head of Sandy
creek, that the reed creek and head of Holston people might know
where to Send to him in case any attack should be made, that he
might waylay or follow the enemy. * * * Yesterday I heard a
report that 50 Indians were seen at Sandy creek but as it came thro
several hands it may not be true."

There were several causes for this change in the disposition of
the men under his command. The day previous, the 8th of July,
Captain Dan Smith, who had a fort at Elk Garden, and who had
charge of the line of defence in the Upper Clinch Valley, wrote to
Colonel Preston, reporting an alarming condition at the head of the
north fork of Clinch and Bluestone. He said: "The constant
Rumor of the Indians being just ready to fall on the Inhabitants
hath scared away almost the whole settlement at the head of the
north fork of Clinch and Bluestone. I am sorry to find that the
people are so scary and that there are so many propagators of false
reports in the country."

Captain Smith then reported that the false rumors were causing
"timorous people to run away." He said: "This the people at the
head of the river did before I got the least notice of their intention
to start. The men have said they will return again after carrying

their wives and children to a place of safety; If they do 'twill be more than I expect. They alledge as an excuse for their going away that there was no Scout down Sandy Creek." Captain Smith admitted the charge was true that there had been no scout down Sandy Creek, but tried to place the responsibility for this neglect upon James Maxwell, to whom he said he had entrusted the duty. Smith charged that, instead of looking after the matter, James Maxwell had "gone down to Botetourt to see his family,—and whose return is not expected shortly;" and that James Maxwell had left the scouting matter in the hands of his brother, Thomas Maxwell. It seems that James Maxwell had notified Smith of the arrangement with his brother and that Smith had acquiesced, for he further reported to Colonel Preston about James Maxwell's non-performance of duty:

"As he lived most convenient to the head of Sandy Creek I consulted him with regard to scouts that should go down that water course. His brother Thomas was the one pitched upon. On their return from the first trip, altho they brought no accounts of Indians, As your letter of the 20th ult. came to hand about that time I sent two scouts down a river called Louisa, and at the recommendation of Mr. Th. Maxwell appointed one, Israel Harmon to act with him down Sandy Creek, for it was natural for me, as I reposed much confidence in Mr. James Maxwell to pay regard to what his Brother Thomas advised. I am now to inform you that Mr. Thomas Maxwell proved Highly unworthy the confidence I reposed in him, so much so that I think his behaviour requires that he should be called to account at the next court martial, as I've just been informed there really is a militia law yet subsisting; for instead of going down Sandy Creek as I strictly charged him to do he went to the head of the river, reported the danger they were in, and assisted Jacob Harmon to move into the New River settlement."

There is no doubt but that Captain Dan Smtih entirely misunderstood the character and quality of the men he was censuring so bitterly, and thoroughly misapprehended their real worth. They had no garrisoned fort at hand, as Captain Smith had at Elk Garden, in which they could easily place their wives and children for safety; and they were living along one of the most frequented and most dangerous trails the Indians used when they made hostile visits to the settlements. The pioneer Maxwells and Harmans were as brave and true as any of the splendid men who were of the first settlers in the Clinch Valley. At least, one of them, the one Smith most severely condemned, Thomas Maxwell, by his future actions heroically disproved the aspersions Smith cast upon his character. Smith was reputed to be a very courageous man; and it may be that he was so fearless that caution and prudence in others to him had the appearance of cowardice. But if Smith ever came in contact with hostile Indians, there is nothing of record to show it.

Thomas Maxwell was no "timorous" man. Dressed in hunting shirt, with tomahawk and scalping knife in belt; and with his trusty mountain rifle on his shoulder, he marched to and fought at King's Mountain. After the battle at that place, which was fought on the 7th of October, 1780, Thomas Maxwell settled on the North Fork of Holston River, near Broad Ford, in the present Smyth County. In the spring of 1781, a small band of Shawnee Indians made an inroad into Burke's Garden and made the wife and children of Thomas Ingles captives. Ingles went immediately to the North Fork of Holston, where he found Captain Thomas Maxwell engaged in drilling a squad of fourteen militia. Maxwell and his men went with Ingles to Burke's Garden, and from that place trailed the Indians until they overtook them on Tug River. In the attack that was made to rescue the captives Captain Maxwell was the only one of the white men killed. The pass where the encounter took place has ever since been called Maxwell's Gap, where the "timorous" man rests in a heroe's grave.

In this letter to Colonel Preston, wherein Smith accuses the Maxwells and other settlers "at the head of the north fork of Clinch and Bluestone" with cowardice and neglect of duty, he makes confession that his own men, in the Elk Garden settlement, were alarmed and asks that a company of soldiers be sent there to relieve their fears. He says: "As the spirits of the men that are yet left in my company Are not in very high flow, I do think that a Company of men stationed on the river if there was not over 20 would greatly encourage the settlers, if they did nothing but Assist to build forts in this busy time of laying by Corn. I really shall be greatly pleased if you should be of the same Opinion." Captain Smith was a little inconsistent, to say the least, in rebuking the Maxwells and Harmans for showing anxiety for the safety of their families, and expressing no condemnation for the timid settlers of his own community.

Subsequent events proved that the pass at the head of Sandy Creek was the most important and dangerous one on the frontier west of New River; and that the Maxwells and Harmans had not been mistaken when they decided it was too dangerous to let their families remain in its vicinity. Consternation prevailed among the inhabitants in Rich Valley, on Walker's Creek, at the head of the Middle Fork of Holston and in the Reed Creek Valley. Captain Robert Doack, who was an officer in the Fincastle militia, and who was then living in the neighborhood of old Mt. Airy, in the present Wythe County, had been ordered to draft a company of men and march them to the heads of Sandy Creek and Clinch. On the 12th of July, 1774, four days after the letter was written by Captain Smith reporting the supposed delinquencies of the Maxwells and Harmans, Captain Doack addressed a letter to Colonel Preston, from which the following is quoted:

"Sir—Agreeable to your Order I Drafted men & was in Readiness to March to the heads of Sandy Creek & Clinch, When some tracts were seen in this neighbourhood supposed to be Indians which Colo. Christian hearing sent Capt. Crockett to where I was, Ordered & Directed me to range near the Inhabitants. We were informd, that sixteen Indians were seen on Walkers Creek which I went down with 25 men but not finding any Signs & hearing the News Contradicted Dischargd them. The people were all in Garison from Fort Chiswell to the Head of Holston & in great Confusion. They are fled from the Rich Valley & Walkers Creek. Some are Building forts they have Began to build at my Father's, James Davis', & Gasper Kinders. I think they are not strong enough for three forts but might do for two. If you thought proper to Order that a Sergeant Command might be Stationed at each of these places on Mischief being Done Or at any two of them I think it would Keep this part of the Country from leaving it & would enable them to save their Crops this I humbly Conceive would be a protection & encouragement & on an alarm when people fled to the forts with their Familys those men would always be Ready to follow the Enemy."

With such conditions of alarm and confusion existing in the more populous settlements of the Holston and Reed Creek valleys, because of the apprehension of Indian raiding parties by way of the Sandy Creek passes, it was the duty of the men on the extreme frontier to remove their families to places of assured safety. At this time there was no reported disquietude or fear in the localities where the Tazewell pioneers had grouped themselves in communities and built forts. The men in the neighborhoods where the Wynne, the Witten and the Bowen forts were located were not calling for help or protection. The Harmans, Peerys, Wynnes, Taylors, Evans' and other settlers in the vicinity of Wynne's fort had confidence in their ability to meet and defeat any Indian bands that came to their neighborhood; the Wittens, Greenups, Peerys, Marrs', and the Cecils, grouped near Wittens fort; and the Bowens, Wards, Martins, Thompsons, and others about Maiden Spring, seem to have been inspired with the same confidence.

In compliance with the orders which Colonel Preston had given him, Colonel Christian marched promptly, with ninety men, to Russell's fort on the Clinch, at Castle's Woods. From that place, on the 12th of July, 1774, he wrote Colonel Preston that he thought it his duty to send Captain Walter Crockett and his company "to cover the inhabitants that lie exposed to Sandy Creek Pass." He further suggested that it was the opinion of the officers of his command that an expedition of 150 or 200 men should be sent to the Ohio, at the mouth of the Scioto, and thence on forty-five miles to destroy the "Shawnese Town."

On the 12th of July, the same day that Colonel Christian wrote to Colonel Preston suggesting that an expedition should be sent to the Shawnee towns in Ohio, Governor Dunmore forwarded an order to Colonel Andrew Lewis, directing him to assemble a force of men from Botetourt, Fincastle and other counties, to go on an expedition to the Ohio Valley for the purpose of bringing the Indians into subjection. Colonel Lewis forwarded Dunmore's order to Colonel Preston, accompanying it with a letter in which he said, in part: "The governor from what he wrote us has taken it for granted that we would fit out an Expedition & has acted accordingly. I make no doubt but he will be as much surprised at our backwardness, as he may call it, as we are at ye precipetet steps in ye other quarter. Dont fail to come and let us do something. I would as matters stand use great risque rather than a miscarrage should happen." Colonel Lewis ordered Preston, as county lieutenant of Fincastle, to enlist two hundred and fifty men, or more, if they could possibly be raised, to go on the expedition. This of course made an end of Christian's proposition for an expedition to the mouth of the Scioto River; and immediate steps were taken to comply with the orders of Governor Dunmore. Colonel Preston on the 20th of July, 1774,

sent by special messenger from his home at Smithfield, a circular
letter to Colonel Christian, in which he said:

"Inclosed you have a Copy of Lord Dunmore's Letter to Colo.
Lewis of the 12th Instant, In Consequence of which, the Colo. has
Called upon me to Attend on the Expedition, with at least, two hundred & fifty Men, or more if they can Possibly be raised; This
Demand if Possible must be Complyed with, as it is not Altogether
our Quota; & indeed it appears reasonable, we should turn out
cheerfully On the present Occasion in Defence of our Lives and
Properties which have been so long exposed to the savages. * * *
We may Perhaps never have so fair an Opportunity of reducing our
old Inveterate Enemies to Reason, if this should by any means be
neglected.   The Earl of Dunmore is deeply ingaged in it.   The
House of Burgesses will without all Doubt enable his Lordship to
reward every Volunteer in a handsome manner, over and above his
Pay; as the plunder of the County will be valuable, & it is said
the Shawnees have a great stock of Horses.   Besides it will be the
only method of settling a lasting Peace with the Indian Tribes
Around us, who on former Occasions have been Urged by the Shawnees to engage in a War with Virginia.   This useless People may
now at last be Obliged to abandon their Country, their towns may
be plundered and burned, their cornfields destroyed; & they distressed in such a manner as will prevent them from giving us any
future Trouble; Therefore I hope the men will Readily & cheerfully
engage in the Expedition as They will not only be conducted by
their own Officers but they will be Assisted by a great number of
Officers & soldiers raised behind the Mountains, whose Bravery they
cannot be Doubtful of, while they Act from the same Motive of Self
Defence."

This circular letter must be authentic, as it was one of the Preston papers turned over to Lyman C. Draper by the descendants of
Colonel William Preston; and which is now possessed and preserved
by the Wisconsin Historical Society as a valuable and precious
document.   The spirit of the paper is not of a character that should
win the approval of the descendants of the pioneer settlers of Southwest Virginia.   It breathes too much of the spirit of the Celtic Rob
Roys and the Saxon Cederics, who thought it not immoral to plunder
and kill their weaker neighbors.   The paper also shows that Colonel
Preston and, possibly, a number of the Trans-Alleghany pioneers,

still held to the idea that there were no good Indians; and were in
sympathy with the policy, which started at Jamestown, of extermi-
nating the aborigines. If the proposed unrighteous features of the
expedition induced any of our ancestors to accompany it, we should
not be proud of the fact. It was an invitation to go with an expedition to Ohio to drive the benighted aboriginal inhabitants from their
lands, to plunder and burn their homes, destroy their crops, and
massacre their women and children. Fortunately these cruel designs
were thwarted by the peace which was made with the Indians by
Lord Dunmore immediately after the battle of Point Pleasant was
won by the gallant Virginia mountaineers.

———

The year 1774 was a very eventful and trying one to the Tazewell pioneers. Though the population west of New River was
sparse and very much scattered, the inhabitants soon became intimately associated in making preparation to repel invasions of the
hostile Indians. Excitement was intense at a most important period
of the year, when the settlers were busily occupied in making and
saving their crops of grain, chiefly corn, upon which their families
were dependent for subsistence during the ensuing year. Small
scalping parties of Shawnees began to invade the regions along and
west of New River; and in making these incursions they showed a
strong disposition to use the passes at the headwaters of Sandy
River, all of which fronted on the Upper Clinch Valley in Tazewell
County.

In compliance with the orders of Colonel William Preston,
five companies were in process of enlistment and organization to
join the expedition of Colonel Andrew Lewis to Ohio. These companies were ultimately organized and marched under command of
Captains William Campbell, Evan Shelby, and Walter Crockett, of
the Holston Valley; Captain William Herbert of the Upper New
River Valley; and Captain William Russell of the Clinch Valley.
While these companies were being enlisted and assembled, a small
band of Shawnee Indians came up Tug River, crossed over to and
down Wolf Creek to New River, and went up the latter stream to
the homes of Philip Lybrook and John McGriff on the east side of
New River, just below the mouth of Sinking Creek, in the
present county of Giles. On Sunday, the 7th day of August, 1774,
they made an attack upon a group of children who were playing on

the bank of the river. Three of Lybrook's children one a sucking infant, a young woman by the name of Scott, and two little girls of Mrs. Snidow were killed; and Lybrook, who was at a small mill he had built near his home, was wounded in the arm. The children were scalped and mangled in a very cruel manner. McGriff shot and mortally wounded one of the Indians. Some years later the remains of the Indian were found under rocks at a cliff near the scene of the tragedy. Three small boys, Theophilus and Jacob Snidow and Thomas McGriff, were made captives and taken away by the Indians. On the following Wednesday night, while camping at Pipestem Knob, in the present Summers County, West Virginia, two of the boys, Jacob Snidow and Thomas McGriff, made a daring and successful escape. Judge Johnston, who gives a very interesting account of the tragic incident in his History of the New River Settlement, says: "Theophilus Snidow, the other captive boy, was carried by the Indians to their towns north of the Ohio, and when he had reached his manhood returned to his people, but in delicate health with pulmonary trouble from which he shortly died."

Colonel Preston had sent Major James Robertson, with a scouting party of twenty men to Culbertson's Bottom, now known as Crump's Bottom, in Summers County, West Virginia, to build a fort and give warning to the settlers on the river above. Robertson wrote to Colonel Preston on the 1st of August, 1774, reporting, in part, as follows: "About three hours ago John Draper came here with thirteen men, which makes our number 33." He then reported that he was keeping scouts out continually, and had seen no fresh signs of Indians for four or five days; but said: "as John Draper came down yesterday he surely seen the tracks of five or six Indians, he says, on Wolf Creek, and they made towards the settlements." This was evidently the same party that made the attack upon the Lybrooks and Snidows, as Colonel Preston reported to Lord Dunmore that there were but six Indians in the band that killed the Lybrook and Snidow children. The Indians had knowledge of the scouting station at Culbertson's and had adroitly avoided Robertson's scouts, by traveling up Tug, crossing over to Wolf Creek and reaching New River about twenty miles above where Robertson was stationed. On the 12th of August he again wrote Colonel Preston from Culbertson's, sayings: "This morning our scouts met with a couple of poor little boys between this and Blue Stone, one a son of John McGriff's, the other a son of Widow Snidows at Burks fort, that made their escapes from the Indians, last Tuesday night about midnight away up towards the Clover Bottoms on Blue Stone or between that and the lower war road on Blue Stone."

Robertson was very much impressed with the danger that threatened the inhabitants of the Upper New River settlements and of Reed Creek, on account of the ease with which the Indians could come up the Sandy route and slip between the outposts on New River and those on the headwaters of the Clinch. This caused him to communicate his fears to Colonel Preston as follows: "Unless you keep your own side of the mountain well guarded there them stragling little partys will do Abundance of Damage. Where People is gathered in forts there ought to be men under Pay Just Ready on any Occasion these Small partys passes Scouts and Companys without Possibly being Discovered."

Fearing that he might be censured for not discovering and driving back the scalping party that murdered the Lybrook and Snidow children, Robertson declared that if his own life and honour, and the lives of all his relations, and the lives of all his well wishers had been at stake he could have done no more than he did do to prevent the horrible catastrophe at Lybrook's. He saw that all the border settlements were greatly endangered, and knew the importance of strengthening the defences on the line from New River to Cumberland Gap. That he and his men were anxious for the safety of their own families, who lived in the Upper New River settlements, was shown by his writing Colonel Preston: "I suppose my helpless family is in great fear, and indeed not without reason."

Major Arthur Campbell, who was in charge of all the military forces and defences west of New River, was so solicitous for the safety of the settlements on the Clinch that, as soon as the news reached him of the Sinking Creek massacre, he sent express messengers to Captains Russell and Smith bearing duplicates of the following urgent orders:

"Royal-Oak Augt. 9, 1774

Dear Sir—I have this moment Received intelligence of several people being killed last Monday by the Indians on Sinking Creek about 10 miles from Colo. Prestons. This makes it necessary that we should be strictly on our guard lest some straggling party should visit us. Therefore endeavour without loss of time to get the inhabitants in your Company collected together in 2 or 3 convenient places for forts, and let them keep up strict and regular Duty until more men can be sent over to assist them which I will endeavor to have done with all possible speed. This alarm will retard the expedition at least a week, therefore all young men that chooses to do regular duty may be taken into pay. I expect an Express tomorrow from Colo. Preston after which you shall have further Instructions. Pray do everything in your power for the safety of the Inhabitants.

I am Dr. Sir, very sincerely yours

Arthur Campbell

On his Majestys service
To Captain Daniel Smith on Clinch."

It seems that Captains Russell and Smith proceeded without delay to execute the orders sent them by Major Campbell. On the 24th of August, two weeks after transmitting the said orders to Russell and Smith, Major Campbell notified Colonel Preston that he had received a petition from the inhabitants of the Clinch Valley requesting that they be regularly employed in the service and also asking that the number then on duty be enlarged. Campbell wrote Colonel Preston that he declined to grant the petition "without orders from you;" but reported: "I let the Gentlemen know, that the inhabitants that strictly did regular Duty might be continued on the Lists until a sufficient Number of Draughts might arrive to complete the Companys and then I would recommend it to the Officers to keep the best Woodsmen of ye Inhabitants in pay for the purpose of ranging in preference to any that might offer themselves from Holston or New River."

Major Campbell's apprehension that the Sinking Creek massacre would delay the march of the Lewis expedition to Ohio was well founded. The enlistment of the number of men called for from Fincastle County had been greatly retarded by jealousies and rivalries among the militia officers of the Holston Valley. These dissensions had given much trouble to both Major Campbell and Colonel Preston; and when they had about succeeded in getting the trouble under control the massacre of the Lybrook and Snidow children occurred. This horrible incident made many of the frontiersmen reluctant to go with the expedition and leave their families exposed to the scalping bands of Indians. The men of the Upper Clinch Valley had been doing much volunteer scouting and ranging service without compensation for such service, other than the protection of their own settlements, while the ranging parties sent out from the

New River and Holston settlements had been receiving pay for their service. The war which was on hand involved the protection and welfare of all the settlements west of New River; and the men of the Clinch Valley very justly held that they should be regularly employed in the service, with compensation, as were the men of the more populous settlements on the Holston and New River.

On the 16th of August, Captain William Russell, who had given his fort at Castle's Woods the name of "Fort Preston," wrote to Colonel Preston from that place, notifying him that he was ready and anxious to march with his company "to the appointed place of Rondezvous" for the Lewis expedition. Captain Russell also said in his letter to Colonel Preston: "I hope Sir you will think it absolutely necessary to have two Captains to Command on Clinch at this Critical season, that ought to be ranging, besides those in the Forts, as Constant Guards to the Inhabitants."

Captain Russell clearly saw that the passes at the heads of the several branches of Sandy River were not being properly guarded at a time which he pronounced a "critical season." And he suggested that Captain James Thompson, who had been appointed to command a company stationed at Fort Blackmore, in the present Scott County, should be transferred to a command "towards the head of the River." The anxiety of Captain Russell for the protection of the inhabitants at the head of the Clinch was so great that he made the following personal appeal to Colonel Preston: "Should I be granted a Command, and it be agreeable to you and Capt. Thompson, should be proud if it could be your pleasure to appoint him towards the head of the River, as that will give him a more Immediate opportunity of securing the Inhabitants about his Father's, and even his own."

Captain Thompson was a very near and dear kinsman of Colonel Preston. Thompson was the grandson of Colonel James Patton, and Colonel Preston was nephew of Patton. But this strong personal appeal to the county lieutenant of Fincastle County did not procure two Captains with companies for the head of the Clinch; and Captain Daniel Smith was retained in command of the upper stations in the Valley.

Colonel Preston surely must have believed that the pioneers had settled on the headwaters of the Clinch with a resolute purpose of remaining there; and that they would not only be able to take care of themselves, but would also afford a strong barrier against Indian incursions into the Holston and Reed Creek settlements. Captain Russell's letter of the 16th of August was well calculated to strengthen this conclusion in Preston's mind. When Russell gave the number he would take with him on the Ohio expedition he said: "There are about thirty that will certainly go with me; and Capt. Smith says Wm Bowen has four that will go with me." These four were, William Bowen and his two brothers, Reese and Moses, and David Ward; and the four made good by going and doing valiant service on the expedition. There were others from the Upper Clinch Valley who were at Point Pleasant, whose names will be mentioned in succeeding pages.

In the meantime Captain Daniel Smith proceeded to carry out the orders of Major Campbell to gather the inhabitants in the forts, and to enlist men regularly for the several stations in his charge. Lists of the garrisons at the Maiden Spring Fort and Thomas Witten's fort at the Crab Orchard were left among the papers of Colonel William Preston; and they are worthy of a place of honor in a history of Tazewell County. I copy them from Thwaites' Dunmore's War:

At The Maiden's Springs Station 26th. Augt 1774.

Mr. Robt. Brown, Sergeant till 23rd Sep^t then Joseph Cravens.

Henry Willis

Joseph Cravens

James MClehany discharged 19th. Oct. 55 days

James Cravens

John Jameson listed 29th Augt disch. 19th Octo 53 days

James Rogers

Thomas Brumly listed 22nd Augt disch. 19th Oct. 60 days

And^w Lammy listed 16th. Augt 4th Sep^t Saml. Fowler came in his room

John Flintham listed 14th. Augt. disch. 19th. Oct. 68 days

James Douglas M. S.

John Newland W. ⎫

Samuel Paxton W. ⎬ listed Sept 14th. discharged 22nd. 8 days

Philip Dutton W. ⎭

John Cravens 23rd. Sept. M. S.

Rees Bowen Aug. 26- Sept. 2

David Ward Aug. 26- Sept. 2

Robt. Cravens Nov. 1st. - Nov. 18

Rees Bowen and David Ward were discharged on the 2nd of Sept. so that they could go with Captain Russell on the expedition to Ohio; and Robt Cravens enlisted as a member of the Maiden Spring garrison after he returned from Ohio.

At The Upper Station
(This was Witten's Fort. — Auth.)

Mr. John Campbell Ensign

listed 15 Augt.
- Isaac Spratt ⎤ Sergeant 25th. Sept. went away
- George Dohorty ⎦ without leave
- Andw. Steel Oct. 18th disch 64 days
- John Hambleton disch 18th Oct. 64 days
- Alexr. Grant deserted 8th. Sept.

29th Augt.
- David Bustar (Bruster)
- Wm. Thompson

Edward Sharp 7th. Sept. listed. disch. 21st. 14 days

Michael Glaves. 6th. Sept. went away without leave 7th. Octr.

James Fullen 5th. Sept. disch. 21st. 16 days

James Edwards 5th. Sept. went away without leave 30th. Sept.

John Williams 7th. Sept. disch. 16th. 9 days

Thomas Potter 5th. Sept. went away without leave 7th. Oct. came back.

Levi Bishop 8th. Sept. Do Do 22d. Sept.

Robert Manford (Moffett) 8th. Sept.

Alexander Henderson 15th. Sept. went away 12th. Oct.

Francis Hambleton 15th. Sept. went out without leave 25th. Sept. came back

John Crafford 15th. Sept. discharged 24th. 10 days

Isiah Hambleton 15th. Sept. 22nd. Sept. went away without leave

Benjamin Rediford 15th Sept. 25th. Sept. Do

George Vant 15th. Sept. 26th. went away, came back Oct. 1st.

Andw Branstead 15th. ⎤ Sept. 26th. Do
James Mitchell 15th. ⎦ Sept. 26th. Do Do

Rowland Williams Do

Mr Thomas Whitten senr appointed Sergeant 26th. Sept.

Thomas Whitten jur Octo. 1st.

John Grinup   Do.

Francis Hynes   Do.

Samuel Doack listed Octo. 1st. went away 12th. Oct.
Thomas Rogers	Do.	Do.
John Lashly	Do.	Do.
Wm. King Octo. 1st.
Tho⁵ Meads	Do.
Jacob Kindar	Do.
Daniel Henderson } Oct. 10th.
Peter Kinder }
Jonathan Edwards in his brothers room 6th. Oct.
Christian Bergman 5th. Oct.
Michael Razor 24th. Octo.
Jeremiah Whitton 27th. Oct.

It may seem strange that so many of the men who were stationed
at the Witten fort "went away without leave." There was but one
man marked as a deserter; and it is, no doubt, a fact that all those
who absented themselves from the post did so because it was necessary to save their corn crops. The officers at the station were evidently without authority to grant leaves of absence, but, knowing
the necessity for the men going home, acquiesced in their departure
and did not class them as deserters. This conclusion is supported
by the fact that some of the absentees returned to duty without
reproof from their officers.

Along with the lists of the men who were stationed at the Maiden
Spring and Crab Orchard forts, was a list of the persons who acted
as scouts in the Upper Clinch Valley during the summer and fall of
1774. This list was also found among the papers of Colonel William Preston, and is as follows:

Scouts.
William Bowen	Aug. 12th
James Fowler
Tho⁵ Maxwell	10 days	June 11th
Rees Bowan
David Ward
John Kingkeid	17 days
Wm. Priest	7 days
John Sharp	10 days
Wm. Crabtree
Samuel Hays
Robt. Davis 15 days of his time to go to Robt. Moffet.

William Wynne's fort at Locust Hill was not garrisoned by a regularly enlisted force. However it was protected by a volunteer garrison, composed of the Wynne's, Harmans, Peerys, Butlers, Evans', Carrs, and other settlers of the neighborhood. This was at that time the most thickly settled community within the bounds of the present Tazewell County; and the fort was so favorably situated that its defence was easy.

CHAPTER IX.

FINCASTLE MEN CALLED FOR OHIO EXPEDITION—INDIANS INVADE CLINCH AND HOLSTON SETTLEMENTS.

After sending his order of the 12th of July to Colonel Andrew Lewis, directing him to raise a body of men and march to the mouth of the Kanawha and build a fort there, Lord Dunmore went to the fort at Winchester, Virginia. From that place the governor wrote Lewis on the 24th of July, 1774, notifying him that conditions were so serious in the Upper Ohio Valley that he had determined to go to Fort Dunmore (formerly Fort Pitt) at Pittsburg, and from that place conduct an expedition down the Ohio River, to strike the Indians a blow that would break up their confederacy. Governor Dunmore directed Lewis "to a raise a respectable body of men" and join him at the mouth of the Kanawha as quickly as possible. He also wrote Lewis: "I wish you would acquaint Col⁰ Preston of contents of this Letter that those he sends out may join you, and pray be as explicit as you can as to the time and place of meeting."

In the last days of August, Captain William Russell began his march with the Clinch Valley contingent, about forty men, to join the other Fincastle troops at a point on New River. About the 1st of September the Fincastle troops, some two hundred in number, under the command of Colonel William Christian took up their march and on the 6th of September arrived at the appointed place for assembling, the Great Levels of Greenbrier, then named Camp Union. The next day, the 7th of September, Colonel Christian wrote Colonel Preston that Colonel Lewis said that the number of men who had come to the camp exceeded his expectations, and that not more than 100 more men should be sent from Fincastle County to join the expedition. John Floyd and others were still engaged in enlisting companies of men to go on the campaign; and Colonel Lewis was afraid he could not secure and convey enough provisions for the subsistence of the number of men that had already assembled. There was another serious trouble upon Colonel Lewis. He had a small supply of powder, only one-fourth of a pound for each man who carried a gun, about six shots to the man. This was a very small supply of powder for such a dangerous expedition, and shows how desperately daring were the mountaineer pioneers. No doubt

Colonel Lewis recalled the Sandy Expedition of 1756, which was under his command and had to endure such terrible hardships from a lack of provisions and ammunition. He wisely determined to take no more men with this expedition, his second effort to reach the Shawnee towns, than could be furnished with ample supplies of provisions and ammunition. From a report made to Colonel Preston, Lewis then had with him about 1400 men. His little army was composed of volunteers and militia from the counties of Augusta, Botetourt and Fincastle, a company of volunteers from Culpeper County, commanded by Colonel John Field, and a company from Bedford County, under the command of Captain Thomas Buford. The men from Augusta were commanded by Colonel Charles Lewis, brother of Colonel Andrew Lewis; the Botetourt troops by Colonel William Fleming; and those from Fincastle by Colonel William Christian, as previously related.

The day the Fincastle troops arrived at Camp Union, the 6th of September, they found that Colonel Charles Lewis had marched with about 600 Augusta troops toward the mouth of the Kanawha. Colonel Christian wrote to Colonel Preston: "His business is to proceed as far as the mouth of Elk & there to make canoes to take down the flour. He took with him 500 Pack Horses carrying 54,000 pounds of flour & 108 Beeves." Colonel Christian then stated that he had been apprised by Colonel Andrew Lewis that he would start with the Botetourt troops in a few days, and leave the Fincastle troops at Camp Union to bring up the rear some days later. Christian thought this would greatly dissatisfy his men, as they were eager to be with the advance troops. On the 12th of September, Colonel Christian wrote Colonel Preston: "Col° Lewis has just marched with Col° Fleming and the Botetourt Troops, with an addition of Capt Shelby & Capt Russell's companies from Fincastle and has left under my care the remaining part of the Fincastle men, a few Culpeper, Dunmore (Shenandoah) and Augusta men, and ordered me to stay for the return of the pack horses that went with Ch: Lewis, which I shall look for along this day week. I have dispatched Mr. Posey towards Staunton to hurry out all the flour possible by that time and several persons are employed in gathering beeves. There is gone on 72,000 wt of flour. There is now here about 8 thousand, and 130 horse loads to be here tomorrow night, 96 loads at the Warm Springs which I have to send back for, & I suppose there is between 30 and 40,000 weight beyond the Springs.

I purpose to march this day week with all that can be had or a day or two after if possible."

This shows that the expedition was amply provisioned; and the future accomplishments of the little army proved that it had sufficient ammunition, received from sources that the records preserved do not disclose.

————

August the 25th, 1774, Colonel William Preston sent the following written orders to Major Arthur Campbell, looking to the defence of the settlements on Clinch River:

"Sir—Agreeable to the Conclusion come to by a Council of the Militia Officers of this County, the second of this month, for the Denfence of the Frontiers, in the absence of the Troops, I ordered Capt. Thompson with sixty men to guard the lower settlements on Clinch, which duty I suppose he is upon by or before this time; & as the upper Settlements are still uncovered, I would have you appoint Capt. Daniel Smith to that Service, with such Officers as you think proper; & there must be thirty men draughted from Capt. Herberts & the late Capt. Doacks Companies. The men are to be disposed of along that Frontier as was agreed on at the meeting of the Officers above mentioned.

"I would also request that you would examine carefully into the number of scouts on that quarter, and, if you see it necessary, to abridge them. You will likewise make enquiry, how they, & each of them, have performed the trust reposed in them, and make report to me accordingly."

Wm. Preston

(To Major Campbell)
    Aug. 25th 1774"

Up to this time no substantial help had been given to the inhabitants of the Upper Clinch Valley for the defence of the dangerous frontier on which they were living. The list of men stationed at Witten's fort at Crab Orchard, published on a preceding page, indicates that a few men were sent from the Holston Valley in compliance with the order of Colonel Preston. It is certain that Ensign John Campbell, who was a brother of Major Arthur Campbell, and Issac Spratt and Levi Bishop were from that Valley as they were then living on the north and south forks, respectively, of the Holston River, within the bounds of the present Smyth County. The inhabitants of the Holston Valley were more in dread of Indian incursions than were the settlers on the Clinch, and there was good reason for their fears. They had no forts on the North Fork of Holston, and there were but two on the Middle Fork of that river, Campbell's fort at Royal Oak, and Thompson's fort at Town House (Chilhowie). If the men from the Holston region had gone to the Clinch to perform garrison duty, they would have been compelled to leave their families unprotected, or to place them in Campbell's or Thompson's fort. Therefore, it is not surprising that so few of them went to the forts on the Clinch for service.

While the Lewis expedition was marching to the Ohio Valley, small bands of Shawnees and Mingos began to invade the Clinch and Holston valleys and make murderous attacks upon the inhabitants. The Indians kept spies hovering about Lewis' little army as it marched to the Ohio; and took advantage of the absence of the men, who were with the expedition, to kill and rob the unprotected people left in the Clinch and Holston settlements. The first attack by the Indians upon the settlers in the Upper Clinch Valley was made on the 8th of September, 1774. On that day a band of 12 or 15 Indians were in Thompson Valley, and about daybreak killed John Henry and his wife and three small children. Bickley, in his History of Tazewell, has related the incident in very interesting style, and his account of the occurrence will be quoted in succeeding pages of this volume, along with his accounts of all the massacres that were committed in Tazewell County by the Indians. Dr. Bickley made a mistake as to the date of the Henry massacre, placing it in May, 1776.

Henry was living in Thompson Valley, on the southside of Rich Mountain, a short distance east of Plum Creek Gap, upon land now owned by Archie Thompson. He had settled there in the month of May preceding. In a letter dated, "Royal Oak, Sept. 9th. 1774," Major Arthur Campbell made a report of the attack upon the Henry family, which he said occurred the morning of the previous day, that is the 8th of September, 1774. Henry was standing in his door when two Indians fired at him, inflicting a mortal wound. He realized that he could do nothing for the protection of his wife and children and Major Campbell says: "He immediately ran to the woods; and shortly after, accidentally met with Old Jno. Hamilton who concealed him in a thicket until he should go and alarm the Fort, and bring him assistance. Hamilton had the courage to go to Henry's House; but saw nothing, either of the Indians, or of the woman and children." The woman and three children had been killed and scalped and piled up a short distance from the house, and in that way escaped Hamilton's notice, which caused him to report their capture. Hamilton was one of the enlisted men at Witten's fort at the Crab Orchard, which was about three miles distant from the scene of the massacre; and his name appears upon the list of the garrison as "*John Hambleton.*"

On his way to the fort, Hamilton met John Bradshaw, whom Bickley says had settled in the valley, two miles west of the present town of Tazewell, in 1771. Bradshaw had been alarmed by discovering some Indian signs in his corn field that morning and had started over to Rich Valley, in the present Smyth County, where his family had gone on a visit. He struck out through the woods, passed by the Henry home, and at a point about three miles from the scene of the tragedy came upon a place where twelve or fifteen Indians had breakfasted, as shown by provisions they had left, and other signs. From that place he followed the tracks of the red men a short distance and found they were directing their course toward the Rich Valley. He made a rapid journey to that valley and gave warning that night to as many of the settlers as possible; and they began to gather at a Mr. Harrison's who lived on what Major Campbell called "the main path to Clinch in the Rich Valley, opposite to the Town-House." Other inhabitants of the valley fled to the fort at Royal Oak; among these was the wife of Ensign John Campbell, who was in charge of the garrison at Witten's fort; and Archibald and John Buchanan with their families. The families of the two Buchanans made a narrow escape from the Indians. These Buchanans were brothers, and cousins of Colonel John Buchanan, the surveyor. John Buchanan lived in the Locust Cove, and his wife was a sister of Colonel Buchanan. Archibald Buchanan, lived near the mouth of Cove Creek that empties into the North Fork of Holston. He afterwards moved to the present Washington County, and is the ancestor of most of the Buchanans who now live in Tazewell County, his brother John being the ancestor of the other Tazewell Buchanans. After murdering the Henry family, the Indians, evidently, crossed Clinch Mountain into Poor Valley and passed over Brushy Mountain into the Locust Cove; and then traveled down Cove Creek to where it enters the North Fork of Holston River. A short distance above that point, about a mile above the mouth of

Cove Creek, they made Samuel Lammey a captive. They must
have come upon Lammey alone, as his family had been sent to Campbell's fort at Royal Oak, after the warning given by Bradshaw to
the Rich Valley settlers. The Indians then started on their homeward journey, crossed the Clinch Valley, with their prisoner, passed
through Roarks' Gap, and followed Dry Fork to its confluence with
Tug River.

The next attack made by the Indians also occurred within the
bounds of the present Tazewell County. There were three Indians
in the attacking party, and they were evidently a part of the band
that massacred the Henrys and went over to Rich Valley. It was
the custom of the Indians when they made hostile visits to the border
settlements to break up into small bands and scatter their attacks
upon the cabins of the most isolated and unprotected inhabitants.
This plan made escape easier from pursuing parties sent out by the
settlers. On the 13th of September, five days after the Henrys
were murdered, three Indians made an attack upon a soldier who
was out hunting or scouting about half a mile from the fort at
Maiden Spring. The Indians shot at the soldier, but failed to hit
him. He shot one of them so severely that the wound proved fatal.
Major Arthur Campbell, in reporting the affair to Colonel Preston,
said: "A party of our people happened to be within 300 yards when
the guns were fired; they soon were at the place of action, and give
the remaining two Indians a good chase. The wounded fellow found
means to get into a large cave or pit within 70 or 80 yds. of the
place where he was shot; in which it is supposed he is dead, as he
fell when he was shot, and bled a good deal. I have one of the
plugs now in my house that burst out of his wound a few steps from
the tree he stood behind when he was shot. The pit is to be searched
by means of letting a man down in it by ropes with lights, as our
men are anxious to get his scalp." This cave is about a half mile
South of Maiden Spring and the Bowen homestead.

Major Campbell also reported that on the evening of the 13th
Captain Smith's scouts discovered the tracks of a party of the enemy
going off with horses and prisoners they had taken. From this it
appears that others besides Lammey had been made captives; but
Campbell still thought that Henry's wife and children had been
made prisoners by the Indians, though Mrs. Henry and all the
children, except one little boy, were afterwards found by a company of men who went to the Henry home, dead, scalped and piled

up on a ridge a short distance from the house. The Indians when
they made their forays always stole as many horses as they could
find, which they used to carry away the plunder they took and their
captives. Captain Smith when informed by his scouts of the invasion set out with a party of twenty-one men in pursuit of them, but
was unable to overtake them. At that time there was a very small
number of men on the Upper Clinch region employed as scouts.
They had to cover and guard a number of passes along a front of

This is a view of the Bowen homestead, and no more beautiful
pastoral scene can be found anywhere. The white cross mark is very
near the spot where Rees Bowen built his fort in 1773. Rees Bowen
the 5th now owns and occupies the splendid estate.

fifty miles; and could not do the work effectively, no matter how
skilled and daring they might be as woodsmen. Major Campbell
knew that these passes were not properly guarded; and in his reports
to Colonel Preston, sent on the 9th and 17th of September, complained, because not a man from Doack's or Herbert's companies
had yet gone to help guard the Clinch Valley frontier, though Preston had ordered, on the 25th of August, that thirty men from these
companies be drafted and sent there.

Small parties of Indians next invaded the Clinch Valley in the
present Scott County, and also the lower settlements on the Holston. The first outrage they committed was at or near Fort Blackmore on the Clinch, when two negroes were captured and a number

of cattle and horses stolen from the settlers. The garrison at the fort was so small that the men were afraid to go out and encounter the Indians, not knowing the number in the party. This so emboldened the Indians, who hoped to capture the fort, that they brought the two negroes in full view of the fort and made them run the gauntlet.

In the afternoon of the following day, the 24th of September, John Roberts and his wife and several children were killed, and the eldest child, James, a boy ten years of age, was made a captive by a band of Shawnees and Mingos under the leadership of Logan, the noted Mingo chief. This massacre occurred on Reedy Creek, an affluent of the North Fork of Holston, and the place was then supposed to be within the bounds of Fincastle County, Virginia; and it was, but afterwards it was found that it had been given to Tennessee through carelessness of the Virginia commissioners when the boundry line was run between North Carolina and Virginia in 1802. Logan left in the Roberts cabin a war club, with a letter tied to the club and addressed to Captain Cresap. The original, when found, was sent to Major Arthur Campbell, and by him forwarded to Colonel William Preston on the 12th of October, 1774. The letter was written on a piece of birch bark and with ink made from gunpowder. It had been prepared before Logan left Ohio with his scalping party; and was written, at his dictation, by a white man named William Robinson, who was captured on the Monongahela River, July 12th, carried to the Indians towns, saved from the stake by Logan, and adopted into an Indian family. Before he sent the letter to Captain Cresap, Colonel Preston made a copy on the back of the letter Major Campbell had written him when he forwarded the Indian chief's letter from Royal Oak. This copy was found among the Preston papers and is as follows:

"To Captain Cressap—What did you kill my people on Yellow Creek for. The white People Killed my Kin at Coneestoga a great while ago, & I thought nothing of that. But you Killed my Kin again on Yellow Creek; and took my cousin prisoner, then I thought I must Kill too; and I have been three times to war since but the Indians is not Angry only myself.

Captain John Logan

July 21st. Day."

In his mention of the killing of his kin at Conestoga, Logan refers to what was called the Paxton riot, which occurred in 1763 in Pennsylvania, when twenty inoffensive, friendly Conestoga Indians were brutally murdered by a mob of border desperadoes.

Further outrages were committed in rapid succession upon the inhabitants of both the Clinch and the Holston. The people in the Holston Valley were so alarmed by Indian marauding bands that the men refused to comply with the orders of Colonel Preston and Major Campbell to send reinforcements to the Clinch Valley settlers to help guard the passes on the frontier. At the same time powder and lead became very scarce, the settlers on the Clinch having been compelled to use their ammunition to protect their crops during the summer and fall from destruction by numerous wild animals. Flour was also wanted badly at Blackmore's and at the head of the Clinch. That powder was dangerously scarce is proven by the fact that when Major Campbell was sending a company of militia, on the 29th, of September. 1774, to repel or pursue a band of Indians, he wrote Colonel Preston:

"I luckily procured one pound & a half of powder before the militia went out. which I divided to such as had none. 3 loads apiece. which they went very cheerfully on. If you could possibly spare me one or two pounds I would divide it in the same, sparing manner, in case of another alarm."

On Thursday, September 29th. a very bold attack was made upon three men by the Indians within 300 yards of Moore's Fort on the Clinch, six miles below Castle's Woods. The attack was made between sunset and dark, and the Indians fired at the men from ambush, instantly killing a man named John Duncan. Though a party of men rushed from the fort and ran to the spot as soon as the guns were fired, the Indians succeeded in scalping Duncan and made their escape. Night came on and prevented any pursuit until the following morning, when it was too late to overhaul the savages. Daniel Boone was then in charge of the fort at Moore's and was supervising all the forts on the Clinch below Elk Garden. Although he was one of the most accomplished of the woodsmen and Indian fighters on the border. he was supported by such small and indifferent squads of men stationed at the several forts that he was unable to cope successfully with the wiley red men, who in most instances were being directed by the daring and intelligent John Logan.

Boone sent an express messenger to Major Campbell on the 30th
of September, to inform him of the killing of Duncan, and also told
him that the Indians were still lurking about Fort Blackmore,
where the two negroes had recently been captured and "coursed"
in front of the fort; and that Captain Looney, who was in charge
of the fort, had only eleven men and could not venture to attack or
pursue the enemy. The situation at Russell's fort, at Castle's Woods,
was also so serious that the people there were crying for help.
Captain Dan Smith, on the 4th, of September, wrote to Colonel
William Preston, saying: "The late Invasions of the Indians hath
so much alarm'd the Inhabitants of this River that without more
men come to their assistance from other parts, some of the most
timorous among us will remove to a place of Safety, and when once
the example is set I fear it will be followed by many. By what I
can learn the terror is as great on Holston, so that we've no room
to hope for assistance from that quarter. * * * * I am just
going to the assistance of the Castle's Woods men with what force
could be spared from this upper district." At the foot of the letter,
Captain Smith made a list of the men he was taking with him to
assist the alarmed garrison at Castle's Woods. They were:

Vincent Hobbs	Wm. McaDoo
Thos. Shannon	John Mares (Marrs)
Robert Brown	Joseph Mares (Marrs)
Saul Cecil	David Pattorn (Patton)
John Smith	Israel Harmon
Wm. Baylstone	Thos. Maxwell
Holton Money (Mooney)	Joseph Turner
Samll. Money (Mooney)	Wm. Magee

From an inspection of the above list it seems that the inhabitants of the headwaters of the Clinch and Bluestone were taking
pretty good care of themselves, and were willing and able to help
protect their more "timorous" neighbors lower down on the Clinch.
Nearly every man on this roll was from the Upper Clinch section,
now in Tazewell County, and a number of the names are still represented in the county—among them Marrs, Brown, Cecil, Patton,
Maxwell, Shannon and Harman. Three months previous to using
the Tazewell men for relief of the garrison at Castle's Woods, Captain Smith had written Colonel Preston, preferring charges against
Thomas Maxwell and Israel Harmon for neglect of duty as scouts

at the head of Sandy Creek. He accused them of cowardice, because they were removing their families from the head of the north fork of Clinch and Bluestone and taking them to places of safety; and Smith was asking that Thomas Maxwell be court-martialed. Captain Smith, evidently, had found that he had made a grievous mistake as to the courage of Maxwell and Harmon; and was trying to make amends for the wrong he had done them, by selecting them to become protectors of the "timorous" inhabitants living in his own section of the Clinch Valley.

About the 1st, of October the people in the Holston Valley and in the Upper New River region were apparently terror-stricken. A man by the name of George Adams, who lived on the Holston, wrote to Colonel Preston and told him that the people about Moccasin Gap had all fled from their homes; and that some of them had gathered at his house. He begged that a few men be sent out to go with the Moccasin people to their homes and guard them while they gathered their crops, which he said were large but being destroyed by the "vermin" (wild animals); and that the men would have to take their families to other forts, if they lost their grain. Adams also said; "ammunition is very scarce with us which is the occasion of abundance of fear."

On the 6th, of October, 1774, Major Campbell wrote Colonel Preston from Royal Oak and very graphically portrayed the state of alarm that then prevailed on the Holston, and on New River. He said:

"The people in the Wolf-Hill settlement, (the present Abingdon) will have the Indians to come up the Valley & North fork, opposite to them, and then make a Right-Angle to their habitations; the people on ye south fork will have the Enemy, to steal Slyly up the Iron Mountain, and make one Grand attack on the Head of Holston, and Sweep the River down before them; The Head of New River will have it, that the Cherokees will fetch a Compass, round Wattago Settlement, and come down New River, on a particular Search for their Scalps. The Rich-Valley and North fork people will have Sandy the dangerous pass, for proof of which they quote former and recent Instances; to wit Stalnaker & Henrys Family being carried out the same road."

This looks like consternation reigned supreme throughout the settlements west of New River, with one exception. The exception

was the settlements on the headwaters of the Clinch, where our
pioneer ancestors were not calling for help, but were remaining
at their frontier homes and forts, resolved to hold them against the
savages, or yield up their lives in their defence. This they were
doing, though some of their best and mightiest woodsmen had gone
with the Lewis expedition to Ohio, and others were being sent to
succor the threatened and alarmed inhabitants lower down the river,
where Logan was still operating with his scalping parties.

The next attempt to inflict damage on the settlers was near the
fort of Captain Evan Shelby, which was located on the site of
Bristol, Tennessee, and which was called in frontier days Sapling
Grove. It happened on the 6th of October, 1774, and when Captain
Shelby was nearing the mouth of the Kanawha with his company of
Fincastle riflemen, who were an important unit of the Lewis expedition. The Indians, who had been prowling and spying in the neighborhood, surprised and captured a negro girl, the property of Captain Shelby, within 300 yards of his fort. Their purpose in making
her a captive was to get information about the fort. They tried to
find out how many guns were in the fort, what amount of supplies
was there, and the relative strength of the place. Several questions
were asked the negro girl by the Indians, but she loyally and bravely
refused to give them any information. Thereupon, the red men
knocked her down twice, and started away with her. After they had
gone about a mile from the fort they heard a boy passing who was
on his way home from mill, and they tied the girl to a tree and
went in pursuit of the boy. During their absence, the girl managed
to get loose, and ran immediately to the fort and gave an alarm.
Whether the boy was captured and taken away is not shown by
accessible records, and the presumption is that he escaped.

On the 6th of October, a very daring murder was committed at
Fort Blackmore, in the present Scott County, when Dale Carter
was killed and scalped within fifty-five steps of the fort. Carter
was sitting alone on a log outside the fort. The Indians had crawled
along and under the bank of the river with the view of making a
surprise attack upon the place and capturing it by a bold push.
Carter happened to discover the enemy and immediately gave the
alarm by "hallooing, murder." One of the Indians fired at Carter
and missed him, but another fired and wounded him through the
thigh. One of the boldest of the red men, possibly Logan, ran up
and tomahawked and scalped the wounded man. A man by the

name of Anderson fired from the bastion of the fort at the daring Indian while he was scalping Carter, but failed to hit him. Dale Carter was the ancestor of the Hon. Henry Carter Stuart, lately governor of Virginia, and of all the Carters of Russell County.

While the revolting incidents that I have recounted were taking place in The Clinch Valley and other sections of Fincastle County, the army of Virginia mountaineers, led by Andrew Lewis, was assembling and marching to the mouth of the Kanawha to join forces with Lord Dunmore at that place, as had been previously arranged. The knowledge the Indians had received of the object of this joint expedition—that is to discipline the hostile tribes in Ohio—no doubt, made the depredations in the Clinch Valley fewer and less violent than they would otherwise have been. It is probable that the small bands of Indians, with the great Logan leading them, were sent here for the purpose of so alarming the inhabitants as to demand a recall of the companies, eight in number, that had gone from that part of Fincastle County west of New River; and in that way so weaken Lewis' army as to give the red men a chance to defeat the "Long Knives" when they crossed into Ohio. In fact, if the Indians were trying to work such a scheme, at one time their purpose came very near being accomplished. On the 26th of September, just after he had been officially informed of the butchery of the Roberts family by Logan and his band, Major Campbell wrote to Colonel Preston an urgent request to send a messenger to Lewis' army to hurry the return of the men from Fincastle County, especially the companies of Captains Russell and Shelby, whose families were in great distress and danger.

A great deal of the alarm felt and shown by the people of the Holston and New River settlements was caused by apprehension that the Cherokees were secretly associated with the Shawnees and Mingos; and that the Southern Indians would come in great force against the Fincastle inhabitants while such a large number of the best fighting men were away on the Ohio expedition. Colonel Preston, however, did not take this view of the situation; but thought it probable "some straggling fellows" from the Cherokee Nation might have joined a party of Shawnees who had lately been at the Cherokee town, possibly Logan's band; and that they had since been committing robberies and murders on the Clinch and the Holston. Colonel Preston also expressed the opinion that the Ohio Indians could not send any number of men at that time to annoy the settlements, as they would be kept busily occupied defending their own homes from attacks by the army which Lewis had taken to the mouth of the Kanawha. He was correct in his conclusions, as after events proved, and very wisely declined to recall the companies commanded by Russell and Shelby, or any part of the Fincastle troops that had gone with Lewis to Ohio.

Soon after sending his orders of the 24th of July, from Winchester, Virginia, to Colonel Andrew Lewis to raise a respectable body of men and to meet him at the mouth of the Kanawha, Governor Dunmore proceeded to Pittsburg. He, as speedily as possible, assembled the Delawares, Six Nations, and such other tribes as were disposed to be friendly, held a conference with them, and called their attention to the cruel treatment the Shawnees and the Virginians were extending each other. This was done, Dunmore said, to secure the aid of the Delawares and other friendly disposed Indians in an effort to restore peaceful relations between the Virginians and the Ohio Indians. The Delawares, and other tribes that were represented at the conference, not only gave assurance of their friendship for the whites, but consented to send delegations to the Shawnees and other hostile tribes, and to urge them to meet Governor Dunmore for a conference at some designated spot on the Ohio. In a report subsequently made to Lord Dartmouth, secretary of state for the colonies, Dunmore gave an account of his course of action after his conference with the Delawares. He wrote to Dartmouth:

"I determined therefore to go down the Ohio; but I thought it Prudent to take a Force which might effect our purpose if our Negotiation failed: And I collected from the Militia of the Neighbouring Country about twelve hundred Men, to take with me, Sending orders to a Colonel Lewis to March with as many more, of the Militia of the Southern Counties, across the Country to Join me at the Mouth of the little Kanhaway, the Place I appointed to meet the Indians at.

"I passed down the river with this body of Men, and arrived at the appointed place at the Stated time. The day after Some of our friends the Delawars arrived according to their promise; but they brought us the disagreeable information, that the Shawnees would listen to no terms, and were resolved to prosecute their designs against the People of Virginia.

"The Delawars, Notwithstanding, remained Steady in their attachment; and their Chief, named Captain White Eyes, offered me the assistance of himself and whole tribe; but apprehending evil effects from the Jealousy of, and natural dislike in our People to, all Indians, I accepted only of him and two or three: And I received great Service from the faithfullness, the firmness and remarkable good understanding of White Eyes.

"Colonel Lewis not Joining me, and being unwilling to encrease the expence of the Country by delay, and, from the accounts we had of the Numbers of the Indians, Judging the Force I had with me Sufficient to defeat them and destroy their Towns, in case they should refuse the offers of Peace; and after Sending orders to Colonel Lewis, to follow me to a Place I appointed near the Indian Settlements, I crossed the Ohio and proceeded to the Shawnese Towns; in which march, one of our detached Parties encountered an other of Indians laying in Ambush, of whom they killed Six or eight and took Sixteen Prisoners.

"When we came up to the Towns we found them deserted, and the main body of the Indians, to the amount of near five hundred, had Some time before gone off towards the Ohio; and we Soon learnt that they had Crossed the river, near the Mouth of the great Kanhaway, with the design of attacking the Corps under Colonel Lewis."

Governor Dunmore's expeditionary force was composed of troops he raised in the counties of Frederick and Dunmore (the latter now Shenandoah County), and forces he found at Pittsburg under the command of Colonel Angus McDonald and Major William Crawford. The combined forces aggregated twelve hundred splendid, trained men. It was known as the northern division of the army that was going against the Ohio Indians; and was under the immediate command of Colonel Adam Stephens. He was a native of Scotland, was an educated physician, and had settled in the Lower Valley of Virginia. Stephens was a noted Indian fighter, was with Washington at Great Meadows, and was badly wounded at Braddock's defeat; but after his recovery from the wound had served throughout the French and Indian War, and commanded the Virginia regiment in Pontiac's War. He served with distinction in the Revolutionary army, first as a brigadier general and then as major general. After the Revolution he returned to his home at Martinsburg, Virginia, now in West Virginia, and for some years was an active and distinguished participant in the civil affairs of the State. The northern division had along as scouts and officers men that were then and afterwards noted characters—among them being Simon Girty, Simon Kenton, Peter Parchment, John and Martin Wetzel, and Daniel Morgan.

As previously related, Colonel Charles Lewis had marched on the 6th of September from Camp Union with the Augusta troops and Captain Matthew Arbuckle's company from Botetourt, taking along four hundred pack-horses loaded with flour, salt and tools; and all the beef cattle that had been collected at the camp. Captain Arbuckle marched at the head of the column with his company, and was the best qualified man then living to act as guide for the advancing army. In 1765, with one or two companions, he had explored the Kanawha Valley to the Ohio River; and was the first white man to pass along that valley, except a few who were prisoners of the Indians. For these reasons he was selected as captain of a company of scouts to guide the Lewis division of the army. The orders given Colonel Charles Lewis directed him to go to the mouth of Elk Creek, to build a small storehouse there, to have sufficient canoes made to transport the flour and other supplies down the Kanawha to the Ohio River; and to remain in camp at that place until he was joined by the other section of the expedition that was to follow.

On the 10th of September, Colonel John Field left Camp Union with his Culpeper men. He was offended because Colonel Andrew Lewis would not recognize him as the ranking officer and yield him command of the expedition. Field had explored the Lower Kanawha Valley the previous year, and had undertaken to make a settlement there; but was prevented from doing so by an attack made by a party of Indians. He made a narrow escape, but his son, Ephraim, and a negro woman, his cook, were made prisoners and taken to Ohio by the savages. Field knew the country pretty well, and pursued a route of his own selection to the mouth of Kanawha, arriving there in time to take a part in the battle that was fought at that point.

Colonel Andrew Lewis marched on the 12th of September, from Camp Union with the Botetourt troops, Captain Evan Shelby's and Captain William Russell's companies from Fincastle, and Captain Thomas Buford's company from Bedford; and took with him all the beeves and pack-horses that had been collected after Colonel Charles Lewis started on his march. On the evening of that day a messenger from Colonel Charles Lewis came into the camp and reported that one of Colonel Field's men, who was out with a hunting party, had been shot and killed by an Indian, but that the Indian had been killed before he could scalp the white man. It seems that Indian scouts and scalping parties hovered about each section of the expedition as it marched to the mouth of the Kanawha, and kept their people in Ohio thoroughly posted as to the movements of the army.

On the 23rd of September, Colonel Andrew Lewis, with his forces, joined his brother Charles and the Augusta men at their camp on the banks of Elk Creek, about one mile above where it flows into the Kanawha. This camp was about 108 miles from Camp Union, according to a computation made by Colonel Fleming, commander of the Botetourt troops. Colonel Lewis had been compelled to move his troops very slowly, making an average of only about ten miles a day after starting from Camp Union. The route he had followed was through a pathless wilderness and very rugged; and he had to cross Gauley Mountain—a difficult and hazardous undertaking, with cattle and pack-horses to handle. The combined forces remained at Elk Creek until the 30th, engaged in completing the storehouse and making canoes to transport the supplies down the river. On the 24th Lewis sent out scouts in different directions to look for the enemy, and on the 25th, one of the scouts that had crossed to the west side of the Kanawha returned, and reported that about four miles from camp a small party of Indians had passed the scouts in the night with horses, and going down the river. The evening of the 25th, Colonel Lewis sent scouts to discover the whereabouts of Lord Dunmore and to ascertain when he would arrive with his troops at the place designated for meeting, the mouth of the Little Kanawha.

Failing to receive any message from Lord Dunmore, Colonel Lewis decided to proceed without delay to the mouth of the Great Kanawha, and began his march to that point on the 1st of October. The troops were formed into two columns for the march, each column being divided into two divisions. The Botetourt troops constituted the right and the Augusta men the left column. Captain John Lewis, a nephew of Colonel Andrew, marched with his company a short distance in front of the two columns, acting as the advance guard. The cattle and pack-horses were placed between the front and rear divisions; and each flank was covered with a guard of one hundred men. This was an admirable formation for protecting the army from surprise attacks by the Indians; and was used each day of the march until the expedition arrived at the mouth of the Kanawha, its excellence being shown by the fact that not a man or animal was lost during the six days occupied in the march from Elk Creek to the Ohio.

This was the first army of a thousand men, composed entirely of frontier hunters and skilled woodsmen, that had ever marched against the Indians. It was not only unique in its composition, but must have presented a rare and imposing spectacle as it marched over mountains and through the trackless wilderness. The men were not uniformed, but their dress was strikingly similar in character and appearance. They wore the frontier fringed hunting shirt— dyed various hues, brown, yellow, and red—girdled by a belt around the waist; and fashioned by their wives and daughters from jeans or heavy flax cloth, which the noble women had manufactured at home with spinning wheel and loom. Their accoutrements were: a leather pouch swung on their left side by a shoulder belt, and a powder horn, similarly carried on the right side. The leather pouch held their bullets and lead, bullet moulds, patching, tow for wiping out the rifle barrel, and such small tools as might be needed for cleaning and repairing their guns. The powder-horn was made from the horn of a cow or ox, scraped so thin and highly polished as to make it transparent, and in which the powder was safely dry in the very worst weather. All the men had either fur caps or soft hats made from the furs of animals they had killed; and they wore moccasins and heavy woolen or buckskin leggings that reached half-way up the thigh. Each man was armed with that "terrible gun," the mountain flint-lock rifle, and carried in his belt a tomahawk and scalping knife. Some of the officers wore swords but each of them was equipped with rifle, tomahawk and scalping knife. As they marched, scouts were kept far out on the flanks and in front, and axemen went in front to blaze the trail and remove fallen trees and other obstacles.

Colonel Lewis and his army reached the junction of the Great Kanawha with the Ohio on the 6th day of October, 1774, and went into camp on the point that lies in the fork of those two streams. A letter from Governor Dunmore to Colonel Lewis was found in a hollow tree, having been deposited there by messengers sent by the

governor, but who had arrived at the place several days in advance
of Lewis' army. Dr. Lyman Draper says the messengers were,
Simon Girty, Simon Kenton, and Peter Parchment. But Samuel
Murphy, an Englishman who was with Dunmore's division, made

The above picture is made from a photograph of the heroic bronze
statue of General Andrew Lewis, that stands at the west side of the
magnificent Washington Equestrian Statue in the Capitol Square,
Richmond, Virginia. It correctly shows the pioneer garb and accoutrements worn by General Lewis and his mountain men at the battle of
Point Pleasant.

the list: Simon Girty, John Turner, and Joseph and Thomas Nicholson. It is certain that Simon Girty, the despised "white renegade," was one of the messengers.

Colonel Lewis sent scouts with a reply to the letter from Dunmore that had been found in the hollow tree. The contents of that letter were never revealed to the public; but it is believed by many that Lewis was ordered to cross the Ohio and join Dunmore, who was then endeavoring to make peace with the Indians; and that Lewis in his reply letter expressed dissatisfaction for himself and unwillingness on the part of his men to comply with the orders of the governor. On the 8th, scouts, led by Simon Girty, came down the Ohio in a canoe, and brought letters from Lord Dunmore to Lewis. The records do not disclose what the orders were, but it is generally agreed by historians that Lewis was directed to take his forces across the Ohio and join Lord Dunmore at the Indian towns near the Pickaway Plains. Though displeased with the change of plans originally adopted, Colonel Lewis made preparations on the 9th to break camp the following morning, the 10th, and join Dunmore, in compliance with the orders given him.

If such was the purpose of Colonel Lewis, he was destined to be foiled in its execution. Cornstalk, the great Shawnee chief, had been kept fully informed by spies and runners of the movements of the Lewis army from the time it started from Camp Union until its arrival at the Ohio River. He had gathered together from eight hundred to one thousand of the bravest and most skillful warriors of the Shawnee, Mingo, Delaware and Ottowa tribes, and marched them rapidly through the forest to the Ohio River, reaching that stream at a point some six or eight miles above where Lewis and his men were camping. During the night of the 9th he transported this large force across the river on rafts, and marched them quietly down the stream with the intention of making a surprise attack at daybreak upon his white foes, before they had been fully aroused from their slumber. Cornstalk's plans were well conceived, and would possibly have been successfully carried out but for the interposition of two men from the Clinch Valley, James Mooney and — Hickman, who were members of Captain Russell's company. They had gotten up before daylight the morning of the 10th, and had started up the river on a hunting or scouting expedition. After going about a mile from the camp they came suddenly upon Cornstalk's warriors, who were already moving towards the encampment of their white foes. The Indians fired at the two men and Hickman was killed, the fatal shot being fired by Tavenor Ross, a white renegade. Mooney ran swiftly back to camp and gave the alarm, reporting that he had seen enough Indians to cover five acres of ground, and that his companion, Hickman, had been killed by the red men.

Thwaites and other historians have stated that the two men who discovered Cornstalk's army were members of Captain Shelby's company; and Thwaites says that the man who was killed was James Hughey. A man with that name does appear upon the roll of Captain Shelby's company; but Thwaites is contradicted by Colonel William Fleming, who, in his account of the battle, says positively that the two men beloned to Captain Russell's company. And Fleming is supported by Isaac Shelby, son of Captain Evan Shelby, and lieutenant of his father's company. In a letter to his uncle, John Shelby, written at Point Pleasant, on the 16th of October, 1774, Lieutenant Shelby said: "Monday morning about half an hour before sunrise two of Capt. Russell's Company Discovered a large party of indians about a mile from Camp one of which men was killed the Other made his Escape & brought in his intelligence; in two or three minutes after two of Capt. Shelby's Comp^y came in and Confirmed the Account." This proves beyond question that the first man killed at Point Pleasant was from the Clinch Valley; and that a Clinch Valley man was the first to announce the approach of Cornstalk and his army of desperate warriors.

CHAPTER X.

THE BATTLE OF POINT PLEASANT—KENTUCKY OPENED FOR SETTLEMENT.

Immediately after Mooney gave the alarm, Colonel Andrew Lewis called his men to arms. He believed the report as to the number of Indians was exaggerated, and that it was only a scouting party. So believing, instead of advancing with his entire force, he ordered two detachments to be formed, to be made up of select men from each company, and each detachment to have one hundred and fifty men. As soon as the detachments were formed they went in quest of the Indians. Colonel Charles Lewis lead the Augusta detachment, and had with him Captains Dickinson, Harrison and Skidmore. Colonel William Fleming led the Botetourt and Fincastle men, and had with him Captains Shelby, Russell, Buford, and Love. When the advance began, the Augusta line marched on the right near the foot of the hills, and the Botetourt and Fincastle line marched on the left, moving up the Ohio River, keeping at a distance of about two hundred yards from the stream. The advance was made briskly, and when about three-fourths of a mile from the camp, the sun being one hour high, the detachment led by Colonel Charles Lewis came in contact with the enemy. The Indians fired a few shots, killing the two white scouts that were in advance of the columns. This was quickly followed with heavy firing by the concealed enemy on the right, which extended instantly to the left; and the two detachments of white men became hotly engaged in deadly strife with their hated savage foes.

The attack made by the Indians was both fast and furious, and was met with equal fury by the enraged white men. Hearing the heavy clash of resounding firearms, Colonel Andrew Lewis realized that he had made a mistake in his estimate of the number of the attacking enemy; and he sent Colonel Field hurriedly to the front with a reinforcement of two hundred men. Early in the engagement Colonel Charles Lewis was mortally wounded, but he remained with his men until the line was substantially formed. He had not "taken to a tree," that is, used a tree for protection, but was standing on a clear piece of ground. cheering his men and urging them to advance, and wearing a scarlet waistcoat—a fine target for the

Indians. Finding that the wound was serious, he handed his gun to a man near him, remarked to his men, "I am wounded, but go on and be brave," walked unassisted back to the camp, and died in a few hours thereafter.

Soon after Colonel Charles Lewis was forced to retire from the field of battle, Colonel Fleming was desperately wounded. Two balls passed through his left arm, and one entered his breast. After encouraging his men with a calm voice to press on to victory, he retired to the camp, and was thought to be mortally wounded. At this time the Indians on the firing line, which extended for more than a mile from the foot hills toward the river, greatly exceeded the Virginians in number; and they succeeded in forcing the white men on the right of the line to retreat 150 or 250 yards. Colonel Fleming had rallied and reformed the line just before he was wounded; and then Colonel Field came upon the scene of conflict with reinforcements. As ranking officer, after the retirement from the field of Colonels Lewis and Fleming on account of their wounds, Colonel Field assumed command of the entire line. He was soon supported by additional troops sent forward by Colonel Andrew Lewis. The additional reinforcements were lead by Captains McDowell, Matthews, and Stuart from Augusta; and Captains John Lewis, Pauling, Arbuckle, and McClannahan from Botetourt. With the lines so substantially reinforced, the Virginians moved forward; and not only recovered the ground they had lost but began to drive the enemy back and up the river. The Indians were forced back until they got in line with the Fincastle troops that Colonel Fleming had left in action when he was compelled to retire from the battle. While the Indians were falling back, Colonel Field was killed. He was standing behind a tree, trying to get a shot at an Indian on his left who was attracting his attention by laughing and jeering at him. While Field's attention was thus diverted, he was shot by two Indians who were concealed behind logs on his right. There being no other field officer in the engagement, the command of all the lines devolved upon Captain Evan Shelby, who was senior captain among the surviving commissioned officers.

From the commencement of the battle, which began about an hour after sunrise, until twelve o'clock the conflict was waged with unceasing vigor by both the white men and the red men. The hostile lines, though more than a mile long, were in such close contact, being separated not more than twenty yards, that numerous single combats were engaged in by the combatants. In these encounters, either the Indian or the white man would single out a foeman worthy of his steel, and the two would join in a hand-to-hand struggle; and with tomahawk and scalping knife fight until one, or both, of the combatants fell. An encounter of this kind took place between William Bowen and an Indian of powerful statue; and the stalwart man from Tazewell vanquished his savage adversary.

After twelve o'clock the fighting became less violent; but Isaac Shelby declared it "continued sharp enough until one o'clock." The Indians about midday tried to slip around the right flank of the Virginians and get to the camp. This effort was defeated by the whites, who in turn outflanked the enemy, and forced the Indians to fall back on their entire line. They used their best men to cover their retreat but were so hard pressed that they had to leave a number of their dead on the field, something very unusual for the red men to do. About one o'clock, while retreating, the Indians reached "a most advantageous spot of ground," from which, as was concluded by Captain Evan Shelby and the other officers, it would be very difficult and dangerous to dislodge them. This resulted in the lines of both the whites and the Indians remaining, as they were then formed, sufficiently near each other to continue the fighting; and the firing was kept up, with advantage to the white men, until sunset. During the night the Indians made a skillful retirement across the Ohio, carrying their wounded with them and throwing many of their dead into the river.

The Virginians, though greatly exhausted, and deeply grieved by the losses they had sustained of gallant officers and men, were content with the result of the battle. They enjoyed the proud satisfaction of knowing that none of their men, save poor Hickman, had been scalped by the Indians; but that the white men had taken nearly twenty scalps from their dead foes.

When a list of the casualties the Virginians had suffered in the battle was made, it was found that of the Augusta line Colonel Charles Lewis, Colonel John Field, Captain Samuel Wilson, Lieutenant Hugh Allen, and eighteen privates had been killed; and that Captains John Dickinson and John Skidmore, Lieutenants Samuel Vance and ——— Laird, and fifty-one privates of the same line had been wounded. It was found that of the Botetourt, Bedford and Fincastle men, Captains John Murray, Robert McClannahan, James Ward, and Thomas Buford, Lieutenants Matthew Bracken, and Edward Goldman, Ensign John Cundiff, and seventeen privates were killed; and Colonel William Fleming, Lieutenant James Robinson and thirty-five privates were wounded.

At the request of Colonel Andrew Lewis, the casualties of the battle, as above enumerated, were forwarded to Colonel William Preston by Colonel William Christian, and are, therefore, official. From this report it appears that eleven officers and thirty privates were killed, a total of forty-six. And that six officers and eighty-six privates were wounded, a total of ninety-two. Lieutenant Isaac Shelby wrote his uncle John that about forty-six were killed and about eighty were wounded. Shelby also reported that "five men that came in Daddy's Company were Killed."

There is an existing roll of Captain Shelby's company, but none of Captain Russell's. But from a daily report of the forces commanded by Colonel Fleming the day before the battle at Point Pleasant, it appears that Shelby had 44 men fit for duty and Russell 41. The brief accounts of the engagement given by Colonel Christian and others do not tell whether any of the men from Clinch Valley were killed. These reports do show, however, that Russell's company was in the engagement from the time the first volley was fired until the fight was ended, and that they were in the thickest of the fray. From available records it is shown that six men from the territory of the present Tazewell County were in the battle. They were the three Bowen brothers, William, Rees and Moses Bowen; and David Ward, Robert Cravens, and Lyles Dolsberry.

After Colonel Andrew Lewis marched from Camp Union, the troops he left at that place were joined by three more companies from Fincastle County. They were commanded, respectively, by Captains John Floyd, James Harrod, and William Herbert, which made the contingent from the county complete. The Fincastle men were so eager to participate in the Ohio campaign, that their commander, Colonel Christian, determined to break camp at Camp Union and follow Lewis down the Kanawha. This course was followed on the 27th of September, and, after an eight days' march, Christian with his troops arrived at Elk Creek on the 5th day of October. On the 6th day of October, he began his march from Elk Creek to the mouth of the Kanawha; and on the 10th, when about twelve or fifteen miles from Point Pleasant, he was met by scouts and informed that the army had been attacked that morning by a large body of Indians, and that the battle was still raging. There-

and Southwest Virginia   315

upon, Colonel Christian pushed on with his troops and arrived upon
the scene about midnight. He got there too late for the battle; but
not too late to assist in giving comfort to the wounded and suffering,
and fresh hope to the men who confidently expected the conflict
would be renewed the following morning.

Colonel Fleming, in a journal he kept of special incidents of the
campaign, thus, in part, describes features of the battle: "The
enemy wherever they met with an advantageous piece of ground in
their retreat made a resolute stand, during which some of them were
employed to move their dead, dying and wounded. In the afternoon
they had gained such an advantageous post that it was thought
imprudent to attempt to dislodge them, and firing ceased on both
sides about half an hour before sunset. From this place the enemy
made a final retreat and crossed the Ohio with their wounded. Some
of their dead were slightly covered in the field of battle, some were
dragged down and thrown into the Ohio, and others they had
scalped themselves to prevent our people. Whilst this passed in the
field, Colo. Lewis was fully employed in camp, in sending necessary
reinforcements where wanted on the different quarters. The troops
were encamped on the banks of the New River and Ohio, extending
up both Rivers near a half mile. The point betwixt the rivers was
full of large trees and very brushy. From the furtherest extent of
the tents on both rivers, he (Colonel Lewis) cleared a line across,
and with the brush and trees made a breastwork and lined it with
the men that were left in camp."

An Englishman, named Smyth, who falsely claimed to have been
a participant in the engagement, in writing about the battle, accused
Colonel Andrew Lewis of cowardice, because he did not adopt the
tactics of Braddock and Grant, rush to the front and fight the
Indians in the open; and others, who were jealous of Lewis, were
disposed to repeat the unjust accusation. The testimony of Colonel
Fleming, and the previous and subsequent record of Andrew Lewis
prove that he was one of the bravest of the brave men of his day.
Roosevelt, in his "Winning Of the West," says: "It was purely a
soldiers' battle, won by hard individual fighting; there was no dis-
play of generalship, except on Cornstalk's part."

With all due respect for Colonel Roosevelt's aptness as a military leader, he is greatly at fault in his estimate of the management
of the battle by the commander of the army and of the leadership
of the officers who executed his orders. From the report of Mooney.

of Russell's company, and that of the two men of Shelby's company, Lewis was uncertain as to the number of Indians that were advancing for an attack, or what the nature of the attack would be. Believing that the attacking force was nothing more than a large scouting party sent across the Ohio to hold him on the south side of the river while Dunmore's division was engaged on the other side of the Ohio, he sent forward two divisions, each having one hundred and fifty picked men, to meet the advancing foe and ascertain their strength. Then, as a wise precaution, he proceeded to fortify the camp, in the manner described by Colonel Fleming; and when he found that a really large body of Indians was making the attack, he quickly sent ample reinforcements to support the two divisions that had been first dispatched to the front. He knew the character of the ground he was camping on, with its many advantages for the Indians in their well known peculiar methods of fighting; and, so knowing, he showed both excellent judgment and the skill of a trained frontiersman in the management of the battle.

That the Indians were confident they would be the victors was manifested by their conduct before they made an attack, and during the progress of the battle. When they crossed the Ohio they carried with them their deer skins, blankets and other kinds of goods; and also brought along their boys and squaws. It was intended that the boys and squaws should follow the warriors as they drove the pale faces back and club the wounded whites to death; and thus help to win the fight quickly. They expected to drive the white men into the Ohio and the Kanawha; and to prevent their escape across these rivers had placed lines of their braves on the opposite sides of the streams to shoot the whites as they attempted to cross. The courage and defiance of the Indians was beyond anything the old Indian fighters had ever witnessed. Their chiefs ran continually along the lines, exhorting their men to "lie close" and "shoot well," to "fight and be strong," while their men over the Ohio called to them to "drive the white dogs in." Cornstalk's splendid voice could be heard above the din of the conflict as he urged his comrades on to battle.

The day after the battle was fought, large ranging parties were sent out to locate the Indians. Finding that the enemy had retreated across the Ohio, the scouting parties returned to the camp. On the 12th the cattle and horses that had been dispersed and that strayed during the fight were collected. Colonel Fleming in his Orderly Book says: "This day the Scalps of the Enemy were collected and found to be 17. They were dressed and hung upon a pole near the river bank & the plunder was collected & found to be 23 Guns 80 Blankets 27 Tomahawks with Match coats, Skins, shot pouches, powderhorns, war-clubs &c. The Tomahawks Guns & Shot pouches were sold & amounted to near 100 pounds."

On the 13th of October, the scouts or messengers that had been sent to notify Lord Dunmore of the battle and victory returned. They brought orders for Colonel Lewis to cross the Ohio and to march toward the Shawnee towns; and to join his Lordship at a certain place, afterwards known to be the Pickaway Plains. The 14th, 15th, and 16th, the men in camp were kept busily occupied finishing a storehouse, and erecting a breastwork, which latter was raised two logs high, with part of a bastion. Leaving the sick and wounded, with a sufficient force to hold and protect the camp against small bands of the enemy, Colonel Lewis crossed the Ohio on the 17th with about one thousand men, and proceeded on his way to join Dunmore and his army.

The defeat they had encountered so completely broke the spirit of the Indians that, as soon as they reached their towns, a council of the head-men and chiefs was called and held, to see if a favorable treaty could not be made with the Virginians. Cornstalk, who had, at the council which met immediately before hostilities commenced, earnestly opposed the war, at the present council as vigorously opposed making peace with the whites. He was a splendid orator, but all his eloquent appeals to his fellow-chiefs were made in vain. He urged them, if necessary, to kill all their women and children, and that they sacrifice their own lives, fighting till the last man fell, rather than yield to the Long Knives. Failing to win their consent for a continuation of the war, disgusted with their cowardice, he struck his tomahawk into the war post, and declared that he would go to Dunmore and make peace for the cravens. To this proposition, prompt and unanimous approval was given; and Cornstalk with his fellow-chiefs repaired to Dunmore's camp.

Soon after the chiefs reached Lord Dunmore's camp, he sent a messenger to inform Colonel Lewis that he was engaged in a peace parley with the Indians, and ordered him to halt with his forces and to go into camp. Dunmore feared that, if the Virginians came to his camp while the Indians were there, Colonel Lewis would not be able to control his men, who were enraged at the loss of such a large number of their esteemed officers and comrades in the recent battle; and that they would murder the chiefs while they were engaged in the peace conference. His Lordship, however, invited Colonel Lewis, and such of his officers as he chose to select, to visit the camp and take part in the peace negotiations.

The invitation was declined in such terms as to convince Dunmore that Colonel Lewis, and his officers, and the men in the ranks, had not made the long and severe march from their distant homes to the mouth of the Kanawha, and fought the bloody battle at Point Pleasant to accomplish nothing more than an uncertain peace with the savages, a peace which Dunmore had been seeking from the moment he left Pittsburg. The mountaineers from Fincastle County wanted to go on to the Shawnee towns and do what Colonel Preston had promised them should be done, that is, plunder and burn the Shawnee towns, destroy their corn fields, take their "great stock of horses," and force the people to abandon their country, or kill them. And the men from the Holston and Clinch valleys were eager to march on and avenge the cruel outrages that had been committed, since they left their homes, upon their neighbors and kindred by Shawnee and Mingo scalping parties.

The governor then concluded a treaty of peace with the Indians. Being disturbed over the attitude of Lewis and his men, his Lordship laid aside his dignity, mounted his horse and rode to Lewis' camp. He informed Lewis that a treaty had been agreed upon, and that its terms were such as would protect the inhabitants of the regions west of the Alleghanies. Then he told Lewis that the presence of himself and army could be of no further service, but might be a hinderance to the conclusion of the treaty; and ordered him to march home with his forces. It is said that Colonel Lewis was greatly concerned for the safety of Governor Dunmore while he was visiting his camp. The soldiers were so angry on account of being ordered to return home just as they had gotten where they could strike and punish their foes, that Lewis thought it best to double or treble the guards about his tent while the governor was visiting him. Dunmore and his party remained in the camp that night. The next day he called the captains together, told them what he had done, and requested them to return home with their men; and that day the return march was begun.

The terms of the treaty, as briefly reported by Governor Dunmore to the secretary of state for the colonies, were: "That the Indians should deliver up all prisoners without reserve; that they should not hunt on our Side the Ohio, nor molest any Boats passing thereupon; That they should promise to agree to such regulations for their trade with our People, as should be hereafter dictated by the Kings Instructions, and that they Should deliver into our hands certain Hostages, to be Kept by us until we were convinced of their Sincere intention to adhere to all these Articles. The Indians finding, contrary to their expectation, no punishment likely to follow, agreed to every thing with the greatest alacrity, and gave the most Solemn assurances of their quiet and peaceable deportment for the future: and in return I have given them every promise of protection and good treatment on our side."

Apparently the provisions of the treaty were reasonable and just for both the Virginians and the Indians; but, for some unknown reason, the Mingos refused to accept its terms. It may be that they were influenced to take this course by Logan, their famous chief, who was not present at the preliminary conference that negotiated the treaty. He had just gotten back to the Mingo towns from his bloody scalping expedition to the Holston and Clinch valleys; and had brought with him the little Roberts boy, captured on Reedy Creek when the Roberts family was massacred, and also the two negroes he had captured at Moore's Fort. From contemporary reports, it is known that he also had a large number of scalps, possibly as many as thirty, dangling at his belt when he returned from this expedition. It is probable the scalps of Mrs. Henry and her children, who were murdered in Thompson Valley, were part of Logan's trophies.

Provoked by the refusal of the Mingos to accept the treaty, Lord Dunmore sent Major William Crawford with a force of two hundred and fifty men to the nearest Mingo town to inflict such punishment upon the recalcitrants as would bring them into submission. A night attack was made upon the town and five of the Indians were killed; and fourteen, chiefly women and children, were taken prisoners, the balance of the inhabitants escaping under cover of the night. The town was destroyed with the torch; and a considerable amount of booty was brought away, which was sold for three hundred and five pounds and fifteen shillings, and divided among Crawford's men. George Rodgers Clark, who a few years later was the leader of the famous expedition that made conquest of the Illinois country, was with Crawford when the disgraceful attack was made upon the Mingo town.

Logan had proudly and defiantly refused to attend any of the peace conferences, or give his assent to the terms of the treaty. Finally he ceased to oppose peace, but declined to avow whether or not he would continue his acts of hostility against the whites. Dunmore made several futile efforts to get an interview with the proud Indian chief; and at last decided to reach him and find out his intentions through a special messenger. He selected for the mission his interpreter, John Gibson, who was the reputed husband of Logan's sister that had been brutally murdered by Greathouse and Baker at the Yellow Creek massacre. Gibson went to the Indian town and Logan agreed to talk privately with his brother-in-law, and took him aside for an interview. The outraged chief, with fervid eloquence, delivered a message for the governor that has since been pronounced one of the most classic and dramatic orations that can be found in the literature of any country. Gibson, who was an educated man, wrote it down while Logan was engaged in its delivery, and it is as follows:

"I appeal to any white man to say if ever he entered Logan's cabin hungry and he gave him not meat; if ever he came cold and naked and he clothed him not? During the course of the last long and bloody war, Logan remained idle in his camp, an advocate for peace. Such was my love for the whites that my countrymen pointed as I passed and said, 'Logan is the friend of the white man.' I had even thought to have lived with you but for the injuries of one man. Colonel Cresap, the last spring, in cold blood and unprovoked, murdered all the relations of Logan. There runs not a drop of my blood in the veins of any living creature. This called on me for revenge. I have sought it. I have killed many. I have fully glutted my vengeance. For my country I rejoice at the beams of peace; but do not harbor a thought that mine is the joy of fear. Logan never felt fear. He will not turn on his heel to save his life. Who is there to mourn for Logan? Not one."

When Gibson returned to the camp with the message, Lord Dunmore assembled his soldiers and scouts, among the latter were Michael Cresap and George Rodgers Clark, and read the speech to them. Its beauty and pathos so impressed the rugged frontiersmen that they constantly strived to remember and repeat it. Cresap, whom Logan still believed was the murderer of his sister and brother, though he was guiltless, was so mortified and enraged by

its recital that he threatened to tomahawk Greathouse, who was
the real perpetrator of the hideous crime.

In after years the genuiness of the speech was assailed, some
writers asserting that it was the production of John Gibson or some
other white man. Thomas Jefferson investigated, with his usual
care, the authorship, and, in his Notes on Virginia, not only attributes it to Logan, but commends the beautiful eloquence of the
Indian chief. Theodore Roosevelt, also a careful investigator, in his
Winning of the West, declares it was spoken by Logan. The style
is entirely distinct from that used by the white men of that period,
and neither Dunmore, nor any white man who was with him, had
the peculiar talent for composing such a production. In thought
and expression it bears the unmistakable impress of the child of
nature.

The Mingo chief, whose life was a tragedy, was the most pathetic
figure among the American Indians that were known to the early
white settlers. His father was a French child that was captured
by the Indians and adopted into the Oneida tribe; and who, when
he grew to manhood, was made a chief by the Indians that lived in
the Susquehanna Valley. Logan's mother belonged to the Mingo or
Cayuga tribe, which was a branch of the Iroquois Nation. His
Indian name was Tah-gah-jute, and he took the name Logan from
his friend James Logan, who was secretary for Pennsylvania, and
for a long time acted as governor of that province. Logan lived in
Pennsylvania until 1770, when he moved to Ohio. At the time of
Dunmore's War he was living at old Chillicothe, now Westfall, on
the west bank of the Sciota River. He had always been the faithful
friend of the white people, but the murder of his kindred made him
an everlasting foe of the white race. His last home was at Detroit,
where he was killed in a drunken brawl in 1780. Quoting from a
historian of the period, Howe says: "For magnanimity in war, and
greatness of soul in peace, few, if any, in any nation ever surpassed
Logan. His form was striking and manly, his countenance calm
and noble, and he spoke the English language with fluency and cor-
rectness."

Dunmore's War and the battle of Point Pleasant were of such
moment to the pioneer settlers of the Clinch Valley, I have felt constrained to write freely about the most important incidents con-
T.H.—21

nected therewith. The treaty of peace made by Dunmore with the Ohio Indians, after they had been vanquished by the Virginia mountaineers, gave assurance to the inhabitants of the Clinch Valley that the red men would not, for a time, molest them in their earnest endeavor to clear away the forests and establish comfortable homes for themselves and their descendants. The Shawnees had pledged themselves to make no more invasions of the territory south of the Ohio for either war or hunting purposes. This pledge was not violated until after the Revolution began, when brutal British agents persuaded the Indians to resume hostilities and murder the border settlers.

Colonel Lewis, after parting with Lord Dunmore, marched rapidly and directly back to Point Pleasant, arriving there with his forces on the night of the 20th of October. The following day a large detail of men was made for the purpose of completing the fortifications that Lewis had commenced the day the battle was fought. The fort when completed was named Fort Blair; and it was a small rectangle, about eighty yards long, with block-houses at two of its corners. During the absence of the army across the Ohio, a number of wounded had died from their injuries. Colonel Christian in a letter to Colonel Preston reported: "Many of our wounded men died since the accounts of the battle came in. I think there are near 70 dead. Capt. Buford and Lieut. Goldman and 7 or 8 more died whilst we were over the Ohio and more will yet die." Colonel Christian also said: "Colo. Fleming is in a fair way to recover and I think out of danger if he don't catch cold."

Colonel Fleming, who was an accomplished surgeon for that day, had been very severely and supposedly fatally wounded. Two balls struck his left arm below the elbow and broke both bones, and a third entered his breast three inches below the left nipple and lodged in the chest. In a letter to a friend he said: "When I came to be drest, I found my lungs forced through the wound in my breast, as long as one of my fingers. Watkins tried to reduce them ineffectually. He got some part returned but not the whole. Being in considerable pain, some time afterwards, I got the whole returned by the assistance of one of my attendants. Since which I thank the Almighty I have been in a surprising state of ease. Nor did I ever know such dangerous wounds attended with so little inconvenience." Colonel Fleming did recover from the wounds, but was disabled for active service in the Revolutionary War. He afterwards served

Virginia in many responsible civil positions, and his death, which
occurred Aug. 24th, 1795, was occasioned by the wounds he received
at Point Pleasant. The sword he wore in the battle is now a cherished heirloom in the possession of Judge S. M. B. Coulling, of
Tazewell, Virginia. Judge Coulling is a great-great-grandson of
the valiant soldier and distinguished surgeon.

Soon after the return of the army to Point Pleasant, the troops
began to make the homeward journey in small companies. They
were eager to get back home, and took the most direct routes to their
respective places of residence. The men from the Clinch and Holston did not return by the route they used when they marched to
Camp Union and thence to the mouth of the Kanawha. They
crossed to the west side of the Kanawha at Point Pleasant and took
the most direct course they could find for their homes. The Tazewell men, so far as is known, all got back about the first of November, safe and sound, except John Hickman, who was the first white
man killed at Point Pleasant, and Moses Bowen who died on the
march home from smallpox. Captain William Russell was left in
command of Fort Blair, with a garrison of fifty men who were to
remain until a regular garrison could be provided by the General
Assembly. It is hardly probable that any of the Tazewell men
remained with Russell, as they were still anxious for the safety of
their families.

The treaty with the Indians being satisfactorily concluded, and
Lewis' men having gone home, Lord Dunmore started on his return
journey to Williamsburg. He arrived there on the 4th of December,
was received with much acclaim by the people, and was presented
with congratulatory addresses by the city, the College of William
and Mary and the Governor's Council. About the time of his arrival,
or shortly thereafter, Dunmore received five dispatches, numbered
9, 10, 11, 12, and 13, from the Earl of Dartmouth, then secretary of
state for the colonies; and dispatch Number 13 gave the governor
very great concern. In this dispatch Dartmouth rebuked Dunmore
severely for permitting grants to be issued for lands west of the
Alleghany and allowing settlements to be made thereon, which was
done in violation of the royal proclamation of 1763, that forbade
British citizens settling west of the Alleghany Mountains.

The announced purpose of the proclamation of 1763, was to prevent continued trouble with the Indian tribes who were the allies of
the French in the war that had just been terminated. A few years

after the royal proclamation was promulgated, the companies that
had obtained from the Virginia Government grants for hundreds of
thousands of acres west of the Alleghany Mountains, and who had
surveyed numerous tracts of land and sold them to prospective settlers, went industriously to work to avoid the terms of the proclamation, by securing an extinguishment of the claims of the various
tribes to the lands in the disputed territory. This induced many
persons to cross to the territory west of New River and settle on
lands purchased from Colonel Patton's representatives, or from the
Loyal Company; and others settled on unappropriated boundaries,
expecting to perfect their titles under what was called the settlers
right or "corn laws." About all the pioneer settlers in the Clinch
Valley had come here and located on waste or unappropriated land.

Over in England the mythical belief that the shores of the Pacific
Ocean were not far beyond the Alleghany ranges had been dis-
sipated; and through the explorations of Christopher Gist and others
it was known that the territory embraced in the charters of Virginia,
lying beyond the mountains, was of vast extent and wonderfully
valuable for agricultural purposes. This information attracted the
attention and aroused the cupidity of certain Englishmen. They
devised a plan for getting possession of the extensive region belonging to Virginia west of the mountains, and enriching themselves
by selling it in parcels to settlers.

In June, 1769, about the time the settlers began to come to the
Clinch Valley and to other localities west of New River, a company
of Englishmen and Americans presented a petition to the King of
England, asking that they be permitted to purchase and colonize the
large boundary in America that had been ceded by the Iroquois
Nation to Great Britain by the Fort Stanwix treaty, negotiated in
1768. The company was composed of men of influence, headed by
Thomas Walpole; but the scheme was so vigorously opposed that
the prayer of the petition was not acted upon until October, 28th,
1773, when the Privy Council ordered that the grant be issued to the
petitioners. A new province was to be established to be called
Vandalia, and the seat of government was to be located at the mouth
of the Great Kanawha, on and about the ground where the battle of
Point Pleasant was fought.

But for the disturbances that arose in the American colonies in
1774, and that culminated in the Revolutionary War, the speculative scheme of Walpole and his associates would have taken legal

shape. This would have invested Walpole's company with title to
all the unoccupied land belonging to Virginia west of the Alleghanies, including the Clinch Valley. And it is more than probable
that all the pioneer settlers of the Upper Clinch Valley would have
been turned out of their homes, or forced to pay Walpole's company
for them, as none of the first settlers had secured regular titles for
their lands, and did not perfect them until after the Revolution. It
would also have taken authority from the Virginia Council to issue
grants for lands west of the mountains; and put an end to the
policy of the General Assembly for pushing the frontiers westward
by the creation of new counties, as was done by the erection of
Botetourt and Fincastle counties.

That Governor Dunmore was secretly favoring the plans of Walpole is shown from his letter to the Earl of Dartmouth, replying to
the aforementioned Dispatch "No. 13." It is possible that this was
the true reason for the indifferent treatment he extended the Virginia
mountaineers whom he had requested to join him in the Ohio campaign. On the 12th of July, 1774, Dunmore wrote a letter to
Colonel Andrew Lewis, directing him to go to Ohio with a force of
men, to destroy the Indian towns and to show the savages no mercy.
The governor said: "All I can now say is to repeat what I have
before said which is to advise you by no means to wait any longer
for them to Attack you, but to raise all the Men you think willing
& Able & go down immediately to the mouth of the Kanhaway &
there build a Fort, and if you think you have forse enough (that
are willing to follow you) to proceed directly to their Towns & if
possible destroy their Towns & Magazines and distress them in
every way that is possible."

In the face of these specific orders to his subordinates, the governor, immediately after his arrival at Pittsburg, began to take steps
to negotiate a peace with all the Ohio tribes, including the Shawnees,
without giving Lewis and his brave men opportunity to accomplish
the ends for which they had made their laborious and perilous march
to the Ohio. Dunmore's conduct in connection with the campaign
was so insincere and vacillating that Lewis and his men strongly
suspected him of treachery. Howe, in his History of Virginia, says:
"Lord Dunmore marched the army in two divisions: the one under
Col. Andrew Lewis he sent to the junction of the Great Kanawha
with the Ohio, while he himself marched to a higher point on the
latter river, with pretended purpose of destroying the Indian towns

and joining Lewis at Point Pleasant; but it is believed with the real object of sending the whole Indian force to annihilate Lewis' detachment, and thereby weaken the power and break down the spirit of Virginia." Howe is strongly sustained in his charge of treachery against Dunmore by Colonel John Stuart, who commanded a company of the Augusta men at Point Pleasant, and who wrote a narrative of the battle. Alexander Withers, in his Chronicles of Border Warafare, corroborates Colonel Stuart's accusations. Colonel Stuart was a fellow-countryman of Dunmore, being a native of Scotland, and this adds greater force to his charges of infidelity against the earl.

In his letter to the secretary of state for the colonies, Dunmore made a very earnest effort to convince Dartmouth that he was not only opposed to extending the settlements beyond the limits of the colonies as they stood in 1770, but that he had done everything possible while governor of New York to prevent any such extension. He also protested that he made ineffectual but earnest efforts to prevent further settlements in the terriory west of New River that the Cherokees ceded to Virginia by the treaty concluded at Lochaber on the 18th of October, 1770. He was certainly not in sympathy with the men who composed Lewis' army, many of whom had already settled in the forbidden territory; and some of whom, Floyd, Harrod, and others, had been preparing to settle in Kentucky. Dunmore showed his contempt for the pioneers by saying: "They acquire no attachment to Place: But wandering about Seems engrafted in their nature; and it is a weakness incident to it, that they Should forever immagine the Lands further off, are Still better than those upon which they are already Settled."

The Tazewell pioneers were not composed of restless rovers, such as Lord Dunmore describes. They, or their ancestors, had left the old countries to secure that freedom of thought and action which later became the inalienable right of every American citizen. The lands they found here and settled on were so rich and attractive that they knew it was useless to seek anything better "further off." So, they remained, and imparted to their descendants a love for Tazewell soil that has almost become an obsession. In his report to Lord Dartmouth, in explanation of the existing conditions on the Virginia frontiers, Lord Dunmore said:

"In this Colony Proclamations have been published from time to time to restrain them (the frontier settlers): But impressed from their earliest infancy with Sentiments and habits, very different from those acquired by persons of a Similar condition in England, they do not conceive that Government has any right to forbid their taking possession of a Vast tract of Country, either inhabitated, or which Serves only as a Shelter to a few Scattered Tribes of Indians. Nor can they be easily brought to entertain any belief of the permanent obligation of Treaties made with those people, whom they consider, as but little removed from the brute Creation."

These utterances of Governor Dunmore very accurately set forth the motives and characteristics of the Tazewell pioneers; but they were not a proper subject for unfavorable comment by an official representative of the government of Great Britain. The British Government, from the time the first settlement was made at Jamestown, had established and followed a policy of aggression and extermination toward the American aborigines. England's title to the immense region now embraced in the United States was based upon the chimerical right of discovery and the brutal principle that might makes right. If treaties were made with the Indians by the British Government, in each and every instance the natives were deceived and defrauded. Such treaties were not made from a sense of moral or legal obligation to the aboriginal inhabitants, but from a selfish desire to make the colonies stronger and prepare them for further encroachments upon the natural rights of the red men. If our ancestors believed that the English King had no right to forbid them taking possession of the Clinch Valley and adjacent territory for their homes, that the treaties made with the Indians were devoid of "permament obligation," and that the natives were no better than "the brute creation," these convictions had been imbibed from the teachings and practices of the British Government toward both the Indians of America and the inhabitants of the East Indies. We should feel proud of the fact that our pioneer ancestors rested their right to make their homes in the wilderness regions of the Clinch upon the theory that the lands were uninhabited, that they were of "no man's land;" and that they did not look for title to a government that claimed the country by right of conquest or discovery.

Dunmore wrote to Lord Dartmouth that there were "three considerations" he wished to offer for his Majesty's approval: "The first is, to Suffer these Emigrants to hold their Lands of, and incorporate with the Indians; the dreadfull Consequences of which may be easily foreseen, and which I leave to your Lordships Judgment. The Second, is to permit them to form a Set of Democratical Governments of their own, upon the backs of the old Colonies; a Scheme which, for obvious reasons, I apprehend cannot be allowed to be carried into execution. The last is, that which I proposed to your Lordship, to receive persons in their Circumstances, under the protection of Some of His Majesty's Governments already established, and, in giving this advice, I had no thought of bringing a Dishonour upon the Crown."

These suggestions offered by the governor of the Virginia province, through the secretary of state for the colonies, to George III., King of England, make it obvious that Dunmore's War was waged more particularly for the benefit of the Royal Government than it was for the protection of the frontier settlers. Dunmore was aware that the principles of democracy were taking deep root in the minds and hearts of the inhabitants of the mountain regions of Virginia; and that open resistance to their eager wishes to extend their settlements into Kentucky and along the southern banks of the Ohio would intensify rather than curb the growing democratic spirit of this liberty-loving people. And he realized that the methods he had used to thwart the main purpose of the Lewis expedition to the Ohio had kindled a flame of resentment among the inhabitants of the three great trans-montane counties, Augusta, Botetourt, and Fincastle. Hence his wise suggestion to the British Government for the adoption of a conservative and compromising policy in its treatment of the frontiersmen, who had shown at Point Pleasant their ability to defeat the confederated tribes of the Northwestern Indians without any assistance from the Royal Government. The battle of Point Pleasant, which was won by the Virginia backwoodsmen, a number of Tazewell pioneers being in the engagement, was virtually the opening battle of the American Revolution.

One of the most important outcomes of the Point Pleasant battle, and one that proved of vital benefit to the inhabitants of the Clinch Valley, was the opening up of Kentucky for permanent settlement. This erected a strong barrier in that direction between the hostile Indians and the Clinch settlements; and during the progress of the Revolutionary War greatly reduced the number of attacks that would otherwise have been made upon the pioneers of this region.

The battle of Point Pleasant was also an event of immense

interest to the American colonies. It not only furnished opportunity for the permanent settlement of Kentucky and the Kanawha Valley, but gave George Rodgers Clark and his intrepid followers inspiration to originate and consummate the expedition that won for Virginia the extensive and valuable Northwestern territory; and extended the northern boundary line of the American Nation from Nova Scotia along the chain of inland seas, and on to the Pacific Ocean. Eventually it gave the United States possession of the lower Mississippi Valley, through Thomas Jefferson's purchase of Louisiana in 1803; brought Texas, the splendid Lone Star State, into the Union; and secured, by conquest, the large territory ceded by Mexico in 1848. The descendants of the Tazewell pioneers can proudly claim that their ancestors were among the participants in the eventful battle. There were other results that flowed from the battle that are not so pleasant to contemplate. It sowed the seeds of life and greed in the broad road the white men afterwards traveled, but scattered the seeds of death and despair along the narrow path the poor American Indians were forced to travel for more than a century.

Soon after the conclusion of Dunmore's War, Daniel Boone, who had been sojourning in the Clinch Valley for more than a year, determined to carry into effect his long coveted plans for planting a colony in Kentucky. The Fort Stanwix treaty had extinguished the ancient claim of the Iroquois to the territory in question; and the treaty that Dunmore made with the Ohio Indians had procured from them an abandonment of the right they asserted to the hunting grounds south of the Ohio. The Cherokees, however, claimed, and justly so, absolute title to Kentucky by the terms of the treaty made at Lochaber, South Carolina; and under a treaty made with the province of Virginia in 1772, which latter treaty provided that the boundary line between Virginia and the Cherokee Nation should "run west from the White Top Mountain in latitude thirty-six degrees thirty minutes."

Boone saw the necessity for getting rid of the claim of the Cherokees before making a further attempt to lead a colony into Kentucky. He remembered how his first attempt to migrate to that country, in the autumn of 1773, had been defeated by a roving band of Cherokees, who set upon and killed his son James, and Henry

Russell, son of Captain William Russell, together with four white men and two negroes who were attending young Russell. This caused him to exercise caution to escape a similar occurrence. John Floyd had made, in the spring and summer of 1774, numerous surveys of large and valuable tracts of land in Kentucky for Patrick Henry, William Preston, William Russell, William Byrd, William Fleming, William Christian, Arthur Campbell, and other Virginians; and all these, no doubt, joined Boone in the scheme to acquire the title of the Cherokees. Boone decided to enter into negotiations with the Indians. Early in the year 1775 he induced Colonel Richard Henderson, Thomas Hart, John Williams, James Hogg, Nathaniel Hart, Leonard H. Bullock, John Lutrell, and William Johnston, all living in North Carolina, to join him in an effort to purchase the Cherokee claim. A company was formed to that end, and Boone, Henderson and Nathaniel Hart went to the Cherokee towns to commence negotiations. They made a proposition to the Indians, and suggested that a general council of the Nation be held to consider the sale of the desired territory to Boone and his associates. A council was held at Sycamore Shoals on the Watauga River, at which about twelve hundred Cherokees were present, more than half of them warriors. On the 17th of March, 1775, a treaty was concluded and signed by the agents of the company and certain chiefs of the Cherokee Nation. In consideration of a large quantity of merchandise, said to be of the value of ten thousand pounds sterling, the Indians conveyed to the North Carolinians and their associates all the lands south of the Ohio and lying between the Kentucky and Cumberland Rivers. Dragging Canoe, the great chief, opposed the treaty and made a strong speech against it. He very earnestly and pathetically called the attention of his tribesmen to the happy state the Nation had occupied before it was encroached upon by the greedy white men, and how other tribes of their race had been driven from their homes by the whites, who seemed determined to drive the natives out or exterminate them. He declared that: "Whole nations had melted away in their presence like balls of snow before the sun, and had scarcely left their names behind, except as imperfectly recorded by their enemies and destroyers." Dragging Canoe saw in this proposition of Boone and his companions to get the remainder of their finest hunting grounds the beginning of a movement of the white men to drive his people from their beautiful homeland in the Southern Alleghanies, and force them into the wilderness beyond the Mississippi. The old chief urged his countrymen to fight to the death rather than submit to the loss of more of their territory. His pleas were unavailing, and the territory sought by Daniel Boone and others was sold to them.

The Cherokees had parted with their acknowledged title to their famous hunting grounds, from which they had in succession driven all intruders, "time out of mind." But instead of the lands becoming the property of Henderson's company, it merely removed the Cherokee cloud from the title which Virginia had acquired and was asserting under the charters granted by James I., King of England; and Kentucky at that time was a part of Fincastle County, Virginia. The Indian chiefs conceded that their title was of doubtful value, because they had never used the territory for residencĕ, but only for hunting purposes. Oconostoto and Dragging Canoe told Henderson that the Northwestern Indians would oppose his occupancy of the territory and would show the white men no mercy. And another old chief told Daniel Boone: "Brother we have given you a fine land, but I believe you will have much trouble in settling it."

Regardless of these warnings, as soon as he was satisfied that the Cherokees would make the sale, Henderson started Boone with a company of thirty men to blaze and clear a trail from the Holston to the Kentucky River. Equipping his men with rifles and axes, Boone immediately started out to prepare the trail, which passed through Cumberland Gap, crossed the Cumberland, Laurel and Rock Castle rivers, and on to the Kentucky River. Boone's party was occupied two weeks in accomplishing its task, and on several occasions they were attacked by small parties of Indians and some of his men killed.

When the treaty with the Indians was completed, Henderson started out to follow the trail that Boone and his men had made. He had a large party of men; and wagons to transport the goods, tools implements and so forth, that would be needed in preparing a permanent settlement. But he had to abandon the wagons in Powell's Valley, because the trail beyond would not permit the use of vehicles; and pack-horses were used for the balance of the journey. On the 7th of April messengers from Boone met Henderson's party with the information that the Indians were proving dangerous, and urging Henderson to hasten on to where Boone and his men had gone into camp. Henderson as quickly as possible joined

Boone, reaching his uncompleted wooden fort on the 20th of April, where he was received with a salute from 20 or 30 rifles; and they proceeded to lay the foundation of the settlement at Boonesborough. Roosevelt says, in Winning of the West: "Beyond doubt the restless and vigorous frontiersmen would ultimately have won their way into the coveted western lands; yet had it not been for the battle of the Great Kanawha, Boone and Henderson could not, in 1775, have planted their colony in Kentucky; and had it not been for Boone and Henderson, it is most unlikely that the land would have been settled at all until after the Revolutionary War."

The purchase from the Indians by Henderson and his associates was made for the purpose of establishing a new province, or colony, to be separated from the colonies of Virginia and North Carolina, and they named it Transylvania. Nearly all of the present Kentucky and a considerable part of Tennessee, then North Carolina, was embraced in the purchase. About the same time that Henderson and Boone took their colony to their new possession, Colonel James Harrod returned to Kentucky with a large party of emigrants, and resumed work on the fort and village he had commenced to build in 1774 on the present site of Harrodsburg. And Benjamin Logan, who was a lieutenant in one of the companies from the Holston in the Point Pleasant campaign, went out with a party and built Logan's Station, ten miles from Boonesborough. It is highly probable that Colonel William Preston, Major Arthur Campbell, and other prominent Virginians were identified in some way with Henderson's Transylvania Company, as John Floyd returned to Kentucky in 1775 to act as surveyor for that company. The scheme may have originated, in a measure, from resentment toward Governor Dunmore on account of his unfair treatment of the Fincastle men who took part in the Ohio campaign; and with the intention of forestalling Thomas Walpole and his speculative company of Englishmen, who were perfecting their plans to found the province of Vandalia.

After his arrival on the scene, Henderson lost no time in putting his plans into effective operation. He opened a land office at Boonesborough, and had boundaries that aggregated many thousands of acres surveyed by Daniel Boone and others; giving certificates of entry therefor to any colonists who wished to become purchasers. A number of the colonists were apprehensive of the legality of Henderson's right to sell and convey these lands. They decided

to rest their right of entry upon the Virginia land laws. The Tazewell pioneers had made their settlements under these laws, as is
shown by the patents issued to them after the Revolution. These
laws gave to every man who settled in the wilderness regions the
right to enter four hundred acres of unappropriated land, if he
built a cabin thereon and cleared and cultivated in corn a small
boundary. The General Assembly of Virginia afterwards confirmed
the claims of the Kentucky colonists who relied upon the Virginia
laws for their titles.

Henderson and his Transylvanians asked the consent of the Continental Congress, then in session, to send representatives to that
body, independent of Virginia and North Carolina. Lord Dunmore
as governor of Virginia, made protest against all the acts of the
proprietors of Translyvania as illegitimate, and claimed that the
greater portion of the mushroom province was Virginia territory and
was a part of Fincastle County. Thomas Jefferson and Patrick
Henry, who were delegates from Virginia to the Continental Congress, made vigorous protest against recognition of Transylvania,
and the Congress refused to admit its representatives to seats in that
assembly. The North Carolina Government adopted the same policy
as that of Virginia. While the Revolutionary War was in progress,
in 1778, the General Assembly of Virginia declared Henderson's
purchase from the Indians null and void, using as authority for the
act a general land law passed in 1705 by the General Assembly.
One of the provisions of the act forbade the Indians from alienating
their lands, "by whatsoever rights claimed or pretended to, to any
but some of their own nation;" and declared all conveyances contrary
to the act void; and imposed heavy penalties on those who should
purchase or procure conveyances from them. However, instead of
inflicting penalties upon Henderson and his associates, the General
Assembly thought it equitable, and sound public policy, to reimburse
them for procuring from the Cherokees a relinquishment of their
actual or pretended claims to the Virginia territory situated in Kentucky. In accordance with that view, the General Assembly in
October, 1778, enacted the following relief measure:

"Whereas it has appeared to this Assembly, that *Richard Henderson and Company,* have been at very great expense, in making
a purchase of the *Cherokee* Indians, and although the same has been
declared void, yet as this Commonwealth is likely to receive great
advantage therefrom, by increasing its inhabitants, and establishing

a barrier against the Indians, it is therefore just and reasonable the said *Richard Henderson and Company* be made a compensation for their trouble and expense.

"1. *Be it enacted by the General Assembly,* That all that tract of land situate, lying, and being on the waters of the *Ohio* and *Green* rivers, bounded as follows, to wit: beginning at the mouth of *Green* river, thence running up the same twelve and a half miles, when reduced to a straight line, thence running at right angles with the said reduced lines, twelve and a half miles on each side of the said river, thence running lines from the termination of the line extended on each side of the said *Green* river, at right angles with the same, till the said lines intersect the *Ohio,* which said river *Ohio* shall be the western boundary of the said tract, be, and the same is hereby granted the said *Richard Henderson and Company,* and their heirs and tenants in common, subject to the payment of the same taxes, as other lands within this Commonwealth are; * * * but this grant shall, and it is hereby declared to be in full compensation to the said *Richard Henderson and Company,* and their heirs, for their charge and trouble, and for all advantage accruing therefrom to this Commonwealth, and they are hereby excluded from any further claims to lands, on account of any settlement or improvements heretofore made by them, or any of them, on the lands so as aforesaid purchased from the *Cherokee* Indians."

As this act declared, the Commonwealth was greatly benefitted through the settlements made by Boone, Henderson and others in Kentucky, in that they erected on the western frontier a strong barrier against the Western Indians. It was of great value to the Clinch settlements, because it largely diverted the attention of the Western tribes from this region, and relieved our pioneer ancestors from hostile invasions by large bands of the red men. But it did not relieve the inhabitants on the headwaters of the Clinch and Bluestone rivers from frequent bloody attacks by small scalping parties. The Sandy River Valley still remained an open way by which the Indians could approach undetected the Clinch and Bluestone settlements.

CHAPTER XI.

THE REVOLUTIONARY WAR.

During the fall, winter and spring following the termination of Dunmore's War the Tazewell pioneers pursued their home-making labors with increased and unabated ardor. They had been here long enough to test the fertility of the soil, and had found they were not mistaken in their first estimate of its excellent quality. The delightful spring, summer, and autumn seasons they knew would more than compensate for the rigorous winter weather that would have to be endured for three months each succeeding year. Health, abundance of the best food, and other creature comforts, were assured to each and every one of the inhabitants that exercised a reasonable amount of intelligence and diligence to obtain these blessings. And the promise of relief from hostile invasions by the Indians gave fresh impulse to the purposes and hopes of the settlers of turning the wilderness country into a great agricultural and grazing region. More horses and cattle were brought out from the eastern settlements to be grazed on the ranges in the summer and to consume the excess of corn and other grains in the winter. Oats, rye and wheat had now been introduced; and the raising of hogs in large numbers became popular, as there was an ample supply of mast every fall in the forests to fatten thousands of porkers. Numbers of new settlers moved into each community; new cabins were built; the sound of the woodman's axe could be heard ringing during the day near every cabin home; and the crash of the falling forest giants as they yielded to the sturdy blows of the axemen reverberated from every adjacent mountain hollow. The horrible cloud that had been hovering over and about the pioneer homes—the frightful massacres by the Indians—had been swept away; but a terrible storm was gradually approaching from the east, that, before many seasons were passed, would find its way into the peaceful valleys where our ancestors were erecting their homes.

In the spring of 1775 the quarrels between England and her American colonies reached a crisis. The British Government was forcing the issue of whether the colonies should become sovereign independent governments, or be compelled to remain and be ruled as dependencies of Great Britain. This question had been agitating the mother country and the colonies ever since, 1765, and had reached an acute stage which precluded any hope of a peaceful settlement. In March, 1774, Parliament passed what was called the Boston Port Bill. It was a retaliative measure to punish the people of Boston for their physical resistance of the tax on tea imported into the colonies. The Port Bill provided that no merchandise of any kind should be landed at or shipped from the wharves of Boston—with the threat that the other ports of Massachusetts, and the ports of all the colonies, would be inflicted with a similar embargo, if they followed Boston's example of resistance to the tea tax. When the news of the enactment by Parliament of the Port Bill reached Williamsburg, the Virginia Assembly, then being in session, immediately made protest against the outrageous measure; and had the protest entered on the journal of the House. Governor Dunmore, who was a repressive royalist, was so provoked that he dissolved the assembly and ordered the members to return to their homes. Howe, in his history of Virginia says:

"On the following day the members convened in the Raleigh tavern, and, in an able and manly paper, expressed to their constituents and their government those sentiments and opinions which they had not been allowed to express in a legislative form. This meeting recommended a cessation of trade with the East India Company, a Congress of deputies from all the colonies, 'declaring their opinion that an attack upon one of the colonies was an attack upon all British America;' and a convention of the people of Virginia. The sentiments of the people accorded with those of their late delegates; they elected members who met in convention at Willimsburg, on the 1st, of August, 1774."

The convention of Virginians gave a detailed review of the grievances that had been imposed upon the colonies, demanded measures of relief, elected delegates to a general Congress of the colonies, and instructed them as to the course they should follow in the Congress. The Congress assembled at Philadelphia on the 4th of September, 1774; and was in session while Dunmore was engaged in his expedition to Ohio against the Indians. It is believed that Dunmore, in part, planned and executed his expedition to Ohio to divert the attention of the people of Virginia, and especially those who lived beyond the Blue Ridge and the Alleghanies, from the exciting and dangerous controversies that were going on between the British Government

and the colonies. If this was his intention, he failed most signally
in its accomplishment.

On the 14th, of October, 1774, just four days after the Virginia
mountain men won their eventful victory at Point Pleasant, the
second Continental Congress, in session at Philadelphia, passed
strong and defiant resolutions setting forth numerous grievances
imposed upon the colonies and demanding redress therefor. The
first clause of the preamble was in the following words:

"Whereas, since the close of the last war, the British Parliament,
claiming a power of right to bind the people of America by statute,
in all cases whatsoever, hath in some Acts expressly imposed taxes
on them, and on various other pretences, but in fact for the purpose
of raising a revenue, hath imposed rates and duties payable in these
Colonies, established a board of commissioners with unconstitutional
powers and extended the jurisdiction of the Courts of Admiralty,
not only for collecting the said duties but for the trial of causes
merely arising within the body of a county. And whereas, in consequence of other statutes, judges, who before held only estates at
will in their offices, have been made dependent on the Crown alone
for their salaries, and standing armies kept in time of peace. And
it has lately been resolved in Parliament, that by force of a statute
made in the 35th of Henry VIII., colonists may be transported to
England and tried there upon accusations for treasons and mis-
prisions, or concealment of treasons, committed in the Colonies; and
by a late statute, such trials have been directed in cases therein mentioned."

The second clause of the preamble referred to the Act passed
by Parliament to discontinue shipping to and from Boston harbor,
and mentioned the several other acts that had been enacted as sup-
plemental of the "Port Bill;" and then declared: "All of which
statutes are impolitick, unjust and cruel as well as unconstitutional,
and most dangerous and destructive of American rights."

In the third clause the dissolving of the legislative bodies by
colonial governors, as had been done by Dunmore in Virginia, was
referred to in disapproving terms; and the fourth clause of the preamble announced that the deputies of the colonies had been called
together in a general Congress for the purpose of asserting and
vindicating their rights and liberties, and to make known to the
British Government:

T.H.—22

"That the inhabitants of the English Colonies in North America, by the immutable laws of nature, the principles of the English Constitution and the several charters of compacts, have the following *Rights.*"

A number of rights were claimed for the American colonies and set forth in the resolutions that followed the preamble. Among the most important of these were: the entitlement of life, liberty and property; the enjoyment of the rights, liberties and immunities of free and natural born subjects within the realms of England; the right of representation in British Parliament, or to be free from taxation by the British Government; the right of Provincial Legislatures alone to legislate in all cases of taxes and internal policy; the right of trial by a jury of their peers; and the right to peaceably assemble and consider their grievances. These and other rights were claimed, demanded and insisted upon as their indubitable rights and liberties, of which they could not be deprived "without their own consent, by their representatives in their several Provincial Legislatures."

After passing these mildly defiant resolutions, the Congress, on the 20th day of October, 1774, adopted certain articles of association, fourteen in number, looking to the future trade relations of the colonies with Great Britain and her dependencies. The first article provided:

"That from and after the first day of December next, we will not import into British America from Great Britain and Ireland, any goods, wares, or merchandize whatsoever, or from any other place, any such goods, wares, or merchandize as shall have been exported from Great Britain or Ireland, nor will we, after that day import any East India tea from any part of the world; nor any molasses, syrups, paneles, coffee, or pimento, from British plantations, or from Dominica; nor wines from Madeira, or the Western Islands; nor foreign indigo."

The second article was one of seeming little importance at the time of its adoption; but if it had been followed strictly after the colonies gained their independence it would have averted the Civil War of 1861-65. That article is as follows:

"That we will neither import, nor purchase any slave after the first day of December next; after which time we will wholly discontinue the slave trade, and will neither be concerned in it ourselves nor will we hire our vessels, nor sell our commodities or manufactures to those who are concerned in it."

All the other articles were directed to the successful enforcement of the embargo against Great Britain. The fourth article emphatically declared that if the obnoxious Acts and parts of Acts passed by the British Parliament were not repealed by the 10th of September, 1775: "We will not, directly or indirectly, export any merchandise or commodity whatsoever, to Great Britain, Ireland or the West Indies, except via Europe," meaning the neutral countries of Europe. One of the articles provided for the appointment by the people of the counties, cities and towns of committees to see that persons within the limits of their appointments did not violate the provisions of the articles; and if violaters were found they were to be published as "foes to British America" and "the enemies of American liberty." These committees were to be known as safety committees. There was also an article directed against profiteering, which said: "That all manufactures of this country be sold at reasonable prices, so that no undue advantages be taken of a future scarcity of goods."

Previous to adjourning, the Congress prepared a petition to the king, addresses to all the several American colonies, and a memorial to the people of England, acquainting them with the work that had been done and the great purposes of the American people. After accomplishing so much for the future good of their country, the memorable body of patriots and statesmen adjourned to meet again in Philadelphia on the 10th of May, 1775.

In January, 1775, at the instance of Lord Dartmouth, secretary of state for the colonies, the troubles between the colonies and the home government were made the subject for a heated discussion in Parliament. It was upon this occasion that William Pitt, the Great Commoner, became the fearless champion of the rights of the colonists, and unerringly predicted the results that would flow from an adherence to the wicked policy inaugurated by the British ministry. The stern demands of the colonies, and their notice that all commercial intercourse with Great Britain and her dependencies would be broken off, unless the demands were granted, so enraged the vicious ministers of George III. that Parliament was constrained to stand by the Crown. And the Government's policy of outrage and oppression was ordained to be continued and mercilessly enforced.

Already the thought of independence had been lodged and was steadily growing in the minds of the colonists; and nowhere had the democratic spirit taken deeper root than with the brave and hardy pioneers of the Virginia mountain regions. Among the first to act upon the address the Continental Congress had sent to the Virginians were the men of Fincastle County. A meeting of the freeholders of that county was held at the Lead Mines, the county seat, in January, 1775, to consider the resolutions and articles of association adopted by the Congress. The first step taken by the meeting was the selection of a committee of safety; and the recorded proceedings, as given by Summers, were as follows:

"In obedience to the resolves of the Continental Congress, a meeting of the Freeholders of *Fincastle* County, in *Virginia*, was held on the 20th day of *January*, 1775, who after approving of the Association framed by that august body in behalf of the Colonies, and subscribing thereto, proceeded to the election of a Committee, to see the same carried punctually into execution, when the following gentlemen were nominated: the Reverend *Charles Cummings*, Colonel *William Preston*, Colonel *William Christian*, Captain *Stephen Trigg*, Major *Arthur Campbell*, Major *William Inglis*, Captain *Walter Crockett*, Captain *John Montgomery*, Captain *James Mc.Gavock*, Captain *William Campbell*, Captain *Thomas Madison*, Captain *Daniel Smith*, Captain *William Russell*, Captain *Evan Shelby*, and Lieutenant *William Edmondson*. After the election the committee made choice of Colonel *William Christian* for their chairman, and appointed Mr. David Campbell to be clerk."

It was also ordered by the meeting, that an address expressing the thanks and congratulations of the people of Fincastle County be prepared and sent to the citizens who had represented Virginia at the recent session of the Continental Congress. The address was promptly written and forwarded, addressed as follows:

"To the Honorable Peyton Randolph, *Esquire*, Richard Henry Lee, George Washington, Patrick Henry, *Junior*, Richard Bland, Benjamin Harrison, *and* Edmund Pendleton, *Esquires, the Delegates from this Colony, who attended the Continental Congress held at Philadelphia*:

"Gentlemen,—Had it not been for our remote situation and the *Indian War* which we were lately engaged in to chastise those cruel and savage people for the many murders and depredations they have committed amongst us, now happily terminated under the auspices of our present worthy Governor, His Excellency the Right Honorable the Earl of *Dunmore,* we should before this time have made known to you our thankfulness for the very important services you have rendered to your country, in conjunction with the worthy Delegates from the other Provinces. Your noble efforts for reconciling the mother country and the Colonies, on rational and constitutional principles, and your pacifick, steady and uniform conduct in that arduous work entitle you to the esteem of all *British America,* and will immortalize you in the annals of your country. We heartily concur in your resolutions, and shall, in every instance, strictly and invariably adhere thereto.

"We assure you, gentlemen, and all our countrymen, that we are a people whose hearts overflow with love and duty to our lawful Sovereign, *George the Third,* whose illustrious House for several successive reigns have been the guardians of the civil and religious rights and liberties of *British subjects,* as settled at the glorious Revolution; that we are willing to risk our lives in the service of his Majesty for the support of the Protestant religion and the rights and liberties of his subjects, as they have been established by compact, law and ancient charters. We are heartily grieved at the differences which now subsist between the parent state and the Colonies, and most ardently wish to see harmony restored on an equitable basis and by the most lenient measures that can be devised by the heart of man. Many of us and our forefathers left our native land, considering it as a kingdom subjected to inordinate power and greatly abridged of its liberties; we crossed the *Atlantic* and explored this then uncultivated wilderness bordering on many nations of savages and surrounded by mountains almost inaccessible to any but those very savages, who have incessantly been committing barbarities and depredations on us since our first seating the country. These fatigues and dangers we patiently encountered. supported by the pleasing hope of enjoying those rights and liberties which had been granted to *Virginians,* and were denied in our native country, and of transmitting them inviolate to our posterity; but even to these remote regions the hand of unlimited and unconstitutional power hath pursued us, to strip us of that liberty and property with which

God, nature and the rights of humanity have vested us. We are ready and willing to contribute all in our power for the support of his Majesty's government, if applied to constitutionally, and when the grants are made by our own Representatives, but cannot think of submitting our liberty or property to the power of a venal British Parliament, or to the will of a corrupt Ministry. We by no means desire to shake off our duty or allegiance to our lawful sovereign, but, on the contrary, shall ever glory in being the loyal subjects of a Protestant prince, descended from such illustrious progenitors, so long as we can enjoy the free exercise of our religion as Protestants, and our liberties and properties as *British Subjects.*

"But if no pacifick measures shall be proposed or adopted by *Great Britain,* and our enemies will attempt to dragoon us out of those inestimable privileges, which we are entitled to as subjects, and to reduce us to a state of slavery, we declare that we are deliberately and resolutely determined never to surrender them to any power upon earth but at the expense of our lives.

"These are our real, though unpolished, sentiments of liberty and loyalty, and in them we are resolved to live or die.

"We are, gentlemen, with the most perfect esteem and regard, your most obedient servants."

There is nothing obtainable from contemporaneous records to show the number of men that attended the meeting. But there must have been a large gathering, with every section of Fincastle County represented, the Clinch Valley included, as two members of the committee, Captains Smith and Russell, were from that valley. Historians, who have published and commented upon the address, have generally abscribed its authorship to Reverend Charles Cummings. They appear to have reached this conclusion from tradition. The phraseology of the paper shows beyond dispute that it was written by a preacher, and not by a soldier or politician. Reverend Cummings was a preacher, the only one on the Committee, and was its most highly educated member. The professions of love and duty for George III. and his "illustrious House" indicate that the man who drafted the address was an extreme Protestant in religion, and found one redeeming virtue in the otherwise repulsive character of King George—the adherence of the House of Hanover to the cause of Protestantism in its terrible struggle with Roman Catholicism. The love and duty which overflowed the hearts of the men of Fincastle and of "the fighting parson," for George III. were made a secondary consideration when they realized that their civil and religious rights were being violated by the English King. Hence their stern intention to defend those rights at any cost, as written in a closing paragraph: "We declare that we are deliberately and resolutely determined never to surrender them to any power upon earth but at the expense of our lives."

The Tazewell pioneers, no doubt, to a man, were in accord with this expressed determination of their fellow-countrymen to resist to the utmost any attempt to abridge their rights as American citizens. They had been made genuinely and religiously responsive to the charm of the freedom they were enjoying in this grand mountain country—a freedom that was then unknown in any European monarchy, and which exists in none of them now. Though the worship of Kingship had not been discarded by all the settlers west of New River, it soon disappeared when there came a clash of arms between the patriot colonists and the armies of England.

Immediately after the news was received in England that the Continental Congress had recommended to the colonies a suspension of all commercial intercourse with Great Britain and her dependencies, Parliament retaliated by ordering that the colonies be forced into acceptance of the obnoxious shipping laws and the tax on tea. General Gage, who had recently been made governor of Massachusetts, was ordered to begin a campaign of subjugation; and a fleet and an army of ten thousand men were sent him from England to aid in the campaign. As soon as his plans were settled upon, Gage seized and fortified Boston Neck, had the military stores in the arsenals at Cambridge and Charlestown removed to Boston, and issued peremptory orders to the Massachusetts General Assembly to dissolve and disperse. Instead of cringingly obeying the commands of the governor, the members resolved themselves into a Provincial Congress to devise plans and furnish means for meeting force with force. They appropriated money for the organization and equipping of an army of twelve thousand men for the defence of the colony. It was a daring and dangerous course of action for a feeble colony to follow, to thus defy the greatest naval and military power of the world. But the patriots of Massachusetts had received assurances from Virginia and her other sister colonies that they would stand faithfully by them in the mighty struggle to preserve inviolate their rights as American freemen.

BATTLES OF LEXINGTON AND BUNKER HILL.

When Gage began to reveal his purpose to use an armed force to suppress the spirit of revolt, the people of Boston decided to take their supplies of arms and ammunition to Concord, sixteen miles distant. This was effected by concealing the ammunition in cart loads of rubbish and hauling the supplies to the desired destination. In some way Gage was informed of the movement of the Boston people; and he secretly sent Colonel Smith and Major Pitcairn with a regiment of eight hundred soldiers, on the night of the 18th of April, for the two-fold purpose of destroying the stores of ammunition and capturing John Hancock and Samuel Adams. These two men were the main leaders of the revolt in Massachusetts. The detachment of soldiers started for Concord about midnight, and the movement was quickly discovered by some of the alert citizens. They gave an alarm to the people of Boston, Cambridge and Charlestown by ringing bells and firing cannon. The fearless patriot, Joseph Warren started Paul Revere on his memorable midnight ride through Charlestown to Concord and Lexington to warn the people of the hostile approach of the British soldiers under Smith and Pitcairn. This ride has ever since been famous in song and story. Revere eluded the enemy pickets and succeeded in arousing the people; and when the British column reached Lexington a company of militia, commanded by Captain John Parker, was formed on the town common to meet the coming foe. Pitcairn was in charge of the advance troops, and when he saw the patriots were prepared to resist his progress, he halted his men, ordered them to load their guns and advanced at the double-quick upon Parker and his men. Riding at the front, Major Pitcairn cried out: "Disperse, ye villains! Throw down your arms, ye rebels and disperse;" but the Americans resolutely held their ground. Major Pitcairn, seeing their purpose not to yield, fired his pistol at them and then ordered his men to fire. The order was obeyed, and the first discharge of the British muskets killed four and wounded nine of the Massachusetts men. This was the first volley that was fired in the Revolutionary War.

Being greatly outnumbered the Americans began to disperse, and four more of their number were killed while retreating. A scattering fire from Captain Parker's men wounded three of the British soldiers and Major Pitcairn's horse. The militia having dispersed, the British column marched on to effect the main object of the expedition; and arrived at Concord at 7:30 o'clock in the morning. They found but little ammunition there, as the inhabitants had moved the larger part of their stores to other places for concealment. Two cannons were spiked and their carriages destroyed, and a small quantity of ammunition was thrown into a nearby mill pond. While the British were engaged in their work of devastation, the surrounding country having been thoroughly aroused, minute-men began to assemble from all directions. The Americans determined to enter the village and drive the British away; and, in carrying out this design, found a company of the enemy guarding the North Bridge that spanned Concord River. On discovery of the British, the American officers for the first time ordered their men to fire, and two of the enemy were killed by this first volley of the Americans. From that moment the colonists became the aggressors in the running battle that has since been called the "Battle of Lexington." The bridge was captured by the provincials, the enemy retired into the town, and then began to retreat along the road to Lexington. Between Concord and Lexington many of the patriots had concealed themselves on the sides of the road; and for six miles along the highway the terrified British soldiers were treated to a galling fire by the men who were hidden behind rocks, trees, fences and barns. Lord Percy met the fugitives a short distance from Lexington with reinforcements, and saved Colonel Smith's forces from a complete rout. The fight was continued, however, until the precincts of Charlestown were reached. As the conflict continued the untrained Americans gained courage and confidence, and would probably have demanded the surrender of Smith's and Pitcairn's forces if they had not feared that the British fleet would bombard and burn Boston. The losses of the Americans in the first battle of the war were forty-nine killed, thirty-four wounded and five missing, while the British losses in killed and wounded numbered two hundred and seventy-three.

The news of the battle of Lexington spread through all the colonies with remarkable rapidity, though the means the provinces had for communicating with each other were very limited. It filled the masses of the people, who had determined to separate themselves from the monarchy of England, with enthusiasm. The victory proved that America had the men, and, if adequate means could be obtained for maintaining her armies, success was assured for the Revolution.

New England was fired with zeal for the American cause, and within a few days after the battle was fought an army of twenty thousand patriots had gathered about Boston. Nearly all the leaders and many of the men of this provincial host were veterans of the French and Indian War. A line of entrenchments was thrown up which surrounded the city from Roxbury to Chelsea, and it was the common purpose of the Colonials to drive Gage with his army from the city. The Colonial forces were constantly increasing in numbers. John Stark arrived with the New Hampshire militia; grand old Israel Putman was plowing when tidings of the battle of Lexington reached him; he left his plow in the field, turned his oxen loose, mounted a horse and rode to Cambridge in one day, a distance of sixty-eight miles. He procured a commission of brigadier general from the provincial legislature, spurned a commission of major general offered him in the royal army, organized a regiment of men, and afterwards joined his compatriots at Boston. Nathaniel Green came with Rhode Island's quota, and Benedict Arnold arrived with the provincials from New Haven.

Events of great interest to the colonies occurred in rapid succession. Ethan Allen and his Green Mountain boys on the 9th of May captured Ticonderoga. With a mere handful of men, eighty-three in number, Allen crossed Lake Champlain and made a surprise attack at daybreak upon the fort. The sentinel at the gate was driven from his post, and Allen's men faced the barracks ready to fire upon the garrison if resistance was shown. Allen, with Benedict Arnold, who had gone along as a private, rushed to the quarters of Delaplace, the commandant, roused him from his slumbers, and called for a surrender of the fort. When Delaplace asked: "By what authority?" Allen flourished his sword and shouted: "In the name of the Great Jehovah and the Continental Congress." The English officer, with his garrison of forty-eight men surrendered a fort which had cost Great Britain eight million pounds sterling. Two days afterwards the Americans took Skenesborough and Crown Point; and all the northern region was wrested from the English.

Generals Howe, Clinton and Burgoyne arrived at Boston on the 25th of May, bringing with them heavy reinforcements from England and Ireland, increasing the British army to more than ten thousand men. The British generals lost no time in preparing plans to bring the Americans into submission. General Gage issued a proclamation in which he pronounced the revolting colonists rebels

and traitors, but offered pardon to all, except John Hancock and
Samuel Adams, who would lay down their arms and renew their
allegiance to England. This arrogant proposition was scornfully
rejected by the patriotic men of New England.

The Americans in some way obtained information that the
British were getting ready to make sallies from Boston, to drive
away the provincial forces and devastate the surrounding country.
Influenced by this information, on the night of June 16th a thousand
men under the command of Colonel Prescott, grandfather of the
great historian of that name, equipped with picks and spades, slipped away from the American camp and threw up entrenchments on
Bunker Hill. A redoubt eight rods square was planned by the
engineers, and by daybreak was nearly completed. The British
ships were so near that the Americans while at work could hear the
sentinels on the vessels calling out, on the hours, "All is well." At
day-dawn the fortifications were revealed to the British, and it was
seen that Prescott's cannon would command the city. General Gage
and his officers decided that the safety of the British army demanded
expulsion of the Americans from the fortifications on the hill. The
guns of the fleet, and the British batteries on Copp's Hill, were
turned loose on the American position, but did little damage. About
noon a British force of three thousand veterans, commanded by
Generals Howe and Pigot, landed at Morton's Point and made an
assault upon the Americans. Prescott had at this time fifteen hundred men, who were weary and hungry, but they bravely stood to
their guns and awaited the approach of the enemy. Generals Put-
nam and Warren entered the trenches and fought throughout the
battle as privates. The British column was ordered to advance at
three o'clock and at the same time, by prearrangement, every gun of
the fleet and the shore batteries of the British was opened upon the
Americans. Prescott directed his men not to fire until an order was
given them. When the enemy got within fifty yards of the trenches
the order to fire was given, and every gun in the redoubt was quickly
discharged. The front line of the British was swept away by the
deadly aim of the Americans; and the enemy recoiled and retreated
beyond small gun range.

As quickly as possible the British lines were reformed and
another advance was made upon the Americans, with the same result
as the first. A third assault was made and the Americans had but
three or four rounds of ammunition per man left, and as soon as this

was exhausted the British host scaled the trenches. The Americans clubbed their guns and still fought the enemy, but were forced to retire from the trenches at the point of the bayonet. The British lost a thousand and fifty-four, killed and wounded, in the battle, while the American losses were one hundred and fifteen killed, three hundred and five wounded, and thirty-two prisoners. Among the American dead was the gallant General Warren. The retreat was effected by way of Charlestown Neck and Prospect Hill, and a new line of entrenchments was made, which left with the Americans command of the entrance to Boston; and the battle of Bunker Hill gave fresh encouragement to the colonists. When the news of the battle was carried to the Southern provinces the spirit of resistance to British tyranny was greatly increased; and the scheme for forming the government of The United Colonies of America was given fresh impulse.

The day that Ethan Allen and his Green Mountain boys captured Ticonderoga the Continental Congress reassembled at Philadelphia, pursuant to adjournment the previous autumn. George Washington, John Adams, Samuel Adams, Benjamin Franklin, Patrick Henry, and others, who were to be conspicuous figures in the Revolution, were members of the august body.

Composed of such men as these, the Congress was still controlled by a conservative and compromising spirit. The delegates were so reluctant to engage in a bloody conflict with the mother country that another written appeal was prepared and forwarded to George III., urging him to recede from his policy of oppression toward his American subjects. In this memorial, however, the king was given to understand that, if necessary, the colonies would fight to the bitter end for the preservation of their civil and religious freedom. Congress recognized the necessity for co-ordinating the military forces of the colonies and took steps for organizing a Continental army. The necessity for having a commander-in-chief was also seen, and John Adams nominated George Washington, of Virginia, for the responsible position. On the 15th of June, 1775, Congress unanimously confirmed his nomination. Washington was so awed by the heavy responsibilities he was called upon to bear that, with tears in his eyes, he remarked to Patrick Henry: "I fear that this day will mark the downfall of my reputation." But the great patriot accepted the heavy task and proceeded to Boston as quickly as possible to take command of the Continental army at that place, which was accomplished fifteen days after the battle of Bunker Hill.

During the spring, summer and fall of, 1775, the authority of England's King was superseded by independent republican governments in all the colonies. The Virginia colonists had kept apace with the colonies of New England. In March a convention of Virginians was held in Old St. John's Church at Richmond. Patrick Henry urged that an army be raised to resist British oppression; and in support of his suggestion made the wonderful speech that would have immortalized him if he had done nothing else to assist in freeing his countrymen from enslavement by England.

The hostile conduct of the colonies caused the issuance of orders to the several colonial governors to place all military stores beyond the reach of the patriots. In compliance with these orders, Governor Dunmore, on the 19th of April, 1775, secretly removed the gunpowder from the magazine at Williamsburg, and stored it on the Magdalen, a British man-of-war, that was anchored off Yorktown. The people of Williamsburg remonstrated with Dunmore and threatened to seize his person if the powder was not returned. Dunmore was so exasperated that he swore if any injury was offered to himself or the officers who had acted under his orders, he would free the slaves and destroy Williamsburg with fire. These brutal threats not only failed to suppress the people, but caused such indignation throughout the colony that thousands of men from all sections of Virginia armed themselves, assembled at Fredericksburg, and offered their services to defend the capital and drive Dunmore from the colony. Patrick Henry was the leader of this movement; and Dunmore was so greatly alarmed that he sent the King's receiver-general to Henry and paid him for the powder.

CONVENTION OF FINCASTLE MEN.

On the 15th of July, 1775, the Committee of Safety for Fincastle County met at the Lead Mines. After protesting against the dishonorable acts of Dunmore, the following resolutions were adopted:

"Resolved, that the spirited and meritorious conduct of Patrick Henry, Esq., and the rest of the gentlemen volunteers attending him on the occasion of the removal of the gunpowder out of the magazine at Williamsburg, very justly merits the very hearty approbation of this Committee, for which we return them our thanks, with an assurance that we will, at the risk of our lives and fortunes, support and justify them with regard to the reprisals they made.

"Resolved, That the council of this Colony in advising and co-operating with Lord Dunmore in issuing the proclamation of the 3rd of May last, charging the people of this Colony with an ungovernable spirit and licentious practices, is contrary to many known matters of fact, and but too justly shows to us that those who ought to be mediators and guardians of our liberties are become the abject tools of a detested administration.

"Resolved that it is the opinion of this committee that the late sanguinary attempt and preparation of the King's troops, in the colony of Narragansett Bay, are truly alarming and irritating, and loudly call upon all, even the most distant and interiour parts of the Colonies, to prepare and be ready for the extreme event, by a fixed resolution and a firm and manly resolve to avert ministerial cruelty in defence of our reasonable rights and liberties."

In this way the people of Fincastle County, including the settlers of Clinch Valley, thoroughly identified themselves with the struggle the American colonies were making for their independence. As soon as the Colonial Convention, which met at Williamsburg on the 24th of July, 1775, made provision for the raising of two regiments of soldiers, to be commanded by Patrick Henry, the county of Fincastle promptly sent a company of its daring riflemen to Williamsburg. The company was under the command of Captain William Campbell, and did valiant service in the struggle which was then taking place between Governor Dunmore and the revolting colonists. Historians have vainly tried to find a roll of the men who composed Campbell's company. Captain Campbell lived in the Holston Valley, and it is reasonable to suppose that most of the members of his company were from that valley. It is more than probable that some were from the Clinch Valley, as this valley furnished men for all preceding and succeeding military expeditions that went from the country west of New River.

Dunmore had, on the 8th of June, fled from Williamsburg and gone on board the warship Fowey at Yorktown. The General Assembly invited him to return to Williamsburg to sign bills of importance to the colony, and perform other necessary duties of his office. He refused to exercise the functions of governor in association with the General Assembly, unless that body would hold its sessions at Yorktown, where he could be protected by the guns of his ship. This proposal was rejected by the Assembly, and all official intercourse between it and the governor was terminated. The last of June, Dunmore sailed down York River, away from the seat of government, and was never again at Williamsburg.

Regarding the royal government in Virginia as ended, the **General** Assembly was dissolved with an agreement that the members would meet in convention at Richmond to organize a provisional government and formulate a plan of defence. The convention met, pursuant to agreement, on the 17th of July, and elected a committee of safety to temporarily direct the affairs of the new government.

The old Magazine, still standing at Williamsburg, from which Governor Dunmore removed the powder.

This committee was composed of the following then distinguished, and afterwards illustrious citizens of Virginia:—Edmund Pendleton, George Mason, John Page, Richard Bland, Thomas Ludwell Lee, Paul Carrington, Dudley Digges, James Mercer, Carter Braxton, William Cabell, and John Tabb. This excellent committee very efficiently and loyally administered the government until the 1st of July, 1776, when the State Government was organized, with Patrick Henry as Governor.

After he sailed from Yorktown in June, 1775, Dunmore remained for about a year at different localities on the Chesapeake Bay, and there were several collisions of minor importance between his troops and the Colonials. He finally located on Gwynn's Island, off the coast of the present Matthews County. From that place he was driven away on the 9th of July, 1776, by General Andrew Lewis, who was then commander of all the Virginia military forces.

It looked like retributive justice for the splendid mountain soldier to enjoy the privilege of chasing the treacherous Scotch Royalist Governor from the soil of the Old Dominion. Lewis felt that Dunmore had acted insincerely and treacherously toward him and his army of mountaineers after they had made their laborious and dangerous march to Ohio in 1774; and the last official act of Dunmore tended to confirm this suspicion of his integrity. His last official act was the issuing of an order for disbanding the garrison at Fort Blair, the fort which Colonel Andrew Lewis had built at the mouth of the Kanawha after he had defeated the Shawnees at Point Pleasant. This order was made in furtherance of a diabolical scheme to turn the Ohio Indians loose upon the Virginia frontiers while the war was raging between Great Britain and the colonies. The plan of execution was to be worked out by John Connolly, the despised Tory agent of Dunmore, who had been the latter's companion and adviser on the Ohio expedition in the autumn of 1774. Connolly was sent to General Gage at Boston, and returned from that place in October invested with a commission of lieutenant colonel of a regiment of loyalists to be raised on the frontiers. The plans agreed upon were to have the various Indian tribes co-operate with the Tories in harrassing the frontiers, then to assemble at Fort Pitt, and from there march to Alexandria, where they would be joined by Dunmore. The plot was for a time successfully advanced, but suspicions were at last awakened that led to the arrest of one of Connolly's emmisaries, upon whose person incriminating papers were found. This was followed by the arrest of Connolly and two confederates, Allen Cameron and Dr. John Smith, both Scotchmen. They were apprehended at Hagerstown, Maryland, enroute for Detroit, where they were going to bribe the Indians and incite them to begin murdering the frontier settlers. When the baggage of Connolly was searched a general plan of the entire campaign was discovered. Large sums of money and a letter from Dunmore to one of the great Indian chiefs were also found. The discovery of the plot saved all the western frontiers for a time from a concerted invasion by the Indians and Connolly's regiment of Tories. Connolly was held a prisoner until 1781, when he succeeded in making his escape to Canada. After his arrival in Canada he plotted a descent upon Pittsburg, and in 1782 conducted a force which destroyed Hannastown.

CHAPTER XII.

FIRST CONSTITUTIONAL CONVENTION—DECLARES UNITED COLONIES
FREE AND INDEPENDENT STATES—DECLARATION OF RIGHTS
AND CONSTITUTION ADOPTED.

In conformity with the requirements of an ordinance passed by the convention held at Richmond in 1775, the Committee of Safety for Virginia directed that the people of each of the counties of the province elect delegates to a General Convention to be held for the purpose of organizing a constitutional government. The delegates to this convention were chosen in the same manner that members of the House of Burgesses had formerly been elected. Fincastle County sent as its delegates Arthur Campbell and William Russell. Though the settlements in the Clinch Valley had been started less than ten years previous, it seems that this great valley had already attained sufficient importance and population to have one of its first settlers represent Fincastle County in the convention that organized the government of the State of Virginia.

The convention assembled in the capitol at Williamsburg the 6th day of May, 1776. On the same day the House of Burgesses, elected under the royal government, also met at the capitol, but concluded that it had no legal existence, as the royal government had been overthrown. The General Convention was organized by electing Edmund Pendleton, president, and John Tazewell, clerk of the body. On the 15th of May, the convention instructed their delegates in Congress to declare the United Colonies free and independent States. The instructions were given by the adoption of a resolution, which is as follows:

"That the delegates appointed to represent this colony in General Congress, be instructed to propose to that respectable body, *to declare the united colonies free and independent States,* absolved from all allegiance to, or dependence on the crown or parliament of Great Britain; and that they give the assent of this colony to such declaration, and whatever measures may be thought necessary by Congress for forming alliances, and a confederation of the colonies, at such time, and in the manner that to them shall seem best; provided, that the power of forming governments for, and the regula-

T.H.—23

tions of the internal concerns of each colony, be left to the colonial legislatures."

The convention on the same day this resolution was adopted also appointed a committee to prepare a DECLARATION OF RIGHTS, and such a PLAN OF GOVERNMENT "as would be most likely to maintain peace and order in the colony and secure substantial and equal liberty to the people." George Mason was added to the committee on the 18th, and on the 27th of May, 1776, Archibald Cary, chairman of the committee, reported the Bill of Rights to the convention, and it was ordered to be printed for perusal by the members.

After it had been printed, the bill was considered in the committee of the whole on the 29th of May and the 3rd, 4th, 5th and 10th of June. It was again reported to the House with amendments on the 11th, the amendments were agreed to, and it was ordered that the declaration, as amended, be fairly transcribed and read a third time. This was done; and on the 12th of June the declaration had its third reading and was unanimously adopted without debate. It has ever since been considered and retained as the most vital part of the organic law of Virginia.

The fathers were confronted with grave issues when they essayed to make a democratic plan of government for themselves and their eager countrymen. They had to cut loose from the monarchical forms under which they and their ancestors had lived for centuries and sever the ties that bound them to kindred and mother country. But, inspired with the spirit of freedom that had been living and growing for more than a hundred years on Virginia soil, they developed a plan of government that will stand unsurpassed in excellence as long as civilization endures.

It is admitted by all persons, who have an intelligent knowledge of its provisions, that the Virginia Bill of Rights is the most comprehensive, compact and perfect charter of human liberty and popular government that has ever been written. Constitutions may have to be made elastic and may need frequent revisions; but the Virginia Bill of Rights requires nothing more than honest interpretation and application to insure for those persons who desire to live under its ægis the purest and best form of democratic government. Its fundamental principles were in perfect accord with the aspirations and purposes that influenced the Tazewell pioneers to seek this beautiful but wild and isolated region for rearing their families.

Immediately after the adoption of the Bill of Rights the convention proceeded to frame a constitution for the new State of Virginia. The constitution was proclaimed on the 29th of June; and the authority of the Committee of Safety, which had been conducting the affairs of the colony for a year, was vacated. Then the convention proceeded to organize the civil department of the government of the Commonwealth as follows:

"Patrick Henry, Esq., governor. John Page, Dudley Digges, John Tayloe, John Blair, Benjamin Harrison of Berkeley, Bartholomew Dandridge, Charles Carter of Shirley, and Benjamin Harrison of Brandon, counsellors of state. Thomas Whiting, John Hutchins, Champion Travis, Thomas Newton, Jun., and George Webb, Esquires, commissioners of admirality. Thomas Everard and James Cocke, Esquires, commissioners for settling accounts. Edmund Randolph, Esq., attorney-general."

Only a few days intervened between the adoption of the Virginia Bill of Rights by the Virginia Convention and the adoption of the Declaration of Independence by the Continental Congress. That wonderful document, which declared all the American colonies were free of British misrule, was drafted by Virginia's greatest citizen, Thomas Jefferson, and on lines that correspond with the resolutions of the Virginia Convention. The Declaration of Independence was adopted on the 4th of July, 1776, was proclaimed the 8th, and as promptly as possible read to each Division of the Continental army, and transmitted to governing authorities of each of the colonies. On the 29th of July it was proclaimed at the capitol, the court house, and the palace at Williamsburg. The proclamation was heard with joy by the people and was saluted with the firing of cannon and musketry.

After Virginia became an independent government, it was necessary to reorganize the civil government of Fincastle County. The first county court under the State Constitution was held at the Lead Mines on the 3rd of September, 1776, with the following members of the court in attendance: William Preston, James McGavock, Arthur Campbell, John Montgomery, and James McCorkle.

The court appointed William Preston sheriff and county lieutenant; William Sayers, deputy sheriff; and Stephen Trigg, deputy clerk.

FRONTIERS ATTACKED BY INDIANS—KENTUCKY, WASHINGTON AND MONTGOMERY COUNTIES FORMED.

While the Virginia Convention was in session at Williamsburg, the fiendish scheme orignated by Dunmore, and managed by Connolly until he was captured at Hagerstown, for uniting the Northwestern and Southern Indians with the Tories to kill and plunder the patriots on the western frontier, was being perfected by the agents of Great Britain. As previously stated, the last official act of Dunmore as governor of Virginia was to order the withdrawal of the garrison from Fort Blair at the mouth of Kanawha River. This left the entire frontier of Virginia bordering on the Ohio without any military post, and left it wide open to invasion by the Indians. As soon as the General Assembly, elected under the Virginia Constitution, met at the capitol the Legislature re-established the garrison at Fort Blair, and had another stockade fort built a short distance up the river. The new fort was named Fort Randolph, and a regular garrison was stationed there, with Captain Arbuckle in command. From the mouth of the Kanawha on down the Ohio as far as the Virginia territory extended there were no stations along the river. The Sandy Valley was unguarded from the Ohio to the headwaters of the three principal tributaries of Sandy River, all of which had their source in the territory afterwards formed into Tazewell County. So, the Upper Clinch Valley and Bluestone settlements were left exposed, as they had been in 1774, to incursions by the Shawnees and other tribes in Ohio.

About the time that Virginia was erected into an independent democratic government, in July, 1776, the Delaware, Shawnee and Mingo chiefs gathered at Fort Pitt and solemnly declared that they would remain neutral in the conflict that had begun between the Americans and Great Britain. The Iroquois had representatives at the council, and, after declaring for neutrality, asserted that the tribes of that nation would not allow either the Americans or the British to march their armies over or through the territory of the Six Nations. They urged the Shawnees and Delawares to adopt the same policy toward the belligerents. This action of the Indians, in proclaiming neutrality, stimulated the agents of the British Government to greater effort for securing the assistance of the red men to exterminate the frontier settlers or drive them from their homes.

Henry Hamilton, who was the British lieutenant governor for the northwestern territory, was selected by his government to seduce the Indians from their pledged neutrality. He was a bold and unscrupulous man, and well fitted for the execution of the wicked purposes of the British Government. His influence with the Indians was on a plane with his unscrupulous character, and he succeeded in enlisting the support of most of the Northwestern Indians on the side of the British. In the fall of 1776, Hamilton summoned the Northwestern tribes to meet him in councils at Detroit. The tribes of that region were strongly represented at the councils; and the Iroquois, who had abandoned their position of neutrality, sent ambassadors to urge the Northwestern Indians to compose their differences, and unite with the Six Nations in their support of the British against the Americans. The fiendish Hamilton made free use of presents and "fire water" to excite the Indians into acquiescence; and succeeded only too well in his brutal designs. By direction of the British authorities, he promised the savages that they should be paid a liberal price for every American scalp they took and delivered to him or other agents of his government, the prices being graduated and fixed for the scalps of men, women, and children. In some instances fifty dollars was the price paid for a scalp; and one cunning Indian divided a large scalp into two parts, receiving fifty dollars for each part. Roosevelt, in "Winning of the West," speaking of Hamilton and his beastly associates, says:

"These were hardened, embittered men who paid for the zeal of their Indian allies accordingly as they received tangible proof thereof; in other words, they hired them to murder non-combatants as well as soldiers, and paid for each life, of any sort, that was taken. The fault lay primarily with the British Government, and with its advisers who, like Hamilton, advocated the employment of the savages. They thereby became participants in the crimes committed; and it was idle folly for them to prate about having bidden the savages be merciful. * * * Making all allowance for the strait in which the British found themselves, and admitting that much can be said against their accusers, the fact remains that they urged on hordes of savages to slaughter men, women, and children along the entire frontier; and for this there must ever rest a dark stain on their national history."

Having won the Indians to the support of Great Britain, Hamilton began to make preparations for attacking the frontiers the following spring. He organized a company of white men, which was made up of French, British, and Tories who had gathered at Detroit. Three members of the band were the despised renegades, Alexander McKee, Matthew Elliott, and Simon Girty. These infamous white men were engaged to lead the savages in the campaign designed to exterminate the white settlers on the borders. Hamilton had been ordered by his superior officers to execute the plans agreed upon by General Howe and Dr. John Connolly the preceding spring, that is, to attack the frontier settlements of Virginia and Pennsylvania, destroy the crops of the settlers, burn their houses, and kill the inhabitants, regardless of age or sex, or drive them east of the Alleghanies. Another pledge was made the Indians to induce them to give their earnest support to the British. Hamilton was ordered to and did promise them that they would not only be paid liberally for the scalps they took, but that they would be given back their former hunting grounds, from which the white settlers were to be ejected.

Maddened with liquor and ensnared by the liberal gifts of the English agents, the poor, ignorant savages indulged the hope that the British would restore to them their hunting grounds south and east of the Ohio. Of course "Perfidious Albion" would never, if it could have done so, made good this pledge to the red men. In October, 1773, the Privy Council had made a grant to Thomas Walpole and a company of Englishmen for all the territory belonging to Virginia situated west of the Alleghanies. Walpole and his speculative associates were to establish a new province to be called Vandalia, with the seat of government located at the mouth of the Kanawha on the Point Pleasant battle ground.

Evidently, it was the intention of the British Government to force the settlers from the regions west of the Alleghany mountains; and, after bringing the colonies into subjection, turn over to Thomas Walpole and his associate Englishmen the extensive territory granted them by the Privy Council. The Revolutionary War first obstructed and then defeated Walpole's scheme. If the war had been won by Great Britain, the pioneer settlers of the Clinch Valley, who had obtained no legal titles to their lands, would have been evicted from their holdings or forced to pay a price therefor to the English speculators.

Early in the spring of 1777, Hamilton collected his motley forces and dispatched them on their mission of bloodshed and devastation. War parties of Indians, accompanied by white leaders, crossed the Ohio, and began to make attacks upon the border settlements from the Monongahela and Kanawha to the Kentucky River. Scouting parties sent out by the whites gave due warning of the approach of the enemy. Though greatly alarmed for the safety of their families, the settlers did not flee from their threatened homes, but made the best preparation they could to repel the attacks of the Indians. The Tazewell pioneers placed their families in the neighborhood forts, several new forts were built, and nearly every strong log cabin was made a block-house with loop-holed walls, heavily barred doors, and other defensive arrangements.

The savages started out by Hamilton were fully supplied with guns, tomahawks, and scalping knives, and an abundance of powder and lead. These supplies had been sent from the British arsenals in Canada; and, thus equipped, the Indians made the year 1777 one full of horrors for the backwoodsmen. Roosevelt says:

"The captured women and little ones were driven off to the far interior. The weak among them, the young children, and the women heavy with child were tomahawked and scalped as soon as their steps faltered. The able-bodied, who could stand the terrible fatigue, and reached their journey's end, suffered various fates. Some were burned at the stake, others were sold to the French or British traders, and long afterwards made their escape, or were ransomed by their relatives. Still others were kept in the Indian camps, the women becoming the slaves or wives of the warriors, while the children were adopted into the tribe, and grew up precisely like their little red-skinned playmates."

This, I believe, is the first recorded instance of the dishonouring of captive white women by the Indians. The awful fate that befell these white women was due, no doubt, to the bestial influence exercised over the savages by their vicious white leaders—the British,

French, and renegade white Americans—who organized and led the Indians in their ferocious attacks upon the frontier settlements.

The first settlers in Tazewell County had the good fortune to escape the frightful experiences that the inhabitants of Kentucky and the region east of the Kanawha had to pass through during the year 1777. There was but one invasion of the Upper Clinch Valley during that year by the Indians, at least, Bickley makes no mention of but one, and none others have been handed down by tradition. This escape of our pioneer ancestors from massacres was largely due to the rapid colonization of Kentucky, under the direction of Boone, Harrod, Logan and others.

The Kentucky settlements were so near to the Shawnees and other hostile western tribes, and the hunting grounds in that region being the finest on the continent, that it was the easiest and most attractive prize the Indians would win under their contract with the British Government. Moreover, the heavy and rapid emigration which was pressing on to the southern banks of the Ohio gave warning to the Indians that the white men, if not obstructed, would very soon cross the Ohio and drive the red men beyond the Mississippi, or into Canada. Consequently, the Indians gave their first and most resolute attention to winning back from the whites the magnificent Kentucky region.

CHAPTER XIII.

KENTUCKY, WASHINGTON, AND MONTGOMERY COUNTIES ARE FORMED.

The permanent settlers in Kentucky had increased to the number of about six hundred by the spring of 1776, and they became ambitious, for sound reasons, to organize their settlements into a distinct county. They were completely detached from the Clinch Valley and Holston settlements in Fincastle County; and believed, or knew, they had no representation in the civil government of either Fincastle County or of the State of Virginia. The people who had refused to accept or recognize Henderson's Transylvania government determined to elect two delegates to the General Assembly of Virginia; and send a petition to that body, asking that a new county be formed, to be called Kentucky. In pursuance of this plan, an election, which continued for five days, was held at Harrodsburg, in June, 1776. George Rodgers Clark, who was then abiding at Harrodsburg, and Captain John Gabriel Jones were elected delegates to the General Assembly. Without delay Clark and his colleague started for Williamsburg, carrying with them the certificate of their election and the petition for the new county.

In their petition the Kentuckians assailed the usurpations of Henderson and his company, and denounced their effort to establish Transylvania as a government independent of Virginia. The petitioners disputed the validity of the purchase made by Henderson and his associates from the Cherokees. They declared that they recognized the fact that the lands they occupied belonged to Virginia territory, and that they were justly entitled to enjoy the privileges and contribute to the support and defence of the State Government.

Upon arrival at Williamsburg, Clark found that the Legislature had adjourned; and he laid the petition of his constituents before Governor Henry and the Privy Council. He requested the council to furnish the Kentuckians five hundred pounds of powder to be used for protecting the border against the Indians. At first, the council declined to supply the powder, but later granted the request.

When the General Assembly convened in October, Clark and his colleague, Captain John Gabriel Jones, were present and asked to be seated, and presented the petition of the Kentucky settlers to the

Assembly. Clark and his colleague were very properly denied the privilege or right to sit as members of the body, but the petition was received and referred to the proper committee. At the same time the following resolution was adopted:

"Resolved, That the inhabitants of the western part of Fincastle not being allowed by the law a distinct representation in the General Assembly, the delegates chosen to represent them in this House cannot be admitted. At the same time, the committee are of opinion, that the said inhabitants ought to be formed into a distinct county, in order to entitle them to such representation, and other benefits of government."

In the meantime the inhabitants of the Clinch, Holston and New River valleys, having heard of the plans of the Kentuckians to procure for themselves a separate county, prepared and forwarded petitions to the General Assembly, praying that the territory of Fincastle County east of Kentucky be divided into two distinct counties. The petitions of the Holston, New River, and Clinch settlers were presented along with that sent from Kentucky. Henderson, as the representative of the bogus Transylvania government, attended the session of the General Assembly, and vigorously opposed the formation of Kentucky into a new county. And, from circumstances connected with the legislation, it may be presumed that there was opposition on the part of leading citizens of the New River Valley to the division into two counties of that portion of Fincastle situated east of Kentucky. The men of the New River and Reed Creek settlements had previously held and received the emoluments of the most desirable county offices, and in fact had dominated the affairs of the county. Finally, opposition of every kind was overcome, and on the 7th day of December, 1776, the General Assembly passed an act which provided for the division of Fincastle County into three distinct counties. In part, the act is as follows:

"Whereas, from the great extent of the county of Fincastle, many inconveniences attend the more distant inhabitants thereof, on account of their remote situation from the court house of the said county, and many of the said inhabitants have petitioned this present general assembly for a division of the same:

"*Be it therefore enacted by the General Assembly of the Commonwealth of Virginia, and it is hereby enacted by the authority of*

the same, That from and after the last day of December next
ensuing the said county of Fincastle shall be divided into three counties, that is to say: All that part thereof which lies to the south
and westward of a line beginning on the Ohio at the mouth of Great
Sandy creek, and running up the same and the main or north easterly
branch thereof to the Great Laurel Ridge or Cumberland Mountain,
thence south westerly along the said mountain to the line of North
Carolina, shall be one distinct county, and called and known by the
name of Kentucky; and all that part of the said county of Fincastle
included in the lines beginning at the Cumberland Mountain, where
the line of Kentucky county intersects the North Carolina line,
thence east along the said North Carolina line to the top of Iron
Mountain, thence along the same easterly to the source of the south-
fork of Holstein river, thence northwardly along the highest part of
the high lands, ridges, and mountains, that divide the waters of the
Tennessee from those of the Great Kanawha to the most easterly
source of Clinch river, thence westwardly along the top of the mountains that divide the waters of Clinch river from those of the Great
Kanawha and Sandy creek to the line of Kentucky county, thence
along the same to the beginning, shall be one other distinct county,
and called and known by the name of Washington; and all the
residue of the said county of Fincastle shall be one other distinct
county, and shall be called and known by the name of Montgomery."

The act also provided that a court composed of justices should
be held in each of the counties as follows: Kentucky, at Harrodsburg, on the first Tuesday in every month: Washington, at Black's
fort (now Abingdon), the last Tuesday in every month: Montgomery, at Fort Chiswell, the first Tuesday in every month."

The act also provided a suffrage qualification for the citizens of
the three counties as follows:

"*And be it further enacted,* That every free white man who, at
the time of elections of delegates or senators for the said several
counties, shall have been for one year preceding in possession of
twenty five acres of land with a house and plantation thereon, or
one hundred acres without a house and plantation, in any of the said
counties, and having right to an estate for life at least in the said
land in his own right, or in right of his wife, shall have a vote, or be
capable of being chosen a representative in the county where his

said land shall lie, although no legal title in the same shall have been conveyed to such possessers; and that in all future elections of senators, the said counties of Montgomery, Washington, and Kentucky, together with the county of Botetourt, shall form and be one district."

At the time this act was passed there had been no separation of the Church and State in Virginia. Hence the act provided for dividing the parish of Botetourt, which embraced all the territory in the then county of Botetourt and the three new counties, into four parishes, to be called, respectively, Montgomery parish, Kentucky parish, Washington parish, and Botetourt parish.

Thomas Jefferson was chairman of the committee to which the bill creating the new counties was referred. He was then recognized as the greatest advocate and exponent of the principles of popular government living in Virginia, as he was later to be acknowledged the greatest in America. No doubt, he was responsible for the peculiar suffrage qualifications imposed upon the men who were to be voters in the counties of Kentucky, Washington and Montgomery. The evident purpose of Mr. Jefferson and his associates was to extend to every free white citizen in these counties the right of suffrage. And the imposition of the freeholder's qualification was merely the application and interpretation of that part of the Virginia Bill of Rights which says: "that all men, having sufficient evidence of permanent common interest with, and attachment to the community, *have the right of suffrage.*"

The line, as established by the act, between the counties of Washington and Montgomery was so uncertain as to location that it was found necessary to have it more clearly defined. In the month of May, 1777, the General Assembly amended the act of 1776, changing the line between Washington and Montgomery as follows:

"Beginning at a ford on Holston river, next above Captain John Campbell's, at the Royal Oak, and running from thence a due south course to the dividing line between the states of Virginia and North Carolina; and from the ford aforesaid to the westerly end of Morris' Knob, about three miles above Maiden Spring on Clinch, and from thence, by a line to be drawn due north, until it shall intersect the waters of the great Sandy river."

The line as located by the original act ran through the present Tazewell County about six miles east of the town of Tazewell, placing the greater portion of the present Tazewell County in Washington County. By the act of May, 1777, the line was located about six miles west of the town, and the larger part of the territory was in Montgomery. In other words, all the country west of the line which ran by Morris' Knob was in Washington, while all east of that line was in Montgomery.

Even after the new line was created by the General Assembly, frequent disputes arose between citizens of Washington and Montgomery as to the true location of the line. In the spring of 1782, the county courts of the respective counties selected Hugh Fulton to run the line. Fulton performed the work promptly and made a report thereof on the 6th of May, 1782, and the report was confirmed by the courts of the two counties. The courses, distances, and so forth, given in the report, are as follows:

"Beginning at a white walnut and buckeye at the ford of Holston next above the Royal Oak, and runneth thence — N. 31 W. over Brushy mountain, one creek, Walker's mountain, north fork of Holston, Locust cove, Little mountain, Poor Valley creek, Clinch mountain, and the south fork of Clinch to a double and single sugar tree and two buckeye saplings on Bare grass hill, the west end of Morris' Knob, fifteen miles and three quarters. Thence from said knob north crossing the spurs of the same, and Paint Lick mountain the north fork of Clinch by John Hines' plantation, and over the river ridge by James Roark's in the Baptist Valley, to a sugar tree and two white oaks on the head of Sandy five miles, one quarter— twenty poles.

"The beginning at said walnut and buckeye above the Royal Oak, and running south, crossing the middle fork of Holston, Campbell's mill creek, three mountains, the south fork of Holston above Jones' mill, his mill creek, four mountains, Fox creek to six white pines on the top of Iron mountain by a laurel thicket, eleven miles, three quarters and sixty poles.

"The distance of said line from the head of Sandy to the top of the Iron mountain is thirty three miles.

Executed and returned, May the 6th, 1783.

Hugh Fulton."

When the Revolutionary War broke out the pioneer settlers of Clinch Valley were in such a perilous situation, on account of the threatened Indian invasions, that they could give no immediate substantial aid to the colonists of the East and South who were resisting the British armies. All the vital energy of the sturdy men of the Clinch had to be conserved and used for the protection of their own settlements. In the previous war, that of 1774, they had to practically take care of themselves; and they would have been compelled to endure many subsequent outrages from the Indians, if it had not been for the crushing defeat they helped to give the savages at Point Pleasant.

The Indians had been previously the only foes encountered by the Tazewell pioneers. In the great struggle for American freedom, begun in 1776, our ancestors had to grapple with the blood-thirsty savages led by the agents and officers of the British Government, the government for which the Virginians had fought so nobly in former wars. Not a man, however, who was living in the Upper Clinch Valley faltered in devotion to the cause of American freedom. There were some of the settlers who regretted to see the ties that bound them to kindred and the mother country rudely broken, but there were no Tories here. The Scotch-Irish, the German Huguenots, and the Englishmen who had come here from Pennsylvania, Maryland and Eastern Virginia had rapidly commingled and developed into true Americans.

Our ancestors were so busily occupied with their home-making pursuits that they neglected to make any written record of their performances in the Revolution. They were extending their clearings into the depths of the forests, were enlarging and making their houses stronger, were building new forts, and block-houses, and getting ready to repel apprehended attacks from the Indians. We are almost entirely dependent upon tradition for knowledge of what transpired in the Clinch Valley during the progress of the Revolution. Dr. Bickley was fortunate enough to write history at a date when a few of the sons and a number of the grandsons of the pioneers were still living. From these he gathered a minimum of valuable information, and, possibly, might have obtained much more, but for undue haste in collecting the data and writing his book. Writing of this intensely interesting period, Bickley says:

"Previous to 1776, the settlers were engaged in erecting suitable houses to protect their families from the inclemencies of the weather, as well as to render them more secure from the attacks of the Indians. Their lands had to be opened, and, consequently, they were much in the forest. As there was an abundance of game, and few domestic animals, their meat was taken mostly from the forest; this likewise took them from home. They were few, and to raise a house, or roll the logs from a field, required the major part of a settlement. This likewise left their families exposed; yet such work was usually executed during the winter months, when the Indians did not visit the settlements. To give further protection to the families of the settlers, in every neighborhood block-houses were, as soon as convenient, erected, to which the families could repair in time of necessity.

"After 1776, forts and stations were built, as it became necessary for many of the settlers to join the army. In these forts, and particularly at the stations, a few men were left to defend them. But the extent of country to be defended was so great, and the stations so few, that there was, in reality, but little safety afforded to the families of the settlers.

"De Hass has given correct descriptions of block-houses, forts, and stations, to which I beg to refer the reader. There was a fort erected by William Wynn, a strict old Quaker, and one of the best of men, on Wynn's branch; another at Crab orchard, by Thomas Witten, and one at Maiden Spring, by Rees Bowen—two men whose names will be cherished in the memories of the people of Tazewell for ages to come.

"There was a station on Linking Shear branch, containing a few men under the command of Capt. John Preston, of Montgomery; another on Bluestone creek, in command of Capt. Robert Crockett of Wythe county, and another at the present site of White Sulphur springs, in command Capt. James Taylor of Montgomery. It is also said, that there was a station in Burk's Garden; I imagine, however, that it was not constructed by order of the Government.

"The following persons, citizens of the county, were posted in these forts and stations, viz:

Bailey, John	Burgess, Edward
Bailey, James	Belcher, Robert
Belcher, Joseph	Brewster, Thomas

Chaffin, Christopher
Connely, James
Crockett, John
Cottrell, John
Evans, John, Sr.
Evans, John, Jr.
Gilbert, Joseph
Godfrey, Absalom
Hall, William
Lusk, David
Lusk, Samuel
Lusley, Robert
Martin, James

Maxwell, John
Maxwell, Thomas
Marrs ————?
Peery, James
Pruett, John
Thompson, Archibald
Witten, James
Wynn, Oliver
Wright, Michael
Ward, John
Ward, William
Wright, Hezekiah

"These men were to hold themselves in readiness to act as circumstances might demand. To make them more efficient, spies were employed to hang upon the great trails leading into the settlements from the Ohio. Upon discovering the least sign of Indians, they hurried into the settlements and warned the people to hasten to the forts or stations, as the case might be. They received extra wages for their services, for they were both laborious and important, and also fraught with danger. For such an office the very best men were chosen; for it will be readily seen, that a single faithless spy, might have permitted the Indians to pass unobserved, and committed much havoc among the people, before they could have prepared for defense. But it does not appear that any "spy" failed to give the alarm when possible to do so. They always went two together, and frequently remained out several weeks upon a scout. Great caution was necessary to prevent the Indians from discovering them, hence their beds were usually of leaves, in some thicket commanding a view of the war-path. Wet or dry, day or night, these men were ever on the lookout. The following persons were chosen from the preceding list, to act as spies, viz:

Burgess, Edward
Bailey, James
Bailey, John
Crockett, John

Maxwell, John
Martin, James
Wynn, Oliver
Witten, James

"The last of whom, was one of the most sagacious and successful spies to be found anywhere on the frontier. His name is yet as familiar with the people, as if he had lived and occupied a place among them but a day ago.

"Such as were too old to bear arms in the government service, usually guarded the women, children, and slaves, while cultivating the farms. Tazewell had but a small population at this time, yet from the number engaged in the regular service, we should be led to think otherwise.

"It is a little strange that the frontiers should have furnished so many men for the army, when their absence so greatly exposed their families. But when we reflect that no people felt the horrors of war more sensibly than they did, and that no people are readier to serve the country in the day when aid is needed, than those of mountainous regions, we shall at once have an explanation to their desire, and consequent assistance, in bringing the war to a close. Beside, the people of Tazewell have ever been foremost in defending the country; showing at once that determination to be free, which so eminently characterizes the people of mountainous districts."

CHAPTER XIV.

CLARK'S EXPEDITION TO ILLINOIS, AND BATTLE OF KING'S MOUNTAIN.

Another event of great moment to the pioneer settlers of Tazewell occurred in 1778. It was the invasion and conquering of the Illinois country by George Rodgers Clark with his small but intrepid army of Virginia frontiersmen. As hereinbefore related Clark had settled in Kentucky, and was one of the two delegates elected to represent that country in the Virginia General Assembly before it was erected into a county. After his return to Kentucky from Williamsburg in 1777 he rendered valuable assistance to Boone, Harrod, Floyd, Logan, and the other settlers in their bloody struggles with the large Indian bands sent by Hamilton to drive the Virginians from Kentucky. Clark realized that the Kentuckians and other border settlers of Virginia would have no rest or safety until the Northwestern Indians were subdued and the British garrisons in that region were captured or driven out. The country beyond the Ohio was occupied by numerous large and warlike tribes; and there were a number of military posts that had been taken from France at the conclusion of the French and Indian War and were still held by the soldiers of Great Britain. From these posts the British commanders were continually equipping and sending out Indian bands to attack, kill, and scalp the settlers in Kentucky and the other border settlements of Virginia.

Clark concluded that it was feasible to make a secret invasion of the country with a small armed force and capture the territory which he knew belonged to Virginia. Early in the summer of 1777 he sent two daring young men as spies to Illinois and the country about Vincennes, without revealing to them his purposes, but to find out existing conditions there. The report which the spies brought back was to the effect, that the French population in the villages where the British had their military posts were not devoted to the cause of England, and were taking no interest in the struggle between Great Britain and the American colonies. This report confirmed Clark in his belief that the Illinois country could be wrested from the British by a small army of resolute border men under his command; and he determined to submit his plans to Governor Henry and seek his official support in the undertaking. To this end, on October 1st, 1777, Clark started from Harrodsburg to Williamsburg. He was engaged for more than a month in making the journey to the capital, where he promptly made known his plans to Patrick Henry, who finally gave Clark authority to raise seven companies of fifty men each, to serve as militia, and to be gathered from the counties west of the Blue Ridge. The governor advanced him twelve hundred pounds to pay the expenses of the expedition, and gave him an order to the authorities at Pittsburg to furnish him adequate supplies and ammunition, and boats to transport them, and such men as he might enlist in that vicinity, down the Ohio. Thomas Jefferson, George Mason, and George Wythe, whom Clark met at Williamsburg, pledged themselves in writing to use their influence with the Virginia General Assembly to grant each man who went with the expedition three hundred acres of land in the conquered territory.

Two letters of instructions, one open, and the other sealed, were given Clark by Governor Henry. The open letter ordered Clark to use his forces to relieve the Kentucky settlers from the distress they were in on account of the frequent attacks made upon them by the Indians. And the sealed, or secret letter, directed him to invade and conquer the Illinois country that was controlled by the British. The men who were then living with their families in the frontier counties were so much engrossed with their home and community affairs that they were loth to engage in an enterprise that would take them far from their homes for a long period. Consequently, much trouble was experienced by Clark when he tried to obtain the quota of men he had authority to enlist for the expedition; but he succeeded in enlisting about one hundred and fifty men in the country about Pittsburg, and determined to start with these to the scene of proposed action. In May, 1778, he started from the Redstone settlements with his soldiers and a number of adventurers and men with families who wanted to settle in Kentucky. They used as transports a flotilla of flatboats, and rowed and drifted down the Ohio to the mouth of the Kentucky. From that point the expeditionary force floated down stream to the Falls of the Ohio, arriving at that place the 27th of May. There the emigrants separated from Clark and his men, and went off to the interior settlements of Kentucky. A considerable number of the Kentucky settlers, and a small company of men from the Holston and Clinch settlements joined Clark at the Falls. By previous arrangement four companies from the Clinch and Holston were to go with the expedition; but only one company, under command of Captain John Montgomery, arrived and reported for service. At the Falls, Clark for the first time revealed to his men the real object of his expedition. Those who had accompanied him down the Ohio, and the Ketuckians, readily agreed to take part in the hazardous adventure; but most of the men from the Holston and Clinch settlements refused to go on the dangerous and necessarily laborious campaign. They left the camp in the night time and started to return to their homes. Though Clark had misled these men, who had gone from Washington County, as to his real objective, he was infuriated by what he considered a desertion; and sent the Kentuckians who had horses in pursuit of the men who had started for their homes, directing the pursuers to kill all who refused to return to the camp. Only a few, however, were overtaken and they returned and went with the expedition. As they passed through the Kentucky settlements on their homeward journey, the men from the Clinch and Holston were treated very rudely and cruelly by the Kentuckians. This was very unjust as they had been deceived as to the nature of the expedition, and were justified in refusing to engage in an enterprise they had not enlisted for—one that would take them so far from their homes and families for a long time. A small number of men who went from the territory which now composes Tazewell County accompanied Clark on his expedition, and were with him when he captured Kaskaskia and Vincennes. Those who were known to have gone from Tazewell, were: William Peery, Low Brown, John Lasly, and Solomon Stratton. To this extent the pioneers of Tazewell participated in the splendid achievements of George Rodgers Clark, who drove the British from the Northwestern territory and put Virginia in possession of the vast domain which was afterwards generously ceded by our State to the United States.

On the 24th of June the expeditionary forces went aboard their flatboats at the Falls and continued their voyage down the Ohio; and upon arrival at a small island near the mouth of the Tennessee River went into camp on the island. Shortly after their arrival they were joined by a small party of American hunters who were returning from a hunting trip in the Illinois country. The hunters gave Clark valuable information about the defensive conditions of the forts at Kaskaskia and Vincennes, and the sentiment of the French and creole inhabitants of the various towns about the British posts. As they were of an adventurous disposition and in sympathy with the revolting American colonists, the hunters gladly accepted Clark's request to accompany him on the campaign. Clark's army of about two hundred men left the island, and made a rapid overland march to Kaskaskia, where, on the 4th, of July, a surprise night attack was made upon the British garrison. The fort and village were captured without the loss of a man by the Virginians. Chahokia and Vincennes in due time were also surrendered to Clark, and the French and creole inhabitants promptly took the oath of allegiance to the United States.

Hamilton was then at Detroit, and was gathering together and equipping large numbers of Indians for other attacks upon the border settlements; but the successful invasion of Illinois by the Virginians forced the beastly British officer to abandon his murderous schemes. He was astounded by the daring, and successful venture of Clark and his wonderful small army of fighting backwoodsmen; and began immediately to make preparation for recapturing Vincennes, and expelling the Virginians from Illinois. For this enterprise he organized a force, which was composed of one hundred and seventy-seven white men and sixty Indians. With an ample supply of arms, ammunition, and other supplies, Hamilton started with his expedition to Vincennes, and reached that place on the 17th of December. Captain Leonard Helm was in command of the fort and his garrison was made up of two or three Americans and a number of creole militia. At the approach of the British the treacherous creoles deserted, leaving Helm with no support but the few faithful Americans, and he was compelled to surrender the fort.

Francis Vigo, a trader from St. Louis and an Italian by birth, had been imprisoned and cruelly treated by Hamilton while Vigo was on a visit to Vincennes. When he was released he returned to St. Louis, and as quickly as possible went to Kaskaskia and gave Clark such information as caused him to take immediate steps for marching against Vincennes. It was midwinter, and it seemed impossible for men to march on foot nearly two hundred and fifty miles through an uninhabited region, where a great part of the ground was lowlands and at the time was flooded by heavy freshets.

But the fearless Clark determined to surmount all difficulties and forestall Hamilton's proposed campaign in the spring. On the 7th of February, 1779, Clark began his march to Vincennes with one hundred and seventy men, part of whom were young French creoles who had remained faithful to the American cause. Clark's march to Vincennes has been related both in history and romance as one of the marvels of the military world.

Clark came in sight of his desired goal on the afternoon of the 23rd, of February, having made the march of two hundred and forty miles in sixteen days. He sent a messenger, a creole whom he had captured, to notify the French inhabitants, and also Hamilton, that he was going to attack the place. The people who were friendly to the Americans were requested to remain in their houses where they would be in no danger; and the friends of the British were told to join Hamilton in the fort "and fight like men." At sundown he marched against the town and at seven o'clock entered its limits. During the night he had his men throw up intrenchments within rifle-shot distance of the fort. At sunrise on the 24th his riflemen began to pour a well directed fire into the loop-holes, and the two small cannon the British were using were soon silenced by the keen-eyed Virginia marksmen. Before noon, Clark demanded a surrender of the fort, but Hamilton haughtily refused to yield. In the afternoon a flag of truce was sent out with the request for an interview between Hamilton and Clark, which resulted in the surrender of the garrison of seventy-one men. Clark and his men hated Hamilton intensely, and spoke of him as the "hair-buyer general," alluding to his payments of large sums to Indians for the scalps they brought in from the border settlements. When Clark assailed him for his brutal acts, he tried to escape responsibility by saying that he had merely executed the orders of his superior officers who had acted under orders given them by the British Government. Soon after Vincennes was captured sufficient reinforcements arrived from Virginia to enable Clark to establish permanent garrisons at Vincennes, Kaskaskia, and Chahokia. He made the Indians sue for peace, or drove them from the country; and the Revolution came to an end without the British being able to regain control of the Northwestern territory.

The permanent settlement of Kentucky had been of great value to the Clinch Valley settlements by attracting the attention of the hostile Indians away from this region. Clark's occupation of the Illinois country was in the same way very serviceable to the pioneers. It prevented any further incursions of the Clinch region by the savages until the Revolution was ended.

BATTLE OF KING'S MOUNTAIN.

The Battle of King's Mountain was an event of far-reaching importance to the cause of American Independence. It was the privilege of a gallant band of the Tazewll pioneers to participate and render valiant service in that memorable engagement, which is generally conceded to have turned the tide in favor of the American patriots in their prolonged struggle for freedom from British oppression.

Major Patrick Ferguson, a Scottish soldier of distinguished lineage, and who won unenviable distinction by many cruel deeds in the British campaigns in New York, had, for a year previous to his defeat and death at King's Mountain, been terrorizing the patriots of the Carolinas. He had first gone to the Carolinas with General Henry Clinton, when Clinton made his expedition against Charleston at the close of the year 1779. At that time Ferguson held the title of major in the British army; but just previous to his death he had been promoted to the rank of lieutenant colonel, having won the favor of his superior officers by organizing the Tories and using them effectively against the Americans. After the capture of Charleston, Sir Henry Clinton began at once to form plans for the complete subjugation of the Carolinas; and he concluded to use for this accomplishment a large Tory element that he knew was to be found in the two Carolinas. For the execution of his designs he selected Major Patrick Ferguson and Major George Hanger, both of whom were intolerant of what they termed disloyalty to the King; and these kindred wicked spirits had already in numerous instances shown a disposition to subject American citizens to inhuman treatment.

The two British officers were clothed with both civil and military authority, and were directed to organize local civil governments as well as subjugate the rebels. They proceeded to organize the Tories into militia companies and regiments; and these were sent out on predatory excursions, greatly to the damage and discomfort of the patriotic Americans. The barbarities inflicted upon the patriots, who refused to renew their allegiance to the British Government, attracted the attention and sympathy of the inhabitants of the Watauga and Holston settlements, known as the "over-mountain region," then a part of North Carolina, but now known as East Tennessee. Colonel John Sevier, who lived on the Watauga, and Colonel Isaac Shelby, residing on the Holston, received urgent calls for assistance from their fellow-patriots who lived in what is now Western North Carolina. Colonel Sevier dispatched a part of his regiment of militia under command of Major Charles Robertson to the assistance of Colonel Joseph McDowell, who with a small force was contending against the large number of Tories that had flocked to Ferguson's standard. A few days after Robertson started Colonel Shelby followed with two hundred mounted riflemen, and joined McDowell near the Cherokee ford of Broad River about the 25th of July, 1780. Robertson and Shelby co-operated with McDowell and other of the Carolinians through the month of August, and participated in the engagement at Cedar Spring on the 24th of that month. The Tories and the Liberty men both claim to have gotten the better of the fight; but, from the accounts given by the respective sides engaged, it was a victory for neither. Shelby and Robertson, with their commands, were in the engagement that followed soon after at Musgrove's Mill, where the mountaineer Americans won a glorious victory. The British loss in the battle was sixty-three killed, about ninety wounded, and seventy prisoners. The American casualty list showed only four killed and nine wounded. The term of service of their men being completed, Colonel Shelby and Major Robertson, with their volunteers from the Watauga and Holston, returned to their homes beyond the Alleghanies.

In a very short while after he returned to his home on the Holston, Colonel Shelby received a message which constrained him to return to that section of North Carolina where he had so recently been fighting the Tory followers of Ferguson. The men from the Watauga and Holston had greatly enraged Ferguson by the part they had played in the recent campaign; and he resolved to make them cease their activities against his forces or treat them as traitors to the British Crown. A man by the name of Samuel Phillips, who belonged to Shelby's command, and who had been so severely wounded in the battle at Musgrove's Mill that he had to be left at Musgrove's home, had been made a prisoner by Ferguson's men.

After his recovery, Phillips was sent across the mountains to tell Shelby and the other officers of the Watauga and Holston valleys, that "if they did not desist from their opposition to the British arms, he (Ferguson) would march his army over the mountains, hang their leaders, and lay their country waste with fire and sword."

Shelby, who was the first to receive the message from Ferguson, sent by Phillips, went immediately to Jonesboro and communicated it to Colonel Sevier. These two fearless men decided to raise as speedily as possible an army of riflemen, and to cross the mountains and make an attack upon Ferguson before he started to execute his presumptious threat. At that time Colonel Charles McDowell and Colonel Andrew Hampton were camping at Colonel John Carter's in the Watauga Valley. They had been forced to retire before Ferguson's large forces of Tories in the Upper Catawba Valley, and cross the mountains for safety. Sevier undertook to enlist the support of McDowell and Hampton and their men for the enterprise, and Shelby engaged to procure the co-operation of Colonel William Campbell, of Washington County, Virginia.

While Shelby was engaged in collecting his own regiment of Sullivan County men, he wrote a letter to Colonel William Campbell, then living at Aspinvale, now Seven Mile Ford, in Smyth County, Virginia, and requested him to raise as large body of men as he could, and to unite with him and Sevier in the contemplated movement against Ferguson. For several weeks prior to the receipt of Shelby's letter Colonel Campbell had been actively occupied with a hundred and fifty men in suppressing a movement of the Tories to seize and destroy the works and stores at the Lead Mines, situated at the point where the county seat of Fincastle had been located, now in Wythe County. Large quantities of lead were then being mined and smelted at that place for the use of the American armies, and the British authorities were exceedingly anxious to have the plant destroyed. Two hundred Tories of the New River region embraced within the present Grayson and Carroll counties, Virginia, and the present Alleghany and Surry counties, North Carolina, had been collected to execute the plans of the British against the Lead Mines. They were well equipped with arms and ammunition, and were commanded by regularly commissioned British officers. The agents of Great Britain were also trying to get the Cherokee Indians to make an invasion of the Watauga and Holston settlements in conjunction

with the British attack upon the Lead Mines. Campbell crossed the
mountains with his Washington County militia in the month of
August and found a large band of the Tories at a place then known
as the Big Glades, or Round Meadows, in North Carolina and near
the line of Carroll County, Virginia. Upon the approach of Campbell
and his men the Tories fled and dispersed so rapidly that only one
of their number was killed by the men from the Holston. Because
of the Tory risings, and for other, possibly personal, reasons, Campbell refused to join Shelby and Sevier in the proposed expedition.

On account of the threatened invasion of the Watauga and Hol-
ston settlements by the Cherokees, both Sevier and Shelby were
reluctant to take all of their men for service against Ferguson.
This induced Shelby to send a second urgent written appeal to
Colonel William Campbell, in which he informed him of the unhappy
situation in which he and Sevier were placed. Shelby also wrote to
Colonel Arthur Campbell, who was then county lieutenant for
Washington County. He told him of the violent threat made by
Ferguson, and also gave him information about McDowell's and
Hampton's party, who had been driven from their homes and families by the Tories. This last appeal had the desired results; and
both of the Campbells announced their willingness to assist in the
expedition. Arthur Campbell afterwards said: "The tale of
McDowell's men was a doleful one, and tended to excite the resentment of the people, who of late had become inured to danger by
fighting the Indians, and who had an utter detestation of the tyranny
of the British Government."

A conference of the field officers of Washington County was
held; and it was agreed that one-half of the militia of the county
should be called out and mobilized at Wolf Creek, just west of the
present town of Abingdon. They were to march from that point
and join the forces of Shelby and Sevier at a designated place, and
to go with them on the expedition against Ferguson. Colonel Arthur
Campbell, in his capacity of county lieutenant, issued a call for the
enrollment of companies from the several sections of the county.
Responding to this call, a company of mounted riflemen was organized in that part of Clinch Valley within the present limits of Tazewell. The county court of Washington had, on the 20th of February,
1777, recommended William Bowen for a captain of militia on the
Clinch; and he had been duly commissioned as such. He was

placed in command of the company of mounted riflemen, and his brother, Rees Bowen, was made lieutenant. When the time arrived for assembling at Wolf Creek, William Bowen was very sick from typhoid fever; and the company had to march with Lieutenant Rees Bowen in command. Unfortunately no roll of the company has been preserved; and, therefore, it is impossible to give the names of all the men from Tazewell who were in the engagement at King's Mountain. Tradition and imperfect records show that David Ward, Thomas Maxwell, James Laird, Thomas Witten, Jr., John Skeggs, and John and Thomas Peery, father and son, were members of the company that went from Tazewell and joined Campbell at Wolf Creek.

Two hundred men started on the 22nd of September, 1780, from Wolf Creek; and on the 26th reached the place of assembly at Sycamore Shoals, at the foot of Yellow Mountain, on the Watauga, three miles below the present town of Elizabethton, Tennessee. Shelby and Sevier were there, according to appointment, each with a regiment of two hundred and forty men; and eagerly awaiting the arrival of Campbell and his riflemen. McDowell had been at the camp with his men, but had joyfully gone in advance across the mountains to announce to his people the coming of their compatriots from the Watauga, Holston and Clinch settlements. On the 26th., just as the army was getting ready to take up its march, Colonel Arthur Campell arrived with two hundred more Washington County men. This substantial reinforcement gave great cheer to the men who had previously assembled. Soon after the arrival of the reinforcements, the gallant little army broke camp and started out on what proved to be a victorious expedition against the insolent Ferguson and his Tory forces. Lyman C. Draper, in his "Kings Mountain And Its Heroes," thus speaks of the equipment of the forces of Campbell, Shelby, and Sevier:

"Mostly armed with the Deckard rifle, in the use of which they were expert alike against the Indians and beasts of the forest, they regarded themselves the equals of Ferguson and his practiced riflemen and musketeers. They were little encumbered with baggage— each with a blanket, a cup by his side, with which to quench his thirst from the mountain streams, and a wallet of provisions, the latter principally parched corn meal, mixed, as it generally was, with maple sugar, making a very agreeable repast, and withal full of nourishment. An occasional skillet was taken along for a mess, in, which to warm up in water their parched meal, and cook such wild or other meat as fortune should throw in their way. The horses, of course, had to pick their living, and were hobbled out of nights, to keep them from straying away. A few beeves were driven along the rear for subsistence, but impeding the rapidity of the march, they were abandoned after the first day's journey."

Roosevelt, who made careful investigation of all records and all the early historians who wrote about the battle of King's Mountain, in his "Winning of the West," says of these soldiers:

"Their fringed and tasseled hunting shirts were girded in by bead-worked belts, and the trappings of their horses were stained red and yellow. On their heads they wore caps of coon-skin or mink-skin, with the tails hanging down, or else felt hats, in each of which was thrust a buck's tail or a sprig of evergreen. Every man carried a small bore rifle, a tomahawk and a scalping knife. A very few of the officers had swords, and there was not a bayonet nor a tent in the army."

The march across the Alleghany and Blue Ridge ranges was accomplished without much difficulty. No enemy except a few bushwhacking Tories were encountered. Lieutenant Larkin Cleveland, who was leading the advance, was shot and severely wounded from ambush while crossing the Catawba on the 30th of September. Sunday, October the 1st, the army arrived at Quaker Meadows; and on Monday, the 2nd, Colonel William Campbell was selected by the corps commanders as commanding officer until a general officer should arrive from headquarters. The expedition was then within sixteen or eighteen miles of Gilbert Town, where Ferguson was supposed to be camping with his army; and Colonel Campbell resolved to hunt down and strike the enemy immediately.

In the meantime, Ferguson had been making plundering expeditions with his Tory marauders in the Upper Catawba Valley, robbing and terrorizing the American patriots. On the 30th of September he was encamped at Gilbert Town, when Crawford and Chambers, who had deserted from Shelby's command while they were camping on the top of Yellow Mountain, arrived at Ferguson's camp. These traitors warned the British commander of the approach of the "Back Water men," a name which Ferguson had given them. The boastful Scotchman was greatly alarmed when he heard of the coming of the men whom he had threatened to hang, and whose homes he had declared he would devastate with fire and sword. On the 1st of October, Ferguson marched his force to Denard's Ford, about eight miles from Gilbert Town, and addressed the following scurrilous and libellous appeal to the Tories of North and South Carolina:

> "Denard's Ford, Broad River,
> "Tryon County, October 1, 1780.

"Gentlemen:—Unless you wish to be eat up by an inundation of barbarians, who have begun by murdering an unarmed son before the aged father, and afterwards lopped off his arms, and who by their shocking cruelties and irregularities, give the best proof of their cowardice and want of discipline; I say, if you wish to be pinioned, robbed, and murdered, and see your wives and daughters, in four days, abused by the dregs of mankind—in short, if you wish or deserve to live, and bear the name of men, grasp your arms in a moment and run to camp.

"The Back Water men have crossed the mountains; McDowell, Hampton, Shelby and Cleveland are at the head, so that you know what you have to depend upon. If you choose to be degraded forever and ever by a set of mongrels, say so at once, and let your women turn their backs upon you, and look out for real men to protect them.

> "Pat Ferguson, *Major 71st, Regiment.*"

Historians, with one accord, have denounced the accusations of brutality and immorality made by Ferguson against the men from the Watauga, Holston, and Clinch regions as fabrications. They were falsehoods, uttered to anger the brutal Tories and arouse them to resistance against the "Back Water men." That Ferguson had no regard for morality and decency was evidenced by the fact that he had two mistresses with him when he was killed. Draper says: "both fine looking young women. One of them, known as Virginia Sal, a red haired lady, it is related, was the first to fall in the battle, and was buried in the same grave with Ferguson, as some assert; or as others have it, beside the British and Tory slain; while the other, Virginia Paul, survived the action; and after it was over, was seen to ride around the camp as unconcerned as though nothing unusual had happened." She was subsequently sent to Lord Cornwallis' army.

On the evening of the 6th of October, Ferguson, who was trying to escape an encounter with the "dregs of mankind," the riflemen from beyond the mountains, who were determined to hunt him down and make him and his Tory ruffians bite the dust, took his station upon the eminence which has since been famous as King's Mountain. The arrogant Briton thought he could there defy and hold in check the Americans until he was reinforced by parties of Loyalists and by Tarleton. Draper, in his description of the mountain, says:

"That portion of it where the action was fought, has little or no claim to the distinction of a mountain. * * * *The Pinacle,* is some six miles distant from the battle ground. That portion of the oblong hill or stony ridge, now historically famous, is in York County, South Carolina, about a mile and a half south of the North Carolina line. It is some six hundred yards long, and about two hundred and fifty from one base across to the other; or from sixty to one hundred and twenty wide on the top, tapering to the south— so narrow that a man standing on it may be shot from either side. Its summit was some sixty feet above the level of the surrounding country."

The same evening that Ferguson took his position on the mountain the Americans were at Cowpens with about eleven hundred men. There they learned definitely that Ferguson was encamped at King's Mountain, and determined to press forward in pursuit of the foe. Colonel Campbell was selected by a council of the field officers to continue in command of the army, and nine hundred and ten well mounted and well armed men were chosen from the entire force to march at once. The march was begun at nine o'clock at night, the 6th, and was continued all night through a drizzly rain; but the men kept their guns dry by wrapping them in their blankets. After daylight the march was continued through the rain until noon, and the sun came out when the army was about eight miles from King's Mountain. Two Tories were captured and they were forced to pilot the mountaineers to where Ferguson was encamped. When they got within a mile of the enemy, they met George Watkins, a Whig patriot, who had been made a prisoner by Ferguson, but had been released on parole and was on his way home. Watkins gave information that induced the Americans to commence the attack upon the enemy without delay. The army was formed into two lines, or divisions, one to be led by Colonel Campbell, and the other by Colonel Cleveland. Following plans that had already been agreed upon in council, the little army encircled the eminence occupied by Ferguson, and at about 3 o'clock p. m. the conflict became fast and furious. Before advancing to the attack, Campbell went along the lines and told his troops: "that if any of them, men or officers, were afraid, to quit the ranks and go home; that he wished no man to engage in the action who could not fight; that, as for himself, he was determined to fight the enemy a week, if need be to gain the victory." The Virginia men were the first to get in position, and, without waiting for the other regiments, they started into the fray. Campbell, when leading his men to the attack, cried out in a loud voice,—"Here they are, my brave boys; shout like h—l, and fight like devils." Draper, in his "King's Mountain And Its Heroes," says:

"Where Campbell's men ascended the mountain to commence the attack was rough, craggy, and rather abrupt—the most difficult ascent of any part of the ridge; but these resolute mountaineers permitted no obstacles to prevent them from advancing upon the foe, creeping up the acclivity, little by little, and from tree to tree, till they were nearly at the top—the action commencing at long fire."

The men from Tazewell were of and among these resolute mountaineers who were thus fighting as they were accustomed to fight the Indians; and it was upon these men that Ferguson turned his best troops to make a charge with fixed bayonets. Draper says that while the Virginia men were making this advance:

"Lieutenant Rees Bowen, who commanded one of these companies of the Virginia regiment, was observed, while marching forward to attack the enemy, to make a hazardous and unnecessary exposure of his person. Some friend kindly remonstrated with him—'why Bowen, do you not take a tree—why rashly present yourself to the deliberate aim of the Provincial and Tory riflemen, concealed behind every rock and bush before you?—death will inevitably follow, if you persist.' 'Take to a tree,' he indignantly replied —'no! never shall it be said that I sought safety by hiding my person, or dodging from a Briton or Tory who opposed me in the field.' " A few moments after uttering these words, the fearless Bowen was shot through the breast, fell to the ground, and expired almost instantly.

The engagement lasted for one hour and five minutes, with alternate advances and repulses by the opposing forces. One historian says: "Three times did the Britons charge with bayonet down the hill; as often did the Americans retreat: and the moment the Britons turned their backs, the Americans shot from behind every tree, and every rock, and laid them prostrate."

Ferguson was as recklessly brave as he was ruthless in his conduct as a soldier. Finding that the "Back Water men" were likely to win the day, he resolved to try to make his escape by charging at the head of his forces, and cutting his way through the lines of the Americans. The mountain riflemen were all eager to have the honor of slaying the hated British leader; and in his last charge Ferguson received six or eight wounds, one bullet crashing through his brain. His death brought consternation to the Tories and Provincial troops, and white flags were raised repeatedly by the discomfited enemy; but the confusion was intense and the Americans continued to shoot and kill until their vengeance was fully satisfied. Campbell and Shelby finally succeeded in getting their men to cease firing and the slaughter came to an end.

From the best information obtainable at the time, it was estimated that the British had about nine hundred men and the Americans the same number in the engagement; and there were several contemporary reports of the losses that each side suffered. Five days after the battle Colonel Isaac Shelby wrote a letter to his father, Colonel Evan Shelby, in which he reported the British casualties as follows: "Ferguson's corps, thirty-seven killed and twenty-eight wounded; Tories, one hundred and twenty-seven killed and one hundred and twenty-five wounded—a total of 157 killed and 153 wounded. Shelby also told his father that 706 prisoners were taken. It is conceded by historians that Shelby's report of the British losses is more nearly accurate than any given.

The final official report made by Colonel Campbell and his associate officers placed the Americans killed at twenty-eight, and the wounded at sixty-two—a total of ninety.

Colonel Campbell's regiment of Virginians were the first to enter the engagement and they were in the hotest and thickest of the fray while the battle lasted. Consequently, they suffered heavier losses than any other regiment engaged. Of the Virginia men, thirteen officers and one private were killed, or mortally wounded; and three officers and eighteen privates were wounded and recovered. The killed were, Captain William Edmondson; Lieutenants Rees Bowen, William Blackburn, and Robert Edmondson, Sr.; Ensigns Andrew Edmondson, John Beattie, James Corry, Nathaniel Dryden, Nathaniel Gist, James Philips, and Humberson Lyon, and private Henry Henigar. Lieutenant Thomas McCulloch, and Ensign James Laird, who had been mortally wounded, died from their wounds a few days after the battle. All of the eighteen privates who were wounded recovered; but the names of the following are all that have been preserved: Frederick Fisher, John Skeggs, Benoni Banning, Charles Kilgore, William Bullen, Leonard Hyce, Israel Hayter, and William Moore.

After the War of the Revolution was over, Colonels Shelby and Sevier were led, or assumed, to believe that Colonel Campbell had not acted courageously in the battle. This provoked a controversy between the friends of Campbell, who was then dead, and the supporters of Sevier and Shelby, that was so rancorous that it did not terminate until after the death of Colonels Shelby and Sevier. A feeling of bitter resentment is still alive among the descendants of the three gallant men who, together, won the splendid victory at King's Mountain. Lyman C. Draper says:

"It is a matter of regret that such patriots as Shelby and Sevier should have been deceived into the belief that the chivalric Campbell shirked from the dangers of the conflict, mistaking, as they did, the Colonel's servant in the distance for the Colonel himself; when well-nigh forty survivors of the battle, including some of Campbell's worthiest officers, and men of Shelby's, and Cleveland's regiments as well, testifying, of their own knowledge, to his personal share in the action, and specifying his presence in every part of the hotly-contested engagement, from the beginning to the final surrender of the enemy at discretion. It is evident that such heroes as Shelby and Sevier had quite enough to do within the range of their own regiments, without being able to observe very much what was transpiring beyond them."

T.H.—25

Nearly half of the Americans who were killed in the battle, and one-third of the wounded were members of Campbell's regiment, while thirteen of the fourteen killed were officers. This shows how the Virginians fearlessly met the foe and that they were gallantly led by their officers, including Colonel Campbell.

The Americans had no surgeon, and of the three surgeons with Ferguson's men only one survived the battle, Dr. Johnson. He kindly gave the necessary surgical attention to the most severely wounded Americans, as well as to the British wounded. The Virginia frontiersmen, however, were accustomed to treating gunshot wounds, having gained experience from their frequent bloody encounters with the Indians. Both the victors and the vanquished camped on the battle field the night following the engagement. One of the Virginians who was in the fight afterwards said: "The groans of the wounded and dying on the mountain was truly affecting, begging piteously for water, but in the hurry, confusion and exhaustion of the Whigs, these cries, when emanating from Tories, were little heeded."

An interesting event that has come down by tradition occurred in this connection. Among Campbell's riflemen from Washington County was a German Huguenot by the name of Philip Greever. He was then living just west of the present town of Chilhowie, in Smyth County. Like all the expert riflemen from Southwest Virginia, he fought from behind a tree, and was the first to fire a shot in the fight. After the battle was over, the Americans rendered what aid they could to their wounded foes, especially those of Ferguson's corps. Greever, while engaged in this humane work, found a wounded Tory lying behind a tree on the hillside, with his hip broken by a rifle bullet and calling for water. Greever went to a spring at the foot of the hill, and, having no cup or other vessel, filled his coon-skin cap with water and carried it back to the wounded Tory. The latter was very grateful for the kind attention given him by the mountaineer, and bewailed his misfortune as unusually trying, because, he said, "the first shot that was fired broke my thigh." Greever was very much interested and astonished, and replied: "Well I was the man who fired that first shot." This incident comes from Greever's son, also named Philip, who moved to Burke's Garden more than a hundred years ago; where a number of his descendants still live. In fact, all the Greevers now in Tazewell county are his descendants. He brought with him to the Garden several relics his father picked up on the battle field at King's Mountain, among them a pair of scissors which were used for many years as a pound weight on the farm steelyards, being the exact weight required for that purpose.

As late as the year 1822 the controversy between the descendants of General William Campbell and those of Shelby and Sevier was still raging. General Francis Preston, a grandson of General Campbell, procured from Philip Greever, who was one of the volunteers from the Holston settlements in Washington County, an affidavit. In this affidavit, Greever swore that General Campbell "behaved as a brave officer and was kind to his men but severe against the Tories." Greever also stated very modestly in the affidavit that he was the first one of Campbell's men to fire at a "Tory I saw behind a tree." As Campbell's men were the first to engage in the battle it necessarily follows that Greever fired the first shot at King's Mountain. This practically substantiates the story handed down by tradition through the descendants of Philip Greever. The affidavit was never published, and the original is now in the possession of Captain John M. Preston, a great-great-grandson of General Campbell, who owns and lives upon a part of the Campbell place, Aspinvale, at Seven Mile Ford, Smyth County.

On the morning of the 8th of October, the army began its return march, with the prisoners strongly guarded, and the wounded Americans conveyed on horse-litters. Colonel Campbell remained behind with a detail of men to bury the American and British dead, but joined his men when they went into camp about twelve miles from the battle ground. Most of the troops had been without food for two days, and near the camp a sweet potato patch was found with sufficient potatoes to supply the whole army. Colonel Shelby said of the homeward journey: "Owing to the number of wounded, and the destitution of the army of all conveyances, they traveled very slowly, and in one week had only marched about forty miles." There is no record which shows when the men from Tazewell arrived at their homes, but it is to be presumed that they all got back safely, except their gallant leader, Rees Bowen, whom they left in a heroe's grave at King's Mountain, and Ensign James Laird, who died from the wounds he received in the battle. He was being conveyed home on a horse-litter, and, when crossing a mountain or stream, was thrown from the litter. The heavy fall opened the wounds afresh and the shock killed him.

———

Very soon after the Tazewell patriots returned from King's Mountain, another call was made upon the men of Southwest Virginia to go to North Carolina. In January, 1781, General Nathaniel Greene was commanding the patriot army in that State, and was being hard pressed by Cornwallis and Tarleton. On the 13th of the month, General Greene wrote to Colonel William Campbell, reminding him of the gallant conduct of himself and his Washington County riflemen at King's Mountain; and requesting him "to bring, without loss of time, a thousand good volunteers from over the mountain." Campbell took immediate steps to comply with General Greene's urgent request; and on the 25th of February he started with about two hundred volunteers from the Washington County militia to join General Greene.

After starting on the march, Campbell wrote a letter to Governor Jefferson in which he said: "A large number would have gone, were it not for the daily apprehensions of attacks from the northward and southern Indians." The British agents were still urging the Cherokees to invade the Holston settlements, and small bands of Ohio Indians were making bloody scalping expeditions to the Clinch Valley. Colonel Campbell proceeded to the Lead Mines with his volunteers, and was there joined by several hundred Montgomery County militia, led by Colonel William Preston and Major Walter Crockett. From the Lead Mines, the united forces were marched to North Carolina and reached General Greene on the 2nd of March, 1781. There was a company of men under the command of Captain James Moore with the Campbell-Preston forces. They were from that portion of Tazewell that was then embraced in Montgomery County. James Moore had been commissioned by Governor Jefferson a captain of militia upon the recommendation of the county court of Montgomery County at its April term, 1779; and George Peery and William McGuire had been commissioned, respectively, First and Second Lieutenant of Moore's company. No roll of the company was preserved, but from tradition and scattered records it is known that, Captain James Moore, George Peery, James Cartmill, Samuel Furguson, William Peery, John Peery, and Thomas Peery were with the Montgomery militia, and participated in the engagement at Whitzell's Mills on the 6th of March, and in the battle at Guilford Court House on the 15th of March, 1781. In both of these engagements the riflemen from Washington and Montgomery counties enacted an important part; and with their "terrible guns" inflicted heavy losses upon the enemy. In this battle at Guilford Court House the men from both of the counties were commanded by Colonel William Campbell; and they were the first to enter the engagement and the last to withdraw from it. Draper says:

"So severely did Campbell's riflemen handle his right wing, that Lord Cornwallis was obliged to order Tarleton to extricate it, and bring it off. By this time Lee had retired with his cavalry, without apprising Campbell of his movement; and the result was, that the riflemen were swept from the field."

In the charge made by Tarleton's men, Thomas Peery was killed and his father, John Peery, was frightfully wounded. He was disabled by a saber blow and fell upon the ground. While prostrate, as Tarleton's troops passed their stricken foe, each brutal Briton gave him a cut with a saber. He received fifty-four saber cuts, and his head and arms were literally cut to pieces. But the hardy Tazewell pioneer survived, recovered from his numerous wounds, and returned to his home on the Clinch, where he lived a number of years in enjoyment of the freedom for which he had given a gallant son and suffered so terribly himself.

There were others of the Tazewell pioneers who were active participants in the Revolutionary War and did service in the Continental army, but the names of only a few of them have been recorded. It is known that Thomas Harrisson fought in the engagements at Brandywine, Germantown, and Yorktown; Archer Maloney was at Brandywine, and Stoney Point; and Isam Tomlinson was in the battles at Brandywine and Germantown.

———

During the entire progress of the Revolution the inhabitants of the Upper Clinch Valley were compelled to rely upon their own strong arms and brave hearts for protection against the hostile Indians. The civil and military authorities of Washington and Montgomery counties were apparently more anxious to protect the settlements in Kentucky and the Greenbrier and Kanawha regions than those of the Clinch Valley. It may be that the Washington and Montgomery authorities were impelled to this course by their absolute confidence in the superior capacity of our pioneer ancestors to take care of themselves—and in this they were not mistaken. At any rate, the Sandy Valley was left wide open, there being no forts or stations established on the Ohio River, from the mouth of the Kanawha to the mouth of Licking Creek. This not only gave opportunity but was seemingly an invitation to the Shawnees to make hostile attacks upon the Clinch Valley settlements. The redskins availed themselves of the opportunity, and made frequent bloody incursions, of which I will write in succeeding chapters.

For the first three years of the Revolutionary period, the Virginia Government gave no attention to the exposed settlements of the Clinch Valley; but at last, on the 23rd of July, 1779, the State Council entered an order directing General Andrew Lewis, Colonel William Fleming, and Colonel William Christian "to meet for the purpose of fixing the Stations proper for the Troops designed for the Defence of the So. Western Frontiers."

In compliance with this order, General Andrew Lewis and Colonel William Fleming met at Botetourt, August 31, 1779; "and on Maturely considering the order of Council, to comply therewith, in forming as compleat a Chain of defence as the number of men allotted for that service will admit of. It is our opinion that at, or as near the following places mentioned as a proper situation will suit—Fifty men with the usual Officers be stationed at or near the Mouth of Guayandot and Fifty Rank & File with the proper Officers at or near the Mouth of Big Sandy River, One Hundred Rank & File at or near the Junction of Licking Creek with the Ohio. And Fifty at or near Martin's Cabin in Powells Valley. We imagine these posts occupied on the Ohio, will be of more service for the protection of the frontier than stationing the Battalion near the Inhabitants." In their report to Governor Jefferson, General Lewis and Colonel Fleming make it very plain that garrisons stationed at the several points suggested, would give excellent defence to the entire Virginia frontier on the Ohio River. If the recommendations of Lewis and Fleming had been adopted and promptly carried out, there would have been no subsequent incursions made by the Indians to the Clinch Valley; and a number of precious lives would have been saved from the tomahawks and scalping knives of the savages.

As soon as the Revolutionary War had terminated in favor of the United Colonies, numbers of new settlers established themselves in the section which later became Tazewell County. They were largely attracted by the fertile lands, splendid springs and mountain streams, abundance of game, and the rich pasturage for domestic animals. And they were also drawn hither from a desire to become the friends and neighbors of the pioneer settlers, who were famous as Indian fighters and had won distinction at King's Mountain, or on other battlefields in the great struggle for American freedom.

The suggestions of Lewis and Fleming that forts should be erected at the mouth of Guyandotte and the mouth of Big Sandy were not carried out; and the inhabitants of the Clinch Valley were left exposed for the next succeeding thirteen years to bloody attacks from the Ohio Indians. This was a great injustice on the part of the State and county authorities to the settlers who were founding a community that would, in the coming years, be recognized as one of the most useful, wealthy, and intelligent within the bounds of our Commonwealth. Regardless of the careless and indifferent treatment extended them, our worthy ancestors wrought on, and within a period of thirty years from the arrival of the first settlers on the Clinch had transformed the wilderness into a substantial community of comfortable homes.

In the meantime, there had been such considerable accessions to the population of the Lower Clinch Valley settlements, and in those sections of Washington County that now compose the counties of Russell, Scott, Lee, and Wise, that the inhabitants were desirous of having a new county erected. To that end a petition was presented to the Virginia General Assembly by the citizens of the said territory; and an act for dividing Washington County into two counties was passed by the Legislature on the 6th of January, 1786. The new county was named Russell, from General William Russell, its then most distinguished citizen; and the boundaries of the two counties were defined as follows: "All that part of the said county (Washington) lying within a line, to be run along the Clinch Mountain to the Carolina line (now Tennessee line) ; thence with that line to the Cumberland Mountain and the extent of the country between the Cumberland Mountain, Clinch Mountain, and the line of Montgomery County, shall be one distinct county, and shall be called and known by the name of Russell, and the residue of the said county shall retain the name of Washington."

The beginning point was at the Montgomery County line, on the top of the Clinch Mountain, about three miles southwest of Morris' Knob. Thus it will be seen that all of Washington County that was located north of Clinch Mountain was constituted and became Russell County; and that all that portion of Tazewell County, as originally formed, lying west of the Montgomery line was made a part of Russell by the act of 1786.

Three years later the inhabitants of that part of Montgomery County lying west of New River, petitioned the General Assembly to erect a new county. In response to the petition, the General Assembly, on December the 1st, 1789, passed an act for dividing the county of Montgomery and creating a new county to be called Wythe. The act declared: "That from and after the first day of May next (1790), all that part of the county of Montgomery, which lies south-west of a line beginning on the Henry line, at the head of Big Reedy Island, from thence to the wagon ford at Peek creek; thence to clover bottom on Bluestone, thence to the Kanawha county line, shall form one distinct county, and be called and known by the name of Wythe."

The new county received its name from George Wythe, the eminent jurist, who was one of the signers of the Declaration of Independence, as a delegate from Virginia. All of the territory east of the line between Russell and Montgomery that afterwards became a part of Tazewell County was placed in Wythe County, where it remained until Tazewell was formed.

The high ambition that brought the pioneers to the Upper Clinch Valley at length reached a concrete form. They had been compelled, even if they had not preferred to do so, to carve out their own destiny as a community, unassisted in this isolated but charming region. Their self-reliance had grown as their duties and numbers had multiplied; and in the closing years of the eighteenth century they began to yearn and clamor for the full exercise of local self-government. In other words, they wanted a county for themselves. This aspiration was at first obstructed and thwarted by certain citizens of the two counties—Russell and Wythe—from parts of which the new county was to be formed. The opposition came largely from the county officers of Wythe and Russell. They did not want to relinquish any of the emoluments of their offices, some of the offices being very lucrative for that day and generation.

In 1799 the movement for a new county became so active and persistent that it brought to pass the long desired event. A petition was prepared, circulated, and signed by hundreds of citizens of the counties of Russell and Wythe praying for the creation of a new county. It was my good fortune recently to find among the archives deposited in the Virginia State Library the original petition sent to the General Assembly one hundred and twenty years ago. Its recitals so graphically set forth the needs of the settlements in Tazewell at that period that it is invaluable from a historic stand-point. Hence, I will give it in full:

"To the Honourable the Speaker, And Gentlemen of the General Assembly of Virginia;

"The Petition of the Inhabitants of a part of the Counties of Wythe & Russell, humbly Represents

——That your Petitioners for near thirty years, have been under the Disagreeable Necessity of traveling fifty miles or upward to transact our own Ordinary Business, besides Regimental Musters, Elections, &c in which cases the Laws of the State Requires our attendance. —Our Roads also are Intolerably bad; many of your Petitioners have to cross four Large Mountains, the least of which chain would in the Interior parts of the State, be considered almost Impassable, And, between each of those Mountains there are Rapid Water Courses, which in common with all streams Among Mountains, are Quickly made Impassable by Rains, and Renders the passage Dangerous, as well as fatigueing & Expensive. Your Petitioners have for many years, not only Experienced the hardships Naturally to be expected from the above Difficulties, but at the same time had to Defend ourselves against the Perpetual Incur-

sions of our Savage Enemies, and that at the Expense of many
Valuable Lives; still hoping and expecting, that when peace would
again Return to our Country, when our Number, and other circumstances would fairly admit, that the General Assembly (on application) would Remove our Local Inconveniences, by granting us A
new County; We however have been thus far Disappointed in our
Expectations, by a small party of Designing men who have from
time to time Opposed our Petition, and by Misrepresenting our case,
have prevented our success; But as we find our Difficulties Increase
with our Population as we wish for nothing more than A Just
Representation of facts, And as we believe, that if the General
Assembly were fully acquainted with the Geography of our country,
it would Insure our success, we beg leave once more to pray that
your Honourable house would be pleased to pass an act that a new
county may be formed of parts taken from the counties of Wythe
and Russell, Beginning at the Kanawha Line and Running with the
Line which divides the counties of Wythe and Montgomery to where
said line Crosses the top of Brushy Mountain, Thence along the
top of said Mountain to its junction with the Garden Mountain,
thence along said Mountain to the Clinch Mountain, Thence along
the top of said Mountain to the head of Cove Creek, a Branch of
the Maiden Spring fork of Clinch River; Thence a straight Line to
Manns Gap in Kents Ridge; Thence North, forty five Degrees
West, till it strikes the Line which Divides the State of Kentucky,
from that of Virginia; Along sd. Line to the Kanawha Line, And
with said Line to the Beginning. — A County bounded as above,
would we humbly Conceive Answer all the purposes contemplated
by your Petitioners without Injuring Either of the Counties from
which it would be taken, as it would leave the court house of Russell County in the Centre thereof, & prevent all Disputes in the
future about the situation of the court house in that county, it would
also Divide the County of Wythe by the Chain of Mountains above
Described & thereby Add to the ease and convenience of both parties. We therefore submit our case to the most serious consideration of the Legislature, in humble confidence that our grievances
will be Redressed and that A New County will be formed Agreeable
to the prayer of our petition. And your petitioners as in Duty
bound shall ever pray &c."

Is it any wonder that the petitioners from Russell and Wythe attained their object? A stronger and more effectively conceived petition was never presented to the Virginia General Assembly. The penmanship of the petition is very fine; and though the paper abounds with capital letters and is defective in punctuation, it is a wonderfully forceful document; and it is unfortunate that the name of the author was not preserved. I have repeatedly asserted that the settlers of the Upper Clinch and Bluestone Valleys were cruelly neglected by the State and county authorities; and this petition verifies my assertions.

When the petition was presented to the General Assembly it met with the usual opposition from "Designing men;" but on the 20th of December, 1799, the act was passed for the erection of a new county, and the act is as follows:

"I. Be it enacted by the general assembly, That all that part of the counties of Wythe and Russell, lying within the following bounds, beginning on the Kanawha line and running with the line which divides Montgomery and Wythe counties to where the said line crosses the top of Brushy mountain, thence along the top of the said mountain to its junction with the Garden mountain, thence along the top of the said mountain to the Church mountain (should be Clinch Mountain), thence along the top of the said mountain to the head of Cove Creek a branch of the Maiden Spring fork of Clinch river; thence a straight line to Mann's Gap in Kent's ridge; thence north forty-five degrees west, to the line which divides the state of Kentucky from that of Virginia; thence along said line to the Kanawha line, and with said line to the place of beginning, shall be known by the name of Tazewell."

The act provided that the county court, which was to be composed of justices appointed by the governor, should hold its terms on the first Tuesday in every month after the county was organized; and that the first meeting of said court should be held at the house of Henry Harman, Junior; that, after taking the oaths prescribed by law, the justices were directed to administer the oath of office to and take a bond from the sheriff who had been appointed and commissioned by the governor; that they appoint and qualify a clerk; "and fix upon a place for holding courts in the said county, at, or near the centre thereof as the situation and conveniences will admit." After they had selected a county seat, the justices were directed to erect public buildings thereon. There were other provisions in the act that it is unnecessary to give in detail.

It seems that the "Designing men," who were opposing the erection of a new county had enlisted the support of Littleton W. Tazewell. He was a young man, twenty-six years old, and was serving his first term in the Virginia House of Delegates as the representative from James City County. Bickley, speaking of the opposition manifested by young Tazewell and the incidents connected therewith, says:

"Tazewell county was named, not in honor of Littleton W. Tazewell, as is generally supposed, but received its name somewhat in the following manner. Simon Cotterel, who was the representative from Russell in 1799, having been authorized to apply for the formation of a new county, drew up a bill, and proposed it on the 18th, of December, 1779, but met with the most violent opposition from Mr. Tazewell, a member from Norfolk county, and a relative of L. W. Tazewell then in Congress. Cotterel rose in his seat, and begged the gentleman to withold his remarks till his bill was matured, to which he assented. Cotterel erased the proposed name and inserted that of Tazewell, and the next day (19th) presented his bill thus amended. Tazewell was silenced; the bill passed, receiving Tazewell's vote. To this stratagem the county is indebted for its name."

It is evident that Dr. Bickley was again misled by relying entirely upon tradition. Possibly some of the features of the story he heard as coming from Cotterel may be true, but in the main they are incorrect. Littleton W. Tazewell was too high a man to be induced to withdraw his opposition to the formation of the new county by such a trivial stratagem as that named by Bickley. After serving in the Legislature young Tazewell was elected to Congress in 1800, but declined re-election in 1802. He served in the United States Senate in 1834-36. In 1829 he declined the mission to England; and in 1834-36 was governor of Virginia.

The county of Tazewell received its name from Henry Tazewell, who was a member of the United States Senate from Virginia when the act was passed creating the county. At that time he was one of the most distinguished citizens of the Commonwealth. From 1775 to 1785 he was a member, in succession, of the Virginia House of Burgesses and the House of Delegates; and served on the committees that drew the Bill of Rights and the first Constitution for Virginia. He was for a number of years a judge of the District Court and the Court of Appeals of this State.

Littleton W. Tazewell represented James City County, and not Norfolk County, in the House of Delegates in 1799. The State records show that Simon Cockrell, not "Simon Cotterel," represented Russell County at the session of 1798-99, with Francis Browning as his colleague; and at the session of 1799-1800, with James McFarlane as his colleague. The patent errors committed by Bickley, through relying on hearsay information, or tradition, make the tale about the stratagem practiced by *Cotterel* insufficiently authentic to be accepted as history.

Appendices---Pioneer Period

A—Sketches of Pioneer Families; B—Massacres by Indians

APPENDIX A TO PIONEER PERIOD

SKETCHES OF PIONEER FAMILIES.

Though it has never been my intention to make this, in any respect, a genealogical history of the families of the first settlers, it has been my purpose to write brief sketches of the pioneers and the first generation born in Tazewell. But even in this worthy design I have been greatly hampered by failure on the part of the descendants of the pioneers to supply me with needed information. Therefore, the sketches must be brief and few in number. As previously stated in this work, I will make no great effort to disclose the antecedents of the pioneers, except for the purpose of showing from whence they came. Thomas Witten was the first white man to take up permanent residence with his family within the limits of the present Tazewell County. For this reason, he and his family will be the first mentioned in these sketches.

THE WITTENS AND CECILS.

These two families were so intermingled by marriage for several generations after they came to the Clinch Valley that I will write of them in a single sketch. The Wittens were of Teutonic origin; but left Saxony and migrated to England as early as the ninth century. There they became identified with the Anglo-Saxons, who had conquered the Britons and gave the name England to ancient Britain. The Cecils were of purely Celtic blood, and natives of the British Isles. Tradition and documentary evidence reveal that the progenitors of the Wittens and Cecils in America came from England with the Calverts, and settled in Maryland, then Lord Baltimore's colony.

In 1766, Thomas Witten and Samuel Cecil, men with large families, and neighbors and kinsmen, moved from Maryland to the region now called Southwest Virginia. Thomas Witten's wife was Elizabeth Cecil, a sister of Samuel Cecil.

Witten located temporarily at what is now known as the "William Allen Place", on Walkers Creek, in the present Giles County, Virginia, on the road between Poplar Hill and White Gate in said

[401]

county. Cecil pitched his tent where the town of Dublin, in Pulaski County, is now located. He lived there until he died, in 1785, and there he and his wife are buried.

John Witten, the eldest son of Thomas, who had married before he left Maryland, stopped on the way out and located near the Peaks of Otter, in Bedford County. Later he came on to the Clinch and located at the place where John C. St. Clair now lives, four miles west of the county seat. The log cabin he used for a dwelling is still standing, and is perhaps the oldest house in the county. He afterwards returned with his family to Bedford, and in 1820 conveyed his valuable farm at the foot of Paint Lick Mountain to his brother, Thomas Witten, Jr. John Witten has a number of descendants in Bedford and Amherst counties, but they spell the name "Whitten."

In the spring of 1767, Thomas Witten moved on from Walker's Creek with his family to the "Crabapple Orchard" tract on Clinch River, and with him came John Greenup, who had married Elizabeth, the eldest daughter of Witten. He also brought out five unmarried sons, Thomas, Jr., James, Philip, Jeremiah and William. The latter was a small boy when his father settled on the Clinch, and James was then only fifteen years old. After attaining manhood, Philip married Ruth Dickerson and moved to Witten's Landing on the Ohio River. William, the youngest son of the first Thomas, married and moved to the Saquatche Valley, in Tennessee.

When trouble began with the Indians, about 1772 or 1773, Thomas Witten and his sons, assisted by their neighbors, built a stockaded fort on the Clinch, near Pisgah. This was one of the first three forts built in the present bounds of Tazewell County, and was a place of refuge for all the inhabitants of the neighborhood when the Indians made hostile incursions to the Clinch settlements.

Two of Thomas Witten's sons, Thomas, Jr., and James, gained much local distinction because of their performances as soldiers and scouts. Thomas, Jr. was not only conspicuous as an Indian fighter, but was also an ensign in the service of the United Colonies in the Revolutionary War. He served as ensign in one of the companies from Montgomery County that protected the border from savage invasions while the Revolution was in progress. In recognition of his services he was granted a pension of $24.00 a month by the

United States Government, which he received until his death. To
show that he was highly esteemed in civil life by his fellow-citizens
he was elected one of the first members from Tazewell, along with
David Ward, to represent the county in the Virginia General Assembly, serving at the sessions of 1801-02 and 1802-03. He married his
cousin, Eleanor Cecil, and fixed his home at the place where Allen
Higginbotham now lives at the east end of Paint Lick Mountain.

James Witten was distinguished while a youth as the first among
his equals as a woodsman and hunter; and even before he reached

Colonel Wilkinson Witten son of James Witten, the scout and
pioneer, born Aug. 12th, 1807, died March 26th, 1878. He was one of
the most esteemed and useful citizens of his day; and represented
Tazewell County several times in both houses of the Virginian General
Assembly.

his majority was recognized as the most skillful and daring scout
employed by the military authorities against the Indians. Bickley
says: "He was brave and generous to a fault. When any duty
requiring bravery, firmness and prudence, had to be performed,
James Witten was the man invariably chosen, as he possessed these
qualities in an eminent degree. Many incidents of interest are
related of him, which should be preserved." These incidents,
unfortunately, were not related by Bickley; and his descendants,
who have been called upon to pass through troublous times, have
failed to preserve the many noble and daring deeds of their gallant
ancestor. He married his cousin, Rebecca Cecil, daughter of

Samuel Cecil, in 1783, and located his home at the place where Colonel Wilk Witten, his grandson, afterwards lived and died, on Plum Creek, three miles west of the county seat. Very near and in view of the spot where he built his first cabin home, the dust of this pioneer hero is resting beneath a bluegrass sod that grows on soil his strong arms reclaimed from a wilderness waste. His grave is marked by a rude marble slab, but cattle and other animals, I am informed, are free to graze and trample upon and about it. His numerous descendents, hundreds of whom now live in Tazewell County, should not permit such neglect of the last resting place of their gallant ancestor, but should erect a suitable monument there to perpetuate his memory.

Jeremiah Witten, though older than his brothers, Thomas and James, held no official rank as a soldier, but he performed faithful service as a private. I have before me certain data which tends to show that he was a member of Captain William Russell's company and was with him at the battle of Point Pleasant. After his return from the Lewis expedition to the mouth of the Kanawha, he performed garrison duty at his father's fort at the Crabapple Orchard, his name being on the roll of the garrison stationed there in October, 1774. He married, and located his home on Plum Creek, at the place where the late, lamented T. E. George lived; and he has many descendants now living in Tazewell County.

William Cecil, son of Samuel Cecil, married his cousin, Ann Witten, daughter of Thomas Witten, about the year 1773. He and his wife made their home on the Clinch at the place where Otis E. Hopkins now lives. I once had in my possession a patent for this boundary of land that was issued by authority of George III. to William Cecil, and which bore date 1774. This is the oldest patent for land in Tazewell County I have ever seen. William Cecil was my great-grandfather and I am named from him. His brother, James Cecil, later, settled at the head of Baptist Valley, where he built the house now owned and occupied as a residence by Fullen Thompson. This is, possibly, the oldest house in Tazewell County that is now used as a dwelling. The two brothers, each, reared a large family of children. They were not conspicuous as soldiers, but, no doubt, did their duty as frontiersmen when the Indians invaded the settlements.

William and Ann Cecil had six daughters and two sons. Susan married Alex Sayers; Rebecca never married; Elizabeth married William Price; Linnie married Crabtree Price; John married Linnie Witten, who was his double first cousin and a daughter of James Witten the scout; Nancy married Buse Harman; Samuel married Sallie Poston; and Sally married James Caldwell. The Prices moved to Missouri; and the Caldwells moved to Tennessee. Cap-

Samuel Cecil, son of William Cecil, the pioneer, born in 1788, died in 1868. He was one of the finest characters Virginia has ever produced.

tain John Cecil, son of William Cecil, was a prominent figure in the civil and military life of the county. He was for many years a member of the county court; and represented the county in the Virginia House of Delegates at the sessions of 1808-09, 1810-11 and 1811-12. While the War of 1812 was in progress he raised a company of volunteers and was made captain of the company, but the Government declined to muster it into service. After he married, Captain Cecil made his home on Little River, known as the Maiden Spring Fork of Clinch River. He there acquired what is now one of the most beautiful and valuable farms in Tazewell County. He sold the place to John Baylor for Confederate money during the Civil War, and thus lost his splendid estate.

Samuel Cecil, son of William, after his marriage with Sally Poston, in 1814 built his home on the north side of and overlooking the Clinch, and opposite the mouth of Plum Creek. The house is still standing, is known as the Mays place, and is now owned by Mrs. O. E. Hopkins, a great-granddaughter of Samuel Cecil. My mother was born, reared and married to my father in this house. Samuel Cecil did not care for public life, and was never an office-holder, civil or military, but was esteemed by all persons who came in contact with him as one of the nicest gentlemen they ever met, and one of the best citizens the county ever produced. His home was among the most noted in the county for its delightful hospitality, where the poor and humble received the same courteous treatment as was extended to the richest and most distinguished

It is apparent that my reason for writing about the Wittens and Cecils in one sketch, because of their intermarrying, is well founded. Thomas Witten's wife was Elizabeth, the sister of Samuel Cecil. Three of her sons, John, Thomas and James, married daughters of her brother Samuel; and two of her daughters, Keziah and Ann, married sons of her brother, Samuel Cecil. This was a pretty liberal exchange in the marriage relation of brothers and sisters already closely related by a previous marriage. And it made the children of each twain double first cousins of the children of all the other twains. By blood they were practically brothers and sisters.

John Greenup, who married Elizabeth, the eldest daughter of Thomas and Elizabeth Witten, remained with his family in Tazewell only a brief while after the county was organized. He had two grown sons, Thomas and Christopher, when the county was formed. When the county court, at its December term, 1800, recommended certain citizens to the governor of Virginia for appointment as officers of the militia, Thomas Greenup was named as one of the captains of the 2nd Battalion of the 112th Regiment.

In 1801, John Greenup and his family, including Thomas and Christopher, moved to Kentucky. The Greenups became prominent in the affairs of the State; and in 1804, Christopher Greenup was made governor. He was inaugurated June 1st, 1804, and served the State four years as its Chief Executive. He was so highly esteemed as a citizen that a splendid county in the Bluegrass State was given his name. Greenup County borders on the Ohio below the mouth of Big Sandy River.

THE BOWENS OF TAZEWELL.

Rees Bowen was the second white man who brought his family
to make permanent residence in the Clinch Valley. Therefore it is
meet that he and his family should be the second considered in the
sketches I am writing of the pioneer families.

The Tazewell Bowens are of Celtic blood. Their immediate
ancestor was Moses Bowen, a Welchman, who married Rebecca
Rees. They came from Wales to America a good many years before
the Revolution, and settled in Lancaster County, Pennsylvania.
Their son John was a Quaker, and he married Lily McIlhany. He
and his wife moved from Pennsylvania to Augusta County, Virginia,
soon after the first settlements were made in the Shenandoah Valley, perhaps as early as the year 1732; and located in that part of
Augusta now embraced in the county of Rockbridge. They had
twelve children and Rees was one of their five sons. He married
Louisa Smith, whose parents then lived in that section of Augusta
now known as Rockingham County. It is said that, after his marriage, he took up his abode on the Roanoke River close to where
the city of Roanoke is now situated.

In some way Rees Bowen learned of the fertile lands and abundance of game that could be found in the Upper Clinch Valley; and
he concluded to abandon his home on the Roanoke River and settle
in this region, where he could locate and occupy, without cost, a
large boundary of fine unoccupied land. It is known from tradition
that when he arrived with his family in the vincinity of the great
spring, to which he gave a peculiar name, he had not then selected
the boundary of land upon which he would settle. After they went
into camp, on the evening of the day he reached the place that has
since been the home of the Bowens, he went out to find and kill a
deer to get a supply of fresh meat. While thus engaged he discovered the spring. Bickley thus tells of the discovery of the
immense fountain and what followed:

"When Mr. Bowen first saw the spring, he discovered a fine
young female deer, feeding on the moss within the orifice from
which gushes the spring. He shot it, and when he went to get his
deer, saw a pair of elk horns standing on their points, and leaning
against the rocks. Mr. Bowen was a very large and tall man, yet
he had no difficulty in walking upright under the horns. He chose

this place for his, and the spring and river have since been known as Maiden Spring and Fork."

The first four years after he and his family located at Maiden Spring were free from any hostile demonstrations by the Indians against the Clinch settlements. He was possessed of great physical strength and was very industrious, and in the four years he erected

General Rees T. Bowen, grandson of Lieutenant Rees Bowen, was born at Maiden Spring January 10th, 1809, and died August 29th, 1879. He was made a brigadier general of militia by Governor Henry A. Wise in 1856; and represented Tazewell County in the Virginia House of Delegates in 1863-1864. General Bowen was elected by the Conservative party to represent the Ninth District in the Forty-third Congress; and served in that body from December 1st, 1873, to March 3rd, 1875. He was the first citizen of Tazewell County that served in the National Legislature.

a large and strong log house, extended his clearings into the forests and added considerably to the number of horses and cattle he brought with him from his home on the Roanoke. Then came trouble with the Ohio Indians, in 1773, when the whole frontier of Virginia was threatened by the red men; and Rees Bowen built a heavy stockade around his dwelling, converting it into an excellent neighborhood fort.

In the meantime, his four brothers, John, Arthur, William and Moses had moved out from Augusta to find homes in the country west of New River. John settled at some point in the Holston

Valley; Arthur located in the present Smyth County, four miles
west of Marion; and William and Moses took up their abode in
the Clinch Valley, but in what immediate locality is now unknown.
When Dunmore's War came on the three brothers, Rees, William
and Moses, went with Captain William Russell's company on the
Lewis expedition to the mouth of the Kanawha River; and were
prominent figures in the eventful battle at Point Pleasant. Moses
Bowen was then only twenty years old; and on the return march
from the Kanawha he was stricken with smallpox, from which
frightful malady he died in the wilderness.

After his return from Point Pleasant, for two years Rees Bowen,
like all the pioneer settlers, was actively engaged in clearing up
fields from the forest and increasing the comforts of his new home.
While thus occupied the war between the colonies and Great Britain
began; and the British Government turned the Western Indians
loose on the Virginia frontiers. This caused the organization of a
company of militia, expert Indian fighters, in the Clinch Valley.
The two Bowen brothers were members of the company, William
being captain, and Rees, lieutenant. This company, composed of
pioneers, did effective service for the protection of the settlers in
the Clinch and the Holston valleys.

When Colonels Shelby and Sevier, in the fall of 1780, appealed
to Colonel William Campbell to join them in the expedition to
King's Mountain, with a volunteer force from Washington County,
Virginia, the company from Clinch Valley volunteered to go. Owing
to illness from a serious attack of fever, Captain William Bowen
was unable to lead his men on the expedition, and the command of
the company devolved upon Lieutenant Rees Bowen. He marched
with his company and joined Campbell at Wolf Hill (now Abingdon), and thence on to the Carolinas, and gave his life for American
freedom, while leading his men in the memorable battle at King's
Mountain.

The widow of the pioneer hero, Louisa Bowen, bravely accepted
the responsibility of rearing eight orphan children, none of whom
had reached their majority. A chart of the Bowen family, which
I have before me, shows that these children were: John, Rees,
Nancy, Margaret, Rebecca, Lily, Louisa and Henry Bowen. The
chart does not disclose anything in connection with John, the first
mentioned among the children of Rees and Louisa Bowen. Rees,

the second, married his cousin Rebecca, daughter of John Bowen, who had established himself in the Holston Valley; Nancy married Major John Ward, who was the first clerk of Tazewell County, and a son of David Ward the pioneer neighbor of Lieutenant Rees Bowen; Margaret married Thomas Gillespie, the first Gillespie to settle in Tazewell County; Rebecca married ———— Duff; Lily married ———— Hildrith, of Kentucky; Louisa married John Thompson; and Henry married Elen Tate, daughter of Thomas Tate, and a neice of General William Campbell. Rees, the second, died without issue; and Henry and Ella Bowen (nee Tate) were the progenitors of all the Bowens who have since lived in Tazewell County. Their two sons were General Rees T. Bowen and Colonel Henry S. Bowen. General Bowen was distinguished in civil life and was a brigadier general of militia before the Civil War. Colonel Bowen was the gallant commander of a regiment of cavalry that did splendid service for the Confederacy.

THE WARD FAMILY.

From the descendants of David Ward, who are now living in Tazewell County, I have been able to procure but very little information about their worthy ancestor. He was one of the most prominent and useful of the pioneer settlers; and I have fortunately found enough in the records of the county and certain publications to enable me to make proper notice of a man who had much to do with giving stability to the Clinch Valley settlements, and the creation and organization of Tazewell County.

The Wards were of Scotch-Irish blood; and came to America from Ulster during the great exodus from Ireland that took place early in the eighteenth century. William Ward, the immediate ancestor of the Wards of Tazewell County, about 1730 left Ireland and settled in Pennsylvania. From that province he migrated to the Valley of Virginia, and fixed his home in the present Augusta County where the village of Greenville is now located, about ten miles west of the city of Staunton. There he passed the remainder of his life and reared a family. In the year 1769, two of his sons, David and William, heard of the splendid country now known as Southwest Virginia, and they migrated to this section. William settled in the Black Lick in the present Wythe County; and David travelled on to the Clinch Valley and located in the Cove, on the place where his great-great-grandson, George Ward, now lives.

David Ward thus was made a neighbor of Rees Bowen, and he at once became a conspicuous figure among the frontiersmen, because of his intelligence and excellent courage. He was known as one of the best Indian fighters on the Clinch, and was a member of Captain Russell's company that participated in the battle at Point Pleasant. When the Revolution began he became a member of the militia company of which William Bowen was captain; and went to King's Mountain with Rees Bowen, where he fought with Campbell's riflemen from the Holston and Clinch valleys.

After Russell County was formed, David Ward was made a justice of the peace for that county. When the county of Tazewell was erected he became, by operation of statute law, a justice of the peace of this county; and he was the first presiding justice of the county court. His son, John, was made the first county clerk of Tazewell. David Ward was chosen, along with Thomas Witten, Jr., to represent the county in the House of Delegates at the sessions of 1801-02, and 1802-03; and represented the county again at the sessions of 1809-10 and 1810-11. His son, John, also represented the county in the same legislative body at the sessions of 1812-13, 1813-14, 1814-15; and 1825-26.

John Ward married Nancy Bowen, and had a very large family, in all ten children, as follows: Levicie, married William Barns; Jane, married Robert Gillespie; Rebecca, married William Crawford; Lily, married John Hill; Nancy, married ———— Hargrave; Henry, married Sallie Wilson; Rees, married Levicie Richardson; Rufus, married Elizabeth Wilson; David and John never married.

THE MOORES OF ABB'S VALLEY.

Bickley says that Captain James Moore settled in Abb's Valley in 1772, but I am satisfied he moved there as early as 1770. Bickley relied on tradition to such an extent that he is at fault in fixing most of the dates in connection with the settlements in the present Tazewell County.

The Moores were of the Scotch-Irish people who lived in Ulster. James Moore, the immediate ancestor of the Moore's of Abb's Valley, left Ireland in 1726, and settled in Chester County, Pennsylvania. He married Jane Walker, daughter of John Walker, who was one of the Scotch-Irish emigrants that came from Ireland and settled in Pennsylvania. After his marriage to Jane Walker, James Moore and his father-in-law moved with their families from Pennsylvania to Rockbridge County, Virginia, then a part of Augusta County, and settled near the Jump Mountain. There Moore reared a family of five sons and five daughters. The sixth child and the second son of the James Moore, of Rockbridge, was Captain James Moore, who was killed by the Indians in Abb's Valley. Captain Moore married Martha Poage, whose parents then lived in Augusta, on the road between the Natural Bridge and the present town of Lexington. After their marriage they lived for several years on the same road, at a place which was subsequently known as Newel's Tavern.

Absalom Looney, a kinsman of James Moore, came to this section of Virginia prior to 1770, on a hunting expedition; and also for the purpose of digging ginseng, which was, even at that time, very valuable for exportation to China and other Asiatic countries. He discovered the valley which has since been called Abb's Valley, and remained there for more than a year, living in a cave to escape discovery by the Indians. When Looney returned to Rockbridge he told James Moore of the rich lands and abundance of game that he saw in the valley. This so impressed Moore that he made an exploring tour to the place, and found it as described by Looney, "the very paradise of the hunter and grazier." He was a breeder of fine horses and saw that the abundance of bluegrass would sustain a large herd, and this, together with other attractions, induced him to arrange for moving his family there. The author of "The Captives of Abbs Valley," who was a grandson of James Moore, says in his Legend of Frontier Life:

"In making his arrangements to take his family there, he went out in the spring accompanied by some labourers, built a cabin, planted a crop, and left an Englishman named Simpson, who had been an indentured servant in his family and was then free, but still remained in his employment, to cultivate the crop and enclose more land during the summer."

In the fall of 1770, James Moore moved his family out and fixed his residence at the place where the massacre of himself and other members of the family afterwards occurred. The place has ever since remained in the possession of his descendants, and is now owned by his great-grandson, Oscar Moore. Captain Moore was accompanied by his brother-in-law, Robert Poage, the latter, with his family, locating about one mile from the Moores. Poage remained but a few years in the valley. When the Indians began to attack the settlements in 1774 he moved back to Rockbridge. This left the Moores completely isolated, their nearest neighbor being ten miles distant from them.

Captain Moore, though aware of the dangers that threatened him and his family from attacks by the Indians, resolved to remain in the valley and face the dangers. When he came there with his family he brought out horses and cattle for breeding purposes, intending to pursue the life of a grazier and breeder of fine stock. He found some parts of the valley comparatively free of forest growth, and on these open spots bluegrass and wild pea vine grew in luxurious abundance. In the summer time his horses and cattle would feed and fatten upon the summer growth of herbage, and even in the winter time they required but little feeding, as there was an abundance of lodged grass to keep them in good condition. His horses and cattle increased rapidly in numbers, and at the time he was killed he had more than a hundred fine horses.

With the purpose of averting any probable danger from attacks by the Indians, Captain Moore converted his cabin into a blockhouse. The doors were made of heavy timber, too thick for a rifle ball to penetrate, and were secured with heavy bars for inside fastenings. The windows were small and placed high in the walls, and had heavy wooden shutters, that could be quickly closed. Like all other frontier houses, this was equipped with loop-holes through which riflemen on the inside could shoot at the attacking enemy.

Ownership of the entire Abb's Valley was one of the fond aspirations of Captain Moore. With this in view, he secured all the land he could under settlers' laws then in existence in Virginia, and formulated plans for acquiring the balance of the valley by purchase. It is said that he was about to bring his cherished plans to a successful conclusion when he was killed by the Indians.

The eager purpose of this brave pioneer to acquire a splendid estate to bequeath to his children did not, however, deter him from a full performance of his duties as a frontier citizen and soldier. His worth was recognized by both the civil and military authorities, and he quickly became a leader among the hardy pioneers who were industriously engaged in converting the wilderness regions of Tazewell into an agricultural and grazing country that would be surpassed in excellence by none on this continent.

James Moore served as a private in the army that Colonel Andrew Lewis marched to the mouth of the Kanawha in the fall of 1774, and did his part in winning victory for the Virginians at the battle of Point Pleasant. He was commissioned captain of a company of militia "on the waters of Bluestone" on the 3rd of April, 1778; and in 1781 he led this company, which went with the riflemen from Montgomery and Washington, under command of Colonel William Campbell, to the relief of General Greene in North Carolina. In the battle of Guilford Court House, Captain Moore, with his mountaineer riflemen, met the first charge of the British infantry; and he and his men won great distinction by their wonderful courage and superior marksmanship.

But three of Captain Moore's children, James, Mary and Joseph, escaped death at the hands of the Indians. The latter was not in Abb's Valley at the time the dreadful tragedy was enacted. A short time prior to the raid made by the Shawnees, Joseph had gone with his father to Rockbridge to visit his grandfather Poage. He became sick with measles and his father had to return to Abb's Valley without him. When James and Mary returned from captivity they found Joseph at their grandfather's in Rockbridge.

James Moore, Jr., was captured in 1784 and remained in captivity until the fall of 1789. In the spring of 1790, he and his sister Mary arrived at their grandfather's in Rockbridge. On the 16th of February, 1797, James married Barbara Taylor of Rockbridge, and very soon thereafter moved with his wife to Abb's Valley and settled upon the lands where his father had formerly lived. He had three children by his first wife, James Ruliford, born in 1799; Martha Poage, born in 1800; and William Taylor, born in 1802. Mrs. Moore died in 1802, shortly after the birth of her son William.

James Ruliford Moore moved to Texas with his family after that State was admitted to the Union. Martha married Rev. Still, who in 1824 went to Kansas as a missionary to work among the Indians.

William Taylor Moore settled at the place in Abb's Valley where his grandfather was killed in 1786. He married twice and had children by each wife. His first wife was Matilda Peery, daughter of George Peery; and his second wife was Mary Barns, daughter of William Barns, of the Cove.

Joseph Moore, son of Captain James Moore, married Rhoda Nicewander, of Rockbridge. He moved out to Tazewell in 1797, and settled in Wrights Valley, near where the present Bailey's Station on the Clinch Valley Railroad is now situated. He had one son, Harvey, and six daughters, Mattie, Mary Brown, Rhoda, Cyn-

William Moore, son of James Moore, the captive, was born in March, 1802, and died in December, 1894. He was one of the best men Tazewell County ever produced.

thia, Julia and Nancy. Harvey married his cousin Jane Moore, who after she became a widow married Charles Tiffany. She was a daughter of James Moore, the captive, by his second marriage. Mattie married her cousin, Joseph A. Moore; Mary Brown married William Shannon; and Rhoda married Elias Hale. Three of the daughters, Cynthia, Julia and Nancy died unmarried.

Joseph Moore remained with his grandfather while his brother, James, and sister, Mary, were in captivity for nearly six years, and during that time had excellent opportunity to obtain a liberal education, as there were good schools in the vicinity of Mr. Poage's. Hence, when he settled in Wright's Valley he was far better educated than most of the men of his age then living in the bounds of the present Tazewell County. He was a skillful surveyor and an excellent scribe.

When the county seat was located he laid the town off in lots; and was made deputy clerk of the county court shortly after it was organized. Hundreds of his descendants are now residents of the county.

When Captain Moore and his family were massacred he had a splendid herd of about one hundred horses. A number of them were colts of Yorick, the Arabian stallion. Joseph Moore, a brother of the Captain, was then living in Kentucky. He came to

Rose, a gray mare 29 years old in 1918, and the last known direct descendant of the famous stallion "Yorick" owned by Capt. James Moore when the Indians massacred the Moore family. Yorrick killed three of the Indians who tried to ride him, and was killed by the Indians when they failed to subdue him. The boy sitting on the mare is Oscar Moore, Jr., and is the great-great-grandson of Capt. James Moore. The photograph of boy and mare was taken near the spot of the massacre of the Moores.

Virginia and administered upon the estate of his deceased brother. When he returned to his home, he took a number of the horses from Abb's Valley, and disposed of them in Kentucky. It has been told, and it is a fact, that the colts of Yorrick had much to do with the production of the fine strain of horses from which Kentucky afterwards became famous. Some of Yorrick's colts were left in Abb's Valley. Above is shown the picture of a gray mare. She was 29 years old when the photograph was made, and is the last known direct descendant of Yorrick. The mare is owned by Mr. O. B.

Moore, and the little boy seated on the mare is Oscar Moore, Jr., the son of O. B. Moore. The photograph of the mare was taken on the grounds of the Moore homestead near where the massacre of the Moore family occurred.

THE HARMANS OF TAZEWELL.

One of the greatest difficulties I have encountered in the preparation of these sketches was in correctly distinguishing the several families of Harmans who were among the pioneer settlers of the Clinch Valley. There are many persons with the name Harman, who are descendants of the pioneers of that name, now living in this county; but they have furnished me with no family records from which I can draw any definite conclusions. Therefore, in writing about the pioneers of that name, I am compelled to rely for information upon the records that exist in the county clerk's office, and such facts as I have found in various histories, together with my personal acquaintance with these people for more than half a century.

The Harmans came to America from Germany. Some of them settled in Pennsylvania, but those from whom most of the Tazewell Harmans are descended settled in North Carolina, near the present town of Salem in that State.

The first Harmans that appear in the annals of this section were Adam Harman and his two sons, who were living on New River in 1755 at the site of the present Eggleston's Springs, in Giles County. They were the men who discovered Mrs. Mary Ingles, after her thrilling escape from the Shawnee Indians, as she was making her way back to Draper's Meadows, an account of which is given in a preceding chapter of this book. Adam Harman first settled in Pennsylvania after he came to America, and from thence came to New River, by way of the Shenandoah and James River valleys. He was a kinsman, possibly a first cousin, of the three brothers, Mathias, Henry and Jacob Harman, who settled in 1771 about one and half miles east of the town of Tazewell, on the lands now owned by the heirs of the late Captain Wm. E. Peery.

Bickley says that another Jacob Harman settled on Bluestone Creek in 1772. Thwaites, in his Dunmore's War, says: "Jacob Harman who settled on Bluestone, in 1771, probably was of the family of Adam, one of the early pioneers of New River." Captain

TH.—27.

Dan Smith, who in 1774 was in command of all the militia forces and military defences on the frontier from Elk Garden to the Bluestone River, reported to Colonel Preston that, through fear of the Indians, Jacob Harman had moved his family "into the New River Settlement." Captain Smith also reported that, upon the recommendation of Thomas Maxwell, he had appointed one Israel Harman to act as a scout down Sandy Creek. These are all of the Harmans I find that came with the first settlers to the Clinch Valley.

Henry Harman, who settled on the Clinch east of the town of Tazewell in 1771, had two sons, George and Mathias that were noted as hunters and Indian fighters. They were with their father in 1774 when he had his terrific encounter with seven Shawnees on Tug River. A graphic account of this encounter, taken from Bickley's History of Tazewell County, is published elsewhere in this history. Captain Henry, as he was afterwards known, received two severe wounds from arrows shot by an Indian in the battle on Tug River. When struck in the breast with an arrow, Harman fell, and the Indians believed they had killed him. They subsequently boasted to whites, whom they had made captives, that they had killed "Old Skygusty," a name they had given the old man, for some unknown reason.

Captain Henry Harman had another son, Henry Harman, Jr., who came to Tazewell with his father in 1771, and was then only nine years old. When he reached manhood he married and built him a home two miles northeast of Tazewell. The place was afterwards known as the "John G. Watts Place." The act passed in December, 1799, by the General Assembly of Virginia creating the county of Tazewell, directed that the first term of the county court should be held "at the house of Henry Harman, Junior," and this mandate was complied with. The late David Harold Peery, of Ogden, Utah, a grandson of Henry Harman, Jr., in May, 1895, wrote a letter to a lady relative who was seeking information about the Harman family; and from that letter the following paragraphs are copied:

"Henry Harman, Jr., my grandfather, was born in North Carolina in 1762, and came to Tazewell with his father in 1771, and married my grandmother, Christina Harman, his cousin, a daughter of David Harman. Grandmother Christina Harman died in 1835. My grandfather, Henry Harman, built a large double log house in which the first court of the county (Tazewell) was held, in 1800. He was a very large man, weighing over 300 pounds, and 6 feet 2 inches in height. To get him out of the house after he died they had to take the door and facing out. He was a man of great intellect, honorable and high-minded; and left an immense estate of lands, negroes and stock. He married my grandmother, Christina Harman, in 1784, and he died in 1808, honored, loved and respected by all.

"The names of their children are as follows: Eleanor, my mother, who married David Peery; Daniel; Rhoda, who married John

Major David Peery was one of the first generations born in the present bounds of Tazewell County. He was the son of John Peery, who settled near the forks of Clinch River in 1772. Major Peery was an excellent man and popular citizen. He was born in 1777, the second year of the Revolution, and died in 1862.

Gillespie; Malvina, who married Alexander Harrison; Nancy, who married Hezekiah Harman, Jr.; Letitia, who married Addison Crockett; Henry Wilburn Harman; Christina, who married Samuel Laird."

The David Harman mentioned by Mr. Peery may have been a brother of Henry Harman, Sr.; and he must have resided elsewhere than in Clinch Valley, as Bickley makes no mention of him. It is very evident that most of the Harmans now living in Tazewell County are direct descendants of the three brothers, Henry, Mathias and Jacob, who settled on the Clinch in 1771; and of Jacob and Israel Harman, who were living on Bluestone in 1774.

THE PEERYS IN TAZEWELL.

Several of the pioneers bore the name Peery; and they were not only valuable co-workers with the Clinch Valley settlers in the pioneer days, but they and their descendants since the organization of Tazewell County have been rated among the most worthy and useful citizens. The Peerys were of the Scotch-Irish blood and came to Pennsylvania during the great exodus of these people from Ulster. From Pennsylvania they moved to Augusta County, Virginia. The Peerys who settled in the Clinch Valley in 1772, or 1773, were all born in that county.

In 1773, Thomas, William and George, who were brothers, moved from Augusta County to what is now Tazewell County. They were sons of Thomas Peery and were raised on Back Creek near Staunton, Virginia. Thomas settled a short distance west of the present town of Tazewell near the place where his son, Harvey G. Peery, afterwards lived, and which is still owned and occupied by his grandson, Squire George Peery; William fixed his home at or near the place where the residence of the late Albert P. Gillespie now stands; and George settled in Abb's Valley. Each of these brothers kept their homes at the place they first located until they died.

Thomas Peery married Margaret Dennis and they raised a family of eleven children, six sons and five daughters. They were: Jonathan, James, William, Thomas (Burke's Garden), Joseph, Harvey George, Mary, Rebecca, Permelia, Eleanor and Nancy. There are hundreds of their descendants now living in Tazewell County and adjoining counties, with many living in other States of the Union. Harvey George Peery, one of the sons of Thomas and Margaret Peery, represented the county of Tazewell in the Virginia House of Delegates at the session of 1844 and 1845.

William Peery married Sallie Evans, a sister of Jesse Evans, whose children were massacred by the Indians in 1779, at the old Buse Harman place, just west of the divide at Tiptop. When the county of Tazewell was created, William Peery gave thirteen acres of land for the county seat; and the public buildings—court house and jail—were erected thereon. During the Revolutionary War he did valiant service for his country in its successful struggle against

British oppression. He accompanied George Rodgers Clark on his expedition to Illinois; and was with Captain James Moore's company in General Greene's campaign in North Carolina, and fought with the splendid riflemen from Washington and Montgomery counties at the battle of Guilford Court House.

William Peery had a large family. Most of his children, after marrying, went West. He had five sons, Robert, Evans, George,

Residence of Major Harvey George Peery, son of Thomas Peery, the pioneer. It was built in 1838, and is located a short distance west of the corporate limits of Tazewell.

Thomas, and Henry Fielding—and seven daughters—Sophia, Emily, Cosby, Polly, Nancy, Olivia and Cynthia. One of his daughters married John Wynne, son of William Wynne. John built the residence where the late Captain Wm. E. Peery lived, a mile and a half east of Tazewell. Wynne sold the place to 'Squire Tommie Peery in 1852, and moved with his family to Missouri. Thomas and Dr. Henry Fielding Peery, sons of William, spent their entire days in the land of their birth. Thomas was one of the most popular and useful citizens of the county. He was its representative in the House of Delegates at the sessions 1819-20 and 1823-24; and he was a justice of the county court for a number of years. Dr. Henry Fielding Peery was one of the most eminent physicians of his day, an assiduous student, and an able writer. Dr. Peery, because of his fine literary attainments, was persuaded to establish the first newspaper published in Tazewell, the Jeffersonville Democrat; and in 1851 he was the leading spirit in the organization of a society known as the Jeffersonville Historical Society.

I have been unable to find much relative to the family and career of George Peery, the brother of Thomas and William, who settled in Abb's Valley. In examining the old records of Montgomery County, I found in the Surveyors "Entry Book" of that county that in the year 1782 George Peery entered 400 acres of land on Bluestone Creek between Jno. Davidson's and Jno. Compton's. And the records of the county court of Tazewell County show that he was a member of the first court held in June, 1800, and helped to organize the county. He had previously been a justice of the peace in Wythe County, before Abb's Valley became a part of Tazewell, and by operation of statute law was constituted a justice of Tazewell County. He was a beautiful penman, as his signature to orders of the county court are so fine as to attract special attention. He raised a family in Abb's Valley, but I have failed to learn the number and names of his children, or what became of them.

In the year 1773 John Peery, a cousin of Thomas, William and George, settled a short distance west of the present county seat of Tazewell, near Plum Creek. Two of his brothers, Solomon and James, settled near him and lived in the community for several years. Solomon moved with his family to some place on Big Sandy River, and James moved to Tennessee. This John Peery was sometimes called "Short Johnnie," to distinguish him from a kinsman also named John, and who lived on the Clinch. In the records of the county court I find that "Short Johnnie" is mentioned as "John Peery, Distillery". He had a distillery where he made apple and peach brandy, and corn whiskey. John and his son, Thomas, went with Captain James Moore's company to North Carolina in 1781, and were in the engagement at Guilford Court House. Thomas, the son, was killed in the battle, and John, the father, was desperately wounded, receiving fifty-four saber cuts that were inflicted by Tarleton's brutal British troopers while he was lying helpless on the ground. "Short Johnnie" had a large family, but I have only the name of one in addition to Thomas, who was killed. There was a son named John, who lived on Clear Fork, and he was known as "John Peery, Silversmith." It is certain that the Peerys who lived on Plum Creek were the descendants of "Short Johnnie."

There was another John Peery who came here in 1773. He tarried for a while on Clear Fork; and then moved on to the Clinch, where he settled permanently near the fork of the river, one and a half miles northeast of the present county seat. There he acquired a large boundary of land, which is considered by many persons the most valuable per acre of any now in the county.

This was the home of Major David Peery, built by him in 1805, and one of the oldest houses now occupied as a residence in Tazewell County. It is now owned and occupied by Samuel C. Peery, son of Capt. Wm. E. Peery.

This John Peery was distinguished by the name of "Long John," and he is also mentioned in the county records as "John Peery, Blacksmith." He was born in Augusta County, Virginia, where he married Nancy Martin in 1772. Their children were all born in the Clinch Valley and their names were: James, David, Catherine, Jane, Archibald, George, and Jonathan. Of these, two of his sons, David and George, remained in Tazewell County and settled on the lands they inherited from their father. The others moved to Kentucky and Missouri. "John Peery, Blacksmith" died at Burksville, Kentucky, at the home of one of his children, about the year 1817.

Major David Peery, son of John Peery, "Blacksmith", was born April 17th, 1778, in the Clinch settlements. In December, 1806, he married Eleanor Harman, daughter of Henry Harman, Jr. Soon after their marriage he built a comfortable log dwelling on the Clinch about one mile east of the railway station at North Tazewell. It is now the residence of Samuel Cecil Peery, and is one of the oldest houses still used as a dwelling in the county. Major Peery has a large number of descendants in Tazewell County and at Ogden, Utah, where his son, D. Harold Peery, died a few years ago at a venerable age.

THE THOMPSON FAMILY.

Bickley, in his history of Tazewell County, says nothing about the coming of the Thompsons to the Clinch Valley; and the male descendants of the pioneers of that name who are now living in the county seem to have little knowledge of when their ancestors came here and what they did after they became settlers. From Mrs. George W. Gillespie, of Tazewell, who is a great-grandaughter of William Thompson, a pioneer; and Mrs. C. W. George, of Albany, Missouri, who is a great-great-grandaughter of the said William Thompson, I have procured very satisfactory information. With this, and such data as the county records supply, I will do the best I can in preparing a sketch of the Thompsons who were of the pioneers.

The Thompsons are of the Scotch-Irish people, who migrated from Ulster and settled in Pennsylvania. They came from that province to the Valley of Virginia, and thence to the Clinch Valley. In the Surveyors "Plot Book" of Fincastle County, which book is now kept with the records of Montgomery County, at Christiansburg, I find that Captain Dan Smith, assistant surveyor of Fincastle County, in the year 1774 surveyed for one William Thompson a tract of 229 acres of land, situated "on the north waters of the South Fork of Clinch River, Beginning at a black walnut at the foot of Morris' Knob." The date of this survey indicates that William Thompson certainly came to the Clinch Valley as early as 1774, and possibly previous to that date. If he ever lived on this tract, which he purchased from the Loyal Company, there is no evidence now in existence of his having such residence. He did, however, acquire under a settlers' right a large boundary of valuable land in the present Thompson Valley, six miles above Morris' Knob and built his home at the place where Milton Thompson, his great-grandson, now lives, about six miles south of the town of Tazewell.

It appears that William Thompson, the first, was twice married. He had two sons, John and Archibald, by his first wife; and three or more sons by his second wife. One of the sons by his second wife was known as "Lawyer James Thompson." He was eccentric, but a man of ability, and was the first Commonwealth's Attorney for Tazewell County. Another son of the second family was named

Col. Archibald Thompson, one of the first generation born in Tazewell County. He was the son of John Thompson and a grandson of Lieutenant Rees Bowen.

William. He was called "Roan Billie", because of the peculiar color of his hair, which was red and gray in spots, somewhat similar to the hair of a roan horse. A third son of the second marriage was Andrew. He lived at the old home place after his father's death; and he erected the tombstones that mark the grave of his father and the graves of other kindred in the Thompson family graveyard. One of these stones records the fact that William Thompson was born in the year 1722, and died in 1798; and another stone gives the date of the birth and death of "Lawyer James Thompson."

John Thompson, son of William, married Louisa Bowen. She was a daughter of Lieutenant Rees Bowen, who was killed in the battle at King's Mountain. Archibald, his brother, married Rebecca

Peery, a daughter of George Peery, who settled in Abb's Valley, and who was one of the justices of the first county court of Tazewell County.

John Thompson, after his marriage, settled in Thompson Valley, about three miles below Plum Creek Gap. He had four sons, William, James, Archibald and Walter, and several daughters. William, son of John, married Matilda Witten, daughter of James Witten, the famous scout. This William Thompson established his home at the foot of Clinch Mountain on the old wagon road which crossed the mountain to Poor Valley, and thence down through Laurel Gap, by Broad Ford, and on to Preston's Salt Works. His three brothers had their homes above his place on the road that then passed up the valley to the Plum Creek Gap. They each had large and valuable boundaries of land, most of which still remains in the possession of their descendants.

Archibald Thompson, son of the first William, after his marriage with Rebecca Peery settled in the upper section of Thompson Valley, at the place where Joseph Neal now lives. Archibald had four sons—William, George, John and James. He acquired an extensive boundary of land in the head of the valley, which he divided between his sons, William, George and James. Nearly all this land is still owned by his descendants. In 1813 he purchased from Captain James Patton Thompson a tract of three hundred acres of land in Burke's Garden, and gave it to his son John. The tract embraced the greater part of the four hundred acre boundary upon which James Burke built his cabin in 1753 or 1754. Rufus Thompson, grandson of Major Archie, as he was called, now owns and lives upon this noted and valuable farm.

THE BARNS FAMILY.

Robert Barns, the progenitor of all the people of that name in Tazewell County, was an Irishman by blood and birth. He was born about the middle of the eighteenth century and left the Emerald Isle when he was a mere youth. Tradition says his departure from the land of his birth was occasioned by an escapade in which he and several mischievous companions succeeded in breaking up an Irish Wake—in that day a very grievous offense with the peasantry of Ireland. The young Irish emigrant located for a brief while in Maryland after he came to America, and then moved on to the present Rockbridge County, Virginia. From thence, he came to the Clinch Valley. His occupation was that of school-master, a class badly needed in that day in these regions. While engaged in teaching the boys and girls of the neighborhood, he took advantage of the liberal settlers' laws of Virginia and acquired what is now a splendid landed estate in the Cove, nearly all of which still remains in the possession of two of his great-grandsons, William O. and Joseph G. Barns.

Robert Barns came here about the time the Revolutionary War was drawing to a conclusion. His wife was Grace Brown, and there was a peculiarity in the structure of her hands that continues to mark many of her descendants, even unto the third generation. Her fingers had no joints below the second, or middle, joints. It is said that her father and brothers and sisters had hands similarly formed.

Robert and Grace Barns had but three children at the time of his death, two sons and one daughter. They were William and John, and the daughter, whose name I have not found, married John Goodwin. Robert Barns died in 1802, and his will is one of the first recorded in the Will Book of this county.

William Barns, son of Robert and Grace Barns, married Levicie Ward, daughter of John Ward, the first clerk of Tazewell County, and grandaughter of David Ward, the pioneer. He inherited a large share of his father's valuable estate. During his entire life, after reaching manhood, he was one of the most prominent citizens of the county; and he represented Tazewell County in the Virginia House of Delegates at the sessions of 1829 and 1830. He lived through the entire period of the Civil War, and gave his earnest sympathy and support to the Confederate cause. Though too old to perform military service, he had three sons who served in the Confederate Army. Clinton Barns had the rank of captain; Oscar was lieutenant of Company D, 23rd Virginia Battalion of Infantry, and John served as a private in the same company.   When the small Federal army under command of General Burbridge, in December, 1864, was retreating after being beaten by the Confederates at the Salt Works, a party of stragglers went to the house of 'Squire Barns for the purpose of securing loot. One of the ruffians, without provocation, shot the venerable man, in the presence of his family. The wound was in the breast and was at first considered fatal, but the old gentleman recovered, and remained active in body and mind until he died in 187-.

William and Levicie Barns raised a very large family which consisted of four sons and six daughters. All of these, except one daughter, Rebecca, married and raised large families. Robert Barns, the pioneer, has more than a hundred descendants now living in Tazewell, among whom are found many of the best citizens of the county.

THE GILLESPIES OF TAZEWELL.

The Gillespies of Tazewell County are of Scotch-Irish ancestry. Their ancestors came from Ulster, and first settled in Pennsylvania. They moved from that province and located in the part of Western North Carolina now known as East Tennessee.

In July, 1780, Colonel Charles McDowell and other Whig patriots of the Carolinas were being hard pressed by Major Ferguson and his Tory and Provincial forces in the Catawba and Broad River valleys. The Carolinians appealed to Colonel Isaac Shelby to come to their assistance with a volunteer force from the Holston and Watauga settlements. He heeded the call and marched promptly with two hundred mounted riflemen to the assistance of his compatriots beyond the Alleghanies. Thomas Gillespie, a very young man, was then living in the Watauga Valley. He was one of the band of two hundred that went with Shelby to the Carolinas, and did valiant service in the campaign against the Provincials and Tories who were under command of Ferguson and were devastating the country.

Gillespie was with Shelby when he captured Captain Patrick Moore and his Tory garrison of ninety-four men at Thickety Fort on the 30th of July, 1780, and he was in the several small battles that Shelby's men had with the Provincials and Tories. In the fight at Musgrove's Mill on the Enoree River, August 18th, 1780, there were some extraordinary feats of marksmanship by certain of Shelby's riflemen. After the Provincials and Tories were routed, and were being pursued across the river, one of the Tory riflemen, who had crossed the stream, sheltered himself behind a tree to shoot at the Americans as they crossed at the rocky ford. The tree, however, did not completely conceal the body of the Tory. Noticing this, Thomas Gillespie quickly leveled his rifle on the Tory's partially exposed body and at the crack of the rebel's rifle the Tory bit the dust.

When Colonels Campbell, Shelby and Sevier, on the 26th of September, 1780, marched from Sycamore Shoals for the Carolinas to answer with rifle shots the insolent message sent them by Major Patrick Ferguson, one of the men who marched with them was Thomas Gillespie. He was at the battle of King's Mountain; and, no doubt, did his duty there as he had at Musgrove's Mill the preceding August. It is more than probable that on the march to and from King's Mountain, Thomas Gillespie was in some way associated with the men from the Clinch, and from them learned of the very fertile lands and other attractions of this beautiful country. A few years after the war he left his home in the Watauga Valley and journeyed to the Clinch Valley; and took up his residence in the immediate neighborhood where David Ward was then living, and where Rees Bowen was living before he marched to his death at King's Mountain.

Soon after he came to the Clinch settlements he married Margaret Bowen, daughter of Lieutenant Rees Bowen; and established his home in the Cove, at the foot of Clinch Mountain, on or near the spot where W. J. Gillespie now has his residence. There he acquired ownership of a large and valuable boundary which has ever since been owned by his descendants; and is now owned and occupied by W. J. Gillespie, his great-great-grandson. Thomas and Margaret Gillespie reared a large family. They had five sons,— John, Rees B., Henry, William and Robert, and two daughters. They have a large number of descendants, perhaps a thousand, in Tazewell, and throughout the United States.

THE WYNNES.

William Wynne, who settled at Locust Hill, one and a half miles east of the present town of Tazewell, and built a fort there, was one of the most interesting characters among the first settlers. He was a Quaker, and he took no part in any offensive movements made by his fellow-pioneers against the Indians. His fort, it seems, was built purely as a haven of safety for his family and the families of his neighbors. Any person who is sufficiently interested to go upon the ground where it stood will find that it was admirably situated for defensive purposes. The stockade that inclosed the fort was so arranged as to bring within the inclosure the head of the splendid spring that gushes from a cave at the rear of Mr.

George A. Martin's residence. This enabled the occupants of the fort to get an ample supply of water without going outside the stockade when the Indians were hanging around.

There is no record obtainable that tells from whence William Wynne came when he moved to the Clinch Valley. Being a Quaker, it is reasonable to conclude that he came here from Pennsylvania, possibly by way of the Shenandoah Valley. His grave, which can be found in the Peery graveyard, immediately adjacent to the spot where his fort stood, is marked by a marble tombstone on which I recently found the following inscription:

"William Wynne
Born August 10th 1729
Died July 8th 1808."

His will is recorded in Will Book No. 1 of Tazewell County and reveals the fact that he was twice married. By his first wife he had three daughters—Ruth, Orphy Edward, and Sallie Jane; and four sons—Jonah, Elkanah, Oliver and Harman. There is no record in Tazewell which tells the maiden name of his first wife. It may be possible that she was a Harman, as that name was given one of her sons; and William Wynne obtained the Locust Hill tract from the Harmans, who first settled there when they came to the Clinch.

In his will, the old Quaker mentions his second wife as "Phillis". Her maiden name was Whitley. By this wife he had eight sons, all of whom are mentioned in his will. There names were: John, William, Samuel, Robert, Harry, Peter, James and Miner; and a number of daughters. He must have been a thrifty and industrious man, as he accumulated a large estate, both real and personal; and made ample provision, either by advancements before his death or by bequests in his will, for each of his numerous children, said to be thirty-two in number. To his son Miner, he gave his "land lying in Burk's Garden." The Burke's Garden Wynnes are the descendants of Miner Wynne. William Wynne in writing his name made 'e' the last letter of the name. Why his descendants dropped the "e" from the name is not known.

John Wynne married Olivia Peery, daughter of William Peery, the pioneer. She was the sister of 'Squire Tommie and Dr. Fielding Peery. Nearly a hundred years ago John Wynne built the house which the late Captain Wm. E. Peery and his widow occupied as a residence for more than sixty years, located one and a half miles east of Tazewell. In 1852, John Wynne sold the place to 'Squire Tommie Peery, who gave it to his son, William Edward. Mrs. Kate Cecil Peery, the venerable widow of Captain Peery made it her home until her death on May 8th, 1919. Olivia Wynne, wife of John, is buried in the Peery graveyard. Her husband, with his remaining family, moved to Missouri in 1852, after he sold the

The above is the first brick house erected in Tazewell County. It was built for John Wynne over a hundred years ago; and in 1852 it became the home of the late Captain Wm. E. Peery. Perhaps it is the most noted place in the county, and many historic incidents cluster about the lovely old home. Wm. E. Peery, Jr., son of Captain Peery, now owns the property; and it is likely to remain a possession of the Peery family for many future generations.

Locust Hill tract. There are none of the Wynnes left in Tazewell, except the descendants of Miner and Oliver Wynne. The latter located in Burke's Garden after his father's death. William Wynne also owned six hundred and sixty acres of land in Powell's Valley in Lee County. These lands he bequeathed to his five sons, Samuel, Robert, Henry, Peter and James. The Wynns now living in Lee County are the descendants of William Wynne, the Clinch Valley pioneer. It is more than probable that William Wynne was the wealthiest man in Tazewell at the time of his death The appraisement of his personal estate amounted to the sum of $2,603.29; and he owned thousands of acres of the choicest lands in this county.

THE MAXWELL FAMILY.

One of the pioneer families that figured prominently in the early history of the Upper Clinch Valley, is the Maxwells. James Maxwell, who was of the Scotch-Irish blood, came from the province of Ulster to America and settled in Pennsylvania early in the eighteenth century. He married a Miss Roberts, and moved to that part of Augusta County, Virginia, now embraced in the county of Rockbridge. Three of his sons, Thomas, James and Robert, were among the first settlers in the present Tazewell County. Thomas and James settled on Bluestone, not very far from the present town of Graham; and Robert located near Plum Creek, about two miles west of present town of Tazewell. They came here about 1771 or 1772.

Thomas Maxwell has been so frequently mentioned in preceding pages of this book that it is hardly necessary to recount his deeds of daring. He not only had frequent encounters with the Indians, but was with Lieutenant Rees Bowen at the battle of King's Mountain, where he acted with such gallantry that he was made a captain of militia in Washington County, he having located on the North Fork of Holston River, after his return from King's Mountain. The brave pioneer lost his life while assisting in the rescue of the wife and children of Thomas Ingles, who had been made captives in Burke's Garden by a band of Shawnee Indians. If Thomas Maxwell left any descendants, there is no record or traditional evidence by which the author can locate them.

James Maxwell moved from the Bluestone settlements and located on Clinch River, somewhere westward of the present county seat of Tazewell. He did excellent service as a soldier and scout in the war with the Indians in 1774, and also in the Revolutionary War. When Tazewell County was organized in 1800, James Maxwell was made the first sheriff of the county. The records of the county show that he was a very active and influential citizen. He had a family but it has been impossible to get any information about his descendants. It is probable that they all left the county.

Robert Maxwell, who settled on Plum Creek, had eight children. Their names were as follows: Robert, Mary, John, Margaret, James,

Jennie, Mattie and Elizabeth. Jennie and Mattie were killed by the Indians when the savages were making one of their bloody attacks upon the Clinch settlements. Bickley says nothing about this tragic incident. Evidently the girls were very young, and the murder must have occurred in 1780 or 1781. The Indians made frequent visits to the Clinch settlements during those years, while numbers of the best fighting men were away, at King's Mountain in 1780, and at Guilford Court House in 1781. Robert Maxwell's cabin stood south of the road, and opposite the residence of the late Captain James S. Peery. Some of the stones of the cabin chimney still remain on the ground.

Margaret, daughter of Robert and Mary Maxwell, married David Whitley. He built a grist mill on the site now occupied by the Star Milling Company at North Tazewell; and he built the stone house for a dwelling that is now a part of the residence of John D. Peery at North Tazewell. Margaret Maxwell was the ancestress of all the Whitley's who have since resided in that vicinity.

James Maxwell, son of Robert, the pioneer, married Mary Witten, who was a daughter of Jeremiah Witten, son of Thomas Witten, the pioneer. He was a scholarly man, and died in 1866, aged eighty-six years. His wife, Mary Witten Maxwell, died in 1873 at the age of ninety-three years. They had three sons and two daughters. Robert, one of their sons, married Margaret Bates, and he died in 1904, at which time he was in his ninety-seventh year. He was the father of the venerable James Maxwell who is now living at Maxwell, six miles west of the town of Tazewell. His residence is the stone house built by Burdine Deskins at about the same time David Whitley built his stone dwelling at North Tazewell.

APPENDIX B TO PIONEER PERIOD

INDIAN MASSACRES

MASSACRES BY THE INDIANS—MANY HORRIBLE OUTRAGES INFLICTED
UPON THE CLINCH VALLEY SETTLEMENTS.

For a period of eighteen years the Upper Clinch Valley settlements were greatly annoyed with repeated attacks by the Indians; and during that time a number of tragic incidents occurred to impair the contentment of the pioneer settlers. Beginning with the massacre of the Henry family, in 1774, the Indians continued, at intervals, until 1792, to make raids into the territory which was later formed into Tazewell County, in many instances inflicting horrible outrages upon the inhabitants. Dr. Bickley in his history has very graphically related all that he could gather from tradition, and from records, about the massacres committed in Tazewell by the red men; and the most diligent investigations on my part have failed to reveal but few other outrages of sufficient moment to warrant mention in this book. I have, however, from records inaccessible to Bickley, found some of the errors and omissions of Tazewell's first historian, and will make the necessary corrections as occasion requires.

MASSACRE OF HENRY FAMILY.

As previously stated, John Henry and his family were the first victims of the hostile savages who invaded the Upper Clinch regions, in what is now known as Tazewell County. Bickley says that Henry settled in Thompson Valley in the spring of 1771, and that he and his family were killed in May, 1776. There are two errors in this latter statement. The tragedy took place on the 8th of September, 1774, and not in May 1776. Major Arthur Campbell, who was in command of all the military forces and stations in Fincastle County, west of New River, on the 9th of September, 1774, made a report to Colonel Preston, county lieutenant, in which he said the attack was made upon Henry and his family the day previous—that is on the 8th of September, 1774.

John Henry was then living on the south side of Rich Mountain, in Thompson Valley, a short distance east of Plum Creek Gap. He had purchased a tract of land at that point from the Loyal Company. In a recent examination of the Fincastle County records, that are kept in the clerk's office of Montgomery County, I found the following recorded on page 79 of "Plot Book No. 1."

"Surveyed for John Henry 167 acres of Land lying in Fincastle County on the north waters of the South Fork of Clinch River (agreeable to an order of Council of the 16th of Decr. 1773, being a part of the Loyal Company grant) & bounded as follows:

"Beginning at a black walnut at foot of Rich Mountain, running thence S 84 E 63 Poles to a Hicory S 36 W 70 to a Hicory on a Hill, S 7 E 57—to a Spanish Oak S 60 W 153—to a Chestnut N 30 W 74 to a small Sugar Tree S 36 W 38—to a white Walnut and Sugar Tree N 40 W 28—to a Sugar Tree & Lynn N 62½ E 276 Poles to the Beginning.   Daniel Smith asst.
5th May 1774   Wm. Preston S F C"

This survey shows beyond a doubt that tradition has located accurately the place where the first massacre by the Indians occurred in Tazewell County. In 1852, when Bickley wrote his history, the Henry land was owned by James S. Witten. It is now owned by Archie Thompson Bickley says:

"The circumstances attending this melancholy occurrence, are not sufficiently clear. The simple fact of the massacre is beyond doubt. But the old gentleman who furnished me with the circumstances, showed such marked evidences of a decaying state of mind, that I fear the tale is not altogether as authentic as we might desire."

It seems that the attack was made by the Indians, who were lying in wait, just after daylight and Bickley details the circumstances as follows:

"Mr. Henry stepped to the door and unbolted it, with the intention, no doubt, of looking abroad, and yawning in the open air. Stepping in the door, he stretched himself up to inhale the sweet odors of the morning breeze, when a party of Indians, who lay near, fired a gun, and he fell on his face in the yard. He wore on the waistbands of his pantaloons, a large metal button, which must have served as a target to the Indian's gun, as the ball passed directly through it, and into Mr. Henry's body."

The savages then rushed over the supposed dead body of Henry into the house, where they tomahawked and killed and scalped Mrs. Henry and all of her children, except one little boy, who was made a prisoner. Henry rose to his feet, and, knowing he could do nothing to relieve his family, ran into the woods and hid; and, according to Bickley, tried to make his way to the house of his nearest neighbor, a Mr. Martin. Bickley says that Martin had started to Rich Valley with his family, and met Mr. Henry, who was so desperately wounded that he was crawling on his hands and knees to warn his neighbors of the presence of the Indians in the community. Martin put Henry on a horse and took him to the Cove where he died in a few hours and was buried on the farm of William Barns, Esq. He further says that:

"A company was soon collected and preparations made to follow the Indians, who, it was supposed, had carried off the rest of the family. But when they arrived at the fatal spot, the family, consisting of a wife and six children, were found murdered, scalped, and piled up after the manner of a log heap, on a ridge a short distance from the house. One child was not found, a little boy, whom it was supposed had been carried off. A large hole was opened, which became a common grave for the mother and her unoffending children.

"The identical spot on which Henry was buried, could not be marked for a number of years—a few years ago, a grave was opened near the supposed place, which accidently proved to be the very spot on which Henry was buried, which was known from the presence of boards and puncheons, which had been substituted for a coffin, and the identical button through which the fatal ball passed. The button is now in possession of some one in this county."

"The old gentleman" who, from tradition, related to Dr. Bickley the circumstances connected with the massacre of the Henry family was pretty accurate as to what he told. He was mistaken as to the person who discovered the wounded man and played the part of the good Samaritan; and was mistaken in the name of the man who was taking his family to Rich Valley in the present Smyth County. Major Campbell reported the tragedy the day after it occurred. He reported "Old John Hamilton" as the person who found Henry after he was wounded; and named John Bradshaw as the man who had sent his family to Rich Valley. The report of Major Campbell has been very freely detailed in a preceding chapter, and it will be useless to repeat it here.

THE EVANS FAMILY.

From the time that John Henry and his family were killed, until eight years after the Revolution was ended, the settlers of the Upper Clinch Valley were in constant dread of attacks by the Indians. But, if Bickley is correct in the dates he gives, no other attacks were made upon the inhabitants of Tazewell after the massacre of the Henry family until the third year of the Revolution. There were two causes for the temporary immunity our ancestors enjoyed from attacks by the savages. One cause was the excellent preparation the inhabitants had made by building block-houses and forts, and the organization of a splendid corps of scouts that was kept constantly on duty to watch and report any invasion by the hostiles. The Tazewell men were known to be the best Indian fighters on the Virginia frontiers, and the savages dreaded and avoided encounters with them. Another cause for the temporary relief was the determined efforts of the Indians to drive the settlers from Kentucky, which compelled them to concentrate all their forces for the execution of that purpose. Occasionally small parties of the red men would slip in for robbery, and sometimes they would take a prisoner, but no other massacre occurred until 1779.

In 1773, John Evans and his son Jesse moved their families from Amherst County, Virginia, and settled at the head of the north fork of Clinch River, some eight miles northeast of the present town of Tazewell. John Evans located at the Locust Bottom and Jesse established his home about one mile east of his father's where Buze Harman afterwards lived, just west of the village of Tiptop.

In 1777, a small band of Shawnees came to the head of the Clinch and made John Evans a captive and took him to their towns in Ohio. From there he was sent to Canada, and either made his escape, or was ransomed, and went to Philadelphia. Jesse Evans heard of his arrival in Philadelphia and went there in the spring of 1778 and brought him home. Bickley says:

"In the summer of 1779, Jesse Evans left his house with six or eight hired men, for the purpose of executing some work at a distance from home. As they carried with them various farming implements, their guns were left at the house, where Mrs. Evans was engaged weaving a piece of cloth. Her oldest daughter was filling quills for her; while the remaining four children were either at play in the garden or gathering vegetables.

"The garden was about sixty yards from the house, and as no sawmills were in existence at that day in this county, slab-boards were put up in the manner called 'wattling' for palings. These were some six feet long, and made what is called a close fence. Eight or ten Indians, who lay concealed in a thicket near the garden, silently left their hiding places, and made their way unobserved, to the back of the garden; there removing a few boards, they bounded through and commenced the horrid work of killing and scalping the children. The first warning Mrs. Evans had was their screams and cries. She ran to the door, and beheld the sickening scene, with such feelings as only a mother can feel.

"Mrs. Evans was a stout, athletic woman, and being inured to the hardships of the times, with her to will was to do. She saw plainly that on her exertions alone could one spark of hope be entertained for the life of her 'first born.' An unnatural strength seemed to nerve her arm, and she resolved to defend her surviving child to the last extremity. Rushing into the house she closed the door, which being too small left a crevice, through which in a few seconds an Indian introduced his gun, aiming to pry open the door, and finish the bloody work which had been so fearfully begun. Mrs. Evans had thrown herself against the door to prevent the entrance of the savages, but no sooner did she see the gun-barrel than she seized it, and drew it so far in as to make it available for a lever in prying to the door. The Indians threw themselves against the door to force it open, but their efforts were unavailing. The heroic woman stood to her post, well knowing that her life depended upon her own exertions. The Indians now endeavored to wrest the gun from her; in this they likewise failed. Hitherto she had worked in silence; but as she saw no prospect of the Indians relinquishing their object, she began to call loudly for her husband, as if he really were near. It had the desired effect; they let go the gun, and hastily left the house, while Mrs. Evans sat quietly down to await a second attack; but the Indians, who had perhaps seen Mr. Evans and his workmen leave the house, feared he might be near, and made off with all speed."

After the Indians left, a man by the name of Goldsby stepped up to the door, but as soon as Mrs. Evans told him of the attack by the savages he ran swiftly away through fear of the Indians. It was told that he exerted himself so violently in making his escape

The old house, that is partially shown behind the stack of wood, is near the spot where Major Taylor's cabin stood, to which Mrs. Evans and her daughter fled for refuge. This old house was built and occupied by Major Taylor after the Revolutionary War. It stands a short distance north of the residence of the late W. G. Mustard, now the residence of his daughter, Mrs. Henry S. Bowen. The persons shown sawing wood are Mr. Mustard and his grandson, Grat Mustard Bowen. The latter is now a grown man and voting citizen of the county.

that he brought on hemorrhage of the lungs, from which he was a long time recovering. Goldsby was one of the very few cowards that were among the pioneer settlers on the Clinch.

Mrs. Evans, armed with the gun she had taken from the Indians, determined to go with her little daughter to Major John Taylor's. He lived two miles west of the Evans home, at the location of the present home of Mrs. Henry S. Bowen, and about the same distance northwest of Witten's Mill. In a short while after Mrs. Evans and her daughter started to Major Taylor's, her husband returned to his house. He supposed his wife and children were somewhere about the premises, and began to read from a book, possibly his Bible. At last he became alarmed at the absence of his wife and children and went out into the garden, thinking it probable that his wife was gathering vegetables for their dinner. There he found four of his little ones that had been butchered by the Indians. Not finding his wife and eldest daughter, he thought they had been made captives by the Indians. He returned to the house, got his gun, and went to Major Taylor's to get assistance, where he was joyfully surprised to find his wife and daughter uninjured. The men of the surrounding country were quickly notified of the occurrence, and the following morning a party of sympathetic friends accompanied the bereaved parents to their home to bury the murdered children. When the party reached the back of the house they saw Mary, a child only four years old, coming from the spring which was at the front of the Evans home. She had recovered during the night from the blow inflicted with a tomahawk, and had wandered around until daylight, and then gone to the spring to quench her thirst. Her scalp had been torn from her skull and was hanging over her face which was smeared and stained with her blood. Mary recovered entirely from the injury, grew up to womanhood, married and became the mother of a large family.

Bickley says that after the horrible calamity, Jesse Evans became dissatisfied with his home on the Clinch and moved to Tennessee. He must have lingered for several years in Wright's Valley after the massacre of his children. In the surveyors entry book of Montgomery County, I find that Jesse Evans in 1782 entered 400 acres of land in Wright's Valley on the headwaters of the North Fork of Clinch River, to include improvements. This was evidently the tract of land upon which Evans was living when his children were killed by the Indians.

MASSACRE OF ROARK FAMILY.

The year following the massacre of the Evans family another frightful tragedy was enacted in Baptist Valley, when the Roark family experienced a fate similar to that which befell the family of Jesse Evans. Tradition is very apt to err in fixing the dates of incidents similar to those of which I am writing, though it be accurate as to the locality where such events take place and the circumstances connected therewith. Bickley, who had to depend on tradition, places the massacre of the Roarks in the year 1789, when it actually occurred in 1780, as I have ascertained from existing records. The following account of the tragedy is given by Dr. Bickley:

"James Roark lived at the gap of the dividing ridge, between the waters of the Clinch and the Sandy rivers, through which passed the Dry Fork road, and which has since been known as Roark's Gap. Early in 1789, a band of Shawnee Indians left their homes in the west, and ascending the Dry fork, fell upon the defenseless family of Mr. Roark and killed his wife and several children. Two sons and Mr. Roark were from home and, it may be, thus saved their own lives, as the Indians were rather numerous to have been beaten off by them, even if they had been at home.

"This is the only instance that I have met with, of the Indians visiting the settlements of Tazewell before the winter had clearly broken. There was a heavy snow upon the ground at the time.

"From this time forward the Roarks became the deadly enemies of the Indians, and sought them, even beyond the limits of the county. Mr. Roark and one of his sons (John), were afterwards killed in a battle, fought at what was then known as the Station bottom, within the present limits of Floyd county, Kentucky."

In a publication of the State Historical Society of Wisconsin, gotten out in 1917, I have found a report which shows that the Roark massacre occurred on the 18th of March, 1780. The report was made by Major John Taylor to Colonel William Preston, then county lieutenant for Montgomery County, and is official. The original report, now in the possession of the State Historical Society of Wisconsin, was procured by the late Lyman C. Draper from the descendants of Colonel Preston. The report made by Major Taylor to Colonel Preston is as follows:

"Sir:

"The 18th Instant the Indians was In this Neighborhood and Fell in at James Roark's where they Scalped seven of his Children And his wife. They are all Dead only one Girl. They took Seven Head of Horses Five of which was the property of Wm. Patterson.

This part of yr. County is In a scene of Confusion And I make no doubt but the Country will Break up without they Can Get Some Assistance. I am as yet Living at home but Capt Maxwell's Compy are Chiefly Gathered together in Small Parties. Corn is very Scarce Here but if a few men could be raised I think they Could be found, Sir if you have resigned yr Commission Pray let the County Lieut. Have this Letter or a few lines from yr. self which I think will Answer a better End. I expected a few lines from you By Capt Moor but Dont hear of any My family is In Health As I hope yours and I am Sir yr. Most Hum Srt.

Jno Taylor

Head Clinch 23rd March 1780
C B the Murder was Committed In seven Miles of here."

Major Taylor was the same man at whose home Mrs. Jesse Evans and her daughter sought refuge after her children were killed by the Indians in 1779. This report, made by letter to Colonel Preston, not only gives the date of the Roark massacre and the number of victims but furnishes valuable information as to existing military and economic conditions in the Upper Clinch region at that time. The military authorities of Montgomery County had given no assistance to the inhabitants of the Clinch Valley in repelling the repeated invasions made by the Shawnees; and the Evans and Roark massacres had resulted, as the forts and stations maintained by the settlers were so widely separated that the Indians were able to steal in between the forts and murder the occupants of the outlying cabins. Evidently there was a serious scarcity of corn in the Clinch Valley, which gave a shortage of food for both men and animals. The scarcity of grain seemed to be general throughout Montgomery, owing, possibly, to a bad season, or to the employment of so many of the inhabitants in the performance of military duties. In a letter written the 15th of Feb., 1780, by Rev. Caleb Wallace, who was then living near the present town of Christiansburg, to Colonel William Fleming, then locating lands under military grants in Kentucky, the Reverend Wallace says: "The Condition of this Country is truly distressing. Corn has risen to 10, 12 & 15 pounds the Bushel, and it is to be feared that Multitudes will not get it at any Price."

James Roark must have lingered for several years upon the scene after his wife and children were murdered by the Indians.

He was living there in 1783 when Hugh Fulton ran the line between Montgomery and Washington counties. The last course in Fulton's survey is from the west end of Morris' Knob, and is as follows: "Thence from said Knob north crossing the spurs of the same, and Paint Lick mountain the north fork of Clinch by John Hines plantation, and over the river ridge by James Roark's in the Baptist Valley, to a sugar tree and two white oaks on the head of Sandy."

Timothy Roark was a juror on the first grand-jury impaneled in Tazewell County, in November, 1800. Whether he was a son or brother of James is not disclosed by any existing record.

CAPTURE AND RESCUE OF INGLES FAMILY.

Of the numerous hostile visits made by the Indians to the settlements in Tazewell County, none was more thrilling than the capture of the family of Thomas Ingles in Burke's Garden by Black Wolf and his band of Shawnees. Relying upon tradition, Bickley fixes the date of this incident in the spring of 1787. It occurred in April, 1782.

Thomas Ingles was the son of William and Mary Ingles, and was one of the captives taken at the Draper's Meadows massacre in 1755. He was carried with his mother and the other prisoners to the Shawnee towns in Ohio, and was adopted into an Indian family, where he remained for thirteen years. His father went to Ohio in 1768, ransomed Thomas by the payment of one hundred and fifty dollars, and brought him to his home at Ingles' Ferry on New River, situated about one mile south of the present town of Radford. His kinsmen, Dr. John P. Hale, in his Trans-Alleghany Pioneers, says of Thomas Ingles: "He was very much of a wild Indian in his habits when he first returned;" and: "Notwithstanding he was petted, humored and caressed at home, a wild fit would overcome him now and then, and he would wander off alone in the wilderness with his bow and arrow, and stay for days at a time, and, when he returned, would give no account of himself, nor explanation of his conduct."

His parents were anxious to have him educated, and sent him to Albemarle County, where he was placed under the care of Dr. Thomas Walker, the explorer, surveyor, and agent of the Loyal Company. There was a school for young men in the neighborhood of "Castle Hill," Dr. Walker's residence. While attending this school young Ingles made the acquaintance of Miss Eleanor Grills, they became sweethearts, and were married in 1775.

Shortly after his marriage his father gave him a tract of land on Wolf Creek, in the present Giles County. It was in the wilderness and suited to the wild disposition of the young man. He and his family remained a year or two on Wolf Creek, and then removed to Abb's Valley, where he settled on the one thousand acre tract his father had purchased from the Loyal Company. After a residence of a year or more in Abb's Valley, Ingles became alarmed for the safety of his wife and children, because of the nearness of their home to the Indian trail up the Tug Fork of Sandy, and Bluestone. This trail had been used by the Indians for the raids they had made to the headwaters of the Clinch and the Upper New River Valley; and was considered one of the most dangerous on the frontier. He then located with his family in Burke's Garden on the tract of land where James Burke had once lived, and occupied the house Burke had built. His father, William Ingles, had secured from Burke the right to four hundred acres of land which Burke had gotten from either Colonel Patton or the Loyal Company. There was but one other white man living in the Garden, Joseph Hicks by name, a bachelor, whose cabin was two miles distant from the Ingles home.

Though Ingles had moved to the Garden for safety, in April, 1782, a large party of Shawnees, led by the noted chief, Black Wolf, entered Burke's Garden. They concealed themselves until Ingles went out on his farm to work, and then surrounded his home; and made his wife, their three children and a negro man and woman prisoners. After taking as much loot as they could carry, the Indians started with their prisoners and booty back to Ohio. The cries of the captives attracted the notice of Thomas Ingles and his negro man while they were plowing in a field. They abandoned their plows, and started on a run to investigate the trouble. Seeing a number of Indians, and having no gun, Ingles realized that he could do nothing for the relief of his family. He and the negro ran back to their plows, unhitched the horses, and started to the nearest settlement to get assistance. Knowing that the Indians would make their way to the head of the Clinch, Ingles decided to go in another direction, and crossed the mountains to the nearest settlement on the North Fork of the Holston.

It happened to be muster day for the Washington County militia and the settlers on the North Fork of Holston River had assembled, and were being drilled by Captain Thomas Maxwell, who had formerly lived at the head of Bluestone, in Tazewell County. Maxwell, with a party of fifteen or twenty volunteers, went with Thomas Ingles to Burke's Garden to pursue the Indians and rescue the captives.

Joseph Hicks and his negro man were on their way to the house of Thomas Ingles the morning the Indians made the attack. As soon as Hicks discovered the Indians, and saw what they were doing, he and his negro retreated rapidly, crossed Burke's Garden and Brushy mountains on foot to a small settlement in the present Bland County for help. There they secured six or seven men who returned with Hicks to the Garden, arriving about the same time that Thomas Ingles and Captain Maxwell got there with their party. The two forces were united, and went in immediate pursuit of the savages. Captain Maxwell was put in command of the whole party, and the trail of the Indians was first struck at the head of Clinch. Some of the settlers from the Clinch and Bluestone joined the pursuing party; and the trail of the Indians was followed with great caution, as it was feared the captives would be killed if the savages found they were being pursued.

On the fifth day after the capture the advance scouts of the white men discovered the Indians, who were encamped for the night in a gap of Tug Mountain. A consultation was held by the pursuers, and it was agreed that Captain Maxwell should take half the men, and, during the night, get around to the front of the Indians, and Thomas Ingles should remain with the other half at the rear; and that at daybreak a simultaneous attack upon the savages be made by the two divisions. The night was very dark and the ground exceedingly rough and brushy. Consequently the party with Maxwell lost their way and did not reach the front by daylight.

Maxwell having failed to get to his appointed place on time, and the Indians beginning to rouse from their slumbers. Ingles determined to make an attack with his men. Dr. Thomas Hale, who was a great-grandson of William and Mary Ingles and who collected his information from the records of the Ingles family thus relates what transpired after the attack was made:

"So soon as a shot was fired, some of the Indians began to tomahawk the prisoners, while others fought and fled. Thomas Ingles rushed in and seized his wife just as she had received a terrible blow on the head with a tomahawk. She fell, covering the infant of a few months old, which she held in her arms. The Indians had no time to devote to it. They had tomahawked his little five-year-old daughter, named Mary, after her mother, and his little three-year-old son, named William, after his father. His negro servants, a man and woman, captured with his family, escaped without injury.

"In making their escape, the Indians ran close to Captain Maxwell and party, and, firing on them, killed Captain Maxwell, who was conspicuous from wearing a white hunting shirt.

"The whites remained on the ground until late in the evening burying Captain Maxwell, who was killed outright, and Thomas Ingles' lttle son, who died from his wounds during the day. Mrs. Ingles and the little girl were still alive though badly wounded."

It was not known definitely whether any of the Indians were killed, but while the whites remained on the scene they heard groans from the adjacent laurel thickets, that seemed to be made by persons who were suffering or dying.

After burying the dead and giving such attention as was possible to the wounds of Mrs. Ingles and her little daughter, Mary, the party began its return march to the settlements. Owing to the critical condition of Mrs. Ingles and her daughter, the party had to move very slowly, and it required four days for them to reach William Wynne's fort at Locust Hill, one and a half miles east of the present town of Tazewell.

William Ingles, father of Thomas, received the news of the capture of his son's family a few days after it occurred, and he immediately left his home on New River for Burke's Garden. Apprehending that there would be dire need of surgical attention, he took with him the best surgeon he could get in the New River settlements. He reached Wynne's fort about the same time that Thomas Ingles with his wife and children arrived there. No relief could be given little Mary, and she died the morning after the rescue party reached the fort. The surgeon was more successful with the case of Mrs. Ingles. He extracted several pieces of bone from her skull, and treated the wound so skillfully that she was able to travel on horseback in a few weeks, when she, with her husband and babe, returned with William Ingles to his home at Ingle's Ferry, on New River. Very soon thereafter, Thomas Ingles, with his wife and infant daughter, moved to Tennessee, and settled in succession on the Watauga River, at Mossy Creek, and at Fort Knox, now Knoxville. There his daughter, Rhoda, who escaped death at the hands of the Indians, grew up to lovely womanhood, and became the wife of Patrick Campbell a prominent citizen of Knoxville. Some time subsequent to his daughter's marriage, Thomas Ingles moved to Mississippi, where he remained until he died.

THE CAPTIVITY OF JAMES MOORE.

The pioneer family that suffered most at the hands of the Indians was that of Captain James Moore, who moved with his family from what is now Rockbridge County to Abb's Valley, in 1772. Bickley says: "In September, 1784, a party of Indians had entered the present limits of Tazewell, and dividing themselves into small parties to steal horses and to annoy the settlers, three had entered the Abb's Valley settlement, in which resided Capt. James Moore and a brother-in-law named John Pogue (Poage). The Indians had been for a day or two lurking round, waiting, and looking for an opportunity to seize horses or murder the settlers."

These three Indians were Black Wolf and two youths about eighteen years old, one of them a son of the Wolf. While they were lurking round in Abb's Valley, Captain Moore one morning sent his son, James, a lad about eighteen years old, to a distant pasture to get a horse to take a bag of corn to mill. While James was on his way to the pasture, he was suddenly set upon by Black Wolf and his companions and made a captive. He was taken by his captors to the Indian town in Ohio and adopted by a half sister of the Wolf, she giving the chief an old horse in exchange for the boy. It was five years before James Moore got back home, and three years after the massacre of his father and his family. He had many thrilling experiences while with the Indians. In the spring of 1775, he was so fortunate as to get away from the Indians, and several years after his return home he related the following incidents in connection with his captivity:

"When we returned from hunting, in the spring, the old man gave me up to Captain Elliot, a trader, from Detroit. But my mistress, on hearing this, became very angry, threatened Elliot, and got me back. Some time in April there was a dance at a town about two miles from where I resided. This I attended, in company with the Indian to whom I belonged. Meeting with a French trader from Detroit, by the name of Batest Ariome, who took a fancy to me on account of my resemblance to one of his sons, he bought me for fifty dollars in Indian money. Before leaving the dance, I met with a Mr. Sherlock, a trader from Kentucky, who had formerly been a prisoner to the same tribe of Indians, and who had rescued a lad by the name of Moffit, who had been captured at the head of Clinch, and whose father was an intimate and particular friend of my father's. I requested Mr. Sherlock to write to my father, through Mr. Moffit, informing him of my captivity, and that I had been purchased by a French trader, and was gone to Detroit. This letter, I have reason to believe, father received, and that it gave him the first information of what had become of me.

"Mr. and Mrs. Ariome were to me parents indeed. They treated me like one of their own sons. I ate at their table, and slept with their sons, in a good feather bed. They always gave me good counsel, and advised me (particularly Mrs. Ariome) not to abandon the idea of returning to my friends. I worked on the farm with his sons, and occasionally assisted him in his trading expeditions. We traded at different places, and sometimes went a considerable distance in the country.

"On one of these occasions, four young Indians began to boast of their bravery and among other things, said that one Indian could whip four white men. This provoked me, and I told them that I could whip all four of them. They immediately attacked me, but Mr. Ariome, hearing the noise, came and took me away. This I considered a kind providence; for the Indians are very unskillful in boxing, and in this manner of fighting, I could easily have whipped all of them; but when they began to find themselves worsted, I expected them to attack me with clubs, or some other weapon, and if so, had laid my plans to kill them all with a knife, which I had concealed in my belt, mount a fleet horse, which was close at hand, and escape to Detroit.

"It was on one of these trading expeditions, that I first heard of the destruction of father's family. This I learned through a Shawnee Indian, with whom I had been acquainted when I lived with them, and who was one of the party on that occasion. I received this information some time in the same summer after it occurred. In the following winter, I learned that my sister Polly had been purchased by Mr. Stogwell, an American by birth, but unfriendly to the American cause. He was a man of bad character—an unfeeling wretch—and treated my sister with great unkindness. At that time he resided a considerable distance from me. When I heard of my sister, I immediately prepared to go and see her; but as it was then in the dead of winter, and the journey would have been attended with great difficulties, on being told, by Mr. S., that he intended to remove to the neighborhood where I resided in the following spring, I declined it. When I heard that Mr. Stogwell had removed, as was contemplated, I immediately went to see her. I found her in the most abject condition, almost naked, being clothed with only a few dirty and tattered rags, exhibiting to my mind, an object of pity indeed. It is impossible to describe my feelings on that occasion; sorrow and joy were both combined; and I have no doubt the feelings of my sister were similar to my own. On being advised, I applied to the commanding officer at Detroit, informing him of her treatment, with the hope of effecting her release. I went to Mr. Simon Girty, and to Col. McKee, the superintendent of the Indians, who had Mr. Stogwell brought to trial to answer the complaint brought against him. But I failed to procure her release. It was decided, however, when an opportunity should occur for our returning to our friends, she should be released without remuneration. This was punctually performed, on application of Mr. Thomas Ivins, who had come in search of his sister Martha, already alluded to, who had been purchased from the Indians by some family in the neighborhood, and was, at that time, with a Mr. Donaldson, a worthy and wealthy English farmer, and working for herself.

"All being now at liberty, we made preparations for our journey to our distant friends, and set out, I think, some time in the month of October, 1789; it being a little more than five years from the time of my captivity, and a little more than three years from the time of the captivity of my sister and Martha Ivins. A trading boat coming down the lakes, we obtained a passage, for myself and sister,

TH.—29

to the Moravian towns, a distance of about two hundred miles, and on the route to Pittsburgh. There, according to appointment, we met with Mr. Ivins and his sister, the day after our arrival. He

This apple tree was carried from Rockbridge County, by James Moore, the captive, to Abb's Valley, and planted near the place where his father and kindred were massacred. Four years ago, when the tree was 116 years old, it bore 116 bushels of excellent apples. Since then large portions of the tree were torn off by a storm.

had, in the meantime procured three horses, and we immediately set out for Pittsburgh. Fortunately for us, a party of friendly Indians, from these towns, were about starting on a hunting excursion, and accompanied us for a considerable distance on our route, which was through a wilderness, and the hunting-ground of an unfriendly tribe. On one of the nights, during our journey, we encamped near a large party of these hostile Indians. The next morning four or five of their warriors, painted red, came into our camp. This much alarmed us. They made many inquiries, but did not molest us, which might not have been the case, if we had not been in company with other Indians. After this, nothing occurred, worthy of notice, until we reached Pittsburgh. Probably we would have reached Rockbridge that fall, if Mr. Ivins had not, unfortunately, got his shoulder dislocated. In consequence of this, we remained until spring with an uncle of his, in the vicinity of Pittsburgh. Having expended nearly all his money in traveling, and with the physician, he left his sister and proceeded on with sister Polly and myself, to the house of our uncle, William McPhaetus, about ten miles south-west of Staunton, near the Middle river. He received, from uncle Joseph Moore, the administrator of father's estate, compensation for his services, and afterward returned and brought in his sister."

MASSACRE OF THE MOORES.

Of the many cruel massacres committed by the Indians within the bounds of the present Tazewell County that of the Moore family was the most tragic and pathetic. Captain Moore had shown such wonderful fortitude as a frontiersman, and proved himself such a gallant soldier in the Indians Wars and in the Revolution, that his death was a grievous loss to his county and State. Dr. Bickley's acccount of the tragedy is based upon information he received from the immediate descendants of Captain Moore, and from contemporary written narratives. Therefore it must be an accurate narrative of the terrible affair, and I will reproduce it in full, as follows:

"In July, 1786, a party of forty-seven Indians, of the Shawnees tribe, again entered Abb's Valley. Capt. James Moore usually kept five or six loaded guns in his house, which was a strong log building, and hoped, by the assistance of his wife, who was very active in loading a gun, together with Simpson, a man who lived with him, to be able to repel the attack of any small party of Indians. Relying on his prowess, he had not sought refuge in a fort, as many of the settlers had; a fact of which the Indians seem to have been aware, from their cutting out the tongues of his horses and cattle, and partially skinning them. It seems they were afraid to attack him openly, and sought rather to drive him to the fort, that they might sack his house.

"On the morning of the attack, Capt. Moore, who had previously distinguished himself at Alamance, was at a lick bog, a short distance from his house, salting his horses, of which he had many. William Clark and an Irishman were reaping wheat in front of the house. Mrs. Moore and the family were engaged in the ordinary business of housework. A man, named Simpson, was sick up-stairs.

"The two men, who were in the field, at work, saw the Indians coming, in full speed, down the hill, toward Captain Moore's who had ere this discovered them, and started in a run for the house. He was, however, shot through the body, and died immediately. Two of his children, William and Rebecca, who were returning from the spring, were killed about the same time. The Indians had now approached near the house, and were met by two fierce dogs, which fought manfully to protect the family of their master. After a severe contest, the fiercest one was killed, and the other subdued. I shall again use Mr. Brown's narrative, it being quite authentic.

"The two men who were reaping, hearing the alarm, and seeing the house surrounded, fled, and alarmed the settlement. At that time, the nearest family was distant six miles. As soon as the alarm was given, Mrs. Moore and Martha Ivins (who was living in the family) barred the door, but this was of no avail. There was no man in the house, at this time except John Simpson, the old Englishman, already alluded to, and he was in the loft, sick and in bed. There were five or six guns in the house, but having been shot off the evening before, they were then empty. It was intended to have loaded them after breakfast. Martha Ivins took two of them and went up stairs where Simpson was, and handing them to him, told him to shoot. He looked up, but had been shot in the head through a crack, and was then near his end. The Indians then proceeded to cut down the door, which they soon effected. During this time, Martha Ivins went to the far end of the house, lifted up a loose plank, and went under the floor, and requested Polly Moore (then eight years of age) who had the youngest child, called Margaret, in her arms (which was crying), to set the child down, and come under. Polly looked at the child, clasped it to her breast, and determined to share its fate. The Indians, having broken into the house, took Mrs. Moore and children, viz; John, Jane, Polly, and Peggy prisoners, and having taken everything that suited them, they set it and the other buildings on fire, and went away. Martha Ivins remained under the floor a short time, and then came out and hid herself under a log that lay across a branch, not far from the house. The Indians, having tarried a short time, with a view of catching horses, one of them walked across this log, sat down on the end of it, and began to fix his gunlock. Miss Ivins, supposing that

The shelving rock under which Martha Evans concealed herself when the Moore family was massacred. Believing she had been discovered by an Indian, who was sitting on a log that rested on the rock, and who was picking the flint on his rifle, she crawled from concealment, was made a prisoner, and became one of the Captives of Abb's Valley.

she was discovered, and that he was preparing to shoot her, came out and gave herself up. At this he seemed much pleased. They then set out for their towns. Perceiving that John Moore was a boy, weak in body and mind, and unable to travel, they killed him the first day. The babe they took two or three days, but it being fretful, on account of a wound it had received, they dashed its brains out against a tree. They then moved on with haste to their towns. For some time, it was usual to tie, very securely, each of the prisoners at night, and for a warrior to lie beside each of them, with tomahawk in hand, so that in case of pursuit, the prisoners might be speedily dispatched.   *   *   *

"Shortly after they reached the towns, Mrs. Moore and her daughter Jane were put to death, being burned and tortured at the stake.   This lasted sometime, during which she manifested the utmost Christian fortitude, and bore it without a murmur, at intervals conversing with her daughter Polly, and Martha Ivins, and expressing great anxiety for the moment to arrive, when her soul should wing its way to the bosom of its Savior.   At length an old squaw, more humane than the rest, dispatched her with a tomahawk.

"Polly Moore and Martha Ivins eventually reached home, as described in the narrative of James Moore.

"Several incidents, in this narrative, have been left out.   When the Indians set fire to the house and started, they took from the stable the fine black horse Yorick.   He was a horse of such a vicious nature, that no one could manage him but Simpson.   The Indians had not proceeded far when one mounted him, but soon the horse had him on the ground, and was pawing him to death with his feet; for this purpose a few strokes were sufficient.   Another mounted him and was served in like manner.   Perfectly wild with rage, a very large Indian mounted him, swearing to ride him or kill him; a few plunges and the Indian was under the feet of the desperate horse, his teeth buried in his flesh, and uttering a scream as if he intended to avenge the death of his master; he had just dispatched the Indian, when another running up, stabbed him, and thus put an end to the conflict.   'Alas! poor Yorick.'

"It is said that Mrs. Moore had her body stuck full of lightwood splinters which were fired, and she was thus tortured three days, before she died.

"When Martha Evans and Polly Moore were among the French, they fared much worse than when among the Indians.   The French had plenty, but were miserly, and seemed to care little for their wants.   The Indians had little, but would divide that little to the last particle.

"A song, in commemoration of the Moore captivity, is sung by some of the mountaineers to this day, but as it is devoid of poetical merit I omit its insertion.   It may be seen in Howe's History of Virginia."

HARMAN AND PEMBERTON BATTLES WITH THE INDIANS.

The story of the encounter of Henry Harman and his two sons with the Indians was obtained by Dr. Bickley from the Harman descendants; and the account of Richard Pemberton's battle with the red men was given Bickley from tradition. There is nothing of record that I have been able to find to throw further light on these thrilling occurrences, and I will adopt Bickley's narrative thereof in full:

HARMAN AND PEMBERTON FIGHTS—BATTLE BETWEEN THE HARMANS AND SEVEN INDIANS.

"In the fall of 1784, Henry Harman and his two sons, George and Matthias, and George Draper left the settlement to engage in a bear hunt on Tug river. They were provided with pack-horses, independent of those used for riding, and on which were to be brought in the game. The country in which their hunt was to take place, was penetrated by the 'war-path' leading to, and from the Ohio river; but as it was late in the season, they did not expect to meet with the Indians.

"Arriving at the hunting-grounds in the early part of the evening, they stopped and built their camp; a work executed generally by the old man, who might be said to be particular in having it constructed to his own taste. George and Matthias loaded, and put their guns in order, and started to the woods, to look for sign, and perchance kill a buck for the evening's repast, while Draper busied himself in hobbling and caring for the horses.

"In a short time, George returned with the startling intelligence of Indians! He had found a camp but a short distance from their own, in which the partly consumed sticks were still burning. They could not, of course, be at any considerable distance, and might now be concealed near them, watching their every movement. George, while at the camp, had made a rapid search for sign, and found a pair of leggins, which he showed the old man. Now old Mr. Harman, was a type of frontiersmen, in some things, and particularly that remarkable self-possession, which is so often to be met with in new countries, where dangers are ever in the path of the settlers. So taking a seat on the ground, he began to interrogate his son on the dimensions, appearances, etc., of the camp. When he had fully satisfied himself, he remarked, that "there must be from five to seven Indians," and that they must pack up and hurry back to the settlement, to prevent, if possible, the Indians from doing mischief; and, said he, "if we fall in with them, we must fight them."

"Matthias was immediately called in, and the horses repacked. Mr. Harman and Draper, now began to load their guns, when the old man observing Draper laboring under what is known among hunters as the 'Buck Ague,' being that state of excitement, which causes excessive trembling, remarked to him, 'my son, I fear you cannot fight.'

"The plan of march was now agreed upon, which was, that Mr. Harman and Draper should lead the way, the pack-horses follow them, and Matthias and George, bring up the rear. After they had started. Draper remarked to Mr. H., that he would get ahead, as he could see better than Mr. H., and that he would keep a sharp lookout. It is highly probable that he was cogitating a plan of escape, as he had not gone far before he declared he saw the Indians, which proved not to be true. Proceeding a short distance further, he suddenly wheeled his horse, about, at the same time crying out, "Yonder they are—behind that log:" as a liar is not to be believed even when he speaks the truth, so Mr. Draper was not believed this time. Mr. Harman rode on, while a large dog, he had with him, ran up to the log and reared himself up on it, showing no signs of the presence of Indians. At this second, a sheet of fire and smoke from the Indian rifles, completely concealed the log from view, for Draper had really spoken the truth.

"Before the smoke had cleared away, Mr. Harman and his sons were dismounted, while Draper had fled with all the speed of a swift horse. There were seven of the Indians, only four of whom had guns; the rest being armed with bows and arrows, tomahawks and scalping-knives. As soon as they fired, they rushed on Mr. Harman, who fell back to where his two sons stood ready to meet the Indians.

"They immediately surrounded the three white men, who had formed a triangle, each man looking out, or, what would have been, with men enough, a hollow square. The old gentleman bid Matthias to reserve his fire, while himself and George fired, wounding as it would seem, two of the Indians. George was a lame man,

from having had white swelling in his childhood, and after firing
a few rounds, the Indians noticed his limping, and one who fired at
him, rushed upon him thinking him wounded. George saw the
fatal tomahawk raised, and drawing back his gun, prepared to meet
it. When the Indian had got within striking distance, George let
down upon his head with the gun, which brought him to the ground;
he soon recovered, and made at him again, half bent and head foremost, intending, no doubt, to trip him up. But as he got near
enough, George sprang up and jumped across him, which brought
the Indian to his knees. Feeling for his knife, and not getting hold
of it, he seized the Indian's and plunged it deep into his side.
Matthias struck him on the head with a tomahawk, and finished
the work with him.

"Two Indians had attacked the old man with bows, and were
maneuvering around him, to get a clear fire, at his left breast. The
Harmans, to a man, wore their bullet-pouches on the left side, and
with this and his arm he so completely shielded his breast, that the
Indians did not fire till they saw the old gentleman's gun nearly
loaded again, when one fired on him, and struck his elbow near the
joint, cutting one of the principal arteries. In a second more, the
fearful string was heard to vibrate, and an arrow entered Mr.
Harman's breast and lodged against a rib. He had by this time
loaded the gun, and was raising it to his face to shoot one of the
Indians, when the stream of blood from the wounded artery flew
in the pan, and so soiled his gun that it was impossible to make it
fire. Raising the gun, however, had the effect to drive back the
Indians, who retreated to where the others stood with their guns
empty.

"Matthias, who had remained an almost inactive spectator,
now asked permission to fire, which the old man granted. The
Indian at whom he fired appeared to be the chief, and was standing
under a large beech tree. At the report of the rifle, the Indian fell,
throwing his tomahawk high among the limbs of the tree under
which he stood.

"Seeing two of their number lying dead upon the ground, and
two more badly wounded, they immediately made off, passing by
Draper, who had left his horse, and concealed himself behind a log.

"As soon as the Indians retreated, the old man fell back on the
ground exhausted and fainting from loss of blood. The wounded

arm being tied up and his face washed in cold water, soon restored
him. The first words he uttered were, 'We've whipped, give me my
pipe.' This was furnished him, and he took a whif, while the boys
scalped one of the Indians.

"When Draper saw the Indians pass him, he stealthy crept
from his hiding-place, and pushed on for the settlement, where he
reported the whole party murdered. The people assembled and
started soon the following morning to bury them; but they had not
gone far before they met Mr. H. and his sons, in too good condition to need burying.

"Upon the tree, under which the chief was killed, is roughly
carved an Indian, a bow, and a gun, commemorative of the fight.
The arrows which were shot into Mr. Harman, are in possession
of some of his descendants.

PEMBERTON'S FIGHT.

"Richard Pemberton, the hero of this battle, lived in the Baptist Valley, about five miles from Jeffersonville. In addition to a
small farm around his cabin, he cultivated a field, now owned by
William O. George, about one and a half miles from his dwelling.

"On a Sabbath morning late in August, 1788, he started to
his field accompanied by his wife and two children, to see that his
fences were not down, and to repair any breach that might have been
made. According to the custom of the times, Mr. Pemberton had
taken with him his gun, which was his constant companion. After
satisfying himself that his crops were safe, the little party started
back. They had gone but a few hundred yards, however, when two
Indians, armed with bows and arrows, knives, and tomahawks, came
yelling toward them at full speed. In an instant the pioneer's gun
was leveled and the trigger pulled; it missed fire, and in his hurry
to spring the lock again, he broke it, and of course could not fire.
Seeing him raise his gun to shoot, caused the Indians to halt, and
commence firing arrows at him. Keeping himself between his wife
and children and the Indians, he ordered them to get on as fast as
possible and try to reach a house at which a Mr. Johnson lived,
and where several men were living. This house was some half mile
distant, but he hoped to reach it, and save those whom he held
dearest—his wife and children. The Indians made every possible
attempt to separate him from his family, all of which proved vain.

They would retreat to a respectful distance, and then come bounding back like so many furies from the regions of indescribable woe. When they came too near, he would raise his gun as if he was really reserving his fire, which would cause them to halt and surround him. But at every attack they shot their arrows into his breast, causing great pain.

"For nearly an hour this running fight was kept up; still the blood-thirsty savages pressed on; at last, he was sufficiently near to Johnson's house to be heard, and he raised his powerful voice for succor; he was heard, but no sooner did the men at the house hear the cry of 'Indians' than they took to their heels in an opposite direction. At last he arrived at the house, closely pursued by the Indians, and entering after his family, barred up the door, and began to make preparations for acting more upon the offensive, when the Indians made a rapid retreat. Pemberton reached his own house the following day, where he resided many years, an eyesore to those who had so ingloriously fled from his assistance. Many arrow points which entered his breast were never removed, and were carried to the end of life, as the best certificate of his bravery and devotion to his family."

DIAL AND THOMAS MURDERED BY INDIANS.

On the 11th of April, 1786, two men were killed by the Indians within half a mile of William Wynne's fort at Locust Hill, and near the house of John Peery. Peery was living near the forks of the Clinch, one and a half miles east of Tazewell. Matthias Harman and Benjamin Thomas were returning from a scouting expedition, as there were reports current that Indians were prowling around the neighborhood. The scouts stopped at John Peery's, near where a man by the name of Dial was living. Dial, it is said, had liquor for sale, and he and Harman and Thomas imbibed so freely that they became intoxicated. Harman and Thomas had come from their scouting expedition very hungry, and they requested Mrs. Dial to prepare dinner for them. She consented to do so, if the men would get wood with which she could cook the meal. Dial and Thomas started to the woods to get the fuel, and when they got to the end of the lane, about two hundred yards from the house, they were fired upon by six or seven Indians, who had been lying in ambush. Three balls entered Dial's body, but he was able to run to his house, pursued by one of the Indians, who was anxious to kill and scalp him. When they got near the house, the Indian saw other men there and he ran swiftly back to his companions. Dial fell against the chimney corner from exhaustion and died in a few hours from his wounds. Only one of the Indians shot at Thomas and he was so close that Thomas struck the gun up when it was fired. The ball struck an oak tree several feet above Thomas' head. He was knocked down with a war club by one of the Indians, and was scalped and left for dead. Harman, a son of "old man Henry," and, like his father, a daring Indian fighter, seized his gun, ran out of the house, mounted his horse and pursued the Indians for some distance. He dared them to stop and fight; but they were too near Wynne's fort to accept the challenge, and made their escape as rapidly as possible.

Thomas was supposed by Harman to be dead, and was left where he had fallen until the next morning, when he was found by the kind old Quaker, William Wynne. Thomas was taken to Wynne's fort and every effort was made to save his life, but he died after lingering several days.

MASSACRE OF WILEY CHILDREN AND CAPTIVITY OF THEIR MOTHER.

Thomas Wiley, with his wife and four children, was living on Clear Fork, just half a mile above the mouth of Cove Creek. A party of Shawnees came up Tug River and on to the head of Bluestone. On the 1st of October, 1789, they crossed over East River Mountain to Clear Fork. Late in the afternoon of that day the Indians suddenly made their appearance at the door of Thomas Wiley's humble cabin. Wiley was away from home, and the Indians easily made captives of Mrs. Elizabeth Wiley and her four children. The savages first plundered the house of its scant contents and then destroyed it with fire. They then started back toward Bluestone; but, after proceeding a short distance up Cove Creek, they killed and scalped the four innocent children and left their mutilated bodies in the wilderness, a prey for the wolves and other carniverous animals that were then numerous in that region.

The Indians took Mrs. Wiley with them to their towns in Ohio, where she was held a captive for nearly three years. In September, 1792, she made her escape in company with Samuel Lusk, a youth some sixteen years old. He had been made a prisoner in July, 1792, when his scouting companion, Joseph Gilbert, was killed on the waters of the Guyandotte River.

The escape of Mrs. Wiley was nearly as thrilling as was that of Mrs. Ingles in 1755. Early in the night, late in September, 1792, Mrs. Wiley and Lusk slipped away from the Indian village, got in a canoe Lusk had placed ready for the escape; and traveled rapidly down the Scioto River fifty miles to the southern banks of the Ohio, which they reached the morning following their escape from the village. They abandoned the canoe, and travelled as speedily as possible on foot up the southern bank of the Ohio. When they reached a point opposite the present Gallipolis, they crossed the river to a small village where they found some friendly French residing. These kind people gave them refuge, and when a party of pursuing Indians reached the village, they made such effectual concealment of the escaped captives that their pursuers failed to discover them. A party of white men came along, traveling up the river in a push boat to Pittsburg, and Lusk joined them. He got to Pittsburg safely, then went to Philadelphia, and from there came back to Virginia, reaching his home in Wythe County about one month after he made his escape from the Indians.

A few days after Lusk left, Mrs. Wiley resolved to try to make her way home by traveling on foot up the Kanawha, and New River. She bravely started on the laborious and perilous journey. Weary and footsore she succeeded in reaching the home of her husband's brother, who was then living with his family at Wiley's Falls, in the present Giles County, Virginia.

INDIANS KILL JOHN DAVIDSON.

Some time in either 1789 or 1790, John Davidson, a man advanced in years, was killed by the Indians on the Clinch River, half a mile above the present town of North Tazewell. Mr. Davidson had been on a business visit to Rockingham County, Virginia, and was returning to his home when the murder was committed at a point near the present residence of Charles H. Peery.

The circumstances connected with the tragedy were afterwards made known by white persons who had been in captivity, and who were told by the Indians, when they were prisoners, how, and why, Mr. Davidson was killed. He had stopped at a deserted cabin to feed his horse, and while thus occupied was shot to death. The

Indians also said that a white renegade was with them when the horrible deed was done. It seems that the crime was a double one, as the Indians and their companion found a considerable amount of specie in the saddlebags of the old man which was stolen by the murderers. Bickley says:

"A few days after, his son, Col. Davidson, became uneasy on account of his absence, and raising a small company went in search of him. Luckily, when they got to the cabin, they found a hatband, which, being of peculiar structure, was recognized as that worn by Mr. Davidson. After considerable search, his body was found stripped of clothing, and somewhat disfigured by birds. As the Indians had too long been gone to be overtaken, Mr. Davidson was taken home and buried."

ANDREW DAVIDSON'S FAMILY MADE CAPTIVES.

In the spring of 1791, Andrew Davidson was living at the head spring of East River, about a half mile below the eastern limits of the city of Bluefield, West Virginia. In addition to himself, his family consisted of his wife, Rebecca, his three small children, two girls and a boy, and a bound boy and girl named Broomfield. The bound children were very young, between seven and ten years old, and were more in the nature of proteges than servants. Mrs. Davidson was a granddaughter of James Burke, from whom Burke's Garden received its name. Mr. Davidson had gone on a business trip to Smithfield, formerly Draper's Meadows, and now Blacksburg, Virginia. It was the sugar making season, and a few days after her husband's departure for Smithfield, Mrs. Davidson was busily occupied gathering sugar water from sugar trees close to the house. While she was thus engaged, several Indians, who could speak English, came upon the scene. They told her that she and her children must go with them to their towns in Ohio. She was in a delicate condition, and unfit to undertake the long and fatiguing trip she was required to make.

The Indians went into the house, and took such plunder as they wanted to carry away, set fire to the cabin, and began their homeward journey with their six prisoners. When they arrived at a point near where Logan Court House, West Virginia, is located, Mrs. Davidson gave birth to a child. After allowing the mother a rest of two hours, the march to Ohio was resumed. The birth of the child must have been premature, as it was drowned by the Indians the next day on account of its feeble condition.

Mrs. Davidson and the captive children were treated with such leniency while they were making the journey, that she became hopeful they would be kindly treated after their arrival at the Indian towns. In this, however, she was sadly disappointed. Soon after they arrived at their towns, the Indians tied the two daughters of Mrs. Davidson to trees, and shot them to death in the presence of their mother. Her son was given to an old squaw for adoption. While crossing a river the squaw upset her canoe, and the boy, who was with her, was drowned. What became of the Broomfield children was never known, and it is possible they shared the same fate of the little girls who were shot.

Mrs. Davidson was sold to a Frenchman, in Canada, in whose family she remained as a servant until she was found and rescued by her husband in the fall of 1794. Two years after her capture Mr. Davidson made an unsuccessful trip to the Shawnee towns in search of his wife. On his second trip, in 1794, he received information from an old Indian as to her whereabouts, and was guided by the Indian to Canada. He stopped one day at a farm house to get dinner, and what followed is thus related by Dr. Bickley:

"When he got into the Canada settlements, he stopped at the house of a wealthy French farmer, to get a meal's victuals, and to inquire the way to some place where he had heard she was. He noticed a woman passing him, as he entered the house, but merely bowed to her and went in. Asking for his dinner, he seated himself, and was, perhaps, running over in his mind, the chances of finding his wife, when again the woman entered. She laid down her wood, and looked at the stranger steadily for a moment, when she turned to her mistress and said: '*I know that man.*' 'Well, who is he?' said the French lady. '*It is my husband!* Andrew Davidson, I am your wife.' Mr. Davidson could scarcely believe his senses. When he last saw her, she was a fine, healthy-looking woman; her hair was black as coal, but now her head was gray, and she looked many years older than she should have looked. Yet it was her, though he declared nothing but her voice seemed to say she was Rebecca Davidson. Soon the French gentleman returned, and being a humane man, gave up Rebecca to her husband, also a considerable sum of money, and next morning sent them on their way rejoicing."

The happily reunited husband and wife returned as quickly as possible to the vicinity of their former home, and settled at the mouth of Abb's Valley on a farm which was owned some ten years ago by A. C. Davidson. They were so fortunate as to have and raise another family of children, and a number of their descendants are now living in Tazewell County, and in Mercer County, West Virginia.

OTHER MASSACRES RELATED BY BICKLEY.

There were other dastardly outrages inflicted by the Indians upon the Tazewell settlers, whereof the dates and circumstances were uncertain. Dr. Bickley wrote briefly about four of the occurrences, and as I have been unable to get any further facts connected therewith I will reproduce what he said of them:

MURDER OF WILLIAM WHITLEY.

"William Whitley lived in Baptist valley, and had been out on a bear hunt. He came home, and finding that a choice dog was gone, started the following morning to look for him. The day passed off and he did not return. His family became uneasy and a company started out to hunt for him. They had not gone far, however, when they met a man named Scaggs, who had passed a murdered man at the mouth of Dick's Creek. The company pushed on and identified the man to be Whitley. He was dreadfully mutilated—his bowels torn out and stretched upon the bushes, his heart in one place, and liver in another. A hole was opened, and the fragments gathered up and interred. This happened in 1786.

MOFFIT'S CHILDREN CAPTURED.

"Capt. Moffit lived near Clinch river, on the plantation now owned by Kiah Harman. Two of his children were attending to a sugar camp, when they were captured and taken off to the Indian towns in the west. Whether the boys ever got back is unknown, as Captain Moffit soon afterward moved to Kentucky, where some of his descendants still reside.

RAY'S FAMILY KILLED.

"I have been unable to learn anything of the particulars of this occurrence, more than the bare fact, that Joseph Ray and his family were killed by the Indians, on Indian Creek, in 1788 or '9. It is from this circumstance that Indian Creek has taken its name.

DANIEL HARMAN KILLED.

"Daniel Harman left his house, on the head of Clinch, on a fine morning in the fall of 1791, for the purpose of killing a deer. Where he went for that purpose, is not known, but having done so, he started for home with the deer fastened to the cantle of his saddle. Harman was a great hunter, and owned a choice rifle, remarkable for the beauty of its finish, and the superior structure of its triggers, which were, as usual, of the double kind. So strong was the spring of these, that when sprung, the noise might be heard for a considerable distance. He was riding a large horse, fleet, and spirited, and had got within a mile of home, and was passing through a bottom, near the present residence, and on the lands of Mr. William O. George, when suddenly a party of Indians sprang from behind a log, and fired on him. He was unhurt, and putting spurs to his horse, away he went through the heavy timber, forgetting all other danger, in his precarious situation. On he went, but his horse, passing too near a tree, struck the rider's knee, breaking his leg, and throwing him from his horse. In a few minutes the savages were upon him, and with their tomahawks, soon put an end to his sufferings. The horse continued his flight til he got to the house, at which were several of the neighbors, who immediately went to look after Harman. Passing near the Indians, they heard the click of Harman's well-know trigger. A panic struck the men, and running in zigzig lines, they made a rapid retreat, leaving the Indians to silently retrace their steps from the settlement."

LAST HOSTILE INDIAN INVASION.

The last invasion of the territory that afterward constituted the county of Tazewell, was made by the Indians in 1792. A band of Shawnees slipped into the settlements on Bluestone, and the head of Clinch, on a horse-stealing expedition. The Indians had found it more profitable to take horses than scalps from the white men.

TH.—30

They would take the stolen horses to Canada, where they always found a good market for the already famous horses that were being bred in the Clinch Valley. There must have been a pretty large company of Indians in this last foray they made to Tazewell, as they occupied but a little while in collecting about eighty good horses and starting on the return trip to their homes beyond the Ohio River.

The first night after starting on their return journey the Indians were encamped a short distance from the settlements; and their

Portrait of 'Squire Thomas Peery, one of the first generation born in Tazewell County. He was born Feb. 25th, 1794, and died July 2nd, 1860. The beautiful boy standing by him is his son, Thomas Ritchie Peery, who was killed in battle at Winchester, Va., in September, 1864, at the age of twenty years.

presence was accidently discovered by a white man who had been out scouting or hunting. He hastened to the Bluestone and Clinch settlements, and gave notice of his discovery to the inhabitants and the garrisons at Bailey's and Wynne's forts. Major Robert Crockett, who was then commanding the military frontier forces of Wythe County, was making his headquarters at Wynne's fort, where he had a small garrison. By noon on the day he got the information about the Indians, Major Crockett had organized two companies of mounted riflemen, one company from Bluestone, and one from the head of the Clinch. He assembled his forces at a point near what is now called the "Round House" which was built in about

1840 by 'Squire Thomas Peery, and occupied by him as a residence
until his death in 1860. Judge David E. Johnston carefully collected the facts connected with this, the last, incursion into Tazewell
by the Indians; and, in his History of the Middle New River Settlements, thus relates what followed the gathering of the men to
pursue the red men:

"Major Crockett moved off with his men to follow the Indians,
having no time to prepare provisions for the journey. They took
the route down Horse Pen Creek, and to the head of Clear fork,
and down to the Tug and on to the mouth of Four Pole, then crossing the dividing ridge between the waters of the Sandy and Guyandotte Rivers. They sent Gilbert and Lusk forward to a Buffalo lick
on a creek flowing into the Guyandotte, to secure if possible a supply of game. It appears by the report of Major Crockett, found
in the Virginia Calendar Papers, that this was on the twenty fourth
day of July that Gilbert and Lusk set out for and reached the lick,
where they found and killed a deer and wounded an elk, which they
followed, some distance; being unable to overtake it they returned
to the lick to get the deer they had killed. On passing along the
Buffalo path, near which they had left the deer, Gilbert in front,
discovered a stone hanging by pawpaw bark over the path. Gilbert
in an instant discerning what it meant called on Lusk to look out.
He had scarcely uttered the words, when the Indians fired, a ball
from one of their guns penetrating the hand of Lusk, in which he
carried his gun, which caused him to drop the same. The Indians
immediately began to close in on them, Gilbert putting Lusk behind
him, and holding the Indians off by the presentation of his gun.
Gilbert and Lusk kept retreating as rapidly as they could with
safety. Lusk's wounded hand was bleeding freely, and he became
sick from the loss of blood, and begged Gilbert to leave him and
get away; this Gilbert refused to do, saying that he promised his,
Lusk's mother, to take care of him. Finally the Indians got close
enough to knock Gilbert down with their tomahawks, which they
did, and an Indian rushed up to scalp him, when Gilbert shot him
dead, but another one of the Indians dispatched Gilbert, and Lusk
became a prisoner. The Indians immediately hurried with their
prisoner down the creek to Guyandotte, and then down the river to
the mouth of Island Creek, and went into camp behind a rocky

ridge called Hog Back at the present day. Major Crockett instead of following the tracks of Gilbert and Lusk to the lick, had turned to the west, and crossed a ridge onto the right fork of Island Creek, and reached and camped at a point within two miles of the Indian camp, but without knowledge of his proximity to them. During the night Lusk suffered much with his hand until an Indian went off and brought some roots which he beat up into a pulp, made a poultice, and bound his hand which afforded relief. Early on the morning of the 25th the Indians took to their canoes, which they had left at this point on their way to the settlements, and rapidly descending the river to its mouth crossed the Ohio. On reaching the northern bank, they placed their canoes in charge of some of their party and taking Lusk with them crossed the country."

Judge Johnston does not mention the fact that Major Crockett and his men overtook the Indians, made an attack upon them, and recovered most of the horses that had been stolen. Writing about what happened after Crockett and his riflemen left the Clinch Valley, Bickley says:

"They made forced marches, and came up with them (the Indians) about one o'clock at night, at what is called the Islands of Guyandotte. Some of the whites were for attacking them immediately, and others wished to wait till morning, when they might see. While thus in parley, the Indians in the meantime, preparing for some movement, a horse neighed; in a moment a fire was opened upon them, but to no effect. The Indians raised a yell, secured a few of the horses, and fled, leaving a good breakfast, and several dozen pairs of moccasins to be taken home as trophies by the whites. The breakfast of bears' meat and turkey was consumed by the whites, whose appetites were too keen to suffer themselves to enter into speculation as to the probable nicety of their runaway cooks."

The period of anxiety and suffering, and sorrow and tragedy, was at last ended for the pioneers. And the phantoms of fear and death, in the shape of a red man, were no longer to disturb the people on the Clinch.

Ante-Bellum, or Formative Period

From Organization of Tazewell County
to 1861

ANTE-BELLUM, OR FORMATIVE PERIOD

CHAPTER I.

ORGANIZATION OF TAZEWELL COUNTY.

Among the many interesting events that occurred in the early history of Tazewell County, the organization of its county government is of supreme importance. The last section of the act which created the county says: "This act shall commence and be in force from and after the first day of May next," meaning the first day of May, 1800. By authority of the act, the justices who composed the county court held their first term at the house of Henry Harman, Jr., on the second Tuesday in June, 1800.

Unfortunately, a few of the first pages of the order book of the court have been mutilated and lost. It is, therefore, impossible to give the names of all of the justices who were present and sitting at the first term, or to detail any of the proceedings, except from hearsay or tradition. From entries on pages of the order book, following immediately those torn off, it is made evident that the first court sitting was composed in part, if not entirely, of the following justices: David Ward, George Peery, Robert Wallace, Wm. Neal, Samuel Walker, Henry Bowen, and David Hanson.

The act of the General Assembly directed the justices to qualify the sheriff and appoint a clerk. It is a reasonable conclusion that the justices promptly complied with these requirements of the act. James Maxwell qualified as sheriff, and John Ward was appointed clerk of the county. If other candidates offered for the clerkship, their names are unknown, owing to the mutilation and loss of the front pages of the first order book. It is also probable that the location of the county seat was selected at this, the first term of the court. Of course there was a contention over the location, as had been the case in nearly every county formed after Virginia became a state. Tradition says there was a very sharp controversy over the selection of a site for the county seat of Tazewell County. Two locations were offered and urged for adoption. One

(471)

was where the town of Tazewell is situated, and the other at or near the forks of Clinch River—one and a half miles east of the present county seat. The justices being unable, or loth, to determine the most suitable location, it is said that the advocates of the two competing locations agreed for each to choose a champion, and have an old-fashioned rough-and-tumble fight to settle the dispute. Tradition affirms that the champion who battled for the present site proved the better man; and here the county seat was located. This story may be a myth; but on the second day of the first term of the court, the following order was entered:

"Hezekiah Harman being appointed yesterday to lay off the land offered by William Peery and Samuel Ferguson for the use of the county made report that he had laid off twenty-three acres and twenty-eight square poles, Ten acres and Twenty eight square poles being of Ferguson's land and thirteen acres of Wm. Peery's land, whereupon the court were unanimously of the opinion that the public buildings should be erected on the land so laid off and that William George, James Witton and John Crockett do lay off and circumscribe two acres for the purpose of building the public Buildings for this county, and the balance of the land remain for the benefit of the County, only saving and reserving to the said Peery four quarter acre lots out of the land he this day conveyed to the County, and reserving to the said Ferguson two quarter acre lots out of the land he this day conveyed to the County."

This order shows that the court had accepted, and unanimously ratified, the result of the fistic battle between the champions of the two communities that competed for the county seat. On the same day other orders were entered by the court, as follows:

"Joseph Moore came into court and proffered to lay of the lots for a town where the public buildings are to be erected in quarter acre lots for the price of 33 1/3 cents each, and it is ordered that William George, James Witton and John Crockett do attend as Commissioners and direct the surveying of the lots tomorrow."

"Ordered that David Ward and Samuel Walker be Commissioners to contract for the building of a jail for this county, and that they do advertise the same in the most public places to be let to the lowest bidder at next court."

"Ordered that Court adjourn until Court in course and they will meet next Court at the place appointed for erecting the public buildings for this County."

It will be observed that no commissioners were appointed to have a court house erected, though the adjourning order of the court stated that the next term should be held at the place appointed for erecting the public buildings for the county. This seeming neglect to provide a permanent building for the courts is explained by the fact that only a temporary structure could be erected in

Col. Henry Bowen, son of Lieut. Rees Bowen who fell at King's Mountain. He was born at Maiden Spring on March 18th, 1770, and died at the place of his birth April 18th, 1850. He was one of the justices of the first county court of Tazewell, was a Captain in the War of 1812, represented the county several times in the House of Delegates, and left a splendid estate to his two sons, General Rees T. and Col. Henry S. Bowen.

the thirty days that would intervene between the June and July terms. It was determined that a temporary building should be provided by recurring to the community system adopted by the pioneer settlers when they built their cabin homes, and when all the men of a community would gather together and build the cabin of a new settler in a day. Tradition further relates that citizens from all sections of the county assembled at the chosen county seat on a certain day. They brought along their axes, broadaxes, and other tools; and cut down trees, hewed the logs and raised them

into position, rived boards and placed them on the roof, hewed
puncheons for the floor, and completed a court house for the already
great county of Tazewell in a single day. Perhaps the building
was rough in appearance and not very capacious, but it was a temple
of justice for our worthy ancestors and served their purposes well
until a permanent building was erected.

William George, James Witten and John Crockett, commissioners, had laid off and circumscribed two acres for the public
buildings, one acre on the north side and one acre on the south side
of the present Main Street of the town of Tazewell. The tem-

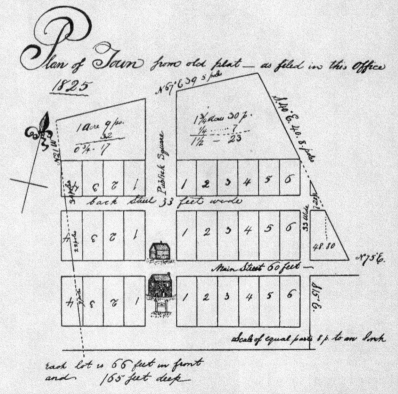

This old plat was made by Joseph Moore who laid off the town
in July, 1800. The author wrote his description of the little log
court house and jail from tradition and imagination two years before
he discovered the plat. It verifies both tradition and his imagination.
I found in the proceedings of the county court the order which directed
the erection of the stocks, shown on plat at rear of the jail.

porary court house was built on the lot where the Lynch building now stands, and which is occupied by Fuller Brothers with their department store. And the jail was located on the south side of the street on the lot where the St. Clair building stands, which is occupied by Will Ed Peery with his hardware store.

It must have been a very proud and happy day for the pioneers who assembled in July, 1880, to witness and participate in the dedication of the new court house, which was emblematic of the heroic struggle they had made for the founding of their county republic. The event, no doubt, brought together the entire male population of the county; and it is almost certain that many of the women and children were also in attendance. This term of the county court opened its proceedings as follows:

"At a court held for Tazewell County, July 1st, 1800, in the new court house according to adjournment of the last court.

"Present David Ward, George Peery, Robert Wallace, Wm. Neal, Saml. Walker, Henry Bowen, and David Hanson."

The justices in those days were appointed for life; and the seven who held the July term of the court had previously been appointed and served as justices of Russell and Wythe counties— David Ward, Henry Bowen, and David Hanson for Russell; and George Peery, Robert Wallace, Wm. Neal and Saml. Walker for Wythe. They, by operation of the then existing statute laws, became a part of the court for the newly erected county; and apparently had authority to organize the county before the justices to be named by the governor and the state council had received their commissions. Owing to the mutilation of the order book, there is but little to be learned about the proceedings of the court at the July term, and nothing whatever of the August term.

At the September term William George, John Crockett, James Witten and Thomas Harrisson, who had been appointed commissioners for the purpose, reported that they had made a sale of the town lots; and they were directed, as commissioners, to convey the lots to the several purchasers.

Leave was granted John Peery, upon the return of a writ of *ad quod damnum*, to erect a water grist mill. After noting the execution of the writ and the verdict of the jury, the order is as follows:

"On consideration whereof & for reasons appearing to the court it is ordered that the sd. Peery have leave to build the sd. mill & Dam agreeable to the verdict returned by the Sheriff on his making good the highway that will be injured by the sd. Dam & making a slope for the passage of fish, which together with the writ is ordered to be executed."

The mill and dam were duly erected on Clinch River about a mile below Pisgah. At that time there was an abundance of fine fish in the river; and the court took the precaution to order that a slope should be placed on the dam so as to give the fish unobstructed passage up the stream.

James Maxwell had been acting as sheriff of the county under temporary appointment, but had not received his commission from the governor. The court had to recommend three citizens for the place, one of whom was to be selected by the governor for appointment. In compliance with this rule the court placed upon the record the following order: "Ordered that James Maxwell, George Peery, & Robert Wallace be recommended to the govn & honl privy Council as fit and capable persons to act as sheriff of Tazewell county." Maxwell was subsequently appointed by the governor and council and acted as the first sheriff of the county.

An order was made appointing David Ward, Samuel Walker, James Thompson and George Peery commissioners to publish notices and ask for bids for building a court house, "the said court house to be completely finished in a workmanlike manner on or before the first day of May, 1802."

Much attention was given to the public roads at this and subsequent terms of the court. The petition sent to the General Assembly for a new county had urged that the highways had been greatly neglected by the authorities of Russell and Wythe counties. So, at the September term, 1800, the county court began to remedy the evil complained of, and at each succeeding term for several years thereafter the roads were made a matter of leading importance. Viewers for new roads and surveyors for those already in existence were appointed. There were no graded roads in the county, and the new roads that were opened were simply cleared of trees and brush, and located on the best natural grades obtainable, while those that crossed mountains and ridges went up a spur on one side and down a spur on the other side.

Orders entered by the court at the October term, worthy of mention, are:

"Ordered that the overseers of the poor do bind William Roberts an apprentice to William Smith according to law to learn the art and mistery of wheelright."

"Ordered that John Powers be appointed a constable in this county."

"John Peery, Joseph Davidson, Thomas Witten, William George, John Thompson, Hezekiah Whitt, Thomas Gillespie, Hezekiah Harman, & John Tollett produced a commission from his Excellency the governor appointing them justices of the peace in & for the County of Tazewell & thereupon they took the necessary oaths of office accordingly."

At the November term the following was the first order entered:

"William Hall, James Thompson, and James Brown, gents, produced a commission from his Excellency, James Monroe, Esq., Governor of this Commonwealth, appointing them justices in and for the County of Tazewell, and thereupon they took the necessary oaths of office, and thereupon they took their seats accordingly."

The county court of Tazewell County then consisted of nineteen justices, twelve of whom had been commissioned by Governor Monroe, and seven of whom had been justices in Russell and Wythe before the territory in which they were living was formed into Tazewell County.

James Thompson, who had been appointed by the court Commonwealth's Attorney for the county, made his first appearance for the Commonwealth at this term. The first grand-jury impanelled in the county was constituted and reported as follows:

"A grand jury, to-wit: Andrew Thompson, foreman, James Witten, William Brooks, Edley Maxwell, James Sloan, Thomas Brewster, William Witten, William Wynne, James Moore, James Cecil, William Cecil, George Asbury, Timothy Rowark (Roark), John Young, James Lockheart, John McIntosh, William Kidd, and John Peery, Sen., being sworn a grand jury of Inquest for the body of this County having received their charge retired to consult of their presentments, and after some time returned and presented as follows."

The list was not preserved, but, from the entries of the Commonwealth's cases in the order book, it is evident there were no indictments made, and only presentments for misdemeanors. Following the report of the grand-jury, the court granted permission for the first tavern opened at the court house, as follows:

"On the motion of William George for leave to keep an ordinary at Tazewell Court House for the term of one year it is ordered that he have leave to keep the said ordinary, whereupon he together with George Peery his security entered into and acknowledged their bond according to law."

When the court convened for the December, 1800, term, "William George and William Peery produced commissions from His Excellency the Governor of Virginia appointing them coroners for Tazewell County."

It appears that between the ending of the November term and the beginning of the December term the name "Jeffersonville" had been given the county seat. In the order made at the November term granting leave to William George to keep an ordinary, the county court had designated the county seat "Tazewell Court House." But in an order entered the 7th of December, 1800, the court says "leave is granted Thomas Peery to keep an ordinary (tavern) at his house in Jeffersonville." The name was given in honor of Thomas Jefferson, who had just been elected President of the United States. He was then recognized as the most conspicuous and potential citizen of the United States in public life; and his splendid principles of popular government had the solid approval of the voters of Tazewell. For eighty years thereafter the county was uniformly steadfast in its support of the party which claimed to stand for the principles of government enunciated by Jefferson.

At this term of the court, Andrew Thompson was appointed Commissioner of Revenue for the year 1801. The assessments within the bounds of the new county had been made for 1800 by the commissioners of Wythe and Russell. Thompson's appointment about completed the civil organization of the county.

A very important duty then devolved upon the court, that of effecting the military organization of Tazewell. This was accomplished by the court entering orders recommending certain citizens to the Governor and Privy Council as "fit and Capable" persons to act as officers of the militia. The court recommended: John Thompson as Major in the 1st Battalion of the 112th Regiment; John Ward as Major of 2nd Battalion of the 112th Regiment; Archibald Thompson, Hezekiah Harman, and Andrew Davidson as Captains in the 1st Battalion of the 112th Regiment; John Davidson, Ambrose Hall, and John Maxwell as Lieutenants in the 1st Battalion of the 112th Regiment; Elias Harman, John Cartmill, and James Peery as Ensigns in the 1st Battalion of the 112th Regiment; George Davidson to act as Captain, William Peery, Jr., Lieutenant, and William Williams, Ensign, in a Company of Light Infantry for the 1st Battalion of the 112th Regiment; Thomas Ferguson, James Witten, and Thomas Greenup as Captains in the 2nd Battalion of the 112th Regiment; Reese Bowen, Abram Eheart, and William Smith as Lieutenants in the 2nd Battalion of the 112th Regiment, Hugh Wilson, John Cecil, and Samuel Belcher as Ensigns in the 2nd Battalion of the 112th Regiment; Samuel Witten as Captain, William Witten, Jr., as Lieutenant, and Reese Gillespie as Ensign of a company of Light Infantry in the 112th Regiment.

The 112th Regiment, when organized, consisted of eight companies, each with fifty men, rank and file, making a very respectable organization of four hundred fighting men. That they were a splendid fighting force is evidenced by the names of the men who were the commissioned officers. They came chiefly from the pioneer families, and some of them were veteran Indian fighters; while most of them were sons of the pioneers, and had used their rifles in more than one encounter with the red men.

A study of the early court records reveals much that bears upon the social, moral, and economic conditions that prevailed in Tazewell at the time the county was organized. This is why I have written thus much and will write more about the proceedings of the first county court. Preachers were few and far between in the frontier settlements in those days; and it became a public necessity for authority to be given other persons than regularly ordained ministers to celebrate the rites of matrimony in Tazewell County. So, I find that the county court on the 3rd of March, 1801, made the following order:

"Ordered that John Tollett be authorized to celebrate the rites of matrimony in this County according to law and thereupon he took the oath of allegiance to this Commonwealth, whereupon he, together with Hezekiah Harman and George Peery his securities entered into and acknowledged their bond in the penal sum of fifteen hundred dollars conditioned for the faithful discharge of the trust reposed in him. Thereupon testimonials is granted him to celebrate the rites of matrimony in this county."

At the same time a similar order was entered authorizing David Ward to celebrate the rites of matrimony in the county, with John Ward and James M. Campbell as his securities. Both Tollett and Ward were justices of the peace and members of the county court.

On the 14th of May, 1801, the court entered four judgments to be paid in pounds, shillings, and pence. These judgments must have been given on contracts that were written in English money, though the Congress of the United States had in 1785 adopted the silver dollar as the unit; and on the 2nd of April, 1792, had enacted that "The money of the United States shall be expressed in dollars or units," the dollar "to be the value of a Spanish milled dollar as the same is now current." and to contain $371\frac{1}{4}$ grains of pure silver. The same act of Congress fixed the weight of the gold dollar at $24\frac{3}{4}$ grains, which made the ratio of value of silver to gold, by weight, as one to fifteen.

When Tazewell County was organized there were no banks of issue in Virginia, and comparatively no paper money in circulation in the frontier counties. A mint had been established at Philadelphia under the coinage act of 1792, but very few, if any, of the minted coins had been brought to the remote settlements on the Clinch. There was, however, sufficient specie in Tazewell to conduct the ordinary business of the inhabitants, most of the local commercial transactions being conducted by barter. The coins in circulation here were mostly of English mintage, with smaller portions of French and Spanish coinage. From 1780 until the close of the Revolutionary War hard money had been plentiful in the United States. This condition was caused by the large disbursments made by the British and French armies and navies during the closing years of the Revolution, together with the loans negotiated by the Continental Congress and our heavy commerce with the West Indies. It is said that the flow of specie from Europe to America was so heavy that the drain was seriously felt in France and England.

The thrifty, industrious citizens of Tazewell had not only become self-sustaining, but had been sending out to the eastern markets large numbers of cattle and horses; and were bringing back in exchange therefor, gold and silver, which did not quickly find its way back to the East. Careful business men in Tazewell did not accept the gold and silver pieces at their face value, but had money scales and weighed each piece to ascertain its actual value. Robert Barns, the Irish schoolmaster, who settled in the Cove, died in 1802; and among his personal effects listed by the appraisers was one money scales. ———

At the July term in 1801, on the 16th day of the month, the sheriff of Tazewell made his first return on an attachment, which had been sued out by Richard Pemberton vs. Solomon Roe. The return is both unique and amusing, and is as follows:

"Executed on one fur hat, two hunting shirts and one close bodied coat." At the August term judgment was given the plaintiff against the defendent for three pounds, twelve shillings and four pence; and the property aforesaid was ordered to be sold by the sheriff to satisfy the judgment.

On the 16th of July the court entered its first order fixing tavern rates in the county as follows:

"Ordered that the tavern rates for this county be as follows, to-wit:

For a dinner	25c
For a breakfast or supper	17c
For lodging in clean sheets (one shilling)	1
For whiskey by the half Pint (one shilling)	S
For rum, French Brandy or wine by the half pt	25c
For Cider, Beer or Mathalgalum by the quart (one)	S
For Peach or apple Brandy by the half Pint	12½ cts
For corn oats or barley by the gallon (one shilling)	S
For stable for hay or fodder for 12 hours	12½ cts
For Pasturage for 12 hours	12½ cts

TH.—31

In fixing the rates to be charged by the tavern keepers the first county court of Tazewell did not exercise arbitrary power, but responded to the requirements of an act of the General Assembly enacted on the 26th of December, 1792. The act was mandatory; and required "every county court in this Commonwealth to set the rates and prices to be paid at all ordinaries within their respective counties, for liquors, diet, lodging, provender, stableage, fodder and pasturage, with authority to increase or lessen the rates at pleasure. This fixing of rates had to be done at least twice in each year.

The first tavern rates fixed in Tazewell were very reasonable, and the bibulous citizens could not complain of the excessive prices charged for liquors. One of the beverages named in the above table of rates, "Mathalgalum," was a peculiar liquor and is unknown in this day and generation. It was something like the nectar of the gods; and was made of honey and water, boiled and fermented, and often enriched with spices. The Roman name for this drink was "methegline." Pliny in his Natural History, published A. D. seventy-seven, declared it has all the bad qualities of wine but not the good ones. It was a very popular beverage in ancient times, both with the cultured nations of Southern Europe and the barbarous tribes of the Northern regions. The Anglo-Saxons introduced it into England, and called it mead. The recipe for this once popular beverage was brought from the old countries by our ancestors, but they found no material in the wilderness with which they could make it when they came here. In fact, the honey or hive bees were not indigenous to America. They are natives to the warm climates of the Old World, that is, Europe, Asia, and Africa; and were brought to America from Europe by the Spanish, French, and English colonists, became naturalized here, and followed the white men into the forests.

David Ward and Samuel Walker were appointed commissioners at the first term of the court to contract for the building of a jail; and at the September term, 1800, David Ward, Samuel Walker, James Thompson, and George Peery were appointed commissioners to advertise for bids for building a court house. I find that William Smythe (Smith) contracted to build the jail and William Williams the court house. Among the first claims against the county allowed by the court were those held by these contractors. All the outstanding claims were as follows and were, on the 11th of September, 1801, ordered to be paid:

William Smythe, for building jail	$220.00
William Williams, for building court house	938.00
Joseph Moore, for laying off lots in Jeffersonville	12.00
Samuel Walker, David Ward, and George Peery, for letting out contract for court house	20.00
Samuel Walker and David Ward, for lettting out contract for jail	6.00
William George, for Brandy at letting out of the building of the court house	1.50
Thomas Harrisson, for Rum and Brandy at selling of the front and back lots	4.16
William George, John Crockett, James Witton, and Thomas Harrisson as commissioners to attend the laying off of the Town lots	16.00
Hezekiah Harman, for surveying the public lands	5.25
Henry Harman, for trouble sustained in holding the first court at his house	2.00

At the April term of the court in 1802, William Smythe, builder of the jail, presented a claim "for extraordinary services done to said jail amounting to forty pounds and sixteen shillings" Thereupon the court "went and viewed the extraordinary services," and were of the opinion that thirty pounds and sixteen shillings was an allowance fully adequate for the services. Smythe at first refused to receive this amount, but subsequently accepted it.

The court house was a frame structure, and must have been a pretty neat and commodious building, as it cost the county about one thousand dollars, though the finest timber in those days was almost valueless. It was erected on the lot where the temporary court house had been built by the citizens in June, 1800, and was used until it was destroyed by fire in the thirties of the last century.

Thomas Harrisson was granted leave at the April term, in 1802, to keep an ordinary at his home in Jeffersonville. This gave the town three taverns, but not more than enough to accommodate the persons who came to town, especially on court days.

The proceedings of the county court of Tazewell, recorded in the first order book, are very instructive as to the character and purposes of the citizenship of the county. That the people were intelligent, ambitious and industrious is proven by the deep interest they took in their local affairs, and the dispatch with which the county government was put in operation. The justices were men of high character and sound common sense—a dignified body of patriotic citizens. The county courts in Virginia at that time were given a very extensive jurisdiction. They had "authority and jurisdiction to hear and determine all causes whatsoever, then depending

The present court house of Tazewell County. It is hardly equal in its appointments to the needs and importance of the county, but is a very imposing structure when compared with the little log house first used as a temple of justice.

or thereafter to be brought, or which should thereafter be brought in any of the said courts at the Common Law or in Chancery, and criminal cases, except such as where the judgment upon conviction would involve capital punishment, and prosecutions for outlawry. This very ample jurisdiction, however, did not inflate the excellent men who composed Tazewell's first county court, or cause them to swerve from what they thought was right in making their judicial decisions. Even when the dignity of the court was involved they were conservative in defending it against contempts, as is evidenced by the following orders entered by the court on the 14th of July, 1803:

"Ordered that David Waggoner be fined in the sum of five dollars for raising a riot in the presence of the Court.

"Ordered that Abraham Davis be fined in the sum of two dollars and thirty four cents for raising a riot in the presence of the Court.

"Ordered that Abraham Davis be fined in the sum of one dollar & sixty six cents for swearing two oaths in the presence of the Court."

CHAPTER II.

BOUNDARIES AND TOPOGRAPHY OF TAZEWELL COUNTY.

A few years after the creation and organization of Tazewell
County, certain citizens of Russell County, who lived on territory
adjoining Tazewell County, petitioned the General Assembly to
have the line between the two counties so altered as to place the
said territory in the limits of Tazewell. The petition was acted
upon favorably by the Legislature, and on the 20th day of December, 1806, the following act was passed:

"Be it enacted by the General Assembly, That all that part of
the county of Russell within the following bounds, to wit: Beginning on the top of Clinch Mountain at the head of Cove Creek on
the line dividing the counties of Russell and Tazewell, and to run
a straight line from thence to Jacob Francisco's Mill, from thence
a direct line to Daniel Hortons, (to include his dwelling house in
Tazewell,) from thence a straight line to the mouth of Cole Creek,
and to extend on the same direction till it intersects the line which
divided the state of Virginia from Kentucky, shall be, and it is
hereby added to, and made a part of the county of Tazewell."

The county, as then formed, was bounded on the north by Kanawha County, on the south by Wythe and Washington, on the east
by Giles, and on the west by Russell and the State of Kentucky.
In 1806 the whole of the present McDowell County, a part of
Wyoming, a part of Mercer County, West Virginia; and about one-
half of Buchanan, and a part of Giles and Bland were embraced
in the bounds of Tazewell County. If Tazewell still possessed all
this territory, she would be the richest county in the world, as she
is now one of the most noted and best in the United States.

Dr. Bickley in his history of Tazewell County, in the chapter
headed: "Formation, And Outline Geography of Tazewell, says
of the county as it then existed:

"The county is bounded on the north by the State of Kentucky,
Logan and Wyoming counties, Virginia; on the east by Mercer and
Giles; on the south by Wythe and Smyth and on the west by Rus-

sell. It has a superficial area of about 1,920,000 square acres, or 3,000 square miles, and is traversed by numerous ranges of the Alleghany and Cumberland mountains. Clinch, one of the principal mountains, passes through it in an easterly and westerly direction, about forty miles. This mountain was named, as will be seen in the chapter on mountains, in consequence of Clinch river. Rich mountain passes through the county about twenty miles; it is a branch of the Clinch. Garden and Brushy mountains are in the southern part of the county, the latter being the county line; they run parallel with Clinch mountain. Paint Lick and Deskins mountains are also parallel and north of the Rich mountain. They are parts of the same range with East river and Elk-horn, being separated by the Clinch, in the valley in which stands the town of Jeffersonville. There are no other mountains deserving of notice, at this place, except the Great Flat Top, in the north-east corner of the county.

"The county is traversed by many streams; some of considerable size; the principal of which are Clinch river, Bluestone, La Visee, Dry, and Tug forks of Sandy river and their branches. The Clinch river rises from three springs; the first on the 'divides' about ten miles east of the town of Jeffersonville; the second in the valley between the Elk-horn (now called Buckhorn) and Rich mountains; the third in Thompson's valley, about eight miles south-east of the county seat. The two first unite about one and a half miles east of Jeffersonville, and flow, in a westerly direction, about twenty-five miles, and unite with the Maiden-Spring fork, and thence flow through Russell, Scott, Lee, and a part of Tennessee, and after receiving the Powell river, empty into the Tennessee about sixty miles above Kingston.

"Bluestone creek rises in the eastern part of the county; flows in a north easterly direction, and empties into the Great Kanawha. The different branches of the Sandy River, rising in this county, flow in a northerly direction and empty into the Ohio."

All the mountains mentioned by Bickley, except the Great Flat Top, still traverse Tazewell County, but they are greatly changed in appearance. They have been practically denuded of the splendid forest trees that crowned their peaks and magnified the wondrous beauty of each mountain side from crest to valley beneath.

Rich bluegrass pastures are now seen, and charm the eye, where giant poplar, walnut, sugar maple, hickory and other magnificent forest trees grew in abundance. Kent's Ridge, which runs through the county north of the Clinch River, as late as 1852 was almost a continuous forest for its entire length; and all the ridges in the numerous valleys were similarly wooded. The rivers and creeks are also greatly altered in their appearance. They are not as transparently clear, nor nearly as large in volume as they were in the early days of the county. The present condition of the streams is due largely to the destruction of the forests.

THE MOUNTAINS.

Bickley in his "Descriptive Geography" of the county writes further about its mountains. In 1852, the Jeffersonville Historical Society, headed by the scholarly Dr. Fielding Peery, was in existence, but its valuable records have been lost. From the papers of the Society, Dr. Bickley gained much of his information, and he thus further describes our mountains:

"The principal mountains of Tazewell are Clinch, Rich, East River, Brushy, Garden, Paint Lick, Deskins, and Flat Top. They have an elevation, above the valleys, of about eight hundred feet, and about three thousand above the level of the sea. For remarks upon their geological formation I would refer the reader to the Transactions of the Jeffersonville Historical Society. The general course of these mountains is N. 67° E.

"Clinch mountain, which receives its name from Clinch river, extends through the entire length of the county. It has several gaps, through which wagon-roads pass.

"Rich mountain, so called from the character of its soil, is a branch or spur of Clinch mountain, running parallel to it, its entire length.

"East River mountain, so called from a stream of that name flowing along near its base, begins a few miles east of Jeffersonville, and runs parallel to the Rich mountain to the county line on the east.

"Brushy mountain, receiving its name from the brushy character of its growth on the south side, runs in the same direction as the Clinch, and forms the southern boundary line of the county.

"Paint Lick mountain is a continuation of the House and Barn mountain in Russell county, and is separated from it by the Maiden Spring fork, of Clinch river. There was once a great elk and deer lick, near its western end, and there are many paintings (still visible), supposed to have been executed by the Shawnee Indians, or perhaps, by the Cherokees. The paintings represent birds, women, Indian warriors, etc. From these paintings, the lick was named, which was soon applied to the mountain. It rises near the western county line and runs in the general direction to near Jeffersonville: it here sinks, to admit the passage of another fork of Clinch river, and again rises, forming Elkhorn mountain.

"Deskin's mountain, so called from an early settler, runs parallel, and near the Paint Lick, for about the same distance.

"The Great Flat Top, rises from a spur of the Cumberland mountains which traverses the county. It is in the north-east corner of the county, and on it, corner Tazewell, Mercer, and Wyoming counties. It receives its name from a large level area on its summit.

NAMES OF RIVERS.

How the rivers and other streams in Tazewell acquired the names they now bear is an interesting matter of history. Bickley, in accounting for the name given Clinch River makes use of the absurd stories told in his day. He says:

"Clinch river heads in this county and receives its name from an incident which occurred on it in 1767. A hunter named Castle, left Augusta and went to what is now Russell county, to hunt with a party of friendly Indians, who were living on it. This tribe made frequent visits to the settlement, carrying off horses, and such other stock as they could get hold of. A man named Harman, who was robbed of some things, and believing Castle to be the instigator to these acts, applied to a Mr. Buchanan, a justice of Augusta, for a writ to arrest Castle and bring him to trial. The writ was issued, and a party raised to arrest him, among whom was a lame man named Clinch. The party went to Castle's camp and attempted to arrest him, but the Indians joined Castle, and Harman's party were forced to retreat across the river.

"In the hurry of the moment, Clinch got behind, and while fording the river was shot by an Indian, who rushed forward to secure his scalp, but was shot by one of Harman's party. The vulgar tradition is, that an Indian was pursuing a white man, who clinched and drowned the Indian in the stream. I had the former statement, however, from a grandson of the magistrate who issued the warrant for Castle's apprehension."

Both of these stories are without foundation. The river was known as the Clinch to explorers and surveyors seventeen years prior to 1767, the date of the Castle incident, as related by Bickley. When Dr. Thomas Walker, made his famous expedition to Cumberland Gap and Kentucky, he noted in his journal on the 9th of April, 1750: "We traveled to a river which I suppose to be that which the hunters call Clinche's River, for one Clinch, a Hunter who first found it." Dr. Walker and his party had that day reached the Clinch at some point in the present Hancock County, Tennessee. They found the stream too deep to carry their baggage across with safety on their pack-horses and made a raft to get it to the north side of the river.

Colonel John Buchanan, deputy surveyor for Augusta County, on the 14th of October, 1750, surveyed for one John Shelton the "Crabapple Orchard" tract of 650 acres, and, in his official capacity, recorded in the surveyor's book of Augusta the tract as situated on the waters of Clinch River. This is the same tract of land upon which Thomas Witten settled in 1767. And on the 16th of October, 1750, Colonel Buchanan surveyed for John Shelton another tract of 1,000 acres located on a "Branch of Clinch River." It is more than probable the second tract was situated on Plum Creek.

The hunters had given the name to the river, "from one Clinch a Hunter," a sufficient length of time before Dr. Walker made his expedition to enable him to recognize it as the Clinch as soon as he came upon it in Tennessee. So it was with Colonel Buchanan when he was in Tazewell in 1750 surveying tracts of land that had been sold by the Loyal Company. He and his surveying party then knew the stream as Clinch River. These two facts, that are of record, not only controvert the mythical stories related from tradition to Dr. Bickley, but show clearly that Tazewell's first historian was in error when he stated that it was in 1766 that the first hunting party came to Tazewell County. It is evident that hunting parties came here some years prior to 1750; and the first party, it is reasonable to suppose, was lead by a man named Clinch, whose companions named the river in honor of their leader or most popular companion.

With these facts in possession, I undertook, by searching the old records in the State Land Office at Richmond, to discover if any man named Clinch was living in Virginia about the time Dr. Walker made his expedition through Southwest Virginia to Kentucky. I found record of only one man of that name, William Clinch. In Patent Book No. 29, I found a patent recorded, for

Residence of the late Col. Wilk Witten, son of James Witten, the scout. It was built in 1838, just in front of where James Witten's log cabin stood, is a brick structure, and of a style of architecture popular in that day.

5,300 acres of land in Lunenburg County, which had been issued on November 3rd, 1750, to Wm. Clinch. It is known, from tradition, and also from existing records, that, previous to and after 1750, hunting parties came from Southside Virginia and also from Tidewater to hunt in the Clinch and Holston valleys. They were called "Long Hunters", because they came prepared to stay for several months each trip; and they hunted for profit, not for sport, nor to procure meat as did the Indians. Sometimes they would kill more than a thousand splendid animals on a single hunting trip—buffalo, elk, bear, deer, and other kinds that were valuable for their hides. They would take great numbers of their hides on pack-horses to Tidewater, where they brought fine prices for shipment to England and other European countries. It is very probable that William Clinch came from Southside Virginia with the first party of Long Hunters that visited the Clinch Valley; and that the river and the mountain that bear the name Clinch received it from him. The Indian name for the river was Pellissippi.

The Big Sandy gets its name from the many sand bars that were found in the bed of the stream. Different tribes of Indians called it Tatteroi, Chatteroi, and Chatterawha. The Miamis called it We-pe-po-ne-ce-pe-we. The Delawares called it Si-ke-a-ce-pe, Salt River. And Little Sandy was called Tan-ga-te Si-ke-a-ce-pe-we, or Little Salt River. Three of the branches of Big Sandy River had

The first residence of Samuel Cecil, built in 1814. It stands north of and overlooking Clinch River, opposite the mouth of Plum Creek, and is three miles west of the county seat. It was originally a two-story double log house, and was later weatherboarded. The floors are made of yellow locust lumber and are as hard as polished metal. The author's mother, daughter and eldest child of Samuel Cecil, was born in 1815 and was reared, and married to my father, in this house. It is now owned by Mrs. O. E. Hopkins, a great-granddaughter of Samuel Cecil, and is used as a tenant house.

their source in Tazewell when the county was first formed. These were the Louisa, Dry Fork, and Tug Fork. Since 1858, when Buchanan and McDowell were taken from Tazewell, only one of the branches, Dry Fork, has its head in the county. Bickley said in 1852: "La Visee (Louisa) has many branches in Tazewell, and is navigable for flat-boats, to the county line. The first white man who ascended it was a Frenchman, who found a well-executed design or painting upon a peeled poplar; hence its name—"la" translated, meaning the, and "visee," meaning a design, aim, or representation. It is sometimes called Louisa fork, from Louisa C. H., Kentucky, near its junction with the Tug River."

This river should be called Louisa. Dr. Thomas Walker discovered and named it "Louisa River," on June 7th, 1750, when he was returning from his expedition to Kentucky. Captain Dan Smith was deputy surveyor of Fincastle County, and made numerous surveys for Dr. Walker, who was the agent of the Loyal Company. Captain Smith made a map in 1774 on which he laid down the headwaters of the Holston, Clinch and Sandy rivers. On this map he placed the headwaters "of a River Commonly called Louisa." As he was then actively engaged surveying tracts of land for the Loyal Company in the present Russell and Tazewell counties, it is evident he was told by Dr. Walker the name of the river, "Louisa." Smith's map shows that it is a branch of Sandy River.

East River was given its name by the white settlers, because it flows in an easterly direction. The Miamis called it Nat-weo-ce-pe-we, and the Delawares named it Ta-le-mo-te-no-ec-pe.

Bluestone River, among the rivers of Tazewell, is second only to the Clinch in historical interest. This river was so named by the white settlers from the deep blue limestone over which it flows, which tends to give a clear blue color to the water in the stream. It also flows in an easterly direction and empties into New River in the present Summers County, West Virginia. The Miami Indians called it Mee-ce-ne-ke-ke-ec-pe-we; and the Delawares named it Mo-mon-ga-sen-eka-ee-pe, or Big Stone Creek.

Wolf Creek rises in Burke's Garden, passes through the gap, which is the only outlet for water from the Garden, flows down through the rugged breaks between Rich and Garden mountains, enters Bland County and runs on to and through Rocky Gap, thence to New River, entering that stream at the Narrows in Giles County. The early settlers found so many wolves along and about the stream, from its source to its confluence with New River, that they naturally gave it the name of Wolf Creek.

There are a hundred or more creeks and branches in the present bounds of Tazewell County that have received their names from their peculiar location, or some traditional incident. Owing to their large number, only the most noted ones can be mentioned in this volume.

Laurel Fork, a branch of the North Fork of Holston River, has its source at the head of Poor Valley, about ten miles southeast of the town of Tazewell. It is a beautiful freestone stream and runs a westerly course down the valley some fifteen miles to the Smyth County line, where it turns south, and, after passing through Laurel Gap, empties into the North Fork of Holston about half a mile from the gap.

Great Indian Creek, in what is called the Sinking Waters, has its head about fifteen miles west of the county seat. Its course is southerly to the Clinch, entering that river at a point about sixteen miles west of Tazewell, where the hamlet known as "Indian"

This old mill is still standing in Plum Creek Gap, about half a mile below the point where the big spring that is the source of the creek gushes from the mountain side.

formerly stood, but where the present thrifty town of Cedar Bluff is now located. A man named Ray and his entire family were massacred by the Indians on the creek in 1788, or 1789; and from this incident the stream got its name. One of the springs at its head petrifies vegetable matter, such as nuts, twigs from trees, etc. I have been shown specimens of these petrifactions.

Clear Fork, a branch of Wolf Creek, heads six miles east of Tazewell. It flows easterly through the narrow, but beautiful Clear Fork Valley for a distance of about twenty miles, and joins Wolf Creek at Rocky Gap.

Plum Creek is one of the most historic streams in the county, and received its name from the large number of wild plum trees the first settlers found growing about its borders. Its principle source is in the gap of Rich Mountain, known as Plum Creek Gap, about three miles southwest of the court house.

In 1852 the creek that rises in Ward's, or Barns' Cove, was known as Cove Creek. Now another stream bears that name. This Cove Creek has its source in Nye's Cove on the south side of East River Mountain, about twelve miles northeast of Tazewell. It passes through a gap in Buckhorn Mountain, and empties into Clear Fork at the old Peter Dills place. On the 1st of October, 1789, a party of Indians entered the home of Thomas Wiley, who lived half a mile above the mouth of Cove Creek, and made captives of Mrs. Virginia Wiley and her four children. As they were going up Cove Creek the Indians killed the four children, but took Mrs. Wiley to their towns in Ohio. She afterwards made her escape in company with a man named Samuel Lusk.

Laurel Creek is now one of the most noted streams in Tazewell County. It passes directly through the town of Pocahontas; and near its banks the first coal was mined for shipment from the Pocahontas coal fields. Dr. Thomas Walker, when returning from his expedition to Kentucky in 1750, camped on Laurel Creek, and made a note in his journal of the coal he found there.

Big Creek also has come prominently into notice in recent years. This creek rises in the southern slopes of Sandy Ridge about twenty miles west of the county seat and near the dividing line between Buchanan and Tazewell counties. It flows in a southerly direction and joins the Clinch at Richlands. There are several large coal operations on its upper waters, from which many thousands of tons of coal are being mined and shipped annually.

CHAPTER III.

That section of a county where the seat of justice is located is generally the most important, because of the location of the county government at that particular point. The valley in which the county seat of Tazewell is placed has added importance on account of its unexcelled physical beauty and unsurpassed fertility of soil. This valley has a length of seven miles and extends from the west end of East River and Buckhorn mountains to the east end of Paint Lick and Deskins mountains. It is bounded on the south by Rich Mountain and on the north by Kent's Ridge; and, with the northern slopes of the mountain and the southern slopes of the Ridge, included, has an average width of about four miles. Within these bounds there are about 18,000 acres of as good land as can be found anywhere on the North American Continent. The main fork of Clinch River meanders through it. Plum Creek heads in a gap of Rich Mountain, about three miles south of the town of Tazewell and flows a northerly course across the valley, joining the Clinch about a half a mile above the place where the first settler, Thomas Witten, built his cabin. Cavitt's Creek finds its source in the southern slopes of Stony Ridge, runs through a gap in Kent's Ridge, and unites with the Clinch, a mile above the mouth of Plum Creek. Scores of limpid branches flow down from the mountains, ridges and hills and find their way into the river, or into one or the other of the two above named creeks. Thousands of crystal springs burst forth from the mountains, ridges and hills and even in the lowlands, and are the sources of the numerous branches that create the creeks and the historic Clinch River. It is impossible to find anywhere on the earth the same quantity and quality of land that is more abundantly supplied with pure, flowing water.

It was in this immediate section of Tazewell that the first settlers—the Wittens, the Harmans, the Peerys, the Wynnes, the Cecils, and others—located with their families. Two of the first three forts built by the pioneers of the Clinch Valley, were erected in this area—Thomas Witten's, at the "Crabapple Orchard," and William Wynne's, at "Locust Hill."

The scenic grandeur of this particular valley and the mountains that encompass it, is beyond description. Its most conspicuous and gigantic feature is Dial Rock. This rock is the face of one of the three heads of East River Mountain that stand at the eastern extremity of the valley. It is composed of several cliffs, which, viewed from a distance, present the appearance of a single rock. How it received its name is not known. There is an old story, handed down by tradition, that in the pioneer days a natural sun-dial, which correctly measured the time of day, was found upon the rock. It

This exquisitely beautiful scene shows the Exhibition Grounds of the Tazewell Fair Association with the Fair in full swing. In the background can be seen the two principal faces of East River Mountain. The tall peak at the right is crowned and faced with Dial Rock.

is more reasonable to believe that it got its name from the man named Dial, who was living in that vicinity, and was killed by the Indians on the 11th of April, 1786.

The summit of the rocks is about fifteen hundred feet above the valley and the Clinch River, which stream flows not very far from the base of the mountain. Dr. Bickley, who scaled the cliffs in 1852, made an estimate of their elevation, and he says: "These cliffs are from one hundred and fifty to two hundred and fifty feet above the common level of the mountain; and seem as if some internal commotion had started them from the bowels of the earth, to awe and affright the eye that should dare look from their tops."

The view from the pinacle of Dial Rock is very extensive and ravishingly beautiful. Bickley, who stood upon the "sixth rock" sixty-seven years ago, thus describes the view one has from the height:

"Mountains rise above mountains, in endless succession, till far in the smoky distance his vision ceases to distinguish the faint outline of the Cumberland and the Tennessee mountains. Looking to the north he sees the great Flat Top, from which others gradually fade into indistinctness, and in imagination seems to say, There,

View of a portion of the town of Tazewell. Wynne's Peak is seen in the background. The location of the town is physically of such a character as to make it impossible to get a complete view of the place in one picture.

there is the valley of the beautiful Ohio—the garden of commerce and industry. To the west, rises Morris' Knob, the highest point of Rich mountain, its summit kissing the very clouds, and seeming to bid defiance to the storms of heaven. To the right, rise Paint Lick and Deskins mountains, and nearly behind them, the rocky peaks of House and Barn mountains, in Russell county. Far in the distance, are seen ranges of Clinch mountain and its various spurs. To the left, is seen Wolf Creek Knob, a continuation of Rich mountain. Close at hand, the rocky sides and top of Elkhorn (Buckhorn), and far in the distance, ridges of the Alleghany range. From this beautiful scene the eye is directed down to the valley when a disposition to shrink back is felt. * * * The scene, in the distance, is beautiful beyond description. The scene around him is sublime beyond conception. It is beyond the power of the wildest imagination to picture half its grandeur."

Dr. Bickley failed to mention "The Peak," which towers above the town of Tazewell. This peak was known in the early days of the county as Wynne's Peak, receiving its name from William Wynne, the pioneer; and the name should be restored. The sum-

View of another section of the town of Tazewell. Rich Mountain is visible at the eastern background of the picture.

mit is 4,250 feet above sea level and has an elevation of 1,716 feet above the town which is nestled at the base of Rich Mountain. From its lofty pinacle the view is equally as far-reaching and entrancing as that one gets from Dial Rock. Persons who have climbed the peak at the end of Paint Lick Mountain, say that the view of the valley from that point is more exquisitely beautiful than it is from either Dial Rock or Wynne's Peak.

The Clinch Valley Branch of the Norfolk & Western Railway runs east and west through the valley its entire length. Two splendid modern macadam roads pass through it from east to west—

one hugging the foot hills of Rich Mountain, and passing through the county seat—and the other running along Clinch River, and passing through North Tazewell. There are two incorporated towns—Tazewell and North Tazewell—in the valley.

When the pioneers came to this valley it was the habitat of a large variety of wild animals. It was the home of the buffalo, elk, black bear, Virginia or white-tailed deer, panther, wolf, otter, beaver, red and gray fox, and many other kinds of small animals. Of the larger animals none but the bear and an occasional deer are now ever found in the limits of the county.

There had existed in this same valley, many thousands of years before the coming of the pioneers, another variety of animals. The mastodon, nearly allied to the elephant of the present age, once lived in this valley and fed upon the abundant herbage that then grew here. This was during what Sir Charles Lyell, the eminent geologist, named the post-pliocene period; but he and other geologists have failed to reckon how many thousands of years have passed since that period ended. Fragmentary fossil remains of the mastodon have been found at several points in this valley. Some years ago when a ditch was being dug near the present residence of Mr. J. P. Kroll, in the town of Tazewell, several fossil teeth of a mastodon were unearthed. In 1893 the late Andrew M. Peery, when having a ditch dug in the meadow near the sulphur spring on his father's, the late Captain Wm. E. Peery's, place, came upon the fragmentary fossil remains of a four-tusked mastodon (tricophodon Miocene). He secured and carefully preserved considerable parts of an upper and of a lower tusk, and also several of the large teeth of the huge beast. They are still kept in the cabinet of the late Captain Wm. E. Peery.

Similiar remains have been found in the recently discovered asphalt pits at Los Angeles, California. The most notable contempary mammals of the four-tusked elephant or mastodon were: the saber-toothed tigers, lions, giant wolves, immense cave bears, large wild horses, camels, mammoths with tusks 15 feet long, and giant ground sloths. These and many other species, large and small, in great numbers, once lived on the plains of Southern California. It is more than possible that the same animals were abundant here at the same period.

BURKE'S GARDEN.

That splendid section of Tazewell called Burke's Garden, though lying outside the great Clinch Valley, is considered by many persons the finest section of the county. It is also a region of much historic importance. In preceding chapters it has been told how the beautiful basin got its name from James Burke, the pioneer hunter; and elsewhere in this volume I have related many interesting incidents connected with its discovery and settlement. Several years ago Mr. E. L. Greever, who is now one of the most prominent lawyers of Tazewell's able bar, wrote an excellent sketch of Burke's Garden, which, for some reason, was never published, though very meritorious and complete. Mr. Greever was born and reared in the Garden, and his ancestors were among its earliest settlers. His knowledge of the Garden is so ample and accurate that I have concluded to adopt his description of its physical beauties and outlines. It is as follows:

"Burke's Garden is not a valley in the ordinary sense of the term. It is rather a basin. Clinch Mountain is an unbroken range for many miles between Thompson Valley and Poor Valley. Towards the east it rises in altitude until it suddenly stops in the jumble of mountains called Bear Town. Here, is one of the highest points in Virginia, nearly 4,800 feet above the level of the sea. From this highest point, the mountain extends away in a grand sweep to the north and east, and away in another grand sweep to the south and east, until the two branches are again united, many miles away, in Round Mountain. Burke's Garden is thus a basin, a cup whose rim is an unbroken range of mountains. From northeast to southeast it is ten miles long, and from southeast to northwest it is five miles wide. Only one natural opening in this massive fence exists, and through it all the water passes out to the sea. This opening is an abrupt, deep notch, cut straight through the mountain. The pass is strewn with great boulders, the wreckage left by the long contest of water and stone. Men have made other roads into the valley, but this is the one mighty gateway constructed by nature.

"Many theories as to the formation of Burke's Garden have been advanced. By many it is believed that in the general upheaval of the country, this place was left much as it is now, that the basin was soon filled with water, and that the water finally broken through the barrier that held it, leaving the fertile bed of the lake to become, in time, a beautiful valley.

"Others maintain that the upheaval broke up the hard sandstone over a large area, but left it intact on the mountain sides, and that erosion has made Burke's Garden.

"It has been suggested that the rim of mountains now marks the outline of the base of what was once an immense peak, and that the top of the peak being soft was gradually worn away.

The Gap which is the only natural outlet from Burke's Garden. When the photo was made of this scene the ground was covered with a deep snow. The stream shown is Wolf Creek, and has its source in the Garden. It was once a fine trout stream, and the author caught his first "speckled beauty," in this creek, about a fourth of a mile below the mill, in March, 1863.

After awhile the hard sandstone was reached and wearing away process on the outside was stopped. The upheavel of the peak having broken up the strata, the process of disintegration went on over the space where the strata were so broken. Thus the hard rim was left while the softer rocks of the interior of the peak, the limestones, gradually wore away until the present state of things resulted. In support of this last theory, attention is called by its advocates to the remarkable fact that the dip of the strata all the way around this mountain rim is toward the outside, very much as if the giant force had pushed up the horizontal strata until they sloped away alike in all directions.

* * * *

"Its altitude, nearly thirty-two hundred feet above sea level, makes the climate cooler ordinarily than the surrounding country, and the seasons in the valley later. The days are seldom uncomfortably warm in summer and the nights are never oppressive. * * * When the first settlers reached the place they found the climate extremely cold. Corn and wheat would not mature. Wheat

Rev. John J. Greever was born in Burke's Garden in 1811 and died in June, 1877. He was a minister of the Evangelical Lutheran Church, was an able theologian and a splendid pulpit orator. He was a grandson of Philip Greever, the man who fired the first shot at the battle of King's Mountain.

bread was a luxury enjoyed only on Sundays and the flour was purchased on Wolf Creek. Frosts came late in the spring and early in the fall. Fruits, such as apples, peaches, &c., were unknown. Rye did remarkably well. The potato found here, its ideal home.

* * * *

"The Indians called Burke's Garden 'The Great Swamp.' The name, as were most Indians names, was descriptive and peculiarly appropriate. The whole expanse of level land, now the very finest of bluegrass pasture, was then wet and almost a bog. This was caused by the dense undergrowth, for the whole country is of limestone formation and is unusually well drained naturally. One man yet living, remembers the time when a bridle path ran through the woods from 'the Gap' to the place where the road to Ceres now crosses the mountain; and he says that the horses had made in the mud a succession of steps which closely resembled a stairway. There existed an idea among the first settlers that this broad expanse of level land was too wet and swampy for farming purposes; in fact, they regarded it as hardly worth clearing and we find many of them, under this delusion, establishing their homes along the central ridge and clearing far inferior lands."

Mr. Greever gives very little credence to some of the traditions that have been handed down through several generations about Burke's discovery of the Garden, especially the one which tells of the hunter's pursuit of a monster Elk from Elk Creek, in Grayson County, on. across Cripple Creek, in Wythe County, over three mountains into the Garden, and thence across mountains and ridges to Elkhorn, in what is now West Virginia. However, Mr. Greever does give credit to the story about Burke and a companion hunter following a very large buck from their camp in Poor Valley into the Garden. And he is of the opinion that Burke, and not Sinclair, piloted Colonel Patton to the place.

The records in the State Land Office at Richmond reveal that patents for two boundaries of land, containing 400 and 500 acres, respectively, were issued on Sept. 20th, 1748, to James Burke. These tracts were situated on Goose Creek in Augusta County; and it is more than probable these lands were obtained from Colonel Patton, under his grant of 120,000 acres. Burke had been intimately associated with Patton in some capacity, as he was one of the first settlers at the settlement made by Colonel Patton at Draper's Meadows in 1748.

There is an old story to the effect that Burke was to be given one thousand acres of the level land in the Garden as compensation for showing Patton the country; and that Colonel Patton and his associates did not comply with their contract. In other words, that Burke was defrauded. It has also been a tradition that Patton made an inclusive survey of all the choice land in the basin, and appropriated it to himself and his kindred. There is no record in existence which shows that any such survey was ever made. In fact no surveying was done in the Garden until 1753, and this was under the grant for 800,000 acres to the Loyal Company. A surveying party composed of Colonel Patton, Colonel John Buchanan, Wm. Ingles, James Burke, and possibly others, in that year surveyed two tracts, one of 345 acres and another of 200 acres, for Wm. Ingles. At the same time a tract of 400 acres was surveyed for James Burke, and was, no doubt, given him by Colonel Patton for services rendered. This was the boundary on which Burke built his cabin and made clearings. It was there that Colonel Andrew Lewis camped for two days in 1756 with his little army that went on the Sandy River expedition; and there his soldiers

This beautiful landscape shows the location of the house of the Floyds when they lived in Burke's Garden. The house stood in the grove of sugar trees at the left of the picture. On the right is seen the handsome residence of Mr. R. M. Lawson, who now owns one thousand acres of the splendid Floyd estate, that consisted originally of about three thousand acres.

found enough potatoes in Burke's patches to supply them with food for two days.

Though it is known that Burke married a widow Griffith, there is nothing I can find of record to show that he had, at the time he was sojourning in the Garden, any children of his own, or that he ever took his family there. His adventurous disposition and avidity for hunting caused him, somewhat like Daniel Boone, to lead a wandering life. He was driven by the Indians from the Garden in 1756, and, when seeking a place of safety, met the Sandy River expedition at, or near, Draper's Valley in the present Pulaski County; and told Colonel Lewis of the visit of the savages to the

Garden. This was why Lewis marched there without delay, hoping that he would get upon the trail of the Indians and destroy them before they got back to Ohio. Burke never returned to the Garden. There is ample evidence in the records of the county clerk's office of Tazewell to show that he disposed of his 400 acre tract to Wm. Ingles who had two tracts of land adjoining. It is probable he exchanged it for the land he afterwards occupied on New River in the present Giles County; and where he had a fort in 1774, near the mouth of Sinking Creek.

When Thomas Ingles moved his family from Abb's Valley to

The black cross is about the spot where James Burke built his cabin in 1763, and where Thomas Ingles' family were made captives in 1782. The land belongs to the estate of the late Rufus Thompson.

Burke's Garden he took up his abode in the house that James Burke had built and had occupied during his brief stay in the Garden. Ingles enlarged the house, and made other improvements in the way of buildings and the clearing of land. The records of the county court of Tazewell County disproves the tradition that the Indians burned the house of Thomas Ingles when they made his family captives in 1782. At the same time that Colonel Buchanan made surveys for Ingles and Burke he surveyed large boundaries of the choice lands in the Garden for Colonel James Patton. As previously related, Colonel Patton was killed by the Indians at the Draper's Meadows massacre in 1755. He was survived by two daughters, Mary, wife of William Thompson, and Margaret, wife of Colonel John Buchanan. By his will, which was probated by the county court of Augusta County, at Staunton, in November, 1755, he divided his estate equally between his two daughters. The splendid Burke's Garden lands were allotted to Mrs. Mary Thompson, and they afterwards passed to her son, Captain James Patton Thompson, grandson and namesake of Colonel Patton.

Col. Peter Litz was of the first generation born in Burke's Garden. He was of pure German blood, was a man of splendid qualities and was one of Tazewell's most highly esteemed citizens. He was born April 25th, 1802, and died April 3rd, 1880.

Mrs. Mary Thompson, or her son James, had, in some way, acquired a right to the Burke's Garden lands belonging to the estate of Wm. Ingles, including the Burke tract of four hundred acres. Captain Thompson moved to the Garden from his former residence at Town House, now Chilhowie, in Smyth County. In 1806 he instituted a chancery suit in the county court of Tazewell to extract from Thomas Ingles his equitable title in the land formerly owned by his father, Wm. Ingles. The style of the suit was James Thompson vs. Thomas Ingles; and on the 27th of May, 1806, the county court of Tazewell entered a decree from which the following extract is taken:

"This court conceiving the holder of an equitable claim, may relinquish the same to the legal proprietor before the same is adjudged to such equitable claimant by adjudication, whereupon the court doth order and decree that, in case the heirs, Executors or other persons representing William Ingles, Decd., should by adjudication or otherwise obtain any lands within the place called Burks Garden, in the bill mentioned, that the Defendent do at his own costs by Deed of conveyance, convey one third part thereof to the said Plaintiff, with general warranty against himself and all other persons; and in case the Heirs, Executors, Administrators, assigns, or any person or persons, claiming under William Ingles, Decd, should by adjudication or otherwise, obtain four hundred acres of

Captain George G. Gose was born in Burke's Garden on January 28th, 1822, and died November 14th, 1889. He served in the Confederate army for about one year as Captain of Company C, 23rd Battalion, Va. Inf. Captain Gose passed all his life in Burke's Garden, and was one of its most substantial and respected citizens.

Land in right of James Burke then the court doth order and Decree that the said defendent do at his own costs convey unto the Plaintiff one third part thereof, in one entire square so as to include the improvements made by the defendant and his father William Ingles, and also *to include the house where Burke, and afterwards said defendant* resided."

This decree proves conclusively that James Burke owned and occupied, and afterwards abandoned and sold to William Ingles, four hundred acres of the best land in the Garden; and that the house that Burke built in 1753 or 1754, plus improvements made by William and Thomas Ingles, was standing in 1806. The decree of the county court of Tazewell was executed to such an extent as to vest the title of the Burke land completely in James Patton Thompson. And on the 26th day of April, 1813, Captain James Thompson and Margaret, his wife, conveyed by deed to Archibald Thompson, "one certain tract or parcel of land in Burke's Garden, including the Old Station, containing 300 acres more or less." The decree and deed, cited, prove beyond question that James Burke was not fraudulently deprived of any land in the Garden, and that Thomas Ingles' house was not destroyed by the Indians when they made his wife and children captives in 1782.

I have been unable to ascertain definitely who was the first permanent settler in Burke's Garden and when he settled there. James Patton Thompson was certainly one of the first, if not the first to take up his residence in the Garden. Among the most prominent settlers from 1800 to 1820 were: Peter Litz, Philip Gose, Philip Greever, Gasper Ritter, John Heninger, George Spracher, Peter Gose, John Day, George Rhudy, Mathias Fox, William Hall, and James Meek. Nearly all these first settlers have many descendants still living in the Garden.

THE COVE.

One of the most attractive and noted sections of the county is the Cove. It is composed of two distinct but contiguous coves. They are known, respectively, as Bowen's and Barns' Cove; and take their name from Rees Bowen, who settled there in 1769; and Robert Barns, who located there in 1784 or 1785. The two coves cover an area of approximately 5 x 4½ miles, and contain about 15,000 acres of as fine grazing and agricultural land as can be found any where on the continent.

In 1852 Bickley wrote about the Cove as Follows: "This is a large area of nearly level land, containing about fifteen square miles, and situated at the west end of Thompson's Valley, between Clinch and Short mountains, which was evidently, at one time connected with the Rich Mountain. The waters seem to have accumulated, (in Barns' Cove) and forced a way through that spot now known as Maiden Spring. The land is very fertile, well timbered and watered, and the surrounding farms in fine order. Add to it the

adjoining lands and residences of Maj. H. S. Bowen and Col. Rees
T. Bowen and I know of no section in Tazewell County, of the same
extent, so desirable. The society is good, and the inhabitants very
hospitable. I hesitate not to call this the garden spot of Tazewell
County. It was settled in 1772 by John Craven, who was followed,
the next year, by Rees Bowen, David Ward, and William Garrison,
the latter, however, settled on its very edge. The descendants of
these men are still in the Cove. The Wards, Bowens, Gillespies,
Barnses, and Youngs, constitute a major part of its population. The
scenery from here is very fine, and the climate warmer than other
parts of Tazewell."

The Wards, Bowens, Barns, and Gillespies, descendants of the
first settlers, still constitute the greater part of the inhabitants
and own nearly all the land in the Cove. George Ward lives where
his ancestor, David Ward, located his home. Rees Bowen, the
fifth, resides at the old Maiden Spring homestead, in view of the
spot where his ancestor, Lieutenant Rees Bowen, built his fort in
the pioneer days. Joseph G. Barns lives near where his great-
grandfather, Robert Barns, erected his cabin in 1785 or 1786.
Jeff Gillespie lives on the spot where his ancestor. Thomas Gillespie,
built his dwelling just after the Revolution. The descendants of
the pioneer families are almost certain to own and occupy this
beautiful and fertile section for many coming generations, as the
present generation are as much wedded to the soil as were their
pioneer ancestors. As each generation comes and goes, their love
for this beautiful land seems to grow more intense.

THOMPSON VALLEY.

Thompson Valley was one of the sections of the Clinch Valley
to first attract pioneer settlers; and in this valley the Indians committed their first diabolical massacre of white people within the
bounds of the present Tazewell County. Joseph Martin, John
Henry and James King settled in the valley in 1871. On the 8th
of September, 1774, John Henry and his wife and three children
were murdered by a band of Indians, led by Logan, the Mingo
chief. If Martin and King have any descendants now living in the
county, they are unknown to the author. William Thompson, with
his family, settled in the valley in 1772, and it received its name
from him.

The area of Thompson Valley is approximately 13 x 2½ miles, and contains about 20,000 acres of valuable grazing and farming land. It lies between Clinch and Rich mountains and runs, from its head, a westerly course. On the south side of Rich Mountain, within this valley, is found some of the very finest grazing lands in Tazewell County. This is the only instance in the county, or in Southwest Virginia, where a mountain is equally rich on both its north and south side, and this, perhaps, accounts for the name given the mountain.

The Maiden Spring fork of Clinch River, which Captain Dan Smith, in surveys he made in 1774 for John Henry and William Thompson, called the "South Fork of Clinch River," has its source at the head of Thompson Valley. This stream flows down the valley a distance of about ten miles, then sinks or enters a cave, flows under Rich Mountain, and gushes out about a mile southwest of Liberty Hill and flows on down by Maiden Spring.

There are a number of excellent farms in the valley. The Thompsons and other descendants of William Thompson, the pioneer, constitute a large share of the population, and own a great part of the most valuable lands in the valley.

POOR VALLEY.

Just across Clinch Mountain, south of Thompson Valley, and running parallel with that valley, is another valley. It lies between Clinch and Brushy mountains, and was named by the early settlers, Poor Valley, because the land is not as fertile as in the other valleys of Tazewell County. But if it was situated in the eastern part of the State, it would be considered both fertile and beautiful. There is very little, if any, limestone in the valley, which accounts for its lack of fertility, as compared with the limestone sections of the county.

Poor Valley constituted a part of Washington and Wythe counties until twenty-six years after Tazewell was formed. Then, upon the petition of the few citizens who lived in the valley, the General Assembly by an act passed on January 4th, 1826, attached it to Tazewell County. The Valley has an area of approximately 17 x 1½ miles, its length being greatly out of proportion to its width, and contains about 16,000 acres, most of the land being level.

At the head of the valley the Laurel Fork of the North Fork of Holston River has its source. This beautiful crystal stream flows down the valley to the line between Smyth and Tazewell counties, passes through Laurel Gap of Brushy Mountain, and enters the North Fork of Holston in Smyth County. The water is free-

Major Otis Caldwell was for many years a resident of Poor Valley. He was born Dec. 12th, 1820, and died Sept. 6th, 1912. He held the rank of major in the Confederate army.

stone and there are many fine springs, some of them of considerable volume. The valley is well adapted to fruit culture, and the inhabitants rarely fail to have an abundant crop of apples.

BAPTIST VALLEY.

Bickley says that Baptist Valley received its name "from the number of persons belonging to the Baptist denomination of Christians, who settled in it." It covers an area of approximately 10 x 1 miles, contains about 6,400 acres; and lies between Kent's Ridge and the ridge that divides the waters of the Clinch and the Dry Fork of Sandy River. Among the first settlers in this valley were: James and Charles Skeggs, Richard Pemberton, ————Johnson, Thomas Maston, Wiliam Patterson, and John Deskins.

The farms, generally, are of small acreage, and were badly and intensely cultivated until some twenty years ago, when the farmers began to handle their land in a scientific manner. At this time there is no part of the county where the lands are more industriously and skilfully cultivated, or where the yield per acre is more abundant. The Tazewell C. H. and Kentucky Turnpike passed through the valley its entire length; and a few years ago a part of the road was reconstructed and macadamized and is now one of the best roads in the county. It is one of the best fruit growing sections of the county, and the apple trees rarely fail to bear heavily. Tourists who travel through the valley are delighted with the scenery, the views from the road being very beautiful.

RICHLANDS VALLEY.

The Richlands Valley, which is in the extreme western part of the county, is not extensive, but has become one of the busiest and most interesting localities in Tazewell. It has an area of 2 x 4 miles, or 5,000 acres of very valuable land. The most of it is bottom land and lies on the north and south sides of Clinch River, which winds its way through the valley. From these fertile river lands the place received its name, and in their midst is located the thriving and coming town of Richlands. The local industrial enterprises, including nearby coal operations, furnish a good market for most of the products of the smaller farmers.

CLEAR FORK VALLEY.

The Clear Fork Valley is situated at the extreme east side of Tazewell County, and extends from the divide at Gratton, six miles east of the Court House, to Rocky Gap in Bland County. That part of the valley which lies within Tazewell County has an area approximately of 8½ x 2 miles, or 11,000 acres. The valley lies between Rich and Buckhorn mountains, and received its name from the beautiful creek that is a branch of Wolf Creek.

When the pioneers came in from the east they traveled up Clear Fork, where they found and followed a trail that had been made by herds of buffalo and that had been used by Indian hunting and war parties in their travels to and from the New River Valley. The farms on Clear Fork are not large, but they are fertile and cultivated with great industry; and the products are bountiful. The farmers of that section always have something to sell, and they are a thrifty and excellent people.

T.H.—33

WRIGHT'S VALLEY.

The valley known as Wright's Valley lies both east and west of the divide at Tiptop. In 1772 Major John Taylor settled at the extreme west end of the valley, near the place afterwards owned by his son Charles, and known as the "Charles Taylor place." Jesse Evans settled the same year just west of the village of Tiptop, at the place afterwards known as the "Buse Harman place." The valley later received its name from a man named Wright; and it was called Wright's Valley as early as 1782. It has an area of about 9½ x 1 miles, or 6,000 acres.

The north fork of Clinch River heads in the western part of Wright's Valley, and one of the branches of Bluestone heads in that part of the valley east of the divide. When the Indians came up Tug Fork to make attacks upon the settlers they always passed through Wright's Valley; and Jesse Evans' children were massacred by the savages in 1779. Evans was then living at the Buse Harman place. There are some excellent farms in the west end of the valley, notably that of the late W. G. Mustard, which is now owned by his daughter, Mrs. Henry S. Bowen.

ABB'S VALLEY.

The valley in Tazewell County that has been written of and talked about most is Abb's Valley. Its area is small when compared with some of the most noted localities of the county, but it has been given extended notoriety from the tragic fate that befell Captain James Moore and his family. The valley received its name from Absalom Looney who discovered it while on a hunting and sang-digging expedition west of New River. It covers an area of approximately 10 x 1 miles, and contains about 6,400 acres of fine grazing and farming land.

When James Moore and Robert Poage moved with their families to Abb's Valley, in 1770 or 1771, they found an abundance of pasturage for their stock, as a considerable part of the valley was destitute of forest growth, and a heavy bluegrass sod covered the open spots. The valley is very cavernous, and, as a result, no running surface stream flows down or across it. All the branches that come down from the hollows or the ridges, and the springs that burst out at the base of the hills sink and enter the caverns.

These create an underground stream that courses down the valley, and gushes out as a big spring near the east end of the valley.

Until the railroad was built to Pocahontas in 1883, Abb's Valley was one of the most isolated and inaccessible sections of Tazewell County. Pocahontas is just across the ridge that bounds the valley on the north, and the water supply of the town is procured from the big spring referred to above. A part of the estate of Captain James Moore is owned by his great-grandson, Oscar Moore, and another part by his great-granddaughter, Mrs. Samuel P. Mustard. The greater part of the valley has passed from the possession of the descendants of the early settlers.

THE BLUESTONE VALLEY.

Of the various valleys in Tazewell County not one is more interesting and important than the Bluestone Valley. In extent it is equal to Burke's Garden, as its area is 13 x 2½ miles, or 20,000 acres. The first settlers in this very attractive section were: Thomas and James Maxwell, Benjamin Joslin, James Ogleton, Jacob and Israel Harman, and Samuel Ferguson. They settled

Charles Fitzgerald Tiffany, whose father, Hugh Tiffany, was one of the early settlers in the Bluestone Valley. He married a daughter of James Moore, the captive. Mr. Tiffany was born June 6th, 1800 and died Feb. 12th, 1876. He was an active and influential citizen and left a splendid estate to his only child, Mrs. Alex St. Clair.

there in 1771 or 1772; and all of them, except Joslin and Ogleton, subsequently became conspicuous figures in the history of Tazewell.

Bluestone Valley lies along the north side of East River Mountain. Beginning at the divide which separates the waters of the Clinch from the waters of the Bluestone, it extends in an easterly direction to a point southeast of Graham. Through the entire length of the valley ran the old Cumberland Gap and Fincastle Turnpike. A splendid modern highway now occupies the location of the old turnpike; and it is, perhaps, the most traveled road in the county.

CHAPTER IV.

DEVELOPMENT OF POLITICAL, SOCIAL AND INDUSTRIAL CHARACTER OF ITS PEOPLE.

A very important period in the history of its people was reached when the county of Tazewell was created and organized. The political, social, and industrial character of the people who then occupied the territory of the new county had to be developed and fashioned. Tazewell County had been made an integral part of the government of the Commonwealth of Virginia; and thereby constituted a unit of the great Federal Government, that eleven years previously had been brought into existence by the adoption of the Constitution and called the United States of America. George Washington had been elected and inaugurated as President of the Nation, in 1779, and had been elected for and served a second term.

Immediately following the first inauguration of President Washington it became necessary for those who had framed the Constitution to interpret its true intended import and spirit; and apply it to the conduct of the splendid Republic which the fathers had conceived from the Virginia Bill of Rights and the Declaration of Independence.

In May, 1784, Mr. Jefferson was appointed by Congress minister plenipotentiary to Europe to assist John Adams and Benjamin Franklin in negotiating treaties of commerce with the several European Powers; and in March, 1785, he was appointed minister to France to succeed Dr. Franklin. He continued as the representative of the United States at the French Court until 1789, when, at his request, he was granted a leave of absence to bring his daughters, who had been with him in Paris, back to their home at Monticello. Upon his arrival at Norfolk, Virginia, he received a letter from President Washington, urgently requesting him to enter his Cabinet as Secretary of State. At first Mr. Jefferson was reluctant to accept the position, as he wished to return to France and witness the struggle that country was making to overthrow the monarchy and establish a republican form of government. This he hoped to see done upon the principles set forth in the Virginia Bill of Rights; and a system of government established similar to

[517]

that embodied in the Constitution of the United States. But, at the urgent solicitation of John Adams, then Vice President, James Madison, and other distinguished patriots and statesmen, he accepted the appointment and became the first Secretary of State under the Constitution.

On the 8th of March, 1790, Mr. Jefferson started from Richmond for New York, then the seat of government, to enter upon the important duties of his office. He traveled by way of Philadelphia to have an interview with Dr. Franklin, who was then languishing from what proved to be his last illness. Franklin and Jefferson were equally earnest advocates of a popular democratic form of government; and were completely in accord in their interpretation of the spirit and letter of the Federal Constitution. After his interview with Franklin he journeyed on to New York, arriving there on the 21st of the month. He found that much important business had already accumulated in his Department of the Government; and was astounded by discovering that a strong desire was being expressed for a monarchical form of government by the wealthy and aristocratic families of New York. This sentiment was not confined to the aristocrats of New York, but was being espoused by such distinguished political leaders as Alexander Hamilton, Fisher Ames, Governeur Morris, and others. Some years afterwards, Mr. Jefferson said:

"Here, certainly, I found a state of things, which, of all I had ever contemplated, I least expected. I had left France in the first year of her revolution, in the fervor of natural rights, and zeal for reformation. My conscientious devotion to these rights could not be heightened, but it had been aroused and excited by daily exercise. The President received me cordially, and my colleagues and the circle of principal citizens, apparently with welcome. The courtesies of dinner parties given me, as a stranger newly arrived among them, placed me at once in their familiar society. But I cannot describe the wonder and mortification with which the table conversations filled me. Politics were the chief topic, and a preference of kingly over republican government, was evidently the favorite sentiment. An apostate I could not be, nor yet a hypocrite; and I found myself, for the most part, the only advocate on the republican side of the question, unless among the guests there chanced to be some member of that party from the legislative Houses."

From these conditions two schools of political and social thought sprang immediately into existence, and were the origin of two well defined political parties that were widely separated on the fundamental principles of civil government. One of these schools, in the main, taught the Jeffersonian creed of popular government, while the other inculcated the Hamiltonian theories of a strong centralized government, to be upheld and conducted by a wealthy and high-born class of citizens. The application of Hamilton's theories would have excluded Andrew Jackson and Abraham Lincoln from the Presidency. Jefferson held rigidly to the doctrine, afterwards enunciated by Lincoln, that "this is a government of the people, by the people, and for the people." Hamilton contended for the doctrine, that this should be "a government of the people, by a part of the people," as William Howard Taft declared it to be in his abortive campaign for re-election to the Presidency in 1912.

It was hardly possible for the Tazewell pioneers, then living, or their sons, to do otherwise than join the great Jeffersonian political legion when the county entered the State and National governments as a political unit. The spirit which led them, or their ancestors, to migrate from monarchical Europe in quest of political and religious freedom, and to leave the eastern colonies, where the colonial governments were dominated by extreme royalists, had grown in intensity after they came into the wilderness to make their homes. His cabin was for the pioneer settler a castle of freedom; and none of the first generation of men born in Tazewell had ever breathed the atmosphere of privilege; but each and every one of these had inhaled the precious ozone of the young democracy that Thomas Jefferson sought to place in charge of the new Republic.

Thus it will be seen that the political thought and characteristics of the people of Tazewell were in perfect harmony with the Popular Government and State Sovereignty theories of Thomas Jefferson. And at the very first opportunity given them as citizens of a distinct county, they so recorded their convictions. This was at the Presidential election in 1804, when Mr. Jefferson was elected President for a second term. The number of votes cast in the county at that election was very small, but the entire vote was given for the electors that were the known supporters of Thomas Jefferson.

From that time until the present day the people of Tazewell have cherished and stood firmly for popular republican government. At the Presidential election in 1828, when Andrew Jackson had become the leader and was the candidate of the Jeffersonian Democracy, a very large vote was polled, and the "Jackson Ticket For Electors" received every vote polled in the county, save three, that were cast for the electors of the Whig party. The Whigs had John Quincy Adams as their candidate for President, and Richard Rush was their candidate for Vice President. I have two of the Jackson Tickets in my possession that were used at the election in Tazewell County. One of these was voted by my father, his name being written on the back of the ballot, as required by law in that day. I have also one of the Adams Tickets which was used by James Mahood, as his name is written on its back. Politicians in 1828 were as apt as they are today in making false and alarmist appeals to the voters. The ballot used by James Mahood was taken from the Lynchburg Virginian, a Whig paper, and at its head is printed the following stirring appeal:

"This Day Fortnight, the great and eventful contest will be decided. All we need say to our friends, is, *Go To The Polls* on that day, and record your votes for *John Q. Adams, Richard Rush,* and *Civil Liberty,* against *Andrew Jackson and Military Rule, John C. Calhoun, and Disunion.*"

The demagogic appeal of the Whigs was repudiated by the freemen of Tazewell, and generally by the voters of the mountain region west of New River. Andrew Jackson was elected President in 1828, and was elected for a second term four years later. He became the political hero of the mountaineers; and it was told, that for some years after his death the older men would frequently vote for Andrew Jackson at Presidential elections. Jackson was a consistent and persistent disciple of Thomas Jefferson.

THE SOCIAL CUSTOMS.

In their social thought and relations the people of Tazewell were, comparatively, as democratic as they were in their political characteristics. The adoption and cultivation by the pioneers of a community feeling and spirit created a social system that has not entirely disappeared from the county. The first settlers had come here to get away, if possible, from the distasteful political and social customs of Europe, that were the spawn of monarchy and aristocracy. In 1774, Governor Dunmore declared, in a report to Lord Dartmouth, that it was the purpose of the frontier settlers "to form a Set of Democratical Governments of their own, upon the backs of the old Colonies; a scheme which, for obvious reasons, I apprehend cannot be allowed to be carried into execution."

Clearly it was the purpose of our pioneer ancestors to exclude from the society they were founding in the wilderness, the old distinctions of caste and privileged classes; and to establish among themselves a condition of wholesome social equality, devoid of unrighteous individualism. They sought to form a community where popular freedom could be exercised on the widest basis consistent with the general good; where each man could say what he thought, unchecked by religious creeds, and untrammeled by despotical government. That they had any desire to fashion a community that would be featured with unlicensed freedom or dominated by ruffianism, is negatived by the excellent social and domestic order that was maintained in the Upper Clinch settlements before they were incorporated with and conducted by the civil government of Virginia.

In a social way all the first settlers stood upon the same plane. They had come here seeking homes and freedom, and they, each, had precisely the same occupation, that of home-makers. Their duties as members of the community were identical—to build cabins for their families, clear fields from the forests, and from the fertile soil win an abundant subsistence for their dependents. They all, alike, had another important common duty to perform, that was to help defend the settlements against the savage enemy. If idlers or criminals tried to fasten themselves upon the community, they were forced to move on into the remote wilderness, or to return to the place from whence they came.

There were no aristocrats among the pioneer settlers; but they were not illiterate boors, as some historians would have us believe. They were intelligent and fairly well educated farmers and artisans, and in many instances combined both occupations. The common purposes, interests and duties of the pioneers invoked amongst them a state of social equality as nearly perfect as it can be found in organized human society. Thus were they and their sons prepared to receive, accept, assimilate, and uphold the great social truths written into the Virginia Bill of Rights by the fathers: "That all men are by nature equally free and independent, and have certain inherent rights, of which, when they enter into a state of society, they cannot, by any compact, deprive or divest their posterity; namely the enjoyment of life and liberty, with the means of acquiring and possessing property, and pursuing and obtaining happiness and safety."

The men of Tazewell came from the people, and, when they became a factor in the politics of the country, they heartily embraced the popular cause.

THE INDUSTRIAL CHARACTER OF THE PEOPLE.

The three physical agents—climate, soil, and the aspects of nature—have been generally accepted as the most potential factors in originating and shaping the industrial character of a nation, or the communities of which it is composed. These agents necessarily fixed for the Tazewell pioneers the vocations they and their children should adopt and follow. They had been attracted to this region by its rich lands, splendid forests, numerous fountains and streams, abundance of game, and magnificent scenery. But the supreme attraction was the fertility of the soil, which naturally produced the most nutritious herbage for both wild and domestic animals; and where heavy yields of cereals could be produced when the forests were cleared away and fields prepared for cultivation. Hence, when each settler moved in, he brought along with his family the necessary implements for making clearings and cultivating the soil—axes, hilling and grubbing hoes, colter plows, and so forth. They came here to be farmers and graziers; and from the time of their arrival all their energy was directed to agricultural pursuits.

It is a singular coincidence that the men of Tazewell not only accepted his political and social doctrines, but adopted the vocation that Thomas Jefferson, the father of American democracy, most highly esteemed. When he was minister plenipotentiary to Europe, with authority to negotiate commercial treaties with the governments of that continent, there was a very grave question connected with his work. It was, whether, in making commercial treaties with foreign countries, the maritime and manufacturing interests of the United States should have first consideration. In a private letter, written from Paris on the 23rd of August, 1785, to John Jay, then Secretary of Foreign Affairs for the Confederated States, Mr. Jefferson gave expression to some very interesting convictions on the disputed question. He said:

"Cultivators of the earth are the most valuable citizens. They are the most vigorous, the most independent, the most virtuous, and they are tied to their country, and wedded to its liberty and interests, by the most lasting bonds. As long, therefore, as they can find employment in this line, I would not convert them into mariners, artisans, or anything else. But our citizens will find employment in this line, till their numbers, and of course their productions, become too great for the demand, both internal and foreign. This is not the case as yet, and probably will not be for a considerable time. As soon as it is, the surplus of hands must be turned to something else. I should then, perhaps, wish to turn them to the sea in preference to manufactures, because, comparing the characters of the two classes, I find the former the most valuable citizens. I consider the class of artificers as the panders of vice, and the instruments by which the liberties of a country are generally overturned."

Mr. Jefferson then tells Mr. Jay, that the people of the United States, at least in those States that had deep water transportation and bordered on the sea, "are decided in the opinion, that it is necessary for us to take a share in the occupation of the ocean." He conceded that this had to be done, and then prophetically announced:

"But what will be the consequence? Frequent wars without a doubt. Their property will be violated on the sea, and in foreign ports, their persons will be insulted, imprisoned, etc., for pretended debts, contracts, crimes, contraband, etc., etc. These insults must be resented, even if we had no feelings, yet to prevent their eternal repetition; or, in other words, our commerce on the ocean and in other countries must be paid for by frequent war."

The resolve of the people of the Eastern States to make this a maritime and manufacturing nation, did provoke war; but not "frequent war," as Mr. Jefferson feared and anticipated it would.

Our war with England in 1812 was occasioned by her gross violation
of our commerce on the seas, and the insults and outrages inflicted
upon our seamen. But we gave Great Britain a sound drubbing in
that war, and no nation has since, until the recent horrible world-
wide war, dared to interfere sufficiently with our rights upon the
seas to drag us into a conflict.

We have a right to presume that the pioneers, in making choice
of a life vocation, were animated by the same spirit that induced
the Sage of Monticello to so dignify agricultural labor, by declaring
that "Cultivators of the earth are the most valuable citizens."
The experience of our country, accumulated during the past hundred and twenty-five years, has confirmed the absolute verity of
Mr. Jefferson's opinions. But, if the pioneers had not become
farmers and graziers from choice, they would have been compelled
to follow these pursuits from necessity. They had established their
homes in a region so isolated and remote from the older settlements,
that they would have found it impossible to furnish their families
with ample supplies of food, except by getting it, with their own
labor, from the rich lands on which they had settled.

The Clinch Valley settlements were then the most inaccessible
west of New River. All approaches from both the New River and
the Holston Valley were rough and dangerous. There were no
roads that could be traveled with vehicles of any kind; and the
bridle paths were steep and perilous. Over high mountains and
along narow paths everything taken to and brought from the distant
settlements had to be transported on pack-horses. Even as late as
1799, when certain citizens of Wythe and Russell petitioned the
General Assembly for the erection of a new county (Tazewell),
the first reason urged in the petition, was, that: "Our Roads also
are Intollerably bad; Many of Your Petitioners have to cross four
Large Mountains, the least of which chain, would in the Interior
parts of the State, be considered almost Impassible, And, between
each of these Mountains there are Rapid Water Courses, which in
common with all the streams Among Mountains are Quickly made
Impassible by Rains, and Renders the passage Dangerous, as well
as Fatiguing & Expensive." The petitioners had to endure these
severe hardships and dangers when traveling to and from their
respective court houses, where they said they were compelled to go
to transact their "Ordinary Business, besides Regimental Musters,

Elections &c, in which cases the Laws of the State Require our attendance."

Thirty years had passed since the first settlers came to the Clinch Valley, and with the population sufficiently increased to warrant the erection for them of a new county, the region still remained isolated and difficult of access. The existing conditions fixed inexorably the industrial status of the people of Tazewell. They were decreed, from choice and by their physical surroundings, to make agriculture their chief business; farmers and graziers they became, and their descendants and successors have wisely continued to pursue the same honorable and lucrative calling.

After the organization of the county, the attention of the land-holders was primarily directed to the breeding and raising of live-stock for market—cattle, horses, sheep, and swine. There were several cogent reasons for the adoption of this plan. One was, that, with the abundance of bluegrass that sprang up in the clearings, and the grass and pea vine that grew abundantly in the forests, it required much less labor to raise domestic animals than to produce grain. But the principal reason for making grazing their occupation was that they had no available markets for their surplus grain, on account of a lack of transportation facilities. On the other hand, they could feed their surplus grain to their cattle and horses in the winter season, and after grazing them in the summer, drive them to eastern markets and get good prices for them. From the very beginning the live-stock raised and grazed in Tazewell has been esteemed as of the best produced on the continent.

Situated four hundred miles from the ocean, and one hundred miles from the nearest navigable stream, the Ohio River, nature decreed that Tazewell County should not be what is known as a manufacturing community. But remoteness from marts, and inadequate means of transportation, made it imperative that the first settlers should be manufacturers for home consumption. They had to make fabrics for their clothing, furniture and furnishings for their homes, farm implements, etc. These articles were really home manufactures, as they were made in the homes and shops of the settlers. Gradually men in each community found it profitable to engage chiefly in mechanical pursuits, and to establish shops for custom work. But weaving, the most important industry, was still confined to the homes, and was done by the wives and daughters of each household. The manufacturing habits of the first settlers were ahered to by their descendants for several generations. Writing in 1852, under the heading, "Home Manufactures," Dr. Bickley said:

"Linsey, jeans, tow-linen, flax-thread, hose, and carpets, are the principal home manufactures of this county: the value of which, according to the census report, is twenty-five thousand four hundred dollars. I have no data from which to estimate the amount of either, but am satisfied that jeans and linsey, stand first in valueation. Tow-linen, which sells for about ten cents per yard, does not cost the Tazewell manufacturer far short of thirty cents. A like statement might be made about the whole list.

"These articles are manufactured at the houses of the farmers, their plantations supplying all the materials, except cotton, which is imported from North Carolina, spun and put up in bales. Wool is carded by machines in the county, and spun by hand. The weaving is done on the common hand-loom. House furniture, of nearly all kinds, is manufactured in the county. Saddles, boots, shoes, iron-work, etc., is also done here. Lumber of the finest quality, may here be had, for the trouble of cutting it."

Bickley thought it was a serious mistake for the farmers to have their wives and daughters give so much of their time to domestic affairs, especially to spinning, weaving, and manufacturing fabrics for clothing and other family uses. He claimed that this was done at the expense of the education of the youth of the county. If that result did follow, of course it was very unfortunate. But, if the manufacturing at home of necessary clothing and other articles for one's family is an economic error, it is also a mistake for a nation to manufacture such things for its own people, if they can be purchased from foreigners cheaper than they can be made at home. At any rate, the people of Tazewell manufactured what they could at home for a period of more than fifty years after the county was erected, and that they were happy and prosperous is beyond dispute.

There were many useful things woven by the pioneer mothers and daughters that Dr. Bickley failed to enumerate. Table linen,

napery, smooth and bleached as white as snow, made from flax
grown on the farms—broken, scotched, and hackled by the men,
boys and girls, and spun into thread as fine as hair—was a part of
the fruits that came from the looms of our foremothers.   And
counterpaines or coverlets, made from cotton or finest wool, and
blankets fleecy white, were woven on these same looms.   Some of
the counterpaines were of as exquisite design and as carefully
woven as any similar piece that ever came from an Oriental loom.

Last large walnut log exported from Tazewell County.

The walnut log shown above was cut and exported from Tazewell about fifteen years ago.   Its size can be estimated from the
horse power used to pull it over well graded roads to the railway
station.   This log, however, was almost a sapling as compared
with the immense trees that were found in the Clinch Valley by the
pioneers.   In the early days of the county a walnut tree stood on
the J. W. Sheffey place at Pounding Mill.   It was hollow at the
butt, and was blown down; and its size was so immense that a
man on horseback rode through the hollow of it.   A poplar tree
stood at the head of Thompson Valley on E. R. Thompson's land

that measured 36 feet in circumference. It was very tall and well proportioned. Some fifty years ago a poplar tree stood on Rich Hill near Pounding Mill. It was hollow at the butt. This tree broke off eighteen or twenty feet above the ground, and it was more than 10 feet in diameter inside the hollow. Isaac and Robert Patrick had a contract with Capt. Jno. P. Sheffey to clear a boundary of land where this tree stood. They were engaged on the job about two years; and they reduced the height of the stump about half, covered it and lived in the hollow for the two years.

See some of the implements the pioneer women used for manufacturing fabrics to make clothing for their families. The woman standing by the loom is Miss Nannie Gregory, one of the very few expert weavers now left in the county. She is wearing the poke bonnet her grandmother wore many years ago. The loom, which was her grandmother's, is a hundred years old, as are also the spinning wheels and reel seen in the picture.

Fortunately weaving had not become a lost art in Tazewell when the Civil War came on. Spinning wheels and old hand-looms were brought into active use during that eventful period. The men from Tazewell who were engaged in military service for the Confederacy were well supplied with clothing made from webs of cloth woven by their mothers, wives, and sisters at home. And the old-time linsey gowns did splendid service for the rosy-cheeked daughters of Tazewell. It was my good fortune to see some of the fair girls wearing these gowns, as pretty as any made from the most gorgeous Scotch plaids.

There was but little change in the industrial habits and conditions of the people of the county when the census was taken in 1850. At that time there were in the county 10 physicians, 8 lawyers, 36 teachers, 22 merchants, 9 clerks, 2 printers, 3 tavern keepers, and one barber, a total of 91 persons engaged in non-productive callings. There were 163 persons employed in mechanical and manufacturing pursuits, as follows: 10 saddlers, 1 painter, 2 hatters, 10 shoemakers, 7 brick masons, 41 carpenters, 9 millers, 11 wagon makers, 21 blacksmiths, 16 tanners, 18 cabinet makers, 2 gunsmiths, 8 tailors, 2 coopers, 1 tinner, and 1 watchmaker. According to the census there were 1,922 farmers in the county in 1850, and Tazewell County was still a pronounced agricultural community.

CHAPTER V.

From the very outset one of the most serious drawbacks to the progress and development of Tazewell was the lack of good roads. Even when the county was formed there were very few, if any, roads in the settlements over which wagons and other vehicles could pass; and there was nothing but bridle paths that crossed the mountains. If one will examine the records of the county court, it will be seen that the roads within the county limits for some years after the county was organized were a very vexing question. One of the most important reasons assigned by the petitioners for the creation of Tazewell County, was: "Our Roads also are Intolerably bad."

The first highway that was built across Clinch Mountain was the road through what was then called Thompson's Gap, and where a bridle path had previously traversed the mountain. This road began at the northern base of Clinch Mountain, at or near the house of William Thompson, in Thompson Valley. It crossed that mountain to Poor Valley, entering the valley at the present hamlet of Tannersville. The grades were very steep and the road-bed was narrow and exceedingly rough. This was for many years the only route persons could use when going from Tazewell to, or coming from, the Salt Works, or other points in the Holston Valley. Before writing his history of Virginia, Henry Howe visited Tazewell County. When he left the county he made his exit by the road through Thompson's Gap. He was so impressed with the grand scenery that he made a picture which showed a section of the road, and which was published in his history. Here is what Howe said about the scenery and road:

"It was late in a November evening that we ascended the lofty Clinch Mountain, after leaving Tazewell C. H. for Abingdon, and put up for the night at a miserable hut on its summit. The next morning the sun shone bright and clear as we buckled on our knapsack and resumed our journey through a light snow which covered the mountain-road that winds with great steepness down the declivity. In about half a mile was presented a scene of which none but a painting in the highest style of art can convey an adequate impression. The whole of a vast landscape was filled with a sea of mountains beyond mountains, in an apparently interminable continuity. Near, were huge mountains, dark and frowning, in the desolation of winter. Beyond, they assumed a deep blue color, and then grew fainter and fainter, until far away in the horizon—fifty or sixty miles—their jagged outlines were softened by distance, and sky and mountain met and mingled in the same light cerulean hue. Not a clearing was to be seen—not even a solitary smoke from some cabin curled up the intervening valleys to indicate the presence of man. It was—

> "A wild and lonely region, where, retired
> From little scenes of art Nature dwelt
> In awful solitude."

When a small boy, the author, in company with his parents and brothers, traveled over this road frequently; and even at an early age was impressed with thoughts similar to those expressed by Howe. It took nearly half a day to cross the mountain with a carriage or other vehicle. We often rested at or near the little cabin Howe mentions; and ate our lunch at the spring, whose waters were highly flavored with the laurel and ivy bushes that grew thickly on the mountain top.

After leaving Tazewell C. H., before reaching Clinch Mountain, Henry Howe had to pass through Plum Creek Gap, where the road was then rougher and more dangerous than the one which crossed Clinch Mountain. It has been a current tradition, that, in the thirties of the last century, Judge Benjamin Estill, then Judge of the Superior Court of Tazewell County, in his general charge to the grand jury at a term of his court, made special mention of the wretched condition of the Plum Creek Gap road. He had been traveling this road from Abingdon to Jeffersonville to hold his courts, and knew what a frightful pretense it was for a highway. The judge directed the grand-jury to indict the overseer of the road for neglect of duty, but took occasion to say to the jury: "You have put a road where God Almighty never intended one to be placed." What would Judge Estill say now, if he could return and view the splendid highway that passes through the Gap, over which automobiles are sped at a rate of fifteen or twenty miles an hour?

A road similar to the one that crossed Clinch Mountain at Thompson's Gap was built across Rich Mountain and through the Gap into Burke's Garden. After passing through the Garden, it connected with a similar road that crossed Garden and Brushy mountains into Wythe County, and from thence crossed Walker's Mountain, and on to Wytheville.

Plum Creek Gap, showing a section of the modern highway built on the route where Judge Estill said God never intended a road to be placed.

All the roads in the valleys were, comparatively, as wretchedly bad as thos that crossed the mountains, and most of them were even worse, especially in the winter season.

The first turnpike road that was built in, or through, the county was the Cumberland Gap and Fincastle Turnpike. It was built by the State; and, starting at Cumberland Gap, passed through the counties of Lee, Scott, and Russell, and entered Tazewell County west of Midway. Passing Midway and Liberty Hill, it ran on to Tazewell Court House. From the Court House it ran by way of

the north fork of Clinch River and through the Bluestone Valley
to the head of East River; and thence down that stream to New
River. From that point the turnpike continued up the river, passed
through the Narrows, on by Pearisburg, and again reached New
River at Ripplemead. There persons traveling the road were
ferried across the river, at the same place the pioneers crossed the
stream when they came to the Clinch. On the east side of New
River the Cumberland Gap and Fincastle Turnpike began again.

One of the most beautiful old homes in Tazewell County. It
was built for Colonel Harvey George in 1832; and is on the old
Fincastle and Cumberland Gap Turnpike, about six miles west of the
court house. In recent years it was the home of the late John Bundy,
and is now owned and occupied by one of his sons, Wm. Rees Bundy.

Thence it passed Newport in Giles County, ran up Sinking Creek
into the present Craig County to Newcastle; and thence to Fincastle. The road was built in the thirties of the last century.

The Tazewell C. H. and Fancy Gap Turnpike, which ran from
Jeffersonville to Wytheville; and the Kentucky and Tazewell C. H.
Turnpike, which ran from Jeffersonville to Grundy, the present
county seat of Buchanan County, were chartered by the Legislature in 1848, and were constructed just prior to 1852. These two
turnpikes are shown on a map in Bickley's History of Tazewell

County, published in 1852; and the Cumberland Gap and Fincastle Turnpike also appears on the said map.

From the time the Cumberland Gap and Fincastle Turnpike was constructed, until about 1850 or 1851, that road was the principal thoroughfare used by the people of Tazewell County for conveying their products to the eastern markets. And all the merchandise and other articles purchased in the eastern markets for consumption in Tazewell were brought here in wagons over this same road. The cattle and horses that were sold from the county were driven east by this route. Sometimes droves of cattle numbering a thous-

This scene is located on what is called "Hubble Hill"; and the modern road is built on the location of the old Tazewell C. H. and Kentucky Turnpike. Looking south Rich Mountain is seen in the distance. All of the mountain visible in the picture is denuded of the heavy original forest, and the sides and top of the mountain are covered with as fine bluegrass sod as can be found in the world.

and, or more, head would be driven to the Valley of Virginia and to Northern Virginia; and there disposed of in bunches to farmers, who would graze and prepare them for the markets, just as the export cattle are now prepared by the Tazewell graziers for exporting.

After the State built the splendid macadam road, which extended in an unbroken line from Buchanan, in Botetourt County, to Seven Mile Ford, in Smyth County, travel and traffic from and to Tazewell was almost completely diverted from that part of the Cumberland Gap and Fincastle Turnpike east of Bluefield. Transportation was then directed across the mountains to Wytheville over the Tazewell C. H. and Fancy Gap Turnpike; and from Wytheville the haul was continued eastward until the advancing line of the Virginia & Tennessee Railroad was reached. The track of this road was slowly laid in the direction of Bristol, and got to Wytheville in 1855. From the eastern part of the county all travel and traffic was then directed to Wytheville, until the Norfolk & Western built its line from Radford to Graham.

In 1858-59 the Tazewell and Saltville Turnpike was built from the Cove across Clinch and Little Brushy mountains to Poor Valley; and from that time the travel and traffic from the west end of the

A view of the Main Street of Tazewell, taken ten or twelve years ago. Since then great improvements have been made to the street and buildings.

county went to Saltville. The branch railroad from Glade Spring to Saltville had been previously built, giving to the citizens of the west end of Tazewell County greatly improved transportation facilities.

Isolation and inaccesibility have always been regarded as two of the most powerful retardments to the progress and development of a nation, state, or community. Against these uncompromising foes of wealth and civilization the Tazewell pioneers and their descendants and successors were compelled to persistently contend for more than a hundred years after the first settlements were made here. But there are other great physical causes which influence and govern the creation and accumulation of wealth and the development of a high civilization in nations or communities. Among these causes are a fertile soil and an invigorating climate. Fortunately both of these—a rich soil and an invigorating climate—were attributes of the Clinch Valley region; and proved ample to mitigate and largely overcome the disadvantages of isolation and inaccessibility from which the inhabitants of Tazewell suffered before railroads came and gave them access to the outside world.

INCREASE IN POPULATION AND WEALTH.

Although the people of Tazewell were greatly hampered by their isolation, there was a steady and healthy increase in the population and wealth of the county from its organization to the beginning of the Civil War. The population was 2,127 when the county was organized in 1800. The census taken by the United States each succeeding ten years placed the population of the county as follows: In 1810, 3,007; 1820, 3,916; 1830, 5,749; 1840, 6,290; 1850, 9,942; 1860, 9,920. It will be seen that there was a decrease of 22 in the population of the county during the ten years that intervened between 1850 and 1860. This was due to the formation of McDowell and Buchanan counties, all of the territory which composed McDowell County and most of that embraced in Buchanan being taken from Tazewell County. McDowell had a population of 1,535 in 1860, and Buchanan had 2,793, a combined population of 4,328. If these two counties had not been created previous to the census of 1860, Tazewell's population would have been about 13,000.

The increase in the wealth of the county during the first fifty years of its existence was normal and satisfactory. Bickley published in his history in 1852 the following table showing the wealth of the county:

"Table Showing The Wealth of The County.

"Value of lands			$3,189,080.00
"	"	farming utensils	36,390.00
"	"	live stock	517,330.00
"	"	agricultural productions	226,579.00
"	"	mechanical productions	7,000.00
"	"	slave property	530,000.00
"	"	stock in trade	85,000.00
Total wealth of the county			$4,591,379.00"

Bickley published another table in his history which showed that there were 58,110 acres of improved, 220,530 acres unimproved, and 1,641,360 acres of land unentered or in large surveys within the bounds of the county in 1852. These figures he must have obtained from the assessors books for that year; and it is evident that most of the unentered land and the large surveys were in the bounds of the present McDowell and Buchanan counties. The improved lands were valued in Bickley's table at $696,320 an average of about $10 per acre. This must have been the assessed value, as many

A bunch of Dorset lambs, over one hundred in number, that were bred and grazed by the late Henry S. Bowen. They had been weighed at the scales of the Packing House at North Tazewell, and averaged 102 lbs. The lambs at that time brought about five or six dollars each. In 1919 they would have sold for fifteen dollars per head.

thousand acres of the improved lands had a much larger actual or sales value at that time, for Bickley said of the lands in the vicinity of the county seat:

"The lands are well improved; and will compare favorably with any in the county. There are many fine farms near the town, among which may be mentioned those of Thos. Peery, Esq., John Wynn, Esq., Col. John B. George, Kiah Harman, Henry, Elias, G. W., and William Harman, Joseph, and Thomas G. Harrisson, A. A. Spotts, Harvey G. Peery, Esq., and Dr. H. F. Peery. 50,000 acres of these lands, are worth from forty to fifty dollars an acre, and little could be purchased for even that sum."

There were other localities in the county where the lands were considered as valuable, even more valuable than those about Jeffersonville. The lands in Burke's Garden were nearer the markets and as fertile as any in the county; and in writing about the Cove, including the lands of Colonel Henry and General Rees T. Bowen, Bickley said: "I hesitate not to call this the garden-spot of Tazewell county." The lands that Bickley wrote about in 1852 now have an average sales value of $200 per acre, or more. Tazewell's first historian compiled from the census of 1850 a table showing the kind, number and value of the live stock in the county. It is as follows:

Specified kinds.	Number.	Value.
Horses	5,150	$309,000.00
Mules and asses	127	8,890.00
Milch cows	4,576	54,840.00
Working oxens	117	2,340.00
Other cattle	10,260	102,600.00
Sheep	19,530	19,530.00
Swine	20,130	20,130.00

Total Value of live stock $517,330.00

In the above table, compiled by Dr. Bickley, it will be seen that cows were valued at $11 per head. The sheep and hogs were, each, valued at $1 per head. These were certainly very low valuations, as wool was then worth thirty cents, and bacon not less than ten cents a pound, and the valuations must have been based on assessed and not on the sales value of the animals.

But if the values given by Bickley, of lands and live stock, be accepted as fair and adequate, still it is evident that Tazewell County had, during the first fifty years of its existence, developed into a community of considerable wealth. This conclusion is strongly sustained by the fact that the economic condition of the county had become so excellent that two banks were established in Jeffersonville as early as 1852. One of these was a branch bank of the Northwestern Bank of Virginia, the mother bank being located at Wheeling, then in Virginia, but now in West Virginia. It was a bank of issue, deposit, and discount. In 1852 its officers were: President, John W. Johnston; Cashier, Isaac M. Benham; Clerk, Rees B. Gillispie.

The Directors were as follows: John C. McDonald, John B. George, Kiah Harman, Geo. W. G. Browne, S. F. Watts, Samuel L. Graham, and Isaac E. Chapman. This bank had a capital of $100,000, and Friday of each week was discount day. It was a flourishing institution and continued to do business until all the State banks passed out of existence during the Civil War.

John Warfield Johnston was born near Abingdon, Virginia, September 19th, 1818. His mother was a sister of Gen. Rees T. Bowen. He received his academic education at Abingdon Academy, and South Carolina College, Columbia, S. C.; studied law at the University of Virginia; and was admitted to the bar in 1839. He located at Jeffersonville, and was Commonwealth's Attorney for Tazewell County in 1844-1846. He represented the county and district in the State Senate at the sessions of 1844-45 and 1846-47. In 1866 he was made judge of this judicial circuit and served as such until 1870. He was elected to the United States Senate from Virginia, and served in that body from October 26th, 1869, to March 3rd, 1883. Judge Johnston died in Richmond, February 27th, 1889.

The other bank was the Jeffersonville Savings Bank. Its officers were: Cashier or Treasurer, Addison A. Spotts; Secretary, William O. Yost. The Directory was constituted as follows: Thomas Peery, Rees T. Bowen, A. A. Spotts, Granville Jones, William Cox, William O. Yost, John C. Hopkins. Capital, by limitation, $100,000. Discount day, Saturday. This bank passed out of existence before the Civil War began.

The religious character of the inhabitants of the county was coexistent and developed along with the social, political, and religious thought of the people. It was my intention to give an accurate and detailed account of the introduction and growth of the various religious denominations that now have church organizations in the county. For the accomplishment of this purpose the ministers and leading lay members of the several denominations were requested to supply necessary data; but the world war so completely engrossed every one's attention that they failed to supply the author with any information in time. Dr. Bickley in his history had a brief chapter on the Church History of Tazewell, which gives some information about the various denominations in the county in the year 1852. It is as follows:

"No portion of my labors, if properly investigated, would be more interesting than this: yet the paucity of material afforded me, makes it quite difficult to give anything like a correct and full church history of this section. The principal denominations in the county are Methodists, Baptists, Presbyterians, and Roman Catholic; each of whom will be noticed.

"The first sermon preached in the county was in 1794, by Rev. Mr. Cobbler, appointed to the New River circuit, by the Baltimore conference. This sermon may be regarded as the budding of Methodism in Tazewell county. The seeds sown by this good man fell upon a genial soil, and he had the satisfaction of seeing Jeremiah Witten and Mrs. Sarah Witten, William Witten and his lady, John and Sarah Peery, Elizabeth Greenup, Samuel Forguson, Isabella Forguson, and two colored persons, flock around the Christian standard, determined that Christ should not be forgotten, even in the mountain-gorges of the wild 'backwoods.'

"Thomas Peery gave them a piece of land, and in 1797 they built a meetinghouse about one mile west of Jeffersonville.

"Between 1794-7, meetings were generally held at the house of Samuel Forguson, near the present seat of justice. Before 1794, prayer-meeting was the only form of worship practiced: this seems to have been coexistent with the earliest settlement. The march of Methodism has been steadily onward; they have, at present, seven churches in regular fellowship.

"The first Baptists in the county, were the Seaggs and Hankins. The first sermon preached to them, was by Rev. Simon Cotterel from Russell county, in 1796. Their first meetings were held in private houses, in the Hankins' settlement. The Baptists seem not to have made as rapid progress as the Methodists; as they have now only two regular churches in the county. I have been unable to learn the number of communicants, but understand that it is greater than would be supposed from the number of churches.

"The first Presbyterians in the county were William Peery, Samuel Walker, and his wife. Prof. Doak preached the first sermon to them, somewhere about 1798. He was soon followed by Rev. Mr. Crawford, from Washington county. The first church organized was in the Cove, in 1833, which was placed in charge of Rev. Dugald McIntyre, assisted by Rev. Mr. McEwin. This church, from some cause, was suffered to go down, and the Presbyterians were without a regular church till the summer of 1851, when a church was organized at Jeffersonville, and placed in charge of Rev. Mr. Naff. They have one church, and about twenty communicants.

"At what time the first Roman Catholics appeared in the county, is not known. Edward Fox, a priest who resided at Wytheville, preached the first sermon to them in a union church at Jeffersonville in 1842. He continued to preach, at intervals, till the close of the controversy between him, and President Collins of Emory and Henry College. Having been beaten from every position, he quit Wytheville, and consequently the Tazewell Catholics were left without a priest. Bishop Whelan coming to this section of the state, took occasion to visit his flock in Tazewell; the Methodists opened their pulpit for him, and in acknowledgment of their kindness, one of his first sentences was not only to insult them, but the house of God. He remarked, he "felt embarassed because he was preaching in an unconsecrated house." President Collins, who had firmly opposed the spread of this doctrine in South-western Virginia, being in the neighborhood, heard of the occurrence and replied to him in a few days. Notwithstanding this, Catholicism began to spread, and preparations were made for building a cathedral, which is now in course of construction."

As to things spiritual, it is questionable whether there has been much progress made on that line in the county since the days of which Bickley wrote. There are more church organizations, more Christian denominations, more numerous and handsomer church buildings, and there are hundreds of professed Christians where there were but tens in the early days of the county.

The people who attend worship are better dressed, and better educated; and thousands of youths and children are being trained in Sunday Schools and other church organizations that have been established for their benefit. The music is of a higher class, but it does not have the same spiritual force and feeling that attended the congregational singing heard at the old camp meetings and within the sacred walls of the old log churches at Pisgah, Concord and elsewhere in the county. It may be possible that the churches are becoming materialized at the expense of their spirituality.

EDUCATIONAL CONDITIONS.

At that time there was one thing, that historians, generally, pronounce as absolutely essential to the welfare, progress, and civilization of a state or community, in which the people of Tazewell were deplorably deficient. They had accepted and made practical use of the social, political, and economic doctrines of Thomas Jefferson; but had neglected to follow his precepts as the champion of popular education. It may be possible that the isolation of Tazewell rendered it difficult to get competent and sufficient teachers to give instruction to the large number of children then in the county. Whatever may have been the cause, it is a fact that from the time the county was organized there was a constant increase of illiteracy among the inhabitants, certainly until 1852, and, possibly, until the present free school system was established by the State Constitution of 1870.

The entire white population of Tazewell in 1852 was 8,832; and there were 1,490 white persons over twenty-one years of age who could neither read nor write. It is likely that there were nearly as many illiterate whites who were under twenty-one years old as there were above that age. There were only 694 children attending the schools, and but fifteen school houses in the entire county. Bickley said these houses were better suited for barns than seats of learning.

This alarming condition of illiteracy aroused the serious attention of the Jeffersonville Historical Society, whose membership was composed of about a hundred of the most influential citizens of the county. The late Major Rufus Brittain was then an accomplished and popular teacher, and was earnestly engaged in educational work in the county. At the request of the Jeffersonville Historical Society he prepared a paper on the educational situation, which was submitted to the Historical Society. It was and is a very valuable paper, and is as follows:

"This cause, so important to the best interests of every well-regulated community, has not heretofore, in this section, received

High School Building at Tazewell. It is very different in appearance and appointments from the few school houses scattered over the county in 1852, which Bickley said were better suited for barns than seats of learning.

that attention it deserves: and as a natural consequence of this neglect, we find the county sadly deficient in the means of training up the children of her citizens for stations of honor and usefulness.

"By the returns of the last census, it is found that out of 3,317 persons in the county over twenty-one years of age, 1,490 are unable to read and write. This is indeed a deplorable picture of the intelligence of our county, and might well cause every intelligent man in it to blush with shame, were it not that we find some excuse for this ignorance when we consider the situation of the greater

portion of our population, scattered as it is over a wide extent of
country, and laboring under great disadvantages for maintaining
schools.

"The early settlers of this region had many difficulties to
encounter in their efforts to procure homes for themselves and their
children, and too frequently education appears to have been of but
secondary importance in their estimation. Yet primary schools
of some sort seem to have been maintained from an early date after
its settlement, in those neighborhoods where children were sufficiently numerous to make up a school, and parents were able and
willing to support a teacher. Instances, also, have not been wanting,
where families not situated so as to unite conveniently with others,
yet appreciating the advantages of a good school, have employed
teachers to instruct their children at home, and thus afforded them
privileges of which the children of their less enlightened neighbors
were deprived. But of late years, since portions of the county
have become more densely populated, and in various ways much
improved, the cause of education here has not kept pace with that
improvement, for even in those parts of the county best able to
maintain schools, no permanent provision has been made for their
continuance; and in those schools that generally have been best
supported, long intervals between sessions so frequently occur, that
pupils forget much of what they acquired during their attendance;
and thus the little time spent by many in school is spent under the
greatest disadvantage for the proper development of their intellectual faculties. Teachers, as might be supposed, under these
circumstances, together with the fact that their compensation is
usually very moderate, are often incompetent for the task they
have assumed, both as respects talents and acquired qualifications.
And though under these circumstances good teachers are sometimes
obtained, yet most generally in such cases the office is only assumed
as an available stepping-stone to some other and more profitable
pursuit. Indeed, it would be unreasonable to expect persons to
prepare themselves for the proper discharge of the onerous duties
of a primary school teacher, unless they hoped to receive some
adequate reward for their services.

"Now, in consideration of the state of our schools, and the
deplorable ignorance in which the children of our county are in
danger of growing up, it must be evident to all who think properly
on these subjects, that we need to adopt and carry out some effi-

cient school system, by means of which, our schools shall be made
more permanent, and sufficient inducements be held out to command
and retain the services of competent and well qualified teachers:
and that the means of a good primary education be brought within
the reach of every child in the community, and for those who desire
it and excel in the branches taught in primary schools, that oppor-

Major Rufus Brittain, was not a native of Tazewell County, but
came there when he was a very young man, to engage in educational
work. In this vocation he performed eminent service, and also filled
many positions of trust and responsibility, among them county clerk
and county treasurer. He served in the Confederate army as Adjutant
of the 29th Regiment Virginia Infantry. Major Brittain was born
June 19th, 1822, and died April 11th, 1899.

tunities be afforded to acquire a knowledge of the higher branches
of a good English and scientific education.

"These important objects, our schools, as now conducted, fail
to accomplish, and the state school-fund for the education of indigent
children, is in a great measure wasted, as by its regulations, it must
depend chiefly on the schools as they now exist.

"But the legislature of the state has provided a Free School
System, which if adopted and carried out with proper energy and
in an enlightened manner, these noble objects, in a great measure,
might be attained. In order to its adoption the law requires a vote
in its favor of two-thirds of the legal votes of the adopting district
or county. Such a vote, we fear, could not be obtained here, until

some effort is made to enlighten our citizens on the subject of education and schools systems; and show them the advantage that would accrue to themselves and their children by having the latter furnished with the proper means of moral and intellectual culture. There would also be a variety of difficulties to encounter in the execution of this Free School System. In some portions of the county the population is quite sparse, and a sufficient number of children could not be included within a convenient school district. This difficulty, however, has no remedy under our present method of keeping up the schools, unless families thus isolated are able to employ teachers to instruct their children at home. But if the schools were established in these thinly-settled districts, by taking in boundaries large enough to furnish a sufficient number of children to each, and some efforts made to overcome the inconvenience of a distant school, by conveying the children to and from school in such a manner as could best be provided: the mere fact of a good school being kept up, would be a new inducement for persons to emigrate to those districts, and in a few years the population would so much increase that a school could be made up within convenient bounds. This system, also, being chiefly dependent on funds raised for its support by taxation, might meet with great opposition from those who have a higher appreciation of the value of money than they have of intelligence; and, again, others who are possessed of large amounts of taxable property and few or no children to send to school, may think it oppressive, unless convinced that it is the duty of every state or community to educate, or furnish the means to educate, the children of its citizens. In a republican government like ours, the permanence of which evidently depends on the virtue and intelligence of its citizens, it might be deemed unnecessary to demonstrate the importance of every child being properly instructed and furnished with the means of acquiring that knowledge which will fit him to perform the duties incumbent on a citizen of a free and enlightened country. Yet there are too many who are slow to perceive or acknowledge the importance of good schools, and the necessity of being at some trouble and expense to keep them up. Hence all patriotic and intelligent members of the community who have tasted the blessings of an education, or felt the want of one, should co-operate with each other, and use their influence for the improvement of our schools, and the increase of the virtue and intelligence of our citizens."

CHAPTER VI.

THE ORIGIN AND DESCENT OF TAZEWELL COUNTY.

Nearly two hundred years intervened between the first settlement at Jamestown and the erection of Tazewell County as a distinct civil organization. And it was more than a hundred years after Captain Newport landed the colonists on the banks of James River before any definite information was obtained of the character of the extensive region that belonged to Virginia west of the Blue Ridge Mountains. It was nearly a century and a half after the settlement was made at Jamestown before Virginians began to explore the country beyond the Alleghany Mountains, "on the waters of the Mississippi."

A detailed synopsis which will show how Tazewell County came into existence as a distinct civil community, and how its present geographical lines were established, will, no doubt, be instructive and useful to many persons. The territory which now constitutes the county of Tazewell was within the geographical lines of the charters granted by James I. for the colonization of Virginia. Previous to the year 1716 Virginians who lived east of the Blue Ridge had not the slightest conception of the extent and quality of the uninhabited part of the province beyond the mountains. The Trans-Alleghany domain remained a vast unexplored, mysterious region, having no civil or military connection with the Colonial Government at Williamsburg. Governor Spottswood's expedition to the Shenandoah Valley in 1716 gave the first partial knowledge to Virginians of the character of the English territory beyond the Blue Ridge.

The first attempt to bring any part of the vast trans-montane region under the Virginia Colonial Government was the creation of Spottsylvania County, by an act passed November the 2nd, 1720. The county was formed from the counties of Essex, King William, and King and Queen. Its boundaries crossed the Blue Ridge, but took in only a part of the Upper Shenandoah Valley. Very few settlers moved into that valley while a section of it was a part of Spottsylvania.

On September, 20th., 1734, the General Assembly passed an act creating Orange County. It was formed from Spottsylvania; and not only took in a part of Spottsylvania east of the Blue Ridge, but it embraced all of Virginia west of that mountain. The act creating Orange provided that its Northern and Western boundaries should be extended to "the utmost limits of Virginia." This made the territory of the present Tazewell County a part of Orange County.

Four years after the formation of Orange, the Virginia Government ascertained that a number of people had availed themselves of the very liberal provisions of the act which created that county; and had "settled themselves of late upon the rivers of Sherrando (Shenandoah), Cohongorton, and Opeckon, and the branches thereof, on the northwest side of the Blueridge of Mountains." This discovery induced the General Assembly to pass an act on December, 15th, 1738, for the erection of two new counties to be taken from Orange, and to comprise all the territory lying west and northwest of the Blue Ridge. These two new counties were Frederick and Augusta. They were named from Frederick, Prince of Wales, son of King George II., and father of George III., and his wife, Princess Augusta. The northern line of Augusta, embraced the present Rockingham County, and part of Page; its southern boundary was the line between Virginia and North Carolina, and the present State of Tennessee; and its western and northwestern boundaries extended to the utmost limits of the province of Virginia. Though Augusta was created by the General Assembly in 1738, it was not organized until 1745. The act provided that it should remain a part of Orange County until the Governor and Council were informed there was "a sufficient number of inhabitants for appointing justices of the peace and other officers, and erecting courts therein." As soon as Augusta County was organized, what is now Tazewell County, and all of Southwest Virginia, became a part of Augusta.

The General Assembly passed an act on the 28th, of November, 1769, for the division of Augusta into two counties. This act declared: "That from and after the thirty-first day of January next ensuing, the said county and parish of Augusta, be divided into two counties and parishes;" the new county taken from Augusta was named Botetourt. The lines between Augusta and Botetourt began at the Blue Ridge and ran north fifty-five degrees west to the confluence of the South and North branches of James River, which point is in the present county of Rockbridge. From that place the line ran up the south branch of the river to the mouth of

Carr's Creek, thence up that creek to the mountain, and thence north fifty-five degrees west "as far as the courts of the two counties shall extend it." All the territory south and west of this line was placed in Botetourt. A Commission of Peace was issued by the Governor of Virginia, appointing the following named persons justices of the peace for Botetourt County: "Andrew Lewis, Richard Woods, Robert Brackenridge, William Preston, John Bowyer, Israel Christian, John Maxwell, James Trimble, Benjamin Hawkins, David Robinson, William Fleming, George Skillern, and Benjamin Estell. On the 13th of February the county court was organized, with Andrew Lewis presiding. John May qualified as clerk under "a commission from Mr. Secretary Nelson," Richard Woods qualified as sheriff under a commission from the Governor; and James McDowell and James McGavock qualified as his deputies. William Preston qualified as surveyor under a commission from the President and Masters of William and Mary College and the seal of the College. Preston also qualified as Escheator under a commission from the Governor. Tazewell County for the succeeding two years was a part of Botetourt County. Settlements had previously been made in the Upper Clinch Valley, and the county court of Botetourt at its May term, 1770, ordered Anthony Bledsoe to make a list of the tithables in the Clinch settlements. The settlers on the Clinch and the Holston then had to go to Fincastle, the county seat of Botetourt, to attend courts and perform the ordinary duties of citizenship. At the August term, 1770, of the county court, Rees Bowen, from the Clinch, and Arthur Campbell, from the Holston settlements, were selected by the litigants to arbitrate a suit in which Thomas Baker was plaintiff and Israel Christian was defendant. Bowen and Campbell a few years later became very distinguished as citizens and soldiers. Israel Christian was a justice of the county court and donated the land whereon the county seat, Fincastle, is located.

Responding to a petition of the inhabitants who lived west of New River, the General Assembly on the 8th of April, 1772, passed an act for dividing Botetourt into two counties. The new county was named Fincastle, and the county seat was located at the Lead Mines in the present Wythe County. Organization of the county government of Fincastle was effected on the 5th day of January, 1773. All the territory west of New River and south of the Ohio, including Kentucky, was placed in the bounds of the new county; and the present Tazewell County became a part of Fincastle County.

About three years after the organization of Fincastle County, in 1776, the people of Virginia revolted against Great Britain, and established for themselves an independent government—the Commonwealth of Virginia. Shortly afterwards, the inhabitants of Kentucky petitioned the General Assembly to form the territory they were occupying into a distinct county. Thereupon the inhabitants east of the Cumberland Mountains addressed petitions to the General Assembly, requesting that the balance of Fincastle County, lying east of said mountain, be divided into two distinct counties. In answer to the said petition, the General Assembly on December 7th, 1776, passed an act which divided Fincastle County into three counties, to be named, respectively, Kentucky, Washington, and Montgomery. When the line between the last mentioned counties was run a part of the territory afterwards erected into the county of Tazewell was put in Washington, but the greater part was assigned to Montgomery.

In 1785 the inhabitants of that part of Washington County situated west and north of the Clinch Mountain petitioned the General Assembly for the formation of a new county. An act was passed on January 6th, 1786, in response to the petition, erecting a county which was named Russell, in honor of General William Russell, the pioneer patriot. The southeastern dividing line between Washington and Russell began on the top of Clinch Mountain, opposite and south of Morris' Knob, and ran along the said mountain to the North Carolina, now Tennessee, line. All the territory now embraced in Lee, Scott, Wise, Dickenson, and Russell, and part of the territory of Tazewell and Buchanan counties was comprised in the original boundaries of Russell County. Pursuant to the act of the General Assembly, the county court of Russell convened at the house of William Roberson in Castle's Woods, on May 9th, 1786, and organized the county government. David Ward, one of the first settlers in Tazewell, was one of the justices commissioned for Russell by Patrick Henry, who was then filling a second term as Governor of Virginia. Captain Ward also qualified as the first sheriff of the county. Part of the present Tazewell County was then within the limits of Russell County.

The inhabitants of Montgomery County who lived west of

New River sent a petition to the General Assembly, in 1789, asking that a new county be erected from that part of Montgomery lying west of New River. On December 1st, 1789, an act was passed for dividing the county of Montgomery into two counties. And the act provided: "That from and after the first day of May next, all that part of the county of Montgomery, which lies southwest of a line beginning on the Henry line, at the head of Big Reedy Island, from thence to the wagon ford on Peek Creek, thence to Clover Bottom on Bluestone, thence to the Kanawha County line, shall be a distinct county, and be called and known by the name of Wythe."

On the 19th of December, 1799, the General Assembly passed an act creating the county of Tazewell, to be formed from a part of Wythe, and a part of Russell. From the foregoing synopsis of the processes by which Tazewell County came into existence it is easy to trace its civil descent from the first colony planted at Jamestown. The following is the line of descent:

"The Grand Assemblie Holden at James City the 21st of August, 1633," passed an act that divided the Virginia Colony into eight shires, which were to be governed as the shires of England, and named as follows:

"James City	Warwick River
Henrico	Warrosquyoak
Charles City	Charles River
Elizabeth City	Accawmack"

"The Grand Assemblie, holden at James Citty the 2nd of March, 1642-3" passed an act which declared in part: "It is likewise enacted and confirmed that Charles River shall be distinguished by this name (County of York)." This meant that Charles River Shire, created by the act of August 21st, 1633, should thereafter be known as York County, and in this manner York County was created in 1643.

New Kent County was formed from York County in 1654.

King and Queen County was formed from New Kent in 1691, the third year of the reign of William and Mary.

Essex County was formed from a part of (old) Rappahannock in 1692. "Old Rappahannock" having previously been a part of York County.

Thus it is seen that the two counties, King and Queen and Essex, were directly descended from Charles River Shire.

King William County was formed from King and Queen County in 1701.

Spottsylvania was formed from Essex, King and Queen, and King William in 1720.

Orange County was formed from Spottsylvania in 1724.

Augusta County was formed from Orange in 1738.

Botetourt County was formed from Augusta in 1769.

Fincastle County was formed from Botetourt in 1772.

Washington County and Montgomery County were formed from Fincastle in 1776.

Russell County was formed from Washington in 1786.

Wythe County was formed from Montgomery in 1789.

Tazewell County was formed from Wythe and Russell in 1799.

By and through the foregoing detailed processes, covering a period of one hundred and ninety-two years, the great county of Tazewell was generated from the first permanent English settlement made upon the North American Continent.

CHANGES MADE IN THE GEOGRAPHICAL LINES OF TAZEWELL COUNTY.

After the formation of Tazewell County, in 1799, various changes were made in its geographical lines before it was reduced to its present limitations. A few of the changes were caused by accretions to the original limits, but most of the alterations were made by taking from the county large areas that have since been disclosed as veritable El Dorados of mineral wealth. The first change that was made in the boundary lines was occasioned by the creation of Giles County. It was formed from the counties of Montgomery, Monroe, Tazewell, and Wythe, by an act passed January 16th, 1806. This eliminated from the eastern side of Tazewell County, a valuable strip of territory east of Rocky Gap, which extended from the top of Brushy Mountain to the Kanawha County line.

On the 20th of December, 1806, the General Assembly passed an act which provided for taking a narrow strip from Russell County, and attaching it to Tazewell. The western line of this boundary has been given in a preceding chapter, and need not be restated.

The General Assembly passed an act on the 12th of January, 1824, creating Logan County. That county was formed from Giles, Kanawha, Cabell, and Tazewell, and was named from Logan, the great Indian chief. The territory taken from Tazewell, has, in recent years, become very wealthy.

A very considerable and valuable addition to the territory of Tazewell was made by an act of the General Assembly, on January 4th, 1826. This act placed Poor Valley in Tazewell. When I began writing the history of the county, I made inquiry of county officers, and the lawyers at Tazewell, and many of the older citizens, and no one could inform me how Poor Valley became a part of the county. I searched for information in the State Library, and found the following passed by the General Assembly as above stated:

"Whereas it is represented to the present General Assembly, by sundry inhabitants of the counties of Washington and Wythe, that in consequence of the great distance at which they reside from their court houses, muster-fields, and other public places, and having in going thither to cross three large mountains, they labour under great inconvenience and difficulty, and the tract of country in which they reside being very thinly inhabited, and not likely soon to be otherwise; wherefore,

"I. Be it enacted by the General Assembly, That all that part of the counties of Washington and Wythe, known by the name of Poor Valley, and within the following boundaries, to wit: "Beginning on the top of Clinch Mountain, at the highest point opposite the plantation of Major John Ward; thence a south course until it strikes the top of little Piney Mountain in the county of Washington, and with the top of said mountain, running east to Wilson's Gap in the county of Wythe, thence a north course until it intersects the Tazewell county line, shall be a part of the county of Tazewell."

On January 9th, 1826, the General Assembly passed an act which took from Tazewell a small boundary of territory and added it to Giles County.

An act was passed on March 12th, 1834, restoring a part of Logan County to Tazewell. The boundary lines of the restored section were as follows: "Beginning at the Dry fork of Sandy river, and running thence a northern course to the top of the ridge dividing the waters of Guyandotte and Sandy Rivers; thence along the top of said ridge to the Flat Top Mountain (so as to include the now residence of James Marshall) to the line of Tazewell County, where it corners on Logan and Giles counties, shall be annexed to and be henceforth a part of the county of Tazewell."

By an act of the General Assembly passed on February 3rd, 1835, Tazewell had another accretion from Russell County. The act is as follows: "I. Be it enacted by the General Assembly, that so much of the county of Russell as lays next to and adjoining the county of Tazewell, and is contained in the following boundary lines, to wit: beginning at the line dividing the counties on the top of Kent's ridge, thence a straight line (crossing Clinch river a short distance below the mouth of Mill Creek) to the forks of said creek, thence up said creek, (the north branch thereof) to the top of the dividing ridge between Sandy and Clinch rivers, leaving the road to the northeast, thence along the top of said ridge to the ridge of mountains dividing the Louisa and Russell forks of Sandy river, and down said ridge of mountains to the Kentucky line, shall be annexed to, and be henceforth a part of the county of Tazewell."

On March 18th, 1836, another small boundary was taken from Tazewell and added to Giles by an act of the General Assembly, and defined as follows: "That so much of the farm formerly owned by Archibald Burdett (and now by George W. Pearis) containing three hundred and thirty-seven acres, as lies within the county of Tazewell, shall be annexed to and be henceforth a part of the county of Giles." This farm was located on East River.

The General Assembly by an act passed on March 17th, 1837, formed the county of Mercer from the counties of Giles and Tazewell. This new county was named from General Hugh Mercer, who was mortally wounded at the battle of Princeton, January 3rd, 1777. He was one of the splendid heroes of the American Revolution, and the county seat of Mercer County was given its name in commemoration of the battle in which General Mercer lost his life. The act of the General Assembly separated from Tazewell County territory that has since been developed into one of the richest mineral sections of the North American Continent. The boundary lines of the new county established by the General Assembly, were as follows:

"Beginning at the mouth of East river in Giles county and following the meanders thereof (East River) up to Toney's mill dam; thence along the top of said mountain (East River Mountain) to a point opposite the upper end of the old plantation of Jesse Belcher deceased, thence a straight line to Peerie's mill dam near the mouth of Alps (Abbs) Valley, thence to a point well known by the name of the Pealed Chestnuts; thence to the top of Flat top mountain; thence along said mountain with the lines of Logan, Fayette and Tazewell counties to New River, thence up and along the various meanderings of the same to the beginning."

An examination of the act creating Mercer County, as printed in the Acts of 1836-1837, reveals the fact that the second line or call, defining the boundaries, was omitted from the printed act. This omission was rectified by an act passed by the General Assembly on March 13th, 1847. The act directed that this omitted line be run by commissioners, commencing at "Toney's Mill dam and run thence a direct line to the top of East River Mountain," and thence for the residue of said lines as prescribed by the act of March 17th, 1837. The omitted line was duly run by commissioners.

There were no further alterations in the outlines of Tazewell County until 1858, when the counties of Buchanan and McDowell were formed. On February 13th, 1858, the General Assembly passed an act creating Buchanan County to be formed from parts of the counties of Tazewell and Russell. And on the 20th of February, 1858, the General Assembly passed an act to form a new county out of a part of the county of Tazewell, to be called and known by the name of the county of McDowell.

The dividing line between Tazewell and Buchanan begins at a point on the Dividing Ridge, about eight or nine miles northwest of the village of Raven; and from thence runs along said ridge to Bear Wallow. And the dividing line between Tazewell and McDowell starts at the point where the counties of Tazewell and Buchanan corner at Bear Wallow. Thence the line runs "eastwardly along the ridge between Clinch and the Dry Fork of Sandy, to a place called the "But of Belsher's ridge;" thence a straight line to the mouth of Horse Pen Creek, and up the same to Jesse Doughtons, and up the left hand fork of said Horse Pen Creek to the Low Gap in Tug Ridge; thence with the same to the ridge between Abb's Valley and Sandy, to the Mercer line."

By the erection of these two new counties, Tazewell had to part with a large territory that abounded with vast natural resources. The extent of the area assigned to Buchanan County is about 300 square miles, and to McDowell about 533 square miles. The territory given to both counties was magnificently timbered and was known to have beneath its surface extensive veins of coal. These natural resources were then but little appreciated, as the possibility of making them available to the markets of the world were believed to be indefinite and remote.

According to the United States census taken in 1860, two years after Buchanan was formed, the county had a population of 2,793 persons. The census of 1910 made the population of the county 12,334 souls. The taxable values of Buchanan County in 1860 amounted to the small sum of $304,506; and the assessed taxable values in 1918 amounted to the large sum of $5,037,721.

The last change made in the boundary lines of Tazewell County was caused by the establishment of Bland County. On the 30th of March, 1861, eighteen days before Virginia seceded from the Union, the General Assembly passed an act to form Bland County from the counties of Giles, Wythe and Tazewell. The dividing line between Tazewell and Bland began at the top of East River mountain at the then county line between Giles and Tazewell; "thence with the top of said East River mountain, westward, to a point two miles west of George Steel's house, on Clear fork; thence across and by a line as near as may be at right angles to the course of the valley between, to the top of Rich mountain, and westward along the top of said Rich mountain, so far as to include the settlement on Wolf creek, thence across the top of Garden mountain; thence along the top of the said Garden mountain, to a point through which the line between Wythe and Smyth would pass if prolonged; thence by said prolonged line, to the said line between Wythe and Smyth."

This left Tazewell County with its present physical outlines, and with an area of 557 square miles.

TAZEWELL'S LOSSES ALMOST INESTIMABLE.

What Tazewell has lost in the way of wealth by the detachment of territory that was incorporated in the bounds of the present counties of McDowell and Mercer, West Virginia, is almost inestimable.

Each year that has passed since the development of the vast mineral and other resources of these two counties was begun has served to enlarge the measure of Tazewell's loss; and the extent of the loss will continue to be augumented for many years to come.

Of the territory that originally constituted Tazewell County, that which has made the most marvelous progress in wealth and population is the present county of McDowell, West Virginia. When McDowell was taken from Tazewell, in 1858, it was so inaccessible and unsuited for agricultural purposes that it was not deemed a loss, but was, possibly, considered a social and economic gain for the mother county.

McDowell County had at the time it was formed, and still has, an area of 533 square miles, 24 miles less than the present area of Tazewell County. In 1859 there were but 282 freeholders in the county, and only about one-third of the land was placed upon the Land Books for taxation—the remaining two-thirds being unentered and still held by the Commonwealth of Virginia. The lands held by private ownership were assessed at 12 cents per acre, and the amount added for buildings on all the privately owned land was the small sum of $3,240, making the total assessed value of the lands and buildings $163,585.00. The taxes collected from these assessments amounted to the meagre sum of $654.38. These figures have been furnished me from memorandums found in the clerk's office of McDowell County. The records in the State Auditor's Office, at Richmond, show that the real estate values returned from the county in 1860 amounted to $93,190, and the personal property to $39,520 —a total of $132,710.

That the wealth of McDowell has been enormously increased is shown by the following tables which are made from the county records:

Assessed Values, 1918.

Real Estate	$30,614,783.00
Personal Property	11,456,892.00
Public Utility Property	12,344,692,78
Total	$54,416,367.78

Taxes Levied for all Purposes for the Year 1917 in
McDowell County.

Real Estate	$432,936.00
Personal Property	152,903.00
Public Utility Property	174,221.00
Total	$760,060.00

These tables show that the increase in the taxable values of McDowell since the county was organized amounted to the astounding sum of $54,252,782.00. They further show that the taxes paid in the county in 1917 amounted to a sum six times as great as the assessed value of all lands and buildings in McDowell in the year 1859.

The source of the stupendous growth in the way of taxable wealth and population of McDowell is primarly found in the extensive mining of the vast deposits of coal that underlie nearly every acre of land in the county. There are a number of coal operations along Tug River, which stream flows through the county from its southern to its northern border. Like conditions are found on the Dry Fork, and on all the other creeks and branches that are tributaries of Tug. Enormous quantities of coal are being mined and shipped to every section of the United States. The coal products in 1917 were: 18,671,942 tons of coal, and 1,415,490 tons of coke—a total of 20,087,432 tons.

It is not surprising that the extensive mining operations have increased the population of the county in proportion to its wealth. The census of 1860 gave McDowell a population of 1,533—all white persons. I have been unable to procure the returns from the census which has been taken this year by the Government, but it is estimated that this census will give the county a population of at least 90,000.

Another evidence of the marvelous progress of McDowell County is found in what she did in the way of supplying men for the service during the late horrible war. The State of West Virginia, from her 55 counties, furnished 55,648 men under the Select Service Act; and McDowell headed the list, by furnishing 3,081 men that were inducted into military service by the Local Boards; and, yet the county had no large cities from which to draw the men. Of the number furnished, 1,578 were white men, and 1,503 were colored. It is also a fact, that a large number volunteered and entered the service through various recruiting offices. With these added, McDowell gave not less than 4,000 soldiers to the Government for service in the late war.

McDowell County has developed into a splendid industrial community, and will continue to progress as such for many years to come, as her vast mineral resources have merely reached an initial stage of development. But she has already attained sufficient industrial standing to make her of great economic value to Tazewell, her mother county.

———

The severance from Tazewell of that portion of her territory which was made a part of Mercer County, by an act of the Virginia General Assembly in 1837, has also proven a heavy economic loss to the mother county. All of the present area of Mercer County situated west of a straight line, beginning at the top of East River Mountain at a point about ten miles east of the city of Bluefield, crossing East River just west of Ingleside, thence to the western limits of the city of Princeton, and thence to the northern line of Mercer, was comprised in the original boundaries of Tazewell County. Within this area as great industrial activity has prevailed during the past twenty-five or thirty years as that which has wrought such astonishing results in McDowell County; and with like results in the way of accumulated wealth and increased population.

The celebrated Flat Top coal fields are located upon territory that was taken from Tazewell; and these fields were the next to be developed after the mining of coal was commenced at Pocahontas. Bluefield, the magic city of this region, is also situated within this area. In fact, about one-half of the territory of the present Mercer County was taken from Tazewell County, and this has made the business and social relations between these two counties very intimate ever since Mercer was erected into a county.

It was my purpose to give as detailed statement of the progress made by Mercer as I have written of McDowell County. I have gotten repeated promises that data would be supplied to that end, but the desired information has not been given. However, I do know that there has been, comparatively, as marvelous increase in the wealth and population of Mercer County as in McDowell. The assessed values of all property—real estate, personal property, and public utility property—in Mercer County in 1918, amounted to the sum of $41,650,020 This, of course, includes the assessed values of the cities of Bluefield and Princeton. It has been estimated that, at least, $37,000,000 of these values are located within the territory that was taken from Tazewell and given to Mercer.

By estimate, the city of Bluefield has about 15,000 inhabitants and Princeton about 8,000. The mining towns in the Flat Top region, and those that are scattered along the Norfolk and Western, and the Virginian Railway, will, no doubt, make the population of Mercer County quite as large as that of McDowell.

Bluefield is bountifully supplied with banking capital, does a large amount of business in the mercantile and manufacturing lines, is rapidly increasing its population, and is constantly extending its improved (building) area toward the line which separates Tazewell County from West Virginia. In fact, the improved limits of Bluefield and those of Graham (Tazewell's largest town) are now nearly united, and may, in the near future, be called the "Twin-Cities." Bluefield is not only the metropolis of the Pocahontas, Flat Top, and Elkhorn coal fields, but occupies the same relation to Taxwell County and the entire Upper Clinch Valley.

War and Reconstruction Period

Detailing the Causes of the Civil War and What
Transpired from 1861 to 1870

WAR AND RECONSTRUCTION PERIOD

CHAPTER I.

PRINCIPAL CAUSES OF THE CIVIL WAR.

The Presidential election of 1860 marked a distinct era in the political thought and practices of the people of the United States. As early as 1818 events began to transpire in the field of American politics that forced the reforming of political parties and threatened to disrupt the Union. It was in December, 1818, that the "Missouri Question," as it was then called, made its appearance through the introduction in Congress of a bill for the admission of Missouri to the Union as a slave State. While Missouri had been a Territory, large numbers of slaveholders from Southern States had moved into the Territory and taken their slaves with them. When the bill for its admission to the Union as a slave State came before the House of Representatives, James Tallmadge, Jr., of New York, moved to amend it by providing that "the further introduction of slavery be prohibited in said State of Missouri, and that all children (negroes) born in the State after its admission to the Union shall be free at the age of twenty-five years." The discussion of the bill, as amended, was marked with great ability and much acrimony. Of course, the members from the South, with Henry Clay as their leader, were violently opposed to the Tallmadge amendment. But the ability of Mr. Clay and the stubborn resistance of the Southern members could not stem the swelling tide of anti-slavery sentiment that was sweeping over the North and Middle West. The bill, as amended by Tallmadge, was passed by the House, but when it went to the Senate the anti-slavery amendment was bitterly opposed by the Southern Senators, and the amendment was rejected. Then the House refused to recede; and for a time Missouri was denied admission to the Union.

At the following session of Congress, in December, 1819, the Missouri question again came to the front, when a bill was introduced to admit Maine to the Union as a free State. The bill for the admission of Missouri was re-introduced immediately following the introduction of the Maine bill. This aroused another fast and furious debate between the pro-slavery and anti-slavery membership of the House. But the Missouri bill with the anti-slavery restriction was again passed, as was the Maine bill, by the House. When the two bills went to the Senate that body refused to concur, and a single bill, uniting Maine and Missouri for admission to the Union, was introduced. Thereupon, Jesse B. Thomas, a senator from Illinois, proposed a compromise feature to the bill, which has since been known among politicians as the "Missouri Compromise." This compromise provision forever prohibited slavery north of 36° 30' in all the territory which President Jefferson acquired from France in 1803 by what has since been known, and shown on the maps, as the Louisiana Purchase. It was passed in the Senate, but the House refused to admit the two States by a single bill. The compromise feature, however, was accepted by the enactment by the House of separate bills for the admission of the two States. Missouri then made a Constitution which forbid the residence of free negroes in the State. This so provoked the anti-slavery members of Congress that they refused at the next session to admit the State. After a prolonged and heated discussion, a compromise was effected by writing into the bill a provision, "that Missouri should be admitted to the Union upon the fundamental condition that no law should ever be passed by her Legislature enforcing the objectionable provision in her Constitution, and that by a solemn public act the State should declare and record her assent to this condition, and transmit to the President of the United States an authentic copy of the Act. The disciplinary condition was grudgingly accepted, and Missouri thus secured admission to the Union.

Thomas Jefferson and the older statesmen then living, the men who had helped to carry the colonies successfully through the Revolution and establish our independence, were greatly distressed and alarmed by the course the Missouri question had taken. The Compromise had established a geographical line between the free and slave States; and they believed this would ultimately generate bitter sectional feeling and bring disaster to the Union. In these gloomy apprehensions, future events proved they were not mistaken. Mr. Jefferson was then living in retirement at a venerable age, but was still in possession of his unusually great mental faculties.

While the Compromise measure was pending in Congress, he gave expression to his fears in a letter he wrote to a member of the House of Representatives. He said, that "the Missouri question is the most portentous one which has ever threatened the Union. In the gloomiest hour of the Revolutionary War I never had any apprehensions equal to those which I feel from this source."

Following the admission of Missouri to the Union the slavery question for a while ceased to be a disturbing issue in the politics of the country. But the heated controversies in Congress over the extension of slavery had compelled a complete reconstruction of political parties. The Federalist party, because of the avowed hostility of its founders to popular government, had steadily disintegrated, and in 1820 had become an impotent organization. And the Republican party, founded by Thomas Jefferson, after his death on July 4th, 1826, was destroyed as an effective organization through the rivalries and jealousies of its leaders. Two new, vigorous organizations, the Whig and Democratic parties, were constructed from the ruins of the two old parties. The rank and file of the Whig party came almost entirely from the Federalists and the anti-slavery men of the North and West, while the Democratic party was composed almost entirely of the followers of Thomas Jefferson. Henry Clay had been a nominal adherent of Mr. Jefferson, but had evinced a leaning to some of the principles of the Federalists, such as the tariff, suffrage, and finance. This caused him to unite his political fortunes with the Whigs and to be made the most brilliant and highly esteemed leader of that party until his death, which occurred June 29th, 1852. Andrew Jackson, who had been all the while a zealous disciple of Mr. Jefferson, naturally became the aggressive leader of the Democrats, and he remained the idol of his party until the day of his death, which came on the 8th of June, 1845.

The new political parties had their first contest in the Presidential election of 1828. Andrew Jackson and John C. Calhoun were the candidates of the Democrats for President and Vice President; and John Quincy Adams and Richard Rush were the candidates of the Whigs. The slavery question was completely ignored during the campaign by both parties, but the Whigs projected two new issues of such absorbing interest that all other questions were cast aside in what was one of the most memorable political struggles that has ever taken place in the United States. The Whigs made their fight on what they termed "Militarism," and "Disunion," charging that General Jackson would turn the Government into a military depotism, if he was made President; and that Calhoun would disrupt the Union, if he was given the opportunity. These new and alarmist issues proved unavailing for the Whigs. General Jackson had received as a gift from the hands of Mr. Jefferson the leadership of American democracy, and this was a potent influence which brought victory for the Democratic ticket.

———

In 1836 an event occurred which, a few years later, made the slavery question a more alarming issue in American politics than ever before. About the same time the Missouri question was agitating the country American citizens began to settle in that part of Texas which lies west of the Sabine River. This part of Texas had been relinquished to Spain by treaty when she ceded Florida to the United States. Many of the settlers had taken slaves with them to Texas; and by the year 1833, eleven years after Mexico had become an independent republic, the number of Americans in Texas had reached twenty thousand. They determined to establish for themselves a republic, independent of Mexico. To promote this scheme, in 1835, a provisional government was set up; and General Sam Houston was made commander-in-chief of the military forces. Houston drove all the Mexicans from Texas. General Santa Anna invaded the country in February, 1836, and invested the Alamo, the old Spanish fort near San Antonio, which was held by a small garrison of Texans under the command of Colonel Davy Crockett. The fort was stormed by the Mexicans and all the garrison butchered by order of Santa Anna. Four days previous to the bloody tragedy at the Alamo, the Texans held a convention and issued a declaration of independence. In September, 1836, General Houston was elected President of the Republic; and a Congress was also elected and held its first session in October, 1836.

In 1837, the independence of the "Lone Star State," as it was then called, was recognized by the United States. The political leaders in Texas then began to advocate annexation of the State to the United States. This scheme was bitterly opposed by the anti-slavery men of the North and cordially supported by the slave-holders of the South. But the leaders of both the great National parties studiously avoided making the Texas question an issue until 1844, when it became the supreme issue in the Presidential election of that year.

John C. Calhoun, then Secretary of State, concluded a treaty of annexation with Texas, which was communicated to the Senate by President Tyler on the 12th of April, 1844. In negotiating the treaty, Mr. Calhoun's purpose was to defeat Martin Van Buren, who was again seeking the nomination by the Democrats for the Presidency; and also to make the annexation of Texas the chief issue between the two National parties.

The treaty was received with great disfavor by the Whigs, as Mr. Clay, who was their leader and their avowed candidate for the Presidency, had declared his opposition to the annexation of Texas. And Mr. Van Buren's supporters also, generally, opposed it, because he had pronounced against annexation. In fact, he and Mr. Clay, believing that they would be the candidates of their respective parties, had agreed that the Texas question should not be injected into the campaign.

When the National Convention of the Democratic party assembled at Baltimore, the 27th of May, 1844, the treaty was still pending in the Senate. Nothwithstanding the fact that a majority of the delegates on the first ballot voted for Van Buren, it became impossible to nominate him, as the delegates from the South insisted upon the adoption and enforcement of the two-thirds rule which had been used at preceding national conventions of the party. The Southern delegates stood for James K. Polk, of Tennessee, and secured his nomination; and the ticket was completed by nominating George M. Dallas, of Pennsylvania, for Vice President. The convention declared for the annexation of Texas; and the Democrats immediately adopted for their battle cry: "Polk, Dallas, and Texas," following the example of the Whigs, who had successfully waged their campaign in 1840 with the cry: "Tippecanoe and Tyler Too."

The Whigs had held their National Convention at Baltimore on the 1st of May, and nominated Henry Clay by acclamation for President; and had chosen Theodore Frelinghuysen as their candidate for Vice President. In a communication written from Raleigh,

North Carolina, on the 17th of April, 1844, and published in the
National Intelligencer, then a Whig organ, Mr. Clay had announced
his opposition to the annexation of Texas. He gave several reasons
for opposing the treaty. One was, that, although Texas had been
a part of the territory acquired by purchase from France, our
Government had parted with that portion of the territory beyond
the Sabine River, by the treaty with Spain in 1819; and that the
Sabine line had been recognized and accepted by the United States
in subsequent negotions with Spain, and with Mexico after that
country became a republic. Mr. Clay did not think it would be
honorable and just for us to regard our treaty with Spain as a
mere "scrap of paper," though he had heartily opposed its ratification by Congress. Another reason he assigned for his opposition was that: "Annexation and war with Mexico are identical."
He declared: "Assuming that the annexation of Texas is war
with Mexico, is it competent to the treaty-making power to plunge
this country into war, not only without the concurrence of, but
without deigning to consult Congress, to which, by the constitution,
belongs exclusively the power of declaring war?"

By the nomination of Mr. Polk the Democrats had forced the
Whigs to accept the Texas question as the paramount issue of the
Presidential campaign, and which Mr. Clay's Raleigh letter had
invited them to do. But the Democrats shrewdly determined to
strengthen their position by coupling the Oregon question with that
of the annexation of Texas. Great Britain was then secretly forming plans to wrest Oregon from the United States upon a fictitious
claim to the splendid territory which now constitutes the two great
States of Oregon and Washington. Our old enemy, Great Britain,
also had her agents actively and offensively at work in Texas to
prevent the Lone Star State becoming a member of the Union. Thus
was General Jackson given excellent opportunity to hurl one of his
terrible javelins at his personal and political foe, Mr. Clay; and to
assail the integrity of the British Government, which he cordially
despised for its treacherous conduct in Texas and its avowed purpose to steal Oregon from the United States. The old hero of
the Democracy did his work effectively through a letter written
from the Hermitage, June 24th, 1844, to a friend in Indiana. In
the letter, he first attacked Mr. Clay's views on the national bank,
system of taxation, and other questions; and then assailed his posi-

tion on the Texas question, as follows: "He says, virtually, that Texas ought not to be admitted into the Union, while there is a respectable and considerable portion of our citizens opposed to it. On such a condition it is obvious annexation can never take place. British influence had considerable and respectable advocates in this country in our Revolutionary War, and our second war with her. Will it ever be without them? Never. As long as there are fanatics in religion, as there are diversities and differences in human opinion respecting the forms of government and the rights of the people, such advocacy will be found resisting the advance of institutions like ours, and laboring to incorporate with them the features of an opposite system.

"Who does not see that the people of the United States are competitors with the people of England in the manufacturing arts, and in the carrying trade of the world? And that the question is soon to be, if it be not already, whether Texas and Oregon are to be considered as auxiliaries to American or British interests? Whether these vast and fertile regions are to be settled by our posterity, blessed by republican government—or are to become the theatre of British enterprise, and thus add another link to the vast colonial claim by which that great monarchy upholds its lords and nobles, and extracts from suffering millions the earnings of their labor?

* * * * *

"The American people cannot be deceived in this manner. They know that the real object of England is to check the prosperity of the United States—and lessen their power to compete with England as a naval power, and as a growing agricultural, manufacturing and commercial country. They know that Lord Aberdeen, in the midst of thousands and thousands of starving subjects of the British monarchy, is more anxious, or ought to be, to relieve the wants of those wretched people than he can be to alter the relation subsisting between the white and black races of this country."

General Jackson closed the letter with an appeal to the American people to not "let slip the opportunity now offered of concentrating their Union, and promoting the general causes of their prosperity and happiness, by the annexation of Texas."

The views of General Jackson, as set forth in this letter, were promulgated throughout the Union as quickly as possible by Mr.

Polk's party managers; and, possibly, it did more to secure success for Polk and Dallas than any other one thing that transpired in the campaign. It gave fresh impulse to the already aggressive policy of the Democatic party for territorial acquisition, a policy which had always been popular with the American people, and all peoples who have a strain of Anglo-Saxon blood in their veins. It also aroused enthusiasm in the young men of adventurous and daring spirit, who were eager to see something of "grim visaged war."

For the first time in his political life, Mr. Clay had placed himself on the hesitating or timid side of any grave question that had arisen in the politics of the country. He had enthusiastically advocated war with Great Britain in 1812; had ardently opposed the treaty of 1819 which ceded to Spain all that portion of Texas west of the Sabine River; and had stubbornly resisted the efforts of the Abolitionists to prevent the introduction of slavery into the territory acquired by the Louisiana Purchase.

The great Whig leader, being put upon the defensive, and believing that he was losing favor with the pro-slavery Southern Whigs, because of his pronounced hostility to the annexation of Texas, was induced to modify his position on the Texas question. This was accomplished through a letter Mr. Clay wrote to Stephen Miller, editor of the Tuscaloosa (Ala.) Monitor, in which he said: "Personally I could have no objection to the annexation of Texas; but I certainly would be unwilling to see the existing Union dissolved or seriously jeopordized for the sake of acquiring Texas." But in the letter, Mr. Clay spoke of the treaty for the annexation of Texas as "Mr. Tyler's abominable treaty." The letter was used with telling effect by the Democrats, who designated it Mr. Clay's "Death Warrant." They insisted that Mr. Clay was playing double, that he was pandering to the Abolition sentiment at the North by expressing opposition to the Texas treaty, and was currying favor with the slaveholders in the South by proclaiming that he was "personally" friendly to annexation.

Apparently, it had been the desire and purpose of both the parties to eliminate the slavery question from the campaign, as each of them had many friends at the North who were earnestly opposed to the extension of slavery. Mr. Clay's letter to Miller completely wrecked the intentions of the Whigs and the Democrats on that line.

There was another concurrent circumstance that made slavery a very eventful issue in the future politics of the United States. The Abolitionists had nominated James G. Birney, of Michigan, as their candidate for the Presidency. In the Presidential campaign of 1840 Birney had been the candidate of the Abolitionists, who posed as the "Liberty Party." At the election in 1840 he received only 6,475 votes; but at the election of 1844 his vote was swelled to 62,127. Birney's followers in the election of 1844 were the rudiments from which the great Republican Party was developed; and that sixteen years later, under the guidance of Abraham Lincoln, gained control of the Nation and preserved the Union.

No more exciting political contest has ever been witnessed in the United States. More than two and a half million American citizens voted at the election. Of these, James K. Polk received the suffrage of 1,336,196; Henry Clay, 1,297,912; and James G. Birney, 62,127, giving Polk a plurality of 38,284 over Clay. The popular vote of South Carolina was not included in the foregoing, as the electors from that State were chosen by the Legislature. There were twenty-six States in the Union, with an aggregate of 275 electoral votes. Of these, 170 were cast for James K. Polk and 105 for Henry Clay, which gave Mr. Polk a majority of 70 in the electoral college. Polk's election was conceded to be a verdict of the people for the annexation of Texas. At the following session of Congress annexation was accomplished by a joint resolution, which was signed by President Tyler on the 1st of March, 1845, three days before the inauguration of President Polk.

The assertion of Mr. Clay, in his letter written at Raleigh, that "Annexation and war with Mexico are identical," was reduced to a certainty two years after its utterance. During the winter of 1845-46 General Zachary Taylor was in command of the United States army that had been sent to Texas as an army of occupation. He was ordered to move westward and take a position on the east side of the Rio Grande; and on the 28th of March, 1846, he arrived at that river and went into camp opposite Matamoras. On the 22nd of April, General Ampudia, who was in command of the Mexican forces at Matamoras, notified General Taylor that he should break camp and march his army eastward beyond the Neuces River, that stream being claimed as an agreed boundary line between Mexico and Texas. General Taylor promptly refused to comply with the demands of the Mexican general; and on the 24th of April, General Arista, who had taken command of the Mexican army, informed General Taylor that, "he considered hostilities commenced and should prosecute them." Immediately following the notification, General Taylor sent a detachment of sixty dragoons—officers and men—up the river as a scouting party, to ascertain if the Mexicans had crossed or were crossing the Rio Grande into Texas. The American party came in contact with a large force of Mexicans, seventeen of the Americans were killed and wounded, and the balance captured. Thus began the war between the United States and Mexico.

On the 11th of May, 1846, President Polk sent a message to Congress "invoking its prompt action to recognize the existence of war" and to place at the disposition of the Executive the means of prosecuting the contest with vigor, and thus hastening the restoration of peace. After the message was read in the House of Representatives, a bill was promptly introduced by an Administration supporter, declaring that "war existed by the act of Mexico," and giving authority to the President to call out and organize an army of fifty thousand men, and to supply them with all necessary equipments. The assertion in the preamble of the bill, that "war existed with Mexico," provoked a heated discussion of the measure by the Whig members of the House. They were reluctant to plunge the country into war with our neighbor republic upon the doubtful pretext that "our country had been invaded and American blood spilled on American soil." After a very brief debate a vote was forced on the measure; but fourteen members of the House had the courage to vote against the bill.

Very soon after the declaration of war, agitation of the slavery question again assumed alarming proportions. From the commencement of hostilities with Mexico, the Whigs and Free-Soilers of the North had claimed that the war was being prosecuted to acquire territory into which slavery could be extended. This charge was reasserted when the President, three months after the formal declaration of war, sent a message to the Congress, suggesting that the chief obstacle to be surmounted in securing peace would be the adjustment of a boundary that would prove satisfactory and convenient to both republics. The President conceded that we ought to give Mexico a just compensation for any territory she would be forced to cede to the United States as a result of the war. And he requested Congress to appropriate two millions of dollars to be "applied under the direction of the President to any extraordinary expenses which may be incurred in our foreign intercourse."

When the bill was receiving very harsh criticism from the Whigs and anti-slavery men in the House, David Wilmot, of Pennsylvania, who was then serving his first term in Congress as a Democrat, offered, on August 8th, 1846, an amendment providing "that as an express and fundamental condition to the acquisition of any territory from the republic of Mexico by the United States, neither slavery nor involuntary servitude shall exist in any part of said territory." This amendment has ever since been called the "Wilmot Proviso;" and it not only became an issue in the Congressional campaign then in progress, but was made the basis of the Free-Soilers' campaign in the Presidential election of 1848.

The two million dollar bill was finally passed by the House, but failed of final action in the Senate by a filibuster which was lead by John Davis, a Senator from Massachusetts. At the next session of Congress the two million dollar bill was enlarged to three millions; and the Administration had gained sufficient strength in both Houses to secure the passage of the bill without the proviso being attached. Though the Administration had gained a notable victory in securing the passage of the appropriation bill free of the Wilmot amendment, the Democrats had met a disaster in the Congressional elections the preceding fall, when a new Congress was elected. At that election the Whigs and Free-Soilers had won a majority in the House of Representatives, and it was certain that the Southern Democrats would be blocked in any effort to extend slavery into territory acquired from Mexico.

The new Congress met in December, 1847, and Robert C. Winthrop, of Massachusetts, was made Speaker of the House by the Whigs. Mr. Winthrop had earnestly supported the Wilmot Proviso in the preceding Congress, and it was thought his election for Speaker would provoke renewed agitation of the slavery question. But the Whig leaders were laying their plans to elect the President in 1848, and very wisely avoided the introduction of the slavery question into the proceedings of that session. The Democrats were alarmed by the success of the Whigs at the election the previous fall, and they, too, remained quiet. Both parties were then looking for their Presidental candidates for the approaching election. Remembering that the only success they had achieved at a Presidential election since the organization of their party was with a military hero for their candidate, the Whigs resolved to win victory in 1848 with a similar standard bearer. General Zachary Taylor had made a great reputation in the war with Mexico, where, by winning a series of victories from Mexican generals and against enormous odds, his soldiers had bestowed upon him the name "Old Rough and Ready." He was a Whig in politics, was a slaveholder, but had not voted for forty years, owing to the fact that he had for all that time been an officer in the United States army. Mr. Clay was eager to be made the candidate of his party again, but the Whigs nominated General Taylor for President and Millard Fillmore for Vice President, and declined to make a platform for their candidates. They thus sought to avoid taking sides with either the anti-slavery men of the North, or the pro-slavery Whigs of the South. When sneered at by the Democrats for failure to promulgate a platform of principles, the Whigs would declare: "The Whig platform is well known and immutable. *It is the broad platform of the Constitution,* with the acknowledged right of the people to do or to demand anything authorized by that instrument, and denying the powers of our rulers to do anything in violation of its provisions." With this exalted declaration, the Whigs prosecuted with much vigor what they called a "Star and Stripe" canvass.

The Democratic party at the North, especially in New York, had become seriously disorganized by factional fights. Mr. Van Buren remained sore and resentful toward the Southern Democrats for procuring his defeat for the nomination in 1844. The party in New York had been divided into two bitterly hostile factions. One faction bore the name "Hunkers," were adherents of President Polk, and were led by William L. Marcy, then Secretary of War. The other was called "Barnburners," were followers of Mr. Van Buren, and were under the leadership of Governor Silas Wright. In fact, the Hunkers represented the pro-slavery wing, and the Barnburners the anti-slavery wing of the Democratic party; and were products of the quarrel provoked by the annexation of Texas.

When the National Convention of the party met at Baltimore the State of New York had two full delegations present, one composed of Hunkers and the other of Barnburners, each delegation claiming the right to sit in the convention to the exclusion of the other. The National Convention attempted to heal the breach in the party by the usual method of admitting both delegations, with power to jointly cast the vote of the State. But the Barnburners would not accede to the compromise and left the convention. The Hunkers wisely concluded that it would be expedient for them to take no part in the proceedings, and refrained from casting the vote of New York State. The convention nominated General Lewis Cass, of Michigan, for President, and William O. Butler, of Kentucky, for Vice President. On the 22nd of June, 1848, the Barnburners held a National Convention at Utica, New York, and nominated Martin Van Buren for the Presidency, and Charles Francis Adams, of Massachusetts, for the Vice Presidency. This Free-soil movement forced the slavery question into the campaign, regardless of the wishes of both Whigs and Democrats to keep it out. The Whigs again won the Presidency with a hero candidate, but their victory was the forerunner of an early dissolution of Henry Clay's great party.

The war with Mexico had been brought to a successful conclusion by the Americans; and on the 2nd of February, 1848, a treaty of peace had been negotiated between the United States and the Republic of Mexico. By this treaty the extensive territory then known as New Mexico and Upper California was ceded to the United States; and it precipitated a struggle between the anti-slavery and pro-slavery advocates for control of the new territory. Previous to the making of the treaty an animated controversy, involving the slavery question, had been going on in Congress over the territorial organization of Oregon. The leaders of both National parties were anxious to eliminate the slavery question from the approaching Presidential campaign; and they thought this could be done by a compromise measure. Accordingly the matter was referred to a committee of eight members of the United States Senate, which committee was representative of every sectional interest involved. A Compromise bill was finally adopted and signed by the President on the 12th of August, 1848. The bill provided that the Legislature of Oregon Territory should enact laws in conformity with the wishes of the people on the question of slavery. As its people had already pronounced against the introduction of slavery, Oregon, necessarily, became a free Territory. As to New Mexico and California, the bill gave to the governors and judges of those two Territories the power to make such legislation as was needed for their temporary government; but restraining them from passing any laws on the subject of slavery; and vesting authority in the Supreme Court to determine, if called upon to do so, whether slaveholders could settle in either of the Territories with their slaves while the temporary governments were in existence.

When this compromise measure was adopted no one anticipated that California would soon be seeking admission to the Union as a full-fledged State. On January 19th, 1848, gold was discovered in such quantities at Sutter's Mill, near Coloma, that emigration to California on a large scale quickly ensued. Most of the gold-seekers arrived in the early part of 1849, and by the end of that year the population of the Territory exceeded 100,000. The people held a convention on the 3rd of September and framed a constitution, in which there was a provision that prohibited slavery in the State. A State government was organized, and a petition was sent to Congress asking that California be admitted to the Union.

President Taylor in his first message to Congress, when it convened in December, 1849, recommended that California, with her anti-slavery constitution, be promptly admitted to the Union. He also made recommendations with regard to New Mexico that were obnoxious to the pro-slavery people of the South. His message provoked intense anger at the South, but largely increased his popularity at the North. As a sequence, the situation on the slavery question became more alarming to the statesmen who wished to preserve the Union.

Mr. Clay, having failed in 1848 to secure a second nomination for the Presidency from the Whigs, had been sent again by his Kentucky friends to the United States Senate. Though grievously disappointed in his Presidential aspirations, the grand old statesman was eager to procure "an amicable arrangement of *all* questions in controversy between the free and slave States growing out of the subject of slavery." He sought to accomplish his lofty purpose by introducing a series of resolutions, setting forth the measures he believed would terminate the sectional animosities that were being aroused by the prolonged agitation of the slavery question. The resolutions were referred to a committee of thirteen, of which Mr. Clay was made chairman. After duly considering the several resolutions, the committee incorporated them in a single bill, which was named the "Omnibus Bill." The Administration was firmly opposed to Mr. Clay's compromise scheme, as it contravened some of the most important recommendations President Taylor had made in his message to Congress. A prolonged and acrimonious debate followed the introduction of the Omnibus Bill, that was not ended until President Taylor's death, which came suddenly on the 9th of July, 1850.

Mr. Fillmore, who had been elevated to the Presidency by the death of President Taylor, was in full sympathy with Mr. Clay's measures of Compromise; but the friends of the deceased President antagonized the Omnibus Bill so vigorously that it could not be passed in its entirety. Mr. Clay and his associates then resorted to the use of separate bills to secure the passage of their Compromise measures. A bill was passed for the organization of the Territory of Utah, and that placed freedom and slavery upon the same plane in that Territory. Other separate bills were then passed, providing for the admission of California; for the organization of New Mexico; for adjustment of the disputed Texas boundary; for the more effective recovery of fugitive slaves; and for abolishing slavery in the District of Columbia.

The leaders of both political parties, with a few exceptions, were well satisfied with the Compromise, and expressed confident belief that the slavery question had been effectually adjusted. But a few prominent Whigs at the North, led by William H. Seward, Benjamin Wade, and others, had persistently opposed the Compromise measures. Subsequently they organized a revolt in their party at the North against President Fillmore's administration that brought crushing defeat to the Whigs in the next Presidental election. On the other hand, the Democrats of all sections of the Union became compactly united in support of the Compromise; and the Southern Whigs were equally earnest in its support.

T.H.—37

The Democrats assembled in a National Convention at Baltimore on June 1st, 1852, to nominate a Presidential ticket. There were three candidates for the Democratic nomination for President—General Lewis Cass of Michigan; James Buchanan of Pennsylvania; and William L. Marcy of New York. Forty-eight ballots were taken without either of the candidates getting two-thirds of the delegates that was necessary to secure the nomination. Franklin Pierce, of New Hampshire, who had been given scattering votes during the balloting, was unanimously nominated for President on the forty-ninth ballot; and William R. King, of Alabama, was nominated for Vice President. The Democrats took a very bold position on the slavery question. In their platform, which was unanimously adopted by the convention, it was resolved that "all efforts of the Abolitionists or others to induce Congress to interfere with the question of slavery or to take incipient steps in relation thereto, are calculated to lead to the most alarming and dangerous consequences." It was then defiantly declared that "the Democratic party will resist all attempts at renewing, in Congress or out of it, the agitation of the slavery question, under whatever shape or color the attempts may be made." All the Compromise measures that had been passed by Congress were enthusiastically endorsed, the fugitive-slave law being given special significance in the platform.

Two weeks later the Whigs held their National Convention at Baltimore; and they were as sharply divided on the slavery question as the Democrats were closely united thereon. There were but three names placed before the convention as candidates for the Presidential nomination. They were, President Fillmore, General Winfield Scott, and Daniel Webster. The first ballot showed that the Southern Whigs were solidly for Fillmore, with the exception of one vote from Virginia; and that the Northern Whigs were for General Scott, except twenty-nine that voted for Mr. Webster. A long and bitter contest was waged by the friends of the rival candidates, but General Scott was nominated on the fifty-third ballot. The ticket was completed by nominating William A. Graham, of North Carolina, for Vice President.

The Whigs had again selected a military hero for their candidate; and they were, in the first stages of the campaign, very hopeful of winning the Presidency. But personal enmities among the leaders and widely divergent views on the slavery question brought humiliating defeat to the Whig candidates. The Whigs carried but four States of the Union—Massachusetts and Vermont in the North, and Kentucky and Tennessee in the South. Of the 296 electors in the electoral college, Franklin Pierce got the votes of 254 and General Scott only 42. Both the great Whig leaders, Clay and Webster, had died while the campaign was in progress; Mr. Clay a few days after Scott's nomination, and Mr. Webster a few days before the election. The Whig party never rallied from this disastrous defeat, but began to disintegrate, and soon ceased to be a vital element in national politics.

Elated with the wonderful victory they gained over their now prostrate rival, the Democrats thought they had secured a lease of power that would last for many years. But there was one portentous incident of the Presidential election which failed to impress the Democrats with the imminent danger that awaited them. The Free-Soilers had again presented a Presidential candidate in the person of John Parker Hale of New Hampshire. He received 157,685 votes, nearly 100,000 more than Birney, the Free-Soil candidate, got in 1844.

By his inaugural address, on the 4th of March, 1853, President Pierce placed his administration squarely upon the principles and policies announced in the platform made at Baltimore by his party. He had no sympathy with the politicians who contemplated a dissolution of the Union, and said: "Do my countrymen need any assurance that such a catastrophe is not to overtake them while I possess the power to stay it." Of the slavery question, which then threatened to break up the Union, he said:

"I believe that involuntary servitude, as it exists in the different States of this Confederacy, is recognized by the Constitution. I believe that it stands like any other admitted right, and that the States where it exists are entitled to efficient remedies to enforce the constitutional provisions. I hold that the laws of 1850, commonly called the 'compromise measures,' are strictly constitutional and to be unhesitatingly carried into effect. I believe that the constituted authorities of this Republic are bound to regard the rights of the South in this respect as they would view any other legal and constitutional right, and that the laws to enforce them should be respected and obeyed, not with a reluctance encouraged by abstract opinions as to their propriety in a different state of society, but cheerfully and according to the decisions of the tribunal to which the exposition belongs."

The views expressed by President Pierce in his inaugural address gave complete satisfaction to the people and political leaders of all sections, except the rank Abolitionists in the North and the extreme pro-slavery men in the South. The latter seemed resolved to tear down the barriers that prevented the introduction of slavery into the new Territories, or to break up the Union. The country continued at repose from the inauguration of President Pierce until Congress convened in the session of 1853-54, when a bill was introduced for the organization of the Territory of Nebraska. Archibald Dixon, of Kentucky, had been sent from that State as the successor of Mr. Clay in the United States Senate. Early in January, 1854, Mr. Dixon gave notice that when the bill to organize the Territory of Nebraska came to the Senate he would move, that "the Missouri Compromise be repealed and that the citizens of the several States shall be at liberty to take and hold their slaves within any of the Territories."

This unfortunate movement of Mr. Dixon for a repeal of the Missouri Compromise and the Compromise measures of 1850, for which his illustrious predecessor, Mr. Clay, had labored so earnestly, was premeditated, and was backed by the extreme pro-slavery men from the South, including Jefferson Davis, Robert Toombs and Judah P. Benjamin. It gave increased momentum to the already infuriated Abolitionist sentiment in the North, and accelerated the growing spirit of Disunion in the South. Stephen A. Douglas was then looming up as an aspirant for the Democratic nomination for President in 1856. He realized that the repeal of the Missouri Compromise for the purposes assigned by Mr. Dixon, "that the citizens of the several States shall be at liberty to take and hold their slaves within any of the Territories"—would disrupt the Democratic party in the free States. To obviate the threatened danger to his party, Mr. Douglas reported a bill in the Senate which provided for organizing two new Territories, Kansas and Nebraska. In one section of the bill it was declared that the Missouri Compromise of 1820 was inoperative and void, because "it was inconsistent with the principle of non-intervention by Congress with slavery in the States and Territories as recognized by

the Compromise of 1850." The bill of Mr. Douglas further declared
that "its true intent and meaning was not to legislate slavery into
any Territory or State, and not to exclude it therefrom, but to
leave the people perfectly free to regulate their domestic institutions
in their own way." This was nothing more than a reutterance of
the Democratic doctrines of "Popular Sovereignty," and "States
Rights."

A stormy debate, which was continued in Congress for four
months, followed the introduction of the Douglas bill; but it was
finally passed by the Democrats, who were assisted by the Southern
Whigs. The measure proved to be the "Death Warrant," for the
Presidential aspirations of Mr. Douglas. A bitter and bloody struggle was begun between the pro-slavery and anti-slavery men for the
organization and control of Kansas Territory. In May, 1854,
emigrants from Missouri and Arkansas commenced to move into
Kansas. They held a pro-slavery convention on the 10th of June,
1854, and announced that slavery already existed in the Territory.
This caused the Massachusetts Emigrant Aid Society, and other
Abolitionist organizations in New England, to send out colonies; and
they established settlements at Topeka, Ossawatomie and at other
points. For a period of five years the inhabitants of the Territory
engaged in bloody strife over the slavery question. Repeated
efforts were made by the rival factions to set up a territorial government. On November 29th, 1854, an election was held to choose a
delegate to represent the Territory in Congress. Armed bodies of
men from Missouri took possession of the polls, and of the 2,843
votes cast, 1,729 were proved to be illegal. The pro-slavery and
the anti-slavery men, each, elected legislatures and held constitutional conventions; and many bloody conflicts were engaged in. One
of the events of the year 1856 was the brutal murder of pro-slavery
men by a party of fanatical Abolitionists led by John Brown, who
was afterwards hung by the Virginia authorities for raising an
insurrection at Harper's Ferry. Finally, the Free-Soilers won, and
on January 29th, 1861, Kansas was admitted to the Union as a
free State.

While the disorders in Kansas were at their highest pitch, and
a few days before the Democrats nominated their National ticket,
an incident occurred in the National Capitol that stirred to frenzy
the Abolitionists of the North. Charles Sumner, a Senator from

Massachusetts, delivered a rancorous speech in the Senate on what he styled the "Crime against Kansas" that greatly incensed the Southern members of Congress. The speech was violently resented by Preston S. Brooks, a hot-headed member of the House of Representatives from South Carolina. On May 26th, 1856, he assaulted Senator Sumner, striking him over the head with a heavy cane while he was sitting in his chair in the Senate Chamber. Mr. Sumner was so severely injured that he had to go abroad for medical treatment, and did not resume his seat in the Senate until 1859. A resolution was introduced in the House for the expulsion of Brooks, and the committee to which it was referred recommended that he be expelled. Brooks resigned, and was immediately re-elected by his constitutents. When the resolution to expel him was being considered in the House, Brooks declared that "a blow struck by him then would be followed by a revolution." This incident greatly accelerated the Abolition movement that had already attained dangerous proportions at the North.

On the 1st of June, five days after the Brooks-Sumner affair occurred, the Democrats held their National Convention at Baltimore. They nominated James Buchanan for President, and John C. Breckinridge for Vice President. In their platform they endorsed the repeal of the Missouri Compromise, and upheld the "right of the people of all the Territories to form a constitution with or without slavery."

The newly formed Republican party, which had been organizing and consolidating its forces during 1854 and 1855, had met in National Convention previous to the Democrats. They nominated John C. Fremont, of California, for President, and William L. Dayton, of New Jersey, for Vice President. In making their platform the Republicans declared that it was "both the right and the imperative duty of Congress to prohibit in the Territories those twin relics of barbarism—polygamy and slavery." The Whigs had nominated Millard Fillmore for the Presidency, and selected Andrew Jackson Donelson, of Tennessee, as their candidate for the Vice Presidency. They made no declarations in their platform on the slavery question. By this avoidance of the most vital issue in American politics, the Whigs made but little showing at the election. Buchanan received the electoral votes of every Southern State except Maryland, which gave its vote to Fillmore. Of the

Northern States, New Jersey, Pennsylvania, Indiana, Illinois and California voted for Buchanan. In the aggregate he received 174 electoral votes. Fremont received the votes of the other eleven free States. The Republicans had developed great strength and spirit in their first National encounter with the Democratic foe. Then began the movement to array a solid North against a solid South.

After the inauguration of President Buchanan, the Democrats had control of every department of the Federal Government; and steps were promptly taken by the extreme men at the South to introduce slavery into Kansas and such other new Territories as should be organized. An event then happened which gave opportunity for the enforcement of this policy. Very soon after President Buchanan was inaugurated the Supreme Court of the United States rendered its decision in the famous Dred Scott case. Dred Scott was a Missouri slave, whose master in 1834 took him to Illinois, a State which prohibited slavery within its bounds. Scott married in Illinois, where he remained, with his master's consent, until 1838. Then he was taken to Minnesota Territory, where slavery had been prohibited by the Missouri Compromise. Later, his master brought Scott to Missouri, where the master asserted his right to treat him as a slave, and whipped him for some offense. Scott brought a suit for damages against his master, claiming that his residence in Illinois and Minnesota had made him a free man. The master denied that Scott had any right to sue, as he was descended from slave ancestors and had himself never been set free. Scott won in the Missouri court, but his master appealed the case to the Supreme Court of the United States. This high tribunal in 1857 reversed the decision of the Missouri court, holding that negro slaves were chattels, mere things, "who had no rights and privileges but such as those who held the power and the government might grant them." The court also declared that Scott's residence in Minnesota and Illinois could not confer freedom upon him, because the act of 1820 (the Missouri Compromise) was unconstitutional and void. The Supreme Court also decided that Congress had no more right to prohibit the carrying of slaves into any State and Territory than it had to prohibit the carrying thither of horses or any other property, holding that slaves were property whose secure possession was granted by the Constitution. The opinion of the Supreme

Court was in harmony with the views of President Pierce as expressed in his inaugural address on the 4th of March, 1853.

Throughout the years 1858 and 1859 there was a bitter struggle, sometimes attended with bloodshed, between the pro-slavery and anti-slavery men for the possession of Kansas. In this momentous struggle Stephen A. Douglas separated himself from the Southern Democracy and thereby disrupted the Democratic party.

CHAPTER II.

THE HARPER'S FERRY INSURRECTION.

The most significant and appalling event that occurred during the prolonged agitation of the slavery question was the insurrection led by John Brown at Harper's Ferry in October, 1859.

John Brown, son of Owen Brown, a New England fanatic, was born at Torrington, Connecticut, May 9th, 1800. When he was five years old his father moved to Ohio. After he attained manhood he met with business failures in Ohio, Massachusetts and Connecticut. In 1855 he moved from Connecticut to Kansas, no doubt at the instance of the Massachusetts Emigrant Aid Society. He became a leading spirit among the Abolitionists who were struggling to prevent the introduction of slavery into Kansas; and was engaged in a number of lawless enterprises against the slaveholders. Brown assumed the role of a religious enthusiast, was a rigid Presbyterian, and pretended to believe he was called of God to give freedom to the Africans held in slavery at the South.

As early as 1857, Brown began to formulate secret plans to invade Virginia for the avowed purpose of liberating slaves. His scheme was to make the line of the mountains which cut diagonally through Maryland and Virginia, down through these States into Tennessee and Alabama, the base of his operations. These plans were formed with associate conspirators in Kansas, Iowa, Canada, Ohio, New England and other places. In 1858 he and his two sons, Oliver and Watson, went to Harper's Ferry, then in Jefferson County, Virginia, now West Virginia, where, under the assumed name of Smith, they pretended to be prospectors hunting for ores. They stayed thereabout several months and then disappeared. After an absence of several months, John Brown returned to the vicinity and rented a farm in Maryland about four miles from the Ferry. He and his sons made frequent visits to Harper's Ferry, where the old man still appeared as "Bill Smith." The invading force, which was composed of John Brown, three sons, and thirteen other white men, and five negroes, was assembled at the rented farm. And large quantities of arms, ammunition, clothing and other supplies, purchased with money supplied by Northern Abolitionists, were deposited at the farm.

About 10:30 o'clock Sunday night, October 16th, 1859, John Brown, his three sons, Oliver, Watson and Owen, and thirteen other white men, and five negroes crossed the Potomac on the railroad bridge and took violent possession of Harper's Ferry. A small party of the desperadoes was sent into the adjacent country to arrest slaveholders, and take possession of slaves. They arrested Colonel Lewis Washington and twelve of his slaves; then arrested a Mr. Allstadt and his sixteen-year-old son, and forced all their negroes they could find to go with them. The prisoners were taken to the Ferry and confined in the engine house of the United States Arsenal, Brown and his band having taken possession of that building. In the morning, when the people came from their houses they found the town in complete possession of the insurrectionists. A number of men in the employ of the U. S. Government at the Arsenal, on going to their work, were arrested and confined in the Armory.

Alarms were sent to Charlestown, the county seat of Jefferson County, and to other nearby towns, calling for assistance; and companies of the volunteer militia were quickly dispatched to aid the citizens of Harper's Ferry. The "Jefferson Guard" from Charlestown arrived upon the scene at 11:30 A. M.; and during the day troops from Shepherdstown, Martinsburg and other points came in. They took possession of the railroad bridge, and occupied houses that commanded the front, rear and sides of the Armory, where Brown and his men had congregated after leaving a small squad in charge of the railroad bridge. Before the arrival of the troops a negro man had been killed by the insurgents, because the negro refused to join them. They had also killed Joseph Boerly, a citizen, while standing unarmed in his door; and had shot and killed Samuel P. Young, a citizen from the country, who was riding in to give assistance to the people of the town. While desultory shots were being exchanged between the soldiers and the insurrectionists, Fontaine Beckham, mayor of the town, was shot by one of Brown's sons and died almost instantly. The troops had captured William Thompson when the bridge was taken from the insurgents, and the indignant populace demanded that he should be immediately executed, because of Beckham's death. Thompson was taken out on the bridge and shot to death, his body being riddled with balls.

By directions of Captain Brown, a squad of insurrectionists had taken possession of Hall's rifle works. They were dislodged by the soldiers and one of the squad killed. Earlier in the day the Martinsburg men, who were mostly railroad employees, tried to force their way into the Armory to rescue the prisoners. In the charge Conductor Evans Dorsey, of Baltimore, was instantly killed, and Conductor George Richardson received a wound from which he died during the day. Colonel Robert W. Baylor, who was "Colonel Commandant" of the military forces, in his report to Governor Henry A. Wise of the operations of the day said: "During this engagement and the previous skirmishes, we had ten men wounded, two I fear mortally. The insurgents had eleven killed, one mortally wounded, and two taken prisoners, leaving only five in the engine house, and one of them seriously wounded." Night came on and operations ceased, but a strong guard was placed around the Armory to prevent the escape of any of the desperadoes.

At 11 o'clock that night a train arrived at Sandy Hook on the Maryland side of the Potomac. The train brought a military company from Baltimore, and eighty-five U. S. Marines sent from Washington by the War Department. General John B. Floyd was then Secretary of War, and he had selected Colonel Robert E. Lee to command the marines; and Lieutenant J. E. B. Stuart, of the 1st U. S. Cavalry, was Colonel Lee's aid. Colonel Lee promptly marched the marines across the river and stationed them within the Armory grounds, so as to completely surround the engine house. Late on Monday, Brown had sent a written message to Colonel Baylor proposing to yield, if he was permitted to cross the Potomac bridge with his men and all their arms and ammunition, and to take along his prisoners who would be released as soon as they got a little beyond the river. This proposition was rejected promptly by Colonel Baylor. It was agreed between Colonel Lee and Colonel Baylor that at daybreak "the volunteer forces should form around the outside of the government property and clear the streets of citizens and spectators, to prevent them from firing random shots. to the great danger of our soldiers, and to remain in that position whilst he would attack the engine house with his marines."

At early dawn the troops were drawn up in accordance with the above arrangement. Lieutenant Stuart then advanced to the engine house and, in a parley with Brown, demanded an unconditional surrender. Brown refused to surrender on any terms, except those he had presented to Colonel Baylor the day previous. Colonel Baylor in his report to Governor Wise says: "The marines were then ordered to force the doors. The attempt was made with heavy sledge hammers, but proved ineffectual. They were then ordered to attack the doors with a heavy ladder which was lying a short distance off. After two powerful efforts the door was shattered sufficiently to obtain an entrance. Immediately a heavy volley was fired in by the marines, and an entrance effected which soon terminated the conflict. In this engagement, the marines had one killed and one slightly wounded. The insurgents had two killed and three taken prisoners. After the firing ceased, the inprisoned citizens walked out unhurt."

At about noon on the same day the Independent Grays, of Baltimore, were dispatched to Brown's house across the river to search for arms and ammunition. They returned at six o'clock and brought with them what had been found secreted by the insurgents. There were two hundred Sharpe's rifles, two hundred revolvers, twenty-three thousand percussion caps, one hundred thousand percussion pistol caps, ten kegs of gunpowder, thirteen thousand ball cartridges for Sharpe's rifles, one Major General's sword, fifteen hundred pikes, and a large assortment of blankets, shoes and clothing of every description. They also discovered a carpet bag, containing documents throwing much light on the conspiracy, printed constitutions and by-laws of an organization, showing or indicating ramifications in various States of the Union. They also found letters from various individuals at the North—one from Fred Douglas, containing ten dollars from a lady for the cause; also a letter from Gerrit Smith, about money matters, and a check or draft by him for $100, endorsed by a cashier of a New York bank. All these were turned over to Governor Wise.

Governor Wise, who had arrived on Tuesday, went with Colonel Lee and others to have an interview with Brown. The Governor said "he was sorry to see a man of his age in that position." Brown defiantly replied, "I ask no sympathy and have no apologies to make." Then, the Governor asked him if he did not think he had done wrong, and he replied, "No." And he declared, that though he had but twenty-two men with him on the raid, he expected large reinforcements from Maryland, Virginia, North and South Carolina, and the New England States and New York. This was an admission that the conspiracy was much more extensive than Brown later claimed it to be; and that he and his associates expected to excite a wide-spread insurrection among the slaves at the South.

On Wednesday, the 19th of October, United States Senator James M. Mason, of Virginia, and Congressman C. L. Vallandingham, of Ohio, sought and obtained an interview with Captain Brown. The object of the interviewers was to persuade him to disclose the names of the prominent Abolitionists who were connected with the conspiracy and had helped to finance the enterprise. A reporter of the New York Herald was present and made a stenographic report of the questions propounded and the answers given by Brown. He either refused to answer or evaded all questions that would accomplish the purpose of Mason and Vallandingham. But he lost no opportunity to magnify his own importance as a Great Deliverer, Philanthropist, and exponent of the Golden Rule; and he tried to justify his many criminal acts during the years he had been engaged in outlawry. Shortly after this interview the prisoners—John Brown, Aaron C. Stephens, Edwin Coppie, Shields Green and John Copeland—were placed in the custody of the sheriff of Jefferson County and lodged in the county jail at Charlestown.

On the 20th of the month a mittimus was issued by Rodger Chew, a justice of the peace, directing the sheriff to deliver the bodies of the prisoners to the county jailer for safe keeping. And on the 26th a grand jury brought in an indictment against John Brown, Aaron C. Stephens, alias Aaron D. Stephens, and Edwin Coppie, white men, and Shields Green and John Copeland, free negroes. The prisoners were indicted: "For conspiring with negroes to produce an insurrection; for treason in the Commonwealth; and for murder."

The prisoners were brought into court under an armed guard, and upon their arraignment each prisoner plead, "Not Guilty." Then the prosecuting attorney announced that, "The State elects to try John Brown first." Thereupon, Brown asked for delay in his trial for various reasons, chiefly because of his physical condition and absence of counsel he was expecting to be sent by his sympathizers at the North; but the court, for sufficient cause, refused to grant the request, and the trial was begun.

The first day was occupied in selecting a jury. When Brown was brought into court the second day, Mr. Botts, of his counsel, informed the court that friends had tried to persuade the accused to put in a plea of insanity, but that he disdained to put in the plea. Brown then said: "I will add, if the court will allow me, that I look upon it as a miserable artifice and pretext of those who ought to take a different course in regard to me, if they took any at all, and I view it with contempt more than otherwise. I am perfectly unconscious of insanity, and I reject, so far as I am capable, any attempt to interfere in my behalf on that score."

This act of the prisoner made it impossible for his counsel to make any reasonable defense for their client. He made no denial that he had committed the offenses charged in the indictment, and persisted in claiming that what he had done with his organized band of outlaws was righteous in the sight of God. The jury could not do otherwise than bring in a verdict of guilty on all of the three charges laid in the indictment, and the verdict was: "Guilty of treason, and conspiring and advising with slaves and others to rebel, and murder in the first degree." Before sentence was pronounced by Judge Richard Parker, the presiding judge, Brown was asked by the clerk if he had anything to say. The condemned man arose and addressed the court in a clear voice. He undertook to justify the criminal conduct of himself and companions, and denied having any sense of guilt; and he said: "I feel entirely satisfied with the treatment I have received on my trial. Considering all the circumstances, it has been more generous than I expected." When Brown concluded, Judge Parker declared that no reasonable doubt could exist of the guilt of the prisoner and sentenced him to be hung in public, on Friday, the 2nd of December, 1859. The sentence was executed and John Brown expiated his many crimes on the appointed day.

The other prisoners were tried in succession, and they shared the same fate that befell their desperate leader. Below is a record of what befell John Brown and his "Men-at-Arms," as they were named by one of Brown's admiring biographers:

General John Brown—Executed at Charleston, Dec. 2nd, 1859.

Captain John E. Cook—Escaped, but was captured at Chambersburg, Pennsylvania, Oct. 25th, was tried, found guilty, sentenced Nov. 2nd, and executed Dec. 16th, 1859.

Lieutenant Edwin Coppie—Tried immediately after John Brown, found guilty, and executed Dec. 16th, 1859.

Captain Aaron C. Stephens—Trial postponed until spring term on account of his severe wounds. Tried, convicted, and executed March 16th, 1860.

Lieutenant Albert Hazlett—Escaped from Harper's Ferry, was captured at Carlisle, Pennsylvania, October 22nd, extradited to Virginia, tried and sentenced at spring term, and executed March 16th, 1860.

Lieutenant William H. Leeman—Killed at Harper's Ferry.

Captain Oliver Brown—Killed at Harper's Ferry.

Captain Watson Brown—Killed at Harper's Ferry.

Captain John Kagi—Killed at Harper's Ferry.

Lieutenant Jeremiah Anderson—Killed at Harper's Ferry.

Stewart Taylor—Killed at Harper's Ferry.

William Thompson—Killed at Harper's Ferry.

Dauphin O. Thompson—Killed at Harper's Ferry.

Charles P. Tidd—Made his escape. Died at Roanoke Island from fever while the battle was going on at that place, Feb. 8th, 1862. He was a soldier in the Federal Army.

Francis J. Merriam—Escaped, and died in New York City, Nov. 28th, 1865.

Owen Brown—son of John—escaped, and died in California, Jan. 9th, 1891. He was the last of the five who escaped to die.

Barclay Coppie—Escaped and was killed in a railroad accident in Kansas, Sept. 3rd, 1861, was then a Lieutenant in a Kansas regiment.

John A. Copeland—(Free Negro)—was tried, found guilty, and executed at Charlestown, December 16th, 1859.

Shields Green—(Escaped slave from South Carolina)—was executed at Charlestown, Dec. 16th, 1859.

Lewis L. Leary—(Free negro)—died from wounds at Harper's Ferry.

Oscar P. Anderson—(Free negro)—escaped, and died from consumption at Washington, D. C., Dec. 13th, 1872.

Dangerfield Newby—(Free negro)—killed at Harper's Ferry.

The prompt action of the Virginia authorities in trying and

disposing of John Brown and his professional outlaw associates was bitterly denounced by the Abolitionists as merciless and unjust. They were so blinded by fanaticism that they did not realize the enormity of Brown's lawless deeds; and they claimed that the incident was magnified in importance by the Southern people through fear of future similar occurrences. Governor Wise and the Virginians were actuated by no vague fear of other similar insurrections; but were resolved to show the people of the North how the South would meet and repel the mightier attack upon Southern institutions that was foreshadowed by the insurrection at Harper's Ferry—the attack that came about eighteen months later.

CHAPTER III.

THE PRESIDENTIAL ELECTION OF 1860.

Agitation of the slavery question was foreshadowed by the admission of Louisana to the Union in 1812; and it became a dangerous issue in American politics when the struggle for the admission of Missouri as a slave State began in 1820. For a period of forty years the agitation continued and grew in violence until the climax came in 1860. The Presidential election of that year transformed the militant National Democracy into a disrupted and powerless minority party—in which condition it remained for twenty-four years—and relegated the scattered remnants of the once great Whig party to political oblivion.

When the Democrats assembled in their National Convention at Charleston, South Carolina, on the 23rd of April, 1860, to nominate a Persidential ticket, it was found impossible to reconcile the divergent views of the delegates who came from the two sections of the Union. The delegates from the free States were enthusiastically in favor of the nomination of Stephen A. Douglas, while the delegates from the slave States were more deeply concerned about the position the party should take on the slavery question than they were in the choosing of a Presidential candidate. Southern extremists, led by Judah P. Benjamin, demanded that there should be written into the platform an explicit assertion of the right of citizens to settle with their slaves in the Territories; and also make emphatic declaration that this right should not "be destroyed or impaired by Congressional or Territorial legislation." The extreme pro-slavery men also insisted upon a declaration that "it is the duty of the Federal Government, when necessary, to protect slavery in the Territories, and wherever else its constitutional authority extends." These demands were resisted by the delegates from the free States, and the Southern men refused to accept any compromise proposition made by the Democrats from the North. Seven of the Southern States—Louisiana, Alabama, South Carolina, Mississippi, Florida, Texas and Arkansas—withdrew from the convention, and organized another assemblage, which was presided over by James A. Bayard,

T.H.—38

of Delaware. The Douglas men then had control of the convention but could not muster enough votes to give him the nomination. Finding it impossible to make a nomination, on the 3rd of May the convention adjourned to reconvene in Baltimore on the 18th of June.

When the Democratic Convention re-assembled at Baltimore on the 18th of June the sectional spirit manifested at the Charleston gathering had not abated but had become more aggravated. The delegates from the South, with those from California and Oregon, and two delegates from Massachusetts—Caleb Cushing and Benjamin F. Butler—nominated John C. Breckinridge, of Kentucky, for President, and Joseph Lane, of Oregon, for Vice President. The delegates from the North, assisted by a few scattering votes from the South, nominated Stephen A. Douglas for President, and Herschel V. Johnson, of Georgia, for Vice President.

William P. Cecil, of Tazewell County, was one of the delegates from the Thirteenth Congressional District of Virginia to the National Democratic Convention; and attended and participated in its deliberations both at Charleston and Baltimore. Knowing that the people whom he represented were in sympathy with the men of the South, who were resolved to maintain their constitutional rights, he co-operated with the Southern delegates both at Charleston and Baltimore, and voted for the nomination of Breckinridge and Lane. The Thirteenth Congressional District was then composed of the following counties: Smyth, Washington, Lee, Wise, Russell, Tazewell, McDowell, Buchanan, Wythe, Grayson, Carroll, Pulaski, and Scott.

During the interval between the adjournment at Charleston and the assembling of the Democratic convention at Baltimore, an organization which styled itself the "Constitutional-Union Party" held a convention in Baltimore, and nominated John Bell of Tennessee for President, and Edward Everett of Massachusetts, for Vice President. The new party, which never again appeared in American politics, was an aggregation of old Whigs and men from the defunct American, or Know Nothing party. They were anxious to preserve the Union, but upheld the Institution of slavery as a guaranteed constitutional right.

And, in the interval between the adjournment of the Democratic convention at Charleston and its re-assembling at Baltimore, the

Republicans had met in National Convention at Chicago. Abraham Lincoln was nominated as the candidate of the party for the Presidency; and Hannibal Hamlin, of Maine, was made its candidate for Vice President. Mr. Lincoln was opposed to the extension of slavery, and favored the enactment of laws to prohibit its extension beyond the States where the institution already existed. Mr. Breckinridge advocated the extension of slavery, and was not averse to the doctrine of secession. The campaign was conducted upon the widely divergent views of Lincoln and Breckenridge on the slavery question, and four years of awful civil strife was the fruit it bore.

As the campaign progressed the rift that divided the Democrats of the two sections of the Union was widened, and the ranks of the Republicans were constantly augmented by accessions from Northern Democrats, who were indignant because of the avowed purpose of the Southern leaders to withdraw from the Union, if necessary, to extend and perpetuate slavery. It soon became evident that the voters of the free States would vote for either Lincoln or Douglas, and that the votes of the Southerners would be cast for either Breckinridge or Bell. When the election returns were canvassed, it was found that Lincoln had carried every free State, and that Breckinridge had won in every slave State except four; Virginia, Kentucky, and Maryland voting for Bell, and Missouri for Douglas. The electoral vote by the colleges stood: 180 for Lincoln and Hamlin; 72 for Breckinridge and Lane; 39 for Bell and Everett; and 12 for Douglas and Johnson. By a plurality of the popular vote, Lincoln carried 18 States; Breckinridge, 11; Bell, 3; and Douglas, only 1. Of the entire popular vote Lincoln got 1,857,601; Douglas, 1,291,574; Breckinridge, 850,082; and Bell, 646,124. Thus it will be seen that Lincoln lacked 930,170 of a popular majority, and was a minority President. The election was purely sectional in character, as all the States carried by Mr. Lincoln were north of what is known as "Mason and Dixon's Line."

When the result of the election was announced the Abolitionists at the North were greatly elated, especially those who had eulogized John Brown and his criminal associates for their conduct at Harper's Ferry. The people of the South were thrown into a state of intense anger and excitement, and felt that no other course was left them but peacable withdrawal from the Union. A political party had gained control of the executive branch of the Federal Government with the avowed purpose of not only preventing the extension of slavery into the Territories, but of eventually securing, through peaceful means, its abolishment from the States of the Union.

The session of Congress that followed Mr. Lincoln's election was stormy and eventful. John C. Crittenden, then a Senator from Kentucky, tried to avert, by compromise, the impending catastrophe. Early in the session, in December, 1860, he presented in the Senate, as the basis for settlement of the slavery question, the famous Missouri Compromise line 36° 30' as a division of the public domain. The proposition of Mr. Crittenden was offered in the form of a constitutional amendment. Large numbers of °petitions were received daily from citizens of the free States urging the adoption of the proposition. Jefferson Davis, Robert Toombs, and nearly all the extremist Southern Senators, together with Stephen A. Douglas and the conservative Senators from the North, were in favor of the Crittenden plan for restoring peace and harmony between the two sections of the Union. But it was found that no Abolitionist, and not a single prominent man of the party that had elected Mr. Lincoln, would accept and stand by the proposed plan for settlement of the momentous question. Thereupon, nearly all the Southern Senators, including Mr. Davis and Mr. Toombs, united in sending a telegram to the people of the South, advising them, as a matter of safety, to withdraw from the Union.

On the night of the 14th of November, 1860, Alexander H. Stephens, afterwards Vice President of the Confederate States, made an address to the Legislature of Georgia and an immense audience at Milledgeville. It was a very conservative and able address; and Mr. Stephens took the position that Georgia ought not to secede from the Union because of Mr. Lincoln's election. In part, he said: "In my judgment, the election of no man, constitutionally chosen, to that high office (the President) is sufficient cause to justify any State to separate from the Union. We are pledged to maintain the Constitution. Many of us have sworn to support it." He urged, that "if the Republic is to go down. * * * Let the fanatics of the North break the Constitution, if such is their fell purpose." Mr. Stephens also called attention to the fact that the opposing parties had control of both Houses of the newly elected Congress, which made the Republican President powerless to carry into effect any unconstitutional principles of his party. Hearing of this speech, Mr. Lincoln wrote to Mr. Stephens for a copy, that he might be more fully informed of its import. On Dec. 22, 1860, Mr. Lincoln wrote to Mr. Stephens a private letter, endorsed at the head "For your eye only", and, in part, saying:

"Do the people of the South really entertain fears that a Republican administration would, *directly* or *indirectly*, interfere with the slaves, or with them, about their slaves? If they do, I wish to assure you, as once a friend, and still, I hope, not an enemy, that there is no cause for such fears. The South would be in no more danger in this respect, than it was in the days of Washington. I suppose, however, this does not meet the case. You think slavery is right and ought to be extended, while we think it is wrong and ought to be restricted. That I suppose is the rule. It certainly is the only substantial difference between us."

Clearly it was at that time Mr. Lincoln's purpose not to disturb slavery in the Southern States, but to prevent its extension beyond those States where it already existed. This, however, was not satisfactory to the ultra pro-slavery men of the South, who had resolved to extend it into the Territories, and to also demand a strict enforcement of the Fugitive Slave Law. They were also demanding that persons committing crimes against slave property in one State, and fleeing to another should be delivered up for trial in the State where the crime was committed, and that: "A person charged in any State with treason, felony, or any other crime, who shall flee from justice and be found in another State, shall, on demand of the executive authority of the State from which he fled, be delivered up, to be removed to the State having jurisdiction of the crime." Executives of certain of the free States had refused to deliver up such criminals; and the Governor of Ohio had actually refused to deliver up to the Virginia authorities men who were engaged in the Harper's Ferry insurrection.

Following the advice of Jefferson Davis, Robert Toombs and other Southern Senators, South Carolina withdrew from the Union by an ordinance of secession, passed by a convention on the 20th day of December, 1860. Later on, at short intervals, Mississippi, Louisiana, Alabama, Florida, Georgia, and Texas passed ordinances of secession. In her ordinance, South Carolina had incorporated an invitation to all the Southern States who might secede to join her in sending delegates to a Congress to meet on the 4th of February,

1861, at Montgomery, Alabama. This invitation was accepted by Alabama, Florida, Georgia, Louisiana, Mississippi, and Texas; and the delegates from those States assembled with the delegates from South Carolina at Montgomery on the day fixed in the invitation. The Senators and Members in the Federal Congress, of each of the seceding States, had resigned their positions, except Mr. Bouligney of Louisiana. He occupied his seat until the expiration of his term on the 4th of March, 1861. The delegates or deputies of the "Sovereign and independent States of South Carolina, Georgia, Florida, Alabama, Mississippi and Louisiana," then proceeded to ordain and establish a Constitution for the Provisional Government of the same.

On Saturday the 9th of February, 1861, the first Congress of the Confederate States of America was organized, the president and each member taking the following oath: "You do solemnly swear that you will support the Constitution for the Provisional Government of the Confederate States of America, so help you God."

The Congress of the Confederate States of America then proceeded to elect a President and Vice President for the Provisional Government. The vote being taken by States, Hon. Jefferson Davis of Mississippi was unanimously elected President; and Hon. Alexander Hamilton Stephens of Georgia, was unanimously elected Vice President of the Provisional Government. And on the 18th day of February, 1861, the inauguration of Jefferson Davis as President and Alexander H. Stephens as Vice President of the Confederate States of America took place. At an early date President Davis announced his cabinet as follows: Secretary of State, Robert Toombs, of Georgia; Secretary of Treasury, Christopher G. Memminger, of South Carolina; Postmaster General, John H. Reagan, of Texas; Secretary of Navy, Stephen R. Mallory, of Florida; Attorney General, Judah P. Benjamin, of Louisiana.

CHAPTER IV.

In the meantime Governor John Letcher, of Virginia, who was as conservative in his opinions on the question of secession as Alexander H. Stephens, became greatly disturbed; and he called the General Assembly in extra session, to meet on the 7th of January, 1861. Upon the recommendation of Governor Letcher, the General Assembly, on the 14th of January, one week after it assembled, passed an act which provided for electing members of a convention to consider the grave questions that confronted the country. This act required a poll to be opened "to take the sense of the qualified voters as to whether any action of said convention dissolving our connection with the Federal Union or changing the

Major William P. Cecil, son of Samuel Cecil and uncle of the author, was born on the Clinch, April 9th, 1820, and died on New River at the mouth of Walker's Creek, July 12th, 1899. For a number of years he was prominent in the affairs of Tazewell County, as a lawyer and in an official capacity. He served several terms as Commonwealth's Attorney; was one of the delegates that represented the county in the Virginia Secession Convention in 1861; and represented the county in the House of Delegates at the sessions of 1874 and 1875 and 1876 and 1877—the Legislature then met annually. In the Civil War, he was first captain of a company in the 22nd Battalion, Virginia Infantry, and was promoted to major of the battalion.

organic law of the State, shall be submitted to the people for ratification or rejection." The election for delegates was held on the 4th of February, 1861, and the question submitted to the people was decided affirmatively by a large majority. One hundred and fifty delegates were elected, apportioned among the various counties and cities of the State. Tazewell County, and Buchanan and McDowell counties that had not been separated from Tazewell by legislative apportionment, elected William P. Cecil and Samuel L.

Judge Samuel Livingston Graham was born September 19th, 1816, and died April 12th, 1896. In early life he was clerk of the courts of Tazewell County; was a member of the Virginia Secession Convention of 1861; captain of a reserve company from Tazewell County, and was engaged with his company in the battle of Saltville, Virginia, in October, 1864. He was judge of the county court for the counties of Buchanan and Wise; and United States Marshal for the Western District of Virginia during Mr. Cleveland's first administration.

Graham as their representatives in what has since been called the "Secession Convention."

When the convention assembled on the 13th of February, it was found to be largely composed of the most prominent leaders of the Whig and Democratic parties in the State. The author, then a boy fourteen years old, was living with his parents in Richmond, and it was my privilege to witness the opening and organization and to frequently attend the deliberations of this splendid Convention of Virginians. I have looked upon many legislative and other deliberative bodies; but, in all my experience, I have never seen an assembly of men, representing the people, that surpassed this convention in ability and earnestness of purpose. It was manifest that a large majority of the members opposed withdrawal from the Union under conditions then existing.

On the 19th of February, 1861, Hon. John S. Preston, Commissioner from South Carolina, made his famous speech to the convention. Mr. Preston was born at the Salt Works, in the present Smyth County, Virginia, and was one of three distinguished sons— William C., John S. and Thomas L.—of General Francis Preston. I sat on a step of the rostrum from which he spoke, and heard him, with burning eloquence, make appeal for Virginia to go to the assistance of her endangered sister States of the South. Secession sentiment was increased by Mr. Preston's speech; and during the weeks that followed, until the ordinance was passed, the question was debated on the floor of the Convention by great Virginia statesmen, ably, earnestly, and sometimes thrillingly.

On the 4th of March, 1861, Abraham Lincoln was inaugurated President of the United States. In his inaugural address, Mr. Lincoln referred to the apprehension that existed "among the people of the Southern States that by the accession of a Republican Administration their property and their peace and personal security are to be endangered." He gave assurance that "There has never been any reasonable cause for such apprehension;" and this assurance was reinforced by quoting an utterance made in one of his speeches when a candidate: "I have no purpose, directly or indirectly, to interfere with the institution of slavery in the States where it exists. I believe I have no lawful right to do so, and I have no inclination to do so."

But, Mr. Lincoln, announced his purpose to "preserve, protect and defend" the Government. He declared: "The Government will not assail you. You can have no conflict without being yourselves the aggressors." These words were addressed to his dissatisfied countrymen at the South. The members of the Virginia Convention, after reading these utterances of the President, were hopeful that the disturbing questions might still be amicably adjusted. So believing, on the 8th of April, the Convention adopted a resolution creating a committee of three to wait upon the President; "and to respectfully ask of him to communicate to this convention the policy which the Federal executive intends to pursue in regard to the Confederate States." It was a committee composed of three very eminent men; William Ballard Preston, of Montgomery County; Alexander H. H. Stuart, of Augusta, and George W. Randolph, of the city of Richmond.

The committee went to Washington on the 12th of April, and the President received them on the morning of the 13th. Unfortunately for the peaceful mission of the committee, on the day of their arrival at Washington bombardment of Fort Sumter was commenced by General G. T. Beuregaurd and war had actually begun. The President handed the committee a written reply to the preamble and resolution of the Virginia Convention, in which he said:

"The power confided to me will be used to hold, occupy, and possess the property and places belonging to the government, and to collect the duties and imposts; but beyond what is necessary for these objects there will be no invasion—no using of force against or among the people anywhere. *   *   *   *

"But if, as now appears to be true, in pursuit of a purpose to drive the United States authorities from these places, an unprovoked assault has been made upon Fort Sumter, I shall hold myself at liberty to repossess, if I can, like places which had been seized before the government was devolved upon me. And in any event I shall to the extent of my ability repel force by force."

Two days after sending his reply to the Virginia Convention, President Lincoln issued his eventful proclamation calling forth the militia of the several States of the Union to the aggregate number of 75,000. This was done to carry out the policy he had announced in his reply to the resolution of inquiry sent from the Virginia Convention. A requisition was made upon the Governor of Virginia for her quota of militia under the proclamation. Governor Letcher immediately issued a proclamation declaring that Virginia would not, under any circumstances, supply troops to aid in any manner in any assault upon the Southern States.

Following these important incidents the Convention went into secret sessions; and, after sitting several days with closed doors, on the 17th of April, 1861, adopted an ordinance which repealed the ratification of the Federal Constitution by the State of Virginia, and resumed all the rights and powers granted by the State to the

Federal Government. The ordinance required that the question should be submitted to the people on the following fourth Thursday in May for ratification or rejection. An election was held on that day, and the action of the Convention was endorsed by a very large majority of the votes cast at the election.

The secret sessions of the Convention, held before the ordinance was adopted and promulgated, were marked with very able and heated discussions of the secession question. There was a strong anti-secession sentiment prevailing among the members, as was shown by their votes when the ordinance was put upon its final passage. It was adopted by a vote of 88 to 55. The minority was made up of a number of the most distinguished men of the Commonwealth. Among these were: Alexander H. H. Stuart, John B. Baldwin. Edmund Pendleton, William McComas, Jubal A. Early, Robert Y. Conrad, James Marshall, Williams C. Wickam, John S. Carlile. Alfred M. Barbour, George W. Summers, John Janney, who was President of the Convention; Waitman T. Willey, Sherrard Clemmens, Samuel McD. Moore, John F. Lewis, Algernon S. Gray. William White, J. G. Holladay, and others.

The men who represented the counties that constitute the present Ninth Congressional District of Virginia in the Convention were as follows: Lee—John D. Sharp; Lee and Scott—Peter C. Johnston; Scott—Colbert C. Fuqua; Russell and Wise—William B. Aston; Tazewell and Buchanan—William P. Cecil and Samuel L. Graham; Washington—Robert E. Grant and John A. Campbell; Smyth—James W. Sheffey; Wythe—Robert C. Kent; Pulaski—Benjamin F. Wysor; Giles—Manillius Chapman. Three of these—Mr. Sharp of Lee, Mr. Fuqua of Scott, and Mr. Grant of Washington—voted against the ordinance; but Mr. Grant changed his vote to the affirmative. The other members from this district—nine in number—voted for the ordinance.

Governor Letcher took prompt steps for organizing and mobilizing the military forces of Virginia. A number of well-trained volunteer companies were already in existence in the various cities and counties of the State, and these were quickly mustered into service. The governor, on the 22nd of April, nominated Colonel Robert E. Lee to be Commander of the military and naval forces of Virginia, with the rank of major general. The nomination was confirmed by the Convention; and on the following day, the 23rd,

the great military chieftain appeared and was introduced to the
august body by John Janney, the venerable President, in a speech
that presaged the fame that Lee would win in the four years that
followed. General Lee s response to the beautiful remarks of Mr.
Janney was brief and characteristic. He said: "Mr. President
and Gentlemen of the Convention—Profoundly impressed with the
solemnity of the occasion, for which I must say I was not prepared,
I accept the position assigned by your partiality. I would have
much preferred had your choice fallen on an abler man. Trusting
in Almighty God, an approving conscience, and the aid of my fellow-citizens, I devote myself to the service of my native State, in
whose behalf alone, will I ever again draw my sword."

A temporary union of Virginia with the Confederate States
was effected through Commissioners appointed by the Convention,
and Alexander H. Stephens, Commissioner for the Confederacy.
And on the 25th of April an ordinance was passed adopting the
Constitution of the Provisional Government of the Confederate
States; and this ordinance was not to be effective until and unless
the Ordinance of Secession was ratified by the voters of Virginia.
Later, a resolution was passed inviting the President of the Confederate States, and the constituted authorities of the Confederacy,
to make the city of Richmond, or some other place in this State, the
seat of government of the Confederacy. Alexander H. Stephens,
Vice President of the Confederate States of America, says in his
History of the United States: "On the 21st of May, after the
secession of Virginia, the seat of government of the Confederate
States was transferred to Richmond, the capital of that State."

Thus did a convention, composed of the most eminent men of
the Commonwealth, separate Virginia from the United States of
America and identify its hopes and fortunes with the Confederate
States.

I have undertaken to relate as briefly as possible the most
potent factors that forced a dismemberment of the Union, and the
consequent four years of tragic strife between the sections. This,
I believed, was necessary before telling what the people of Tazewell did as their part in the Civil War.

If one cares to search for the causes of the war between the
States, they can surely be found in the series of events that attended
the agitation of the slavery question—beginning with the Missouri

question in 1818, and culminating in the Presidential election of 1860. To whom shall be alloted the fearful responsibility of originating the causes that provoked the terrible catastrophe? This, up to the present time, has been largely a matter of individual or sectional opinion. Conservative thought may, possibly, eventually find that the fault was dual—divided equally between the fanatical Abolitionists of the North and the uncompromising slaveholders of the South. The Abolitionists so abhored slavery that they violated the Constitution, defied the decrees of the highest judicial tribunal of the Government, and employed the most barbarous agencies for its abolition. And its extreme advocates at the South claimed, as did John C. Calhoun, that slavery was a benevolent institution and should be perpetuated. Others at the South contended that its economic value transcended all questions of morality and righteousness. From these two extremes there was developed an irrepressible conflict that could not be concluded except by war.

CHAPTER V.

WHAT TAZEWELL DID IN THE WAR.

There was practically no difference of opinion among the people of Tazewell as to what they ought to do in the conflict between the North and the South. At the election held for ratification of the Ordinance of Secession the vote of the county was practically unanimous for ratification of the ordinance. This attitude was not evoked by a desire to extend or perpetuate slavery. According to the census of 1860, the entire population of the county, after the formation of Buchanan and McDowell counties, had been reduced to 9,920 souls. Of this number 8,625 were white persons, 1,202 were negro slaves, and 93 free negroes. There were not more than two or three hundred slave-owners in the county.

From the day that Tazewell became a political unit of the State of Virginia and of the Federal Union, the people of the county had remained steadfast in their devotion to the political creed of Thomas Jefferson. They were thoroughly indoctrinated with his theories of States-Rights and Local Self-Government. Hence, when the North undertook to violate the constitutional and reserved rights of the Southern States, the men of Tazewell stood heartily with Virginia in her resolute support of the Southern people. It was not to extend or perpetuate slavery that Tazewell sent two thousand of her devoted sons to do service for the "Lost Cause."

The sublime spirit that animated the Clinch Valley pioneers to defend their homes and loved ones from assaults made by the savage red foe, and to do much splendid service for their country on numerous battle fields while fighting Great Britain's red-coated veterans during the Revolutionary War, was reawakened in the breasts of their descendants when the tocsin of war was sounded in 1861. Immediately following the withdrawal of Virginia from the Union, volunteer companies were rapidly organized in Tazewell County, so rapidly that it was almost impossible to supply them with equipments for service. But this did not stay the ardor of the brave and eager men of Tazewell. Most of the men and boys of the county had guns of their own, and they knew how to use them quite as well as did their pioneer ancestors. Many of the soldiers went to the front armed with their own guns and pistols, and the cavalrymen furnished their own horses. Twenty companies—ten of infantry and ten of cavalry—did valiant service for the Confederacy.

Bodies of Confederate troops were on several occasions encamped in the county while the war was going on. The first of these was a small army under the command of General Humphrey Marshall, of Kentucky, that camped in the spring of 1862 east of the county

Captain William Edward Peery, son of 'Squire Thomas Peery, and grandson of William Peery the pioneer, was, possibly, the most universally beloved man that Tazewell County ever produced. He was born July 7th, 1829, and died March 15th, 1895. It can be safely said that he lived and died without an enemy on earth. His home was the centre of the lavish hospitality for which Tazewell in his day was so noted. He was educated at Emory and Henry College, and was a man of fine literary taste and attainments. The first year of the Civil War he served on the staff of Gen. Jno. B. Floyd. In the spring of 1862 he became lieutenant of a company of cavalry, of which company the gallant Col. W. L. Graham was captain. This company was attached to the 16th Virginia Cavalry Regiment in the fall of 1862, and he was made captain. On the retreat from Gettysburg he lost his right arm and was made a prisoner at the battle of Boonesboro, Md., in June, 1863. He was imprisoned at Johnson's Island until March, 1865, when he was exchanged, and returned home after an absence of two years. Captain Peery would never accept a public office, though often solicited by his friends to stand as a candidate. However, he held and expressed decided and intelligent convictions on all public questions, and had much to do with shaping the political and economic thought of the people of the county.

seat, then Jeffersonville. General Marshall had his headquarters at
the home of the late Captain Wm. E. Perry, and most of his men
were quartered on Captain Peery's farm. His army was composed
of the 5th Kentucky Infantry, commanded by Colonel A. J. May;
54th Virginia Infantry, under Colonel Trigg; 29th Virginia Infan-

This old walnut tree is one of the most noted trees in Tazewell
County. It stands near the west end of the residence of the late
Capt. Wm. E. Peery; and many hundreds of his friends were greeted
and socially entertained by him under its delightfully refreshing
screen. Tradition affirms that Dr. Thomas Dunn English wrote the
sweetly pathetic ballad, "Ben Bolt," within the precincts of its cool
shadows. He certainly wrote "The Logan Grazier," one of his poems,
under this tree. Dr. English was then sojourning in Tazewell and
was frequently the guest of Captain Peery.

try, under Colonel Moore; a small battalion of infantry, commanded by Major Dunn; a battalion of Kentucky cavalry, under
Colonel Bradley; and a battery of artillery, commanded by Captain Jeffries. General Marshall had been ordered to assemble these
forces at Tazewell to co-operate with General Henry Heath, who

was stationed at Dublin, in Pulaski County, and Colonel Gabriel C. Wharton who was encamped at Wytheville with his regiment, the 51st Virginia Infantry. The three commands—Marshall's, Heath's, and Wharton's—did co-operate in May, 1862, against the Federal army under General Cox that was advancing up New River, aiming to reach the Virginia and Tennessee Railroad, now the Norfolk & Western Railway. General Marshall had made a fine record in the Mexican War, but in the operation against Cox he showed such inefficiency that he had to retire from active military service.

The next body of men that encamped for a season in the county was a battalion of Georgia artillery. There were three or four companies and it was a splendid body of men. They camped here during the winter of 1862-63, and came more especially to get supplies of food for the men and feed for their horses, there still being an abundance of grain, hay, and meat in the county. The encampment was made in a basin at the head of a hollow just west of the present fine orchard of Samuel C. Peery, on land then belonging to the estate of Major David Peery, and now owned by Ritchie Peery. Comfortable cabins were built for the officers and men, logs cut from trees on the site of the camp being used for that purpose. The place was afterwards called by persons living in the locality the "Georgia Camp." It is about two miles northeast of the town of Tazewell. Early in the spring of 1863 the Georgians left their winter quarters and went South for active service.

Very soon after the Georgians left, the 45th Virginia Battalion of Infantry, known as Beckley's Battalion, occupied the camp that had been vacated. This battalion was composed of four companies, and was made up almost entirely of men from the border counties, most of them from Boone and Logan. Several of the Hatfields and McCoys belonged to the battalion, Ans. Hatfield being a lieutenant in one of the companies. It was as fearless fighting body of men as could be found in the Confederate service. Lieutenant Colonel Henry Beckley, son of General Alfred Beckley, of Raleigh County, commanded the battalion; Major Blake Woodson, of Botetourt County, was second in command; J. G. Greenway, who afterwards became distinguished as a physician at Hot Springs, Arkansas, was adjutant; and Dr. Jno. S. Pendleton, brother of the author, was surgeon. In the spring of 1864 the writer enlisted as a private in Company A, which was commanded by Captain Stallings, who

T.H.—39

was clerk of Logan County. At the battle of Piedmont, on the 5th
of June, 1864, the 45th Virginia Regiment and the 45th Virginia
Battalion were near each other on the fighting line, only one regiment, the 60th Virginia, intervening.

The Tazewell men in the 45th Regiment suffered heavily.
Colonel William Browne was mortally wounded; Captain Charles
A. Fudge, was severely wounded and fell into the hands of the
enemy; Captain James S. Peery was captured, and several other
men from the county were made prisoners, among them Jesse White.

Captain Charles A. Fudge entered the service of the Confederate
States early in the spring of 1861 as second lieutenant of Company
H, 45th Regiment, Virginia Infantry. And in the spring of 1862 he
became captain of the company. He commanded his company in
numerous battles; but at the battle of Piedmont, on June 5th, 1864,
he was desperately wounded and captured by the Federals. He was
confined in prison until the war ended. Though he lived to a venerable
age he never recovered fully from the terrible wound received at
Piedmont. He was born March 7th, 1834, and died November 2nd, 1912.

General William E. Jones, who commanded the Confederate forces,
was killed just about the time the Federals made a successful
breach in the Confederate lines and flanked the 45th and 60th
Regiments, and the 45th Battalion. Colonel Beckley was wounded
early in the action, a minnie ball passing through his left wrist;
and Major Woodson was shot through the left arm, between the
shoulder and elbow. The author was captured in this battle, and,
after being a prisoner for two days, was paroled at Staunton.

There were other encampments of Confederate soldiers, at various times, in the county. Colonel A. J. May camped for a time with his Kentuckians at Indian, now Cedar Bluff; and in July, 1863, he had a small force of cavalry camping on Colonel Henry Bowen's place in the Cove. The 16th Virginia Cavalry, commanded by Colonel William L. Graham, wintered at Camp Georgia in the winter of 1863-64.

The losses incurred by Tazewell as a result of the Civil War were not confined to those that came from the death and disablement by wounds of so many of her best men. Her financial losses were very heavy. All the coin, and paper money, of any future value, that was in circulation in Tazewell when the war began had disappeared, or was valueless, when the struggle was over. Gradually but unceasingly for four years, the thousands of horses, cattle, sheep and hogs, that were owned by the farmers and graziers had been reduced to mere hundreds by home consumption and the generous supplies furnished the Confederate Government. The production of grain in the county was largely diminished by the absence of so many men who had been actively engaged in farming before they became soldiers. But the old men and the boys labored faithfully, and enough grain was produced to feed all the people at home and to furnish considerable quantities to outsiders in exchange for depreciated Confederate money. The faithful negro slaves also toiled on uncomplainingly, and did their part nobly in caring for the wives and children of their masters and the families of the soldiers who had no slaves. Nothing more worthy of commendation transpired during the Civil War than the faithful service performed by the slaves in Tazewell County. In proportion to their condition and opportunity they did as excellent service as the gallant men who fought for the Confederacy.

Too much cannot be said in praise of the splendid service rendered by the good women of Tazewell while the war was in progress. There were no Red Cross organizations in the county, and none anywhere in the South, to do such work as was performed by the Red Cross organizations in the recent World War. But every precious mother and daughter of Tazewell while the States of the Union were engaged in fratricidal strife was in herself an

impersonation of the modern Red Cross heroine. They could not
go to the battle grounds to attend the wounded and dying; but
at home they were one in thought and purpose to do all they could
for the comfort of the men who were marching, fighting and dying
for the cause they loved.

The old spinning wheels and looms were brought from the
garrets and lumber-rooms and put into active use. During the
last two years of the war, in 1863 and 1864, it was very seldom
that fabrics of any kind suitable for clothing, either for men or

The above picture is reproduced from a daguerreotype made at
Lynchburg, Va., in March, 1864. I am using it to show the excellent
quality of the woolen cloth woven by the good women of Southwest
Virginia to supply their boys and kindred with clothing while they
were fighting for the "Lost Cause." At the right of the picture is
the author, dressed in a suit which was made from jeans woven by
his aunt, Mrs. Kate Cecil Peery. On the left is my brother, Dr. Jno.
S. Pendleton, and he is clothed in a suit of jeans for which our mother
wove the cloth. My brother was surgeon of the 45th Battalion, Virginia Infantry, and I was a private in Company A of the same battalion. This is the only picture of a Confederate soldier clothed in
jeans I have ever seen, and that is why I use it here.

women, except such as were manufactured at home, were obtainable.
All the country stores were closed, because the merchants could
not buy any goods to continue business; and the stocks of the two
or three stores that tried to continue business in Jeffersonville
would hardly have made a load for a four-horse wagon.

Nearly all the farmers, large and small, had flocks of sheep which they carefully conserved, and the cultivation of flax was resumed. In this way enough raw material was produced in the county, when used with cotton thread, to provide ample clothing for the people at home, and keep the soldiers from Tazewell comfortably clad. Bales of cotton thread were procured from North Carolina mills and used for chains in the webs of jeans, linsey, and flannel that the women skilfully wove on their hand-looms.

There were no commercial dyestuffs then procurable. The daughters of Tazewell had not only inherited their skill as weavers, but had retained the ingenuity and adaptability to conditions that made the pioneer mothers pre-eminent. They found in the forests and gardens vegetable dyes, from which they got very pleasing color effects. The colors were not as brilliant as those produced by the modern chemical dyes, but they were satisfactory. Black and white walnut bark, hickory bark, sumac berries, wild indigo plants, and madder roots grown in the gardens, were the chief materials used. The colors produced from these were black, brown, blue, red, and sometimes by making two separate colorings a very pretty green effect was gotten. The linsey gowns worn by the girls and the jeans coats and pants of the men and boys were neat and comfortable.

FEDERAL RAIDS THROUGH TAZEWELL

Tazewell's isolated location was a great protection against devastations by Federal armies while the war was going on. There were no permanent or even temporary occupations of any section of the county by the enemy; but there were four invasions by raiding parties, three of which were made by large forces. All of the raiders came by the same routes the Indians travelled when they made their murderous forays to the Upper Clinch settlements. Three of them came up the Tug Fork, and one the Louisa Fork of Big Sandy River.

TOLAND'S RAID.

In July, 1863, Brevet Brigadier General John Toland. in command of about one thousand Federal cavalry, suddenly invaded Tazewell County. He came up Tug River and entered Abb's Valley on the afternoon of July 15th, crossed Stony Ridge and camped that night on Mrs. Susan Hawthorne's place about midway between the present residence of Mrs. Henry S. Bowen and the old Charles Taylor place, which is about half a mile west of Mrs. Bowen's house. At daybreak on the morning of the 16th, Toland resumed his march. Some of his men burned Lain's mill, which stood on the site now occupied by Witten's mill. For some reason the Federals applied the torch to and totally destroyed Kiah Harman's dwelling, which stood about one-fourth of a mile north of the Round House.

General Toland camped about three hundred yards west of the beautiful home of Mrs. Henry S. Bowen, shown above, and situated seven miles northeast of the court house. This is one of the most attractive of the many lovely homes in Tazewell County.

Just after sunrise the head of the column arrived at Captain Wm. E. Peery's, one and a half miles east of the court house. Thomas Ritchie Peery, brother of Captain Peery, Samuel L. Graham, John Hambrick, and the author, the latter then sixteen years old, were sitting in Mrs. Peery's room, waiting to get their breakfast, which was being hastily prepared. We had left our guns on the porch at the back of the room in which we were sitting. The floor of the porch was, as it now is, on a level with the ground, and paved with brick. Suddenly two Yankee cavalrymen rode on to the porch and picked up our guns; and the house was then completely surrounded by troopers.

Mr. Graham and Mr. Hambrick slipped out into the hall and went into the ell part of the house, which Mr. Hambrick, as manager of the Peery farm, was then occupying with his family. By a clever ruse, Graham and Hambrick avoided being made prisoners. Mr. Hambrick went quickly to bed, pretending to be sick, and Mr. Graham assumed the role of his physician. When a couple of troopers entered the room Mr. Graham was feeling Hambrick's pulse, and told the intruders he was a very sick man, urging them to retire as a shock might kill the patient. The trick was successful, as the kind-hearted soldiers promptly left the room.

In the meantime Tom Ritchie Peery, who was then nineteen years old, and the writer, who was sixteen, had been ordered to join a bunch of prisoners that were out in the barn lot. There were some fifteen or twenty youths and old men, who had been captured along the line of march from the head of the Clinch.

General Toland was moving his force very rapidly so as to reach Wytheville as quickly as possible; and his men did not have much opportunity to plunder houses on the line of march. They took eight or ten horses from the Peery farm, among them two fine dapple iron-gray mares that belonged to Mr. Hambrick. Only two horses were left on the place. One of these was "Bill", 'Squire Tommie Peery's old riding horse, over twenty years old; and the other a beautiful young sorrel horse my grandfather Cecil had given me. The Yankees couldn't catch old Bill and my horse. These two horses jumped fences and ran into the brush at the west end of Buckhorn Mountain.

There were several boxes of old Kentucky rifles in the granary, that had been left there by General Marshall's men in 1862. The guns were brought from the granary, broken up and piled with pieces of wood, and burned. Some of the guns were still loaded, and as the barrels became heated the sharp cracks of the rifles made the Yankees scatter. During this time of confusion, the writer quietly walked away from the guards and slipped back into the house, seated himself, and remained there until all the troops had passed up the road on their march to Wytheville. The other prisoners were taken as far as Burke's Garden and were there paroled. While passing through the Garden, a storehouse that belonged to D. Harold Peery was set on fire by the raiders and destroyed. It was where the late Henry Groseclose had his store.

About 10 o'clock the morning of the 16th, some four hours after Toland's men passed, Colonel A. J. May, who was camping with a small force of Confederates on Colonel Henry Bowen's place in the Cove, passed Captain's Peery's with about fifty mounted men in pursuit of Toland. Colonel May was riding rapidly at the head of the column, and was carrying a pennant or small flag.

Colonel Andrew Jackson May was a Kentuckian by birth, but was so closely associated with what transpired in Tazewell County during the entire Civil War, that he made it his future home, and was recognized as one of Tazewell's Confederate soldiers. In the spring of 1861 he was living at Prestonsburg, Kentucky, and entered the service of the Confederacy as lieutenant colonel of the 5th Kentucky Infantry. In the fall of 1862 he organized the 10th Kentucky Cavalry, and was made colonel of the regiment. He was its commander until the war closed.

From his manner, he seemed to say with his flag: "Follow me!" They were following him compactly and eagerly. The Colonel was every inch a soldier, and his men were as fearless as their leaders. A little later, Colonel Vincent Witcher, another daring soldier, passed Captain Peery's with a small force of mounted men pursuing the Federals. Colonel May and his men on the morning of the 17th came in contact with the rear guard of Toland's forces at Stony Creek, some six miles northwest of Wytheville,

where several of the Federals were killed, and, perhaps, a few
prisoners taken.

From Stony Creek, General Toland pushed on rapidly to Wytheville, reaching the head of what is now called Tazewell Street on
the 17th of July, 1863, about ten o'clock A. M. The people of
Wytheville had been notified of the approach of the enemy, but
no Confederate troops were then stationed at that point. There
was a home guard organization of about fifty youths and men, all

Captain David G. Sayers entered the Confederate army in the
that was commanded by Captain Elias V. Harman. In the fall of 1862,
spring of 1862 as second lieutenant of a company of Partizan Rangers
Lieutenant Sayers was made captain of a company that was attached
to the 37th Battalion of Virginia Cavalry, known as Witcher's Battalion. He was with the detachment of Witcher's men that pursued
Toland's regiment when it made its raid to Wytheville. Captain
Sayers was born September 15th, 1840, and died April 12th, 1902.

of whom were under or over military age. A small detachment
of reserves, possibly fifty in number, was sent to their assistance
from a Confederate training camp at Dublin, in Pulaski County.
The command of the one hundred men was placed with Colonel
Joseph L. Kent. He had entered the Confederate service as Captain
of the Wythe Grays, in April, 1861. That company was a unit
of the 4th Virginia Infantry, Stonewall Brigade. He had served
as Colonel of the 4th Regiment in 1862, but on account of ill health
had been forced to retire from the service. Colonel Kent, being

an experienced military man, made excellent disposition of his small but fearless force. Some youths and men concealed themselves in and behind houses along the east and west side of Tazewell Street and performed desperate feats as sharpshooters, or snipers, as they are now called, while the enemy was advancing along that street.

For some reason an attempt was made by the invaders to fire the town, or, at least, certain houses. At the time it was said or thought that the burning was done in revenge for the killing of Gen. Toland by a sniper. He was killed immediately in front of the beautiful residence of Captain William Giboney, which fronted on Tazewell Street and stood where the High School building is now located. The torch was applied to the Gibboney residence, and all its valuable contents were destroyed, except a few articles that were appropriated by the raiders. Among these articles was a dictionary that fell into the hands of Captain Fortescue, who was in charge of the advance guard of Toland's troops. The dictionary was afterwards recovered by Captain Gibboney, and on its blank pages the following entry was found:

"Camp Piatt

Aug. 1st, 1863.

"This book (an old Webster's Dictionary) was the only article saved from the buildings and residence of Wm. Gibboney, in Wytheville, Va., destroyed by order of Brevet Brigadier Gen. John Toland on the 17th day of July, 1863. It was entrusted to Thos. O'Brian, who in attempting to cross New River was drawn under the current and drowned—it was afterwards recovered & lost in a skirmish—& recaptured & carried to Wytheville, where it was again in the hands of the enemy—& again recaptured & carried over four hundred miles by the troops, being under fire the entire trip, lasting nearly eight days—& arrived at Gauly Bridge, W. Va. in an almost exhausted condition and immediately engaged with Gen'l McCausland of the Rebel army & reached Camp Piatt after 15 days of tedious hardship & heavy loss of Men.

Wm. H. Fortescue,

Capt. Commanding Squadron."

Several years after the conclusion of the Civil War, Mr. Albert H. Gibboney, son of Captain Wm. Gibboney, received a letter from Captain Fortescue in which he made the following statements:

"In reference to your Father's property, will say the order to burn it was given to me by Gen. Toland *in person.* When Gen. Toland gave me the order I asked him if he had better not make it written. He replied that it could be done quicker than he could write the order." Captain Fortescue also wrote Mr. Gibboney:

"I was in charge of the advance that entered Wytheville & had as Junior, Captain Delaney—who was one of the first officers killed. Gen. Toland had just ordered a sabre charge & Col. Powell, 2nd in command, rode up & gave me the order. I had just given the order when Gen. Toland was struck and died instantly. Col. Powell was the next one to fall. And though I was afterwards on many hotly contested fields I was never upon any that was more so than Wytheville."

The fighting began at about 10 o'clock, and was continued for about an hour. Of course such a small force of citizens and soldiers could not successfully hold back one thousand, or more, splendidly armed and mounted men. The Federals by repeated charges forced the Confederates to retire and scatter; but the enemy had been defeated in their plans for doing extensive damage to the railroad. As soon as the Confederates withdrew, the Federals sent detachments towards the railroad station to begin the work of destruction. But they heard the loud whistling of a locomotive that was pulling a train from the east and that was approaching Wytheville. They thought the train was bringing Confederate reinforcements, and made a hasty return to the main body of Toland's men; and the demoralized command commenced its retreat to West Virginia.

After setting fire to Captain Gibboney's dwelling the torch was applied to several houses on Tazewell and Main streets. The dwelling and printing office of David A. St. Clair, situated opposite Captain Gibboney's home, were totally destroyed. A storehouse on Main Street that was used for medical supplies by the Confederate Government, and the Cumberland Presbyterian church on Main Street, that stood a short distance east of the present Episcopal church, were also burned down. The women and children in the other houses that were fired, put out the flames as soon as the Yankees retired from the buildings. If the Federals had not retreated so hastily it is likely that much more serious damage would have been done to the town.

The Federals' losses amounted to seven killed and thirty wounded. Among the killed were General Toland and Captain Delaney. Lieutenant Colonel Powell, second in command, was severely wounded and was made a prisoner. He was riding one of John Hambricks' fine gray mares that had been taken from Captain Peery's place on the morning of the 16th. The mare was restored to Mr. Hambrick a few days thereafter, being ridden from Wytheville by Colonel Jas. F. Pendleton, father of the author.

There were only three whites and one negro killed on the Confederate side. Captain Oliver was mortally wounded near the stone house on Tazewell Street, then owned and occupied by Mrs. Haller, mother of the late Colonel Charles Haller; and now owned and occupied as a residence by Miss Frances Gibboney and her sister, Mrs. Kate Campbell. Pat Helligan, an Irishman, was standing in his house and declined to surrender on account of his nationality; he was shot and died instantly. Clayton Cook was mortally wounded, just as he walked out of Crockett's Hotel. He was very deaf and did not hear the demands the Federals made upon him to surrender. George, a faithful negro slave of Mr. Ephraim McGavock, was shot while trying to save his master from capture. A number of citizens were made prisoners, among them Colonel Thos. J. Boyd, Dr. Gage, Alfred Sult, James Corvin, Frank Slater, James Miller, Wash Leshy, Ephraim McGavock and Robert Bailey. The prisoners were taken as far as the top of Big Walker's Mountain, about ten miles northwest of Wytheville, and there released.

General Toland was shot through the heart and expired instantly. It has never been positively known who fired the shot that killed him. Some said it was Bob Bailey, a youth in his teens, son of Jesse Bailey. Others said it was Andrew Parish, also a youth, who fired the fatal shot; and still others claimed it was a woman who killed him. Well might Captain Fortescue declare: "Although I was afterwards on many hotly contested fields, I was never upon any that was more so than Wytheville." Nothing more desperately daring was done during the Civil War than the defence that was made at Wytheville by the old men and boys, and, possibly, the women of the town.

The Federals were very much demoralized by their experience at Wytheville. After arriving at the top of Walker's Mountain, instead of retreating by the same route by which they had advanced, they left the turnpike road and went down a mountain spur called "Ram's Horn", and entered the valley in Bland County, and turned their march eastward. When they came to the place of William Stowers they turned their horses into his wheat field and entirely destroyed his crop. From that point they went east as far as Charles Grayson's place. There they turned back and went through the gap of Brushy Mountain over what is known as the Laurel road, and followed that road down Laurel Creek to Frank Suiter's place in the Hunting Camp Valley. They stole all Mr. Suiter's horses, and followed a path across Round Mountain and came into the Wolf Creek Valley at the now Isaac Stowers farm. Then they proceeded up Wolf Creek to Crabtree's Gap, and crossed Rich Mountain into the Clear Fork Valley. Turning down Clear Fork, they proceeded down the valley to the Henry Dill's place at the mouth of Cove Creek, and turned up that creek. A small detachment of Confederate soldiers and Tazewell citizens charged upon the rear guard of the Federals as they were going up the creek, killing several of the enemy, and captured several men and a number of horses. The raiders crossed East River Mountain at the George Gap, which is at the southwest corner of the Walter M. Sanders farm. From thence they passed through "Pin Hook" (now Graham). crossed the Stony Ridge and camped that night in the meadows near Falls Mills. The next morning they proceeded by way of the mouth of Abb's Valley to a gap in the Laurel Ridge, just above the big spring. There they were attacked by a part of the 10th Kentucky Cavalry. In the skirmish two of the Kentuckians. Thomas Fletcher and ——— Tutz were killed; but the Federal losses are not known. Continuing their retreat, the Federals passed just east of Pocahontas, and on by way of the Peeled Chestnuts; and at last gained safety in the mountains of West Virginia.

A very interesting incident occurred while the Federals were retreating, in which a Tazewell girl proved herself a heroine. A Federal trooper stopped at the home of Jonathan Hendrickson, who lived about two hundred yards west of the present Graham furnace. He ordered his supper, which was promptly served him. When he arose from the table he was looking into the muzzle of his own carbine, which was pointed at the Yankee by Miss Mattie Hendrickson. She politely told him he was her prisoner; and she held him as such until a squad of Confederates came along and took him in charge.

The second raid by Federals through the county was made by a very small detachment. They travelled at night, on foot, and kept away from all thoroughfares and houses. The object of the raid was to get to the Virginia & Tennessee Railroad near Marion, and to destroy bridges, burn depots, and so forth. This raid was made in the latter part of August, 1863. Toland's unsuccessful raid to Wytheville was made about six weeks previously. There were about twenty-five or thirty men in the second raid, and they approached Tazewell by the Sandy Valley route and entered the county in the Horse Pen Cove. There they concealed themselves to await nightfall, when they would resume their journey over ridges and mountains.

Several peach trees, laden with ripe fruit, were standing about a deserted cabin near where the men were in concealment. Some of the hungry men were lured from their hiding by the tempting red peaches. While they were gathering and devouring the fruit, Charles Taylor, who lived half a mile northwest of Witten's Mill, and about the same distance west of the present residence of Mrs. Henry S. Bowen, came suddenly upon the raiders. Mr. Taylor was out looking for lost cattle, which he thought had strayed into the Horse Pen Cove. The officer in command of the expedition made Mr. Taylor a prisoner; and required him to make oath that he would not reveal the presence of the raiding party to anyone, which Mr. Taylor faithfully observed. Later on, they were discovered by an old woman named Patsy Hall, who did weaving for people in the surrounding neighborhoods. They made Patsy take an oath similar to that administered to Mr. Taylor. She did not consider the oath binding, and forthwith travelled to the home of Robert Graham, who lived where Robert Tarter now resides, and told Mr. Graham and others in the neighborhood that the Yankees were coming by way of the Horse Pen Cove. Of course Patsey, like the old woman who saw a thousand squirrels in a tree, imagined there were hundreds in the raiding party, and so related.

Runners were sent out immediately to notify the people, just as the pioneers were warned of the approach of Indians, and before sundown the approach of the enemy was made known to all persons along the route the raiders were expected to follow. A detachment of the Tazewell Troopers were doing scouting duty, and were encamped in Abb's Valley, under the command of Lieutenant Joseph S. Moss. Judge S. C. Graham, then a youth seventeen years old, son of Robert Graham; and J. R. East, a youth about the same age, were sent as couriers to Abb's Valley to warn Lieutenant Moss of the presence of the enemy. He immediately brought his squadron to the head of the North Fork of the Clinch, and during the night sent out scouts to discover the whereabouts of the raiding party. About daylight the trail of the party was discovered just east of Witten's Mill. It was seen that they were traveling on foot, through the woods and fields, and in a staight line toward the railroad at or near Marion. Lieutenant Moss dismounted about a dozen of his men, and with them followed the trail. He had mounted troopers take the horses of himself and his dismounted men by the usual horseback route in the direction of Marion; and the trailers got their horses in one of the valleys between Marion and Tazewell. From Witten's Mill the raiders made a bee line, evidently by use of a compass, to Marion, crossing Rich, Clinch, Brushy and Walker's mountains. They reached the southside of Walker's Mountain, about five miles north of Marion, some time during the night of the next day following their discovery in Horse Pen Cove. They again went into concealment, with the purpose of striking the railroad in the night time.

A courier had been sent hastily from Jeffersonville to Marion to warn the citizens and any Confederate force that might be in that vicinity. As soon as the messenger arrived at Marion, Hon. James W. Sheffey and about twenty more citizens armed themselves and started out to hunt for the raiders. They found them on Hungers Mother Creek, about six miles north of Marion, and about two miles east of the Chatham Hill road, at a place then belonging to John Allen, but now owned by Elkana Ford. The hungry Yankees were feasting on roasting ears they had roasted at a fire, hiding and waiting until night time, when they could slip to the railroad and destroy bridges. The smoke from their fire attracted the attention of the squad of citizens and they closed in upon the raiders. When they saw the citizens, the raiders began to scatter and run. Two or three of them were captured but the balance made their escape.

AVERILL'S RAID.

Brigadier General W. W. Averill, with a brigade of cavalry, composed of 2,479 officers and men, made the third Federal invasion of Tazewell County, in May, 1864. It was the privilege of the author to view this raiding army, but under more fortunate circumstances than he had seen Toland's raiders in July, 1863.

General John S. Williams, who was in command of the Confederate forces stationed at the Salt Works, had received notice of

Major Thomas Peery Bowen was the eldest of the four gallant sons of Gen. Rees T. Bowen who served in the Confederate Army as members of the "Tazewell Troopers." He was mustered into service in May, 1861, his company being designated Co. H of the 8th Regiment, Virginia Cavalry. In the fall of 1861 he became captain of the company; and early in 1863 was promoted to major of the regiment for gallantry in action. Major Bowen was severely wounded in battle, but remained in active service until the surrender at Appomattox. He was born at Maiden Spring, August 2nd, 1838, and died October 6th, 1911.

Averill's advance through West Virginia. General Williams dispatched the 8th Virginia Cavalry, under command of Colonel Abe Cook, and with Major Thomas P. Bowen second in command, to ascertain the strength of the Federals and to impede their advance to the Salt Works, if that place should prove to be Averill's objective. Two companies of the 8th Cavalry had previously been sent to Abb's Valley to perform picket service. Colonel Cook reached Tazewell late in the afternoon of the 7th of May with the remainder of his regiment; and about the same time Averill entered Abb's Valley, where he encamped that night. Colonel Cook camped with his regiment in the meadow, now owned by Joseph S. Gillespie, at the west end of Tazewell.

At about noon the 8th of May the head of Averill's column arrived at the Round House ('Squire Tommie Peery's former home) and there halted. The advance regiment filed into the meadow opposite the Round House, and the men dismounted and held their horses while they grazed upon the grass, which was luxuriant and about knee deep. They sent out pickets, but the main body did not advance beyond the Round House until late in the afternoon. These pickets went as far as the Brittain place, a mile west of the court house.

In the meantime Colonel Cook, acting upon orders sent by couriers from General Williams, fell back towards the Salt Works. Colonel Cook's retirement left Averill's advance unopposed.

Some time ago the author heard Mr. Alex St. Clair relate what he knew of Averill's movements after he left the Peery place. Mr. St. Clair was a member of Company I, 16th Virginia Cavalry, that met Averill's army on the 10th of May, 1864, in the battle at Queen's Knob, or the Gap of Crockett's Cove, in Wythe County. Upon request, he has furnished me his recollections in writing, and they are as follows:

RECOLLECTIONS OF MR. ST. CLAIR.

"About the 1st of May, 1864, Gen. Averill left his winter quarters near Charleston, W. Va., with about 2,500 cavalry, his objective being Wytheville, Va., where he would strike the Va. & Tenn. R. R., one of the main arteries by which the Army of Northern Virginia was supplied. Advancing by way of Logan and Wyoming counties he reached the head of Abb's Valley on the evening of the 7th, where he surprised two companies of the 8th Va. Cavalry, on picket duty, and captured 20 men. Camping in the Valley that night, he pro-- ceeded the following day toward Tazewell C. H. At Five Oaks he was met by a small force of Confederates. In the skirmish that followed a Federal soldier was killed and buried in the garden of C. H. Greever, Esq. A few days after a neighbor asked the Esq. if he was not sorry to have the Yankee buried so near his house. His reply was, 'No ding it, I wish they were all in there.'

T.H.—40

"Averill reached Tazewell Court House on the afternoon of the 8th, and encamped on the farm of the late Capt. W. E. Peery, one and a half miles east of the Court House. For some unaccountable reason, he abandoned the advance on Wytheville, by way of Burke's Garden, broke camp about midnight, and at daybreak on the 9th was at the residence of the late Charles F. Tiffany on Bluestone. At this place the Federals took quite a number of horses and negroes and destroyed the wagon train of the 16th Va. Cavalry, capturing W. P. Whitley, Wm. Gose, and others. Averill continued his march by way of Cross Roads, Mercer County, and Rocky Gap and camped the night of the 9th near Bland C. H.

"The 16th Va. Cavalry, which had wintered at 'Camp Georgia' near the residence of S. C. Peery, two miles north of Tazewell C. H., was ordered east May 4th, arriving at a point near what is now the city of Bluefield. Col. Wm. L. Graham, who was in command of the regiment, learned that a strong Federal force was advancing from Princeton. This proved to be Gen. Crook with about 7,000 men, who was acting in conjunction with Averill, and had for his objective Dublin, Va., which he reached after the battle of Cloyd's Farm. This battle was fought May 9th.

"After Crook had passed Rocky Gap, Colonel Graham led the 16th to Wytheville. On the morning of the 10th Gen. John H. Morgan reached Wytheville, in advance of his command, and ordered Col. Graham to take his regiment to the gap at Crockett's Cove, six miles from Wytheville, and to hold the gap till reinforced. Passing through the gap, the 16th emerged into the Cove beyond. In a very short time we saw our advanced guard coming pell mell with two Yankee regiments in hot pursuit. Mounting our horses we dashed back into the gap. Col. Graham's command was: "Dismount boys and follow *Grimes*", which we did with a will, and poured a withering fire into the charging Yanks, emptying many saddles, and sending the rest scurrying to cover. Col. Graham, not being a West Pointer, gave many unique commands, but which always meant, "go for them boys", with *Grimes* in the lead. The 8th Va. Cavalry, having arrived, occupied the gap. The 16th was deployed and moved east along the top of the mountain. The Yankees dismounted a regiment and attempted to turn our right flank by crossing the mountain and striking our rear; but the 16th met them on the mountain top, drove them down the mountain, thus

hrowing us on their left flank. Just at this time, Gen. Morgan, who
ad gone around the mountain west of the gap where the fight
began, advanced on Averill's right flank. Seeing this, Averill began
o withdraw, which he did in a most skillful manner, forming his
egiments in Echelon, each one when driven back forming in the
ear of the others, thus maintaining a stubborn resistance. But with
ll his skill and bravery, night alone saved him from utter rout and
apture. Averill lost many in killed and wounded, himself among

Colonel William L. Graham was one of the most fearless soldiers
and commanders that Tazewell County gave to the Confederate army.
He was a grandson of Colonel John Montgomery, who was a noted
Indian fighter, and who served with George Rodgers Clark in the
Illinois campaign. Colonel Graham was not a trained military man,
but a natural born fighter and leader. He always led his men into
battle, calling on them to "Follow Grimes." He was born near Chatham Hill, Smyth County, Virginia, in October, 1820, and died in
April, 1908.

he latter. The Confederates losses were very small. In this
engagement about 2,500 men on each side took part, but I doubt
f a more systematic and skillful fight took place during the Civil
War. Averill retreated to the neighborhood of Blacksburg, where
he joined Crook, who fell back to Meadow Bluff in Greenbrier
County. After resting a few days, he moved along the C. & O.
R. R., destroying the same, and joined Hunter at Staunton. The
united armies then began the advance on Lynchburg, by way of
Lexington, Buchanan, Liberty, etc. McCausland, skirmishing at

every point of vantage, burning bridges, blocking roads, etc., so delayed the advance that Early reached Lynchburg in time to save the city. On the 18th of June, Hunter became alarmed and commenced an ignominious retreat, fleeing through the mountains of West Virginia, to the Kanawha, thus leaving the way open for Early's advance on Washington City."

BURBRIDGE RAID AND BATTLE AT SALT WORKS.

The fourth, and last, Federal raid through Tazewell County was under command of Brigadier General Stephen G. Burbridge; and was made in the last days of September and the first days of October, 1864. His object in making the expedition was to get to and destroy the Preston Salt Works, situated on the North Fork of Holston River, in Smyth County. From these works the Southern States were getting their principal supplies of salt.

General Burbridge assembled an army of five thousand men at Pikeville, Kentucky. From that place he marched to the Louisa Fork of Big Sandy River, and up that stream to Grundy in Buchanan County. Then he proceeded up the Louisa River, using the Kentucky and Tazewell C. H. Turnpike, crossed the Dividing Ridge, and entered the Clinch Valley at the present village of Raven, in Tazewell County. He then moved up the Clinch, passing Richlands, and arrived at Cedar Bluff on the 30th of September. There he came in contact with a body of Confederates, mostly Kentuckians, who were commanded by that splendid soldier, Colonel Giltner, of Kentucky. Burbridge pressed on from Cedar Bluff toward the Salt Works, marching through the Cove, crossing Clinch and Little Brushy mountains, and passing through Laurel Gap. Giltner and his small force could do nothing more than place obstructions across the roads and delay the advance of the Federals.

Burbridge passed through Laurel Gap on Saturday evening, October 1st, 1864. Instead of pressing on to the Salt Works, where Giltner had gone and joined the Confederate forces, he encamped for the night in the river bottoms, just south of Laurel Gap, now owned by Thomas E. George. Some military critics have ventured the opinion that Burbridge committed a serious blunder by not rushing on to attack the Confederates in the night time, and before they received reinforcements. It is more than probable that the Federal General found his troops so exhausted by their long and difficult march that he deemed it safest to rest them before making an attack.

On the morning of the 2nd of October, he broke camp and marched to the scene of battle, arriving there at about 9:30 o'clock. About the same time General John S. Williams got to the Salt Works, bringing with him nearly a thousand men. The Confederate General had three thousand men, including seven hundred reserves from the counties of Tazewell, Washington, Wythe, Grayson and Carroll. The reserves were men over forty-five years old and youths under eighteen.

The Confederates had formed their line of battle along the tops of the bluffs and cliffs on the south side of the North Fork of the Holston, reaching up the river from Buffalo Ford, and down the stream to where the chemical plant of the Mathieson Alkali Works is now located. When Burbridge arrived at 9:30 o'clock he promptly formed his lines on the north side of the river, fronting the Confederate forces, and the battle began about 10 o'clock. Each army was commanded by a Kentuckian, and both of the armies engaged were composed very largely of Kentuckians. The battle was continued from 10 o'clock in the morning until sundown, when victory perched upon the banner of the Confederates. Summers in his history of Southwest Virginia, says:

"The Federal loss in killed and wounded in this battle was about three hundred and fifty, the number of prisoners captured is variously estimated at from three to twelve hundred. The Federals left upon the field one hundred and four white and one hundred and fifty-six negro soldiers.

"The Confederate loss was eight killed and fifty-one wounded. among the killed being Colonel Trimble and Lieutenant Crutchfield. of the Tenth Kentucky Regiment."

Among the reserves, who acted with great valor was one company from Tazewell County, that were a part of the 13th Battalion of Virginia Reserves. That battalion was commanded by Colonel Robert Smith of Tazewell County, with Major Henry Smith of Russell County second in command, and was composed of the following companies:

Company A, Smyth County, commanded by Captain Robert Brown.

Company B, Tazewell County, commanded by Captain Samuel L. Graham.

Company C, Washington County, commanded by Lieutenant J. S. Booher.

Company D, Smyth County, commanded by Captain Evan D. Richardson.

Company F, Washington County, commanded by Captain William Barrow.

Colonel Robert Smith was born at Jacksboro, Tennessee, March 1st, 1819. In 1839 he married Miss Dorinda Cecil, daughter of Samuel Cecil, and took up his residence in Tazewell County in 1848. He was commissioned lieutenant colonel of the 13th Battalion, Virginia Reserves, in 1864, and commanded that battalion at the battle of Saltville on October 2nd, 1864, where he and his men won fame for their gallantry. In 1871, Colonel Smith moved with his family to California, where he died at a venerable age in December, 1899.

Company G, Russell County, commanded by Captain A. P. Gilmer.

Company H, commanded by Captain George E. Starnes.

Company I, Washington County, commanded by Captain Thomas E. Patterson.

The 13th Battalion held the line in front of the residence of "Governor" (James) Sanders. Every attack made by the Federals was repelled, and the battalion did such valiant service that Summers, writing about the part the reserves took in the battle, says:

"It was thought at the time that the bravery exhibited in this
contest by the reserves from Southwest Virginia was equal to the
bravery exhibited by the citizens of this county at King's Mountain
in 1780."

Burbridge began to retreat very soon after the battle was ended;
and returned to Kentucky by the same route he had used in making
the advance to the Salt Works.

After four years of heroic struggle and awful sacrifice the
depleted armies of the Confederacy were compelled to ground their
arms and furl the "Stars and Bars."

Tazewell County had sent forth nearly two thousand of her best
and bravest sons to do service for their country. Many of them
had fallen on battle fields, and were resting in heroes graves; many
had been maimed and physically impaired for life; others were in
Federal prisons and their home-coming was delayed; but those who
were still fit returned speedily to their homes and dear ones. It
was not a land made desolate by the iron-hoof of war to which they
returned. The rich soil, gushing springs and beautiful streams the
pioneers found when they came to the Clinch Valley were still
here. It was springtime when the Tazewell soldiers got back home.
The pastures on the hills and mountain sides, and the meadows along
the streams were carpeted with that exquisite verdure which had
made and still makes Tazewell almost world-famous. The returned
soldiers went earnestly to work to further develop and beautify the
land they had inherited from the pioneer fathers and mothers.
How faithfully they and their sons have performed that service is
now to be seen on every hand.

RECONSTRUCTION AND REORGANIZATION OF COUNTY GOVERNMENT.

Upon the downfall of the Confederate States, the State government of Virginia, that had been exercising at the capitol governmental functions during the war, was necessarily overthrown.
Francis H. Peirpont had been elected Governor of Virginia on the
20th of June, 1861, by a bogus convention that assembled at Wheeling. He established his seat of government at Wheeling; and kept
it there until the State of West Virginia was admitted to the Union
and the government of the new State was organized. On the 20th

of June, 1863, Governor Peirpont removed his seat of government to Alexandria. And, on the 9th of May, 1865, Andrew Johnson, President of the United States, issued a proclamation recognizing Peirpont as Governor of the Commonwealth of Virginia.

In this proclamation, President Johnson ordered: "That all acts and proceedings of the political, military, and civil organizations which have been in a state of insurrection and rebellion within the State of Virginia, against the authority and the laws of the United States, and of which Jefferson Davis, John Letcher, and William Smith were late the respective chiefs, are declared null and void. All persons who shall exercise, claim, pretend or attempt to exercise any political, military or civil power, authority, jurisdiction or right, by, through or under Jefferson Davis, late of the city of Richmond, and his confederates, or under John Letcher or William Smith, or civil commission or authority issued by them or either of them, since the 17th day of April, 1861, shall be deemed and taken as in rebellion against the United States, and shall be dealt with accordingly." The President also declared that the Federal Government would aid Governor Peirpont, "in the lawful measures which he may take for the extension and administration of the State government throughout the geographical limits of the said State."

Following the issuance of President Johnson's proclamation, Governor Peirpont, with his executive officers, removed the seat of government from Alexandria to Richmond, and occupied the governor's mansion and the capitol. The first entry in the Executive Journal was made on the 23rd of May, 1865, and is as follows:

"His Excellency the governor, in pursuance of the authority in him vested by the laws of the Commonwealth, and upon due information of the suppression of insurrection and domestic violence within the limits of the Commonwealth, ordered that the seat of government be restored to and re-established at the city of Richmond, from and after this date, and issued his proclamation accordingly."

By the mandate of the President's proclamation, every civil office in Virginia—State, county, and municipal—became vacant; and it was incumbent upon Governor Peirpont to see that all such offices were refilled with capable men.

The last term of the county court of Tazewell, while the Confederacy was in existence, was held on March 1st, 1865. S. W. Cecil presided, and the other justices sitting were, W. H. Buchanan and S. F. Watts. For nearly seven months thereafter the county was without any court or county officers; but the affairs of the county remained as orderly as when the pioneers lived here without any justices or constables to maintain order.

The first term of the county court, held under the restored, or Peirpont, government was on the 27th of September, 1865; and the first orders entered were the following:

"Be it remembered that on this the 27th day of September, in the year 1865, at Tazewell Court House appeared William O. Yost, William H. Buchanan, Adam Hedrick, Rees B. Higginbotham, Reizin R. Steel, Samuel H. Chiddix, Joseph C. Brown, Mark T. Lockhart, James Hankins, Henry Hunt, Jonathan Smith, Hugh D. Dudley, James Davis, Granville Jones, and David G. Yost, who presented commissions from F. H. Peirpont, Governor of Virginia, as justices of the peace for said county from this day till the 1st day of August, 1868, who took and subscribed the oath prescribed by the Constitution and the oath of office before Washington Spotts, one of the Commissioners appointed by said Governor for the said county of Tazewell."

William O. Yost was elected presiding justice for the term to expire the 1st day of August, 1868.

Rees B. Gillespie, who had been elected sheriff on the 17th day of August, 1865, by the qualified voters of the county, qualified to serve from the 27th day of August, 1865, until the 1st of January, 1867.

Sterling F. Watts, who had been elected at the same election as Commonwealth's Attorney for Tazewell County, qualified by taking the necessary oaths.

Rees B. Gillespie, sheriff of the county, appointed H. R. Bogle, William Hankins and Mathias Harrisson his deputies, and they qualified as such.

David A. Daughtery, who had been elected Commissioner of Revenue for District No. 1, and Charles J. McDowell, who had been elected Commissioner of Revenue for District No. 2, appeared and qualified.

Simon W. Young, William Hankins, James Allen, and Ransom S.

Dudley qualified as constables; and Thomas B. Crabtree qualified as overseer of the poor.

James W. Thompson, who had been elected clerk of the county at the election in August, qualified—his term of office to extend until the 30th of June, 1870.

Thus was the county government of Tazewell reorganized without any carpetbag element in it.

The President of the United States having, by proclamation, declared the government of Virginia restored, an election was held in the fall of 1865 to elect members of the General Assembly; and George W. Deskins was elected as the representative of Tazewell County. At the session held during the winter of 1865-66 the General Assembly proceeded to elect the various State officers and to enact such laws as were made necessary by the results of the war.

The Fourteenth Amendment was passed by Congress in July, 1866, and its ratification by the Southern States was made a condition precedent to their readmission to the Union. The Amendment was indignantly rejected by the Legislature of every Southern State, except Tennessee. In the Virginia Legislature, at the session of 1866-67, only one member voted for its acceptance. The rejection of the Amendment gave Thad Stevens and his radical associates in Congress rare opportunity to vent their hatred for the unhappy South. They began immediately to formulate their Reconstruction measures.

On the 2nd of March, 1867, Congress passed an act which provided for establishing military governments in the "rebel States". Under its operation Virginia was designated "Military District No. 1." The act also provided that the people of the "rebel States" should frame acceptable constitutions and adopt the Fourteenth Amendment before they could have representation in Congress; and the act further provided: "That until the people of any of said States shall be by law admitted to representation in Congress, any civil government which may exist therein shall be deemed provisional only, and in all respects subject to the paramount authority of the United States, at any time, to abolish, modify, control or supersede the same."

The act of March 2nd, 1867, also provided for the election of members to a convention to frame a constitution for Virginia, and authorized the voters of the State to vote for or against a convention to form a constitution. An election was held on the 3rd of December, 1867, a convention was voted for by a majority of the people, and delegates elected thereto. Colonel James Milton French, of Bland County, was elected to represent Tazewell and Bland counties in the convention. The convention met at Richmond on the 3rd of December, 1867, and framed what has since been known by the name of the "Underwood Constitution."

Thereupon, Congress passed an act on the 10th of April, 1869, authorizing the submission of the Constitution of Virginia to the people for ratification or rejection, and provided for the election of State officers and members of Congress at the same election. The act also prescribed that the President of the United States should submit the Constitution to the people of Virginia at such time as he deemed best, and should also submit to a separate vote such provisions of said Constitution as he deemed best.

There were several clauses of the Constitution that were obnoxious to all the white people and many of the negroes of the State; and President Grant ordered that the obnoxious clauses, each, be submitted separately. He issued a proclamation on the 14th of May, 1869, ordering that the election for ratification or rejection of the Constitution be held on the 6th of July, 1869. The election was held at the designated time, and the Constitution was adopted, the affirmative vote being 210,555, and the negative vote 9,136. The obnoxious clauses were rejected by a majority of more than forty thousand votes.

At this same election Gilbert C. Walker was elected Governor of Virginia, John F. Lewis, Lieutenant Governor; and James C. Taylor, Attorney General. Governor Walker was inaugurated on the 21st of September, 1869; and the General Assembly, elected under the Constitution, met at the capitol on the 5th of October, 1869. On the 8th of October the Legislature ratified and adopted both the Fourteenth and Fifteenth Amendments to the Constitution of the United States. In this manner civil government was restored in Virginia, and the State again became a member of the Federal Union.

In the meantime, while the State was under military rule, the terms of the justices who were appointed by Governor Peirpont, and who constituted the county court for Tazewell County, had expired. General George Stoneman, who was then in command of

Military District No. 1, appointed a new list of justices. The new
court held its first term on the 31st of March, 1869, when the
following business was transacted, as shown by the order book of
the court:

"Be it remembered that on the 31st day of March, in the year
1869, at Tazewell Court House, in the County of Tazewell, appeared
Henry F. Hunt, Jacob Wimmer, William T. Doak, James Albert,
Crockett Stump, Jeptha Fallen, John G. Prater, George T. Falkner,
William B. Yost, William J. Tabor, Absalom J. Hall and William
Lester, who severally produced commissions from Bre't. General

Captain Henry Bowen was the most distinguished son of Tazewell,
certainly the most highly honored by his people. He was born at
Maiden Spring on December 26th, 1815, and died in view of the old
homestead—the place of his nativity, on the 29th day of April,
1915. In May, 1861, he entered the service of the Confederate
States as a member of the "Tazewell Troopers;" and at the age of
twenty-one became captain of that gallant company, and led it in
the frequent battles in which it was engaged until he was captured
at the battle of Winchester in September, 1864. In this battle Tazewell lost several of her brave boys. Captain Bowen's distinction in
civil life began when he was elected to represent Tazewell County in
the Virginia General Assembly in 1869. He served at the sessions of
1869-70 and 1870-71; and had the distinction of being a member of the
General Assembly that restored Virginia to the Union by the adoption
of the Fourteenth and Fifteenth Amendments to the Federal Constitution. In 1882 he was elected to Congress by the Readjusters, as
the representative of the Ninth Congressional District. And again
in 1886 he was elected a member of Congress by the Republican Party.
Upon his retirement from Congress, he returned to the vocation of
his pioneer ancestors—that of grazier and farmer—which noble calling
he followed to the end of his life.

George Stoneman, Commanding the Military District of Virginia, who took and subscribed to the oath prescribed by the Congress of the United States by act passed the 2nd day of July, 1868, before Henry F. Hunt a justice of the peace for said County, and a majority of the justices being present they proceeded to election of one of their body for presiding justice, and Henry F. Hunt was declared duly elected presiding justice of this Court."

David Lester, who had been appointed by General Stoneman sheriff of Tazewell County, qualified as such.

Rees B. Gillespie, who had been appointed clerk, qualified.

John G. Lester qualified as Commissioner of Revenue for District No. 1, and John S. Moore qualified as Commissioner of Revenue for District No. 2.

Mathias H. Beavers qualified as constable for District No. 1, and Rees B. Lester qualified as constable for District No. 2.

The justices and county officers that were appointed by General Stoneman served for one year. Under the provisions of the Underwood Constitution the old county court system was abolished; and the last term of that court was held in Tazewell County on the 30th of March, 1870. James P. Kelly was elected judge of the county court of Tazewell by the General Assembly at its session of 1869-70.

The first term of the county court of Tazewell, under the new system, was begun on the 27th day of April, 1870, with Judge James P. Kelly presiding.

Rees B. Gillespie was appointed clerk of the court, Henry C. Alderson was appointed Commonwealth's Attorney, and Charles A. Fudge was appointed sheriff of the county. He appointed Hamilton R. Bogle, Alexander St. Clair, F. P. Spotts, and William H. Barnett his deputies. All of these were qualified by the court and entered immediately upon the duties of their respective offices. It was necessary for Judge Kelly to make these temporary appointments; and the several appointees served until their successors were elected by the voters of the county.

The despised military rule under abhorred Reconstruction was thus completely terminated in Tazewell County. This county, however, had escaped the evils of the much hated carpetbag government, for during the entire Reconstruction period the affairs of the county were administered by men who were "natives here and to the manner born."

APPENDIX TO WAR AND RECON-STRUCTION PERIOD

Containing the Names of Tazewell Men Who Served as Field and Company Officers In the Confederate Army

LIST OF FIELD AND COMPANY OFFICERS.

It was my intention to procure for publication rolls of the twenty companies from Tazewell County that were in the service of the Confederate States. This scheme has been impossible of accomplishment, as very few of the rolls have been preserved. Only four or five have been obtained, and these are two few to publish.

A friend of the author informed him that valuable information about the Confederate soldiers from Tazewell County could be secured from 'Squire S. M. Graham, son of the gallant Colonel William L. Graham. From Mr. Graham I have received information of great value. He has furnished it in such excellent form that I will make no alterations, but publish as it came from his pen. It is as follows:

Graham, Va., Jan. 8th, 1919.

Col. W. C. Pendleton,
　　　Marion, Va.

Dear Colonel:

I have just received your letter of the 6th inst., asking for information as to the companies organized in Tazewell County, that served in the Confederate Army. I regret that I cannot give you all the information you desire. I remember well all the Field Officers and Captains that went from this county into the Confederate Army; but I cannot recall the Lieutenants—some of them I remember, but very few.

I have no record of these companies, nor the officers, except a short one, I compiled from memory about two years ago.

There were twenty companies organized in Tazewell County,

that served in the Confederate Army—ten companies of infantry and ten companies of cavalry.

The first four companies were organized early in the spring of 1861, and were incorporated in the 45th Regiment Va. Inf. as Companies A, G, H, and K.   Joseph Harrisson was the first Cap-

Colonel Joseph Harrisson was among the first of Tazewell's sons to enter the service of the Confederate States as a soldier. He was elected captain of Company A, 45th Regiment, Virginia Infantry, in May, 1861, and served as captain of that company until the spring of 1862. For the remainder of the war he was continually engaged in other branches of the service. Colonel Harrisson was born within the present limits of the town of Tazewell in 1830, and died here in 1905. He was a man of undaunted courage and was an excellent soldier.

tain of Co. A. He served until the spring of 1862. John Thompson was the second Captain and served until the end of the war. William Browne was the first Captain of Co. G.   He served as Captain until the spring of 1862, when he became Colonel of the regiment. He was mortally wounded at the battle of Piedmont in June, 1864. He was a West Pointer, and an accomplished officer. After the promotion of Colonel Browne, James S. Peery became Captain of Co. G. He was captured at the battle of Piedmont and was not released from prison until the war ended.

Edwin Harman was the first Captain of Co. H.   Robt. H. Taylor 1st. Lieutenant. C. A. Fudge, 2nd Lieutenant and Armour Bailey, 3rd Lieutenant. In the spring of 1862 Captain Harman became

Lieutenant Colonel of the 45th Reg. and was mortally wounded at the battle of Cloyd's Farm in May, 1864. When promoted to Lieu. Col. he was succeeded as Captain of Co. H. by Charles A. Fudge. Capt. Fudge was desperately wounded and captured at the battle of Piedmont in June, 1864, and was not released from prison until the end of the war. He never fully recovered from the wound. Lieutenant Bailey remained with the company until the end of the

Colonel Titus Vespasian Williams was born in Tazewell County, June 2nd, 1835, and died at the home of his son, Emmett, at Valena, Iowa, on May 7th, 1908. He graduated at the Virginia Military Institute on July 4th, 1859. In the fall of 1859 he opened an academy at Jeffersonville and was conducting that school when Virginia seceded from the Union in June, 1861. He immediately organized a company of volunteers which entered the service of the Confederacy, with him as captain, and was attached to the 45th Regiment, Virginia Infantry. Very soon after entering the service he was promoted to the rank of major and transferred to the 37th Virginia Infantry. For gallant conduct in the seven days battle below Richmond, in 1862, he was promoted to colonel of the 37th Regiment and remained its commander until the close of the war. Colonel Williams was a splendid soldier and received wounds in several engagements.

war. Lieutenant Taylor resigned and afterward became a captain in the cavalry service.

Titus V. Williams was the first Captain of Co. K. He was a graduate of the Virginia Military Institute, and soon after his election to the captaincy of Co. K he was promoted to the rank of Major and was transferred to the 37th Regiment Va. Inf. After the seven days battle around Richmond, in the summer of 1862, he was promoted to Colonel of the 37th Regiment and commanded it until the end of the war. He was wounded in two or three different engagements. After the promotion of Captain Williams, John H. Whitley, who was 1st. Lieutenant of Co. K, became Captain. He served until the reorganization, in the spring of 1862.

Colonel Edwin Houston Harman was born February 13th, 1835, in the Bluestone Valley, Tazewell County. He was the son of Erastus Granger Harman, one of the first-born generation of that section of the county. On the 2nd of April, 1861, he was married to Miss Jennie King at the bride's home on Back Creek, Pulaski County, Virginia; and a few days thereafter entered the service of the Confederate States as captain of Company A, 45th Regiment, Virginia Infantry. In the spring of 1862 he was promoted to lieutenant colonel of the regiment. He was a daring and accomplished soldier and officer; and it was strangely decreed by fate that he should fall in battle but a few miles distant from the place where he won his bride three years previously. On the 9th of May, 1864, Colonel Harman was mortally wounded at the battle of Cloyd's Mountain, and died from the wound two days later. His dust now rests in a heroe's grave in Thorn Spring Cemetery, about six miles west of where he fell in battle.

He was succeeded by Captain Henry Yost, who commanded the company until the end of the war. Captain Whitley, after leaving the 45th Regiment, became a Lieutenant in Co. I, 16th Reg. Va. Cav., and served in that capacity until the battle of Monocacy in July, 1864, where he was captured. He remained a prisoner until the war ended.

T.H.—41

The 45th Regiment Va. Inf. was a fine body of troops, but was cut to pieces by overwhelming numbers at Cloyd's Farm in May, 1864, and in the following June was almost annihilated at the battle of Piedmont.

The next company organized in Tazewell was a cavalry company, known through the war as the "Tazewell Troopers." This company was organized in the spring of 1861, and became Co. H, 8th Reg. Va. Cav. John C. McDonald was the first Captain. He served a few months and resigned. He was succeeded by Geo. W. Spotts who served a short time and resigned on account of ill health. T. P. Bowen succeeded Captain Spotts and served until he was promoted to major about the beginning of the year 1863. Captain T. P. Bowen was succeeded by his brother Henry Bowen, who served until he was captured near Winchester, in the fall of 1864. He was not released from prison until the war was ended. The Lieutenants of this company, serving the last year of the war, were 1st Lieutenant Abbott, of Raleigh County, West Virginia, 2nd Lieut. Joseph S. Moss; 3rd Lieut. Austin Peck, Mercer County, West Virginia. There were quite a number of Mercer County men who joined this company after its organization and served in it until the end of the war.

In May, 1861, there were three other companies of infantry organized, one of which became Co. C, 50th Regiment Va. Inf. This company was commanded by Captain Frank Kelly throughout the war. John D. Greever of Burke's Garden was a Lieutenant in this company and beyond all question it passed through a greater number of big battles than any other company from this county. They fought from Fort Donelson to Appomattox. Captain Kelly and the most of the 50th Regiment were captured a short time before the war ended.

The captains of the other two companies were W. P. Cecil and D. B. Baldwin. These companies were attached to the 23rd Battalion, Va. Inf., afterwards known as "Derrick's Battalion". Baldwin's Company was Co. D, and Cecil's Company Co. C. Capt. Cecil was promoted to major of the battalion and was succeeded as captain by George Gose. Major Cecil and Captain Gose both resigned in the spring of 1862. Captain Gose was succeeded by F. M. Peery. Both Captain Baldwin and Captain Peery served until the end of the war. Oscar Barns and James H. Gillespie and William Witten were lieutenants in Baldwin's company. H. G. Peery was a lieutenant in Peery's company and had command of the Sharp Shooters of the battalion.

In the early spring of 1862, there were four more companies organized. Two of these companies were attached to the 29th Regiment, Va. Inf. as Co. I and Co. H. Co. I was commanded by Cap-

Captain D. B. Baldwin was born at Christiansburg, Virginia, in August, 1832, and died at Bluefield, W. Va., in August, 1916. He came to Tazewell in 1857, and for more than twenty years was one of the most active and popular citizens of the county. In May, 1861, he entered the Confederate army as captain of Company D, 23rd Battalion, Virginia Infantry, and served faithfully and gallantly in that capacity until the war was ended. Captain Baldwin located at Bluefield, West Virginia, in 1885, when that now thriving city was nothing more than a village; and from that time until a brief while before his death he was actively engaged in the real estate business. He accomplished much in the way of boosting Bluefield, where his memory is cherished by many devoted friends.

tain Thomas Peery and Co. H by Captain Ebenezer Brewster. Captain Brewster was promoted to major and was succeeded as captain by William Hankins. Both Captain Hankins and Captain Peery served until the end of the war.

The other two companies were organized as Independent Partizan Rangers. One of them was commanded by Captain William L. Graham and the other by Captain Elias V. Harman. The lieuteanats in Graham's Company were: 1st, W. E. Peery; 2nd, Joshua

Day; 3rd, John Woods. In Harman's: 1st, D. H. Harman; 2nd,
D. G. Sayers. These companies rendered valuable service to Tazewell County during the summer of 1862 by disorganizing, exterm-
inating or driving away bands of freebooters that infested some of
the border counties. In the fall of 1862, Captain Graham's company was divided into two companies and attached to the 16th
Regiment Va. Cavalry as Co. F. and Company I. Captain Graham
was made Lieut. Colonel of the regiment. He was wounded near

Captain John H. Whitley entered the service of the Confederacy
as first lieutenant of Co. K, 45th Virginia Infantry, in May, 1861.
Owing to the promotion of the captain of the company, Lieutenant
Whitley was made its captain a few months after he went into service;
and he served in that capacity until the spring of 1862. He then
joined the cavalry as a lieutenant in Co. I, 16th Virginia Cavalry; and
served as such until he was captured at the battle of Monocacy in
July, 1864. He was kept in prison until the end of the war. Captain
Whitley was born January 1st, 1842, and died September 17th, 1918.

Winchester in June, 1863. and captured in Moorefield Aug. 7th,
1864, and was not exchanged until a few days before Gen. Lee
surrendered.

Lieutenant W. E. Peery was made captain of Co. I. His lieutenants were Joshua Day (afterwards resigned), J. H. Whitley, John
Woods, Samuel Thompson (killed in Maryland, summer of 1864)
and Ferdinand Dunn. Captain W. E. Peery lost his right arm and
was captured at the battle of Boonesboro, Md., in June, 1863. He
was imprisoned on Johnson's Island until March, 1865. The com-

pany was commanded by one of the lieutenants until the end of the war.

Robt. H. Taylor was made Captain of Co. F. The lieutenants were William Bailey, J. H. Flummer and W. H. H. Witten. Captain Taylor served with the company until July, 1864, when he disappeared and did not return. The company was commanded by Lieutenant Wm. Bailey until the end of the war.

Captain Jonathan Hankins was born in Tazewell County in 1840, and died April 8th, 1894. He organized a company of cavalry in the summer of 1862, and in the fall of that year his company was attached to the 16th Regiment, Virginia Cavalry. Captain Hankins commanded the company until the war ended, and was an excellent officer and soldier.

In the fall of 1862, Captain E. V. Harman, being past military age, resigned. His company, together with some State Line troops, was divided into three companies and attached to the 37th Battalion Virginia Cavalry, known as "Witcher's Battalion." Captain David G. Sayers, Capt. John Yost and Captain Crockett Harrisson (son of Sandy Joe) commanded these companies. D. H. Harman was 1st Lieutenant in Sayers' company. Some of the men in these companies lived in McDowell and Buchanan counties.

Another company was organized in the summer of 1862, and that fall it was attached as Co. C, to the 16th Regiment Va. Cav. Jonathan Hankins was Captain and served through the war. The lieutenants were Julius C. Williams, Milburn Linkous and Milburn Barrett.

There were three companies of cavalry organized in the summer of 1863. Two of these companies formed a part of the 22nd Regiment Va. Cav. and were commanded, respectively, by Captains Balaam Higginbotham and W. W. Brown. Both of these captains served until the end of the war. Jesse Bailey was a lieutenant in Brown's company. The other company formed a part of the 10th Reg. Ky. Cavalry, and was commanded by Captain Elias G. W. Harman until the end of the war.

There was a company organized in the spring of 1864, composed of boys between the ages of seventeen and eighteen years and men between the ages of forty-five and fifty. This company formed a part of the 13th Battalion Va. Reserves Inf. and was commanded by Captain Samuel L. Graham. The 13th Battalion Va. Reserves was commanded by Lt. Col. Robt. Smith, of Tazewell County. This battalion became famous at the first battle of Saltville, fought Oct. 2nd, 1864. They held their ground, with the grim determination of seasoned veterans, against many savage attacks of the enemy. They received great praise for their heroic conduct from the veterans engaged in that battle. The conduct of this company is specially mentioned because it was composed of boys and old men who had never been under fire before and had but very little military training. John Rutherford was 1st Lieutenant in this company.

After the fall of Fort Donelson, General John B. Floyd retired from the regular Confederate Army. The State of Virginia commissioned him Brigadier General of State Troops, and authorized him to raise a brigade from the classes not included in the conscript laws of the Confederate Government. Pursuant to this authority he organized a Battalion of Infantry as a nucleus to the brigade. This battalion was commanded by Lieutenant Colonel Stuart Hounshell, who was at that time a citizen of Tazewell County, and had been major of the 51st Reg. Va. Inf. This battalion was encamped at Wytheville for some time, in the latter part of the summer of 1862. They moved from Wytheville to this county and encamped for about a month in Abb's Valley. This battalion was composed of men from most all the European nations and men from every section of the United States. It was truly a motley crew, the equal, in that respect, to the French Foreign Legion. Some of the greatest criminals of the time were in it. Elegantly refined and highly educated gentlemen were there—two nephews of President Jefferson Davis, the Balfour boys, were captains in this battalion. Some of these men had been with Walker on his ill-fated expedition to Nicaraugua. Some of them had been soldiers in the last war between France and Austria, and most all of them, had belonged to Wheat's famous battalion, the "Louisiana Tigers." This

Captain James S. Peery was the son of Harvey George Peery, and grandson of Thomas Peery, the pioneer. He was born June 6th, 1837, and died September 7th, 1905. In May, 1861, he entered the Confederate service as first lieutenant of Co. G, 45th Virginia Infantry; and in the spring of 1862 became captain of that company. Captain Peery was captured by the Federals at the battle of Piedmont, June 5th, 1864, and was confined as a prisoner at Johnson's Island until the conclusion of the war.

battalion had disintegrated since the death of their commander, Colonel Wheat, and the most of them had joined this State Line Battalion.

From Abb's Valley the battalion moved down the Tug Fork of Big Sandy to a point below Warfield and fought, successfully, some small battles while on this expedition. In the meantime there was great activity in organizing a battalion of State Line troops in Tazewell County. Several companies were enrolled, captains and lieutenants elected. These companies were organized into a battalion. But about the time of the organization the conscript laws

of the Confederate Government were extended so as to include all
the men in the State Line service, and it was reported that the men
of this battalion scattered, in every direction, from their encampment, the first night after its organization. The sole result of this
organization was the dissemination of numerous empty military
titles. The men, who had joined this battalion, were absorbed by
different regiments in the regular Confederate Army.

Captain A. J. Tynes was not a native of Tazewell County, but was
living there when the Civil War began. He entered the service of
the Confederacy as a member of the Tazewell Troopers and served
with that company until he was commissioned captain in the Field
Commissary Department and attached to McCausland's Brigade.
Captain Tynes was with his brigade in a number of campaigns and was
with it at Petersburg and at Appomattox. He was born in Campbell
County, Virginia, Nov. 29th, 1833, and died at Tazewell on Nov. 11th,
1914.

I have never made any effort to post myself as to the officers
of this State Line Battalion, from the fact that they saw no service,
while in this organization, to entitle them to be classed as soldiers.

In the spring of 1864 there was organized at Falls Mills a
Home Guard company, composed of boys from 15 to 17 years of
age, and men from 50 to 65 years old. This was done to protect
the community against threatened invasions and outrages. Two
Union Home Guard companies had been organized and were operating in the counties of McDowell and Wyoming. These companies

were a constant menace to the neighborhoods of Abb's Valley and Falls Mills. There were no regular Confederate soldiers left in that section of the county and these Union Home Guards had already committed several serious outrages on defenceless families, so it was up to the old men and the boys of the neighborhood to put on a bold front or else tamely submit to being robbed by a gang of cowardly thieves.

Captain John Thompson was a great-grandson of William Thompson, and was born in Thompson Valley, July 8th, 1837. He enlisted in the Confederate army in May, 1861, as a lieutenant in Co. A, 45th Virginia Infantry; and in the spring of 1862 was made captain of the company. He commanded that company in all subsequent campaigns until he was captured by the Federals in the Valley of Virginia in the spring of 1865; and was confined at Fort Delaware until June, 1865. Captain Thompson was elected Sheriff of Tazewell County in 1867; and moved to California in 1870, where he died in February, 1882.

About 30 old men and boys met at Falls Mills and obligated themselves in the most solemn manner to defend the communities of Abb's Valley and Falls Mills against invasion by these Union Home Guards. Dr. R. W. Witten, an ex-army surgeon, was elected Captain, James H. Tabor, 1st Lieutenant, Theopholis Arms, 2nd Lieutenant, Isaac O'Donnell, 3rd Lieutenant, W. Scott Witten, Orderly Sergeant. These officers did not ask for commissions from the government, nor did they ask that the company be recognized as an organization of the Confederate Army. They realized that the

Confederate Army was unable to protect them, so they determined to protect themselves, and the results show how well this company performed its duties. There was not another robbery committed by those Home Guards near Falls Mills or Abb's Valley until after the war ended. About a week after the war ended, one of these Union Home Guard companies appeared, just at daylight, in the

Captain James P. Whitman is the only Tazewell man now surviving who held the rank of captain in the Confederate army. At the beginning of the war he was a student at the academy of Col. Titus V. Williams at Jeffersonville, and was made a lieutenant in Company K, 45th Virginia Infantry, of which company Col. Williams was the first captain. Captain Whitman served as a lieutenant until the spring of 1862, when he enlisted as a private in the cavalry company of Capt. Wm. E. Peery, which later became a part of the 16th Virginia Cavalry as Company I. He was made adjutant of this regiment, and served as such until the end of the war. He was at Gettysburg, and in all the campaigns in which his regiment participated, including the retreat from Petersburg and the surrender at Appomattox. His surviving comrades pronounce him a daring and faithful soldier. Captain Whitman is the present Inspector General of the Grand Camp of Virginia Confederate Veterans.

mouth of Abb's Valley, at the homes of Wm. H. Witten and John Calfee. They took 10 or 12 horses and robbed the homes of all the household plunder they could carry away, and then made their escape as rapidly as possible. The Falls Mills company, before the war ended, had made several efforts to get in contact with this Union Home Guard Company, but was never able to catch up with it.

T. V. Williams, Colonel, 37th Regiment Va. Infantry, wounded 1862-3.

Henry Bowen, Colonel, 22nd Regiment Va. Cavalry.

William Browne, Colonel, 45th Regiment Va. Infantry, killed Piedmont, 1864.

A. J. May, Colonel, 10th Regiment Ky. Cavalry.

Edwin Harman, Lieutenant Colonel, 45th Regiment Va. Infantry, killed Cloyd's Farm, 1864.

W. L. Graham, Lieutenant Colonel, 16th Regiment Va. Cavalry, wounded 1863, captured 1864.

Stuart Hounshell, Lieutenant Colonel, 51st Regiment Va. Infantry and Floyd's State Line Battalion.

Robt. Smith, Lieutenant Colonel, 13th Battalion Va. Infantry Reserves.

T. P. Bowen, Major, 8th Regiment Va. Cavalry.

Ebenezer Brewster, Major, 29th Regiment Va. Infantry.

W. P. Cecil, Major, 23rd Battalion Va. Infantry.

E. A. Holmes, Major, Staff Officer, captured 1864.

Rufus Brittain, Adjutant, 29th Regiment Va. Infantry.

J. P. Whitman, Adjutant, 16th Regiment Va. Cavalry.

Eli Steel, Adjutant, 22nd Regiment Va. Cavalry, killed 1864.

A. J. Tynes, Captain, Field Comissary Dept., McCausland's Brigade.

Dr. W. P. Floyd, Surgeon.

Dr. J. M. Estill, Surgeon.

Dr. Jas Peery, Surgeon.

Dr. Thos. Cecil, Surgeon.

A. J. May was a resident of Prestonburg, Kentucky, at the time the war began. He joined the 5th Kentucky Infantry at Prestonburg, and became Lt. Col. of the regiment. This regiment remained in the infantry service until late in the fall of 1862, when, from some cause, it was disbanded. The most of the men who had belonged to this regiment were organized into the 10th Ky. Cavalry. Colonel May became Colonel of this regiment. In the meantime, soon after the beginning of the war, he moved his family from

Prestonburg to Tazewell, where he resided until his death, which occurred about forty years after the war.

———

If there is a neighborhood in Tazewell County that deserves a separate page in history for the part it took, and the sacrifice it made, in the Civil War, it is the section of the county around Falls Mills, inside of a radius of two miles.

There were thirty-seven men from this section who went into the Confederate Army; the most of them were small farmers or the sons of small farmers, two or three of them were mechanics— there was but one man among them who belonged to the slaveholding class.

These men were scattered among eleven different regiments. Eleven of them belonged to the 16th Va. Cav., six to the 29th Va. Inf., six to the 50th Va. Inf., five to the 8th Va. Cav., two to the 23rd Bat. Va. Inf., two to the 45th Va. Inf., one to the 4th Va. Inf., Stonewall Brigade, one to the 24th Va. Inf., one to the 54th Va. Inf., one to the 51st Va. Inf., and one to the 13th Bat. Va. Res. Inf.

Eight of these men were killed in action, five of them died of disease in the service, and thirteen of them were wounded, making a total casualty list of twenty-six, which equals a fraction over seventy per cent of all those in the service.

THE NAMES OF THESE SOLDIERS WERE AS FOLLOWS:

Alexander Arms, 8th Va. Cav., killed near Staunton, Va., Nov. 1864.

W. J. Buckland, 50th Va. Inf., wounded at Wilderness, May, 1864.

Hugh Buckland, 50th Va. Inf., wounded at Chancellorsville, May, 1863.

John W. Buckland, 16th Va. Cav., wounded at Gettysburg, July, 1863.

Robert Belcher, 16th Va. Cav., wounded near Wayne, W. Va., Jan., 1864.

Obediah Belcher, 29th Va. Inf., killed at Drewry's Bluff, May, 1864.

I. Green Belcher, 23rd. Va. Inf. Battalion.

James Bargar, 29th Va. Inf.

W. E. Butt, 13th Bat. Va. Reserves.

Bullard P. Compton, 16th Va. Cav., wounded at Moorefield, Aug. 7th, 1864.

Elihue Compton, 16th Va. Cav., wounded at Gettysburg, July, 1863.

Thos. Dangerfield, 16th Va. Cav., killed near Wayne, W. Va., Jan., 1864.

Ransom Dudley, 4th Va. Inf., wounded (lost arm), Gettysburg, July, 1863.

Frank Dudley, 8th Va. Cav.

James Dudley, 8th Va. Cav.

A. J. Dudley, 8th Va. Cav.

William Dudley, 29th Va. Inf., died in summer of 1862.

Thos. Ferguson, 50th Va. Inf., killed at Chancellorsville, May, 1863.

W. L. Graham, Lt. Col., 16th Va. Cav., wounded near Winchester, June, 1863.

Jno. A. Hambrick, 29th Va. Inf., died in summer of 1862.

C. A. Hale, 8th Va. Cav.

Madison Mullin, 50th Va. Inf., killed at Chancellorsville, May, 1863.

Austin Mullin, 54th Va. Inf.

William Prunty, 23rd Bat. Va. Inf., died in spring, 1862.

Jesse Poe, 24th Va. Inf., killed at Malvern Hill, July 1, 1862.

William Poe, 50th Va. Inf., died in summer of 1862.

Kiah Poe, 29th Va. Inf., wounded at Drewry's Bluff, May, 1864

Zach Poe, 16th Va. Cav., wounded in camp, accident, 1864.

David Shufflebarger, 51st Va. Inf., wounded (lost leg) at New Market, May, 1864.

Elbert Tabor, 16th Va. Cav., killed near Wayne, W. Va., Jan. 1864.

Andrew Tabor, 16th Va. Cav., killed at Moorefield, Aug. 7, 1864.

John A. Tabor, 50th Va. Inf., wounded at Chancellorsville, May, 1864.

Thomas E. Tabor, 29th Va. Inf.

Henry Tabor, 45th Va. Inf., wounded at Fayette C. H., Sept. 1862.

W. J. Tabor, 16th Va. Cav.

Daniel Wagner, 45th Va. Inf., died in 1861.

George Williams, 16th Va. Cav.

The casualties sustained by the troops from all over the Northeast corner of Tazewell County were almost as great as those sustained by the Falls Mills neighborhood. Many of these men died of typhoid fever, among them were Trigg Tabor, Augustus Tabor, Hugh Tabor, Jefferson Tabor (died in prison), Wm. Dillon, Ransom Prunty, David Crockett, William Crockett, Jordan Harless, Charles McDowell, Giles Parker, Dennis Stowers, Geo. Doughton, Harrison Tiller, David Workman and Hugh Wilson.

Among those killed in action and died of wounds, were Thomas Dillon (son of Jeff), Robt. Moore, William Moore, Montgomery Faulkner, Jesse Osborne, George Gill, Robt. Gill, Lt. Col. Edwin Harman, Gordon Carter, Augustus Carter and Thomas East. There were a number of others wounded.

There was an unfortunate condition of affairs that prevailed in the extreme Northeast corner of the county during the last year of the war. A few soldiers from that section were at home, absent from the army without leave. Two factions sprang up among them, and the result was a bitter feud, in which four men lost their lives. Mark Perdue, a well-behaved, harmless young man, was the first victim of this feud. The next men killed were John Fletcher and Osborne Dillon. The last victim was Samuel Hamill, who lost his life about the time the war ended.

To the credit of both parties to this feud, it can be truly said that neither faction gave any trouble to people outside of the feudists themselves, and but one or two individuals among them ever affiliated with the Union Home Guard marauders, who were a standing menace to this section during the last year of the war.

Post Bellum or Development Period

Showing the Progress Made by Tazewell
County Following the Civil War
and Reconstruction

POST BELLUM OR DEVELOPMENT PERIOD

CHAPTER I.

COUNTY RECOVERS FROM EFFECTS OF CIVIL WAR.

The period of recovery and readjustment from the evil effects of the Civil War and Reconstruction actually began as soon as the new Constitution of Virginia was put in force and reorganization of

Residence built by Thomas Witten, third, in 1838. Situated four miles west of Tazewell, on Cumberland Gap and Fineastle Turnpike. Now residence of John C. St.Clair.

the county government of Tazewell was effected. And the recovery was given increased momentum when the public free schools were recognized as a valuable asset for the county rather than a burden to the taxpayers. Despite the retardments occasioned by the war, and the heavy financial loss suffered from the freeing of 1,200 slaves in Tazewell, the wealth of the county was not seriously impaired. As soon as the war was over the farmers commenced to clear up for cultivation and grazing purposes boundaries that had

T.H.—42   (657)

been left covered with virgin forest growth, and thus added largely
to the area of improved lands.

The population had increased from 9,920 in 1860 to 10,701 in
1870. Although the assessed value of real estate in the county was
but $1,790,425 in 1870 as against $3,104,524 in 1860, this anomalous condition was evidently induced by heavy increases in tax rates,
and a consequent inclination on the part of the landowners to have
their lands assessed as low as possible. The assessors were generally in sympathy with this low assessment idea, and there was
no actual depreciation in the sales values of lands in Tazewell
County, resultant from the Civil War. A disposition to keep
assessments low is still manifest in Tazewell, and in all the counties
of Southwest Virginia. In fact, the disposition prevails in nearly
all the rural sections of the State. There are several good reasons
that can be assigned for this disposition of the landowners of Tazewell County, and of Southwest Virginia, to cling tenaciously to the
idea of low assessments. One potent reason is, that in Tazewell,
and in many sections of Southwest Virginia, a very large percentage
of the improved lands have advanced in price until fancy values have
been placed upon them; and at prices very far beyond their actual
value for purely agricultural purposes. If they were assessed at
approximately these fancy values, they would cease to be paying
investments. But the chief reason for a continuance of low assessments is the enormous increase in the cost of government. The
Federal Government now spends billions where it formerly spent a
few hundred millions; the State Government costs the taxpayers
three or four times as much annually as it did fifteen or twenty
years ago; and all local governments in Virginia—municipal, county,
and district—have increased their expenditures in like proportion.
The taxpayers very reasonably apprehend that an increase in the
assessed value of their real estate to its actual value would not
lower the tax rates now imposed; but would serve to swell the
revenues and stimulate the extravagance and waste that prevail in
the several governments they are compelled to help maintain.

As early as 1852 the people of Southwest Virginia became
deeply concerned about railroads. The Virginia & Tennessee Railroad had been chartered by the Virginia General Assembly in 1847,
to be built from Lynchburg to the present city of Bristol, a distance
of 204 miles. The route had been surveyed and the road bed was

being graded in 1851-52. When Dr. Bickley wrote and published
his history in 1852, he tried to direct the attention of the people of
Tazewell to the important matter of securing railway facilities for
the development of the agricultural interests and mineral and other
natural resources of the county. At that time the farmers of Tazewell were not cultivating their land in a scientific way; and did

Dr. George Ben Johnston was born in the town of Tazewell, then
Jeffersonville, on July 25th, 1853, and died in Richmond, Virginia,
December 20th, 1916. He was descended from hardy pioneers, who
were prominent as daring soldiers and distinguished citizens—the
Bowens, Prestons, Floyds, and Johnstons—and who helped to prepare
Southwest Virginia as an ideal home for American freemen. And he
is recorded as the most noted professional man who was a native son
of Tazewell. His great skill as a surgeon placed him in the front rank
of his profession. He was so highly esteemed by his fellows that he
was elected, without opposition, President of the "American Surgical
Association," the highest and most coveted honor to which an American
surgeon can aspire. His devotion to Tazewell was so intense that he
kept on the mantel of his private office a bottle of rich soil procured
from the old Floyd estate in Burke's Garden, which he told his friends
was to be deposited in his grave when he was buried. I have been
informed by his sister that his wishes were complied with.

not seem to be eager to have a railroad penetrate the county. Bickley said:

"Give us railroads, and let the press make known the claims of
Southwestern Virginia, and the 'gee up' of the New England plow-
boy will soon be heard upon our mountain sides. Our mountaineers

will soon be seen trading in Richmond. Baltimore, Philadelphia, New York, and Boston. Our neglected fields will bloom under the hands of scientific agriculturists, till wagons will no more be seen passing westward with men to build States on the ruins of those they have left."

During the year 1852 a number of families—some of the Wynnes, Peerys, Wittens, and others—moved from Tazewell to Missouri. Lands were then very cheap in Missouri, while such land as the "movers" left in Tazewell was worth from forty to fifty dollars an acre. Therefore, it must have been Missouri's cheap lands and not dissatisfaction with conditions in Tazewell that caused the migrations of which Bickley complains.

In writing of the minerals, Bickley said they were "both numerous and important—silver, iron, lead, arsenic, sulphur, salt, niter, gypsum, and large quantities of coal." Speaking of the coal he said:

"Coal exists everywhere, though wood is so plenty that it has not been used as fuel to any extent; hence, no search has been made for it. Bituminous, and, probably, cannel coal, exist in great quantities. The nearest to Jeffersonville that has yet been discovered, is on the lands of G. W. G. Browne, in Poor Valley, about four and a half miles from Jeffersonville. It is thought that coal does not exist on the head branches of Clinch River, but I imagine the supposition has no foundation. It has been found below, and in every direction around, and, no doubt, exists generally through the county. When shall we have an outlet for this coal?

Dr. Bickley had very imperfect knowledge of the coal bearing sections of Tazewell County; but his confident expectation that these coal deposits would prove of great value and ultimately be placed in the markets of the world were well founded. An answer to his question: "When shall we have an outlet for this coal?" was made just thirty years afterward by shipments of coal from Pocahontas.

———

In 1871, General G. C. Wharton was representing Montgomery County in the Virginia House of Delegates. He was acquainted with the extensive deposits of coal in the Flat Top Mountain region; and for the purpose of developing the coal beds of that country obtained a charter from the Legislature on March 7th, 1872, incorporating "The New River Railroad, Mining and Manufacturing Company." The incorporators named in the act were: John B. Radford, John T. Cowan, Joseph Cloyd, James A. Walker, William T. Yancey, William Mahone, Charles W. Statham, Joseph H. Chumbley, A. H. Flannigan, Philip W. Strother, John C. Snidow, Joseph H. Hoge, William Eggleston, G. C. Wharton, William Adair, James A. Harvey, A. A. Chapman, Robert W. Hughes, A. N. Johnston, Elbert Fowler, David E. Johnston, John A. Douglas, W. H. French, R. B. McNutt, James M. Bailey and A. Gooch.

The charter gave the company authority "to construct, maintain, and operate a railroad from New River depot, a point on the line of the Virginia and Tennessee division of the Atlantic, Mississippi and Ohio Railroad Company, in the county of Pulaski and State of Virginia, to such a point as may be agreed upon at or near the head-waters of Camp Creek, in the county of Mercer and State of West Virginia."

The charter also empowered the company to engage in mining coal, and iron and other ores, to acquire ownership of land for mining and manufacturing purposes, and to build branch roads for bringing out ores in certain counties of Virginia and West Virginia.

Deep interest was awakened in Tazewell by the chartering and organizing of the New River Railroad, Mining and Manufacturing Company. It gave promise of a realization of the long indulged hope that an outlet by rail would be obtained for shipment of the abundant products and minerals of the county. Schemes were promptly devised and projected by interested citizens to have a branch road built to Tazewell. But such enterprises in that day were very slow in reaching a practical form.

There was then very little capital that could be gotten in Virginia for such work as was contemplated by General Wharton and his associates; and they were compelled to seek assistance from capitalists in Philadelphia and other places at the North. Certain shrewd financiers and promoters in Philadelphia in this way learned of the mineral riches of the great Flat Top coal region. They immediately sought to identify themselves with the New River Railroad, Mining and Manufacturing Company, with the intention of getting control of its franchises and displacing the original incorporators. Their schemes were cunningly devised and were worked out successfully. They got control of the franchises of the company and reorganized it under the name of The New River Railroad.

General William Mahone, after several years of strenuous effort, got the Virginia General Assembly to pass an act on June 17th, 1870, for merging and consolidating the Norfolk & Petersburg Railroad Company, the Southside Railroad Company, and the Virginia & Tennessee Railroad Company into a single line, and forming it into the Atlantic, Mississippi & Ohio Railroad. The merging of these three roads, giving a through line from the Seaboard at Norfolk to Bristol, a distance of four hundred and eight miles, was of immense value to Southwest Virginia; but it was bitterly opposed by many citizens of this section.

At the organization of the new company, General Mahone was made president and became its active and efficient manager. He raised money by mortgages, purchased new rails from English manufacturers, paying for them with bonds of the company; and put the line in excellent condition. The rails proved to be of very inferior quality, the British manufacturers having perpetrated a base fraud upon General Mahone. An awful financial panic came on in the United States in 1873. It so greatly reduced the earnings of the Atlantic, Mississippi & Ohio Railroad, that the company failed on October 1st, 1874, and on April 1st, 1875, to pay the semi-annual interest on its mortgage indebtedness.

These delinquencies caused the bondholders and other creditors to institute proceedings in the United States Circuit Court for the Eastern District of Virginia, asking for the appointment of a receiver. Philadelphians engineered the movement, and a Philadelphian was appointed receiver. He conducted the affairs of the company until the road was sold under a decree of the court. The sale was made on the 10th of February, 1881, and Clarence M. Clark and associates, of Philadelphia, became the purchasers.

On the 9th of May, 1882, the New River Railroad Company of Virginia, the New River Railroad Company of West Virginia, and the East River Railroad Company of West Virginia were consolidated into the Norfolk & Western Railroad Company.

Surveys having been completed the Norfolk & Western Railroad

Company, on the 3rd of August, 1881, commenced the construction
of its New River branch line from the main line at New River
Depot to Pocahontas. The grading of the road down the western
banks of New River to the mouth of East River—thence up that
river to where the city of Bluefield is now located; and thence to
Pocahontas—was both difficult and expensive. But the work was
carried on rapidly; and the grading and track laying were completed
to Pocahontas on May 21st, 1883. The first shipment of coal from
the Pocahontas mines was made on the — of June, 1883.
Although the road ran but a short distance on Tazewell soil, along
the northeastern border of the county and in sight of the Mercer
County line, it was well understood that another line would soon be
built to and down the Clinch Valley. A charter was obtained for
this line on the 6th day of April, 1887; and, at a meeting of the
stockholders of the Norfolk & Western Company, held subsequently,
authority was given the directors of that company to consolidate the
Clinch Valley extension with the Norfolk & Western. Work was
begun on the Clinch Valley line on the 20th of June, 1887, and
before the end of the year 1888 trains were running along the
Clinch through the entire length of the county.

The whistlings of the locomotives and the rumblings of the
heavily laden trains, as they moved up and down the Clinch Valley,
not only brought joy and increased comforts to the inhabitants of
Tazewell, but were destined to be the carriers of vast wealth to
the county. Extensive developments of the Pocahontas and Flat
Top coal beds brought thousands of miners and thousands of other
consumers to that region, and established good markets for many
farm products that previously had not been transported from the
county on account of their perishable nature. Eggs, fowls, butter,
fruits, vegetables, and Tazewell's famous bacon found ready sale
in the coal fields. Bluefield and Pocahontas became busy hives of
industry, with thousands of inhabitants.

What was known as "the boom," when men became wild with
their schemes to build towns and cities, and gambled recklessly in
town lots, came in 1890. The towns of Graham and Richlands in
Tazewell were laid off, and their founders aspired to make them
industrial centers. Things moved along nicely until the year 1893.
Then came the direful panic and industrial depression that brought
business disaster to every section of the Union and calamity to the

laboring men of the country. The coal mining industry became stagnant throughout the United States; and it was almost discontinued in the Pocahontas fields and in Wise County. Norton, the boom town at the western terminus of the Clinch Valley Railroad, was turned into a deserted village; and Graham, at the eastern terminus, presented an air of desolation. The coke ovens at Pocahontas were idle and abandoned; and it was told that calves were grazing about and hogs sleeping in the coke ovens. Many of Tazewell's farm products became valueless, except for home consumption. Eggs sold for five cents a dozen; navy beans for sixty-five cents a bushel; butter for ten cents a pound, and some of the farmers used it for axle grease.

CHAPTER II.

PROSPERITY RETURNS TO TAZEWELL COUNTY.

In 1897 the rainbow of prosperity once again hovered over the Clinch Valley; and its gracious influence has remained here until the present time. A new era for the county seems to have been ushered in; and since the year 1897 Tazewell has been progressing on every line. Her population, as shown by the census of 1890, had grown to 19.889, as against 12.861 in 1880. In 1900—notwithstanding the hard four years, 1893-96—the population had increased to 23,384, and in 1910 it was 24,946. Thus, it is seen that the population of the county within a period of thirty years had increased nearly a hundred per cent. The heavy increase of the population was chiefly due to the building of railroads into the county and the development of its mineral resources.

During the twenty-two years following 1890, the wealth of Tazewell increased in greater proportion than the population. In 1890 the assessed taxable values of the county amounted to $2,015,075 of which $1,447,090 was real estate, and $567,985 was personal property. By 1912 the taxable values had grown to $7,237,566, composed of $4,713,155 real estate, $1,483,136 tangible and $1,041.275 intangible personal property. The increase in assessed taxable values in twenty-two years was over three hundred and fifty per cent. But the growth of the wealth of Tazewell County during the six years following 1912 is truly amazing. The assessed taxable values for 1918 are shown by the following table which has been kindly supplied by H. P. Brittain, county treasurer:

"Assessed Taxable values, for county purposes, in Tazewell County for the year 1918.

Personal Property, Tangible and Intangible	$ 6,073,017.00
Real Estate	5,065,630.00
Railroads and Electric Railways	1,191,516.00
Telegraphs, Telephone and Express Companies	20,886.00
Heat, Light and Power Companies	95,390.00
Total	$12,446,439.00

A very large part of the assessed taxable values of the county was composed of live stock. The animals listed for taxation for county purposes were: 4.274 horses, 20.234 cattle, 14.154 sheep, 7,749 hogs, and 151 goats. A conservative estimate of the value of the live stock sold from Tazewell County in 1918, places the amount at one and a half million dollars.

Dr. Samuel Cecil Bowen has been pronounced one of the finest all-around characters Tazewell County has given birth to. He was born at the old Maiden Spring homestead on May 15th, 1881, was the son of Rees Tate and Mary Crockett Bowen, and the great-great-grandson of Lieutenant Rees Bowen, the hero of King's Mountain. Dr. Bowen obtained his academic education at Hampden-Sidney College and the Ohio State University. He graduated with distinction as Doctor of Medicine at the Virginia Medical College in 1905, was resident physician at Memorial Hospital, Richmond, Virginia, for eighteen months; and, after engaging several years m the general practice of the profession, spent three years at the New York Eye and Ear Infirmary as house surgeon of that noted institution. In 1912 he located at Richmond, where he became associated with Dr. R. H. Wright as a specialist in the treatment of diseases of the eye, ear, nose, and throat. Very soon after he commenced to practice as a specialist he aroused the attention of eminent men of the profession as a skillful and successful operator; and previous to his death, which occurred Dec. 20th, 1918, had won a State-wide, and even National reputation as a specialist.

Further proof of the great increase of wealth in the county is evidenced by the increased number of banks, the large aggregate capital of these banks. and the heavy deposits they show.

There are now nine banks in the county. with an aggregate capital of $855,600. Three of these—Bank of Clinch Valley, Taze-

well National Bank, and Farmers National Bank—are located in the
town of Tazewell; two—First National Bank of Richlands, and
Richlands National Bank—are at Richlands; two—First National
Bank of Pocahontas, and Bank of Pocahontas—are at Pocahontas;
and two—First National Bank of Graham, and Bank of Graham—
are at Graham. The sworn statement of these nine banks, published in November, 1919, showed that the aggregate deposits then
amounted to the sum of $3,012,205.58.

The population of Tazewell County by the recent census is
27,840. There are no cities, but there are five substantial towns
within its borders. The census of 1920 gives the population of the
towns as follows: Richlands, 1,171, increase 428; Tazewell, 1,261,
increase 31; North Tazewell, 626, increase 284; Pocahontas, 2,591,
increase 139; Graham, 2,752, increase 835. There was an increase
in the population of the county, during the decade just closed, of
2,894 souls. Of this increase, 1,717 persons were found in the five
incorporated towns, and only 1,177 in the balance of the county.
The increase in the wealth of the county was much greater in proportion than the population.

Educational conditions in the county have been greatly improved
during the past twenty-five or thirty years. Previous to the introduction of the public free schools by the Constitution of 1870, the
people of Tazewell had relied entirely upon private schools for
the education of their children. That class of schools could be
maintained only in the communities that were thickly populated,
and where the wealthiest citizens were located. There was a
meager provision made by the State for the education of indigent
white children; but this provision proved of little value to the
cause of popular education.

In 1852 there were but fifteen school houses in the county—all
of them one-room buildings—and Bickley said they were "better
suited for barns than seats of learning." Then the area of the
county was much greater than at present, as it included a part of
Buchanan, all of McDowell County, and a part of Bland. The
census of 1850 disclosed the existence of a shameful state of illiteracy within the bounds of Tazewell. There were but 3,311 white
persons in the county over the age of twenty years, and of these
1,490 were unable to read and write. And there must have been
a large number of white persons between the ages of ten and twenty

who could not read and write. It is probable that more than fifty per cent of the white persons in the county were illiterate. The percentage of illiteracy was reduced considerably by taking Buchanan and McDowell counties from Tazewell in 1858.

No marked improvement in educational conditions was observable in Tazewell until about thirty years ago, when the people of Virginia became interested in popular education. There was first hostility, and then indifference to the public free schools. The taxpayers were reluctant to be taxed for the support of the common free schools, and many citizens refused to send their children to these schools. But the people of Virginia, including those of Tazewell County, were at last awakened to the fact that the education of the masses was an essential need for the preservation of a progressive civilization in the Commonwealth, and for the perpetuation of our republican form of government.

Private schools were practically abandoned, and every attempt to establish academies or colleges in the towns and communities proved futile. The entire purpose of the citizens was then directed to the upbuilding of the free school system. That this effort has been attended with great success is evidenced by what was accomplished through the free schools in the scholastic year of 1918-19. During that scholastic year the sum of $116,517.49 was expended in Tazewell for General Control, Instruction, Operation, Maintenance, Auxiliary Agencies, and Improvements of school property. Of this sum $73,705.00 was paid in salaries to the teachers, and $15,109 for new buildings. There are now 73 white and 7 colored plants or school houses in the county; and for the last school year there were 150 white and 14 colored schools, each room being counted, technically, a school. These schools are classified as follows:

Four-year High Schools, 4; Junior High Schools, 2; Graded Schools, meaning three-room and four-room, 3 white and 3 colored; Common Schools, one and two-room, 68. The number of teachers employed was 150 white and 14 colored. A school census was taken in 1915, and the school population was:—white, 7,173; colored, 693—a total of 7,899. The enrollment of pupils for the year 1917-1918 was—white, 6,080; colored, 693—a total enrollment of 6,773.

That illiteracy in Tazewell County has been rapidly disappearing is shown in the report of the State Superintendent of Public

Instruction for the school year 1914-15. His report states that, according to the school census of 1915, Tazewell stood third among the counties having the lowest rate of illiteracy in that part of the population between 10 and 20 years of age. Illiteracy with that part of the population between 10 and 20 years old had been reduced to about one per cent. This is a splendid showing for Tazewell and is very encouraging to the friends of Popular Education. Culture has ceased to be the privilege of classes in Tazewell County.

GOOD ROADS.

In the matter of improved highways the county has made most creditable progress. This has proved an important contributing cause for the increased taxable values of the county. On the 18th day of April, 1911, a bond issue of $625,000 was voted for by the three magisterial districts, to be expended under the direction and supervision of the State Highway Commission. The magisterial districts voted separately as to the amount each would expend on its roads. Jeffersonville District voted $200,000; Clear Fork District $250,000; and Maiden Spring District, $175,000. Another election for issuing additional bonds was held and carried on the 4th of April, 1916.

Under the provisions of the second bond issue Jeffersonville District received $96,000; and Clear Fork District $155,900. Maiden Spring District voted in the election but declined to participate in the proceeds of the bond issue. At a later date Clear Fork District issued bonds to the amount of $9,000 without authorization from the electorate of the county. The sum total of the bond issue for road purposes is $885,900.

Tazewell County's Bond Issue system is, perhaps, the most satisfactory that could be devised, certain of the bonds maturing one year after date, some in two years, some in three years, et cet., the last maturing in 1946. The county does not provide for nor carry a sinking fund, the current levies being sufficient to retire the bonds as they mature and pay the interest on balance of issue, the tax burden being fairly distributed over the years from date of issue to maturity of last lot of bonds. This system has proved to be most satisfactory.

Soon after the first bond issue was carried, active work on the county roads was begun; and nearly all the proceeds of the several bond issues has been expended. As a result, the county now has

135 miles of macadam roads, and 100 miles of improved dirt roads, or a total of 235 miles of improved roads. There still remains 285 miles of unimproved roads, there being a total of 520 miles of public roads in Tazewell County.

A splendid macadam road has been completed from a point five miles east of the Russell County line to the eastern line of Tazewell County at Graham. This road practically follows the route of the old Cumberland Gap and Fincastle Turnpike, but with greatly improved grades. At the regular session of the Virginia

Scene in valley about a mile west of the court house, showing the modern road built on the location of the old Fincastle and Cumberland Gap Turnpike. In the background Morris' Knob is visible. The photo from which the half-tone cut is made was made by A. M. Black, Tazewell's splendid photographer. It won first prize in a contest for prize of $1,500 offered by the Ladies' Home Journal, under the heading: "An Old Virginia Road."

General Assembly in 1919 the road from Cumberland Gap to Graham was designated as one of the State highways by the act passed at that session of the Legislature. The road is now completed, with the exception of the five miles in the west end of Tazewell County and a few short sections in Scott County.

Another modern highway follows the route of the Tazewell C. H. and Kentucky Turnpike to the head of Baptist Valley, and has been macadamized down that valley a distance of four miles. Similar roads have been built in other sections of the county; one from Cedar Bluff by Steelesburg, to intersect with the Cumberland Gap and Graham road at a point west of Midway; another from Witten's Mill to Tiptop; and one from Pocahontas to the head of Abb's Valley. Perhaps, the best road in the county follows the

route of the old Tazewell C. H. and Fancy Gap Turnpike, from
the forks of the road opposite the residence of the late Captain Wm.
E. Peery, up the south branch of Clinch River to Gratton; thence
crosses Rich Mountain, and passes into and through Burke's Garden.
This is one of the most travelled and attractive roads in the county.
In a few more years Tazewell will have one of the most complete
and splendid systems of highways in our State.

In former years the county was celebrated for its number of
saddle and draft horses. The improved highways have already
nearly made travel on horseback obsolete, and the splendid saddle
animals that for more than a hundred years had attracted buyers
from all regions have nearly disappeared. Hundreds of automobiles
have taken the place of saddle and carriage horses, and auto trucks
are rapidly displacing the fine draft teams that were so long the
pride of this people.

———

Buckle and other historians, who made civilization a theme,
have expressed the conviction that climate, soil, and food are the
three essential physical agents for creating a high degree of civilization in a community or nation. And these writers have affirmed
that the most important product evolved from the essential physical
agents is the accumulation of wealth. Their contention is, that
without a wealthy leisure class there can be no large measure of
knowledge and no intellectual class.

When the pioneer fathers came to the Clinch Valley they found
here amply provided by nature the three basic essentials for erecting a highly civilized community—that is, climate, soil, and food.
They utilized very successfully these natural agencies for establishing comfortable homes for themselves and their families; and
secured to their posterity the most priceless attributes of civilization, political and religious freedom. While accomplishing this,
they were laying a firm foundation upon which their descendants
and successors might erect the best type of civilization.

Class and caste were the disintegrating elements in the moral
force and national character of all ancient civilizations. A similar
defect was the controlling instrumentality in modern European
civilization, which during a period of four recent years turned Continental Europe into a bloody shambles; and threatened to uproot
the excellent social fabric constructed by the fathers of our own
beloved land.

The extremes of wealth and poverty do not now exist and have never been existent in Tazewell. There are many comfortably wealthy men in the county; and, perhaps, half a dozen millionaires. But, with a population of 27,840 souls in the county, as shown by the census of 1920, there are only 53 paupers here. The paupers are of a class that are unable to work on account of the infirmities of age, or other physical causes, and mental deficiency. Fifteen are entirely dependent and are maintained at the county farm, while thirty-eight are partially dependent and receive aid from the public funds. The county owns a valuable farm, situated one and a half miles east of the county seat, its estimated value being seventy-five thousand dollars. During the fiscal year which ended the 1st of July, 1919, the products of the farm amounted to $4,890; and the live stock on hand at that date was valued at $8,760. The annual expense for conducting the farm and maintaining the paupers is, approximately, $6,000. As long as present conditions continue society here will be contented and prosperous; and, apparently, it will be best for the county to remain, as it always has been, primarily an agricultural community. Adherence to this system will give comfort and security to the energetic worker, and will not furnish asylum to the idler. God forbid, that Tazewell shall ever have a system with paupers at the base and idle rich at the top of the social scale. May its social system never be like that of modern England, of which Matthew Arnold affirmed: "Our inequality materializes our upper class, vulgarizes our middle class, and brutalizes our lower class."

Wealth, great wealth is now collectively possessed by the people of Tazewell. What will they do with it? Under the spell of modern civilization, shall the rising generation be trained to place a negligible value upon the instrumentalities of civilization that were recognized and utilized by the pioneer fathers; and be taught that money, position, power, idleness, and luxury are the prime essentials of an advanced civilization? This is the gravest question the Christian world has to solve. What part will the people of Tazewell enact in its solution? Shall civilization continue to advance here on definitely true lines, or retrograde into a refined barbarism? Shall we continue to teach but neglect to practice the great social and political truths of Thomas Jefferson, embodied in the Virginia Bill of Rights and the Declaration of Independence?

APPENDIX TO HISTORY OF TAZEWELL COUNTY

Names of Tazewell County men who served in the military and naval service of the United States during the World War, as shown by the Muster Roll of Tazewell County, which is made up from records of the Local Board of said county, and the list of volunteers furnished the clerk of said county by the Adjutant General of Virginia.

Quite a number of men outside of draft age volunteered, and up to the present time no record has been obtained showing the names of these men.

ARMY.

WHITE.

Thomas Albert Adison, Robert Samuel Angles, Willis Carl Anderson, Marion Calvin Asbury, James Riley Able, William B. Absher, Gus Asbury, John Johnson Asbury, Joseph Andrew Amos, Edd Kelly Adison.

Charles Arthur Billips, John Robert Birklebach, Shade Creed Baldwin, Charley Wm. Blankenship, James Barnett, David Carl Beavers, Charlie Mose Beavers, Dan Brodskie, Charles Oata Bowman, Homer Beavers, Steve Boray, Robert A. Billips, Nelson Henry Barker, Paris Brown, Sam Buchanan Bogle, Wm. Jasper Blankenship, Arthur Marvin Buskill, Posy Earl Burcham, James Robert Burress, Marion Bowman, J. Raymond Barnett, Martin Luther Bowling, Isaac C. Buchanan, Geo. W. Belcher, George Walter Beavers, James Brooks, Eugene Newton Burroughs, Pola Andrew Brooks, George Beavers, Shelburn G. Bruster, John Ward Baylor, George Thomas Baumgardner, William Benson, George Bandy, Peery Boothe, Roy Thomas Barrett, Roy Boyd, Charles G. Brown, Watts Baldwin, George Dewey Bowman, Arthur Samuel Beavers, Sidney Isaac Bowman, James Fred Brown, W. D. Brown, Gilbert Brinegar, Sidney Blankenship, Lawrence W. Blankenship, Cecil Calloway Bane, Erwin Bane, Tazie Belcher, Fayette Beavers, Grover Cleveland Barnett, Jesse Marvin Boyd, John George Blackwell, Bandy Boggess, Riffe Boggess, Stanley Lee Bowman, James Luther Belcher, Howard S. Bowman, Otis Lee Boothe, Lee Barrett, Sidney Bloch, James Bryant Burton, David Lonzo Bowman, Enoch Bayles, William Frank Baylor, Glenn Everett Beavers, Charles Thomas Boone, Sylvester Blankenship, Bryan William Barnett, James William Bowser, Earnest Brown Bales, Trube T. Bourne, Rees Richard Boone, Lawrence A. Barrett, William J. Bowser, Jasper Brewster.

Lewis H. Carbaugh, James Allen Clark, Joe Conley, John Clinton Coleman, Arnold Coles, John Carter, Nick Crist, William Arthur Coleman, William Otis Caldwell, Walter Preston Creasy, Robert Samuel Crabtree, James Robert Cregar, Alva Brittain Cregar, Chester Carter, Vinton Victor Christian, Jesse Lee Coen, Claude Chrisman, Robert Marvin Crabtree, Samuel Clark, Daniel Frank Collins, Thomas Cochran, Jesse Ben Clark, Aaron Carter, Wiley Robinson Compton, William Cordill, William Carter, Fred B. Cordle, James Raleigh Compton, Roy Alexander Cohen, Vance Witten Carter, John Willie Christian, Creed Frazier Catron, William Cebard Cox, John Ed. Crockett, Jesse Walter Cregar, Avery M. Crabtree, Lewis R. Coulling, Edward Charles Clark, Charles R. L. Cruey, Arthur Cordle, Grover Campbell, Albert del. Castello, James Thomas Crouse, William Henry Cole, S. M. B. Coulling, Jr.

William Deskins, Luther Henry Dunnigan, Samuel Dillow, Charles Davis, Joseph Elliott Deaton, James Miller Davidson, Henry Albert Davis, George F. Deaton, Charles Smith Dalton, John Frank Daniel, James Henry Davis, Will Allis Dillon, Hasten Dingus, J. P. Davidson, Hugh Cornelius Davis, George Thomas Dillow, Robert Samuel Davis, Baxter Duncan, Alfred V. Dennen, Arthur Blaine Dunningan, James Dawson, Marshall Deaton, Charles Hugh Dudley.

Leland S. Edwards, Jesse Lee Epperson, Frank Chalmers Ellett, Walter Clinton Edwards, M. E. Eagle, Newton Harman Edwards, Haz. Eagle, William Ray Edwards, John Gideon Epperson, Fielden Kirk Earls.

Albert Pendleton French, Joseph Farris, Andrew Sid. Franklin, Charley Farmer, James Edgar Fields, Emory Lee Flanary, Wm. Chafe Faulkner, Jr., Robert Guy Flanary, Clinton Farmer.

William Cosby Greever, Harvey George Gillespie, Charles
Joseph Gose, George Thomas Gentry, Samuel William Green,
Robert Griffith, Samuel Walton Graham, Hal Gordon Graham,
Robert B. Gross, Robert R. H. Gillespie, Frederick William Glen-
ville, John Arthur Graham, William G. Gillespie, John A. Graham,
Charles M. Gillespie, Harvey Eli Green, Reuben Pendleton Green,
Benjamin H. Griffith, Joseph W. Guess, Thomas Walter Gillespie,
Julius Goodman, George Gydosh, Andro But Gussian, George
Benoni Gose, Robert Felix Gillespie, Earnest Burton Gravely,
Carnie J. Gillespie, Irby Gillenwaters.

Daniel Clayburn Hogston, James Stanley Horne, Roby Kellis
Hill, Robert P. Harman, Edward Albert Holmes, Luther Hall, Ira
Edward Horton, James Robert Harless, Lee Harman, Cary John
Hodge, Hampton Hutson, Thomas Hankins, John Edd. Howery,
Will Herald, George H. Harman, Frank R. Henderson, Roy Lee
Hagy, Henry Thomas Haley, Harry A. Humphrey, Edward W.
Hill, John Hunnel, Henry Mullins Hanshaw, Lee Helmandollar,
Arthur Hunnel, Amos Hess, George C. Hooker, Ira E. Helton, Wil-
liam Harman, Otto Herald, James Bishop Hays, Bryant Harman,
Thomas T. Hewson, Hugh R. Hawthorne, Reese Hall, James Frank
Hopkins, Thomas Albert Howery, William Harman, William Henry,
Charles Dale Harman, Earl Preston Hall, Frazier Harman, Henry
Hunt, Walter Lee Hankins, Charles Hughes, David Paul Harris,
Charles Chester Hindley, Daniel Robert Harman, Timothy Hankins,
Andrew J. Hall, Albert Claude Hankins, James Hess, William H.
Harrison, Joseph Brown Heldreth, Irvin Ben Hodges, Paul Perry
Hunter, John Clarence Heldreth. Lee Hoops, William Hall, Thomas
Milton Harris, Sid. Harry, Robert L. Hoops. William Prevo Hager,
Robert Arthur Harris, Thomas Hughes, Walter Helmandollar,
George B. Houchins, J. E. Hurt, Harvey G. Harrison.

Henry Ingle.

George Raymond Jennings, Herbert Jackson, James William
Jones, Walter I. Jenkins, Burl Jones, Marion I. Jackson, Eugene
Johnson, John R. Jones. Thomas A. Jackson. Joseph C. Jones,
Chesley Albert Jeter, Taylor Jackson, Joseph Elbert Johnson,
Robert Lee Jones, Edward Lewis Jackson, Henry Alexander Jones,
Robert C. Jackson.

Joseph Frazier Kitts, William Gent Kiser, Fletcher Kiser, William Thomas Keesee, Walter E. Kiser, Newton Roy Kinder, Claude G. Kitts, Oscar John Kachelries, Charles George Kinder, James Robert Kinder, William Frank Kinder, Johan Kenevar, Christian Thomas Kirk, Alonzo Hyatt Kelly, James G. Kelly, Jesse Moore Karr, Roy Howard Keister, Oscar Heath Keister, John Tyler Keesee, Grover Leo Kinder, David Clyde Keister, Joe S. Kish, Jr.

James Crockett Lester, Charles Lawrence, Samuel Erastus Leffel, Robert Lockhart Lefler, William Allen Lee, Thomas H. Lambert, Adam Bittle Lambert, James Robert Lawrence, Jr., Clarence E. Lawrence, Christopher Lockwood, Titus Lambert, William Eli Lockhart, Seldon Crockett Lambert, Robert Andrew Lethcoe, Abb Lambert, John Wyatt Lawrence, Robert Thomas Long, Robert Frazier Lambert, Channel A. Lawson, Crockett Lowe, Ewing Waters Lawson, Paris H. Lambert, Beverly D. Litz, John Cleveland Lambert, John W. Lawrence, William Whitt Lowe, James Truby Lambert, William S. Lockhart, Luther James Lankford, Walter D. Lovell, William Jordan Luke, William Albert Lawson, Arthur W. Lawson, Victor Hugo Lewis, Edd Herman Lowe, Sylvester Lowe, Fred Lambert, James E. P. Lockhart, George W. Lowe, Vess C. Lowe, Lindsay Lowe, T. O. Laird.

Robert Leslie Maxwell, William Music, Arthur Price Morton, Vinton Robert Moss, Hubert Pontell Meredith, Glenn White Martin, Joseph Anthony Macaro, Isaac Drayton Maxwell, Robert H. Mahood, Will Rees Murray, Thomas Lee May, Joe Melfa, Lee Myers, Edward A. S. Mitchell, William Leece May, Charles D. Mattox, James M. Moore, Paul Mallory, John M. Mobray, Walter Monk, William Mitchell, Jr., Thomas Augustus Marrs, Robert Meadows, David Acuff Mahone, Mark S. Mallory, Rees Munday, Marvin Edward Meadows, Columbus Moore Mothena, George W. Mitchell, James Archabald Moore, Samuel Davidson May, George Spotts Moore, Thomas T. Moore, Charles Walter Moore, Morris Magrill, William Dudley Marrs, George Clarence Martin, Louis Cleveland Marshall, John Martin, Robert Owen Morgan.

Henry J. McGlothlin, Lindsay T. McGuire, Frazier Buford McMeans, Henry Guy McKinney, Albert Lester McMeans, Eugene Lanoy McGinnis, Ellis V. McFarland, Archie Patton McKenry,

John McGuire, Samuel E. McMullin, William E. McCall, James Okey McNeely, Lawrence W. McFarland, George Peery McGuire, Robert Daniel McCall, Charles Grant McGlothlin, Lorenzo A. McGlothlin.

Gordon Thomas Neel, Guy Henry Nash, Suddeth Walton Neel, Wiley Stuart Neal, Henry Clarence Neel, Fred Thomas Nash, James Corbett Neel, Ira Lacy Neel, James Henry Neal, Levi Walker Neel, William Henry Neel, Kyle Nipper, John H. Newman, Robert Sidney Neel, George C. Nicewander, John Estil Neel, James Thornton Neel, James Alderman Newton, Wiley Newberry, George Nichols, Henry Guy Norman, William Herald Nixon, Lawrence O. Nelson.

William Harvey Osborne, Vista Osborne, Isiah Osborne, Neely Osborne.

Bart Edwin Pruett, William Henry Phillips, Charles George Powers, Howard Lacy Peak, Clarence Eugene Peery, Henry Porter, William Albert Peery, Kenneth C. Patty, Archie Lee Pruett, Maxwell A. Pruett, John Richard Peery, George E. Pruett, Walter Stuart Patrick, Charles Clarence Peery, Robert A. Pack, Bane Gustaff Peery, Walter Sherman Patrick, Lewis Parker Pruett, Robert C. Pack, William Pierce, Augustus Peery, Rush Floyd Pauley, Robert Pack, William C. Pruett, Walker Puckett, Walter Price, Mustard Pruett, Peter William Peterson, Leftridge C. Patton, Oscar Brown Pruett, Archie S. Powers, Garland Peery, Thomas Allen Peery, Clarence Henry Peery, William E. Peery, Jr., Archie Riley Pruett, Frank Pierce Pickle, Andrew McDonald Peery, William Proffit, James Prophet, J. O'Keefe Peery, Lawrence S. Peak, Roscoe Pack.

Byron Franklin Quillin, William L. Quesenbury.

Rees Melvin Russell, William Everett Riley, James Arthur Riley, Witten Rucker, Floyd Repass, James William Rich, Creed Rose, Henderson J. Ruthledge, James Madison Roark, Jesse Marvin Rye, Walter Thompson Rye, Frank Ratcliff, Guy A. Rosebaum, John Gibson Repass, Carlile T. Rees, Charles B. Rosseau, Arthur Reedy, Leonard M. Reedy, John Thomas Roten, Sam P. Riley, Lacy Johnson Repass, Herbert Henry Rosenbaum, Maxwell A. Riley.

James Alma Sluss, Ben Stacy, Norman Clarence Smith, Robert Cline Sparks, Thomas Lewis Shawver, Dudley Gratton Shrader, Luther Arch Settle, James Claude Sayers, Washington Lee Sayers, Walter Stuart, Curtis L. Shufflebarger, Sam Riley Smith, Sidney H. Shell, Horton Shepherd, William John Selney, Samuel S. Summers, Milton T. Simmons, Elisha Earl Stevenson, Everett Sluss, Charles Arnold C. Salyers, Hugh Thomas Stevenson, Louis Jackson Scott, Jonah F. Southern, Charles Whitt Sparks, Pearl Henry Shreve, John William Shawver, John Robert Saunders, John C. Steele, Alexander G. StClair, Floyd Henry Stevens, John Short, Jackson Sluss, James Clinton Sturgess, George W. Steele, Wash Lee Sayers, James Allen Smith, Ballard N. Short, William Newton Shufflebarger, Robert Lee Spurgeon, Daniel Gratton Shrader, Clay Scyphers, Charles J. Stephenson, Joe R. Switalski, Meredith Strouth, Edgar Marion Steele, Frederick Wm. St.Clair, Robert Edgar Simpson, Rex E. Steele, Lucien Snodgrass, Lucian Smith, Thomas Ford Shamblin, Charles Russell Stinson, Geo. W. Simms.

Leck Andrew Thompson, Clarence Kenny Turner, Roy Martin Triplett, Mercer Elliott Thomas, John Henry Tabor, John Davis Tabor, William Andrew Turley, William Erastus Tickle, William James Tiller, Roy Ashland Thompson, Adam Stephen Tabor, Greever Taylor, C. W. Thompson, Pose William Thomas, Robert Samuel Taylor, Walter Lee Taylor, Brown Taylor, Emory Lee Taylor, Foster J. Thompson, Benjamin H. Thompson, James Raleigh Twigg, Raleigh Totten, Oday C. Thompson, Sidney Taylor Tickle, Samuel Eli Turner, Eugene Thompson.

Flem Vandyke, Pearl Vance, Charley Crockett Vance, Thomas Vandyke, Jesse W. Vernon, Doak Vandyke, John Alexander Vandyke.

Martin Wilson, Dale West, Leck Evans Whitt, Charles Waldron, William Walter Watkins, Edward Whitman, Roby F. Wiles, Beverly Wade, Robert Johnson Wimmer, Samuel Henry Wimmer, Adam Greene Wagner, James Widner, Emory Wilson, Arthur Wimmer, Clarence Edwin Watkins, Joseph Shannon Wynne, John Thomas Worsham, George R. Walker, James Thomas Wilson, Thomas Marion Waldron, James Robert Whitley, Kent W. Witten, Roscoe Riner Wall, Fugate Campbell White, Lilburn Benjamin Wilson,

Will Samuel Witt, Spencer B. Warner, Samuel Luther Whitehead, William Welch, Kelly G. Wright, Andrew J. (of Robert) Witten, Frank Estil Williams, David Oscar Williams, John Clarence Whitt, Wilk Otis West, John Carl Witt, Elias Whitt, John Aaron Waldron, Arthur Monroe Woody, Archie Zack Whitt, Albert Glenn Wynn, Tom Wilson, Robert A. Walker, Joseph E. Whitt, Hobart William Webb, McKinley Wiles, W. P. Wyatt, Jesse Andrew Woods, Eugene B. Witten, Jack W. Witten.

Charles W. Yates, James Richard Young, David William Yost, Henry Peery Yost, Clarence Kelly Yost, James Harvey Yates, Edward Roy Yost, Charles George Yost, Levi Jesse Yates, Paul Richard Yost.

George L. Zimmerman, Ignatz Zachosky.

Total 628.

NAVY.

WHITE.

Charles R. Brown, Jr., William Jefferson Brown, William Arnold Burton.

A. J. Collins, Samuel William Carter, Bishop Hicks Coon, Paul Crockett.

James R. Doak,

Jesse F. Earnest.

Willie Guy French.

Jesse Samuel Gillespie, Charles Greer, Paul Gydosh.

Will Neal Hurley, Eugene Claude Harman, Rufus Crockett Harrison, John Jasper Henkle, Daniel Henry Harrison.

James Vernon Johnson, Everett Johnson, Roscoe Kelly Jones.

David Roscoe Kitts, Robert Ernest Kitts.

Robert Lee Longworth, Sam. J. Lubliner, Thomas Lawrence Lowe.

Charles Franklin Medley, Robert Henry Moore, Thomas Fairfax Martin, Cecil Martin, Clarence Myers.

Walter McGhee, George Gordon McBride, George William McCall, Harvey Grat McMullin, Henry L. McCall, William Lewis McMullin, George O. McGuire.

Bud Neal, Vance Clayton Neeee, James Curtis Neel.

James Walter Peery, Haynes Graham Preston, Raymond Surface Peery, George Armstead Pobst, Cornwell A. Peverall, Samuel C. Peery, Jr., Earl McMinn Pruett, Charles Fudge Peery.

Grady Lee Ross.

Sherman Lee Slaughter, Robert I. Sarver, Thomas Monroe Sayers, Rees Bowen Thompson, John Thompson, Arthur Taylor.

Everett Woods, Beverly Walton White.

Total 53.

MARINES.

WHITE.

Wm. Byrd May Chapman.

Henry Franklin Gilmer.

Thomas Robert Harrison, Mathew Butler Hammit, Robert Smith Hopkins.

Cecil Addison Mowles, John Earnest McMullin.

James Beverly Neal.

Eugene Pierce, Wm. Donreath Poindexter, Joseph Everett Porter.

Alderson Sexton, Kennerly Sexton, Gillespie R. Smith.

Andrew J. Witten.

Total 15.

S. A. T. C.

WHITE.

Wm. Gordon Bottimore, Benjamin Elbert Bates, Rufus Brittain, Samuel E. Baylor.

William Pamplin Crabtree, Thomas Healy Campbell, Robert V. Crockett.

Tyler McCall Frazier.

Charles Dewey Garland, Robert Gratton Gillespie.

James Hudson Hufford, Walter Henry Hankins, Joseph N. Harker, Jr.

Joseph N. Johnson.

Hubert Elmer Kiser.

James Ed. Litz, Thomas Wright Lawford.

Harry Fleming Macom, Barns Thompson Moore.

Victor W. McCall.

John Milton Newton, Jr., William Alexander Neel.

Joseph Elmo Peery, Lawrence Russell Painter, Russell Barns Painter, James Sidney Peery.

John Charles Scott, S. Houston St. Clair, Tom Ganaway Spratt.

Lacy Paul Wallace, Robert B. Williamson, James Albert Wagner, Dewey Clyde Wynn, Thomas Rawl Witten, Herbert Ward.

Total 35.

ARMY.

COLORED.

Burnett Armstrong, Irving Armstead, Lee Alexander, Argro Armsteard, George Allen.

Clarence Blackstone, John Robert Baldwin, Herbert Odis Bane, Arthur G. Bradshaw, Will Bradford, Robert Brooks, William Boatman, Yoeman Braxton, Otis Butler, Emory Bailey, Charley Barnes, Sonny Branson, John Burford, Jim Ballinger, F. J. Brown, Kirt Bailey, Oscar Edward Brown.

Herbert Cox, Rufus Conner, Henry Crockett, Emerson Carson, John Coulter, Levi Clark, Clarence Charlton, John Warren Carroll, Frank F. Carroll, Herbert B. Cross, Dan Crider, Robert Davis, Eugene Franklin, Frank Fuller, Leigha Ford, William Fleming, William McKinley Ford.

Ben Glenn, Aubray John Gant, Charles Green, Edward Gatewood, Clarence Gant, Stuart Gillespie, Lacy George, Clarence W. Goodman, Forace Gallman, Edd Graham, Sellers Gilliam, Walter Green, Lacy Goodman.

Raish Hodge, Hampton Holly, James Haskins, Will Hall, Willie Hightower, Wm. A. D. Hickmond, Johny Howe, Earl Horton, Raleigh Holly, Otey Wm. Hunter, Robert Harber, Frank Harber, Van June Holland, Charles F. Hobbs, Andrew Hairston, Allen Harper, John Johnson Holly, Simon P. Holly, Roscoe McClure Harman, Harman Harris, Ulyses Higginbotham, James Harris, James Higginbotham, Hobart Harris.

Sam Ingram.

Charles Robert Johnson, Timothy Elias Johnson, Granville Jackson, Jefferson S. Jordan, Grant Johnson, Eddie Jeffries.

Henry King, Rolen Kee.

Lacy Benjamin Lewis, James Leece, Ira Lanier, John Wyatt Lawrence.

James Molton, Lee Moseley, Jesse M. Morris, James Mack, Simon Maddox, Thomas Elbert Matney, Andrew Morehead, Joseph Moore, William Edward Morris, Charlie Morgan, William Murphy, Lura Morton.

Robert A. Nickerson, Trevalyn Milton Nash.

Lacy Owens.

Robert Preston, James Poindexter, Lacy Preston Peery, Joseph Jethro Pratt, Henry Phillips, Charles Pepper.

Jack Robinson, Walter Rippey, Robert Robinson, Ernest Reynolds, Sam Robinson, Eddie Roberson, Will Roland, William Ples Robinson, Roy Rose, George Robinson.

Governor Walker Smith, Tom Stiff, George Allen Saunders, Charles A. Sinkford, Raymond Streets, Charles Smith, Raymond B. Steele, Roy Scott, William G. Smith, John Steeples, Ballard Sanders, Boykin Stone, George Marion Staley, Charles George Steele, Roy Stuart, Richard Sinkford, Walter Franklin Smith, James Saunders, Elmer Sandy.

Marvin Thompson, Robert Thompson, George Turpin, Wm. Lawrence Thompson, Isaac Turpin, Fess Thompson, Alexander Toliver.

Lewis Williams, Harry White, Telfair Washington, William Webster, Ben Worley, Walter J. Ward, Thomas E. Warren, Felix Walker, Henry Wilson, Charley Walker, Lee Williams, John Rufus Webb, Snooks Willis.

Total 158.

S. A. T. C.

COLORED.

Walter W. Jackson.
Horace Bowser Logan.
Thomas H. Mitchell.
Cecil F. McCollum.
Dewey Rowden.
Arthur Scales.
James Lightburn Woody.
Bernard Isom Witten.
Total 8.

The following is a list of men from Tazewell County who were killed in action, or died from disease, or other causes, in France and in the training camps in the United States:

WHITE.

Pola Andrew Brooks, George Dewey Bowman, Martin Luther Bowling, Ervin Bane.

Paul Crockett, S. M. B. Coulling, Jr., William Henry Cole, Aaron Carter.

Fielden Kirk Earles.

Joe Farris.

Carnie J. Gillespie, John A. Graham.

David Paul Harris, William Henry, William Harman, Carey John Hodge, J. E. Hurt, Reese Hall, Henry Ingle, Thomas A. Jackson.

Robert Frazier McMeans, Thomas D. McCracken.

Henry Clarence Neel, Robert Sidney Neel, Wiley S. Neal.

Augustus Peery, William E. Peery, Jr., Joseph Everett Porter, Lawrence S. Peak, Roscoe Pack.

Leonard M. Reedy.

John Short, Wash Lee Sayers, Thomas Ford Shamblin, James Clinton Sturgess, William John Selney.

Roy M. Triplett, Samuel Eli Turner, Benjamin H. Thompson.

Doak Vandyke.

Samuel Henry Wimmer, Emory Wilson.

James H. Yates.

COLORED.

Elmer Bandy.

James K. Haskins, Harman Harris.

Roy Rose.

Charles Arthur Sinkford.

LOCAL BOARD.

S. S. F. Harman, *Chairman.*
C. W. Greever, *Secretary.*
Dr. P. D. Johnston, *Medical Examiner.*
Nye Britts, *Chief Clerk.*

MEDICAL ADVISORY BOARD.

Dr. W. R. Williams, Dr. M. B. Crockett, Dr. H. B. Frazier, Dr. Isaac Pierce, Dr. R. P. Copenhaver, Dr. W. E. Ritter.

GOVERNMENT APPEAL AGENT.

James W. Harman.

INDEX

(685)

688

INDEX

696

INDEX

696

INDEX

696

INDEX

696 INDEX

Page

Quapaw Tribe ... 24
Village ... 25
Quebec, Can ... 87, 89
Taken from France ... 197
"Queen Anne," Indian Queen ... 52
Quiltings ... 241–246

R

Raleigh, Sir Walter 93, 95, 98, 100, 101
Randolph, Edmund ... 355
Randolph, Hon. Peyton ... 340
Rapidan River ... 147, 148, 158
Ratcliffe, John ... 105, 106, 112, 113, 115, 118
Ray, Joseph, Family Killed ... 465
Raymbault, Chas., Jesuit Pioneer ... 186
Red Men, Origin of ... 3
Reed Creek 174, 184, 273, 283, 362
Settlement ... 286
Valley ... 278
Reedy Creek ... 297, 319
Settlement ... 174
Religion—
Indian ... 65
Persecution ... 69, 157
Services in Virginia Colony 108, 119
Denominations in Tazewell County ... 540–542
Representative, Government ... 122
Republican Party, Origin of ... 571
Reservations, Indian—
Sioux ... 26
Comanches ... 27
Qualla, N. C. ... 40
Pamunkey ... 52
Tulalip, Wash ... 62
Revolutionary War ... 267, 305–388
First Battle ... 328
Campbell Expedition to N. C. ... 388
Spies ... 368
Ribault, John ... 88
Rich Mountain, Va ... 56, 57, 293
Battle of ... 55, 671
Rich Valley 169, 278, 294, 295, 300
Richlands, Tazewell County, Va ... 513, 663, 667
Richmond, Va 109, 117, 138, 168, 349, 351, 353
Confederate Capital ... 604, 660
Ridpath, (Historian) ... 195
Roanoke (Lick), Va ... 60, 159
Colony ... 96, 113, 146
Indians ... 97
Island (Wocoken) ... 94–97
River ... 159
Valley ... 168, 173, 184
Roark, James ... 365
Roark Family Massacre ... 440

Page

Roberval, Lord of ... 87
Rockingham County ... 164, 167, 179
Rolfe, John ... 120, 121, 122
Rolfe, Thomas (Son of Pocahontas) ... 121
Roads in Tazewell County ... 530–536
Roosevelt, Theodore, 64, 176, 242, 243, 246, 265, 315, 321, 322, 357, 359, 380
Roque, Francis de la ... 87
Round Meadows ... 378
Royal Councils ... 104–105, 107, 109
Royal Government in 1776 ... 37, 328
Royal Oak, Smyth County, Va ... 36, 268, 283, 293, 294, 295, 297, 300, 364, 365
Russell, Wm., 257–260, 263, 274, 281–291, 302–316, 323–342
Russell Co. ... 257, 258, 302
Formed ... 391–392, 670

S

St. Augustine, Fla ... 24, 77, 83, 84, 120
St. Croix River ... 186, 194
St. Helena Sound ... 78
St. John's River, Fla ... 69, 82, 88
St. Joseph River ... 186
St. Lawrence, Gulf of ... 85, 91
St. Lawrence River, Discovery of ... 86, 186
St. Louis River ... 86
St. Pierre, Gen ... 188, 189
Salling, John ... 60, 159, 160
Saloop (Sassafras) ... 110
Salt Pond ... 183
Salt Pond Mountain ... 183
Salt Works, Battle of ... 628–631
Sandy Expedition ... 218–223
Sandy River ... 271, 281, 283, 285
Savannah Indians ... 44
Scalps, Commercialized ... 204
Price of ... 357
Schools for Indians ... 62–63
Scioto River ... 205, 210, 211
Scotch-Irish Pioneers ... 156
Origin of Name ... 157
Immigrants ... 157
Scott County ... 257, 285, 296, 301
Sea Venture, Ship ... 117, 120
Secession ... 596–605
Seminole Indians ... 19, 22–24
Origin of Name ... 22
In War of 1775 ... 23
In War of 1812 ... 23
Treaty with U. S., 1832 ... 23
Reservation in Arkansas ... 24
In 1916 ... 24
In Oklahoma ... 24
Seneca Indians ... 17, 18, 199, 204

Printed in the USA
CPSIA information can be obtained
at www.ICGtesting.com
LVHW050830300524
781525LV00007B/493